Starting an
Online Business

ALL-IN-ONE

6th Edition

D0770415

by Shannon Belew and Joel Elad

for
dummies®
Wiley Brand

Starting an Online Business All-in-One For Dummies®, 6th Edition

Published by: **John Wiley & Sons, Inc.**, 111 River Street, Hoboken, NJ 07030-5774, www.wiley.com

Copyright © 2020 by John Wiley & Sons, Inc., Hoboken, New Jersey

Published simultaneously in Canada

For general information on our other products and services, please contact our Customer Care Department within the U.S. at 877-762-2974, outside the U.S. at 317-572-3993, or fax 317-572-4002. For technical support, please visit https://hub.wiley.com/community/support/dummies.

Wiley publishes in a variety of print and electronic formats and by print-on-demand. Some material included with standard print versions of this book may not be included in e-books or in print-on-demand. If this book refers to media such as a CD or DVD that is not included in the version you purchased, you may download this material at http://booksupport.wiley.com. For more information about Wiley products, visit www.wiley.com.

Library of Congress Control Number: 2020931514

ISBN 978-1-119-64846-8 (pbk); ISBN 978-1-119-64845-1 (ebk); ISBN 978-1-119-64848-2 (ebk)

Manufactured in the United States of America

V9AA8745A-EB95-47EF-A2C7-A2F964365B99_022820

Contents at a Glance

Table of Contents

Introduction

Online businesses have finally found a permanent foothold in today's marketplace, leaving little doubt that the Internet is not only the conduit for a viable online business model, but is often a necessary tool for building, managing, and growing any type of business. Even traditional retailers are increasingly seeing their e-commerce sales eclipse in-store sales throughout the year, and especially during major shopping holidays, such as Black Friday.

We are excited about the potential that an online business holds and the fact that e-commerce and digital marketing are now thought of as necessary components of almost any business. Since beginning our own online endeavors, we have had the privilege of meeting and working with a variety of entrepreneurs — people who, much like you, share a dream of finding economic independence by running their own businesses. As you might have guessed, many of them found success on the Internet.

The Internet provides not only a legitimate resource for starting a business that will offer a steady source of income for your family, but also a nearly endless source of ideas and opportunities to market and grow your company. It can even give you the flexibility to work from home, the freedom to work part-time, or the ability to earn an additional source of income to help make your life more enjoyable. And maybe your online business could be the next Amazon, eBay, or Facebook! Almost anything is possible with the Internet, but the pursuit of success starts with a good idea, a solid business foundation, and an endless amount of determination and hard work.

In this book, we help get you started by sharing with you the knowledge and tools we've picked up along the way and by providing you with a few shortcuts to help further your own online endeavors.

About This Book

Much has changed since we wrote the first edition of this book in 2006, but much has stayed the same. Our number-one goal for the book — to cover the many ways you can start or expand a business by using the Internet — is still the same. Likewise, many of the basic principles for starting your online business are still tried-and-true methods. For this sixth edition, we took great care to update all the key information that has remained valid in the past few years. Our second goal for the book is to expose you, the reader, to new trends and tools that can be utilized by all types of businesses from nonprofit organizations to traditional retailers. We searched out many of the new opportunities that have recently evolved. For example, the expanding use of mobile applications, smart home devices (such as Alexa), virtual reality (VR), and video and voice search, all of which are forever changing the way businesses must operate online.

Mobility, alone, has affected almost every area of online businesses, from site design principles and shopping cart features to downloading mobile applications and making mobile payments. In 2019, mobile devices accounted for more than 52 percent of all web traffic, and some researchers anticipate that number to expand to 90 percent by 2022. Similarly, where most online searches are currently originating from mobile devices, it's anticipated that *voice search* (saying the words as opposed to typing them into your mobile device or smart home device) will eventually be the leading way to find information online. Those same smart home devices, from Alexa to Nest, along with VR, are making the consumer experience even more personalized, connecting customers to online brands, in some cases without even needing the consumer to say a word! Although this seemingly futuristic state of shopping online may seem intimidating to some, for entrepreneurs it all leads to new ways to make money online, which we delve into in depth in this edition of the book.

Similarly, another change that continues to gain momentum and provide online business opportunities is social commerce. Social media networking sites, such as Twitter, Facebook, Pinterest, Snapchat, and Instagram, are now staples for both promoting your business and making money. Industry giants such as Amazon pioneered the way in which online shoppers can make purchases directly through Twitter by using special hashtags, and even nonprofit organizations are realizing significant boosts in fundraising dollars thanks to the power of donations through social media. Powering all these platforms and online businesses is the use of content to help drive website traffic (customers). Google continues to emphasize the importance of quality content and rewards those online businesses that follow suit and produce with better search engine rankings. Knowing what type of content visitors want to see and understanding how to deliver it for the best results are now critical parts of managing and growing an online business. It may seem like a lot of information, but don't worry! All these changes (and more!) are captured in this newest edition of our book.

The book also provides you with details regarding specific online business strategies and moneymaking opportunities but also covers basic offline information. It's the stuff that every small-business owner needs to understand, such as how to apply standard accounting principles and keep up with the legal side of running a business.

Of course, using this book doesn't guarantee that you will make a lot of money — or any money, for that matter. We provide you with just enough knowledge and inspiration to keep your online business dreams on track. Running a business is hard work and requires persistence, dedication, and perhaps an equal mix of patience and luck.

Foolish Assumptions

While we wrote this book, we assumed a few things about you:

» You're a smart, inquisitive person who is seeking information about running a business on the Internet.

» You have an entrepreneurial spirit and are a bit of a risk taker — at least in the area of starting a business.

» You may be looking for ways to use the Internet to build an existing bricks-and-mortar business or to increase online donations for a nonprofit organization.

» You're comfortable using computers and browsing the Internet.

» You use email regularly.

» You're willing to find out about new technologies.

» You want to use websites and online technologies to build a brand.

» You're open to the idea of reaching out to others on the Internet using social media, such as Facebook, LinkedIn, Instagram, and Snapchat.

» You want to use the Internet to make money.

» You've bought items online and maybe even sold a few things.

Icons Used in This Book

Throughout the book, icons call attention to important details.

REMEMBER

This friendly reminder serves up important information. Whenever you see this icon, know that this information is something worthwhile to keep in mind as you move forward.

TECHNICAL
STUFF

You can usually understand an idea without having to know its behind-the scenes details. Even when we point them out with this icon, feel free to skip them and move on.

TIP

Check out this helpful hint. We picked up this information somewhere along the way.

WARNING

Pay special attention when this icon appears. It could save you from making a fatal error — at least in your online business!

Beyond the Book

In addition to what you're reading now, this book also comes with a free access-anywhere Cheat Sheet that gives you even more pointers on how to build a loyal online customer base and promote your business through social media. Also check out our list of web resources for online businesses as well as our handy checklist when launching your online business. To get this Cheat Sheet, simply go to www.dummies.com and type **Starting an Online Business All-in-One For Dummies Cheat Sheet** in the Search box.

Where to Go from Here

You can start reading any section of the book that most interests you or that you think is helpful to you and your business. For example, if you're starting a business for the first time, you might want to begin with Book 1. For those needing a boost in marketing or expanding an existing business, you probably want to go directly to the books that discuss those specific topics. However, you should at least browse through *every* section of this book.

Even if your e-commerce skills are more advanced, it never hurts to have a refresher course on some business basics. Considering that the Internet touches many different aspects of people's lives, you never know what unexpected tidbits of information you might discover.

If you have questions or comments, you are welcome to share them with us on Twitter (www.twitter.com/shannonbelew and www.twitter.com/joelelad) or connect with us on LinkedIn.

1

Start-Up Essentials

Contents at a Glance

Chapter **1**

Starting from Scratch

It's sometimes difficult to remember a time when we didn't have instant online access to almost anything desired, from finding a phone number for a new business (no phone book necessary!) to buying a hard-to-find bottle of your favorite wine (even if it's located in a vineyard across the country!). The Internet has replaced or supplemented trips to the library, grocery store, travel agency, bank, auto dealership . . . the list is almost endless. You name it; there's little you cannot find, access, or buy online. Behind each of these unique and convenient online retailers are entrepreneurs that started out just like you — with a good idea for an online business and the motivation to turn it into a reality.

Of course, it doesn't hurt that everyone from consumers to investors now recognizes the legitimacy of online businesses. It was once considered risky to shop online. But an Internet-based business model has proven to be a worthwhile investment time and time again, with the same potential risks and rewards as any other type of business. Add to the mix that technology has also come a long way, and shopping online using everything from a desktop computer or laptop, to a tablet or a web-enabled mobile phone (smartphone) is as easy as ever. And individuals are not the only ones spending more on online transactions. Increasingly, businesses of all sizes are also buying products and services online. Those same companies are also spending money to advertise on the Internet and reach their customers through traditional websites and social media sites. All these interactions represent a business opportunity by which people earn a living on the Internet. Why shouldn't one of those people be you?

Online revenues continue to grow — for all types of products and services in almost every industry. Even during challenging economic conditions, when traditional retail stores have struggled with growth, online retail sales continue to surge. Increasingly, retailers are seeing more revenue come from their websites, accounting for more than 10 percent of total retail sales in the first part of 2019, according to the U.S. Department of Commerce. More than 270 million consumers are expected to browse and buy online by the year 2020, generating $523 billion in online sales, according to research and advisory firm Forrester. U.S. companies selling services online to other businesses (B2B) are also seeing impressive growth. Companies adopting an online software as a service (SaaS) business model are experiencing two times the revenue growth and three times the customer growth, according to research from management consulting firm McKinsey and Company. Even social media sites are providing an avenue for making and increasing online sales, with revenue from social commerce reaching $14 billion in the United States and $30 billion worldwide, according to eMarketer, an independent market research company.

Speaking of worldwide sales, consider that North America represents only a small portion of potential online consumers. The international market is growing, with Europe accounting for more than 20 percent of Internet users and Asia accounting for close to half, according to Internet World Stats. Some European countries continue to have double-digit growth in online sales, and $53 billion in online sales will come from Southeast Asia, alone, by 2023, according to Forrester. These statistics represent substantial potential from online shoppers around the world. Isn't it time you join this generation of online entrepreneurs and take advantage of these rapidly growing markets and start an online business? In this chapter, we describe the kinds of businesses that exist online, and motivate you to get started.

What Are You Waiting For? Start Your Business Now!

You might have dreamed for years about starting an online business. Or perhaps you woke up just yesterday with a brilliant idea. What are you waiting for? The truth is that the most difficult part of beginning a new endeavor is making the decision to do it. You can easily get bogged down with excuses for why your business won't happen. To keep you motivated and on track, here's a list of the top reasons to start an online business *now*:

>> **You can gain financial freedom.** One major incentive for owning any business is the potential for a better income. The Internet offers the opportunity to create your own wealth.

» **You have unlimited customer reach.** No geographical boundaries exist when you run a business over the Internet. You can choose to sell your products or services in your community, in your own country, or to the entire world.

» **It's affordable.** You can now create a website inexpensively and sometimes for free. The cost to maintain your site, secure products, and cover related expenses is often relatively low. This low start-up cost is especially evident when you compare the start-up costs of an online business and a traditional *bricks-and-mortar business* (a physical building from which to sell retail merchandise).

» **Your schedule is flexible.** Part time, full time, year round, or seasonal: Your schedule is up to you when you operate your virtual business. You can work in the wee hours of the night or in the middle of the day. An online business affords you the luxury of creating a schedule that works for you. (Of course, the more time you invest, typically the greater your earnings potential!)

» **Novices are welcome.** As the Internet has grown, *e-commerce* (or electronic commerce, a type of business activity conducted over the Internet, such as sales or advertising) applications have become increasingly simple to use. Although you benefit by having experience with your products or services, the process of offering those items for sale online is easy to understand. You can set up shop with little or no experience under your belt!

» **You can start quickly.** From online auction sites such as eBay to storefronts powered by Amazon.com, the tools that can help get you started are readily available, essentially overnight. Many of these sites (such as Amazon) handle all the details for you — they set up the website infrastructure, manage the payment and shopping cart system, and even provide easy access to merchandise.

» **You can expand an existing business.** If you already own a business, the Internet provides you with the most economical and most efficient way to expose your business to a huge new group of customers and increase sales.

» **No age barriers exist.** You might be retired and itching for extra income, or perhaps you're a teenager who's only beginning to consider career opportunities. Online businesses provide economic opportunities for entrepreneurs of all ages.

» **A variety of ideas qualify.** As proven time and again, the Internet supports a broad range of business concepts. Although some ideas are better suited to long-term success, almost all your ideas have potential.

» **Niche markets hold unlimited potential.** Thanks to the reach of the Internet, unique or custom products and services have a potentially lucrative home in e-commerce. These products and services may not generate a large enough demand in a local market to sustain an offline business, but can find a significant niche customer base through the broad reach of an online audience.

>> **Everyone else is doing it.** Okay, maybe your parents wouldn't approve of using this logic. It's certainly true, though: People around the world are finding success and more financial freedom by starting businesses online. It's one leap you should be proud to take!

If you're still hesitant, consider this bonus reason: The information you need to take your business online is *right at your fingertips* — literally. This book gives you most of what you need to get started. Whatever else you require, such as information about conducting business in your specific state or regulations for your specific industry, is on the Internet (put there by some other enterprising entrepreneur, no doubt). You have no more excuses!

Choosing Just the Right Business

After you decide to start your own online business, you should look at the different categories of online businesses from which you can choose. In this section, we conveniently provide those categories.

REMEMBER

Not all online businesses will explode like Amazon, eBay, LinkedIn, or Facebook. But even if your business never grows into a megabrand, you need to plan for the long haul. You want your business to succeed and survive. Also, selecting the right type of online business is just as important. Losing interest or lacking an understanding of your chosen business area can hinder the growth of your new online business. Putting some thought into the type of online business you want to pursue pays off.

Creating online businesses for today and tomorrow

The secret to e-commerce success is to create a business that will stand the test of time. Sure, some people take advantage of relatively short-lived trends and make a mint (from Pet Rocks to Neopets, for example). The odds that you could create the same magnitude of buying hysteria with a product or service, however, are small. Instead, hundreds of thousands of entrepreneurs are quietly and steadily making a respectable living by using the Internet, and their ideas will find a market for many years. They're not making millions of dollars a month, but they're paying their bills and making a profit.

The widely used term *online business* can be used in different ways. It sometimes refers to a company that operates only over the Internet and has no other physical location from which to sell goods or services. It can refer to a traditional bricks-and-mortar business that also sells over the Internet. And we sometimes use it to reference a segment of revenues generated from the web for traditional businesses or organizations. In this book, an online business is any entity (or person) using the Internet, in whole or part, as a source of income for itself, its business, or its organization (such as a club or a nonprofit agency).

Finding a business that's your type

You can pursue a variety of businesses to earn money online. Almost all types of income-generating opportunities fall into one of two categories:

>> **Business to consumer (B2C):** Customers are typically the individual consumers who make up the general public. They buy products or services designed for personal use.

>> **Business to business (B2B):** Customers are most likely other businesses. They might buy hospital equipment, steel by the ton, employee uniforms, or anything that would be used primarily by a company.

Crossover between the two categories can occur. Sometimes, either type of customer can use the products or services you offer, as is the case with office supplies. And with more businesses now shopping online, this crossover occurs frequently.

TIP

Knowing whether your primary customers are individuals or businesses helps you to create more effective marketing campaigns. Typically, these two groups buy from you for very different reasons. By marketing to each individual group, you can better target your advertising messages for increased sales. You may find that your primary customers require (or respond better to) one type of marketing and that your secondary customers require another type.

Within the two primary categories, you find the different types of businesses you can operate. Here are a few examples of the ways in which you can generate revenue online:

>> **Online retail:** When you have a bricks-and-mortar (or traditional retail) store and offer your products for sale online as well, you enter the world of online retailing. You're responsible for hiring the resources and purchasing the tools needed to sell your wares over the Internet. One example of an online retailer is the Barnes & Noble bookstore — you can buy your books online or visit the bricks-and-mortar store. As mentioned, most traditional businesses now have some component of revenue that comes from online sales.

>> **Pure e-commerce:** E-commerce is a broad term used to describe the transaction of business via the Internet. E-commerce can also refer to any website where you sell merchandise but lack a physical location for customers to visit in person (bricks-and-mortar store). For years, the term commonly used for this type of online business has been an e-commerce *storefront*. (Offline, the retail industry uses this term to describe the outside of a building, which includes its signage, front door, and overall image.) As online businesses, and e-commerce, have matured, the term *storefront* isn't used as often. Instead, you may hear someone simply refer to a business as an e-commerce site (regardless of how it's structured) or online merchant. In this book, we continue to use *storefront* to refer to a one-stop shop for setting up an online presence to sell products. Amazon Marketplace (www.amazon.com), CafePress (www.cafepress.com), and Etsy (www.etsy.com) are examples of storefronts. These storefront sites provide you with a custom page that displays all your wares. Etsy allows you to customize the page from which you sell your handcrafted or vintage wares. Amazon allows you to set up a presence or page to sell your items through its broader website. Your page on CafePress has a structure that matches the overall CafePress site. Think of it as a flea market or one of those small kiosks you see in the mall — you get your very own little shopping area that you can customize, and visitors to your page see your merchandise and can learn a little about you if you choose to include personal information about yourself or your business.

We discuss e-commerce fundamentals, including simplified solutions for storefronts, in more detail in Book 8. For now, you need to know that good storefront providers offer the following:

- *Templates for your website:* You don't need to build a site from scratch. Many storefront providers offer wizards or HTML files that you can customize for your storefront.

- *Hosting options:* Many storefront providers have a variety of options for you, some free and some for a fee. These options might include shopping cart systems, phone support for your storefront, and discounts on fees if you pay rent by the year rather than monthly.

- *A shopping cart solution:* When selling items on your website, online customers need a place to hold items as they shop, and then complete the purchase process. This virtual shopping cart is actually a back-end solution that enables customers use to buy products from you.

- *Payment options (possibly):* The capability to accept online payment (credit card or debit card) is an absolute must. But other options allow payment to be deferred or even allow financing of purchases.

- *Products (in some cases):* Your preferred storefront solution may offer you everything but the kitchen sink, as the saying goes. Increasingly, you have the option to use a provider that also supplies the product. Your contribution is providing unique artwork or content (as with CafePress), or simply providing traffic, or customers (as with an Amazon storefront).

- *An auction (in some cases):* The way your customers buy products is somewhat different when you auction items. Your customers can bid on the final purchase price, as opposed to buying at a price you set. (eBay, the daddy of all online auction sites, has become so popular, however, that it has blurred the lines among auction, storefront, and online retail. We discuss eBay in Book 8, Chapter 4.)

» **Service business:** You don't have to sell products to have an online business. From doing taxes to writing brochures, most professional services can be sold online, just like physical products. Web-based services or applications, also called software as a service (SaaS), is another type of service business and is often sold B2B.

» **Content site:** Charging a fee for content and information products has become an accepted business model, provided the content has sufficient perceived value, whether informative, educational, or entertaining. And as a content site becomes more popular with visitors, options such as paid advertisements on the site can also generate income. The growing use of electronic readers (such as the Kindle and Nook) as well as Apple's iPad is helping create more acceptance and demand for paid content of all types, from e-books to podcasts. Similarly, the popularity of YouTube and other social media sites is driving interest in video. When you consider types of content to offer for sale, include video as an option for your paid content offerings.

» **Social commerce:** A growing online moneymaking opportunity is found in a category labeled *social commerce.* People are discovering ways to earn revenue from Facebook, Pinterest, Instagram, and other *social sites* (online venues that connect and engage consumers). Whether it's selling games and apps through social media sites, opening an online boutique on Instagram, or boosting online sales of products and services through engagement in social networks, one thing is certain: Social commerce is a real opportunity for a viable online business.

» **E-commerce applications:** If anything lends itself for sale over the Internet, it's technology. E-commerce applications continue to provide lucrative growth for innovators. Think of e-commerce as any type of technology product that makes doing business online (and offline) easier. Inventory programs, shopping cart solutions, and payroll management software are all examples of innovations that fit nicely in this category.

TIP

In Book 4, we explain how to create a revenue model for your business; you can apply this model to any of the types of businesses in the preceding list.

As you can see, you have no shortage of opportunities to satisfy your urge to start a business. After you officially decide to take the plunge, you can narrow the field and get started.

Getting Started

Even after reading this entire chapter, you might still consider having an online business to be a dream — a vision for your future. You might want to take small steps, testing the water to see whether an online business is right for you, just as you dip your toe into a pool before diving in. At some point, though, you have to decide to go for it. To that end, this checklist describes what you need to do to begin wading into your own online business:

>> **Make the decision to commit.** Although you don't have to quit your day job, you need to acknowledge that you're ready to pursue your goal. Say aloud, "I want to start an online business!"

>> **Set clear goals.** Write down *why* you want this business and what you expect to gain from it. These goals can be related to financial objectives, lifestyle goals, or both. If you know what you're looking for, you can also more easily choose the right business to meet your needs.

>> **Talk with your family.** After you commit to your idea and establish your goals, share your plan. If you're married or living with a partner, talk about your vision for the future. After all, your dream for an online business affects that person's life too. Discussing your plans with family is also a helpful step in making your business a reality.

>> **Create an action timeline.** Unlike the broad goals you set in the first item in this list, writing down specific action steps can help you realize tangible results. From researching business ideas to obtaining a business license, assign a targeted date of completion to further ensure that you make each step happen. (Figure 1-1 shows an example of an action timeline to use with your business.)

>> **Identify a business.** As we show you in the preceding section, you can choose from different types of businesses to operate online. Before going any further, however, you have to decide which business to pursue. Narrow your choices by thinking about what you enjoy doing or which specific qualifications you already possess. Consider your professional experience and your personal desires. You might even have a hobby that can be developed into a moneymaking business.

>> **Develop your business idea.** Define your idea and determine how you will turn it into a profitable online business. (Read Book 1, Chapter 2 when you're ready to evaluate whether your idea is feasible.)

After you make it through this checklist, you're ready to go to work and transform your dream into a legitimate business.

(Sample) Start-Up Action Timeline for Your Online Business

Start date: January 15
Estimated start-up date: June 30

Action	Completion Date	Status/Comments
Finalize/validate business idea	1/30	
Write formal business plan	2/15	
Select business name	1/30	
Register business name	2/15	
Choose domain name	1/30	
(if different from corporate name)		
Register domain name	1/31	
Identify business location	2/01	
Check zoning laws (if home-based)	2/05	
Set up office (computer, telephone, and so on)	2/15	
Decide organization status of company	1/30	
(sole proprietor, corporation)		
Legalize business structure	2/28	
(file incorporation papers)		
Obtain business license	2/05	
(and other necessary permits)		
Set up business bank account	2/05	
Meet with accountant to review tax requirements	2/10	
Obtain Employer Identification Number (EIN)	2/15	
Secure business insurance/health insurance/other	2/28	
Secure funding (if using outside sources)	3/31	
Apply for sales tax certificate (if applicable)	3/01	
Select:		
Hosting service	3/02	
Web developer	3/02	
Distributor or drop shipper (if applicable)	3/30	
Create content for website	4/29	
Select products, or finalize services, or both	5/20	
Develop website	6/10	
Add shopping cart or other e-commerce applications	6/15	
Obtain merchant account	6/15	
File trademarks and/or copyrights	6/16	
Submit site to major search engines	6/17	
Initiate marketing plan	6/20	
Test (and correct) all site functions	6/28	
Launch site to public!	6/30	

FIGURE 1-1:
A timeline for starting your online business.

Chapter **2**

Turning Ideas into a Viable Internet Business

Congratulations! After you make the emotional commitment to get started, you have to shift gears and concentrate on the next set of actions that will make your Internet business a reality. From evaluating the potential success of your idea to identifying who will buy your products, in this chapter you gain the tools to help get your idea off the ground. In the process, you begin thinking like an online entrepreneur and find out how to start your business on the right track.

Thinking Like an Online Entrepreneur

Using the Internet to conduct business is similar in many ways to operating a traditional company. In fact, many traditional offline businesses now conduct part of their business online. Today, consumers research products and services online and expect to be able to buy products or services online, even from bricks-and-mortar stores. For those reasons, the lines between online and offline businesses are increasingly blurred.

Profitability (or how much money you make after subtracting your expenses), taxes, marketing, advertising, and customer feedback are other examples of factors that affect your business whether it's online or offline. However, some exceptions set apart an online business, particularly in regard to how you deliver products and service your customers. Even the most experienced entrepreneur can get caught in the trap of forgetting those differences. Your attitude and how you approach the business as an online entrepreneur can make a huge difference in how successful you are online.

Adjusting your attitude slightly and viewing business from behind the lens of an online entrepreneur isn't difficult. Doing so is simply a matter of recognizing that the Internet changes the way you can and should operate your online business.

When you think like an online entrepreneur, you

>> **See the invisible storefront.** Although the doors, walls, and even the salesclerk for your online business might be invisible, they definitely exist. In fact, every part of your web business leaves a distinct impression. Yet rarely do you hear or see the response to your storefront directly from customers. Consequently, and contrary to popular belief, a website demands your continual care and attention — adding products, fixing bugs, replying to email, and more.

>> **Understand who your customers are.** Even if you don't personally greet your online visitors, don't be fooled: The Internet offers the unique opportunity to learn and understand almost everything about your customers. You can learn where else they shop, how much time they spend on your site, what products they're interested in, how they prefer to shop (on a desktop computer or on a mobile device, for example), what triggers or offers they respond to best, where they live and work, how much they earn annually, and on what other websites and social media networks they spend their time. Online entrepreneurs collect and use this information regularly in an effort to increase sales and better serve their customers. (When you're ready to meet your customer, turn to Book 6, where we explain the basics on how to get and use this wealth of customer information. We go into even more detail on understanding the online buyer's journey in Book 11.)

>> **Respond to fast and furious changes.** The way people use the Internet to buy, sell, or search for products and services changes rapidly. Also, the rules for operating an online business as imposed by both the government and the business world in general are modified almost daily. Sustaining success online means that you must take the initiative to keep up with new trends, laws and regulations, safety and security concerns, technology, and even marketing and social media tools.

>> **Speak the language.** Communicating to your customers through a website can be challenging. Your buyers want and expect quick and easy access to information. Because attention spans are limited, content should always be relevant, easy to find, and to the point.

>> **Communicate visually.** Equally important to the words you choose are the images and videos you incorporate into your site. Whether you use purchased stock photos or pictures that you take yourself, you want images to be crisp and clear. Videos, whether professionally produced or ones that you film yourself, are best when the quality is good, the video length is short, and the content is relevant to the message you are communicating. In addition, product images and videos should be the best quality possible.

REMEMBER

As an entrepreneur, you must choose your words, images — and even music — carefully. Your site's content, including the words and pictures you use on your web, will

- Help sell your products or services to visitors.

- Serve as interesting and useful content to share on social media, which is an important method of marketing your online business.

- Play a big role in *search engine optimization (SEO),* or the way you can increase visits to your site by placing higher on the list of rankings by Internet search engines. (Yes, images, like words, are searchable and can help increase your rankings in search engines!)

>> **Know when (or whether) to innovate.** You might be able to develop a new or different method for doing business online, although it's probably not necessary. Innovative tools already exist, and you can often find them on the Internet quickly and cheaply. You don't need to reinvent the wheel — you just have to know how to find and apply the tools that are already out there.

>> **Reap repeated rewards.** Establishing multiple streams of revenue or maximizing a single source of revenue is a common practice online. For instance, you might have an outstanding information product for sale on your site. The same product can just as easily be sold on other websites in exchange for a small percentage of earnings. Or you can choose to add a product from another website to your site and pay that site a percentage of earnings. (To begin increasing your earnings, read about affiliate programs in Book 4.) Similarly, you may decide to sell cloud-based or web-based services to other businesses on a monthly basis. This Software as a Service (SaaS) online business model provides recurring revenue for your online business. (If this is your preferred route, we delve further into running a SaaS business in Book 10.)

Putting Your Business Idea under the Microscope

Every successful business begins with that first idea. From fast-food restaurants to selling cosmetics from home, Ray Kroc first dreamed of hamburgers at McDonald's and Mary Kay visualized selling makeup door to door. When the Internet first provided similar opportunities, Jeff Bezos visualized a way for consumers to buy everything from books to clothing and have it delivered straight to their doorsteps through Amazon. Your dream for an innovative new business is no exception — and the Internet has continued to make it easier than ever to launch a successful business. Maybe you have several unique concepts to choose from or are firmly set on a single one. Either way, how do you decide whether you should quit your day job and focus on your brilliant idea? You have to pick apart the idea, observe closely, and determine whether it merits a full-time (or part-time) business.

One question often asked is whether or not the idea has to be original. Innovative, never-before-broached ideas for an online business certainly exist. But being the first to have and implement an original idea is not a guarantee for success. Likewise, there may be exceptional opportunities for updating or modifying an existing business to an online format. Consider that Netflix became an online streaming version of bricks-and-mortar video rental stores. The video rental concept was not new, but Netflix took video rental online and eventually became part of the reason for the demise of the leading offline video rental giant, Blockbuster. Ultimately, your concept for the business, whether it's a new idea or a twist on an existing idea, must be well thought out to increase your probability for success. This section describes the three methods you can use to decide whether your idea has potential.

Using informal research to verify your idea

The best place to begin gathering information is from sources closest to you. Be prepared to receive varying opinions — both positive and negative. Use this input as a general gauge of whether to continue reaching out to the next source of information. You and your idea are in the center, surrounded by three rings from which to collect input, as shown in Figure 2-1. If the ring closest to you provides mostly positive input, proceed to the next ring.

Ring 1 consists of your friends, family, and coworkers. Ask them these questions:

>> Have you ever heard of this type of product or service?

>> Would you buy this product or service?

>> Do you think it's a good idea?

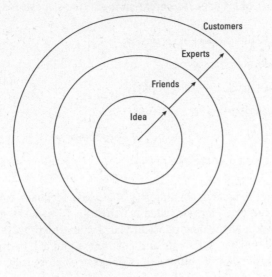

Three Rings of Decision

Customers

Experts

Friends

Idea

FIGURE 2-1:
Using your close
contacts and
moving outward
is a good method
for gathering
information.

>> What challenges do you think I will encounter?

>> What are the benefits?

>> Can you envision me selling this product or service? Why or why not?

In Ring 2, seek input from industry professionals, investors, other entrepreneurs, and organizations that offer support to small businesses. Ask questions similar to those listed for Ring 1. Because of the experience of the people in Ring 2, you should give more weight to their responses. Small–business support resources include the following:

>> **Small Business Administration (SBA)** (www.sba.gov): The SBA, a government-sponsored organization, helps small-business owners with loans, paperwork navigation, free seminars, and other services.

>> **Small Business Development Center (SBDC)** (www.sba.gov/sbdc): The SBDC is a partnership between the SBA and universities. Together, they provide support, mentoring, training, and educational services to both new and established small businesses. SBDCs are available through local branches, often located in a partnering university or Chamber of Commerce.

>> **Chamber of Commerce** (www.uschamber.com): From small towns to large cities, all local chambers help owners develop their small businesses.

>> **SCORE** (www.score.org): This network of retired executives matches small-business owners with business-exec retirees who volunteer their time to help small businesses develop and prosper.

In Ring 3 are your potential customers. Ask them these questions:

» Would you use this product or service?

» Have you used something similar?

» How much would you be willing to pay?

» How often would you use it?

» Where would you normally go to buy this product or service?

» Would you order it over the Internet?

If you find that you're receiving a majority of positive feedback from sources in all three rings, you can consider your idea worthwhile. Or at least you have enough validation to continue to the next phase of your evaluation process. Later, you may want to return to this list of friends and customers and ask them to "beta" test, or try out an early version of your product or service before it is fully available to the general public.

Applying a SWOT analysis to your idea

Another popular method for determining the pros and cons of an idea is referred to as *SWOT analysis*. (SWOT is short for strengths, weaknesses, opportunities, and threats.) Companies use it for several reasons, including as a decision-making tool for product development. The simple process also lends itself to a more thorough investigation of your business idea. This section covers how you can put your idea to the SWOT test!

Create your own SWOT chart by following these steps:

1. **On paper, draw a cross (or a box divided in half both horizontally and vertically) to create four quadrants, and label them as shown in Figure 2-2.**

   After you draw and label the chart, you can begin to fill in the details.

2. **In each quadrant, write down the factors that influence or contribute to each of your four SWOT categories.**

TIP

   Strengths and weaknesses are considered *internal* factors that control or specifically contribute (good or bad) to the business concept. Opportunities and threats are *external* factors that are influenced to some extent by the environment or are otherwise outside of your control.

SWOT Chart

Strengths	Weaknesses
Opportunities	Threats

3. **Analyze the information you filled in. Ask yourself the following questions to start developing your SWOT analysis:**

Strengths

- What advantages does the product or service offer?
- Do I have expertise in this business or industry?
- Can I get a patent to protect the idea?

Weaknesses

- How much does developing the product cost?
- Is getting suppliers difficult?
- Am I learning a new industry from the ground up?

Opportunities

- Does my idea take advantage of a new technology?
- Is my product or service in demand?
- Have changes in policies or regulations made my idea necessary?

Threats

- Does my product or service have established competitors?

- Do my competitors sell the product or service for less than I can?

- Will changes in technology make my product obsolete?

TIP

Use the feedback you receive from your informal research (during the Three Rings exercise) as factors in your SWOT quadrants. Combining other people's opinions with your own provides a more comprehensive — and useful — SWOT analysis.

4. **After you fill in the categories of your first SWOT analysis, take a look at which quadrants contain the most factors or the most significant factors.**

The listed strengths and opportunities indicate the advantage you might have in the marketplace. If you're lucky, they outweigh your weaknesses and challenges. Perhaps you can now see what you must do to offset those disadvantages if you really want your idea to work.

Whatever the outcome of your analysis, you should have a better feel for the value of your business idea after viewing the completed SWOT analysis.

Creating a feasibility study to validate an idea

After your idea gains a nod of approval from friends and family and the SWOT analysis indicates that your product has merit, your idea must jump through one more hoop for complete validation. A *feasibility study* is a somewhat formal, written process that helps you determine whether your idea is realistic. The goal of the study is to provide you with final proof that your business concept is viable.

A feasibility study answers these basic questions:

>> Will the product or service work?

>> How much will it cost to start?

>> Can your idea make you money?

>> Is the business concept *really* worth your time and energy?

CHOOSING THE BEST IDEA FOR *YOU*

Perhaps you have no trouble dreaming up new ideas for a business. Instead, your challenge is deciding which one to pursue. Unlike the SWOT analysis or feasibility study, no established test determines which of your many pursuits is best suited for you. This decision is much more subjective and personal. When deciding which idea is best for you, consider the following questions. Use your answers to help gauge such things as how passionate you are about a particular idea or which ideas may be better suited for your current skills or lifestyle.

- Does this idea interest you?
- Does this product or service *excite* you?
- Do you have experience with this product or service?
- Does it require a large investment?
- Do you have money readily available to fund the concept?
- Will starting this business require you to alter your lifestyle?
- Are you willing to change your lifestyle for this idea?
- Does this business reflect your personal goals?
- Does this idea reflect your professional goals?
- Can you imagine owning this same business in 10 years?

Turning Ideas into a Viable Internet Business

A feasibility study kicks your analysis up a notch. It relies on in-depth research to provide more detailed answers to questions in five primary areas:

» Your product and service

- What is the product or service?
- How will my customers use it?
- Where or how will my customers buy it?
- How is it designed, and how is it delivered to my customers?
- Am I testing to ensure that my product works correctly? (Describe these tests in detail.)

» Your experience (including your management team's experience)

- Who is my management team?

- What experience do I (and my employees) have?

- What are my specific skills and credentials?

- Which skills am I missing, or in which areas am I weak?

- How much time can I devote to my business?

» The market in which you're competing

- What is the demand for my product?

- Who are my customers? (What is the target market?)

- How big is the market I'm selling to?

- What is the status of the market? Is it growing or stagnant?

- Where and how can I reach those customers?

» Your competition

- Who are my primary and secondary competitors? (Describe each of your competitors in detail.)

- How do my competitors market their products or services?

- What makes me different from or better than my competitors?

- Is my product easy to copy? How can I prevent copycats?

» Your costs

- How much does it cost to make my product or produce my service?

- What other business costs do I have?

- How much money do I need to start?

- Do I have access to funding?

- When will I make a profit?

Now you know how much information you have to gather in your feasibility study. As you answer all these questions, make sure that you back up those answers with detailed research. Then write your results in a one-page summary that discusses what you discovered. Your summary should answer all the questions in each category and provide proof of whether you have a viable idea. After the validation process is complete, you can turn your attention to the next piece of the business success puzzle: potential customers.

Identifying Your Market and Target Customer

The terms *target market* and *target customer* are defined as the entities that buy your product or service. Although these phrases are sometimes used interchangeably, *market* is often used to describe a collection of individual target customers. The term *buyer persona* is also used as a way of providing a detailed description (or persona) of your typical customers. You most likely have several types of customers, each with a unique persona — and you mostly likely have several buyer personas that make up your target customers.

Classifying your customer

Knowing your target customer is an important advantage when you begin marketing. As we explain in earlier sections in this chapter, recognizing your primary customers lends credibility to your business concept. The more you know about your target customers, the more easily and cost-efficiently you can build your business and market to these folks.

How do you decide who this person is or who the groups of people are? You can create buyer personas by describing or segmenting your customers based on different traits or classifications. The two most common classifications are

>> **Demographics:** Age, income, gender, and occupation are examples of common factors used to describe your customers.

>> **Psychographics:** Music choices, hobbies, and other preferences make up this category. Usually, psychographics reflect lifestyle choices.

You can describe your customers in other terms as well, such as these categories:

>> **Benefits:** Describe why customers use your product or service. For example, customers might need it for medical purposes. Or they might receive a luxury benefit, where they don't *need* the product or service but choose to invest in it for perceived benefits.

>> **Geographic preferences:** Point out where people live. The location can include a specific neighborhood, city, state, region, or even country. Customers can also be segmented according to home (or residential) locations versus business locations.

Technology has made it easy to target your customers by location. Knowing where your customers are in terms of geography can be a critical competitive advantage.

>> **Use-based preferences:** Specify how frequently customers want or need your product.

Typically, your target market includes customers described by a mixture of the terms and categories in this list, which you use to develop your buyer persona. For instance, if you sell trendy men's clothing at discounted prices, one buyer persona for your target market might be described this way:

Male

Age 25 to 30

Professional

Owns home or rents high-end apartment, with a total annual household income of $50,000 or more

Lives in urban area or major metropolitan city

Buys clothing at least monthly and updates style seasonally to enhance appearance

Depending on what type of product you sell, your target market most likely includes a wider mix of customer types — not just one.

Going to the source

In the preceding section, we talk about the components of a market description. Where do you get the information to build this type of description, though? You can use any or all of the following methods to gather information for your customer profile:

>> **Survey potential (or existing) customers.** Conduct a focus group in which you interview a small group of likely customers. Or distribute a survey or registration form online to gather the data.

>> **Observe competitors' customers.** Stake out your competitors by visiting them online. You can often discover exactly what competitors think about their own customers by reading through their sites. (This information is often readily available on competitors' websites in sections labeled About Us or Company Information.) For competitors with retail locations, visit their stores and observe the customers and their habits in person.

>> **Use published market research.** To identify the types of customers most likely to buy your products, read about trends in reputable market reports. You can find much of the research for free online. Larger research firms charge a fee (which can range from several hundred dollars to several thousand dollars per report) for detailed reports. If this type of research interests you, start with companies such as Forrester (`https://go.forrester.com`), Gartner (`www.gartner.com`), or IDC (`www.idc.com`).

Use this information to pinpoint who your customer is.

Competing to Win: Analyzing Your Competition

If you're serious about developing a successful online business, you need every advantage possible. That means getting to know not only who your customers are but also who else is after their business. Start by writing down a list of your top three to five competitors.

Keep this list on hand, and document basic information, such as

>> Website address

>> Physical address (if they have one) and number of locations

>> Annual sales (if publicly available)

>> Number of employees

>> Types of products or services offered (with full description)

>> Strengths and weaknesses

>> Copies of ads, flyers, and brochures

>> Special promotions (especially online offers)

>> Pricing information for products or services similar to yours

TIP

As a quick and easy way to keep up with your competition, visit their websites and sign up for their newsletters and other promotional offers by email. You can also follow them on social media sites such as Facebook, Instagram, and Twitter.

Be sure to maintain a list of your secondary competitors, too. These companies don't sell your exact products or services but come close enough to compete for your customers' dollars.

Hooray! You completed your due diligence and have a fat file of information about your stiffest competition. What now? This kind of data does you no good when it just takes up space in a filing cabinet. Use it to your advantage.

Sift through your collected information again to refresh your memory (because you probably have lots of information), and then follow these steps:

>> **Compare apples to oranges.** Using the information you collect, compare both your strengths and weaknesses to that of the competition. (You can even do a complete SWOT analysis on each of your competitors!) This comparison identifies where you fit in the marketplace relative to other players in your area of interest.

>> **Plan your marketing strategy.** You have access to your competitors' marketing material, so use it to define your own marketing strategy. Play up your company's strengths in ads; advertise in markets that your competitors missed; and plan to educate your customers on the benefits that separate you from your competition.

>> **Create a competitive pricing model.** Maybe you discovered that you could beat a competitor's price. Or perhaps your research shows that you *must* price lower to survive. Use a competitor's pricing data to map out the best pricing model for your product or service.

>> **Determine growth models and financial requirements.** Suppose that a major competitor is ready to partner with a big distributor. Although you might not be able to compete immediately, this information helps you plan for growth. Use this knowledge to better understand your competitor's growth and financial strategies, and then adjust yours accordingly.

REMEMBER

The old cliché is still accurate: Knowledge is power. Don't let good information go to waste. Use what you learn to differentiate yourself and win points with your customers.

IN THIS CHAPTER

» Understanding the purpose of a
business plan

» Organizing the pieces of your dreams
into tangible goals

» Determining when you need help and
what to expect

» Getting long-term value from the
plan you make today

Chapter **3**

Getting Real: Creating a Usable Business Plan

O ne big complaint from entrepreneurs, especially those running small companies, is "Why do I have to write a business plan?" Quite honestly, you don't. Some entrepreneurs who choose to forgo a business plan do just fine, but others struggle.

In this chapter, we tell you why having a business plan is a good idea and show you the benefits you can reap from not only having one but also reviewing and updating it regularly.

Understanding the Value of a Plan

Starting and managing a business without a business plan is, like it or not, the same as searching for a buried treasure without a map: Although you know that the gold is in the ground somewhere, you're wasting an awful lot of time by randomly digging holes in the hope of eventually hitting the jackpot. Without a plan, the odds of success aren't in your favor.

Why, then, do people resist using this tool? They resist it for two reasons:

>> **Having a plan involves a great deal of work.** Don't despair: You can minimize the amount of work involved, which we get to momentarily.

>> **They don't understand the importance of having a plan.**

To help you overcome your business plan angst, we provide these reasons for having a plan — you can decide whether to take another step without one:

>> **You can more easily secure money.** This goal is probably the most common reason for the creation of a business plan. If you decide to ask strangers to lend you money, whether those strangers are bankers or private investors, they want to see a plan. Lenders have a better chance of protecting (and recouping) their investments when a formal strategy documents your projected income and profits. Even if you're counting on family members for a loan or are using your own funds, having a business plan confirms that you have thought about how to use the money wisely.

>> **A plan creates a vision that gives you a well-defined goal.** Coming up with a great idea and transitioning it into a viable business opportunity can be challenging. Having a written plan forces you to fully develop the long-term vision for your product or service. With those clearly defined goals in place, you stand a much better chance of accomplishing your vision.

>> **A plan can provide timeless guidance.** Done correctly, this document provides a concrete plan of operation for your business — not only during your start-up phase but also for three to five years down the road. Keep in mind that the plan might need occasional tweaking (as discussed at the end of this chapter). However, investing the time now to create a strong foundation ensures that you have a barometer to help you make decisions for managing your company.

Chances are that at least two of the three reasons on this list are valuable to you. Even if you don't plan to attract investors, you're already forming a picture about what your company looks like, and you're setting goals to make sure that you get there. The only remaining step is to make your thoughts more permanent by writing them down in a business plan.

Recognizing That the Parts of the Plan Make a Whole

A traditional business plan is sectioned into seven or eight major parts. At first, that number of parts might seem a bit overwhelming. Consider, however, that most experts recommend keeping a finished business plan to fewer than 20 pages. (You can usually get by with many fewer pages.) When you break down that recommendation, each section becomes only 2 or 3 pages long, which translates to 5 or 6 paragraphs per page. It's not so much after all.

REMEMBER

Each part plays a critical role in your overall plan. Although each section can almost stand alone, the sections work together to present a complete picture, or vision, of your business. Don't even think about omitting one of them.

TIP

Depending on your main purpose for having a business plan, you can develop sections with more diligence. For example, if you're seeking outside funding, make sure that the financials section is as thorough and accurate as possible.

Before you start writing, get a sense of the scope of your plan by reading these brief descriptions of the basic parts you need to cover:

>> **Executive summary:** Although this part comes first in your plan, you typically write it last. This brief page does just what it says: It highlights the major points from each of the other parts of the plan. This page is usually the first one that investors and other advisors read, and how well it's written can determine whether they turn the page or show you the door.

>> **Business or product description:** This section provides a detailed description of your overall business and your product or service. You should include a *vision statement* (or *mission statement*), which summarizes your goals for the business. When you describe your product or service, don't forget to pinpoint what makes it a unique and viable contender in the marketplace.

>> **Market analysis:** Provide a thorough description of your target market. In this case, discuss both the overall industry in which you're competing and the specific customers to whom you're marketing. Don't forget to include a description of any market research you conducted.

>> **Competitive analysis:** In much the same way as you describe your target market in the market analysis, in this section you provide an in-depth view of your competitors in that market. The more detail you can provide, the better, to show exactly how well you understand (and are prepared for dealing with) your competition. Address your competitors' weaknesses and also state how you can counter their strengths.

Don't double up on your work. Use information you gather during your SWOT analysis and feasibility study (see Chapter 2 of this minibook). Adapt the research and results of both to include in the market analysis and competitive analysis sections of your business plan.

>> **Management team:** Whether you're flying solo on this operation or working with a team, highlight the expertise that you and your executives bring to the table. Include summaries of your key professional experience, educational and military background, additional certifications and completed training programs, and all other relevant accomplishments. Remember to include a copy of your full résumé.

>> **Operations:** Here's where the "rubber meets the road." Use this section to describe your marketing and operations strategies. Then detail *how* you plan to implement these strategies in your business. Think of the operations section as your chance to prove that you know how to convert innovative ideas into a successful business.

>> **Financials:** Start talking money. In this section, you include projections (or estimates) of how much money the business will earn and your expenses, or costs of doing business. This combination is typically referred to as a *profit-and-loss (P&L) statement.* For the first year, break down this information for each month. (This listing demonstrates how far you must proceed into your first year before you start making money and indicates where seasonal slow points might occur, with smaller amounts of income coming in.) After the first year, show your projections annually. (See Book 2 for complete descriptions of legal and accounting requirements.)

When you're pursuing outside funding, try to be optimistic about your financial projections. Don't be unrealistic, but don't be too conservative, either. If you're using the plan only internally, you can play it safe and estimate your future profits toward the lower end.

>> **Appendix:** Consider this area a catchall for important documents that support portions of your business plan. Place copies of your loan terms, patent or copyright documentation, employee agreements, and any other contracts or legal documents pertaining to your business.

You might wonder whether you can use an easier, or shorter, business plan format with an online business instead of the traditional format. No, not really. As you can see from the descriptions in the preceding list, each part or section of the plan is generic. You can use almost any business plan template, tailor it slightly to your specific type of business, and achieve the same results.

TIP

Having a sample plan written for an organization similar to your online business is helpful. Check out one of the business-planning resource centers on the web, such as Bplans (www.bplans.com), to locate a sample plan specifically for online businesses to use as a guide. Free resources and tips are available to help create your plan, or you can pay for additional tools and software.

Getting Help to Write the Plan

Even though you will probably feel better about writing a business plan after you read the rest of this chapter, more options can help make writing one easier. When creating a plan feels like more than you can handle alone, the solution is to hire a professional to write it for you or purchase business plan software that walks you through the process.

Don't think that a business plan template or other software package is cheating. Your goal is to get your business off the ground — don't close any doors or turn away any help. The money you spend on your business plan is an investment that has the potential to pay back many times. The time you spend on your business plan can likewise shorten the time you must spend later in preparing your business for success.

TIP

Several good options for business plan software exist, including buying an off-the-shelf version, such as BusinessPlan Pro from Palo Alto Software. You can also use LivePlan (www.liveplan.com), an online version of Palo Alto Software's business plan software, which offers a monthly billing option in its pricing plans. If you need limited guidance on developing a plan, check out the free business plan builder from LawDepot (www.lawdepot.com/contracts/business-plan) and from the U.S. Small Business Administration (SBA) (www.sba.gov/tools/business-plan).

Determining when to hire a professional

Not everyone needs outside help to construct a solid business plan. If you're starting the business part-time or you plan to be a one-person company for a while, the plan doesn't necessarily have to be lengthy and complicated.

TIP

As a *sole proprietor* (one-person company), part-time operator, or home-based business owner, you might write a condensed version of the business plan, with the same sections but less detail. Rather than use a 20-page document, you might be able to achieve the same objective in only 8 pages.

Alternatively, if you need to secure a large amount of money for your online business start-up, it just might pay (literally) to get help — especially if you plan to *pitch* (sell) your business idea to savvy investors, such as venture capitalists. Bringing in a seasoned business plan writer helps you

>> Add polish to your plan

>> Remember to include pertinent information

>> Phrase the wording of your business plan in the best possible way so that you speak the language of investors

If you're pressed for time, getting assistance might also speed the process for you. Additionally, if you commit to using the business plan to its full potential (as a long-term operational guide), hiring an experienced consultant almost guarantees that your plan is a top-notch piece of work.

Knowing what to expect from a business plan consultant

After you decide to seek assistance with your plan, you might be surprised to find that you're still expected to contribute information. Business plan writers are often referred to as consultants, and for good reason: You consult these folks to get advice and guidance on how to make the most of your plan.

REMEMBER

A consultant translates your thoughts into the final written document. Consultants aren't mind readers, though: You're still responsible for providing all the initial information, often in written form.

You might be wondering how much this service costs. After you realize that you're still doing a good bit of the work, your expectations on price might change. Regardless of the amount of work you must contribute, however, writing the plan still takes a great deal of time, and you're paying for the consultant's expertise. Expect to pay the minimum national average of $1,500 to $5,000 for a business plan written by a professional, with consultants' fees ranging from $50 to $150 per hour, on average.

Keep in mind that wide variations might still exist, on both ends of the price scale, for this service. Much of the final price depends on

>> Your requirements for the plan

>> What you can contribute (to save the consultant time)

- » The consultant's experience level
- » The complexity of the business concept
- » The amount of research required to substantiate the plan

Although more knowledgeable consultants might charge a higher hourly fee, they could complete the project much sooner because of their experience. A consultant who lowballs the price of the project might not fully understand the amount of time involved and might try to increase the quoted price later.

When you're working with a professional, the length of time to complete your plan depends on several factors. Here are some examples:

- » How much information you can provide
- » How quickly you can provide the information
- » How extensive a plan you need
- » The availability and accessibility of the facts about your business

TIP

If you decide to hire a professional, check first with experienced advisors who offer free assistance. Your local Chamber of Commerce or SCORE, an organization that offers guidance to new and established businesses, might provide enough to support writing the plan yourself. In addition, the SBA offers online videos, including one for writing a business plan called "How to Write a Business Plan." You can access it at https://sba.gov/videos.

TIP

When you're ready to hire a professional, keep these points in mind:

- » Look for someone with experience in your product or service industry.
- » Find a consultant who's comfortable with, and knowledgeable of, online businesses.
- » Review samples of other business plans the consultant has written.
- » Ask for written testimonials and references you can contact.
- » Get a firm price quote.
- » Agree on a reasonable timeline for completing the plan.
- » Put your final terms into a written contract, including specifics of what you're responsible for providing.

Using a Business Plan Today, Tomorrow, and Always

Ignoring your business plan or forgetting to maintain it is the same as failing to plan. To ensure that your business plan passes the test of time, consider these suggestions for ways to use it:

>> **As reference material:** Refer to your plan often. Rereading your original plan is a good way to make sure that you're staying on track.

>> **As a decision-making tool:** When major operational issues occur or expansion opportunities arise, turn to your business plan. Decide whether the issue at hand fits your original goals and timeline before taking action.

>> **As a troubleshooter:** When problems surface, minimize your frustrations. Use your own words of wisdom to resolve your problems. Take a look at your plan to see where the hiccup is. More than likely, you addressed potential problems in the operations section of your business plan.

>> **As a hiring tool:** When you're ready to expand your executive team, or add any other key staff positions, a business plan can show prospective employees that the company's course has been carefully charted. Having proof of a game plan for growth and showing you have been sticking to it is particularly important when trying to hire executives or recruit advisors and a board of directors.

>> **As a vision guide:** After your business is running, you can easily lose sight of the big picture. Concentrating on daily tasks and problems can derail your overall progress. Check your plan frequently and refocus your vision.

TIP

Every January, schedule at least two business plan preview sessions for the coming year. If necessary, pencil in a date and time on your calendar. (Block out 3 or 4 hours.) Do this task semiannually or quarterly, depending on whether you made, or will make, significant changes to your business.

Chapter **4**

Funding Your Online Business

One of the most important choices you make when you're creating a company is how to fund your brave new endeavor. The amount of money you have available and where it comes from truly helps you begin defining the rules by which you must operate the business.

If you borrow $25,000 from a bank, for example, right away you know what's at stake. Each month you *have* to come up with at least enough money to cover that loan payment or else you risk jeopardizing your personal credit record (if you're a sole proprietorship and aren't incorporated). On the other hand, if you borrow $5,000 from your in-laws, you're potentially inviting additional decision-makers into your business because there's no such thing as "silent" in-laws.

Whether you need $500 or $500,000 to get your business going, this chapter shows you various financing options and describes what each one means to the future of your business.

Bootstrapping the Low-Cost, No-Cost Site

We won't lie to you: Just like starting a political campaign, starting a business is easier if plenty of money is available. Fortunately, having a lot of money isn't a requirement to start an Internet business. If you don't have access to megabucks, you can always *bootstrap* your new business. (The term comes from the idea of pulling yourself up by your own bootstraps, or making your own way.) In the case of financing your entrepreneurial dream, bootstrapping is a matter of making a little money go a long way.

Making the leap to the bootstrapping lifestyle

One of the first rules of bootstrapping is to hang on to other sources of income for as long as possible. In other words, keep your day job! You might have to design your website during lunch breaks or work past midnight to prepare customer orders for shipping. Although keeping a regular job while starting a business can mean a grueling schedule, it provides you with much-needed financial security in the early stages of building your company.

TIP

Try something between maintaining a full-time job and starting a business. Many entrepreneurs worked part-time jobs at night so that they could dedicate themselves to their new businesses during the day.

If you're the all-or-nothing type, perhaps you want to throw yourself completely into the business. Or maybe you're confident enough in your idea that you just *know* success (cash!) will materialize. However, you should still plan for alternative sources of income. Look for freelance work, short-term consulting jobs, or whatever else it takes to keep money coming in while building your business.

Saving money to make money

Making sure that cash is coming into your business is only your first step. Learning to conserve your cash is the second rule of bootstrapping. Controlling the *outflow* of money, or how that money is used, is quite important.

Here are some ways that any good bootstrapper can conserve cash:

>> **Become frugal.** Spend only when absolutely necessary, and then buy on the cheap. Rather than buy brand-new office furniture, for example, find what you need by shopping garage sales, thrift stores, and eBay.

» **Budget wisely.** Create a financial plan that helps you track income, expenses, and projected sales. By monitoring the money you have coming in and going out every day, you're less likely to get into trouble. Book 2 shows you how to establish this type of budget and set up your accounting procedures.

» **Use other people's money.** Rather than borrow money from banks or investors, "borrow" money from your suppliers and customers. You can negotiate terms with vendors that allow you to pay for supplies 30, 60, or 90 days out (in other words, after you receive them). Then ask customers to pay for your product or services up front or in net 15 days. This strategy lets you use your customers' money, rather than cash out of your pocket, to pay your expenses.

» **Sacrifice for the business.** The cash coming into your business should be just that — money for your business. If you're using revenues to support your personal lifestyle, the business doesn't stand a chance. Bootstrappers commonly forfeit luxuries and even downgrade their living circumstances while growing a company. Could you live in a smaller house for a while or drive a less expensive car?

» **Inspire, don't hire.** The early stages of building your company can be overwhelming, with lots of hats for you to wear. Rather than hire full-time employees, inspire others to work with you *gratis* (for free). Not everyone wants or needs immediate compensation, so sell people on your skills as a leader and get them excited about where your company is headed. College interns are a good source of free or inexpensive labor for your business. When the economy is weak and jobs are scarce, even out-of-work professionals are willing to accept internships in an effort to improve or expand their marketable skills. The promise of a job (after you're on more stable financial ground) may be enough to get someone working 5 or 6 hours a week right now. Some individuals are also willing to work for free, in return for a recommendation from your company. For example, a lot of people design complementary websites in exchange for using those websites as client referrals. By seeking out this type of synergistic swap, you can avoid hiring employees in the beginning.

» **Find a mentor.** Hiring a consultant can break the bank before you even open your doors for business. Mentoring is an alternative way to get advice from established professionals that costs you absolutely nothing. These experts probably won't do the work for you, but they can advise you on critical decisions, introduce you to other professionals and suppliers, and sometimes even help you find your first customers. People are generous with their time, especially when you ask them to share their personal expertise with you.

Getting resourceful

In addition to locating experts or finding cash, you need to identify other means of getting what you need. Check out these resourceful alternatives to help you jump-start your online business:

>> **Barter and trade:** One way to keep a lid on your spending and still acquire supplies and services is to trade with other companies. Rather than pay a professional to write copy for your web pages, for example, barter with a writer for her service. *Barter,* or trade, is a method of paying for products or services without using cash. When you barter, you exchange your services or products for those of another person (or company). This method of conducting business has become so popular that you can now join formal barter-exchange organizations. Membership is usually free. You can find barter organizations online that serve your specific state or region or find one that has a national reach. You can learn more about bartering and find organizations near you from the International Reciprocal Trade Association (IRTA; `www.irta.com`).

TIP

The Internal Revenue Service (IRS) doesn't mind bartering, as long as you record on your taxes whatever you receive as income. Any transaction involving the exchange of a product or service that doesn't involve cash changing hands is considered "barter" by the IRS. The IRS has guidelines and reporting requirements for individuals and formal barter exchanges. For example, barter amounts should appear as income for both parties when you complete Form 1099. You can read the complete guidelines for how to report bartering as income on the IRS website (`www.irs.gov`).

>> **Try out trial versions before you buy.** When you stock up on necessary software for your online business, don't rush to buy expensive off-the-shelf products, which can cost several hundred dollars. Instead, use free demonstration (demo) versions that are good for a specified period. Eventually these free trials run out of time, so budget accordingly if you anticipate needing to make a more permanent software purchase.

>> **Use free tools.** Lots of free business-related software (called *freeware* or *open-source software*) and free or almost-free applications are accessible over the Internet. Independent software developers and small companies typically offer software applications, graphics, games, and developer tools at no cost to you, and with no strings attached. Other apps cost just a few dollars. And even if you don't find a recognizable brand-name product, you might find one that has similar features. Be aware that freeware and free business apps may have no technical support or very limited support. If you are using open-source software, there is usually a community of developers on forums who help answer questions, but it is not support in the traditional sense of the term.

TIP

If you find a software solution you really like, but there's not a free version publicly available, consider contacting the company directly. Sometimes you can get a 2-week or 30-day trial with all features enabled if you ask for it!

Looking at the pros and cons of bootstrapping

Bootstrapping may sound like you're flying by the seat of your pants (or your boots), but it's quite the opposite. It requires adopting a rigorous thought process that includes detailed and innovative planning.

Although bootstrapping may seem painful, consider the alternative of bringing in other investors or borrowing money. Is it worth the sacrifice? Take a look at how a bootstrapping approach can affect your business now and down the road, and then decide for yourself:

>> **You retain ownership.** Keeping full ownership or controlling interest of the business is one of the most important benefits of bootstrapping. You get to make all the decisions, without having to run them by investors or shareholders or even lenders first. You also choose how and when the company grows. And if you need to bring in capital (money) down the road by selling shares of your company, you don't jeopardize your control. You can sell off a minority interest and maintain controlling interest.

>> **You can make quick decisions.** Typically, you don't have layers of departments or managers in a bootstrapper organization. You can make decisions without getting bogged down by bureaucratic red tape. The ability to make agile decisions is an important advantage over competitors, especially when you're heavily into the research-and-development (R&D) process. Your organization can offer new products or make other changes much faster than many of your competitors can.

>> **You assume minimal risk.** Without putting much money on the line, your risk (or what you can afford to lose) is greatly reduced. You also have the most to gain because your investment and your risk factor are small. This motivating aspect can spur you to success.

>> **You maintain a cash-is-king mindset.** Being frugal pays off now and later. Initially, your conservative decisions will assist you in building a positive cash flow for your business. As a bootstrapper, you'll tend to hold on to those same decision-making philosophies in an effort to maintain your cash reserves as the company expands. This mindset may help to keep your online business debt free.

Finding the Perfect Investor

Not everyone has what it takes to grow a successful company from nothing or while operating on a shoestring. Or maybe your business concept requires a significant injection of capital right from the start. If so, you have other alternatives to bootstrapping. The most popular approach is to find an investor.

Investors, either individuals or a group of individuals, buy into your idea and provide the money you need in exchange for stock (or a percentage of ownership) in your business. You can choose from several types of investors; each type comes with its own pros and cons, of course. The trick is to find the best type of investor for your needs.

Turning to your friends and family

You're probably familiar with the idea of turning to your friends and family (F&F) network for start-up funds. A major advantage of this strategy is that you have a lot of flexibility in how you structure the terms of the agreement.

The simplest method is to simply ask for a loan. You need a certain amount of cash, and your mom or best friend is happy to oblige. As a bonus, the interest amount on the loan is usually minimal or nonexistent, and the time for repaying the money is often more flexible — not a bad deal.

An alternative is to take on your friends and family as investors. In other words, you give up a percentage of shares or stock in the business for the amount of money they agree to provide. On the upside, you don't repay that money. However, if you no longer want those people to own a piece of your business, you have to buy back their stock to get rid of them.

TIP

Websites that offer free or low-cost legal documents, such as Nolo.com (www.nolo.com), sometimes offer promissory note templates or other sample loan agreement documents that you can use to define lending terms when borrowing money from friends and family.

Here are some advantages of acquiring investors from your F&F network:

>> **You can easily obtain the money.** You have an established circle of friends and family members who already know and trust you. Sometimes, you don't even have to sell them on your business idea — let alone show them your business plan. They just want to help you.

>> **You can get cash quickly.** Unlike going to a bank or venture capitalist, you don't have to jump through any lending hoops or participate in a series of drawn-out meetings. Friends and family may be able to get their hands on cash quickly and hand it over to you sooner.

>> **You have a potentially large pool of investors.** You can easily find small amounts of money from lots of different sources. If you need $50,000, you can get ten friends to contribute $10,000 each rather than try to find one person who can contribute the entire amount.

This method has a few disadvantages too, of course:

>> **You can have problems with unstructured terms.** Because you know each other, you tend to keep things informal. That opens the door to uncertainty and inconsistency and big misunderstandings. Be wary of taking on friends and family members as investors without structured, written agreements that clearly define the terms of their investments in your company or the payback terms of your loan.

>> **You may give up too much stock.** You want to gratefully reward those who take a chance on you, especially when you're close to them. For that same reason, however, you can end up giving away too much interest in your company. Or if you turn to a large group of friends to invest, you may have to ante up a large block of stock for a small amount of cash. This uneven exchange can put you in a precarious position as the company grows.

>> **The business can interfere with relationships.** Taking on your most trusted circle of friends or family as investors can lead to heated disagreements, hurt feelings, and your fair share of misunderstandings. Damage to these friendships or to relationships with family members isn't easy to repair.

Finding angels

If the uncertainty and lack of structure of the F&F network bothers you, turning to an angel may be more appealing. An *angel* investor can be an individual investor or a group of investors who are willing to put money into start-up or young companies.

Several important differences separate angels from other types of investors. Angels are private investors and usually bridge the funding gap. Raising more than $100,000 or $200,000 from friends and family is tough, yet a venture capitalist usually isn't interested in investing less than a million dollars, especially in a company without a track record. An angel meets midlevel funding needs.

Another important difference is that an angel investor typically doesn't take an active role in a company. An angel wants to provide capital, not run the business, although that person sometimes becomes a member of an advisory board or board of directors. (We discuss the board of directors as part of your formal business structure in Book 2.) In addition to taking this hands-off approach toward your business, an angel is less likely to demand an immediate return on an investment. Whereas your father-in-law may expect to recoup his money in a couple of years, an angel's target return may be 5 years.

This network of investors has become more careful and savvy, performing due diligence and examining every aspect of proposed businesses. As with any type of investor, angels invest in businesses they believe will give them a good return on their money. For that reason, angels are influenced by fluctuations in business trends, or what's considered hot at a given time. One year it could be something as general as social media networks (like Snapchat and Instagram) and the next year it could be mobile apps for the healthcare industry. Regardless what types of businesses are popular investment targets, generally angels are more willing to take risks on new, unproven businesses. But keep in mind that the overall requirements for investing are increasingly the same as those used by venture capitalists (as outlined in the next section).

A hands-off approach to long-term lending sounds great, right? It's not all roses, though. Among the negative factors in seeking money from angels is that they often require a larger stake in a business. Having a higher percentage of ownership in a company offsets their risk. When the return on investment comes, it equates to a significant amount of money for your angels. Also, acquiring money from angel networks is getting tougher. Increasingly, angels are using the same or similar funding guidelines as those of venture capitalists. Angels expect you to have a polished business plan, an experienced management team, and an *exit strategy* (a way for the angels to recoup their initial investment and then some).

If the negative side of working with an angel doesn't bother you, how do you locate one? Examine your own network of colleagues, friends, and family — ask if they have any contacts that might be interested. If that strategy doesn't provide any leads, search for angels at the regional or national level. Here are some places to begin your search:

» Chamber of Commerce or other local business-support organizations

» Professional associations (local and statewide) focused on technology

» Your accountant, banker, or attorney (who often works with or knows angels)

» Investment clubs

Online resources for angel networks and entrepreneurs, including crowdfunded sites that match entrepreneurs with prospective angel investors, include

>> **EquityNet:** www.equitynet.com

>> **Funded.com:** www.funded.com

>> **Gust:** www.gust.com

>> **Social Venture Circle:** www.svcimpact.org

Venturing into the world of venture capital

Venture capital (VC) funding isn't the easiest route for securing money for your business. Maybe you remember the stories of the dot-com era when millions of dollars were thrown haphazardly into Internet start-ups. Well, in spite of that bursting bubble, venture capitalists are still out in force. In the first half of 2019, $55 billion of VC funding was raised in the United States, according to the *MoneyTree Report.* By comparison, $120 billion was raised in a full year during the record-setting year of 2000. Even though VC money is being raised at near-record levels, getting their money is still challenging.

To be honest, we don't recommend even considering venture capital as a resource for a brand-new company. This type of funding is designed for businesses that need an aggressive (or very large) amount of money to support the next level of business growth. Venture capitalists are institutional investors (professionally managed funds) that invest anywhere from $500,000 to $10 million or more in a company. Most often, this investment is made in preparation for an initial public offering (IPO) on the stock market, a sale, or a merger with another company.

Suppose that you're thinking big and are intrigued by venture capital as a funding source. How do you know whether your company is ready to pursue VC money? Although the funding criteria vary among venture capitalists, most of them generally expect the following from your company (and you):

>> **The company has already used seed money.** Your company is long past the point of obtaining money from friends and family as part of its start-up stage. Seeking money from a venture capitalist means that you have already received additional rounds of financing from angel investors and are now ready for a more substantial investment boost.

>> **The company has a proven track record.** Establishing a history of success is a necessity for venture funding. Investors expect your company to have experience under its belt and proof of the underlying business concept. Having an offline (bricks-and-mortar) business that has verifiable financial records greatly increases your success of finding funding.

>> **An experienced management team is in place.** Being the sole employee of a company isn't a good thing when you're seeking venture capital. Instead, you *must* have a seasoned team of executives with the experience to take your company to the next level.

>> **The company is in a hot industry.** Venture capitalists invest in more than a company — they invest in an industry. And some industries or markets are hotter than others at any given time. Your business doesn't have to be in the top three industries of interest, although it certainly improves your chances for funding.

>> **The company is in a high-growth stage.** Securing venture capital means that your company is no longer in an early growth stage. It's now positioned for significant earnings. Although the amount can vary, a good rule is that your company can achieve annual revenues of $25 million within a 5-year time frame.

>> **You're willing to relinquish control.** If you don't have in place a top-notch team of heavy hitters (including yourself), relinquishing executive control may become a condition of funding. If you previously held the title of CEO and president, you can expect to be replaced by an outsider of the venture capitalist's choosing.

If you're serious about pursuing venture capital, you should do a few things first:

1. **Start making connections early.**

Go to seminars on venture capital funding (usually sponsored by professional organizations in your community) and meet the venture capitalists involved in giving the presentations.

2. **Contact other companies that have recently secured funding.**

Seek out other small businesses and ask for referrals to VC firms. In addition, ask questions and get a general understanding of what the process may be like for a company similar to yours.

3. **As you're building these networks, start your own form of recordkeeping.**

Securing venture capital is a tedious, time-intensive process. The sooner you begin to understand the process, the more likely you are to be successful.

4. **Begin making a list of potential venture capital firms.**

Keep track of the companies in which they invest, how much they invest, and in which industries they most actively invest.

When you're ready, two established resources can assist you in locating and learning about venture capital firms that might be a good match for your business:

>> **Guide to Venture Capital & Private Equity Firms, 2019 Edition**: This extensive guide, at www.greyhouse.com/guide-to-venture-capital-and-private-equity-firms, offers direct access to more than 3,000 venture capital and private equity firms worldwide. In addition to presenting basic overview information about each firm, the guide also lists extensive contact information, including phone numbers and email addresses. Grey House Publishing, the publisher, offers a hardbound copy ($395) and includes free access to an online version.

>> **MoneyTree Report:** This quarterly report lists detailed information about venture capital funding in the United States. It's a collaborative effort between PricewaterhouseCoopers and the National Venture Capital Association with data from Thomson Reuters. For information, and to review the quarterly reports, visit the website at www.pwcmoneytree.com.

TIP

Check your local library and used books sold through Amazon for a copy of either resource on this list. Although you may get a slightly older edition of the book, you can save the out-of-pocket cost of several hundred dollars that you would spend for a more current edition, and many of these resources stick around for a while.

REMEMBER

During economic downturns or when the economy is generally weakened, both venture capitalists and angel investors become increasingly selective about where and how they invest. Having a solid business plan with a strong road map to a return on investment becomes even more important.

Checking Out Alternative Financing

When all else fails, a diligent online entrepreneur still has a few alternative financing options, although they are not necessarily your best choice. These options can help you open your doors for business, so to speak. Many times, you end up combining a variety of these sources to fund your great idea:

>> **Credit card:** For better or worse, a credit card is a popular choice for funding a business. More than 80 percent of small businesses have used personal and business credit cards as a source of money, according to the Small Business Administration (SBA). Especially during economic periods when lending tightens from banks and other traditional resources, credit cards can sometimes provide the only source of fast cash for a new or growing business. Although credit cards may be a quick and easy alternative, they can also be

expensive. Some credit card companies charge interest at 20 percent or more, even during times when interest rates are historically low. In addition, they can slap you with hefty fees for late payments or for exceeding your credit limit. Financial advisors also caution that fully paying down the balance of your credit cards can take decades when you're making only the minimum monthly payments.

TIP

Consider moving balances with high interest terms to another card. Credit card companies often offer limited introductory low- or no-interest rates for transferring your balances from other cards. If these offers don't come in the mail, don't be afraid to call credit card companies (including your existing one) to negotiate for a better rate.

» **Crowdfunding:** An amazingly successful fundraising alternative hit the Internet in recent years that helps generate money for individuals, businesses, and non-profit organizations. *Crowdfunding* works as its name indicates and allows almost anyone to invest in a creative project or business. Establish how much funding you want to raise and a period of time in which the project must be funded. You can allow people to fund anywhere from a few dollars to a few thousand dollars. Funding investments are typically paid out only if the project is fully funded in the specified time period. You may also provide a return on the investment based on the funding level, such as a product prototype, early access or beta access to a solution, or even a small number of shares in the company.

Several crowdfunding sites make it easy to set up funding projects. Some popular sites are Kickstarter, Indiegogo, and GoFundMe. Typically, the site takes a small percentage of your total funds raised if the project is successfully funded and may charge additional processing fees. Although these sites expose you to a much wider audience of potential investors, often the investments still come largely from people you know. Unless you have a very unique business idea or interesting way of pitching the idea and get picked up by the national media, in most cases it is up to you to promote the funding campaign through your social networks. That means crowdfunding, while still a terrific alternative source of funding for your online business, is largely dependent upon your ability to promote the campaign.

» **Retirement cash:** A personal savings plan, such as a 401(k), has long been a source of money for someone opening a start-up business. Before draining your account, consider the penalties for early withdrawal and seek advice from your accountant on the pros and cons of this source of funding.

» **Home equity loan:** Depending on the state of the housing market and interest rates on various types of home loans, you may be able to use your home as a funding source for your business. As a homeowner, you can cash out the equity in your house, use it for other purposes, and pay it back at a fixed interest rate over 5, 10, 15 or more years. Similarly, you can refinance your home and use the additional funds for starting the business. Another option is to open a home equity line of credit, which gives you a fixed amount of money that you're approved to borrow. You take out the money only as you need it, rather than in one lump sum. As is the case with any type of loan, you must have solid credit scores, among other things, to qualify.

REMEMBER

Borrowing money against your house is always risky! Many business experts hesitate to recommend this method as an option because you could lose your home. Consult with your accountant, or other financial advisors, before making this decision.

>> **High-interest loan:** Some specialized lenders finance loans (even high-risk ones if you have poor credit) at high interest rates. These rates are usually similar to, or higher than, credit card rates. When all other options fail, this method may be a possibility; be cautious, though, about taking this route.

>> **Microloan:** If you're looking for a smaller amount of capital, the SBA has a microloan program for amounts up to $50,000. The average loan size is approximately $13,000. The loans are backed by the SBA but are distributed and managed by local, approved community lenders. As with any loan, there are collateral requirements, but funds can be used for working capital, equipment, inventory, and supplies. To find out who offers loans in your area, contact your state or regional SBA office or visit www.sba.gov.

>> **Online lenders:** There are a host of non-traditional lenders now offering loans online to new and existing businesses. These lenders are known for having quick, easy application processes with flexible terms, and are thought to be generally open to working with start-ups and e-commerce businesses. Lenders like Kabbage (www.kabbage.com) are ideal for new businesses that need smaller loan amounts. On the flip side, OnDeck (www.ondeck.com) provides loans to businesses that have been around at least a year, and need larger amounts of capital. PayPal's Working Capital program (www.paypal.com/workingcapital) allows businesses flexible terms for borrowing money without a credit check, but you must be a PayPal business.

>> **Grant or award:** If your business concept is innovative, you may want to search out grant opportunities or contests offering financial rewards. *Grants* are monetary awards that you don't have to repay. Some organizations — such as business magazines, office-supply chains, and other large retailers — sponsor business-plan-writing contests with financial payoffs or award cash and prizes as part of their general business contests. No all-in-one resource tracks all sources of grants and awards. You have to do your homework by diligently searching the Internet and thumbing through business publications for opportunities. However, the shot at free money may be well worth your time.

WARNING

Be wary of websites that charge for a list of "free money" resources from government grants. Although legitimate grants are available, you don't have to pay for them: You can obtain a list for free from the Catalog of Federal Government Assistance at the U.S. government's grant site (www.grants.gov). You can download a free app from the site to easily track grants from your mobile device.

» **Incubator:** This type of entity or organization, established to support entrepreneurial development, usually provides shared resources for businesses. Sometimes, a *shared resource* refers to a physical location (such as an office building) or access to volunteer or hired professionals who are shared by the organization's entrepreneurs. Although incubators don't traditionally provide start-up money, they're still considered an alternative funding source because they provide your business with a range of tools, resources, and services. Many types of incubators with different levels of services are available. Examples range from offering free support (such as educational workshops and training for entrepreneurs) to providing shared workspaces or office space for a reduced fee. Depending on the arrangement, incubators may require a small percentage of ownership in your business, ask for stock options, or charge a small fee for services. In most cases, this situation results in a nominal expense to you compared to other funding options. The amount of savings and the invaluable assistance (which can accelerate the growth of your business) translates into a wise investment of your start-up dollars.

TIP

Locate technology and small-business incubators in your area by contacting InBIA, previously known as the National Business Incubation Association, at www.inbia.org.

Taking a Shortcut: Purchasing an Existing Site

Securing financing for an online business takes time and persistence — no doubt about it. If you're interested in a completely different path, you can take a shortcut. Have you considered purchasing an existing website? Don't get excited — you don't have to march up the virtual steps of Amazon or eBay and put an offer on the table. (To be realistic, you'd be laughed right out the door.) Somewhere between the people dreaming of starting a business and the giants dominating the Internet, hundreds of thousands of other mom-and-pop businesses have already established a small presence online. Many of them are doing quite well, others are struggling, and some just don't have any sense of direction.

Those latter categories provide you with the largest opportunity to jump-start your online dreams. Check out the following sites, which provide lists of online businesses for sale:

>> **BizQuest** (www.bizquest.com): Claiming to be one of the original business-for-sale websites, BizQuest has a healthy number of business listing in all categories. To get the most relevant list of available online businesses, use its search tool to search for the term *Internet*. Last time we checked, this search term returned nearly 20 pages of results for available Internet businesses for sale.

>> **Website Properties** (www.websiteproperties.com): Unlike traditional business brokers, Website Properties specializes in just that — websites. You can search a list of available sites directly from its site, and you can easily and immediately view a great deal of information about available sites, without having to request access to the details from a broker.

WHAT MAKES AN EXISTING SITE A SMART PURCHASE?

Buying an existing online business is basically the same as purchasing any other type of business: You have to do your homework and determine whether the purchase is a wise one. Find answers to these questions about a business before you sign on the dotted line:

- Is the online business a viable business model?
- Does the purchase include existing inventory or customer contracts?
- Even though the site is established, does its concept pass your feasibility test?
- Is the site generating revenue? How much? (Ask for financial statements verified by a certified public accountant.)
- What expenses does it incur?
- Can you reduce the amount of overhead by making different management decisions?
- Can you increase the percentage of profit by making different management decisions? If so, how long would it take to implement these changes?

(continued)

(continued)

- When was the site established?

- What is the annual percentage of revenue growth? (How much more money does it make over the previous year?)

- How many people visit the site each day? (Ask for verification.)

- Does the owner maintain any logs or records verifying the number of visitors and other stats?

- What are the site's popularity rankings in all the major search engines?

- What, if anything, has the owner previously done to increase rankings?

- Has the site been featured in any magazines or other websites?

- How many other websites link to this site, and vice versa?

- If a product is being sold, does the site use a dedicated supplier? Are other supplier sources available?

- If the site sells an information product or is a service business, do you have the skills and staff to duplicate it?

- Does the site have a poor reputation or many unhappy customers?

- Is the site in good standing with the Better Business Bureau and other organizations?

- Does it have a current business license?

- Are its taxes current?

- Has its URL expired, or is it about to?

- Does it have a valid Secure Sockets Layer (SSL) certificate to allow protected, properly encrypted transactions over the Internet?

- Which hardware and software, if any, are included with the sale?

- Do you gain any proprietary software in purchasing the site?

- Why is the current owner willing to sell?

- Can you create your own site and generate similar results in a short time for less than the selling price?

Stop dreaming, and take a look at the benefits of scooping up an existing site to launch your business. You can

TIP

>> **Override start-up costs:** Finding an existing online business means that you don't have to worry about all the initial costs and hassles of getting the site started. Maintaining or building an existing site is usually cheaper than starting from scratch.

>> **Eliminate time to market:** Although you may have a business up and running in just a few weeks, establishing yourself in the market and gaining a presence in the search engines takes much longer. Buying a ready-made site (even a fledgling one) removes at least some of this concern.

>> **Gain established customer base:** The "build it and they will come" theory has repeatedly been disproved when applied to websites. Purchasing an online business with existing customers is a definite perk.

To make sure that the site you're considering buying has real value when it comes to customers, ask to see proof of a current email list or database of customers or members (not just a log of daily visitors).

>> **Get a site for a steal:** Do your homework and you can purchase a site for little money. Look for businesses in which the owners

- Are tired or bored of the site

- Have no time to maintain it

- Ran out of money after putting the basics in place

- Are in a cash crunch

These factors don't necessarily mean that the business is bad — just that it was under poor management.

>> **Negotiate payment terms, with no out-of-pocket costs:** Even if you end up with a large (but reasonable) price tag, you still have a money-saving alternative. For instance, offer to make a small down payment on the site. Then let the owner know that you will make monthly payments until the balance of the sale price is paid in full. (If the site is producing revenue, you can use a portion of that income to cover the payments, so only the deposit comes out of your pocket.)

>> **Lease to own:** In this strategy, the seller retains ownership of the site and you manage it. You pay the owner a set monthly fee, plus a percentage of the profits, until the sale price is paid.

Funding Your Online Business

Chapter **5**

Creating Policies to Protect Your Website and Customers

Customers are the reason you're in business. All too often, though, their role in your success is an afterthought. Even though you spend a great deal of time thinking about what they can do for you, sometimes you forget about what they expect of you, until a problem surfaces.

In this chapter, we show you how to invest the proper time into the "care and feeding" of your most important business asset — your customer.

Taking Care of Customers

Consider the process of starting your business. You think about your future customers, right? You anticipate who will buy your product. You research their needs and painstakingly detail how to meet those needs in your business plan. You develop a marketing plan that explains how to reach your customers, and you calculate, dollar for dollar, how their spending translates into profit for you.

Something is missing, though: Where in all that research and planning is your pledge to your customers — your vow of how you will treat them? Most business plans don't include this type of pledge, unless one of your company's competitive advantages is defined as an unprecedented level of customer service.

I pledge to you

What is a customer pledge, and how do you develop one? A *pledge* to your customers is a *written* guideline of what they can expect when doing business with you. The pledge should be the basis of your overall customer service philosophy.

Start your customer service pledge internally, and make it something used only by you. From there, you can create an external (public) customer service pledge.

Put it in writing

How do you create a customer pledge? Here are a few simple steps you can follow to get going:

1. **Answer a few general questions about how you really feel about customers (be honest!):**

   - How do you view your customers? Do you know them personally or speak with them on the phone, or are they anonymous?

   - How important are customers to you and your business?

   - How important is repeat business?

   - What are you willing to do for customers every single day?

   - What are you *not* willing to do for your customers?

2. **Define realistic parameters of how you plan to communicate with your customers every day, as shown in these two examples:**

   - *How can customers contact you? Can they*

     - Send email 24 hours a day?

     - Call a toll-free phone number and leave a message 24 hours a day, or call a long-distance number during set business hours?

     - Send or post a message on any social media platform 24/7?

     - Write a letter and send it by snail mail (through the U.S. Postal Service)?

- *When and how will you respond to customers?*
  - Immediately when you respond by email?
  - Within 24 hours (or less) when you respond by phone or email; or within 30 minutes when you respond on social media?

3. **Identify what, if anything, is special about the way you treat customers.**

   For example, do you call customers personally to make sure that they received their orders? Or do you invite them to regular online sessions to discuss how your products or services could improve?

4. **Draft a written document detailing your customer service pledge for your internal use.**

   The document can consist of a short list of bullets or several paragraphs based on your previous answers. This guideline is your personal reminder of how you incorporate customers into your business every day.

5. **Write a pledge to your customer.**

   The pledge, which can be as general or specific as you choose, should reflect your internal customer service philosophy but be a written document that can be read and judged by the customer about how your business responds. You can find sample pledges online from other companies, including one from Zappos at https://zapposforgood.org.

Putting Policies in Place

As you might expect, creating your customer service pledge is only the beginning of the customer care policy. To manage your online business successfully and legitimately, you have to put several policies in place. The government mandates some policies, and others are the result of common sense to minimize confusion for yourself, your employees, and the people with whom you do business. For example, when working with franchise organizations, one of the most critical components of doing business is the *policy manual,* a small booklet filled with written policies establishing an unwavering set of guidelines and procedures for operating. The policy manual serves as an easy reference tool when you have questions about how to operate.

Policies are equally important to customers, employees, and vendors. Although you don't have to create a formal manual filled with your policies, you must write them down somewhere. In many cases, you should also publish them on your website, to protect yourself from misunderstandings and reassure your customers about how you do business.

Privacy policy

A *privacy policy* details how you collect, treat, and use the information you receive from customers and from other people who visit your website. This policy not only covers information that customers knowingly provide but also applies to the use of *cookies,* or the information files that web servers create to track data about people and the online sites they visit.

In some cases, online businesses are opting to blatantly expose the fact that the website tracks cookies so there is no misunderstanding that data is being collected. For example, the very first time the user visits the site, a pop-up message appears, explaining that the site is tracking cookies and what that means. The visitor must exit out of the message before continuing to the website.

Even if you choose not to use this type of tactic, your privacy policy should clearly state your commitment to customer privacy and data security. It should also include information about options or choices visitors and customers have in how their data is used. When operating a contest or any type of prize giveaway, the rules of the contest would be added to your privacy policy. The Better Business Bureau offers tips for writing an effective privacy policy, and provides a sample policy to use as a template, such as this one from the BBB in St. Louis, Missouri: `www.bbb.org/stlouis/for-businesses/understanding-privacy-policies/sample-privacy-policy`.

REMEMBER

A privacy policy is a requirement for your online business if you're based in the United States. The U.S. Federal Trade Commission (FTC) mandates this policy. The policy must be properly labeled on your website and easily accessible within your site.

Your privacy policy should include these elements as well:

>> A description of *how* you collect information from your site visitors and customers

>> Details of *what* information you collect

>> An explanation of what you do with the information and how and where you store it

>> A disclosure of with whom you might share customer information

>> Instructions for how visitors or customers can change their information or remove it from your records

Your policy on how you handle a customer's credit card data should be in line with the requirements of the Payment Card Industry Data Security Standard (PCI DSS). As an online retailer, you're required to comply with certain regulations for handling and storing sensitive customer data under the PCI DSS, or else you could face a steep financial penalty. The PCI Security Standards Council provides up-to-date information for online retailers. To find out more, visit www.pcisecuritystandards.org.

User agreement or terms and conditions

Increasingly, sites are implementing user agreements. Just like a written contract, this agreement specifies terms or conditions by which you allow visitors or customers to use your site. You might choose to post on your site a static (unchanging) page that simply lists these points. A more legally binding version of this agreement, however, requires visitors to acknowledge that they have read the terms and agree to abide by them. Usually, before visitors are allowed to go to certain areas of your site, download an application, register for a service, or make a purchase, they're forced to click a button verifying that they agree to the terms.

When you're creating your site's terms and conditions, you should include this information:

>> **How visitors or customers can or cannot use your site:** Rules that apply to not only your customers but also your employees, such as posting personal information (phone numbers or physical addresses, for example) on a discussion forum

>> **Who is allowed to view your site:** Whether visitors meet age or U.S. citizenship requirements, for example

>> **Which other policies are in place:** Shipping, returns, or complaint procedures, for example

>> **Legal and liability issues:** For example, details of responsibility by you and third parties for providing information and taking actions, and for specifying geographic location where legal disputes will be settled

Shipping policy

Your shipping policy should clearly explain the details of how and when customer orders are handled and shipped. Although you can determine some conditions of this policy, you must also comply with the FTC's mail or telephone-order merchandise rule.

According to the FTC, your online site must

REMEMBER

>> Ship an order within the time frame you promised at the time of ordering or as stated in your advertising or on your website.

>> Ship a product within 30 days after it's received, unless you specify an earlier time frame.

Most online retailers ship products within 5 to 7 business days at the longest. The exception is when a product is on back order, out of stock, or available for pre-order (in which case, an approximate shipping date is given). The FTC rule sets the maximum limits of what's acceptable for shipping products.

>> Give notice to a consumer as fast as possible whenever you cannot ship that person's product when promised.

>> Include a revised shipping date in the delay notice you send to a customer.

>> Allow a customer to agree to a delay or to cancel an order and provide a description of the time required for a refund.

Return policy

Include in your return policy the conditions under which you allow customers to return a product or decline a service. Will the customer receive a full or partial refund from you? A good policy should protect both you and your customers. Be specific about your return policy so that customers clearly understand (and aren't surprised by) your rules. Your policy should include these elements:

>> **Time limit:** Set the maximum number of days within which a return will be accepted.

>> **Conditions of use:** Maintain the right to reject a return if an item shows obvious signs of use, for example.

>> **Restock fee:** Explain any fees incurred by restocking a returned item.

>> **Exceptions:** Specify any items that cannot be returned.

>> **Shipping responsibility:** Determine who pays for the cost of shipping when a product is returned.

>> **Refunds issued as cash or credit:** Decide whether to issue store credit rather than give cash back.

>> **Third-party rules:** Direct customers to consult the return policies of third-party vendors if you sell their items.

TIP

As e-commerce grows, so does the problem of customers taking advantage of online retailers. Let your return policy protect you by limiting the number of days you agree to accept returns. Customers must have enough time to evaluate products (3 to 5 days is a reasonable length of time) but not use it indefinitely before demanding their money back.

REMEMBER

When you're selling products through a third-party vendor, such as a storefront or an auction site (for example, Etsy.com or eBay), be sure to check whether the company has a mandated return policy. The vendor site's policy can override your internal return policy.

Safety for young users

Whether or not you plan to sell to children, establish a policy about minors. If your site is targeted to children under 13 years old, has a separate section for kids, or is a general site but you know kids access it, your website must comply with the FTC's Children's Online Privacy Protection Act, or COPPA. The policy was updated in 2013 to expand the definition of the types of sites and businesses that must comply. COPPA also specifies additional permissions that must be obtained from parents, especially involving the use of video, social media, and online games or apps. In 2015, the organization initiated the process to further update the parental consent requirements. As you see, COPPA is an evolving standard and it's up to you (and it's absolutely critical) to ensure your website continues to meet all guidelines and legal requirements. See compliance details at `www.business.ftc.gov/documents/bus84-childrens-online-privacy-protection-rule-six-step-compliance-plan-your-business`.

Generally speaking, the COPPA rule requires you to

>> Post a clear and comprehensive privacy policy on your website.

>> Notify parents about how you collect information.

>> Get parental consent before collecting information.

>> Allow parents to see the information you collect about their children and let the parents change or delete details.

>> Maintain the confidentiality, security, and integrity of the information you collect.

Other online policies

Following are other polices you may want to include on your website:

>> **Forum or chat room policies:** In these areas of your site, visitors and customers can share their opinions, ideas, and concerns. If your site offers these communication options, set up some basic guidelines for how you operate each one. Your policy should specify such items as who can partici-pate and whether someone must register (or sign in as a member) first. Also, indicate who is monitoring these activities and in what manner. The policy should clearly specify which type of material is inappropriate for posting, and how and when you might remove it.

>> **Social media:** When you ask customers to engage with you through social media sites, such as Facebook and Twitter, or even on your blog, these external sites should be considered an extension of your business presence. After all, on these sites you might obtain information about your customers, such as contact information upon registration for contests and polls. We recommend that you develop a social media policy that explains how your customers' personal information will or will not be used after it is collected.

>> **Exporting:** If your site sells to customers outside the United States, you might be subject to special government regulations by the Commerce Department and Defense Department and possibly other departments. What you sell (or export) and to which countries you sell might be tightly regulated. If you believe that this is the case with your business, seek advice from your attorney about developing an exporting policy.

>> **Spam:** Depending on your type of business, you can include a spam policy in your privacy policy. This policy states whether or not your site distributes marketing email and how you respond to it.

>> **Endorsement and linking to other sites' policies:** Whether you sell prod-ucts or services from other sites, provide links to sites not owned by you, or allow other sites to link to yours, you're smart to notify customers about it. Your linking policy should simply state how external links are used and whether you endorse the information found on these linked sites. Provide customers with a way to notify you of problems with external sites or violations to your policy.

TIP

As privacy laws increase, countries outside the United States are often leading the way in protecting consumer data. If you have consumers in other countries, you need to understand privacy laws. Even if you're based in the United States, you must comply with privacy laws in any region of the world where your customers live. For example, in 2019, the European Union (EU) implemented the General Data Protection Regulation (GDPR), which gives consumers more power in how and when personal data can be used. Businesses that fail to comply with the policy face steep fines. We provide detailed information on how to comply with the GDPR policy in Book 5, Chapter 1.

Delivering on Your Promises

After you establish your basic principles of operation, you have to deliver on them. *Executing,* or following through, on the policies you create isn't easy, but it's essential for several reasons. These policies represent promises to your customers and determine what customers come to expect from you. Failing to meet these expectations compromises your reputation and, ultimately, eats away at your sales.

Equally important are the consequences when you fail to deliver and then incur a legal liability. The government mandates and monitors several policies. Even a small oversight can land you in hot water with both your customers and federal laws.

Nobody's perfect, and you might fail to deliver on a promise now and then. If you fail, be sure to follow these steps:

1. **Notify your customer immediately.**

2. **Apologize for your mistake.**

3. **Correct the problem.**

4. **Offer a partial or full refund, a free gift, or a discount on future purchases.**

TIP

Get help creating a privacy policy for your website, including shipping and return guidelines, using the privacy policy generator tool from Shopify (find it at www.shopify.com/tools/policy-generator).

Chapter **6**

Setting Up Shop: What You Need for Online Efficiency

For some of us, setting up a new office is part of the fun and excitement of starting a new business. It makes it "real," so to speak. But you should plan your office space also for the practical reasons of budgeting start-up costs, gaining a more efficient and functional work area, and ensuring that you have the adequate tools to build your online business and service your customers. From the chair you sit in to your filing system, you need to spend a little time setting up your office with the correct equipment and software, as well as Internet access. (That last one is obvious, eh?) Spending time up front on your workspace options and business requirements can save you plenty of time — and money — later.

A Floor Plan for Success

You might work from a cramped bedroom in your modest home or in a spacious high-rise office complex. Either way, maximizing your workspace can be an important step toward obtaining true efficiency in your business.

Follow these steps to create a floor plan for your office space:

1. **Make a list of how you will use your space.**

Ask yourself these questions:

- Do I need a desk? If so, how much desk space do I need? What about a standing desk? They're good for posture and they provide storage space beneath, which is often in short supply in smaller startup offices.

- Will I store paperwork and files in a central filing system or use some other method?

- Do I need storage space for inventory? Do I have a dedicated space for packing and shipping products?

- Will customers visit my office?

- Do I need working space for employees?

2. **Make a list of all your office furniture, equipment, and accessories (including office supplies and other items that should be stored but remain accessible).**

REMEMBER

If you're sharing the space with others, make sure that you account for their belongings too. Or, if your office performs double duty as a bedroom or dining room, include on your list the non-work-related furniture that will remain in the room while you work. This is important at tax time when you want to take advantage of a home office deduction. The IRS wants to know exactly what percentage of your home is used exclusively for business purposes.

3. **On a sheet of paper, sketch out the dimensions of the room with lines that represent your walls, and then draw all your furniture and large office equipment in position within those walls.**

Rather than literally draw your furniture, you can draw different shapes and label them to help plan the placement of furniture, equipment, and designated work areas.

4. **Arrange the furniture and office equipment in a way that best meets your needs, based on the list you created in Step 1.**

This arrangement should be based on function.

After your room has been put on paper, based on how you want it to function, you can put the measurements to the test to confirm your furniture and equipment fit (see Figure 6-1). This level of detail may seem like overkill, but it's particularly important if you plan to lease office space (in which case, the less you need, the lower your overhead).

REMEMBER

When you arrange your furniture, address storage needs for your office supplies. If you don't have designated architectural space (such as a closet or built-in bookshelves), you'll have to bring in storage (for example, file cabinets, baskets, and removable shelving).

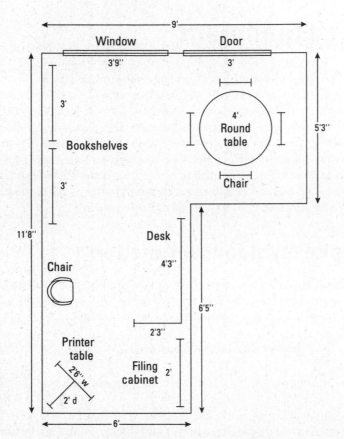

FIGURE 6-1: Precise measurements ensure that everything fits in your space.

5. Measure all pieces of furniture and major equipment.

Using the room dimensions listed on your paper, compare measurements to see whether everything fits. If you run out of room, keep trying different arrangements until you find a floor plan that fits both your needs and your measurements.

TIP

Instead of working from a cramped home office all the time or leasing expensive office space, consider a shared coworking space, such as Regus (www.regus.com) or WeWork (www.wework.com). Often found in larger cities (but quickly spreading to cities of all sizes), coworking spaces have open office areas designed for technology start-ups and other small businesses. These low-cost and flexible alternatives include standard needs, such as meeting spaces and Internet connectivity, and also boast extras, such as access to networking events with peers and investors, and are usually available on an as-needed basis.

Must-Have Equipment

You no longer have to invest several thousand dollars in big, clunky pieces of equipment because both the size and the price of these items have dropped tremendously. For example, cloud-based offerings are readily available, which provide access to web-based products and services at low monthly (or annual) rates. Typically, you don't sign a contract, so you have the flexibility to drop or change services. In addition, free and low-cost applications (apps) for mobile devices such as smartphones and tablets can replace some standard office equipment or services. All this serves as further testament to the power of the Internet, and how easy and affordable it is to start an online business.

Make form follow function

Rather than think about your office equipment in terms of a collection of cartridges and cords, think of each piece in terms of the function it provides. You need access to some key functions (equipment) to run a business.

This list describes the functions most businesses need access to most often:

>> **Printing:** Although most of your correspondence can be conducted online, you still need to print invoices, offline marketing materials, and hard copies (printouts) of items for your files. You can choose from different types of free-standing or desktop printers with various capabilities. Printers can range from $20 to $250. You can eliminate the need for printing invoices entirely by using low-cost online services such as Zoho (www.zoho.com) or PaySimple (www.paysimple.com), that let you invoice customers and manage and collect payments entirely online.

Rather than compare only printer functions, be sure to also compare ink cartridge requirements before you buy a printer. An ink cartridge is often almost as expensive as the printer itself; a $50 printer can require a $30 ink cartridge, for example. Be sure to find out whether the printer requires a particular brand of cartridge and how much the cartridges for that printer cost.

>> **Faxing:** The use and legal acceptance of electronic signatures has decreased dependency on faxes. But some industries and businesses still require a fax. Rather than purchase a separate fax machine, consider signing up for a web-based fax service and receive faxes as attachments to your email. Services such as eFax (www.efax.com) and MyFax (www.myfax.com) offer complete fax solutions for as little as $10 to $17 a month. A business phone system with unified communications features can also handle your fax needs entirely through your phone system.

When comparing online fax services, make sure that you can send and receive faxes from your iPhone, Android, or other smart device. Also be aware of fees charged for overages of incoming and outgoing pages, fees for additional users, and limits on storage time frames and volume for faxes sent or received.

>> **Copying:** Having access to a small copier can be a good investment for your office. When you shop for a copier, decide which features you need:

- Do you want color printing, or is black-and-white print suitable?

- Will you use a *duplexing* feature, which prints both the front and back of the page?

- Is *collating* (automatically stacking and binding papers as they print) a big deal?

Also look for copiers that

- Add large amounts of paper to trays at one time so that you're not continually refilling them

- Have a quick warm-up time (the time it takes the equipment to prepare to print) so that you can start copying quickly

- Are suitable for small to mid-size print job volumes

>> **Scanning:** A scanner enables you to scan images or documents into your computer for manipulation or storage or to send as files or faxes to others. This piece of equipment isn't as much of a requirement as it once was for many types of businesses, but is still particularly useful when you frequently work with photos and other images. Most scanners come with custom software you must install. (Or try the Windows Scanner and Camera Wizard, in the Windows Control Panel.)

TIP

If you need a scanner for only documents or for limited use of image scanning, consider downloading a scanner app for your mobile phone. Apps are available for the iPhone, iPad, and Android smart devices and provide the capability to scan documents or images and then email, fax, or print directly from your phone. You can also share scanned files to Dropbox, Google Drive, or Evernote. (Use this method to track business receipts, too.) Try DocuScan, Scanner Pro, or Tiny Scanner Pro. The apps range in price from $2 to $8. Or you can get a less robust version of a scanner app for free.

» **Mobile communications:** Cellphones have gone from being nice-to-have to being a must-have. Specifically, you need a smartphone that's capable of accessing various applications for maximum efficiency, whether or not you're in your office. You might even require a tablet (such as an iPad), too. These devices are important tools to help you manage your online business. Moreover, online consumers are researching and purchasing products and services directly from mobile devices, so you need to be able to test functionality and accessibility of your website from those devices. Not to mention, one of the benefits of having an online business is that you aren't necessarily hemmed into a certain geographic location; a smart device helps you stay mobile and work from anywhere.

» **Business communications:** Today, you have several options for using a phone in your business. For example, some business owners opt to go without a landline (traditional phone line) and use only a cellular (or mobile) phone. Others save money by sharing a residential line with both their home and business. (This option can be tricky and can come across as unprofessional.) You may consider opting for VoIP (Voice over Internet Protocol), an IP-based option that allows you to share data and voice over a single line. Web-based options, such as Google Voice, Skype, and WebRTC applications, also allow you to make calls over your computer. Most cable companies are offering to bundle your Internet service and voice service. (We discuss Internet connectivity options in more detail at the end of this chapter.) Going this route is often much less expensive than using traditional phone lines and can provide a wider range of functionality. Traditional business phone system vendors also offer cloud-based versions so that you get advanced features without the cost or hassle of managing a complex system. At the end of the day, know that you have lots of options when it comes to how you communicate with your customers.

» **Digital photography:** You might not be used to including a camera in the category of business tools. Yet, in building and maintaining an online business, a digital camera and a video camera might be a requirement, especially if you have an eBay store or any other online retail type of store. Cameras are increasingly important with the growing use of social media as a marketing tool. Sharing pictures on social networks such as Pinterest or Instagram or uploading videos to YouTube, for example, is almost a necessity. At the very least, you need a camera to take product pictures that you can upload to your site. (Some smartphones may be suitable for taking video or pictures to share on social media, but a better quality camera is preferable for high-resolution product pictures for use on your website.)

» **Shredding:** Considering the rise in identity theft (we discuss this in Book 5, Chapter 1), disposing of documents that contain sensitive information — such as billing statements with account numbers or credit card numbers — is more important than ever. Shredding these documents is an easy way to protect your business — and cuts down on storage. A small, portable shredder can be purchased for less than $50; a shredder designed to handle large volumes of paper may cost several hundred dollars or more. It may be worth the extra expense to get a shredder that's hefty enough to dispose of credit cards. Data thieves consider both items to be valuable finds. Alternatively, consider using a mobile shredding service, such as Shred-it (http://www.shredit.com), for particularly large amounts of documents.

REMEMBER

Before destroying all your documents, be mindful of any business records that the IRS requires you to keep for tax purposes. In Book 2, Chapter 4, we review which type of documents must be kept and for how long. Consult a tax advisor if you're not certain about how long you should keep some business records.

TIP

If you can't afford to purchase all your equipment right away, locate a small-business service center close to your office. These centers offer fax, printing, binding, and other services at competitive prices. You can find these service centers in copy stores, such as FedEx Office, or in retail office–supply stores, such as Staples. If you rent a shared office space, or coworking space, these business tools and services are often included as part of the monthly rent.

Revving up with a powerful computer

One important piece of equipment for your new online business is a computer. It's the heart and soul of your office because all your valuable data resides on it and you use it to communicate with folks in all kinds of ways. How do you know whether your existing computer makes the grade now that you're an online entrepreneur? Should you upgrade or buy new? If you buy a new one, how can you be sure that you're investing your dollars wisely? And most importantly, should you buy a PC or a Mac? Although those questions are tricky, they have simple answers.

Jumping into the upgrade-versus-purchase debate

Overall, the cost of purchasing a basic PC computer is outrageously low. You probably receive promotions advertising new desktop computers for $299 — or less. By the time you calculate your time or pay somebody else's labor fee and buy parts, can you truly upgrade an existing computer for that price?

Not so fast. You have to compare apples to apples by looking at more than just the price tag. Compare capabilities. That off-the-shelf computer for $299 may be a bare-bones, stripped-down model — probably no more powerful than that old machine you used for the past couple of years. Sure, the new one might work a bit faster; to get comparable features, though, you most likely have to add memory, hardware, and other applications to truly address your needs. By the time you upgrade your new computer, you may have sufficiently passed its original $300 off-the-shelf price threshold to make you reconsider buying new. Whether or not it's truly a bargain depends on the functionality and power you need.

REMEMBER

If you have the skills and the comfort level to take apart your computer, add components, and then put Humpty Dumpty together again, upgrading can be a cheap and relatively easy solution.

Taking the plunge: Buying new

You might be more comfortable buying a computer with all its parts already assembled. You can still design a custom computer by choosing the options you want and letting a computer retailer customize it for you. Or you can purchase an off-the-shelf machine that's already loaded and ready to go.

How do you decide which computer is right for you? The simplest way to approach this decision is by backing into it. Follow these general guidelines:

1. **Decide how you will use the computer.**

    You're running a business with it, of course. Be specific about which type of activities you're using it for, such as accounting, word processing, keeping a database of customer records, or storing digital photos of your products.

2. **Identify the specific software applications you're using for each of those activities, such as QuickBooks, Microsoft Word, Microsoft Access, or Photoshop.**

    Each of these applications recommends system requirements, including available memory and processor speed.

DESKTOP OR LAPTOP: DECIDING ON A COMPUTER

Even if you're sold on the sleek, compact size of a laptop, consider the following four Cs before you make a final purchase:

- **Cost:** Although desktop computers can be bulky, they're packed with options at rock-bottom prices. Comparatively, you pay for the convenience and size that a laptop offers. It's usually double the price of a desktop with similar capabilities.

- **Capability:** You can run the same applications on both a desktop and a laptop. If you work with a lot of graphics, though, the laptop screen might not do them justice. When you're working in one location, you can connect your laptop to a larger monitor, of course — just remember that the monitor costs extra!

- **Convenience:** Putting a price tag on convenience is difficult. Whether you need to tote your computer from room to room or from city to city, a laptop is your best portable solution.

- **Comfort:** Adjusting to a smaller screen size, a button-size mouse, and a more compact keyboard isn't always easy. Although you can attach a USB mouse or keyboard to a laptop to overcome this problem, you might be more comfortable with the larger components offered on a desktop.

Some laptops are just as powerful and full-featured as desktops. They're slightly larger and heavier, with wider screens and full-size keyboards. Although they can be considered portable, the size and weight put them closer to desktops than laptops.

3. **Match and compare the requirements in Step 2 to the computer you're considering purchasing.**

Look closely at not only the computer's processor but also the hardware and features that come with the computer, including these items:

- Hard drive space
- Operating system (Windows, Mac, Linux/Unix)
- Memory capacity (RAM)
- Networking card (preferably wireless-ready)
- USB (2.0 or 3.0 compatibility)
- Monitor (with the option for a flat screen)

- Keyboard and mouse (wireless, to avoid clutter on your desktop)
- External speakers
- Installed software

4. **Compare the support service and warranties.**

Does the manufacturer or retailer offer customer support? Be sure to find out whether this service is included in the cost of your purchase, and whether it limits the amount of support you can receive before a fee kicks in. Find out exactly what is covered under the warranty and for how long. You might have to purchase an extended warranty to cover some computer parts. Keep in mind that some manufacturers require you to ship back your hardware versus sending a repairperson to your location. Before making a purchase, determine whether on-site support is important to you.

What about a Mac?

Computer users are always debating which personal computer is better for business owners: a PC or a Mac (Macintosh). The PC is usually associated with an operating system (OS) that runs Microsoft Windows; the Mac OS was created by Apple. For a long time, PCs seemed to be the preferred appliance for businesses, and Macs were favored by graphic artists. Today, either is acceptable for business use. With software compatibility for the Mac expanding, and Apple's explosive growth from the popularity of the iPhone and the iPad, business folks seem less reticent to use a Mac.

We don't want to get into a debate of which is better — that's for you to decide. But we do want to make you aware that you have options when purchasing a desktop computer.

Tools for Your Desktop

Your computer is unpacked. You're ready to explore a world of business opportunity. Before you dive in, make sure that you have these basic — but necessary — applications on your desktop, ready to run.

REMEMBER

Inventory the built-in (supplied) programs to determine which ones work for you and which ones don't. Using the built-in software can save you money, but don't sacrifice your need for functionality by using an inferior product. Buy what you need to get your jobs done.

Searching for a web browser

Your *web browser* is the software that lets you travel from site to site across the Internet. You enter a site's address, or *URL (Uniform Resource Locator)*, and the browser displays the site or page on your computer screen. For an online business, having a good web browser is an absolute requirement.

Keep in mind that a browser is typically already included when you purchase a computer, although which browser varies based on your operating system. You can always download a different browser to your computer or update an older version of your existing browser. Get started downloading the browser of your choice by going to these websites:

>> **Google Chrome:** www.google.com/chrome

>> **Microsoft Internet Explorer:** https://windows.microsoft.com/en-us/ internet-explorer/download-ie

>> **Microsoft Edge (for use with Windows 10):** https://www.microsoft.com/ en-us/windows/microsoft-edge/microsoft-edge

>> **Mozilla Firefox:** www.mozilla.org

>> **Opera:** www.opera.com

>> **Safari:** www.apple.com/safari

TIP

Put access to all the major browsers on your desktop, especially as you begin creating and maintaining your business website. Then you can check for consistency among page views displayed with different browsers. For example, Internet Explorer might display your web page in a slightly different way than Mozilla. The difference might be subtle, or it might cause the loss of pertinent product information or graphics. (We talk about these and other web design details in Book 3.)

Sending and receiving messages with email

Email is a painless way to communicate with customers, vendors, and employees. Unfortunately, the popularity of this communication tool has led to a bigger problem: How do you keep up with, sort, store, and reply to all these messages? And what's the best way to combat spam, viruses, and other harmful or annoying applications to your inbox?

You can resolve these issues by finding a good email program. In addition to acting as an organizer and a system for filtering junk mail, your email system should be simple to use and pack a few added features.

One of these email programs might meet your communication objectives:

>> **Thunderbird:** The email program designed by Mozilla automatically detects and sorts junk mail. Packed with features, it also offers an enhanced three-column view of your email. Download Thunderbird for free at Mozilla.org (www.mozilla.org/products/thunderbird).

>> **Gmail:** Google Gmail is a popular, free, web-based email option. Gmail boasts one of the highest storage capacities (which means you don't have to delete old mail to make room for new mail) as well as offers some other cool features. In addition to one of the best spam-blocking capabilities, it can automatically sort messages based on conversations and uses tabs to further sort and categorize messages. Gmail also includes built-in chat. You can access your Gmail from your mobile phone by redirecting your phone's web browser to a Google app.

TIP

For an additional charge ranging from $6 to $25 per year (per user), Gmail offers businesses access to a suite of other business applications. You get a business domain for your email, plus voice and video services, calendar functionality, and document-editing capabilities, for example. You can find all the details at http://gsuite.google.com.

>> **Outlook or Outlook Express:** Microsoft created two versions of its email messaging system:

- *Outlook 365:* Part of the Microsoft Office 365 suite of applications designed for businesses, Outlook 365 is the more advanced email program that is suitable for larger businesses.

- *Outlook:* A personal version of Outlook is available if you have basic requirements. The program's limited functions are suitable for your small or start-up business.

To compare features and download the most recent version, go to the Microsoft website (http://products.office.com/compare-all-microsoft-office-products).

Using document-viewing software and other useful applications

As you begin using the Internet and your computer to communicate, you might find that several programs come in handy. Frequently, you receive a document as an attachment to an email message. Depending on the program the sender used to create the document, it can be in any of a number of formats: a Word file, a PDF (Portable Document Format) file, or an image saved in one of a slew of formats, such as a TIF, GIF, BPM, or JPEG. Even if you don't have exactly the same program as the sender of the file, you can still open and view these files if you have the right software.

We suggest installing the following programs on your desktop so that you're prepared to receive and view information in a variety of formats:

» **Adobe Acrobat (Reader):** *PDF files* are electronic documents that you might receive in email or download from a website. To view, print, or search PDF files, you must have the free Adobe reader software loaded on your computer. Depending on your needs, you may benefit from other services offered as part of the Adobe solution, including Creative Cloud for business (which starts at $34 per month). To get the free reader software, download it at the Adobe Acrobat website (www.adobe.com).

» **File compression:** When you send or receive large files, you should have the capability to compress the files so that you can more efficiently send them by email. You can purchase a tool such as WinZip, which allows you to zip (compress) and unzip files and complete folders and is available for $29.95. But both Windows and Mac OS X come with a compatible compression program built-in.

» **File storage and sharing programs:** You'll want to back up your important files as well as access files from remote locations. In addition, you may need an easy way to share files between employees or with clients and vendors. For cloud-based storage, check out Apple iCloud, Google Drive, or Microsoft OneDrive. One of the most popular solutions is Dropbox (www.dropbox.com), which has a basic free service and a for-fee service (starting at just over $100 per year per user, which can be paid monthly) that has more storage, additional features, and increased security.

» **Movie and audio player:** If you ever visit news sites, such as CNN, you probably come across video or audio clips in news stories that you can view or listen to online. More websites are offering audio and video clips, whether as part of an online small-business training course or a preview of a newly released Hollywood movie. To hear and see these clips, you must have a viewer or player installed on your computer. Microsoft includes Windows Media Player as a built-in player for the Windows operating system.

REMEMBER

Apple makes the easy-to-install player QuickTime Player, which works on either a PC or a Mac. To install the player, follow the download instructions at the Apple website (www.apple.com/quicktime/download). Or try RealPlayer, which also works on multiple platforms. It's available at www.real.com. Adobe Flash Player is another browser plug-in that you may need, if it's not already installed (for example, Google Chrome has Flash Player built in and will automatically update new versions). To install it, visit www.get.adobe.com/flashplayer.

Your Essential Software Toolkit

Most businesses require some robust software programs to handle their core business activities, such as generating printed letters and invoices, juggling finances, designing marketing pieces, and making sales presentations. As you might expect, your choice of business software is almost endless. Some essential programs, however, are important to add to your computer now.

TIP

When you buy a new computer, be aware that some basic software packages, such as Microsoft Works, are often included with the system. If the included software isn't your first choice, negotiate with the salesperson to trade for different software. Or if you order online, look for deals that let you add software programs at the time of purchase for less than the full retail price. If you're currently enrolled as a student or an educator, you may also qualify for a discounted version of some software packages.

This list describes some core software packages you should consider:

>> **Word processing software:** Working with documents, either creating or reading them, is standard procedure in business. A few word processing software solutions are available. For instance, your computer might come with WordPad, a simple, easy-to-use program. For extended features, however, try a more advanced program, such as Microsoft Word (`www.microsoft.com/office`) or Microsoft Office 365 for business, which is available as a cloud-based solution for as little as $5 per month, per user. WordPerfect (`www.wordperfect.com`) is another affordable option, as is the popular Google Docs (`http://gsuite.google.com`).

>> **Graphics or imaging software:** Any time you work with images, graphics software becomes a necessity. You can use this software for everything from creating logos to editing digital photo images. Your computer might come with a paint program that allows you to draw images and do basic photo editing. Depending on your needs, though, you can also explore more advanced graphics software, such as Paint Shop Pro (`www.paintshoppro.com`) or Adobe InDesign (`www.adobe.com/indesign`). Free alternatives are available, including GIMP (`www.gimp.org`), which is available for the PC and the Mac.

>> **Presentation software:** This type of software allows you to create a professional presentation by using text and graphics and applying special effects to the content. PowerPoint (`www.office.microsoft.com/powerpoint`), part of Microsoft Office 365, is one of the most recognized presentation software products. Its ease of use makes it a good match for use in your business. You can create information on individual slides that can be viewed one by one or run in sequence in a slide show. Good alternatives to PowerPoint are Keynote for Mac (`www.apple.com/mac/keynote`) and Prezi (`www.prezi.com`), which is easy to use and includes animation and sound.

TIP

Many of these software programs can be expensive. Before investing, look for trial versions, which allow you to use the full program for free for a limited time, or a cloud-based option, which provides an inexpensive, monthly pay-as-you-go plan. In this way, you can find out if you really need the program before spending a lot of money on it.

Connectivity: Today's Internet Options and More

Considering the variety of Internet service choices you have and the number of providers in business, now is certainly a great time to start an online business. You can select a plan that truly meets your needs and doesn't break the bank. One area that you should *not* skimp on for your online business is your Internet service. After all, it (along with hosting for your site) is the backbone of your business.

An Internet broadband connection works by carrying many different channels of data over a single wire, or source. The continued growth in e-commerce is credited to the ever-expanding number of consumers who have access to a broadband connection in their homes, which makes shopping online faster and easier.

Three types of Internet connections are commonly available:

>> **DSL:** Digital Subscriber Service gives you a high-speed connection by using a normal phone line and digital modem capabilities. Don't worry about your phone line being constantly busy, though: After special equipment is installed on your end, your phone line can be used simultaneously for accessing the Internet and for regular voice communication. Because other options, such as fiber and cable, are more common, DSL is used less frequently.

>> **Fiber:** Fiber is one of the fastest and most advanced connections available. It uses fiber-optic cable as opposed to copper cable. Similar to DSL, not all areas have fiber-optic cable as part of the infrastructure, so availability is still limited in many areas. However, Google Fiber is making its service options available in more communities. You can get 1 gigabit of speed, with unlimited data, for $70 per month. It also includes one terabyte of storage. This is an incredible option for any online business!

>> **Cable:** Much like DSL and Fiber, cable provides a very high-speed connection. Typically considered faster than DSL, but nowhere close to the speed of fiber.

Cable modems use *shared* bandwidth, whereas DSL and fiber use *dedicated* bandwidth. The shared cable network is associated with a higher security risk. We discuss these and other security issues in Book 5.

REMEMBER

Although pricing plans for cable and DSL fluctuate, plan to spend at least $40 to $60 per month. With the increasing demand for faster service, companies are charging more, but bundled services (that combine connectivity for the web and voice service) may offer a break in pricing. Shop around for the best deal before you settle on a service provider, and check to see if Google Fiber is available in your city for an even better deal.

2
Legal and Accounting

Contents at a Glance

Chapter **1**

Minding the Law

One of the first things you discover in owning a business is that you cannot avoid certain specific legal requirements. An Internet business is subject to not only traditional laws imposed on any company but also further regulation. As with the rest of the Net, these rules change quickly, and the burden to keep up is on you.

In this chapter, we review the basic laws so that you can start setting up shop.

REMEMBER

We're not lawyers, and laws differ from state to state. So if you're the least bit concerned, consult a local attorney to answer any of your questions.

Keeping Your Business Legal

Whether you have an online business or an offline business, you must do certain things to set yourself up and operate legally. If you already have a business that you're taking online, this advice is probably old news. But if you're starting your online business from scratch, read on.

Admittedly, quite a few business-related laws exist. As an online business, you must comply with any government regulations specific to e-commerce, as determined by the Federal Trade Commission (FTC). In addition to all federally imposed regulations, you're also subject to any applicable state, county, and city laws. If you're selling to companies or individuals outside the United States, you must also comply with International Trade Law. On its website, the U.S. Small Business Administration (SBA) provides good information about business law and regulations, including specific legal requirements when launching your business and then ongoing requirements after you're up and running. You can find this information as part of the site's many resources, including the "Business Guide," when you visit www.sba.gov/business-guide.

At first pass, these legal obligations can be a bit overwhelming. Like everything else in business, though, you take one step at a time and, before you know it, you have a handle on the situation. The same is true with the legalities of operating an online business. Start out on the right foot by getting up to speed with these basic requirements.

TIP

Depending on the type of business you're conducting over the Internet, additional laws or regulations might apply to you. Several good sources to help you research this information include

>> A trade association in your industry

>> Your local Chamber of Commerce

>> State and local government websites

HEALTH DEPARTMENT PERMIT

If you manufacture, package, or distribute food-related products as part of your online business, you need a permit from the health department. The permit (along with any necessary on-site inspections) is handled by your city or county health department. There may be additional regulations or restrictions concerning the type of facility from which you make and package your food, including home kitchens. Sometimes regulations are based on sales volume of the food product. The legalities of selling food are specific. It is important to complete your due diligence and adhere to the requirements. You might also be subject to certain regulations of the Food and Drug Administration (FDA). For instance, if you're making homemade jelly and selling it over the Internet, you might be required to meet certain labeling standards that detail ingredients and nutritional information. You can obtain a complete food-labeling guide, along with other information about starting and operating an online food business on the FDA website (www.fda.gov/food).

You can get a small-business food-labeling exemption if you don't exceed certain annual sales levels or if you don't make nutritional claims in your advertising.

Federal tax identification number

If you have employees or your business is a corporation or partnership, you need a federal tax ID. Officially known as an employer identification number (EIN), this 9-digit number is used to identify a company whenever its owner files certain forms and tax returns.

TIP

You can apply for a federal tax ID via the online EIN application at the Internal Revenue Service (IRS) website at www.irs.gov/Businesses/Small-Businesses-&-Self-Employed/Employer-ID-Numbers-EINs. It's free to apply online and you get an EIN immediately — no waiting! Or if you prefer, you can download the required Form SS-4 and submit the application by fax or regular U.S. mail.

REMEMBER

The EIN is requested on many different types of business documents, from bank accounts to loan applications. If you don't have a federal tax ID number, you can use your Social Security number instead.

THE $500,000 QUESTION: HOW DO YOU PROTECT CUSTOMER DATA?

The Payment Card Industry Data Security Standard (PCI DSS) is a set of guidelines for all merchants who accept credit cards, including e-commerce merchants. PCI DSS helps ensure that merchants keep customer data secure when they're collecting, processing, and storing personal and financial information.

The release and continued maintenance of this standard is in response to the ongoing increase in identity theft and stolen credit card numbers obtained from Internet sites. Credit card companies, under pressure to tighten security measures, collaborated to issue this worldwide security standard.

Failure to comply with the standard can result in some outrageous penalties, including fines of up to $500,000 per incident or possible cancellation of your merchant account. Overall, the measure to increase the protection of your customers' data is a good one. Unfortunately, it's one more regulation that even very small companies must comply with to avoid penalties. Among the requirements of the standard, companies must

- Install and maintain a firewall configuration to protect data
- Not use vendor-supplied defaults for system passwords and other security passwords

(continued)

(continued)

- Protect stored data

- Encrypt the transmission of cardholder data and sensitive information across public networks

- Use and regularly update antivirus software

- Develop and maintain secure systems and applications

- Restrict business access to data based on job description and needs

- Assign a unique ID to each person who accesses the computer used for financial data

- Track and monitor all access to network resources and cardholder data

- Regularly test security systems and processes

- Maintain a policy that addresses information security

The PCI Security Standards Council (www.pcisecuritystandards.org) manages and publishes the most current guidelines for compliance with the standards, including guidelines for small merchants and for accepting mobile payments with smartphones and tablets. Payment card companies, however, are responsible for enforcing compliance with the standards.

As a merchant, and as part of the validation process, you might have to complete a PCI DSS Self-Assessment Questionnaire (SAQ). You can access the questionnaire by visiting www.pcisecuritystandards.org/pci_security/completing_self_assessment. For specific information about compliance, including information on specific payment card company requirements, go to www.pcisecuritystandards.org/program_training_and_qualification/payment_application-qsa_certification.

Resale certificate

If you sell any type of product, your state might require that you collect and pay a sales tax on every sale. If so, you need to apply for a resale certificate (often associated with buying wholesale). Be aware that the amount of sales tax to collect, the dates the tax is due, and the rules of collection vary by state. For that reason, you should check the regulations for the state in which your business is physically located. Because exceptions to the rules often exist or other details can be difficult to understand, also consider talking with a certified public accountant.

Business bank account

When you first begin to operate a business, you might be tempted to run all your money through an existing personal account. Trust us: This technique happens quite often and is rarely a good idea. Why do people do it? If you're just testing out your business idea, opening a separate account might seem unnecessary. Or perhaps you view it as a way to save some money on bank fees. Unless you plan to maintain your idea strictly as a hobby, however, you need to open a business bank account immediately. Otherwise, it becomes too easy to commingle personal and business expenses. How can you possibly separate them if they share a bank account?

When you open a business account, the bank needs specific information, such as a copy of your business license, your federal tax ID number or Social Security number, and, possibly, proof of incorporation if you want your legally incorporated business name on the account.

TIP

Consider opening two bank accounts: one for all your daily transactions and the other for dealing with sales tax, employee withholding, and other regular tax payments. Keeping these items separate and using simple money transfers from one account to another can help you keep your payroll and employee finances separate and easier to manage. Meet with your bank's manager to find out what perks may be available when opening one or more business accounts.

Employee forms

When you hire others to work for your company (even if you are your only employee), the IRS wants to be in the know, and that involves forms, of course. You should be familiar with several forms required by the IRS:

>> **Form W-9:** When you hire independent contractors (nonemployees), consultants, or self-employed individuals to perform work, have them complete IRS Form W-9. This form provides you with the information you need to report earnings to the IRS and generate a Form 1099 (see the next bullet point) that reports their earnings at the end of the year.

TIP

When you're hiring independent contractors, be sure to check the IRS definition of what constitutes a contractor (versus an employee). For instance, if you have workspace available at your office for the contractor or require the person to work a set schedule, you could cause an independent contractor to be considered an employee. If that's the case, you're responsible for withholding taxes. You can even be fined (with interest) if you don't withhold wages and the mistake is discovered later.

REMEMBER

>> **Form 1099:** If you hire someone (other than an employee or a corporation) to do work for your company, you need to send that person a Form 1099 at the end of the year. (You are legally mandated to provide a copy of the form to the recipient by January 31 of the following year.) You're required to complete this form only if you made one or more payments to the individual totaling $600 or more within the tax year. If you're not incorporated and provide a service for another company, you receive a Form 1099.

If you barter or trade services or products with another company, the IRS expects you to report, on Form 1099, the value of that trade as income.

>> **Form W-4:** If you have employees, they must fill out Form W-4s so that you can withhold, report, and deposit their correct amount of employment-related taxes. You're responsible for *withholding,* or taking out, money for income tax, Social Security, Medicare, and federal unemployment taxes (FUTA).

>> **Form W-2:** By the last day of January following the end of each calendar year, you're responsible for sending this form to your employees. A W-2 reports the total income an employee earned from you during the preceding calendar year, along with the amount of money you withheld for various taxes during the year.

Zoning for Business (at Home)

Your home is the ideal place to start an online business. Working out of your house makes business setup quick and easy, and it equates to low overhead. Before you convert that spare bedroom into an office, however, you need to determine whether you're allowed to operate a business from your home.

The answer typically comes down to a single word: *zoning.* Most cities and towns have zoning ordinances that define how a particular piece of land or group of properties can be used. They further specify which types of activities can occur there. For example, some neighborhoods are zoned for residential, which means that only single-family homes can be built in that area. Other areas might allow multifamily (apartments) residential. In the area of commercial or business use, the zoning becomes more complicated because businesses are often separated by types of industry. An area might also be labeled *mixed use,* which allows both residential and some types of limited commercial activity.

How do you decide whether your residential neighborhood is zoned for business? Check with your city's licensing or planning department. When you provide your address, the city clerk can tell you whether your neighborhood has any restrictions that would prevent you from opening your business.

Some cities and counties make zoning maps, along with a detailed list of city ordinances, available online. If your city has a website, start there first.

Assuming that all goes well and you find no restrictive ordinances, you'll be in business quickly. But sometimes this isn't the case and your home-based business isn't allowed. Then you have to ask for a *variance,* or an exception to the zoning ordinance. Fortunately, because millions of people are working from home now, many cities have already established criteria for such exceptions. Even if your neighborhood isn't specifically zoned for business, therefore, your city might allow small home-based businesses if they meet certain conditions.

To grant a variance, cities and counties want assurance that your business doesn't have

>> High-volume street traffic

>> Increased activity (by customers) in and out of the home

>> Large trucks on-site (delivery trucks or company vehicles)

>> Required additional parking

>> Exterior signage

>> The use or storage of harmful chemicals

>> Warehousing of a large number of products

>> The on-site sale of products to the public (such as what takes place at retail locations)

>> Employees (usually more than three or four) working on-site

These conditions are in place primarily to ensure that your business activities do not adversely affect your neighbors nor have an effect on residential property values. Luckily, most Internet-based endeavors don't create such nuisances. Be sure to reiterate this point with city planners when you're pursuing a variance request for your business.

If your business involves storing and shipping large numbers of products, you might want to lease an off-site storage facility or arrange to have your products shipped from a distribution facility. It not only eases concerns from city officials initially but is also a good preventive measure to keep your neighbors happy.

Increasingly, zoning isn't the only concern when you're starting a home-based business. Many cities are now requiring home occupational permits. If you want to operate from your home, you're required to have this permit — no matter what your business. The good news is that certain occupations or business types are often automatically granted permits (and computer or Internet-related businesses are almost always included). However, you might have to qualify for a permit based on a long list of conditions that are similar to the criteria used in seeking a zoning variance (noise, traffic, on-site sales, and employees, for example). When you apply for a home occupational permit, you might also be asked to provide a list of all your neighbors and their addresses. The city then sends notice of your intent to operate a business from your home and gives your neighbors an opportunity to object. Even with this caveat, obtaining a home occupational permit can be much easier (and faster) than having to get a zoning variance granted. When you apply for the permit, expect to pay a small fee, ranging from $1 to $75.

WARNING

A home occupational permit doesn't take the place of a business license. To operate legally, you must have both. See the next section to find out how to obtain the all-important business license.

Is that all you have to do? Not quite. Even if your home clears municipal zoning ordinances and home occupational permits, other obstacles can stop you from operating a home-based business, or alter the way in which you operate:

>> **Your homeowners' association:** Residents of subdivisions, condominiums, and some neighborhood communities often have homeowners' associations. If you're in this group, some restrictive covenants (or rules) probably govern your home and what you do to it, with it, and in it. The rules might also cover operating a business from your house. Read your covenants or bylaws carefully because even if your city doesn't restrict your business use of your home, these covenants might. If a problem exists, you can always go to the board of directors that manages your homeowners' association and try to obtain an exception.

>> **Landlords:** If you lease an apartment or house, the rental agreement might prohibit you from conducting any business activity on the property. Review your lease thoroughly for clauses that specify how you can use the property.

WARNING

If you choose to ignore legal restrictions concerning how your property can be used, you're taking a considerable risk. If your business activity is discovered, city officials could shut down your business, your homeowner's association could impose steep fines (and even put a lien on your home), or your landlord could evict you.

Obtaining Business Licenses

Regardless of where your business is located, you need a license to operate it. A *business license* is a piece of paper granting you the right to do business within a city, county, or state. Licenses are typically valid for a one- or two-year period and are nontransferable. (If you sell the business, the license is void.) You have to pay a fee when you apply for your license. The amount is often based on the type of business you operate and can range from $25 to several thousand dollars.

TIP

You (and not a city clerk) should specify which business category you fall under when you apply for your license, because a category specifically for an Internet-based, or *e-commerce*, business might not exist. Instead, you have to select a broad category based on the specific activity conducted through your site. Some categories can require steep licensing fees and might not, in fact, apply to you. Scour the entire list and the accompanying fees. Then choose the one most related to your business and with the lowest fee.

In addition to obtaining a city-issued license, you might be required to have a license for the county in which you're operating your business. This license is similar to a city license but is often less restrictive and less expensive. Be aware that some occupations (building contractors, realtors, and other professional service providers, for example) might further require that you obtain a state license. Although you probably don't need a state license to operate your online business, you can double-check by visiting your state's website.

TIP

To help you find out where to go for your city and county licenses, the SBA offers an online list for all 51 states, plus Puerto Rico, Guam, and the U.S. Virgin Islands. You can find the Where to Obtain Business Licenses list at the SBA.gov site: www. sba.gov/starting-business/business-licenses-permits/state-licenses-permits.

Minding the Law

IN THIS CHAPTER

» Deciding which business form is best suited to you

» Establishing yourself as a sole proprietorship

» Evaluating alternative legal structures

» Operating by the rules of incorporation

» Modifying your ownership structure

Chapter **2**

Choosing the Right Foundation: From Partnerships to Corporations

At the top of every start-up checklist is a line item that reads "Establish the formal structure of your business." This line means that you start by deciding how you want your company legally organized. You can be the sole owner or have 2 partners or 50 shareholders. Each form of business has definite advantages and disadvantages, depending on your goals for the business.

Read the information we provide in this chapter about all these options before making your final decision.

Strategizing for the Best Organization

Choosing how to set up your business is easier than you might think. Considering that you have only four primary choices, the odds of narrowing the selection quickly are in your favor. Yet one of the most frequently asked questions when someone is starting a business is "Which structure is best for me?" To get started, you need to resolve four key issues:

>> **Ownership:** Deciding who ultimately owns or controls your company is a primary influence on your choice of legal structure. A second factor is the number of people who control the business. Some forms of business are limited by both the number of owners and the type of owner (individual or corporation) it can have.

>> **Liability:** You must choose where you want the legal responsibility for the business to reside. Deciding whether you're comfortable accepting full liability for the actions of the company or whether you need the protection (or veil) of a corporation is an important choice.

>> **Taxes:** Each of the business structures is subject to various forms of taxation. For instance, you might pay a self-employment tax based on your earnings. Or you could be taxed on the dividends paid out to all owners from the business. In the case of one type of incorporation, you might even experience *double taxation* — paying tax as the business and again as an individual stockholder.

TIP

Because the tax issues are so complex, talk with a tax attorney or certified public accountant to determine which option best fits your specific circumstances.

>> **Funding:** The way in which you finance the growth of your company can play a significant role in determining its structure. If you're *bootstrapping* (self-financing) the company, any of the structures might work for you. However, if you seek outside financing from angel investors or venture capitalists, you need the option of having stock available for distribution. If another business entity plans to own stock in your company, your choice of business structure is severely limited. See Book 1, Chapter 4 for more info on how to fund your business.

Now that you understand these four primary areas of concern, you should have a better idea of where your specific requirements fit in. To make your final decision, read the detailed descriptions in the following sections for each business entity.

Operating Alone as a Sole Proprietor

If you're interested in simplicity, look no further. A *sole proprietorship* is recognized as the quickest, easiest, and least expensive method of forming a business. The main caveat is that only one person can operate as a sole proprietor. You and the business are literally the same entity. The upside of that arrangement is the ease of getting up and running. With the mere act of conducting business (and obtaining a license), you're considered a sole proprietor.

The downside of being a sole proprietor is the potential legal ramifications. Because you and the company are one, you're fully accountable for the losses of the business along with any legal matters. Whether the business is involved with lawsuits or problems with creditors, you're personally liable. No corporate protection is available — your personal assets (such as your home) can be sold and your personal bank accounts used to pay off creditors.

As a sole proprietor, you're also responsible for all taxes. The profits and losses of the business are listed on Schedule C on your personal tax return. And you pay self-employment tax (Schedule SE), which is a combined Social Security and Medicare tax. The self-employment tax is calculated as a percentage of your earnings; as of the 2019 tax year, the percentage is 15.3 percent (12.4 percent for Social Security and 2.9 percent for Medicare). Up to $128,400 of your self-employment income is subject to the Social Security tax, and all your income is subject to the Medicare tax.

In addition to obtaining a business license and paying taxes, you must address two other topics if you're considering operating as a sole proprietor:

>> Registering your company name

>> Forming a sole proprietorship with your spouse

We discuss these topics in the next two sections.

Fictitious name registration

Unless you choose to operate your company under your exact legal name (or use your last name), you need to register a *fictitious* name with the state. The name of your company is different from that of its legal owner (you). Suppose that your name is John Smith and you decide to name your company Online Information Services. By registering that fictitious name, you become John Smith *dba* (doing business as) Online Information Services. Your business name should then appear on your checking account, business license, and any other legal documents.

TIP

Check with your city and state governments to determine how you should register your fictitious name. Some states require only that you submit an application and pay a small filing fee. Others mandate that you publish in a newspaper your intent to use the fictitious name before you begin to use it.

Marriage and the sole proprietorship

Togetherness is a wonderful thing, as you and your spouse might have found out when you got married. You and your spouse might even want to operate a business together. Does this mean that you no longer qualify for the simplified structure of a sole proprietorship? That depends.

The IRS legally recognizes a sole proprietor as having only one owner. If a spouse is working for the company, the IRS expects you to treat that person as an employee (which means that you have to pay payroll taxes). Alternatively, if your spouse has an active ownership role in the company, the IRS treats the business as a partnership (which means that both of you are taxed separately on the income). However, some tax advisors suggest that you can still file as a sole proprietor even if your spouse participates in the company. When you file a Schedule C on your joint tax return, all business income is viewed as one sum for both of you, although the IRS still views your business as belonging to a single owner.

To avoid paying payroll taxes, you may choose to classify your spouse as a *volunteer.* Your spouse is then only occasionally active in the business and doesn't get credit toward Social Security.

WARNING

If the IRS determines that your spouse works regular, consistent hours, it could mean instant classification as an employee. At that point, you might be responsible for paying a hefty sum of back taxes and penalties. Always consult a professional tax advisor to ensure that you're operating within the allowable classifications designated by the IRS.

Sharing the Load with a Partnership

In some ways, a *general partnership* is similar to a sole proprietorship: It's relatively simple and inexpensive to form. Issues of liability and taxes reside fully with its owners. The primary difference with a partnership is that it allows you to have multiple owners.

Although the terms of this type of partnership can be based on a verbal agreement, you should spell out the conditions in writing, for two reasons:

>> **Dispute resolution:** Having the specific details of your original agreement in writing is handy if a dispute arises between you and your partner (or partners).

>> **Proof of partnership:** If something happens and a written document cannot be produced, you and your partners are assumed to share equally in all aspects of the business. Proving otherwise in a court of law, or to the IRS, could prove difficult.

When you define your partnership, the basic agreement should address these areas:

>> **Structure:** Shows what percentage of the company is owned by each partner

>> **Control:** Defines which partner is responsible for which part of the daily management of the company

>> **Profits:** Details the division of profits and losses and the time frame for distributing profits to the partners

A partnership arrangement brings up certain questions that you must consider at the beginning of a partnership:

>> How much money and time will each partner contribute, and how will decisions for the company be made?

>> What happens if one partner stops contributing, can no longer be actively involved, or wants out of the partnership?

>> Can you buy out the interest of another partner, or will the partnership be dissolved automatically when a dispute cannot be settled?

>> How will ownership be transferred if one partner dies or is involved in a divorce (especially if the partners are married to each other)?

>> How will an owner's share in the company be redistributed?

These questions are tough to answer. You probably don't want to believe that anything will go wrong between you and your partners. Unfortunately, for one reason or another, partnerships go sour all the time.

The most successful partnerships are those in which issues such as these were openly discussed and agreed on up front. Likewise, individual owners who have survived a failed partnership have done so because a written agreement was in place. Considering that you and your partners are personally liable for the actions of your company, a formal partnership agreement is your best chance for avoiding problems.

Choosing the Right Foundation: From Partnerships to Corporations

Limited Liability Company

If you prefer entering into a business using an entity that offers a bit more legal protection to you and your partners than a partnership, a *limited liability company (LLC)* might interest you. (Although some states also recognize a limited liability partnership, or LLP, the LLC is more common.)

The LLC combines the flexibility of a partnership with the formal structure and legal protection provided by a corporation. As in a general partnership, income is passed through to the individual partners, and profits can be distributed according to your agreement. (Note that profit doesn't have to be split equally among partners.) An LLC allows you to have an unlimited number of partners, and permits you to raise money for the business by taking on investors (including other corporations) as members. Additionally, members or partners of the LLC aren't personally liable for the actions of the corporation.

If you choose to form an LLC, you have to file with the state, although the requirements typically aren't as stringent as they are in a corporation. (You're not required to maintain bylaws or keep minutes of annual board meetings, for example.) However, the requirements for forming an LLC vary by state, so you have to research those requirements for the state in which you file.

Making It Official with Incorporation

One option to consider when you're establishing a business is whether to incorporate. A *corporation* is a legal entity that's separate from the individuals who create or work for it. Stock in a corporation is issued to individuals or to other business entities that form the ownership of the company.

Different flavors of corporations

Depending on your situation, you can choose one of two types of corporation:

>> **C corporation (or C corp):** This traditional form of a corporation typically offers the most flexibility when you're seeking investors. A C corp is allowed to have unlimited shareholders, usually with no restrictions on who they are. The downside is the way in which this status of corporation is taxed. In a concept commonly referred to as *double taxation*, the business is taxed first on its income and then its individual shareholders must also pay tax.

> **» S corporation (or S corp):** Electing to have Subchapter S status, or to become an S corp, is an option for your company if you have a limited number of shareholders (as few as just you and usually no more than 35). The shareholders must all be individuals (they cannot be corporations or other business entities), and they must be legal U.S. residents. You also have to agree to operate the business on a calendar year for tax purposes. The advantage of becoming an S corp is that you avoid double taxation. (Profits and losses are passed through to shareholders.)

The choice to incorporate

The biggest advantage to incorporating is that it offers legal protection to its owners. As an individual shareholder, you're not personally liable, as you are with a sole proprietorship or general partnership. You might find that a corporation offers significant tax advantages, too. If you're seeking investment capital or plan to take the company public with an initial public offering (IPO), a corporation gives you the most flexibility to do so. Even if you have no plans to go public, being incorporated provides the opportunity to build your personal wealth in the form of an individual or one-participant 401(k) plan, which is also referred to as a solo 401(k) plan. Saving for retirement using a traditional 401(k) plan can be a big advantage of incorporating as an S corp.

Incorporating has a few disadvantages, too. For starters, you must file or register your corporation with your state. This process involves a large amount of paperwork, which takes some time. To file, you have to submit articles of incorporation that state (among other information)

> » The purpose of your business
>
> » The name of the company
>
> » The name of the owner
>
> » The company's location

You also have to submit bylaws, which describe how the company is run, and a list of officers, or the people who direct the company in its daily decisions, such as a president, secretary, and treasurer.

After your corporation is approved by the state, your responsibilities don't end there. To maintain the corporation's status, you're required to issue stock, hold annual board meetings (with its officers), and record minutes of these meetings. These formal requirements of a corporation can be cumbersome for you, especially when you're starting a new business. In addition, a corporation has to file separate tax forms, which are typically more complicated than an individual return. You could be doubling your efforts — and your expense — while trying to comply with taxes.

WARNING

If the corporate veil is pierced, you can be held personally responsible for the debts and legal concerns of your corporation. This situation happens when you don't properly uphold the requirements of your corporation. Any protection offered by the corporation is therefore forfeited.

Forming a corporation isn't the cheapest method of starting a business, either. If you hire an attorney to file the necessary paperwork with the state, expect to spend close to $1,500 or more in legal expenses and filing fees. Even if you elect to incorporate yourself or do it through an online service, it can still cost several hundred dollars. You pay, at the least, an initial filing fee with the state and then an annual fee to maintain your status.

Changing Your Organization as It Grows

Just because you select one form of structure when you're starting your business doesn't mean that you're stuck with it forever. As with other decisions you make along the way, you might find that your growing company warrants a different legal structure at some point. The ideal situation is to select a structure that gives you the most flexibility at the time you start up. Sometimes, though, that's not reasonable. The next-best plan of action is to understand when and how you should change your organization.

Perhaps the best indicators are those related to money and ownership. As a small-business owner, if you use your money better through different tax strategies, waste no time making the transition. Many businesses start out as sole proprietorships because that option is simple. When the owner hits a certain level of income, however, it makes sense to incorporate based on the amount of self-employment taxes being paid. The advantage of saving several thousand dollars outweighs the compliance burden of incorporation. As they say, it's a no-brainer!

Then there's the matter of owner status. As a sole proprietor, if you take on an additional owner, you have to convert to a partnership or some form of corporation. Similarly, if you're operating a general partnership and then decide to seek out other owners for investment purposes, forming a corporation and offering stock might make sense.

REMEMBER

You can much more easily switch from a sole proprietorship or partnership to a corporation than vice versa. After you incorporate a business, you're expected to meet payroll and wage-related tax requirements as defined by the IRS, and you're expected to hold shareholder meetings. If you decide that you cannot maintain a formal corporation or that it's no longer the best structure for your company, you cannot simply stop meeting these requirements. Instead, you must follow certain procedures to legally dissolve the business.

REMEMBER

Before changing the status of your business, *always* consult with your certified public accountant, attorney, or other trusted business advisor. Consider your options carefully!

Chapter **3**

The Trademark-and-Copyright Two-Step

Your business is important to you, and protecting your hard work and assets is probably high on your list of concerns. From your company logo to your business documentation to your website, making certain your intellectual property (IP) is protected from improper use, plagiarism, and defamation is a never-ending process.

In this chapter, we show you how to protect your investment by registering for trademarks and filing your copyright.

Understanding Why Trademarks and Copyrights Matter

Creating a distinctive name, symbol, or phrase for use in your business can involve a lot of work. After all, branding companies are paid tens (or hundreds) of thousands of dollars to come up with the right names for new products or services. The same hard work and amount of time invested applies to a written work of art, a clever body of text used on your website, or an original piece of artwork: If you go to the trouble of developing unique content, it's probably worth protecting it as your own.

To understand how to protect yourself, you have to enter the Land of Legalization. Start by wrapping your brain cells around some extremely important words, as defined by the U.S. government:

>> **Copyright:** A form of intellectual property law that protects original works of authorship, including literary, dramatic, musical, and artistic works, such as poetry, novels, movies, songs, computer software, and architecture. The Library of Congress registers copyrights, which last for the life of the author plus 70 years.

>> **Patent:** A property right granted by the government of the United States to an inventor that excludes others from making, using, offering for sale, or selling the invention throughout the United States or importing the invention into the United States, in exchange for public disclosure of the invention when the patent is granted.

>> **Trademark:** Protects words, names, symbols, sounds, or colors that distinguish goods and services from those manufactured or sold by others and that indicate the source of the goods. Trademarks can be renewed forever, or as long as they're being used in commerce.

Obtaining one of these legal stamps to claim something as your own is a fairly painless process. Taking this precaution can eventually translate into dollars gained. Not having a product or logo protected makes it easier for someone to copy or steal your idea. That's money out of your pocket. Although having a trademark or copyright might not prevent others from infringing on your work, it certainly makes it easier to go after them in court if they do.

REMEMBER

Although the rules for these protective marks are the same whether you're conducting business online or off, the Internet has increased the stakes in some instances. Having your information readily accessible by millions of people around the globe makes it much easier for others to "borrow" from your hard work. That's all the more reason to make the effort to officially protect your information.

Making Your (Trade)Mark

Do you have to register your work to be protected? No. You might be surprised by this answer, but a federal trademark isn't a necessity. Suppose that you design a symbol to be used as the logo for your online business. By placing that logo on your site, and using it there and on any other business materials, you have established rights to it. So, why bother to officially register it? Obtaining federal registration acts as a notice to the public that you own the mark. It can also assist you if you decide to take action in a federal court to stop someone else from using your work. Also, if you want to register your logo outside the United States, the official registration provides the basis for you to do so.

Even if you choose not to formally register your work, you can use the trademark symbol anyway. After you establish that brilliant tagline or artistic logo, go ahead and place the trademark symbol (TM) near your work. However, you cannot use the symbol showing that the work is officially registered until you apply for registration and receive final notification that your mark is registered. At that time, you can use the registered symbol (®).

REMEMBER

Having a registered trademark doesn't prevent others from infringing on its use. After your work is registered, it's up to you to enforce it. This means you may have to pay an attorney thousands of dollars to prove your trademark was violated. It's up to you to decide whether it's worth the investment or your time and resources to fight infringement. If you don't fight the illegal use of your trademark, you may wonder why you should bother trademarking at all. It's similar to having a lock on your door. A trademark helps thwart a thief, but it doesn't always stop him!

Protecting Your Investment with Copyrights

As with trademarks, you don't have to file for copyright protection to claim your written work as your own. Copyright protection is in place at the time you create your work. However, if you choose to file a lawsuit against someone for using your information, the U.S. Copyright Office advises that you need the formal certificate of registration as proof of ownership.

The good news is that copyrighting your information yourself isn't expensive. Online filing fees for a basic registration at the time of this writing are $35 to $55 per work. The fees can escalate depending on the type of work and the amount being registered. A group or work of published content can be registered for as much as $85, for example. You may also require a copyright search for a fee of $200 per hour. The purpose of a copyright search is to identify if anyone else already owns the right to the content. However, copyright searches are sometimes tricky because not all files have been digitized and made available online (a current digitization project is underway, but not yet complete). This means that searches of copyrights prior to 1978, approximately 45 million cards of information, must be sorted through the old-fashioned way — offline, in the U.S. copyright office in Washington D.C. You can learn more about the copyright search process online at www.copyright.gov/circs/circ23.pdf.

THE DIGITAL MILLENNIUM COPYRIGHT ACT

The Digital Millennium Copyright Act (DMCA) became law in 1998. This legislation provides enhanced copyright protection, specifically within electronic media (the Internet). Generally, the DMCA makes illegal the use of technology to copy or pirate digital material, such as software, music, and video. The DMCA further prohibits you from selling or distributing technology that could permit this type of activity.

How does the DMCA affect you? The answer depends on your type of business. If your website distributes music in any way, this law requires that you, as a webcaster, pay appropriate licensing fees for that right. If you're a nonprofit organization, a library, or an Internet service provider (ISP), you gain some added protection if someone uses your system to distribute copyrighted material. If you're the owner of copyrighted material and discover an infringement, you can report it to the ISP that's transmitting the information and request that the material be removed. Other than in these situations, the DMCA might not be a concern for you. You should be aware of it, though, because this piece of legislation continues to be controversial. Potential changes to the legislation are on the table because some technology companies view the DMCA as being too restrictive and interfere with business. Opponents also claim abuses of the legislation are commonplace and must be stopped by the courts. As court cases evolve and changes occur, you might discover that you're more affected than you thought.

If you choose to register, certain rules pertain specifically to websites and other material distributed online (such as documents you offer for download). For instance, you can copyright any original information you include on your site.

Here are some other variables:

>> You can protect computer programs you have written.

>> You can protect entire databases.

>> You *cannot* copyright your domain name for your site (such as www.mysiteisgreat.com).

>> If you decide to send out an electronic newsletter to your customers each week, it's protected under copyright laws, as long as the information is original.

The rules become more complicated when you discuss the period over which a work is protected or the amount of work that can be copyrighted. For instance, the original words on your website pages are protected. However, if you make updates to any of your pages and change that information, it isn't protected. In other words, you aren't given an unlimited copyright to your site's content. If you change the information (which you should do to keep your site fresh and current), you must file another application and pay another filing fee.

Here's an exception to this rule: An online computer program may be treated separately. Online work that's continuously updated can be classified as an automated database, which can have a single registration that covers updates over a 3-month period (in the same calendar year). Or if you have material, such as an e-newsletter, that's updated daily or weekly, you might qualify for a group registration (or a single registration that covers multiple issues).

For more flexibility when allowing others to use and share your online content, such as blogs, website copy, and images, consider a Creative Commons license. Creative Commons is a nonprofit organization that provides different types of licenses for digital content that extend the way your copyrighted content is used while remaining within the legal boundaries of copyright law. You can, for example, grant users the right to share, edit, remix, or build upon your content based on certain conditions. You choose to extend licenses based on the types of attribution and whether it is for commercial or noncommercial use. A Creative Commons license works alongside a legal copyright and is not a replacement or an alternative to copyrighting your work. Copyright laws can be inflexible, but a Creative Commons license allows widespread digital sharing while enabling you to retain ownership of your work. You can learn more at www.creativecommons.org.

TIP

For complete details about copyrighting your online work, specifically as it applies to your website, check out the official site for the U.S. Copyright Office and its information about electronic content, "Copyright Registration of Websites and Website Content," at www.copyright.gov/circs/circ66.pdf. As with all advice in this book, when it comes to legalities, we highly advise you to consult an attorney if you have any questions or concerns about any actions you need to take.

Establishing Registration Yourself

As we point out in the preceding section, establishing your work as your own is as simple as creating it and using it. When you're ready to take the extra step to obtain proof of ownership, you can easily file for a trademark or copyright yourself.

Getting your trademark

You can apply for a federal trademark all on your own. Follow these steps to work through the registration process:

1. **Go to the website of the U.S. Patent and Trademark Office (USPTO) at** www.uspto.gov.

   The main page of the site lists current news and information about trademarks and patents. In the upper-right section of the page is a Find It Fast box with a list of topics from which you can choose more information.

2. **Under the Trademarks category in the main site navigation, click the Apply Online (TEAS) link.**

   This step takes you to the Trademarks Electronic Application System (TEAS) Online Filing page. The left side of the page contains links to detailed information about enhancements to the system and important notices. The center of the page contains important warnings, along with descriptions of filing options and links to the application forms.

TIP

   You can click on any of the Form links, which takes you to a new page with a Note at the top which links you to information about *What you should know before filing*. It provides complete filing information for first-time filers. You can also access a link to an online video tutorial (https://www.uspto.gov/trademarks-getting-started/process-overview/trademark-information-network#heading-2) that shows you each step in the registration process so that you know exactly which information you need to file. You should visit these links before you start the registration process.

3. **Under the Apply Online section, click the Initial Applications Forms link.**

   A new page opens with information about form options and filing fees. It also has links to begin the filing procedure.

4. **Click the Start Filling Out TEAS Regular link to start the application process.**

5. **Complete all steps.**

   After you complete the application tutorial, your mark is officially submitted for approval.

TIP

Have your credit card ready when you file online. A filing fee, ranging from $225 to $400 per item, must accompany your online application.

REMEMBER

Filing for a trademark can be tricky. You must be precise in the information you provide, follow instructions to the letter, and complete the process within a specified time frame. The USPTO prefers that you get professional help and issues a warning from the start, encouraging you to hire an attorney. If you are uncertain about the filing process, it may be worth paying for a few hours of time for a trademark attorney.

When the online registration is processed, you'll receive a serial number for your application. Use this serial number to check the status of your application by calling 800-786-9199 or by using the Trademark Status and Document Retrieval (TSDR) system at http://uspto.gov/trademarks-application-process/check-status-view-documents.

Filing for copyright

To file an application for obtaining a federal copyright of your work, follow these steps:

1. **Go to the website of the U.S. Copyright Office at** www.copyright.gov.

   The home page shows you a list of choices to get information.

2. **Click the Register a Copyright image below the gray menu bar at the top of the page.**

3. **Register with the Electronic Copyright Office by clicking the Log in to the Electronic Copyright Office (eCO) Registration System button and then the If You Are a New User, Click Here to Register link below the login boxes at top left of the page to create an account.**

4. **Select the Standard Application link under the Register a Work section of the Copyright Registration menu tab on the left side of the page.**

   The resulting page provides a list of specific steps of how to register a copyright.

5. **Follow the three steps as outlined on the site.**

   These steps include completing an online application, paying the filing fees, and uploading your work using an accepted file format. Tutorials for each stage help you complete the filing process successfully.

TIP

If you have trouble filing electronically, you can instead send the completed application and copies of your work, along with the designated filing fee, to this address:

Library of Congress Copyright Office
101 Independence Ave., S.E.
Washington, D.C. 20559-6000

After your registration is approved, you receive a certificate of registration (usually in 4 or 5 months).

Retaining Professional Assistance

Hiring an attorney who specializes in trademarks, patents, or copyrights can be a good idea if your situation is complex or you're not comfortable handling the applications on your own. If you're pursuing registration in foreign countries, hiring an attorney who's familiar with international laws is invaluable. Because U.S. copyright and trademark laws are recognized in some, but not all, countries, using an attorney can ensure that you're fully protected.

You can expect to pay big bucks for the expertise of a professional. An experienced attorney might charge anywhere from $125 to $250 (or more) per hour for his or her service. This money is in addition to any filing or application fees you might have to pay. For this fee, you can expect a trademark attorney to conduct a thorough search of existing and pending marks that might conflict with yours. The attorney should also complete all forms on your behalf and act as the primary point of contact with the U.S. Patent and Trademark Office or the U.S. Copyright Office.

TIP

To protect your investment, follow these tips when you're hiring a professional:

>> Look for an attorney who specializes in intellectual property or trademarks, copyrights, and patents.

>> Get referrals from others you know who have used attorneys to register their businesses.

>> Clarify which portion of the work is conducted by the attorney and which part is handled by legal aides (or junior partners).

>> Discuss the attorney's rate and whether you're billed up front.

>> Ask for a written statement or estimate of how much you can expect the process to cost.

>> Confirm that the attorney is licensed.

TIP

You can search for an attorney in your area by using the referral guides on these websites:

>> **American Bar Association (ABA):** Visit www.americanbar.org to locate attorneys in your area who can help you with your specific legal needs.

>> **FindLaw:** FindLaw, at www.findlaw.com, can also help you locate local attorneys who specialize in various legal subjects, including trademark policies.

IN THIS CHAPTER

» Keeping up with IRS expectations

» Tracking your profits and losses

» Finding software to make accounting a snap (or as close as it gets)

» Choosing a professional to protect your pocketbook

» Deciding what paperwork stays and what goes

Chapter **4**

Accounting for Taxes (and Then Some)

U nless you have a penchant for numbers, along with a love of crunching them, accounting is probably the least fun part of owning a business. Even so, we also recognize that it's one of the most necessary business functions. Why? It boils down to these two issues:

» **Taxes:** The Internal Revenue Service (IRS) demands that you keep accurate records of the monetary side of your business. That way, you're sure to contribute your fair share of taxes to Uncle Sam.

» **Profitability:** IRS aside, *you* need to understand how well (or not so well) your business is doing financially. Then you can make good strategic decisions for its future — and yours!

Dread it as you may, you have to embrace accounting. Okay, perhaps not embrace it, but you can at least learn to appreciate its value and commit to keeping up with it. To help prepare you for that financial road ahead, we start by introducing you to some basics of accounting. Before long, you may even look forward to balancing your checkbook. (Hey, anything is possible.) If you find that you just can't hack the accounting life, check out our advice on how and when to choose a professional to help you out.

The Tax Man Cometh — Again and Again

You've probably heard the saying that nothing in life is certain except death and taxes. Suffice it to say that the latter is at least predictable. As a business owner, you can count on the tax man regularly showing up on your doorstep. Rain or shine, without fail, taxes come due at certain times of the year whether you like it or not.

In Book 2, Chapter 2, we give you a glimpse of what to expect of the tax man when we discuss the pros and cons of various ownership structures for your business and how each form is taxed. Regardless of which type of business structure you choose, you face many tax-related requirements when you run an online business.

For starters, several types of federal and state taxes are likely to apply to you, as we describe in the next few sections.

Income tax

You pay income tax on the money your business earns. Almost every type of company has to file an annual income tax return. (The exception is the partnership, which files only an information return.)

The important thing to know is that federal income tax is a pay-as-you-go system — the IRS doesn't want to wait until the end of the year to receive its cut of your money. Instead, you must pay the amount of taxes that are due every quarter. Because you don't always know the exact amount to pay in time to file by the IRS deadline (maybe an overdue invoice comes in at the last minute or a refund has to be issued), you can *estimate* the tax amount for each quarter and then submit that dollar amount. Table 4-1 lists the appropriate IRS form to submit when you're estimating taxes, along with many other forms that the IRS says you need, according to the type of organization you create.

Employment tax

Your tax responsibilities don't end, of course, with reporting your income. Employees play a role, too. Whether you have one person (even if that's you!) or 100 people working for your company, if you hire employees to work in your online business, you're responsible for paying certain taxes on behalf of those employees. Even if they work only part-time, you still have to keep up with the paperwork and pay up.

TABLE 4-1   **IRS Tax Forms Based on Business Type**

Organization Type	Potentially Liable for This Type of Tax	Form or Forms Required
Sole proprietor	Income tax	1040 and Schedule C1 or C–EZ (Schedule F1 for farm business)
	Self-employment tax	1040 and Schedule SE
	Estimated tax	1040–ES
	Employment taxes: Social Security and Medicare taxes and income tax withholding	941 (943 for farm employees)
	Federal unemployment (FUTA) tax	940
Partnership	Annual return of income	1065
	Employment taxes	Same as sole proprietor
Partner in a partnership (individual)	Income tax	1040 and Schedule E
	Self-employment tax	1040 and Schedule SE
	Estimated tax	1040–ES
Corporation or S corporation	Income tax	1120 (corporation) 1120S (S corporation)
	Estimated tax	1120–W (corporation only)
	Employment taxes	940, 941, or 943
S corporation shareholder	Income tax	1040 and Schedule E
	Estimated tax	1040–ES

These obligations are commonly referred to as payroll taxes. You must file *withholding forms* (along with the accompanying payment) to both the IRS and your state treasury department. The types of taxes you pay on behalf of your employees include

>> Medicare and Social Security taxes (as part of the Federal Insurance Contributions Act, or FICA)

>> Federal income tax withholding

>> Federal unemployment tax (FUTA)

Calculating the withholding amount can be complicated. You start with the information submitted by your employee on a Form W-9 and then use the tables in IRS Publication 15, *Employer's Tax Guide* (Section 9), which is available at www.irs.gov/publications/p15/index.html. Withholding guidelines are updated sometimes, so it is important to review the tax guide. The most recent changes occurred in December 2017, as part of the Tax Cuts and Jobs Act, and has some additional provisions that were effective through April 2019. If you are still not sure how to calculate this amount or are uncertain of changes to requirements and how they might apply to you, your financial advisor (bookkeeper or accountant) can easily make the calculations for you and confirm any extensions or updates to withholding guidelines for 2020 and beyond.

With calculated withholding amounts in hand, you need to fork over payroll taxes every quarter. You must file Form 941, *Employer's Quarterly Tax Return*, by the last day of the month that follows the end of the quarter. Table 4-2 shows the payroll due dates for both paper filing and electronic filing.

TABLE 4-2

Due Dates for Payroll Taxes

Quarter Ends	Normal Due Date	Extended Due Date
March 31	April 30	May 10
June 30	July 31	August 10
September 30	October 31	November 10
December 31	January 31	February 10

In addition to providing payroll dates, the IRS website for small businesses offers easy access to almost every other type of tax form you need to submit. The site even contains an online learning center so that you can further educate yourself about all tax and business start-up issues. You can see instructional videos online at www.irsvideos.gov/smallbusinesstaxpayer.

WARNING

The rule of filing quarterly has some exceptions. Always check with your accountant or CPA to confirm that you're filing properly. Otherwise, the IRS can slap you with hefty penalties and interest (never a good thing).

TIP

If you believe that your employment taxes are $1,000 or less (and your liability for Social Security, Medicare, and withheld federal income taxes is less than $2,500 for the year), you may be eligible to submit payroll taxes annually. To do so, request Form 944.

You might want to file electronically. (Come on — if you're running an online business, you ought to be set up for filing online, right?) Although the process is fairly easy, some paperwork is involved. In other words, don't assume that you can wait until the day before your taxes are due to sign up.

To start making online payments, go to the official Electronic Federal Tax Payment System (EFTPS) website at www.eftps.gov/eftps. EFTPS is a free service to business and individual taxpayers. Before you can file your taxes electronically, however, you must enroll online. Click the Enroll button at the top of the page and then follow the instructions to submit your information. Getting set up to make electronic payments generally takes a few days. You must make payments the day before the due date in order to be on time.

REMEMBER

Before you can complete the online application, you must have an employer identification number (EIN) and provide your bank account number and bank routing number.

Sales tax

Another tax responsibility is that of tracking and collecting sales tax from your customers and then submitting it to the appropriate state and local agencies. If you sell (or manufacture) products, you probably have to deal with this issue.

You may be wondering whether you can avoid sales tax because you're selling products online and not in a particular state. Generally, online businesses have always followed this guideline:

> If you sell to people in any state where you have a nexus, or physical presence (a store, a warehouse, and sometimes that can also be the tiniest remote office), you must collect tax from customers originating from that same state.

Increasingly, individual states are becoming more aggressive about collecting sales tax from Internet-based companies, and that means the current ruling on when to collect tax is changing on a state-by-state basis. For example, 21 states have enacted *economic nexus standards,* which require online businesses to collect sales tax if they have any connection to a state, and not only a physical presence. Other states have enacted similar economic nexus standards that are based on reaching gross revenue thresholds within the state. If your online business reaches more than $10,000 in sales in Pennsylvania or Oklahoma, you're required to collect sales tax in those states. Keep in mind that some states do not collect any sales tax.

Bottom line: It's complicated, and the laws are changing quickly! Our advice is to stay on top of the most current information at both the state and federal levels and to have your accountant continually keep you updated. Using a good shopping cart solution (which we discuss in Book 4) for your website may also help make it easier to keep up with which online customers to tax and when.

You're also liable for filing and paying other state-related taxes (not just sales tax). Because the amount varies greatly across states, check with your accountant to find out which taxes apply to your online business. Or you can contact your state's revenue department to learn more.

The Federation of Tax Administrators (FTA) website has a direct link to the appropriate agency websites for each state. Find the link at www.taxadmin.org/state-tax-agencies.

By the Numbers: Accounting Basics

Although we freely admit that accounting isn't our favorite activity, some elements of it are enjoyable. For example, at the end of every month, you have the opportunity to look at the profit-and-loss (P&L) statement to see how well your business is doing — on paper. It's like getting a checkup (for better or worse) and viewing a summary of every activity you performed during the month, as it relates to the bottom line of your business. If all is well, yippee! If you encounter problems, a P&L statement is bound to expose your points of weakness.

If you're still not sure what a P&L is, let alone what it means to your business, don't worry. You'll soak up the idea of a P&L in no time, along with several other important pieces of financial information in the following sections.

Determining periods and methods

Before you can walk, you have to crawl. When you're starting a business, one of the first things you have to do is select your *tax year*, or the defined period that you use to provide an annual snapshot of the financial state of your business.

You can choose from several types of tax year:

>> **Calendar year:** This method is defined by the wall calendar you buy at the beginning of every year. The 12 months start January 1 and end December 31. Your calendar-year accounting system follows the same pattern: Move from month to month and then start all over again on the next January 1.

>> **Fiscal year:** Although this type of tax year also has a fixed 12-month period, it never ends on the last day of December — any other month, but not that one. For example, you could choose to run from October 1 to September 30 of the following year. Why bother? If you have a seasonal business, this method provides an opportunity to adapt your operational schedule to an accounting and tax schedule. If your peak season is at the end of the year, having to worry about reporting or paying taxes can be cumbersome.

>> **52 or 53 weeks:** In this variation of the fiscal year, you operate on a 52- or 53-week period rather than on a 12-month schedule. The catch is that your tax year must always land on the same day of the week (close to the end of a calendar month), thus requiring that an extra week be added to the period to end on the same calendar date each time.

A calendar year is probably the easiest reporting method for you to adopt. Depending on which type of business you form (an LLC or S corporation, for example), you may have difficulty getting the IRS to approve anything other than a calendar year. The IRS refers to it as a *required tax year*.

TIP

If you have good reason to think that the calendar year is a problem for your business, you must file a request with the IRS to change your tax year. For this request, you want to use the Application to Adopt, Change, or Retain a Tax Year. Unless an IRS code provides for automatic approval, be prepared to pay a filing fee for the change request.

Your next decision is to choose an *accounting method* for your business. You use this method to arrive at your income and expenses. Just as you choose your tax year, you select your preferred accounting method when you start your business. You're then expected to stick with it, unless the IRS approves a change.

Here are the two most common accounting methods for a business:

>> **Cash basis:** Simply put, you report earnings when they're received and report expenses when they're incurred. The IRS says that you *cannot* use the cash method if any of these conditions applies:

- You're a corporation (other than an S corporation) with average annual gross receipts of more than $5 million.

- You're a partnership that has a corporation (other than an S corporation) as a partner, and the partnership has average annual gross receipts of more than $5 million.

- You're a tax shelter.

- You have inventory.

Special circumstances and exceptions to the rules always exist. Be sure to check with your CPA regarding which basis is best for your business.

» **Accrual basis:** In this method, your revenues can be reported when you earn them rather than when you receive the money (cash). Likewise, your expenses can be reported on the date they're owed, as opposed to the date on which you pay them. If you produce items or have inventory, accrual is considered the best way to provide an accurate picture of your financial status from year to year. Of course, that rule has some exceptions! You can use another method, even if you deal with inventory, if you are

- A qualifying taxpayer who passes the gross receipt test (with less than $1 million in gross sales for each year of the test period)

- A qualifying small-business taxpayer who passes the gross receipt test (with less than $10 million in average annual gross receipts for each year of the test period)

- An eligible business as determined by the IRS

Also, you must *not* be

- A tax shelter

- Prohibited from using the cash method

And now, your balance sheet

No matter which accounting method you choose, you need to know how to make sense of your company's financial statements. A *balance sheet*, which is one of those statements, is a detailed summary of your business's financial status.

To understand your balance sheet, here are some terms you need to know:

» **Assets:** Everything of value that your business owns. Assets typically include

- *Cash:* Available money in your bank accounts

- *Accounts receivable (A/R):* The money that your customers owe you

- *Inventory:* The monetary worth of whatever merchandise you have on hand

- *Fixed assets:* Land, buildings, furniture, and equipment

- *Miscellaneous:* A catchall term for anything that doesn't fit into any other category

» **Liabilities:** All the debts of the business. Liabilities can include

- *Accounts payable (A/P):* The money that you owe suppliers, vendors, or credit card companies

- *Accrued expenses:* Wages, payroll taxes, and sales tax, for example, that have been collected but not yet paid

- *Noncurrent:* Notes payable to shareholders and the portion of long-term debt that isn't yet due, for example

» **Net worth or capital:** The amount of your ownership or equity or the amount you invested in your company

» **Revenue or sales:** All the income your business has earned, usually recorded over a specific period

» **Expenses:** Everything spent by your business, typically recorded (or totaled) for a specified period

Now you know all the essential terms that relate to a balance sheet. The next important point is that when a balance sheet is put together correctly, the bottom line must "balance" by using the following equation:

Assets = liabilities + net worth

That's it. See? It's not that confusing! To help you grasp how a balance sheet should look, check out the sample shown in Figure 4-1.

A quick glimpse: The P&L

Unlike a balance sheet, an *income statement* (commonly referred to as a profit-and-loss statement, or P&L) provides a quick snapshot of your revenues and expenses. It's made up of *line items*, a sequence of items providing a monetary total for every category of revenues or expenses. When you compile the statement, you can see how much money your business earned (or lost) for that specific period.

TIP

You can create P&Ls on a quarterly basis. Looking at P&Ls monthly is more useful, however, because you can more easily spot any unusual fluctuations in your sales or expenses.

Suppose that you earn $750 in a month, which is deposited in your checking account. Then you withdraw (or spend) $800 that month. The bank also charges you $40 in overdraft fees for two bounced checks that were paid from your account. You have lost $90 for the month (you were short $50, plus $40 in overdraft fees).

Your P&L shows you the same type of information as your bank statement. If you pull up a record of your bank account online, you can see a list showing where your money went that month. By looking at your initial balance, and the checks you wrote against your deposits, you see whether you ended up with a positive balance (a profit) or a negative balance (a loss) over that period.

```
Balance Sheet
Ending December 31, 2016

                                                        2016
ASSETS
Current Assets
Cash                                                   $2,500
Accounts receivable                                     2,800
Inventory                                               5,500

Total Current Assets                                   $10,800

Fixed Assets
Buildings                                              $      0
Land                                                          0
Furnitures and fixtures                                   1,200
Equipment                                                 7,000
Accum. depreciation                                        (200)
Miscellaneous                                                 0

Total Fixed Assets                                      $8,000

TOTAL ASSETS                                           $18,800

LIABILITIES AND SHAREHOLDERS' EQUITY
Liabilities
Accounts payable                                       $3,300
Taxes payable                                             500

TOTAL LIABILITIES                                       $3,800

Net Worth                                               15,000

TOTAL LIABILITIES & NET WORTH                          $18,800
```

FIGURE 4-1:
A sample
balance sheet.

Check out Figure 4-2 to see what a P&L statement looks like.

In the example shown in Figure 4-2, notice two important characteristics of a P&L:

» **The dollar value for each line item is shown as a percentage of your gross revenues (total earnings before anything is deducted).** Using percentages gives you a clearer picture of how much (or little) you're spending from your total earnings. For example, if you find that you're spending 32 percent for banner advertising and only 5 percent on keywords, consider whether that's how you intended to spend your advertising budget.

Regularly review your P&L statement to track whether you're staying within your budget for the year.

TIP

```
Income Statement (P&L)
For month ended July 31, 2016
                                                                  07/31/16
Income:
                                                                 $9,115.00
Gross Sales:                                                        (0.00)
Less Returns                                                       (0.00)
Less Other Discounts
                                                                 _____
                                                                 $9,115.00
NET Sales

Cost of Goods Sold:
   Beginning Inventory               $500.00
   Add:       Purchases               250.00
             Freight                   50.00
                                     _____
                                                                    800.00
   Cost of Goods Available

   Less:      Ending Inventory       (400.00)
                                                                   -400.00
   Cost of Goods Sold

                                                                 $8,715.00
Gross Profit (Less)

Expenses:
   Advertising                        150.00
   Amortization
   Bad Debts
   Bank Charges                        50.00
   Commissions
   Credit Card Fees                    55.00
   Depreciation
   Dues, Subscriptions (Books)         15.00
   Insurance                          145.00
   Interest
   Loans
   Maintenance
   Miscellaneous                       40.00
   Office Expenses – General          137.28
   Operating Supplies                 124.56
   Payroll (Wages & Taxes)          2,800.00
   Permits and Licenses
   Postage                            95.00
   Professional Fees                 275.00
   Property Taxes
   Rent                               650.00
   Telephone
              Landline               289.00
              Cell                    150.00
   Training/Workshops                 20.00
   Travel
   Utilities                         280.00
   Vehicle Expense
              Gas/Mileage             42.14
              Maintenance
   Web Site Fees                     355.00

Total Expenses                                                   5,672.98
Net Operating Income:                                            3,042.02

Other Income:                            0

*NET INCOME (LOSS):                                              $3,042.02

*This is pre-tax income.
```

FIGURE 4-2:
A sample income
(P&L) statement.

> **» The total dollar amount and percentages from the preceding month and for the year to-date are included.** It's all on the same page. If the line item shows that your company's water fee jumped 50 percent in one month, you might want to investigate. It could indicate a leak or other problem. Or the reason might be as simple as you having accidentally made a double payment. Don't laugh: You might be surprised at how easily events like these can slip past you.

Think of a P&L as a tool for keeping track of your business. Like the balance sheet, it provides an important glimpse of your business, over a specific period. If you review your financial statements regularly, you can catch mistakes and identify positive trends and then use that information to make critical decisions about the financial well-being of your online endeavor.

Choosing Software to Make Your Tasks Easy

Accounting software allows you to enter your daily financial activities, press a few keys at the end of the month, and — voila! — print your balance sheet and P&Ls. It's just a matter of picking the right software.

QuickBooks, the accounting software from Intuit (www.intuit.com), is a favorite among many small-business owners because it simplifies the recordkeeping process for your business and is *extremely* easy to learn and use. Many people are already familiar with it, simply because they use it for personal accounting, too. Popular brands such as QuickBooks and Sage (www.sage.com) offer many versions of accounting software based on size, industry, and specific features.

Our purpose isn't to sell you on a particular brand of software. Instead, we want to help you understand which benefits and features to look for so that you can choose the best accounting software for your online business.

Going online?

The first consideration for choosing software is whether you want to use a web, or cloud-based, service provider. Many vendors provide online accounting services. FreshBooks, Zoho Books, and Xero are some of the popular cloud-based options available today. Traditional accounting software providers also offer online versions of their products, including QuickBooks and Sage.

One big advantage of a cloud-based product is that the data is stored off-site and is easily accessible from any computer. Why does this matter? Well, if something happens to your office (such as a fire or a flood), you can still access your data from another location. Or if you travel, you can manage your accounting details while you're on the road.

Another perceived advantage is pricing. Rather than pay several hundred dollars out of your pocket in one whack, you pay it out every month (sometimes as little as $10 a month). After a full year or two, of course, you've paid almost the full price of a box of software. But that monthly fee can also include support and other benefits that over-the-counter accounting software might not offer. Additionally, you have a pay-as-you-grow option. In other words, you can easily upgrade to the next level of service as your business grows or choose certain add-on services, as your needs change — instead of investing upfront for services that you may not need yet.

What size are you?

Speaking of a growing business, when you're shopping for accounting software, one size doesn't fit all. The amount of revenue your business pulls in, along with the number of employees you hire, has a lot to do with which accounting program you should choose. For that matter, solo entrepreneurs may not have any employees! If you run a small business, you'll want to find entry-level software that is designed for very small businesses. If you have a larger company, you may need an enterprise edition that has more robust features.

How much do you want to pay?

Ah, it's everyone's favorite question: How much do you want (or are you willing) to invest in your accounting program? You probably prefer leaning toward the lower side of the price scale. Luckily, most over-the-counter software packages suited to truly small businesses range from $30 to $400 for single users. The price fluctuation largely depends on these factors:

>> **Brand:** As with most business products, you usually pay more when you're using a more widely recognized brand of software. Our experience is that QuickBooks and Sage are a little pricier than the Bookkeeper brand of software (by Avanquest Software), for example.

>> **Features and users:** Price is affected by not only the number of features offered with various accounting software programs but also the complexity of those features. The number of licenses you need, or number of users with access to the program, often affects price. Keep these questions in mind:

- Do you want software that easily integrates with your online banking system, even if it costs more?

- Must the software communicate with your offline point-of-sale system, your online inventory system, or your payroll service? Or do you just want to track your invoices and expenses and spit out occasional reports to pass along to your CPA?

  The more you expect from your accounting software, the more you can expect to pay for it!

» **Industry:** Similar to the issue of the type of features that are offered, some accounting software is designed for your particular type of *industry*. Consultants, manufacturers, retailers, and construction businesses are examples of some of the most common industries that use specific software. If you want accounting software designed for your kind of business, you can probably expect to pay closer to $400 (or higher).

Do you need support?

Another important part of your purchasing decision is the issue of support. One advantage of choosing software that has been around for a while is that the company is usually capable of providing decent support, both online and by phone. Access to support is also an advantage of using a cloud-based solution. Not all versions of a particular product or solution include the same level or type of support, so it is important to understand what is included with your monthly fee.

TIP

Before purchasing your software, find out the terms for receiving ongoing support and compare the product across brands. Some software comes with unlimited online support, and others offer only 30-day support and then charge a fee after that.

In addition to being able to turn to your software vendor for support, you should know that your accountant and other financial advisors are better prepared to help you when you use software that they know how to use. For that reason, don't hesitate to ask for their advice before making your final purchase.

Hiring a Professional

Regardless of the type of accounting software you install or your own ability to number-crunch, at some point you might need or want to hire outside help. An array of tax and accounting professionals are available. In the following sections, we tell you how to determine which one is right for you.

Recognizing that it takes all types

Start by reviewing the types of professionals who can help you. They include

» **CPA:** These initials after a person's name, which stand for certified public accountant, indicate that the person has passed a state-regulated exam and is recognized by the IRS as a paid preparer for submitting your tax returns. Typically, a CPA fully understands accounting methods and is well versed in tax regulations. Because tax laws are cumbersome and continually changing, a CPA might even specialize in a particular area. Examples of industry-based specialization are government, retail, and small business. Specialization can also be classified according to function, such as a CPA who specializes in mergers and acquisitions. Additionally, a CPA can legally conduct audits, whereas other accounting professionals cannot.

» **Accountant:** Except for the lack of a state-issued license or certificate, an accountant has the same basic skills as a CPA. Even so, an accountant can assist in preparing your taxes and file them, too. And like a CPA, a reputable accountant can advise you about financial decisions and should be up to date on changing tax laws.

» **Bookkeeper:** Someone in this category can manage the basic recordkeeping activities for your small business, including these tasks:

- Make deposits

- Log in accounts receivables

- Handle account payables

- Manage payroll

- Send out appropriate forms, such as W2s and 1099s, to employees and contractors

In addition to being able to keep the books, this person should be comfortable with creating an income statement and a balance sheet each month. Of course, bookkeepers come with all levels of experience and education. (Some are professionally certified with a college degree, and others aren't.) A basic bookkeeper is usually the most affordable outside help.

» **Tax consultant:** This catchall term includes both independent advisors (who can range from accountant to CPA) and tax preparers, such as the folks at your neighborhood H&R Block office at tax time. Similar to a bookkeeper, this person's range of experience, knowledge, education, and certification varies.

» **Enrolled agent:** This type of federally licensed professional understands both state and federal tax laws. In addition to completing an exam issued by the U.S. Department of Treasury, an enrolled agent has also passed a federal background check. He or she can also gain licensure after having worked for the IRS for at least 5 years. An enrolled agent is certified in the eyes of the IRS to

- Prepare your taxes

- Assist you in long-term financial planning

- Represent you in dealing with the IRS

>> **Tax attorney:** Most tax attorneys don't handle general accounting functions. Instead, you hire an attorney specifically to deal with issues pertaining to the tax law — for example, to handle an audit requested by the IRS or to file corporate bankruptcy (which we hope you never do). Larger corporations might also keep a tax attorney on retainer or hire one in-house, if the company continually deals with complex tax issues. Your small business is less likely to need the services of a tax attorney regularly.

REMEMBER

Attorneys, enrolled agents, and CPAs are the only professionals authorized to represent you with the IRS.

As a general rule, you need a full or part-time bookkeeper. If you're up to the task (and many small-business owners like it this way), you can wear that hat, too. If you aren't adept at follow-through or if numbers just plain scare you, consider hiring someone.

Depending on the experience (or inexperience) of the professional and the market rate in your community, you can hire a basic entry-level bookkeeper (often referred to as a *bookkeeper clerk*), for a fairly low hourly rate. (The rate can start in the range of $10 to $20 an hour, depending on experience.) A more experienced person, such as a professional full-time bookkeeper or a professionally certified bookkeeper, charges a much higher hourly rate — or a mid-to-upper-end management-level salary if you hire the person full time.

TIP

When you interview bookkeeper candidates, use the free Bookkeeper's Hiring Test, available from the American Institute of Professional Bookkeepers, to qualify them. You can find and print the test at www.aipb.org/testrequest.php.

Knowing what to expect from your tax professional

In addition to having someone handle your daily financial recordkeeping, you should establish a relationship with a CPA, an accountant, or an enrolled agent. This type of professional should be available to assist you with these tasks:

>> Prepare and file your taxes

>> Set up your accounting system

>> Advise you on the legal organization of your company (and other start-up issues)

>> Compile (or review) financial statements

>> Assist you in long-term financial planning for your business

>> Address specific tax-law questions and concerns as they arise

>> Ensure that the proper amounts and types of taxes are being filed

>> Guide you in the completion of (or submit on your behalf) all quarterly tax documentation and other forms that might be required annually

>> Answer questions and advise you about other general tax- and finance-related concerns

REMEMBER

These professionals typically charge a high hourly rate. (A CPA's rate can start at $125 an hour.) Make sure that you clarify how you're charged for time. (Some professionals don't charge for questions asked by way of email, and others do, for example.)

TIP

Before you consult with an outside professional advisor, make a list of the specific questions or issues you want addressed. This list keeps you on track and ensures that you maximize the time spent with your advisor while avoiding running up steep bills.

Finding likely candidates

After you decide which type of professional you want to hire, your next step is finding one. Fortunately, you have lots of places to turn to for a head start on this task:

>> **Referrals:** Ask business peers and family members whom they use or recommend. Ask for specific information, such as

- What do you like about the way this person does business?

- What expertise does the professional have?

- How long have you known this person or used his or her services?

- How much does this person typically charge?

>> **Local organizations:** Area Chamber of Commerce chapters and other local business associations often make their membership databases available to the public. Although the organizations typically don't endorse one member

over another, they can suggest which professionals might be best suited for your specific requirements and tell you whether any complaints have been registered against them.

» **Professional associations:** Industry or professional groups are a terrific place to start your search for a CPA or other accounting professional. You can check out this list of organizations to get started:

- American Institute of Certified Public Accountants: www.aicpa.org

- National Association for Enrolled Agents: www.naea.org

- American Academy of Attorney-CPAs: www.attorney-cpa.com

- CPA Associates International: www.cpaai.com

- American Institute of Professional Bookkeepers: www.aipb.org

» **Classifieds:** When you're hiring a bookkeeper or an accountant, feel free to place an ad in local newspapers, online career or job sites, or on social media sites, such as LinkedIn. These are all good resources for finding the best candidate.

TIP

When you place a help-wanted ad, you'll hear from better-qualified candidates if you're specific about the required job functions. We also recommend requesting that job candidates forward their salary requirements or salary history, along with their résumés.

» **Search engines:** If all else fails, a quick search on Google or Yahoo! will also return a healthy list of local options.

TIP

Narrow the field of reputable contenders by skimming advertisements for professionals who list specific certifications, licensures, and memberships in professional associations.

Choosing the best person for you

After you create a short list of possible candidates, how do you decide which one is best suited for your business? In addition to checking for proper accreditations and confirming hourly rates, you have to consider a few other issues when you're choosing a CPA, an accountant, an enrolled agent, or even a tax attorney:

» **Experience:** You want to know whether the person specializes in particular areas of accounting or tax law. You should also find out, however, what type of work now takes up the majority of the professional's time and also the type of work performed in the past. Two critical questions to ask are

- What areas do you most enjoy handling?

- In which areas do you have the most up-to-date knowledge?

Because definitive rules of taxation and the Internet are still somewhat up in the air, you're not as likely to find a professional who specializes in this area. Instead, look for someone who's eager and willing to stay informed on new issues and changes to the tax law. Preferably, choose someone who's committed to tracking down the answers to difficult or lesser-known tax questions.

Ask your CPA about changes in the tax law to determine whether you're affected. The IRS provides a quick summary of those yearly changes on its website at www.irs.gov.

» **Availability:** A highly qualified independent professional often has a waiting list of clients. Although that's a helpful situation for the accountant, it doesn't help you. You need a professional who can work with you now. No matter what, it doesn't hurt to ask what the person's client schedule is like. For example, some professionals work part-time or have a 4-day workweek. Others are eagerly growing their businesses and are available to answer your questions 7 days a week. Nothing is wrong with either schedule; just find the one that you can live with as a client.

» **Firm size:** Size does matter, and sometimes a smaller firm is the better option. Even though some folks think that a large, recognizable accounting firm is the way to go, that's not always the case. If you have a small company, you might find yourself at the bottom of the totem pole when the firm prioritizes its clients. Your company's needs might get passed off to a junior accountant or other staff person. Unless your business is large enough to support individual departments (HR and marketing, for example), working with a large firm may mean less attention and higher rates. A smaller firm or an independent professional may give you more dedicated attention and be available immediately to answer your questions.

» **Philosophy:** Your financial advisors are ultimately your partners in business. Their professional views *must* complement yours. We're referring to not only ethics but also strategic philosophies. For example, if you're an aggressive risk taker in business, you may think that a conservative accountant will hold you back. Alternatively, you may prefer a conservative outlook as a means to provide a system of checks and balances to your liberal financial outlook.

» **Work style:** This term refers to how professionals interact with you and service your needs. For example, does the CPA insist that his firm file all required paperwork with the IRS, at a steep hourly rate? Or does he prefer to help you get started and then encourage you to take care of everything yourself to keep your expenses in check? What are his preferred methods of communication? If your tax professional isn't a fan of email, he might respond to your questions only by phone. Or an assistant might serve as a middleman, so the tax professional is rarely available to talk with you unless you schedule a formal appointment. Again, none of these issues has a right or wrong answer. Find a style that best meshes with your preferences.

Spending the time to determine these concerns means a lot to the future of your online business. After all, this professional plays an integral part in your business as a trusted financial advisor. That's why we suggest taking your time to select the best match for you and your new business.

Following the Rules of Recordkeeping

After you find a CPA or another financial professional, that person no doubt instructs you on the rules of good recordkeeping. In the meantime, take our crash course to help you get started doing things right!

Dealing with all the paper

When we refer to *records* in the remainder of this chapter, we don't mean your account logs. Instead, we're talking about the physical records (the dreaded *paper trail*) that the IRS expects you to maintain. The thought of accidentally throwing out the wrong receipt or losing a copy of a questionable invoice can send chills up the spine of any well-meaning entrepreneur if the IRS comes calling. At the same time, your office space probably doesn't come with unlimited storage space.

How do you balance the need to hang on to important receipts with the need not to be overrun by the growing mounds of paper? The good news is that the IRS now recognizes electronic versions of financial records. You can therefore scan copies of receipts, invoices, logbooks, and other proof of financial transactions and save them as files on your computer or, better, back up these files online (in the cloud) or to a DVD. Then you get to throw out the hard copies! That's the easiest way to avoid the clutter that builds up with months and years of business transactions.

WARNING

If you lose the electronic file and are audited, the IRS isn't sympathetic. The loss could cost you thousands of dollars — and possible jail time (in the worst-case scenario). We highly encourage you to make multiple copies and store one or more sets at another location or in a fireproof safe, or have a backup copy saved online but off-site.

TIP

You can avoid the time it takes to scan and save critical documentation by hiring a company to do it for you. In addition to making electronic copies of your paper trail, these digital documentation specialists store the electronic files for you. You can also purchase digital documentation software that makes scanning records yourself easy.

Storing records: How long is long enough?

Whether or not you "go digital" with your recordkeeping, one critical question remains: How long should you keep records? We should have a straightforward answer for you, but we haven't found one yet. That's because the IRS states (in Publication 583):

> You must keep your records as long as they may be needed for the administration of any provision of the Internal Revenue Code. Generally, this means you must keep records that support an item of income or deduction on a return until the period of limitations for that return runs out. The period of limitations is the period of time in which you can amend your return to claim a credit or refund, or the IRS can assess additional tax.

Huh? Well, the IRS says that you should keep records for as long as there's a possibility that it might audit you. We always heard that 7 years is a safe bet. However, the true issue isn't the type of *documentation*; rather, it's the type of *situation* you encounter with the IRS.

For example, if you have employees, the IRS says that those tax records must be kept for at least 4 years from the period the tax becomes due or is paid, whichever is later. On the other hand, records about assets, such as property, should be kept until the period of limitations expires for the year in which you dispose of the property. Even tangible guidelines such as those, however, could be null and void if you're audited for a fraudulent tax return. In that case, all bets are off and you had better have ready access to *all* your records, from the beginning of time!

All these situations make up what the IRS refers to as a *period of limitations*. Table 4-3 gives you an overview of the rules for these time restrictions, as defined by the IRS.

TABLE 4-3   IRS Periods of Limitations

If You Do This	The Period Is This Long
Owe additional tax and the other situations in this table don't apply	Three years
Fail to report legitimate income that's more than 25 percent of the gross amount on your return	Six years
File a fraudulent return	Unlimited
Fail to file a tax return	Unlimited
File a claim for credit or a refund after filing your return	Two to three years after tax is paid
File a claim for a loss from bad debt or worthless securities	Seven years

KEEP THESE EMPLOYEE RECORDS SAFELY FILED AWAY

The IRS advises that you retain any information related to employee taxes. Even if a record relates to someone who no longer works for you, keep the following documents for at least 4 years:

- Amounts and dates of all wage payments (including annuity and pension)

- Amounts of tips reported by your employees and records of allocated tips

- Fair market value of in-kind wages paid to your employees

- Employee information, including name, address, Social Security number, job title, and dates of employment

- Copies of Forms W-2 and W-2c that were returned to you (undeliverable, if mailed)

- Records of sick pay or other pay due to injury or absence (including the amount and weekly rate of payments that you or a third-party payer made)

- Copies of employees' income tax withholding allowance certificates — Forms W-4, W-4P, W-4(SP), W-4S, and W-4V

- Dates and amounts of tax deposits you made, along with confirmation numbers for deposits made by Electronic Funds Transfer Protocol (EFTP)

- Copies of filed returns, including 941 TeleFile tax records and confirmation numbers

- Records of any fringe benefits provided to employees, including expense reimbursements paid

TIP

To play it safe, embrace the philosophy "When in doubt, hang on to it." This technique is especially manageable if you have limitless storage capacity for electronic documentation.

REMEMBER

Businesses of all sizes may be eligible for certain deductions or tax breaks, specifically those designed to provide monetary incentive to help stimulate the economy through job growth and expansion. Tax incentives may be available for a limited time period or have exclusions and other stipulations. Take the time to discuss available deductions or incentives with your accountant or tax advisor. After all, these types of tax breaks could mean additional money in your business bank account!

We hope that you never have to worry about an audit from Uncle Sam (the U.S. government). The thought that it's always a possibility, though, is certainly incentive enough to keep all your records in order!

3

Website Functionality and Aesthetics

Contents at a Glance

Chapter **1**

What's in a (Domain) Name?

In the offline world, the mantra of success for business is "Location, location, location!" It's not much different for your online business. Rather than use a numerical address on a building, though, you now use a virtual address or *domain name.* Usually, your online address includes your company's name or initials or some other derivation. Whereas your traditional business address was once listed in the Yellow Pages, your online address is now listed with search engines.

As you might guess, securing the best possible domain name is an important piece of your overall online strategy. The name you select can provide an indication of what your company does, give a hint of your brand personality, and potentially influence how easily customers can find you.

How do you get the perfect name to drive customers to your online place of business? Not to worry: After using the information in this chapter, you'll find that choosing and registering your address is only a few clicks away.

Choosing Your Online Identity

Let's start with the basics. A *URL*, or *Uniform Resource Locator*, represents the unique address for each page on a website or document posted online. Your website might be made up of several web pages, each with a unique URL.

Before you start creating web pages, your first order of business is to determine your domain name, or the part of the URL that specifically identifies the name of your website. We break down a typical URL in Figure 1-1.

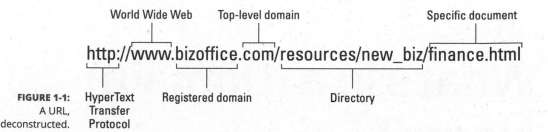

FIGURE 1-1:
A URL, deconstructed.

TIP

You no longer have to enter the entire URL (as shown in Figure 1-1) to get to a website. You can omit both the `http://` and `www.` when entering the site URL in your browser.

REMEMBER

Although your website usually has only one domain name, it has more than one URL. The URL for the *home* page, or *entrance* page, of your site often looks the same as your domain name. Every page of your site, however, has a unique URL, such as

>> `www.myveryfirstwebsite.com`: The home page

>> `www.myveryfirstwebsite.com/index.html`: Also, the home page (the same as omitting the `index.html` portion of the URL)

>> `www.myveryfirstwebsite.com/services.html`: The web page that contains information about the services you offer

REMEMBER

As an online business, it's beneficial to get a valid SSL Certificate. This ensures your website is secure and that data is properly encrypted when a visitor's web browser is communicating with your site. In this case, the URL will contain `https`, which translates to *Hyper Text Transfer Protocol Secure*. In addition, there is also a small icon of a lock that shows up next to the URL in the web browser's address bar. Visitors can click the security icon to see details about your website, like the example shown in Figure 1-2. We discuss this further in Book 5, Chapter 1.

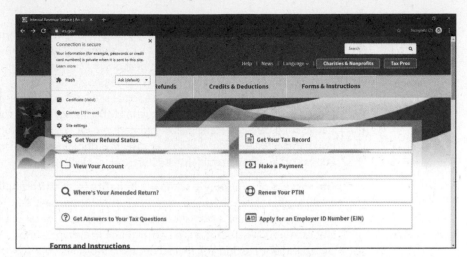

FIGURE 1-2:
A secure URL with HTTPS allows you to see information about a website.

Approaching your domain name carefully

You can take one of several opposing approaches when you select your domain name:

>> **You have an existing business or have already named your start-up.**
If that's the case, you usually should match (as closely as possible) your company's name to the domain name. Using your existing business name is simple, straightforward, and often quite effective. It's possible that your exact name is not available, in which case you have to use some form of the name or add descriptors to the name.

>> **You want to gain traffic by matching popular search phrases.** This was once considered an effective domain naming strategy because it served as a shortcut for directing organic (or free) search traffic to your website. Referred to as an *Exact Match Domain (EMD)*, this is a domain name that's a duplicate of an exact phrase that lots of people use to search for a product or a service. For example, if you sell running gear for women, you might use the domain name www.bestrunningshoesforwomen.com because you know a lot of people type in "best running shoes for women" when searching for that product. With your domain name matching this exact phrase, your site will show up higher in search engine results because it is the best match for that search query. Due to the popularity of EMD, it's often difficult to find a domain that's not already in use. Other popular phrases for EMD are available for sale, but they're typically very expensive. But if you find an available EMD that works for your business, it can be helpful in gaining traffic.

However, Google consistently updates its search engine algorithms (how search results are determined). It has since determined that some EMDs are "spammy" and don't always have the best quality content, despite the domain name (in other words, Google realized some people were trying to scam the system to get more traffic, even if the actual sites weren't completely relevant to the search phrase). You can still try the EMD strategy to gain some boost in traffic, but if Google determines the content on your page isn't top quality or truly an exact match of the search phrase, this domain naming strategy might not pay off at all (and could instead hurt your rankings).

» **The success of your online company benefits from the domain name itself.** Maybe you're starting an Internet company that sells e-books (electronic, downloadable information) telling readers how to start a business. In that case, your legal company name might be irrelevant. A more important consideration is to find a domain that clearly indicates your type of business or the customers you're targeting. In this scenario, your company name might be John Smith dba JS Enterprises. A more effective domain name for your business, however, might be www.bizstartuptips411.com because it tells visitors exactly what you do. This approach is different from EMDs in that you may use one or more keywords, or specific search terms, in your domain name, but you do not try to exactly replicate a phrase someone might use in search, such as "helpful business tips for startups."

Optimizing your domain name for better results

How much does your URL matter when it comes to search engine optimization (SEO)? This topic is always hotly debated by SEO experts. Most agree that your URL once had a big impact on a website's search engine ranking position. But Google is constantly adjusting the algorithms it uses to rank websites in search — and that means the weight it gives to a URL in search results has changed, and may likely change again!

A factor that always seems important is having HTTPS in the URL to verify that the site is secure. The value of using keywords in the URL and the length of the URL may vary in the future. We recommend that you take SEO strategy into account when picking a primary domain name and the URL naming structure for your *subpages* (pages other than the home page) but don't get too wrapped up in determining the perfect searchable URL. Instead, also consider what makes sense in a URL to your customers. No matter what approach you take to choosing your online business name, consider the following list of common denominators in determining the best possible domain for you. A good domain name should generally have these characteristics:

>> **Easy to spell:** As anyone who depends on a computer's spell checker can testify, the average person doesn't do well in a spelling bee. That's why we're firm believers in avoiding hard-to-spell words in your domain name. Although www.BriansBodaciousRibs.com seems harmless enough, it's fairly easy to flub. Why not try www.briansgoodribs.com or www.goodeating.com? The easier your domain name is to spell, the more likely customers are to find you without a hassle. (And, when they do find you, the more likely they'll be in the mood to buy some of your bodacious eats!)

>> **Simple to remember:** Your domain name doesn't have to be catchy or trendy to work. Simplicity goes a long way in our crowded, overhyped world.

>> **Relatively short:** A shorter name is easier for customers to remember than a longer one, and shorter URLs often have some benefit in search engine rankings. Consider the (fictitious) law firm Brewer, Mackey, Youngstein, Yale, and Associates. Its URL might be

www.BrewerMackeyYoungsteinYaleandAssociates.com

Wow! That name takes a while to type, not to mention that you have to spell everybody's name correctly. Instead, consider the name www.Brewerand Associates.com. See the difference?

>> **Contains important keywords:** This characteristic is generally important for two reasons:

- Using descriptive words in the domain clearly says what you do and is helpful to your customers.

- Using relevant words that frequently show up in search engines is potentially beneficial to your site's rankings, but don't try to stuff too many keywords in there. One or two is plenty! (We explain search engine optimization further in Book 6, Chapter 6.)

The law firm used in the preceding example can easily use *keywords,* or words that might be easily associated with the type of business, to create one of these domain combinations:

- www.legalfirmforhire.com

- www.breweryounglawyers.com

- www.attorneysbmyy.com

>> **Intuitive to customers:** You want a domain name to provide, ideally, a sense of who you are and an indication of the type of products or services you're selling. You don't need a *literal* translation, such as www.isellbooks.com — depending on your business, that approach could be detrimental to sales. What if you're selling to a highly targeted or specialized market (such as teenagers or radical sports fans)? A straightforward domain name is labeled as boring and

undermines the image of your company, whereas an edgy or more creative name can win customers. For example, a bookseller specializing in romance novels might use a domain name such as www.romancingthepages.com or www.steamyreads.com. The point is that your customer base, whoever it consists of, should be responsive to your domain name.

TIP

In the examples we use, you notice that the domain names usually end with .com, but that *domain extension* isn't your only option. Today, you can choose from a long list of specialized domain extensions that reflect your type of business (an LLC, for example), type of organization (such as a non-profit), or even your specific industry (like technology or auto dealerships). This is an alternative way to get a name that is already taken, but it may not significantly help with search engine rankings. We discuss these options in more detail at the end of this chapter.

Registering the Perfect Name

Congratulations! You chose your domain name, and you're ready to make it official. The next step is to register the name with a domain registrar. You can sign up using any company that specializes in domain registration. The registrar takes care of all the paperwork that's required to activate your new domain name, including these tasks:

>> Submitting contact information

>> Determining the duration of the registration period

>> Listing your domain in the official Internet list of domains maintained by the Internet Corporation for Assigned Names and Numbers (ICANN) at www.icann.org

TIP

If you're launching an e-commerce store, the storefront solution you use may include free domain registration, in which case it's best to register through that solution provider.

You have a choice: Domain registration options

Who registers domains? Your ISP (Internet service provider) might do it because many now provide this service along with hosting options. Or you can use any other company or website that acts as a third-party affiliate for registrars. If you're creating a website or blog in WordPress, you can register your domain there. In other words, now you can register a domain name with almost anyone!

Although finding a place to sign up is a piece of cake, the annual price for a domain registration varies from a single dollar to more than $30. Several factors influence pricing, including the number of years for which you're registering the domain, the provider, and the type of extension (such as .com, .net, .biz, or .tv). If you add features such as private registration (which restricts the registration details available to the public), the price goes up. Or you can wind up paying nothing for domain registration if you buy several services at one time. (Most domain registrars also offer services such as hosting, email, websites, and blogs.)

TIP

Most domain registration sites regularly offer discount domain pricing. Shop around for the best deal.

Let's make it official

After you make a decision about where to register, it's time to get down to business. The registration process is similar regardless of the service you use. To show you how painlessly you can reserve your domain name, we walk you through the process using the GoDaddy service. Note, though, that we aren't recommending GoDaddy over other services.

Follow these steps to quickly register your domain name:

1. Go to the Go Daddy website at www.godaddy.com.

2. Enter the name you want to register in the domain search box on the home page of the site.

Type only the name you want, and don't preface it with www. The registrar adds that part automatically. (Some registrars' domain search boxes place the www. in front of the search box to remind you that typing that part isn't necessary.)

3. To the right of the search box, click the Search icon.

A page appears listing the results of a search for the default extension, .com, along with additional options.

4. If your domain name isn't available, start over at Step 2.

Read the rest of the chapter first for tips on finding a domain name.

5. If you want to register an additional name, select the Add to Cart button next to each name you want.

REMEMBER

You can have multiple working domains even when you have only a single website. Simply *forward,* or redirect, the domain by pointing all other extensions to the designated domain of your choice.

6. **If you want to register an extension other than .com, select it from the list.**

When you're registering a .com extension, you may also want to register the matching `.net` or `.biz` version if it's available. These extensions are still among the most common, even though there is an ever-growing list of alternatives. If your site is successful, a savvy competitor is more likely to snatch up the .net version over any other. This statement is especially true if the domain name is descriptive with a wide appeal (such as `partygoods.com`) or falls in a popular search category (such as `starwarsfans.com`). If the .com version of your domain isn't available and you're registering another extension, one domain is plenty for starters. After your site grows, you can determine the value of registering other names.

7. **Click the Cart icon at the top of the page.**

You see a list of add-on products, including private registration, hosting, and email. At any point, you can skip these add-on suggestions and continue with the registration process.

During the process of registering your domain, GoDaddy tries to get you to buy other services, from privacy protection to web hosting. If you do not want any of these additional services, you can skip the offers by scrolling down to the bottom of each page and clicking the Continue to Cart button.

8. **Select the term, or number of years for which you want to register the domain.**

Your order's total appears.

9. **Log in to an existing account (as a returning customer), or set up an account as a new customer.**

If you're a new customer, you provide basic information (your name, address, and email address) to set up your account.

To set up your account, the information you provided in the initial domain registration process is automatically used by GoDaddy to fill in your technical, administrative, and billing contact information, unless you specify otherwise. Use these default settings for now. You can always change this information later.

10. **Click the Continue button.**

You see a page summarizing your order information.

11. **Review your information and place your order.**

A thank-you page appears. Congratulations — you now have a domain name that's all yours!

Finding Out What to Do When Somebody Gets There First

We hope that the domain you want is the one you get when you register. Sometimes, though, your first choice for a domain isn't available. Nothing bursts a bubble faster than having this sort of event happen. Don't let it frustrate you, though. You still have several options.

Exploring your domain name options

When you initially search for your domain (as described in the preceding section), the registrar might tell you that it isn't available. Below that notification is typically a box containing a list of suggested alternative domains that the registrar has available. Don't be surprised if the automated system returns a few decent alternatives. At this point, you can choose one of the suggested runners-up generated by the registrar.

If you don't find a perfect match on the suggested list, the next-less-appealing choice takes you right back to the drawing board. Yep, you can start a brand-new search for an entirely different name.

WARNING

There may be a charge for some of the suggested names that are automatically shown to you if your first choice is not available. Read carefully when alternatives are displayed to determine if that alternative is "available" only for a set fee or as part of a domain auction. Some alternatives shown to you are available — but only if you pay hundreds, or even thousands, of dollars!

Getting what you want — at a price

Starting from scratch again usually isn't your preference. After all, you might have fallen head over heels for a domain name and no substitute will work. In that case, you should know that you can pursue that domain name, even though it's already taken.

Here are the ways you can go in hot pursuit of your dream domain name:

>> **Put the name on back order.** Think of this strategy as the official waiting list of domain names. A registrar keeps your name on file and notifies you when the domain you want expires and becomes available. The back-ordered domains go to auction, and you can bid for the opportunity to buy (or register) it. You usually pay a non-refundable fee for this service.

>> **Make an offer.** You might be too impatient to wait and see whether a domain expires. The owner can decide to renew it, and then it's gone for at least another year. That's why several registrars will contact the owner on your behalf and try to confirm whether they are interested in selling, and if so, negotiate the purchase of the domain name. For this service, you pay a flat fee plus commission. Using this technique makes sense for a couple of reasons:

- *You can find out quickly whether an owner is willing to give up a domain name.* The seller must respond within a specified time.

- *Your name and personal information are kept private.* If the offer is accepted, you pay the registrar by credit card and the money is transferred to the seller. The registrar handles the entire process, including the transfer of the domain name.

>> **Contact the owner.** If you prefer to negotiate directly, contacting the domain owner in person is another option, provided the owner's registration information is open to the public. Even though you lose your anonymity in this process, you avoid paying service fees. Better yet, direct contact provides the opportunity to plead your case and use personal charm to try to get a good price for the name. (Okay, that's not always enough to sway a seller, but it might help.) Many companies have negotiated directly with sellers with much success. One domain owner, who no longer had an active site for the URL, gave away the domain. The moral of this story: It never hurts to ask.

TIP

If a domain owner has chosen a private registration, you may still be able to locate him or her. If the website for the domain is *active* (you can view it), search the pages for contact information (a phone number or an email address). If you find a name, you may also be able to find the person on social media, such as LinkedIn, and make contact that way.

REMEMBER

Finding the owner of a domain name is easy to do when you use the WHOIS feature sometimes offered by registrars after a name is shown as already taken. Or, you can go directly to the source and conduct a search for a domain owner via the Internet Corporation for Assigned Names and Numbers (ICANN) WHOIS lookup service at `https://lookup.icann.org`.

All the Good Ones Are (Not) Taken

You might think that all the good domain names have been taken (or are being held hostage for a huge ransom). Not true! Plenty of great domain names are available. The continued popularity of the Internet has prompted lots of acceptable and creative alternatives for domain registration.

Varying the extension

One of the easiest ways to find a good domain name is to use an alternative extension, although we can't deny that the old favorites .com, .net, and .org (for nonprofits) remain the most recognizable. Thousands of extensions, referred to as general top-level domains, or gTLDs, including specific country codes, are now in use and growing in popularity. Using these alternatives is no longer considered a stigma.

In fact, ICANN (the organization responsible for domains) released new gTLDs that are based on business industries and professions (such as .accountants) and other recognizable categories (such as .TV and .coupons). The decision to offer new extensions was made in an effort to address demand overflow for domain names using the .com and .net extensions, and make it easier to get the right domain name for your business or organization. Because ICANN understands that the new gTLDs may also soar in popularity, business owners with trademarked names get preference for reserving or obtaining the domains over owners without a trademarked name. So, if you own the trademark name "Crazy Cats," you can get first rights for reserving the domain name www.CrazyCats.pet instead of someone who may want to have a site that shows videos of crazy cats submitted by pet owners.

How do you get one of these new domains? It's no different than the registration process for any other domain. You simply choose the extension you prefer when registering for a domain name (in keeping with our previous example, you choose .pet instead of .com). The exception to this rule is for any new gTLD that is not yet publicly available.

Table 1-1 lists some of the most common U.S. extensions. We also list some additional extensions by country (but note that more are available, including the popular .asia, for example), and some of the new gTLDs. Don't shy away from any of these. Looking through the list is a simple way to find the domain name of your choice.

TABLE 1-1

Sampling of Extensions Used in Domain Registration

Extension	Generally Used For
.com	General business (.com stands for *commercial*)
.net	Internet business (.net stands for *network*)
.org	Nonprofit and trade association (.org stands for *organization*)
.info	Resource

(continued)

TABLE 1-1 *(continued)*

Extension	Generally Used For
.biz	Small business
.tv	Entertainment, media
.name	Personal use
.mobi	Mobile business sites
.travel	Travel industry use
.media	Magazines, reality channels, digital publishers, graphic designers, and so on
.author	Writers and published authors
.shop	Retailers
.ws	Web (former country code)
.bz	Business (former country code)
.cc	Miscellaneous (former country code)
.us	United States
.vg	British Virgin Islands
.co.uk	General business in United Kingdom
.org.uk	Nonprofit and trade association, United Kingdom
.me.uk	Personal, United Kingdom
.de	Germany
.jp	Japan
.be	Belgium
.at	Austria
.com.mx	General business, Mexico
.com.nz	General business, New Zealand
.net.nz	Usually Internet provider, New Zealand
.org.nz	Nonprofit and trade association, New Zealand
.gs	South Georgia, South Sandwich Islands
.tc	Turks, Caicos Islands
.ms	Montserrat

Getting creative

Acquiring the domain name you view as most suitable for your business may involve a little creativity on your part. As you have probably seen, most general names (applying to wide or popular categories) were scooped up during the first Internet craze of the 1990s. All the gems — `Business.com`, `Politics.com`, `SportsFan.net` — are long gone.

Don't let this information stop you. Keep in mind that plenty of domain names are as effective as those first category-busters. Here are four creative ways to find an outstanding domain name:

>> **Make the domain name specific.** One recent trend is that of niche (or specific) sites. You can find out more about growing a niche on the Internet in Book 10. For now, we want you to know that the same trend applies to domain names. Creating a more specific and telling name, rather than one that's broad, serves you well in search engine rankings and with your customer base. For example, `www.ilovecheese.com` is specific about its subject and audience.

>> **Make the domain name creatively telling.** Ever hear that saying about thinking outside the box? Even though it's a cliché, it holds true with domain names: Sometimes, you're trapped into seeing only one way to describe something, and that usually means being literal. If you sell food and toys for cats, you're tempted to find a domain that says exactly that: `cattoys.com`. Rather than continuously circle around the same type of name, think about other ways that your products, services, or target audience are viewed. Make a list of terms and phrases that people use when they talk about these items. You can still be specific but with a more creative tone. That cat site may do extremely well using a domain name like `mouseloversonly.com` or `thescratchingpost.com`.

>> **Make the domain name perfectly meaningless.** Have you ever stumbled across a website with an outrageously different but perfectly applicable name (like Google and Yahoo!)? Websites with extremely odd, fun, or funky domain names can grow a following like any other site. This advice is best if you're in a business that lends itself to a less conservative approach.

>> **Use add-ins.** If your domain name uses common words, finding an exact match available isn't all that easy. Not to worry: Just mix it up a bit. Abbreviate your words or use a few initials rather than spell out the whole thing. Or break up the name with a hyphen or two (`Pearl-Earrings-For-You.com`, for example). You can also add *inc* or *corp* to the end of your company name (only if you're incorporated, of course) or add another word that indicates the industry you're in — for example, `SmithJewelersInc.com` or `SmithPearlsandDiamonds.com`. Another trick is to include words such as *official*, *favorite*, *original*, or *popular* to the domain name (`FavoritePearlEarrings.com`, for example).

IN THIS CHAPTER

» **Understanding customer-friendly design**

» **Preparing for profitability**

» **Gauging goals and traffic flow**

» **Considering timeless design options**

» **Doing away with fluff**

Chapter **2**

Designing for User Experience

You might have put most of your efforts into dreaming about and planning for your business. As you begin designing your website, though, you see your ideas come to life for the first time. Creating that first site is exhilarating! You have to stay focused, though. Otherwise, you risk becoming distracted by bells and whistles that can waste your time and money and diminish the effectiveness of your site. One of the best ways to avoid a low-performing website is to design it with the user (your customer!) in mind. Taking this approach is part of designing for user experience (also referred to as UX).

Taking a user-centric approach has taught us that you can easily avoid certain common mistakes. The key is to develop a goal-oriented site plan, keep it simple, get user feedback, implement necessary changes, and then repeat as needed! If you follow these ground rules, you're rewarded with a website that's functional, timeless, and customer friendly.

Mapping the Customer Experience

Think back to one of your recent visits to a website. Maybe the site is one of your favorites or one you visited for the first time. How would you rate your experience? Did you find what you wanted quickly and easily? Did you glean the information you needed? Did your browsing lead to a purchase? Or were you frustrated by the whole thing and chose instead to move on to another site? Well, guess what? Your customers think about the same issues every time they visit your site. Even if they don't set out to rate or judge your website on these issues, customers' behavior while visiting the site — and whether or not they complete the actions you intend for them to — is a vote for a positive or poor user experience.

Ultimately, user experience leads them to make two important decisions:

>> Whether to make a purchase from you

>> Whether to return to your site

When it comes to creating the best possible user experience, it's important to map out the journey your customer will take and then test to confirm that the end result you're looking for is achieved. The key to mapping an ideal UX is focusing on functionality as a critical part of the website design process. Below, we point out several examples of functions (such as quick-loading pages, a site search function, and live customer service) that make a difference in user experience.

Basic functionality

When you consider what's at stake with your business when you design your own site, you have to figure out how to use function to influence customer decisions. We suggest attacking function at three levels.

At the first level are *basic functions.* Customers expect this lowest, or base, level of functionality. Basic functions include these features:

>> **Quick-loading pages:** Customers don't have the patience to wait for pages to load. Even if they're still using slower dial-up connections (yes, there are still people who do!), you're expected to ease that problem for them. If you don't anticipate customers having varying speeds of Internet access and account for that difference in your web design, you just missed a potential sale.

TIP

To decrease the need to load new pages in the site, consider using overlays or pop-up content boxes. These elements display additional information without the need to leave the page.

Customers aren't the only ones who benefit from fast load times. Google also likes pages that are fast, and it rewards that behavior with a potential boost in search engine rankings!

>> **Ease of navigation:** When customers go from page to page in your site, the navigation tools you provide should allow customers to

- Readily find and identify navigational buttons and links.

- Immediately return to the home page, regardless of what page they're on.

- Return to the preceding or last-visited page by clicking a link.

- See pages and sections they have visited on the site by using a link history, usually found at the top of the page.

>> **Working links:** All internal and external links to pages on your site should be valid and working. In other words, customers don't want to click a link only to find a *Page Not Found* message. Broken links that go nowhere also diminish the credibility of your site and indicate that you don't update or maintain it.

>> **Viewable images:** When you include photos and graphics on your site, be sure that the images — especially product images — load correctly and quickly. Additionally, avoid using grainy pictures or tiny images that are difficult for customers to see. When shopping online, customers increasingly expect to see multiple views of a product, or have the ability to manipulate the image for a closer view (we discuss this more in Book 7).

>> **Shopping carts:** Yes, this is a category unto itself (and we discuss it in detail in Book 4, Chapter 5). We list it as an interactive function because all too often small websites continue to make the mistake of not even using shopping carts on their sites. Instead, customers are asked to call the company to place orders, or to print, fill out, and fax order forms to the website owner. That's a fatal mistake! You *must* provide a method for shopping and paying for items over the Internet.

>> **Mobile-ready:** Today, more websites are viewed on a mobile device than on a desktop computer! That may not come as a surprise to you if you are as attached to your smartphone as we are, but it does come with special considerations when designing your website. In addition to customers using mobile devices to research, compare, and buy products, mobility is also increasingly important in search results. Google penalizes your site's rankings if it does not meet its mobile-friendly requirements! As a result of this changing emphasis on mobile from search engines and consumers, your website *must* look good and function well on all types of mobile devices, including tablets and smartphones. The best way to approach this is to make sure your website is *mobile responsive*, which means your site automatically (with the use of the right code) resizes itself to fit the type and size of screen your customer is on — whether that's a desktop, a laptop, a small smartphone, a large smartphone, or a tablet. As a part of responsive design, for

example, the site's navigation bar may shift from running across the top of the page when viewed on a desktop to being viewed as a drop-down menu on a phone; or images may appear smaller; or the text may be repositioned to make it easier to read on a smaller screen by scrolling vertically versus horizontally. In the world of UX, the idea is to take a device-agnostic approach to design. Assume that your website could be viewed on *any* device!

Interactive functionality

At the second level of site functionality are *interactive functions*, which actively engage customers with your site. Although this type of functionality isn't necessary to place an order, it can increase value and sales for your site. Samples of interactive functions include

» **Site search:** Give customers a tool that enables them to quickly search for information on your site. This function might not be as useful if your site is small. However, if you have a site filled with products or layers of data, customers appreciate having search capability.

» **Reviews:** Consider offering your visitors the option to review or rate the products and services you offer. This feature is particularly helpful, and almost expected, if you have an e-commerce site. Research shows that customers' buying decisions are heavily influenced by online reviews.

» **Community forums:** *Forums* (or types of discussion areas) provide options that let visitors interact with you and with one another. Many people consider forums a free form of technical support; if your community area or forum boards stay active and updated, this added function might keep customers coming back to your site.

» **Blogs:** These extremely popular online journals provide another opportunity for customers to interact with you and others.

» **Member registration:** You can make registration free or make it a condition of accessing certain sections of your site. In return for signing up as members, visitors can receive newsletters, site updates, or email messages announcing new products. Registration provides members with benefits and provides you with customer contact information — a win-win situation for both parties.

Enhanced functionality

The third level of site functionality is reserved for tools and features that offer customers an *enhanced* experience on your site. Items of enhanced functionality often include

>> **Video, online demonstrations, and tutorials:** Depending on the complexity of the products or services you sell, online demos and web-based tutorials can be useful. Customers receive the value of trying out the product or discovering how it's used, which often increases the likelihood of a purchase. Offering online learning options is easy and affordable by using videos (especially through YouTube). And videos of any type, from customer testimonials to interviews with employees, can be a simple way to add value and increase visitor engagement on your site.

>> **Live or 24/7 customer support:** The Internet never sleeps, and neither do some of your customers. Your customer service is greatly enhanced if you can offer unlimited support. Although it isn't necessarily *technical* support, your customer might need to ask a question before making a decision to buy your service or product. Some research indicates that offering live support can increase online sales by as much as 20 percent.

TIP

You don't have to set up a full customer call center to offer live or 24/7 support. Several companies have developed the service for even the smallest online retailers. Try LiveEngage from LivePerson (`www.liveperson.com/liveengage/messaging`) to add live customer support to your website. This tool offers various pricing plans based on the features you choose and the size of your business, including a pricing plan that charges only when someone uses the chat function on your site.

>> **Geographic locators:** Okay, if you have physical locations in addition to your web presence, geography-related tools are a plus. Your customers appreciate access to maps and driving directions, store locators using interactive maps of the United States (or other countries), and even product-locator searches based on zip codes.

TIP

Customizing a map for your site is easy with the Google Maps API. Visit `https://developers.google.com/maps` to get started. This free tool lets you create maps and driving routes that you can add to your site immediately. Another free Google resource, Google My Business (`www.google.com/business`), allows your offline store to be found more readily by customers searching on Google. Of course, this is useful only if you also have a physical location.

>> **Second-language viewing options:** Not all your customers speak fluent English. Savvy website owners offer customers the option to view sites in other languages. (For example, Spanish is one of the most popular alternatives in the United States.)

>> **Podcasts:** Giving access to information by using several different forms of media is much more common than ever before, yet it is still considered an unexpected bonus. Try adding *podcasts* (self-published broadcasts over the Internet) as a helpful way to share more information about your products or services. You can also use podcasts to conduct short interviews with authors,

Designing for User Experience

designers, trend watchers, analysts, or anyone else your site visitors might find interesting (as they relate to your site). Because podcasts are available through third-party providers, such as Apple iTunes, Google Play, Spotify, and others, you have a chance to reach visitors through your podcast who might not otherwise know about your website.

As you see, understanding the value of functionality and the subsequent choices you make regarding function are major parts of developing a customer-friendly site. Building off functionality is also an opportunity to set yourself apart from your competition. You just need to take the time to plan.

Maximizing Performance for Profitability

When thinking about website design, you (or a designer) can suffer from tunnel vision and focus only on creating a beautiful site that pleases visitors. Let's not forget you're in business to make a profit; so how does your website fit into that goal? Although the answer to this question might seem obvious, you can easily forget that your website is both a marketing tool and a vehicle for obtaining profits. The common denominator between those two points is a site that's functional for customers. As we discussed, when you maximize your customer's ease of use and experience with your site as part of UX design, everyone wins. But part of knowing how to make a site functional for visitors also requires that you understand what it is you need a customer to do while on your site. Defining those user actions starts with identifying which online actions lead to revenue.

To get the most from your site, we recommend creating a *profitability plan*, which is all about efficiency. Start by strategically identifying the features, technologies, services, and products for sale that increase revenue and enhance profitability — and getting rid of those that don't. You may be asking, "What if I don't have an e-commerce site with products sold online?" If your sales are indirect or generated offline, it's still important to prioritize your revenue streams and identify which pieces of online content and calls to action (such as Schedule a Consultation or Contact Sales) best support and lead to offline sales.

TIP

Ideally, you want to develop this plan before your first site goes up. Then you can address profitability in every page of the site as it's built. Not to worry, though: You can apply the same methodology to an existing site. The process just might take a little more time if you need to restructure the flow of your site, or the pathway you want visitors to take to meet your goals. Either way, maximizing your profit is worth the effort.

When you're ready to create a plan that maximizes your potential for profitability, follow these steps:

1. **Define the purpose of your site.**

   The purpose should reflect your site's role in your overall business. Voice that purpose in only one or two sentences. If you have trouble getting started, try answering these questions:

   - My website exists because _____.
   - I am creating (or planning) a website because _____.
   - When my site is complete, I want it to _____.

2. **Evaluate your revenue streams by listing all the ways in which you earn, or plan to earn, revenue from your site.**

   Be specific when you list the ways in which your site contributes to your revenues. For example, divide the list into two categories: direct revenue and indirect revenue.

3. **After you list your profit sources, assign a numeric value to them.**

   The numeric value is based on both sales volume and profitability. Of course, if your site isn't developed, you don't have a sales history. Instead, you rank items according to expected profitability. (You can go back later and cross-reference them by both profitability and bestsellers.)

4. **Determine which applications or functions on your site contribute most to your revenue sources and which indirectly support revenue growth.**

   This step helps you not only understand the purpose of each site element but also prioritize where to spend your time and resources. Some components are essential to building sales, but others are just nice to have. For instance, a shopping cart or payment-processing method directly affects sales because customers use it to purchase products. Similarly, call-to-action buttons (to register for a free trial), forms (to contact sales), or links (to download a white paper) are important because they prompt a desired transaction. Social media sharing buttons, and a registration box to sign up for a newsletter or get the latest blog articles are examples of indirect contributors. (Although social sharing and the newsletter don't lead to immediate purchases, they help future sales by creating continued awareness.)

5. **Compare your remaining list of products, services, and features with your site's purpose (as defined in Step 1) and omit the ones that don't directly contribute to it.**

   Items that don't directly reflect your site's original intent can cannibalize it down the road and eat away at your profits. By streamlining your revenue sources, you keep the site tightly focused on its target customer.

   You should understand now what adds value to your site (and to what degree).

6. **Strategically place features and revenue sources on your site map, which becomes your profitability plan.**

Usually, a site map represents all the pages that make up your website. The layout indicates the placement of the pages. In this step, you're simply creating a site map, or visitor pathway, based on profitability. In other words, specify where you want those "opportunities to purchase" to be placed on pages in the site. Is your largest revenue generator promoted or clearly visible from the top of your home page, or do customers have to click through five pages to see it? Which of your pages are top *landing pages* (pages other than your home page where visitors are likely to enter your site)? Do these landing pages contain the right information or calls to action to lead to a purchase? If you receive indirect revenue when customers agree to submit a form page for more information, can they access the form from your home page or from the top landing pages?

Now you have a plan! With your profitability plan in hand, you have a guide during the technical stage of building your site. (We address the technical aspect of site development in Chapter 3 of this minibook.) The profitability plan helps make clear your objectives for the site based on revenue. Next, you want to define specific goals and conversion points on your website pages to determine how visitors should move through your website and ultimately buy from you.

Establishing Page Goals

In the past (and we mean years ago, when businesses first started getting online), websites had a very simple structure. There were usually three to five main sections of a site (Homepage, About Us, Products, Services, Contact Us) with few total pages — usually less than a dozen. Today, websites, especially e-commerce sites, can have hundreds of pages, or more.

There are also lots of different ways people can find or enter your site — directly (by typing your domain name in a web browser), through a link in social media, by responding to an online ad from Google Ads, in response to a call to action in a video on YouTube, or through organic search (because they're searching for information or products and your site shows up in search results). Not to mention, new visitors can start their experiences with your site from your home page or from any other page in your website (this is considered a *landing page* because visitors "land" on it first).

With so many different pages and options for what and when (or where) a visitor first sees on your site, it's critical to help define the path you want visitors to take. Just as you want a profitability plan for your site, you need to map out and control, or heavily influence, how traffic flows through the pages of your website. Ultimately, you want that traffic flow or "visitor pathway" to result with an action — making a purchase, requesting a quote, watching a video, downloading a white paper, registering for a webinar . . . the list of actions is nearly endless and totally dependent upon what *you* want your visitor to do.

Let's start by defining exactly what we mean by website goals and conversions. A "goal" is an end result you want to achieve, and it must be specific and measurable. You might have a goal to increase traffic to a particular product page on your website by 20 percent over the previous 30 days and have a bounce rate (whether or not visitors immediately leave or *bounce off* that page) of 40 percent or less. A "conversion" is the completion of an action, such as clicking a call-to-action button or actually buying a product.

REMEMBER

We sometimes talk about conversion rates to determine how successful an online offer is on a particular page. One way to calculate the rate is by dividing the number of clicks on a call-to-action button by the number of visitors on the page over a certain period of time. A Buy Now button on a product page may have a 2 percent conversion rate, for example. We go over conversions in more detail in Books 6 and 11.

Before you can map out how you want traffic to flow through your website, you need to define the goals and conversion points for each page of your website. And all these decisions are critical to successful website design! Obviously, you cannot physically control what actions website visitors take and which pages they view, or in which order. However, knowing the goal of a specific page helps you determine which calls to action you need on the page, and further helps you determine what type of content you need on that page. Figure 2-1 shows an example of a visitor pathway based on goals and conversions.

FIGURE 2-1:
Guide the traffic flow through your site based on defined goals and conversion points.

Page ⟶ Goal ⟶ Conversion

/Pricing ⟶ Engage sales ⟶ Request quote

TIP

Use the information from the profitability plan you create to determine what type of conversions you need on each page. This ensures you are directing visitors to click on offers that help generate the highest possible revenue for your online business.

Designing for User Experience

Each page of your website should have a goal associated with it. What is the purpose of the page? What do you want visitors to do when they are on that page? Where do you want visitors to go next? For example, the goal may be for visitors to read information about a common problem they may be having and learn more (which could be measurable by the bounce rate and time spent on the page). The conversion point may be to click a link within the text to a product or service page that solves the common problem they just read about; or it might be to watch a video for more detailed information. Knowing the goal for each page also helps you determine the most appropriate conversion points on the page. (Yes, you can have more than one conversion point!)

Once you have goals, conversions, and visitor flow mapped out, you have a good starting point to determine your site's structure. But don't relax just yet. Next, it's time to wrap up all your goals, flows, and functionality with some attractive design elements.

Putting Your Best Site Forward

First impressions are lasting ones, or so the old saying implies. In the first few seconds of viewing your site, visitors first decide what they think about it. Often, a favorable impression is based entirely on the design elements you use. From classic to vintage or from plain Jane to modern, establishing that look sets the tone for your entire site. Design options are also part of the UX process because it influences customers' response to your site and can directly impact their buying behavior.

Following design trends and UX principles

When you're thinking about site design, consider the following major elements that contribute to a winning look:

>> **Structure:** The foundation of your site's design is its structure, or *layout*. Determining the layout of your site requires that you make decisions about these elements:

- *Number of pages:* Consider the depth of the site (the number of pages that are necessary).

- *Placement of the navigational toolbar:* The series of buttons or links that people use to visit different areas of your site — referred to as a toolbar, navigation bar, or menu bar — is commonly placed along the left (or right) side of the site, along the top, or in in both places. Making your site *responsive,* or adaptive to viewing on mobile devices, is a critical part of site design today. Simple, fixed menu bars or drop-down menu bars are popular style choices when building a responsive website.

- *Buttons, tabs, and links:* Buttons you can use on the navigation bar come in unlimited designs, shapes, and colors (depending on the software you use). Additionally, you can use text, rather than a button, as a link.

>> **Color:** An influential design element is the color scheme for your site. Do you go bold and bright or soft and understated, or do you stick to plain white or neutral colors? Another consideration is how to incorporate those colors (or lack thereof) into the site. You can use a color as a background for your entire site, to highlight sections of text, or to separate segments within your site.

>> **Font:** The font type and size you use throughout your site makes a statement. And with thousands of font styles to select from, you can send a variety of messages to your customers in the blink of an eye. Additionally, the text size you use contributes to not only the look of the site but also its readability. For example, text that's too small might not be easy to read. *Serif* fonts, which have hooks and loops on the letters, are also difficult to view when used online. Sans serif fonts remove the extra detail and can be more easily viewed online.

Font type is an element of web design that changes often, based on current design trends. For example, using creative, artistic, or graphical fonts became popular in 2014. In previous years, a simpler font style was preferred by most designers. The popularity of mobile devices is influencing font styles today. For readability with mobile responsive design, we've seen a return to simple, easy-to-read fonts. No matter which style you choose, it's important to find a design that works for your brand and to be consistent across the site. To stick to the basics, see the following table for a list of some basic web fonts.

Font	Message It Sends
Arial	I'm common and nondescript.
Comic Sans	I'm choosing whimsy over seriousness.
Courier New	I'm old-fashioned, from the era of newsroom typewriters.
Georgia	I'm classic and professional and layered with style.
Times New Roman	I'm quite traditional.
Trebuchet	I'm professional yet relaxed (similar to casual Friday in the workplace).
Verdana	I emit a friendly, modern vibe.

>> **Images:** The use of photos and graphics (animated or otherwise) can complement your site if they're used correctly. The style and type of images that are on trend for UX changes from year to year, but using images has become a design staple. Images draw readers' eyes to specific areas of your site and can help illustrate information and ideas. High-quality images have always been a necessity if you're selling products. But now images are must-have elements for *all* types of sites — not just e-commerce. When you're designing your site, think about how many images you'll use, their size, and which location will produce the best effect.

>> **Social media:** Unless you've been in a cave for the past few years, you know that social media sites such as Facebook, Twitter, Pinterest, Instagram, and LinkedIn continue to increase in popularity and that businesses of all types are expected to embrace them. (You discover more about social media and how to use it in your online business in Book 7.) Social media gets your customers more involved with your brand by encouraging them to comment and share information, which in turn could lead to more customers and more sales. To promote this type of activity, a decent amount of space throughout the website is used to persuade customers to "like" you on Facebook or "follow" you on Twitter. Other common social media tactics include offering customers the ability to *pin,* or share, images and product pictures from your website on social media sites such as Pinterest or Instagram. You need to consider where and how you place these opportunities on your site.

DOES YOUR SITE DESIGN WORK?

Before finalizing your site's design, ask yourself these questions to determine whether your site makes a winning first impression:

- Does the design reflect your defined purpose for the site?

- Will the look of the site appeal to your customers and encourage them to buy from you?

- Does the site's design (especially colors and fonts) allow information and products to be easily seen? Or do your eyes strain to look at text and images?

- Does the choice of layout, specifically the navigational bars, make it easy to locate information and move between pages?

- Is the site consistent with all other marketing and promotional tools you use?

- When customers first view the site, will it promote the image you want them to have of your company?

» **Media:** Video has become a common element that you should consider in the design of your website. The soaring popularity of YouTube, its influence in search engine rankings, and the amount of times it is shared through social media have contributed to the widespread acceptance and use of online video for all sorts of purposes. For some sites, this capability becomes an intricate design element. For others, it may be considered only as a marketing tool. Research supports the idea that video increases customer engagement (how the customer interacts with your site and brand) and can increase product sales (when using video for product reviews or testimonials, for example). You must weigh the pros and cons of video and decide where and when it will be used across your site, along with how to use it in a way that supports, rather than detracts, from your site's usability.

Making design choices

You must make a number of decisions when you develop the look and feel of your site. How do you choose which options make the most sense for you? Generally, one or more of these characteristics dictate a site's look:

» **Your industry or line of business:** If you're in a conservative industry, such as accounting or financial services, consider that subdued colors with a simple layout might appear to be more professional. Alternatively, if a potential customer is searching for a graphic designer, the customer might expect to see a bright, funky design with lots of colorful images.

» **The types of products or services you offer:** Selling products or services that have a serious message (such as medical equipment) begs for a low-key design approach. And the information your site contains might require many layers of pages to provide research or product information. On the other hand, products that are fun or made for recreational purposes might sell better if the site is light and whimsical and filled with product images rather than with product data.

» **An existing brand:** Particularly if you have an established business, your site's style or look might be predetermined by your company's store or product base. You want your site's image to be consistent with your established brand. In that case, you should pull design elements for your website from a logo, marketing materials, or the design of the existing bricks-and-mortar location.

» **Your customers' demographics and psychographics:** Age, gender, education, and geographic location are examples of *demographics*. Attitudes, opinions, and values are considered *psychographics*. In general, the more you know about your customers, the more likely you are to create the appropriate feel for your site. Consider designing your site to fit the image of your target customer, especially with niche (or highly specialized) markets.

>> **Your personal preferences:** Sometimes, your choice of design elements depends on which ones most appeal to your taste. (You get a say in this process, after all.) Okay, you shouldn't design a site based entirely on personal preference, but nothing is wrong with throwing in a few elements that make your heart sing.

The final consideration in designing your website is to create a timeless look — but we don't mean that you design a site once and never touch it again. A common pet peeve is a site on the Internet that's outdated and looks like an early-generation "brochure" site. We instantly feel as though the company doesn't care about its business or its customers. The company probably has a website only because someone told the company's owner that one was needed, so he or she turned a sales brochure into a basic three-page site, launched it on the web, and never thought about it again.

If you want to create a website that's considered timeless, keep these three suggestions in mind:

>> **Keep it simple.** Whether a site was developed in 2001 or 2021, trends change. Trust us when we say that trying to keep up with every new web design feature becomes expensive and time consuming. By keeping your design elements simple and by using only one or two trendy features, however, you increase the design lifespan of your site.

>> **Keep the information updated and relevant.** This advice includes everything from text and photos to hypertext links and copyright dates. Keeping the substance of your site current offers value. Also, you can easily overlook a graphical design that might make a site seem dated, but having incorrect or outdated content is an e-commerce sin.

>> **Avoid images or graphics that visually date the site.** For instance, if you use seasonal or current event photos, your site can quickly become dated. (However, these types of images are suitable in a blog or an area of the site that you plan on updating frequently.) Similarly, photos of people can be telltale signs of an outdated site because of clothing and hair. The exception is if you intentionally use graphics or photos that evoke a retro feel or provide relevant historical information.

TIP

Before designing your site, do your homework. Search the Internet for competitors' sites, and evaluate which design elements work and which don't. You can even gather a small group of prospective customers and ask them which sites they respond to most.

Testing Your Design Assumptions

In case your head is filled with hot design ideas, we should mention that a good site doesn't function by design alone. In fact, sometimes you can make your site even better by sacrificing trendy design elements. As we always say, sometimes it pays to put function first! The question is how can you tell if your site is going to achieve the ultimate goal of making your money?

Lots of factors play into the monetary success of your site, some of which you have little or no control over. The good news is that when it comes to designing the best possible site for success, UX is an area where you have ultimate control. The challenge is deciding what you *think* is good design and functionality versus what your customer actually experiences. This is why you should always test your ideas (and design).

TIP

How do you test your site for a good user experience? You probably guessed it: You get feedback from your users! UX testing can be as simple or as complicated as you want. Here are the steps you should take when conducting a test:

1. **Involve customers and visitors.**

   If you have an existing site, or an existing business, create a *focus group* (a group of testers) that consists of the following:

   - **Customers:** Customers are able to give input that's specific to their prior experience with your products and services, as well as your website (if you've had one for a while). Their responses to the design choices for your site are important because they already have certain expectations as to how they need your site to function in order to enhance their buying decision.

   - **Noncustomers:** These folks may know absolutely nothing about your business. They may provide unexpected feedback. For example, you may use certain descriptive language on your site's navigational bar that is specific to your business but may not be commonly used in the industry or by your competitors. To you and your customer, it may make perfect sense. To a prospective customer, who knows nothing about your business, it may read like jargon that is meaningless or confusing as they try to search your site. Understanding this is an issue may lead you to use descriptions that are in line with your industry to make it helpful to everyone who visits your site, and in turn help you build sales with new customers.

2. **Identify buyer personas for test groups.**

   Not only is it important to solicit feedback from customers and non-customers, but you also want to identify different types of customers, or *buyer personas*. After all, not all personas (or customers) need the same information or pathway through your site to make a purchase. The buying experience could be quite different for each persona or for a group of personas. Having these various customer types represented in your UX testing helps you determine if your site is meeting the needs of your most important groups of customers.

3. **Design your test.**

This may seem obvious, but to create a test, you need to understand exactly what you want to test. You can test for many different things on your site, but it's best to limit it. We like to test for no more than 10 to 12 items at a time. These test items, often referred to as *tasks,* may be actions like, "Can the user find how to buy a specified product when coming to our site on the home page?" or "Can the user discover how or where on the site to watch a tutorial video or demo on how to use our most profitable product?" Developing this list of critical actions is one of the first steps in designing an effective UX test.

4. **Determine test metrics.**

In addition to defining the types of tasks you want a user to test, you need to decide which metrics to use to measure success. It's one thing to test if a user can find a certain video, but it's another to understand how long it takes the user to find that video. Make a list of *metrics* (or measurements) that are important. Common UX task metrics include

- Time to complete a task

- Goal fulfillment (did they accomplish what you asked)

- Task performance (the way the task or goal was accomplished)

We also like to provide an opportunity for testers to give open-ended feedback or general comments (written or verbal) to their experience with each task. Some testing software uses video and allows you to capture verbal and nonverbal feedback from the user. This is helpful in that it lets you document users' thoughts as they try to complete the task (provided they verbally express those thoughts!).

5. **Implement the test.**

There are a couple of ways to administer or give a test to a focus group, and you're not limited to only one method. You may prefer to have a focus group of five to seven users who come together in person to answer interview questions. This is a great way to get open-ended feedback on your website. A focus group may also perform designated tasks while you watch and take notes. In this setting, you ask them questions about the site, or give them instructions and watch as they complete the task from either (or both) a desktop or mobile device.

You may also choose to offer site visitors (or others) an online survey to answer questions about your site's performance or ease of use. In the past, this has been a popular method for existing websites by showing a pop-up window that asks the site visitor to participate in the survey. Although this has proven an effective method, especially if you offer a small incentive (such as a product discount) for taking the test, we think website users are becoming used to seeing these offers and they may become distractors from actually buying products on your site. A controlled testing environment may yield more meaningful results.

One other testing option is to use software that administers the test and uses keystroke capture, video, and even eye-tracking to record the users as they complete the tasks. Some vendors not only provide the tool, but can also recruit users (non-customers) to take the test and then provide a summary of the results.

6. Analyze your results.

It's not much of a test if there aren't measurable results that can be observed and reported. Perhaps the most important part of testing, next to the test itself, is deciphering the results and summarizing key take-aways. This means you sort through all the raw data and look for common responses or behaviors to tasks to find meaningful trends. For example, if 60 percent of your test takers couldn't complete a particular action, or if it consistently took them a long time to complete, then that's an indicator that you need to change something on your site, either in design or functionality, that's making it difficult to achieve the intended goal.

As you can see, there are many things to consider when you undertake UX testing. The results can be incredibly useful, but that's dependent upon a standardized approach to the test. UX testing may not be something you want to do on your own. Not to worry! There are plenty of companies that can assist you with it, but it can get expensive. Alternatively, here are some online tools to help with UX testing:

» Loop11 (www.loop11.com)

» UserTesting (www.usertesting.com)

» UserZoom (www.userzoom.com)

» Validately (www.validately.com)

TIP

There's lots to understand about user experience and usability testing, and it can be overwhelming if you're new to the topic or don't have a background in it. Whether you want to learn a little bit more to help make your site better, or you truly want to dig in to the details of UX, check out the resources available from the Interaction Design Foundation at www.interaction-design.org. The membership-based organization offers a range of UX design and testing classes, along with articles and best practices.

IN THIS CHAPTER

» **Planning a well-structured business website**

» **Finding out how to build your own website**

» **Using HTML commands effectively**

» **Building web pages with specific software tools**

» **Hiring the right professional to help you design your site**

Chapter **3**

Building a Site Without Spending a Fortune

n the early days of the Internet, simply having a website was a way to differentiate your business from the competition. As interest in the web developed and grew, companies of all shapes and sizes focused their efforts on capturing people's attention with websites. Because of this growth in online competition, planning a site and building a distinctive design and proposition became increasingly important. After all, an outstanding site encourages current customers to stay with your business and promotes your site's presence to the new shoppers who come online every day.

The same basic principles of website design apply as much now as they did when the web took off in the mid-1990s. Technologies used on the web might come and go, but you don't have to include the latest and greatest technology on your site. Customers are drawn to sites that are simple, focused, easy to use, well organized, and *useful.* Everything else is just sound and fury.

In this chapter, we present the steps for creating a website that serves your business and your customers. We direct you to spend some time defining exactly what you want on your site, and then we show you ways to implement your ideas, either by yourself or with the help of a professional. In either case, we specify the issues you need to consider and the traps you need to avoid so that you can focus on designing your website and then move on to the next phase of your business.

Mapping Your Route to a Successful Site

When people opt to build a new house or commercial building, they don't just hire a contractor, bring over the concrete and tools, and say "Go for it." Before construction even begins, they craft a carefully detailed plan that they review, edit, and approve. Your website should be treated the same way. The best sites aren't dreamed up by eccentric designers and thrown together quickly. Good sites require a clear road map from the people who run the business to ensure that the focus of the business is never lost.

Thinking about your website before you start its design is important. Start by making a list of all the functions you want to provide on your site. If you're tempted to believe that your site has just one function — to *sell stuff* — we encourage you to break down that function into subfunctions, by answering these questions:

>> **What kinds of products do you want to sell?** The number and organization of pages you have on your site depends on the makeup and complexity of your products or services. For example, you should have at least one page for each type of service that you offer.

>> **How many distinct categories of products will you sell?** You might need a separate page for each product category. Think about splitting up categories such as consumer electronics and computer products, for example.

>> **Will customers be able to create an account on your site?** If so, you need to provide a page where customers can log in, update their personal information, view their orders, and enter payment information.

>> **Will you provide customers with additional content, original or not?** Some websites make money by offering a subscription for their customers to read premium content such as special articles, interviews, and video, audio, and photo excerpts.

>> **How will customers pay for their orders?** You need to be able to take credit card orders, as well as consider popular online payment methods such as PayPal, Venmo, or Google Wallet. In extreme situations, you may consider providing a mailing address if you accept personal checks or money orders.

>> **Will you tell people about you and your business mission?** Some companies think that having a web page about their mission statement isn't important, whereas others use this page as a way to connect with customers.

>> **Will you provide instructions for using your website?** It has been a common practice for websites to create a page for frequently asked questions (FAQs) to help their customers use the site properly and find everything that's available.

After you come up with your list of site functions, the next step is to draw a map showing the web pages you need to accomplish those functions and showing how the pages relate to one another. At this point, don't even think about how the website or the individual pages will look; just identify the different pages that need to exist on your site. Assign each page to a box on your map, and check off the function that the page will handle. When you're done, you should have a map of your site that looks like a flowchart.

SITE-BUILDER CHECKLIST

Most e-commerce websites have a basic list of pages that they provide to their customers. As you're designing your own site, take a look at the functions that most sites provide and decide which types of pages are right for your business:

- Home
- Catalog
- Customer account
- Order information
- Privacy policy
- Frequently asked questions
- Website and social media content
- Map and directions (if you have a retail site)
- Checkout
- Payment processing
- About Us or company history (describes mission, purpose, or employees, for example)

At the top of your map is the *home page,* which is your launch pad to the rest of the website (see Figure 3-1). This page answers all the basic questions that customers have about your business, just like the friendly receptionist in the lobby of a 50-story building. Whether this visit is the first — or the fiftieth — for your customers, the home page has to answer their questions in a clear, concise, organized way or be able to point them in the right direction quickly.

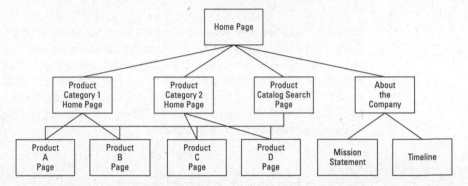

FIGURE 3-1:
The home page on your website leads into all your categories.

TIP

You can build a web page that holds a text version of the map you created and make it available to your customers. Just like a road atlas helps drivers follow their route, this *site map* helps your online customers find anything available on your site without taking a wrong turn — or, in this case, a wrong click.

Below the home page are your main category pages. Although your first draft might look like the one shown in Figure 3-1, the beauty of such a simple map is that your site plan can expand and grow from that basic model. As you design more complex and function-intensive websites, you can add more levels to your website map. When you build your site map this way, you can visualize how your entire site operates, because you capture how your pages support each other.

Setting reasonable expectations

When your website is in the paper-and-pen phase of design, you might find that you're adding a bunch of boxes (pages) and dreaming up the ultimate website. After all, you haven't designed or written the pages yet, so creating a gigantic, robust, fully functional site for any customer is easy — *on paper.*

Although we don't want to take the wind out of your sails (or is that *sales?*), we definitely advise you to keep these expectations and guidelines in mind as you begin to turn your road map into your virtual store:

>> **Don't put too much stuff on one page.** Avoid tying together several product lines. If a page become bloated — too filled with information and graphics, for example — it becomes too long for customers to read and takes too long to load and display on their screens. More important, as a growing part of the population uses mobile devices like smartphones and tablets to surf the Internet, your pages need to be optimal for mobile devices to load quickly.

>> **Position key information at the top.** Keep your pages short, and put key information at or near the top of the page. Newspapers place key articles *above the fold* (the top half of the newspaper page) because not all readers take the time to flip over the paper to read the bottom half. On the Internet, if you're asking your customers to scroll down the page to see something important, you're taking the risk that they won't do it and might leave your site without seeing your business's main functions.

>> **Keep the number of steps to a minimum.** One reason why customers come back to a site such as Amazon is that they can find an item, click once, and have the item shipped to them. Customers turn to online shopping for convenience, so offer them a quick or smooth process to navigate the critical areas of your site. Even though some customers stay to look around, take advantage of your content, or use other functions, your site needs to appeal to the customers who want to get in, get what they want, and get out.

TIP

One way to check the complexity of your website is to look at your road map. If you have too many levels between the home page and a finishing point for placing an order, consider revamping your plan to provide a smoother path.

>> **Remember that good design takes time.** Don't expect to have your site up in a day. Although the broad strokes of creating a website (such as creating the navigation bar and home page layout) can happen quickly, the refinement and fine-tuning of the site (such as defining button colors or the number of columns) can take much longer. Then again, fine-tuning can separate you from the competition in your customers' eyes. Give your designer enough time to do good work but not free reign to create a masterpiece.

Avoiding common holdups in developing a site

The last part of any website design process involves looking at the site map and page count and then estimating how much time you need to create the site. Expert designers typically estimate a number (of hours, days, or weeks, for example), and then pad that number by adding extra time to complete the project. You might ask, "Why pad the estimate?" After all, if someone is just implementing your well-structured plan, what can go wrong?

Developing your site can take longer than you expected for a variety of reasons. As you move from website design to implementation, beware of these traps:

>> **Trying to design and build the site at the same time:** People like to dive in with only a few pages on their maps (*before* the design is complete) and then add pages as they build out their sites. The constant starting, stopping, and thinking about which extra pages are needed can slow you down when you're trying to build the site.

>> **Not having the right capabilities for your site:** Some people envision having a graphics-rich, interactive, advanced website and then find out in the design process that their Internet service provider (ISP) can't support certain programs or supply bandwidth to display video properly. Careful planning helps you create specifications, which you can verify with your site provider to make sure that your site capabilities are what you want — before you buy.

>> **Not updating the entire site when you make a change:** Even the most carefully laid website plans can require some modification when you implement them. Remember that good sites link back and forth between different sections. The last thing you want is to update one section without updating the links in the rest of your site. If this happens, your customers can get lost while surfing around — and might leave for good.

>> **Forgetting about the message:** As your website grows and expands, you can easily lose focus on what the site should accomplish. At any time, you must be able to go back to your home page — or any other page — and determine the site focus by viewing the page for a few seconds. If you spend longer than 10 or 15 seconds interpreting the message, you're off track.

No matter how many changes you make, never let the message of your site get lost or obscured.

REMEMBER

>> **Not having the content ready:** You can have the plan built and promise to deliver your data or content to your website developer by a certain date. If you miss this date for some reason, you throw the developer's plans — not to mention the project's workflow — into chaos.

>> **Not having a reliable developer:** The best-laid plans are just *plans* until someone turns them into a website. If you're depending on someone with specialized skills, make sure that he or she has the time available to deliver your site when you need it.

You Can Do It! Making a Build-It-Yourself Site

The thought of turning site maps, content lists, and other plans into a full-blown website can intimidate almost anyone — especially someone who has never created a web page. To create web pages in the early days of the Internet, you had to know the specialized computer code *HyperText Markup Language (HTML)* and be able to write that code by using a program such as Notepad. Nowadays, you can find many tools to help you design your own site without having an extensive knowledge of HTML, but you can also benefit from knowing how to implement some of the helpful features in the current HTML5 version of markup language.

Therefore, knowing how to use some HTML (specifically, HTML5) is still a good idea because this knowledge gives you more control over the site-building process. Although website tools can create a lot of HTML code and help you build functions quickly, you might have to edit the work those tools do to make your site faster, smoother, and easier for customers to use. You have to direct these efforts to make sure that your site is an effective communications tool for your customers to do business with you. These website tools can help you get something done, but *you* have to provide the "why's" of the web page: Why is it being built, and why should customers use it?

TIP

A good first step is checking with your web-hosting company to find out which site development tools it provides. Most hosting companies have site design tools and templates that work with their servers, and can get you up and running with basic web page designs. You can update those basic designs with your own content, labels, and products.

If your web host doesn't provide any site-building tools or you're not happy with its offerings, don't worry — you have more options, as outlined in this list:

» **Free tools online:** You can find a number of free or inexpensive site builder tools on the Internet, such as the following:

- **GoDaddy:** www.godaddy.com/offers/gocentral/free-website
- **Squarespace:** www.squarespace.com
- **Weebly:** www.weebly.com
- **Wix:** www.wix.com

» **Your payment processor:** Sites such as PayPal offer the functionality to add buy buttons to any regular website, so you can turn any website into an e-commerce-capable website with some simple additions of PayPal generated code.

>> **Site builder software:** Later in this chapter, the section "Going modern with WordPress, Wix, and more" introduces some superfunctional programs that can help you build a rich, complex site for your business.

Using HTML: The old-fashioned way to build a page

Regardless of the web design tool you use to build your website, it can help to have a basic understanding of how HTML works. This understanding helps you edit your pages and figure out what your tools are creating, if necessary.

Unlike software code that has to be translated, compiled, and otherwise prepared before a consumer can use it, HTML code is written, saved as a file, and then interpreted by the program that reads the file. Usually, the software program that reads the HTML file is a web browser, such as Microsoft Internet Explorer. The web browser opens the HTML file and finds these two elements:

>> **Text** represents the titles, headings, paragraphs, links, and other elements that you want customers to see when they visit your website.

>> **Commands, or *HTML markup tags*,** tell the web browser how to *mark up*, or format, the text that's in the file and, therefore, control how the text looks to customers.

The browser reads all the instructions that you place in these markup tags and draws the web page on the computer screen according to your specifications. Because this language is uniform and structured, most web browsers interpret the commands in the same way. Your customers see the same design regardless of the computer or operating system they're using.

Commands are marked in the HTML file by command–start and –stop symbols: the ‹ and › signs. They look like this:

```
<command>
```

Typically, HTML commands are implemented by indicating, in this order:

>> The start of the command

>> The text that will be affected by the command

>> The end of the command

For example, if you want a word to appear bolded on your web page, you write

```
<STRONG> word </STRONG>
```

The `<STRONG>` command indicates that you're turning on (starting) the Bold command. Adding a slash (/) to the ending command tag indicates that you're turning off the command. Your web browser looks at this code and creates an effect as though you're holding down the Bold key, typing a word, and then releasing that key and moving on to the next section.

REMEMBER

If you don't provide the command tag to end a particular command, the web browser continues to format the rest of the file by using that command. If you put a `<STRONG>` command in your file and then forget to end the command, the rest of the text in your web page appears as bold text.

Your web page HTML file has three basic elements:

>> **The `<HTML>` tag:** This tag goes on the first line of your HTML file. It tells the web browser that it can find HTML code inside your file.

>> **The header section:** This section is marked by the `<HEAD>` tag.

>> **The body section:** This section is marked by the `<BODY>` tag.

Your header section should contain all the information that defines your web page, which includes — but isn't limited to — these elements:

>> **Title:** Your website title appears on the browser's title bar and should instantly tell customers the purpose of the web page.

>> **Function definitions:** For example, if you're creating a web page for customers to search your catalog, make sure to define the function as a search page.

>> **Author information:** Fill in the author's information, whether it's you, your business name, or your web designer. That way, customers know whom to thank for a well-planned website, interesting content, and a creative design.

>> **<META>tags:** This type of tag tells your web browser the definition and keywords of your web page. See Book 6, Chapter 6 for more information on these tags.

The body section contains everything else related to the web page, especially anything visible to your customers, such as

>> **Your content:** For example, a description and photographs of your products or services, and any information you're displaying for your customers, might appear in this section.

>> **Navigation information:** Usually, every web page has a consistent set of links that can take your customers to every main section of your website with one click.

>> **Links to other parts of your website:** If your web page needs to reference another part of your website, make sure the link is present in the page.

>> **Links to other websites:** Many times, a website offers links to other websites that are complementary to it or partners with them for co-promotion efforts.

>> **Forms asking customers to fill in information:** For example, you need the name and shipping address of any customers who decide to order something or join your mailing list.

Sometimes, designers put all the information in the body and very little in the header section. Although your web page still loads and presents itself to your customers, the lack of a divider between header and body information makes it harder to update your web pages properly (for example, when you need to change some functions on your website) and maximize your outreach to the Internet community. Similarly, putting main content inside the header section can distort the display of your web page because some web browsers try to condense the header to the top of the screen.

Going modern with WordPress, Wix, and more

Web pages have many elements you can specify, and keeping track of them all is hard when you design pages using only HTML. The growing number of commands available in HTML fueled the need for software programs to help organize all these elements. These programs create the HTML commands automatically so that you can focus on the layout, design, and content of your web page rather than worry about whether you defined all your table cells properly.

One of the most popular software applications for web page design is WordPress (www.wordpress.com), which was initially developed by a core set of volunteer programmers. Preprogrammed templates and plug-in applications that work with WordPress enable those with little coding skill to quickly develop a dynamic website. Another easy-to-use solution that a growing number of people use is

Wix (www.wix.com). This service provides a free website builder to help you design and build your own website. The service prompts you for specific information and then displays a sample of what your web page will look like as you're building the page, from an array of pre-programmed templates. This way, you can try something to see how it will look and then change it right there, if necessary, before continuing with your development.

The pros and cons of using automated site builders

You can use a website builder tool or application, such as WordPress or Wix, to create sophisticated web pages without having much specific knowledge, which is why millions of people use these tools every year. However, using automated site builders isn't without a downside, and you can fall into certain traps if you rely solely on these tools.

Here are some reasons to use a site builder tool:

>> **Ease of use:** A builder tool is designed to make the process of creating web pages as easy as possible. It looks like any other software program you're familiar with using and offers either templates or buttons, menus, and wizards to help you construct the building blocks of your web page.

>> **Wide array of options:** A builder tool is programmed with every available HTML command as well as with functions that combine these commands. This combination gives you many options for creating your web pages, and the tool's ease of use ensures that you don't have to search through documentation to figure out a specific name and definition for a function.

>> **Total control:** You can rely on the code that a builder tool generates (or can be purchased) or insert your own code whenever it's needed. Site builder tools help you easily validate your work by color-coding the commands in your file for easy visibility, for example.

Despite the attraction of these features, you should also see the drawbacks of relying on a builder tool:

>> **Unneeded code:** These programs have a particular way of inserting code into your HTML files, and sometimes they insert too much code or unnecessary code that web browsers can interpret incorrectly. You should optimize your code after a builder tool creates it so that your pages load faster and cleanly. You can use a tool such as the W3C Markup Validation Service (validator.w3.org) to help you go through your HTML files.

>> **Exclusive functions:** Some builder tools offer powerful functions that you can insert into your web pages. These functions are sometimes written with special commands that can be interpreted by only specific web server programs. Web servers advertise this capability as including *extensions*, and whoever is hosting your website has to have the right extensions file for your web pages to work properly.

>> **Portability:** When you build a website using a specific template on one of these sites, moving your website to another provider down the road may prove to be difficult because the look and feel of your website is tied to the template and work you put into designing your site in the first place.

Creating Your Site with the Pros

One way that entrepreneurs get ahead is by understanding their strengths and weaknesses: They focus on their strengths and have other people handle their weaknesses. Many people who want to operate their own online businesses aren't necessarily skilled website designers, and nothing is wrong with that. In the earlier section "You Can Do It! Making a Build-It-Yourself Site," we outline tools and technologies that can help you create your own website. You can choose another approach, however: Make the investment to have a professional website designer create your business site. The right interactions and communications with a professional designer can fuel an excellent site, and can even improve your overall business model so that increased orders and higher visibility help you recover the time and money you spent.

Some people consult with professional designers to create their sites and then give the business owners the tools to maintain their sites without any additional help. Other business owners contract with professionals to create and maintain their sites so that the designers can introduce new styles and functions as their businesses progress. Either approach can be beneficial for your business. You should decide how much help you want, as either a one-time investment or an ongoing expense.

Seeking experience: Choosing the right website designer

Half the battle of finding a website designer is deciding that you need to hire one in the first place. The other half of the battle involves knowing where to look and talking to potential candidates until you find the right fit. Finding the right designer is similar to finding other specialists you need to solve specific problems.

Whether you're looking for an auto mechanic, a plumber, a dentist, or in this case, a web designer, consider these methods for finding a qualified professional:

>> **Listen to word-of-mouth advice.** Talk to your friends, business associates, partners, or anybody you do business with online or in person. Find out which website designers they have used and solicit their opinions of these professionals.

>> **See the designer's work.** Look at websites that you like or enjoy. Most of the time, a small link or reference at the bottom of the home page or About Us page mentions whether a professional designer created the site. Follow the link back to the designer's site for more information.

>> **Evaluate the designer's portfolios.** Use search engines, read relevant magazines in your area, or look around on freelancer sites like Upwork (www.upwork.com) or review sites like Yelp (www.yelp.com) to find a few companies. Then evaluate the samples or references they provide, to see whether their work for other people is good enough or fits the style you want for your own business.

Hooking up with a web design firm

From the early days of the Internet, some web design companies have focused on providing quality work for their clients. Going to a design firm gives you specific benefits for completing your project:

>> **Reliability:** If a particular designer is having a bad day, week, month, or even year, a design firm can shift the workload away from that person and find backup or additional resources to cover the job. Design firms typically have contacts with freelance designers who come into the firm when needed to help tackle a big problem.

>> **Coordination:** If several designers are working on your project, a design firm can coordinate the work and give you a single point of contact who communicates your ideas and tasks to the design team.

>> **Experience:** Design firms have a portfolio of past projects and experience that lends itself to your project. They can bring their know-how and expertise to your project without having to navigate a large learning curve.

Going with a freelancer

When you ask around to find the right website design professional, you might be pointed toward talented individuals who work on a freelance basis and take on specific clients and projects that fit into their schedules. Some freelance professionals take assignments outside their full-time jobs, as a way to make some extra money. Others have enough clients to make their freelance jobs become their full-time careers.

Choosing a freelance designer over a design firm has several benefits. A freelancer

>> **Costs less to hire:** When you hire a design firm, part of the cost goes toward maintaining the overhead costs of the company. Although that overhead is beneficial to ensure the reliability of your project, a freelance designer typically charges less per hour or per project than the average design firm.

>> **Works more nimbly:** You might find that a design firm you choose requires decisions and work to be done in various committees, with approval required at all stages by the firm's managers. This system can slow the progress of a website's development, and if speed is a top concern, a freelance designer who can focus on your project can produce a quicker result because the only approval that's needed is yours.

>> **Provides a unique style:** Although designing a website is definitely a mixture of art and science, the creativity you want might not come from a firm that has developed procedures and processes for cranking out its various clients' websites. An individual freelance designer can bring his or her own quirky, creative, unique style to your project, which is what might draw you to this designer in the first place.

TIP

You can use a website such as Upwork to find the right freelance designer for your project. Simply go to `www.upwork.com` and choose from qualified professionals. After you create a client account with Upwork, you can click the Post Job button to post your time and cost requirements and then receive bids from freelancers.

Comparing apples to apples

While you're deciding whom to hire as your website designer, comparing quoted prices is a natural consideration for making up your mind. If you don't consider certain factors, however, they can skew the math and thereby make your comparison invalid.

For example, a price for designing a website is normally determined in one of two ways:

>> **Flat fee:** One price covers the complete site development.

>> **Per-hour pricing:** You're billed a rate per hour of development time.

Knowing a few key items from your designer or firm can help you compare prices more evenly. In this section, follow the advice that applies to your situation to find out the specific details.

If a designer or firm charges a flat fee for the entire project:

>> **Ask for a specific list of what's provided for that fee.** You might assume that the price you're quoted is the only fee you have to pay but find out at the end of the project that the flat fee excludes extras that you assumed were included.

>> **Ask what happens if someone has to spend overtime hours to complete the project.** One benefit of having a flat fee is knowing that you don't have to worry about the number of hours your designer is spending to build your website. This way, someone can't dawdle on a function to run up the bill, for example. Some design professionals offer a flat fee on the assumption that the project will take a maximum number of hours to complete. In this case, the contract stipulates that if the project exceeds that maximum number, the client pays more.

If a designer or firm charges by the hour:

>> **Ask for time estimates on the various pieces of the project, function by function.** Website design professionals might give you different numbers for the total number of hours needed. Rather than compare total numbers, you can compare detailed quotes to know whether one firm is spending more time on specific functions or one person is forgetting to factor in pieces that other designers know are essential.

>> **Ask for limits to be put into place.** A website designer can easily quote a specific number of hours and then exceed that number and keep the bill running while you pay for his or her excesses. That's why you must establish limits for various pages, especially less complicated pages. The designer should be forced, at the least, to call you if he or she needs to spend more time than quoted so that you can hear an explanation and make the decision.

REMEMBER

Regardless of how you're charged, find out who pays if you find a bug or an error in the work after the fact.

Sometimes, web designers can offer a lower quote because they refuse to cover the cost of fixing the work when the project is complete. Although the initial price is low, you could pay more if a lot of reworking or correction is needed, and then you don't save anything. Request assurances that the designer will spend the time necessary at the end, and specify that no one will be fully paid until the project is completed to your satisfaction.

Your best bet is to ask your designer to provide a full checklist of every action that's necessary to build your website and then to review that checklist as your site is being designed. To ensure that the review takes place, many people tie their designer's payments to the completion of the checklist. For example, when the designer can show that 50 percent of the items were completed, he or she receives 50 percent of the payment. This strategy helps prevent someone from receiving a full payment upfront and then quitting before completing all the agreed-on tasks.

Speeding up the process

Regardless of whom you choose to be your website designer, take the time to get the following "ducks in a row" to ensure that your designer is working as efficiently as possible — and costing you less in the end:

>> **Prepare site specifications upfront.** First and foremost, you should have a clear idea of what your site should contain before your first meeting with the designer. Prepare a written road map of your site (as discussed in the section "Mapping Your Route to a Successful Site," earlier in this chapter) and notes on the various web pages that you feel are essential. You can brainstorm with your web designer about your website, but starting with your road map and making small changes is quicker and easier than starting with a clean sheet of paper and spending hours writing down the basics.

>> **Have your content ready.** Make sure that the content you want for your site is typed and available in electronic format. You're paying the designer by the hour, most likely, and you don't want to pay a skilled professional to type reams of data for you.

TIP

If necessary, hire a copywriter separately from your web designer, and give that copywriter the sole responsibility of creating electronic text or Word document files with your information. You can use sites like Fiverr (www.fiverr.com) to hire people to do quicker, smaller tasks for you.

>> **Establish firm milestones.** When you meet with your web designer, work to establish rough dates for checking the progress or various milestones, which can be the end dates for specific portions of your site. Although some web designers don't like specific hard-and-fast dates, you can reasonably expect to see portions of the project completed by certain dates. This way, you can see the progress of your site, make changes (if necessary) before everything is done, and ensure that the project is progressing.

>> **Be readily available to assist the designer.** Make sure that you're available to answer questions and feed information to your website designer. The designer shouldn't be stuck waiting days (or weeks) to receive specific and necessary information from you. Even if you're incredibly detail oriented and spell out everything in advance, your designer might need to ask you a question, get approval for a change, or find out more information about your business before proceeding.

Keeping an eye on your business interests

When you hire a website design professional, the expectation is that you don't need to know how to use HTML or have any design skills. That is, after all, why you're hiring the professional. However, your design professional will have expectations about how you participate in the project, how your business operations are reflected in the site, and who owns the rights to the resulting site and its content. You must know your role in this process so that you can contribute to a successful site that contributes in turn to your business success.

Keep in mind the concept of scope when you're hiring someone to develop your site. *Scope,* in this case, refers to the amount of information and areas of concern that affect your website developer. She should operate within her role as specified in the contract or agreement between you and her. Don't involve your developer in other aspects of your business or create expectations that she will contribute to your business plan. Keep the developer's activities focused on the job at hand so that she can deliver your site as specified.

REMEMBER

Drawing up your contract or agreement with a website developer provides a learning exercise for both parties. Spell out exactly what you need, and specify whether other people, yourself included, are providing pieces of the puzzle (such as product databases) that interact with their work. This way, you both know the extent of the site developer's responsibilities.

Staying true to your business and customers

As the business owner, you determine how your site fulfills your business goals. Although an eager website developer might want to build something to highlight his specialties, they can conflict with your business purpose. If you're focusing on a pure e-commerce site with little extra content, you need to communicate that fact so that your designer doesn't hand back a content-rich, bloated site.

Know your customers and the audience you want your site to attract. Talented designers can build your site in different ways to appeal to different audiences, and you must point them in the right direction to "hook" the right people. Without any specific targets, your designer might produce something that speaks to every group but says nothing of value to any of them.

Supplying the designer with the right stuff

You can't just drive your car into a service station, toss the guy the keys, say "Fix it," and then walk away and expect to get a fully repaired car hours later. The same situation applies to designing your website: You must provide the right information to your designer, and at the right time during the process, so that your site is built correctly from the start. Here are some tips:

REMEMBER

>> **Outline your business practices.** Your website designer isn't necessarily a businessperson and can't be expected to understand the intricacies of your business. You need to explain how your site should operate and why. If you have certain rules or exclusions for how you sell your goods and services, spell them out before development begins. For example, if you need to enforce a minimum order or disallow certain product combinations in the same order, those business rules must be a part of the proposal. Don't expect your designer to implicitly know how your business operates or understand its specific requirements.

>> **Supply all relevant content.** At some point, you need to provide the content that will fill your website. This content consists of not only the names and descriptions of products but also any product databases, pictures, pricing information, or other data that has to interact with your site. Unless your designer is creating your company logo, you have to provide your logo, mission statement, contact information, and anything else that needs to appear on your site. Some of this information is spelled out in your agreement; other pieces, such as a customer database, can be handed in down the road or even at the end of the process.

>> **Make your systems available when needed.** Your developer also counts on having you and your computer systems available while building your site. This statement is especially true for more complex sites that operate on a web server and communicate with programs such as a database, a supplier's inventory system, and a third-party payment solution. The quicker you can provide access, and the more documentation and notes you can provide about these interlocking programs, the quicker the designer can turn around and build you the correct website.

Clarifying who owns what

When you're hiring someone to design and build your website for you, establish the ownership of this work after it's complete. You might assume — because you're paying a professional to do the work — that this constitutes a work-for-hire agreement where you automatically own full rights to the resulting site and its content.

WARNING

Never assume that you have a work-for-hire situation, and — as part of your contract — spell out the ownership rights of everything the web developer provides to you. In addition, make sure that items such as photos, graphical images, and functions don't carry any unexpected royalties or licenses that you have to pay to use.

After the job is done, ask the web designer for a copy of your website, either available online as a backup copy on a cloud storage service like Dropbox, or on a DVD or USB drive. This way, if something happens to your web server or you have a falling-out with your designer, you still have a full copy that you can use to keep your site running. Make sure that all the images, icons, logos, buttons, and other types of graphics — not just the HTML files — are included in your copy. If your web designer also designed your company logo, ask for the logo in different file formats and sizes.

IN THIS CHAPTER

» **Understanding the different types of hosting**

» **Breaking down the pros and cons of various hosts**

» **Reading the legal fine print**

» **Deciding whether you're ready to be your own host**

» **Paying attention to security**

Chapter **4**

Serving Up Your Site

One of the many decisions you make when you're starting a website is where to host it. You might be wondering what a host does and why you even need one. A *host* site provides a place (a *server*) for your website and all the files that make up your site to reside. That host provides an address so that others can access it by using the Internet.

There are many different options available when choosing how to host your website, including doing it yourself. The biggest concern usually comes down to the amount of access you want or need to the server and the additional services provided. An increasingly critical part of any hosting solution is the security of the server. It's essential that your website's host, your business, and your customers are protected from cyber intrusions and other vulnerabilities (such as a natural disaster that could take down your host — and your website!). This is just one of the many reasons to understand hosting and find the best way, or place, to host your site.

In this chapter, you discover what to look for in a powerful hosting service, the different types of hosting options (including the popular choice of cloud hosting and the less common option of becoming your own host) and the security concerns you must address with any host.

Determining What Makes the Difference for High-Performance Hosting

When you're gearing up for a high-performance website, you must decide how much horsepower — er, *hosting* power — you really need for the site. Horsepower translates into fast loading speeds, video and sounds playing without interruption, and images loading quickly. Most reputable hosting services include most, if not all, of these items for top-of-line hosting, but there may be variations that impact the price you pay for those services. Before weighing your options, it's good to understand these common requirements in a hosting plan and how it affects your site. Consider the following hosting options:

>> **Disk space:** The size of your website files dictates how much disk space, or storage, you need from a host. If you plan to have a lot of pictures, self-hosted videos, or graphics, count on needing more storage space. Typically, disk space is measured in megabytes (MB), and 500MB is usually enough for a basic commerce site — although special features such as high video usage or Flash files may bump this minimum requirement up quite a bit.

>> **Bandwidth:** This capability controls how much data, or information, a server can send and receive at any given moment. The higher the amount of bandwidth your host's server has, the more traffic (visitors) your site can support at one time.

To give you an idea of how important bandwidth can be, consider this real-life example. Pop artist Lady Gaga launched one of her singles for sale on Amazon.com at the special limited price of 99 cents. Her fans rushed to take advantage of the exclusive midnight offering. The result? The site's available bandwidth was exceeded, and Amazon's server crashed — an almost unheard of occurrence for an Internet heavyweight like Amazon. And many disappointed customers were instantly unhappy Amazon customers. There are plenty more of these types of stories where megabrands, such as Victoria's Secret, and other pop culture giants host events that cause a bandwidth blackout. Your site most likely won't hit this amount of bandwidth squeeze (yet!), but it's good to understand the constraints it can put on your site.

TIP

Web hosting is an extremely competitive business. Now, many top hosting providers offer unlimited disk (or storage) space and unlimited bandwidth. These services often throw in free domain name registration, too. Take the time to shop around for the most benefits at the lowest monthly price — the time you invest will be worthwhile.

>> **Data transfers:** Every time someone views information from your site (including text, images, and video), that's considered to be a transfer of data. Think of it as traffic (or data) leaving your site. Hosting plans used

to allow for a specified number of transfers per month and then charged additional fees if you consistently exceeded the limit. Now, most plans no longer mention data transfers in their service description because it is unlimited. To be on the safe side, confirm that data transfers are unlimited.

>> **Allowable languages:** Depending on which scripting language you use to create your site, you might have to find a host that supports that specific type. For instance, support of HTML5 (HyperText Markup Language 5) is standard for all hosting services these days, as is the PHP: Hypertext Preprocessor scripting language. However, if you use Ruby on Rails or Python, you might want to confirm that they are supported without hassle.

TIP

If you hire an outside developer to create your website, be sure to ask which scripting language is being used to design the site. Or ask whether you can specify which language is used. Then confirm that your hosting solution supports that language. Some add-ons for shopping cart applications, for example, require a specific programming code or OS (operating system) to customize the application. Although an entire site is rarely built in a scripting language not supported by your hosting provider, we have seen it happen. Better safe than sorry.

>> **Database access:** If you plan to incorporate a database on your site (for inventory management, for example), the server must allow for it. Typically, you should ensure that SQL (Standard Query Language) or MySQL is available, which means that the server is set up to use this language to access and transfer information from your database. Don't be surprised if you're asked to pay extra for this feature or if it's free only to a certain extent.

>> **E-commerce enabled:** Save yourself a headache later and confirm that your hosting plan supports e-commerce software, such as a shopping cart program, and that it supports the one you want to use. Many companies bundle hosting with a specific e-commerce solution (because they get a cut of the fees from those merchant programs). Either way, you're likely to pay more in hosting fees when you add an e-commerce feature to your site.

TIP

In addition to obtaining e-commerce software, you need a Secure Sockets Layer (SSL) certificate. It ensures that you can safely transmit data over your website when customers make purchases. Check to see whether your hosting plan offers a *shared* SSL certificate, which covers all websites located on its server — in which case, it's probably free. Otherwise, expect to shell out more bucks to purchase an individual SSL for your site. If the hosting company doesn't offer the option, you can check www.symantec.com for more information on purchasing your own SSL. Several kinds of SSL certificates are available, so weigh all your options before making a final decision.

>> **Operating system:** Similar to your desktop computer, a server has an operating system, too. Deciding which one is right for you depends on

what operating system you're using for your website. Two popular server options are:

- *Windows:* When you're using Microsoft Access, Active Server Pages (ASP), or any Microsoft-specific scripts, a Windows-based server is more suitable.

- *Linux:* This server software supports almost any type of scripting language. It's definitely a better match for your website if you use MySQL, PHP, or Perl.

The type of operating system you have on your own computer doesn't influence which server is best suited to host your website.

>> **Redundancy and backups:** Let's get straight to the point — if your server crashes, you're up a creek without a paddle. You must back up your website, which means that your data is copied and saved to another location so that if one server goes down, your data is still available from the second source. Your hosting plan should include frequent, and preferably daily, backups to derail any impending crisis. We discuss this critical component of web hosting in more detail at the end of this chapter.

>> **Web analysis:** To understand who your customers are and how they're using your site, chances are good that you need to know how many people visit your site each day, which parts of the site they frequent, and maybe even which other sites these visitors came from (based on IP addresses). To find out, you need some type of web analysis software. If this feature isn't included with your hosting plan, ask whether any restrictions exist on the type of software you can use with the site, and whether you pay an additional charge for using it.

You can embed a small bit of HTML code into your home page (and other pages) and use Google Analytics for free. Google also has a terrific resource center, including online tutorials, for using analytics. Visit the center at `www.google.com/analytics`.

>> **Support:** No matter who you are, there comes a time when you need a little help. Although it's not easy to determine the quality of a host's support until you experience it, you can compare some basic features. Is support offered 24/7 (24 hours a day and 7 days a week)? If not, what are the hours of the host's customer service center? Are both online support and phone support available? If online support is offered, make sure that it offers access to answers in real time, as opposed to waiting as long as 24 to 48 hours for a response to email. Always confirm whether you're charged for live tech support and whether the charge is based on use by the minute, hour, or month. Those bills can rack up fast, even for a seemingly simple question.

>> **Other:** A host can choose to make *beaucoup* (*lots* of) extra features available with your plan. If all other factors are equal, don't hesitate to compare this assortment of small prizes to find the host with the most. For example,

mailboxes (for your email) are always included, although the number of mailboxes offered varies greatly. However, mailboxes might not be a big deal to you. Some competitive hosting plans offer free tools that allow you to set up a blog; easy content-management programs; polling or voting features that allow you to take surveys of your customers; calendars; access to free stock photos, and more — lots more!

Although comparing features and choosing a hosting plan can be overwhelming, after you begin researching all the options, you find that most hosts make it easy to understand the differences. To ensure competitiveness, hosts often break down their plans into several categories and offer month-to-month agreements, which means you don't have to sign a long-term contract!

TIP

The monthly pay-as-you-go plan for services such as web hosting is now standard, and you can usually get a price break for paying a full year ahead or for signing a multi-year contract. We don't advise the latter, because the price break isn't usually large enough to warrant staying with a service provider for two or three years. It's more important to have flexibility and be free to switch providers if something goes wrong. However, paying upfront for 12 months of service is a great compromise.

With a quick glance, you can determine whether a plan has all the elements you want. For example, most hosting solutions offer a basic or starter package with bare-bones necessities — enough to get, and keep, a simple site with minimal images up and running. You may even find some free hosting options that include very minimal features but could get your basic site up and going! However, when this level is all you need, you end up making your decision strictly on price. (We see it happen all the time.) What we consider to be the other *forced* option is when you require e-commerce capabilities. No matter what, you have to choose the plan that provides for this need. (Typically, no more than one e-commerce hosting plan is available from one source — so you need to shop around to get the best deal.) Again, when you're selecting among providers, your decision comes down to price and which e-commerce program is partnered with (or offered by) each host. Other hosting plans include a mid-tier level (which we think is usually the best option for starting an e-commerce site) and a premium level that is typically loaded with more features than you need.

TIP

The difference in price between a basic plan and a midlevel plan is often only a few dollars.

Ultimately, your best bet is to look for hosting providers that distinguish themselves based on reliability, support, and security. Those that offer extra features or buying incentives (such as free advertising credits on Google AdWords or Facebook) are nice, but you really want a provider that will help keep your business up and running — and secure.

Putting Your Site in the Cloud

An important factor in choosing a host is considering *where* the server is hosted. A traditional option is having a single server that hosts your site or that can be divided and shared with other websites — for simplicity, think of this as a physically located piece of hardware. Increasingly, the more popular option is a hosted service in the cloud. A cloud-based solution is a grouping of servers that are virtually connected together, and there are multiple clusters of these servers. Those clusters are what make up the cloud. You may wonder why this is a big deal. Cloud-based hosting has several advantages:

>> **Scalability:** In the cloud, it's easy to access additional features, including bandwidth. If your site grows quickly, you can quickly turn on or expand the new tools you need to support enhanced requirements or demands on the server (because you now have access to multiple clusters of servers, not just a single server). The scalability benefit also works in the opposite direction. Let's say your website or a product you sell is featured on the *Today* show as a "must-have" holiday gift. You're likely to quickly see an extremely high influx of site traffic! On a traditional server, it would take a lot of time and effort to provide the amount of bandwidth you need to support the new volume of traffic. A cloud solution can scale at lightning-fast speed to handle the spike in traffic. When the holiday season ends, your site's traffic volume is reduced. A cloud solution makes it simple to shift resources back again, or scale down.

>> **Security:** Just as a cloud-based solution can shift resources to accommodate changing traffic requirements, it can also take advantage of the clusters of different servers to protect against cyber threats, such as distributed denial of service (DDoS) attacks. If a cluster of service is under siege, it shifts to a different cluster. Similarly, it offers protection from natural disasters and other threatening events (like hardware failures or fire) that could destroy or severely impact a physical location. In other words, data can quickly be virtually moved to or pulled from a different cluster of servers, without requiring any downtime for the transfer of resources. That means your customers never even know that you've experienced a problem — they get to your site with no interruptions!

>> **Performance:** When your site is hosted in the cloud, it may realize the benefits of increased speeds (website load times) and overall better performance, so there are no lag times in serving up large image files and data-hogging videos. That's not to say that traditional server sites can't be fast and reliable, too. Cloud-solutions just have more options to load-balance or shift the resource needs to various server clusters.

>> **Pricing:** Typically, cloud solutions are somewhat less expensive than other service offerings. As we mention earlier, hosted cloud services also provide

affordable monthly plans with no contract commitments. If you need to scale services up or down, it's cheaper and easier to do so in the cloud.

» **Reliability:** Another potential benefit of a cloud solution is that the hosting company may offer a guarantee of service or protection against an outage. Sometimes you see this described as "uptime" and "availability" of the cloud service. When cloud-based solutions first became available, providers sometimes struggled to keep their servers from going down or being unavailable; this was called a *cloud outage,* and it's one of the reasons that cloud hosting services used to be considered unreliable. Today's leading cloud providers have gotten much better and are now thought to be more reliable and secure than traditional server options. Even so, cloud services began offering a guarantee of service uptime. In some contracts or terms of service agreements, you find a clause that says a refund of a specified amount is provided if a cloud outage exceeds a certain time period (this can be anywhere from several hours to a couple of days). An outage of any sort is still a disruption to your business and equates to lost revenue, but having an uptime guarantee clause is a small way to offset the loss.

REMEMBER

Whether you sign a contract or legally accept an online Terms of Service agreement, *always* read the fine print. You may find that some contracts limit what you can and cannot do on a website, or you may be financially penalized for some actions related to operations of your site.

Serving Yourself: Don't Overlook Other Server Options

Cloud-based hosting options are popular, but they aren't your only option. You may want to skip a hosting plan and rent your own dedicated server. To help you better understand what you might be getting into, we explain the different types of server options:

» **Shared server:** The hosting plans we explain earlier in this chapter are examples of how you use a shared server. In essence, you're using the same computer (or server) along with many other websites. Although that arrangement translates into lower costs, you have less flexibility in the types of applications you can run, because the server is configured with the same settings and applications for all who use it.

» **Dedicated server:** Gaining complete control over the type of server you use and the programs you install on it requires that you have a dedicated server.

As its name implies, the bandwidth, memory, and storage space on this computer are dedicated entirely to *you*. You also typically gain root access, which means that you can configure the server to your specifications. This more expensive option is often used when you need to run special programs or when you have multiple sites or extremely high-traffic sites. The downside of using a dedicated server (in addition to the expense) is that you're usually responsible for installing software, handling regular maintenance, and fixing any unexpected problems or system failures that occur. We recommend tackling this server arrangement only if you're an experienced web master or computer technician.

» **Colocation:** You might like the idea of owning a server but aren't in a position to manage or repair any problems that arise. If that's the case, colocation might be the answer. You provide the hardware (or the computer) and lease space *(rack space)* for it with a host company. The host company then installs the server and ensures that you have consistent access to the Internet, which is a big advantage of colocation. Depending on your physical office space, this situation is ideal for another reason: A server requires certain environmental conditions, such as being kept in a dry, cool (or temperature controlled) room, and colocation providers maintain data centers that meet or exceed these conditions. Because you own the equipment and are responsible for all other aspects of maintaining it, this option also requires that you have advanced skills.

» **Managed server:** Sometimes referred to as a *virtual server,* this option is a compromise to a dedicated server. Unlike with colocation, with a managed server you lease the equipment and the hosting company takes care of most server functions, including installing software and updates; handling security and maintenance; and acting as a troubleshooter for problems. If you have specific needs for your site and aren't proficient in maintaining a server, managed servers work well.

» **Virtual dedicated server:** Another take on limited maintenance but increased flexibility is what some hosts refer to as *virtually dedicated.* As with shared hosting, others use the server with you, but access is limited to a small number of customers. You gain dedicated space and control because the host uses walls or partitions on the computer to separate it into several virtual dedicated servers. Although your site is on a shared server, it has been configured to appear as a stand-alone, dedicated server with no other users.

As with hosting, the price and services offered with each server package vary. You're usually required to sign a long-term lease agreement, so make sure that you understand what the price covers and the responsibilities for both you and the host company. Also, make sure that cancellation terms are clearly spelled out so that you can get out of the agreement if you're unhappy with the provider.

Keeping Your Customers and Your Site Secure

Regardless of how you choose to host your website, you're still responsible for the safety and security of your company's data and that of your customers. When you own an online business, you don't get a free pass on culpability when it comes to the privacy and security of data, from personal information (such as birth dates and passwords) to financial data (such as credit and debit card numbers and expiration dates). How do you best protect against data vulnerabilities?

TIP

It's critical to have a Secure Sockets Layer (SSL) certificate for your site. This certificate enables data to be securely encrypted when transferred or exchanged across the Internet. Basically, it helps prevent hackers and other cyber thieves from accessing sensitive data. Some hosting plans offer an SSL certificate at a reduced price, but you don't have to purchase it through the provider of your hosting plan or the company that provides your server. We explain how to purchase an SSL certificate in detail in Book 5, Chapter 1.

Another security concern is simply making sure your website data is properly backed up. In other words, you need to know if the files that make up your website get compromised or destroyed, there is a way to access duplicate copies of the files. If not, you could lose your entire online business in a flash! Of course, to prevent backups from becoming necessary in the first place, you need a reliable server — not to mention a responsible host. When you're purchasing a hosting plan, determine which precautions a provider has in place to prevent its server from going down. Don't forget that the problem isn't always a matter of equipment failure. Power outages, maintenance checks, and other man-made or environmental conditions (such as severe weather incidents) can cause a server — along with your website — to go out of commission. Redundancy is the best contingency plan because it means that your host has dual systems in place that allow information to remain accessible from a secondary source, even if the primary source goes out. (If you want to know more about redundancy and business continuity for your site, we discuss these issues in detail in Book 5, Chapter 2.)

Chapter **5**

Developing Content That Satisfies Visitors and Search Engines

C ontent is king! This mantra remains popular (and accurate!) when discussing what it takes to shine the spotlight on your website. The words you choose, and how and where you use them, are critical to the online sales process. Now, thanks to Google, the value of content is at an all-time high for helping your website rank well in search engines, too.

Content was officially promoted to royalty when search engines (specifically, Google) began placing significantly increased importance on it as part of *search engine optimization,* or SEO. In short, Google decreed a site's search results ranking is affected by the quality of the site's content and its relevance to website visitors.

To achieve that goal of a good ranking, business owners often depend on someone else to find the right words for their websites. Don't worry: When you're creating content for your own site, you don't have to hire a professional writer. You do have to understand what turns ordinary words into good web copy, which is why we devote this chapter to choosing the right words. In addition, knowing how to write good web content helps you perform well in searches — and get more sales.

Words Are Words — Right? Wrong!

How do you know what works when it comes to describing your products, welcoming your customers, and engaging in any other communication that requires the written word? Effective web copy helps you accomplish these five objectives:

>> Help search engines notice your site

>> Convince customers to visit your site

>> Educate customers about your products and services

>> Elicit in your customers a desire to act (to buy stuff!)

>> Entice customers to come back and do it all over again (buy more stuff!)

When discussing content for the web, you might often hear another term, *content marketing*. This popular term encompasses all five of the preceding objectives as well as the development of lots of different types of content (from website copy and white papers to infographics and videos) and the way you promote and distribute that content to attract customers to your site. In this chapter, we focus on a segment of content marketing, specifically the words or copy used on your website pages. In Book 6, we discuss in more detail how to create various types of content and how to use content as part of a marketing strategy.

REMEMBER

The wider term *content marketing* includes more than just words or text. The broader definition of content in the world of digital marketing includes images, presentations, video, and just about any type of information that can be consumed by online customers.

Words that are "key" to search

Now that you understand the five objectives that help earn the official stamp of approval on your web copy, it's time to introduce another important term when writing for the web: *keywords*. As we mentioned, the first objective of online writing is to get the attention of search engines so that they can direct traffic to your website. More important, you want the search engines to send you the *right traffic*, or rather the people who are most interested in your products and services or the problems they solve. Fortunately, search engines want this, too — especially Google.

As we mention throughout this book, Google has come a long way in how it prioritizes and matches the content on websites to the search queries it receives. Without getting into the nitty-gritty details of Google's search algorithms (or as much as Google reveals about those algorithms!), essentially what Google wants to do is understand the *intent* of the search and match that to the best possible *quality* content. One way search engines accomplish this is by depending upon clues in the form of keywords, or specific words that help indicate what the site and content are about. If someone is searching for bicycles and you sell bicycles, you want to use keywords and keyword phrases related to bicycles, such as bicycle helmets, men's bicycles, racing bikes, peddles — you get the idea. In the past, the more times you used a particular keyword in your content that matched those same words used in search queries, the better chance you had of ranking high in the search engine results.

Google wants you to focus on writing the best quality content possible that matches the searcher's intent — the information your potential customers need to make a buying decision. Keywords and keyword phrases are still important, but Google doesn't want you to stick keywords in your sentences simply for the sake of having keywords in your content (as we just did in this sentence using the word *keywords*). Having your keywords appear four or five times in one sentence does not make the sentence better; rather, it makes it sound forced and awkward. Instead, write your content using natural sentences that reflect the way people actually talk or explain things. Mastering this technique is a big deal because Google continues to get better at not only understanding the *intent* behind the search query but also *predicting* the type of content the searcher wants to see or will find useful.

WARNING

Some website owners and SEO specialists learned ways to trick the search engines by doing something called *keyword stuffing* — adding lots and lots of keywords to their content just to rank higher in search results. Today, Google penalizes you for these types of tricks, and your website could completely fall out of the rankings!

Rather than focusing on a single keyword, use other strings of words that people are more likely to use in search: complete questions or more lengthy descriptions (called *long-tail keyword searches*). For example, if you want to learn about keywords, it's doubtful you will enter only the word "keywords" in Google search. You are more likely to enter phrases like "using keywords to improve search engine rankings," or "how to choose the best keywords when writing for the web." When writing content for your website, it's important to think about what someone really wants to know (intent) and answer that question with useful information (quality content).

TIP

Search engines such as Google evaluate and consider both the quality and usefulness of your content. Using good grammar, proper punctuation, and well-constructed sentences is all part of what earns your content the search engine's seal of approval. It's also important that you not duplicate sentences or paragraphs — search engines want to see that you have original content throughout.

When you're ready to gain a thorough understanding of how to master search engines, check out Book 6, Chapter 6. For now, we simply want to make you are aware of the importance of thinking about search engine rankings while you're writing the initial content for your site.

To review, when you're writing content that's search-engine friendly, remember these two rules:

>> **Think like a customer.** Include content that provides answers to the type of questions your customers are asking.

>> **Avoid saturation.** Keywords should be a natural part of your content, not overly obvious.

TIP

Before writing your content, do your own search using a popular search term for your product or service. Then visit the top five sites in the returned rankings. Note which words or phrases your competitors use, and consider finding a logical place for them in your content.

Beyond keywords

You won't find us downplaying the importance of keywords and keyword phrases, but we would be remiss if we overlooked other important types of words to use when writing online content. After all, not all words are created equal. Some words pack a wallop when they're delivered. Others hang in the air unnoticed.

With millions of words in the English language, choosing the *right* ones for your website might seem daunting. Not so. Writing for the web is easy if you use words, phrases, and sentences that are

>> **Attention-getters:** *You're fired!* Real estate tycoon and the 45th president of the United States Donald Trump gave new meaning to this phrase when he used it to oust participants on his reality television show. He certainly knows how to keep a viewer's attention anytime he delivers the now infamous line. You have to do the same online. Visitors to your website are unforgiving. If you don't catch their attention quickly (and keep it), they desert you in a heartbeat. Choose words, especially in headlines, that command attention and pique interest — all in a blink of the eye.

REMEMBER

The average person looks at a web page for less than a minute (as little as 8 seconds, according to some research) before deciding to move on. The decision your customer makes to stay or leave depends on the information you provide. Make that information

- *Meaningful:* Don't waste words. Be brief and choose words that matter and that reflect the customer's needs.

- *Easy to read:* Use short sentences. Don't bog down readers with too much detail.

TIP

Give customers a choice in seeking more in-depth information. If someone wants *all* the details, you can provide either a hypertext link to another page or an expanded viewing window. There, visitors can find complete product descriptions, case studies, tips for using the products, or other background research.

- » **Self-explanatory:** It's best to avoid using abbreviations, catchy product names, and industry lingo. If you can't avoid using jargon, keep in mind that customers may not understand what you mean on the first read-through. When you use these types of words, define them in parentheses or offer an expanded view that contains the complete information. Be *clear.*

- » **Simple:** Say what you mean. Don't make your customers read between the lines or try to guess what you intended.

TIP

Although this chapter is about choosing the right words, we would be remiss to overlook the value of images as part of your content. Using images and videos is critical today. Images and graphics support your web copy and even help draw attention to it. Videos can bring your web copy to life and gives customers an alternative way to consume information. Plus, images and videos can also help in search engine rankings. We discuss marketing with videos in Book 4, Chapter 3.

Getting Ready to Write for the Web

Words are catalysts that move people to action. With that in mind, what do you want your customers to do when they visit your website? If you said "Buy stuff," think again. That's a given. You need to be more specific: On each page of your website, determine which *action* or series of actions you want customers to take to lead to the decision to make a purchase (as we discuss in Chapter 2 of this minibook). If you can answer that question, you can write words that sell.

Understanding buyer personas

To start writing for the web, you have to determine these factors:

- » **Your audience:** Before you write a single word of copy, take a moment to understand to whom you're writing and why. Content marketers refer to this as your *buyer personas* (we show you how to create personas in Book 11). For now, consider: Who are your potential customers? Why are they visiting your site? What are they searching for — information or products? Specifically, what problem are they trying to solve, and how can you help them solve it?

>> **Your customers' motivation:** In addition to knowing about your customers, you need to understand what motivates them to take action. Do they want to be entertained? Educated? Are their purchases based on emotional decisions? Or do they simply want enough facts to validate their buying decisions? To some degree, their motivation might be dictated by what type of product you're offering, the age of your target customer, or the standard offering in your industry. Even so, understanding motivation helps dictate your writing style and the words you use. It also guides the tone of your writing. Your tone can be serious, whimsical, or no-nonsense. Your tone itself can motivate people to action.

>> **Your customers' solution:** When you understand your customer's desires, needs, and motivations, you can provide a solution. Simply naming your product or showing a picture of it doesn't do the trick. You need to explain *how* your specific product solves your customers' specific problem and tell (or show) *why* your product provides the best solution. If it's the most efficient, cost-effective, or reliable one on the market, let the customer know. These benefits are all part of the solution you offer to influence a customer's final decision to buy.

Okay, so you're convinced that your product answers the needs of your customers, and you're pretty sure you know which features move customers to action. The next part of the equation is packaging the information in a way that customers can easily absorb and mapping it to how they buy.

Tracking the buyer's journey

The first part of what we refer to as content packaging is *specifying the outcome* you want. The next part is matching your content to a particular stage in the buying process, which is referred to as *content mapping*.

Let's start by taking a look at content packaging. Every single page of your website serves a specific purpose. For example, a home page might convince a visitor to stay long enough to click a specific product link. Or it might provide a source of information that prompts your customer to register as a member of your site. You may have a testimonial or case study page that shows how a product solved another customer's problem or compares your product to that of a competitor. A product page on your site has a very clear goal: getting the customer to purchase the product. After you define the expected outcome or goal for a page, it becomes easier to determine whether your content serves that purpose.

Another key to packaging your website information is making the content skimmable. Designing *skimmable* text simply means that you allow a customer to look over chunks of data rather than have to read every single word to get your message. People have short attention spans when surfing the web. The growth of social media sites, such as Facebook and Twitter, has only shortened the already-short attention span. The increasing use of mobile devices for viewing websites makes short copy even more important. Customers reading your content on mobile phones want to get to the specific details, quickly. In short, folks are now used to super-abbreviated communications.

By using a few simple tricks, you can still draw customers' eyes to details, even if they're speed reading.

Follow these suggestions to make your text skimmable:

>> Use short paragraphs.

>> Highlight, or **boldface,** important words and phrases.

>> Use bullets (like the ones in this list) to call out details.

>> Include hypertext links to draw attention to a source of more information.

>> Increase the font size of text to put emphasis on certain words.

>> Incorporate graphics or images that complement the text and call attention to it.

TIP

Because space is often limited on your home page, you can rotate different messages at the top of your page, similar to running a banner advertisement, every 10–15 seconds, for example. Your customers will be quickly exposed to multiple offers or messages, and you won't be cluttering your home page with static content. In fact, you can use this same technique on just about any page of your site, or at various places within the page (but the top half of the page usually gets seen the most which makes that valuable real estate for important information and offers).

Getting organized

After you create killer copy that's skimmable, you might think that you're ready to transfer your final thoughts onto your web page. Wait! You must complete one more step: Organize the information on the page in a way that makes sense. Your message should be simple, concise, and easy to understand. The most important factor is the order in which the information appears on a page. The text should lead visitors to take action (the specific outcome you identified earlier).

Alexa (a company now owned by Amazon that provides commercial web traffic data and analytics) tracks the popularity of websites. We used this online tool to find high-ranking examples of sites that use effective content strategies to drive traffic. Figure 5-1 illustrates how one site, Constant Contact, incorporates some of these content strategies. The desired outcome on the page shown in the figure is to have customers create a free trial account. The bottom of the page provides options to direct visitors based on their intent, including exploring specific product features, viewing templates, or watching a video to learn more. All of the content is organized in a way that leads customers to that final action — clicking to create a free account or move to the next page for more information.

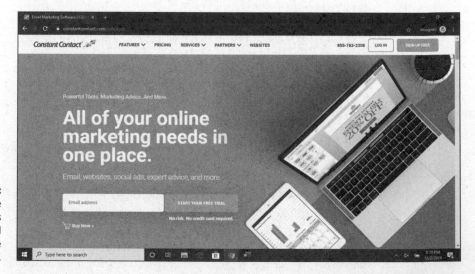

FIGURE 5-1:
This site organizes its content to lead viewers to create a free account.

Figure 5-2 shows the next page a customer might click to dig deeper for information. The first features page about email marketing uses a similar strategy as the home page, by first encouraging visitors to get started with the free trial. It also uses bold words that reinforce how their product solves its customers' needs. In this case, the company addresses the desire a customer has for a simple, easy solution.

Now that you see how to organize your content on different pages, the next step is to map your content and web pages to the stages of a buyer's journey. When mapping content, we like to bucket content into one of these key buying stages:

>> **Awareness:** In this stage, the buyer is realizing that she has a problem that needs to be solved and is exploring ways to address her pain point. Content in this stage should be very high level or talk to a specific issue.

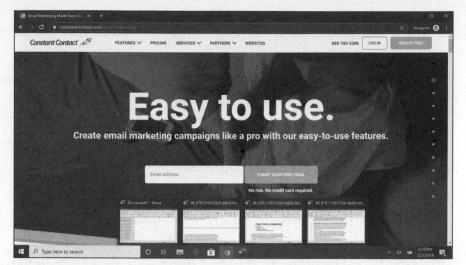

FIGURE 5-2:
Choose headlines
and content
that clearly tell
customers what
problems your
product solves.

>> **Consideration:** In the next stage, the buyer is ready to compare solutions or products from various companies and learn more about specific features. Your content at this stage needs to discuss the product in detail, or provide videos and case studies that also show how other customers have used your product to solve similar problems.

>> **Decision:** The final stage is where the buyer is making her decision. Usually this is when the buyer wants to know specific things about your company, the reliability of delivering the product or service, and detailed pricing information. The content at this stage must convince the buyer to get off the fence and take that final step and officially become your customer.

TIP

As you think about the type of content you have, take note of where it fits within the buyer's journey. As you match content to one of these three stages, you're likely to see a gap where you're short on specific content. This is a helpful (and necessary) exercise to make sure you're addressing all the concerns or questions a buyer has before becoming a customer.

Mapping content where it counts

A single web page can have an unlimited amount of information and choices — filled with lots of links, buttons, and page sections. Your visitors can then choose from several possible actions on that one page. What do you do then?

You have to make a choice: Decide which actions take priority. You can do so by following these simple steps:

1. **Make a list of all possible decisions visitors can make when they're viewing your web page.**

2. **Prioritize the different choices or actions, from most to least desired.**

   For example, it might be more important for visitors to click a page filled with products than to click a link to sign up for a newsletter.

3. **Map the content on the page in such a way that customers view the information in your preferred order (according to your prioritized ranking).**

Our next example, shown in Figure 5-3, is from SugarCRM, a high-ranking business solutions site, which organizes its content in one of two ways, depending on the page and desired outcome. The first goal of the Products page is to encourage visitors to request a personal demo of the solution. To support this goal, there is also an offer to first *watch* a free demo. This call-to-action (CTA) button is clearly showcased at the top of the page in the main navigation. The other goal of the page is to educate site visitors (who aren't ready for a demo or pricing) about product features. To support this goal, visitors can scroll down the page and see short descriptive content blocks with more information about the product's features, as well as link to learn more about each particular feature. The site does a good job of balancing images, offers (or calls to action), and content. The information is easy to understand and site visitors can readily see their options.

FIGURE 5-3:
Prioritize and organize your content using short descriptions and images that support your words.

The site also provides more detailed information targeted to a specific type of user, or customer. It maps each solution offering to the different parts of a business, such as marketing, sales, and support. This content strategy enables visitors to see information on how to use the product based on their specific needs and provides the option to click through to certain pages to learn more through case studies and feature examples. The goal of this type of page is to educate a particular customer segment, giving visitors enough detailed information to make them comfortable with taking a *buying* action (request a demo or contact sales, for example).

REMEMBER

Visitors to a website read information by starting at the top of the page and moving downward. As they do with printed offline text, they also read from left to right. Therefore, content you place at the top and to the left of your pages often is noticed first, unless images or large calls to action are used to draw attention elsewhere on the page.

Moved to Purchase: Turning Words into Action

After you identify the actions you want customers to take, it's time to choose the words that elicit those responses. Choose words and phrases that accomplish these tasks:

>> **Evoke a feeling:** Decisions to make a purchase are often influenced by emotions. Words that help conjure those emotions and feelings are more likely to get a response. Keep in mind, however, that someone shopping for plain paper napkins isn't emotionally connected to the purchase. In this case, a straightforward explanation of the product or its primary benefit (inexpensive cost, for example) probably works best.

>> **Grab attention:** Some words naturally cause people to momentarily pause when they read them. *STOP! Don't go further until you read the next sentence,* for example, is an effective way to get your customer's attention long enough to introduce the next level of information. And don't forget *FREE!* — one of the most popular attention-grabbers.

>> **Identify a problem:** Customers are looking for products and services that answer a need. They're drawn to words that describe the problems or needs that they too are trying to solve.

>> **Contain buzzwords.** Every industry and consumer market has keywords or key phrases that are part of that market's lingo, such as *cross-platform* or *solution-driven*. When you talk the language, your customer is more likely to hear what you're saying and respond. However, be sure to use common, helpful phrases, not confusing abbreviations or acronyms. If you must use acronyms or highly technical terms that are not common, be sure to define the terms.

>> **Offer assurance:** Customers want to feel good about their decision to buy your products or use your services. When you use words that offer comfort or reinforce the buying decision, customers are often encouraged to make a purchase.

EYE-CATCHING WORDS

Use the following list of words and phrases to grab a customer's attention, provide assurance, or ask a customer to take action.

Grab Attention	Provide Assurance	Take Action
Stop	Guaranteed	Buy now
Listen	Trial version	Order here
Urgent	Risk free	Click to order
Sale	No risk	Get more information
Half off	Free sample	Request information
Clearance	No obligation	Contact us
Reduced	Money-back guarantee	Email us
While supplies last	Success stories	Join today
Almost sold out	Testimonials	Subscribe
Secret	Loyal customers	Buy now, pay later
Confidential	Quality	Act now
Hot	Validated or tested	Request a demo
Limited time only	Approved	Get a quote
Connect	Referrals	Like us on Facebook or follow us on Twitter

>> **Request a purchase or action:** If you don't ask customers to make a purchase, your chances of them doing so are greatly diminished. The same goes for any type of action you want the customer to take, such as requesting a product demo, downloading a guide, or watching a video. The type of wording used to get a customer to do something is often referred to as a *call to action* or *CTA*, as we reference throughout this book. The words or phrases ask the customer to make a decision at that point. A call to action is particularly effective when it immediately follows words that offer assurance.

WARNING

Making unsubstantiated or false earnings claims or false promises about products or services can subject you to fines and prosecution. For more information and legal guidelines, visit the Federal Trade Commission at www.ftc.gov.

TIP

Instead of using commands such as *Click here* or *Next* to get folks to click your links, use descriptive terms that are also useful in search engine rankings. For example, use *Learn how to incorporate your business now* or *Get started planning your own water garden* as the link text. Even in your CTAs that appear as buttons, you can get creative with the text.

Chapter **6**

Going Beyond Beta and Launching Your Site

After taking the trouble to design a site, fill it with quality content, and find the perfect place to host it, you would think that that's the end of the story. We don't want to disappoint you, but you have to deal with another major phase before you launch.

In this chapter, we break this final stage into smaller segments to make it easy to follow. For one moment, let us summarize what all those segments mean in layman's terms: Test, test, and test again. Then, and only then, blast off!

Some Things to Know Before You Start Uploading

Both *launching* and *uploading* your site are terms used to represent the point when you finally make a site viewable by the public over the Internet. Before you upload your site for the world to see, though, it should be fully functional. Keep in mind, there may be some plug-ins, features, or backend functionality that may not fully work until your website is live for the universe to see, but these components should be the exception, not the rule. Your site design and content should be complete, your navigational tools should work properly, and all parts of your website, even the smallest parts and pieces, must be in place and working (or ready to start working!).

Okay, you can throw caution to the wind and launch an incomplete site. We don't advise it, though. Why not? Doing so isn't professional, and your customers will become easily frustrated when form falls short of function.

REMEMBER

An incomplete site diminishes your business's credibility.

A haphazardly constructed and prematurely launched website can cause you to lose customers. If a section or feature of your site isn't fully developed or functional, frustrated customers may never bother coming back again.

If you take away anything from this chapter, remember these two points:

>> Fully complete your site before launching it.

>> Make darn sure that every element works.

You should know about a few other helpful concepts before launching:

>> **Little details count.** Bring out the magnifying glass when you're reviewing your site for mistakes before launching. Check for misspellings, broken links, malfunctioning applications and widgets, and other problem points.

>> **Some functions are limited until after the launch.** As we mention, a few features might function *fully* only after your site is live. For instance, forms frequently can be activated only after the site is up for good. These components should still be in place and ready to test once you launch. Remember to check all forms after the site goes live and correct problems immediately.

>> **Third-party data takes time.** If your site must integrate with any third-party applications or widgets, or you use a newsfeed or syndicated content or another type of data from outside sources, the application might not be instantly available when the site launches. Your site might have to wait several hours or even a full day before it is entered into a customer database, the switch is flipped, and the site goes live. If the information isn't accessible after two business days, contact the service provider to report the problem.

>> **Rankings aren't immediate (or guaranteed).** After your site goes live, you can submit it to be reviewed and possibly included in various search engines. (We go into the art of optimization in detail in Book 6, Chapter 6.) Right now, all we ask is that you remember that it takes a while for a search engine to

scan and rank your site after it's up, so don't expect it to show up in the search engines right away. Even after your site is *spidered,* or reviewed, by the search engines, it may not appear anywhere near the top 100 listings. Outside of any advertising or promotion, initially, only people who type your URL in the address field or your company name in a search engine may be able to find your site.

>> **Automated web builders are different from designers.** If you launch (or your web designer launches) your site, it's immediate. In other words, all the files are uploaded to the server at one time. Within minutes, you're finished and the site is online. With some automated web builders or template programs, you might be required to publish your site page by page to the Internet rather than upload a complete file. You can remove a page later if you see a mistake. Be careful, though: Correcting problems to buttons or to the site's menu bar is sometimes difficult after the site is published. Be sure to account for different timelines for publishing a site or pages in a site.

Here's one last thing you should know: Sites look different to different people. We're not talking about personal style preferences. Instead, realize that the code or language used to design your site appears differently when it's viewed with various browsers. Your job is to test your content with every browser you can get your hands on and minimize the differences so that the site looks its best in any browser. In the next section, we suggest ways you can test for optimal conditions before launching your site.

Taking the Compatibility Test: Testing Screen Resolutions, Browsers, and Platforms

Compatibility testing is the fun part of launching a site — if the process doesn't require code changes to improve the way your site is displayed on various devices. Otherwise, this testing might be tedious because any slight variation between code and the way each browser interprets the code can make a noticeable difference on the screen. Even small differences can lead to big issues when it comes to website usability and customer experience.

People can view your site in many ways, and it's up to you to make sure that it looks good and functions well in the most popular browsers and devices. Many free and low-cost tools make it easy to check your site's compatibility in different versions of various browsers and devices, including mobile devices, such as

Android, iPhone, and the iPad or other tablets. For example, we used the testing tools at SauceLabs to test how a website appears in a popular browser (see Figure 6-1) and on an Android phone (see Figure 6-2). Sometimes the differences can be subtle, such as how much information appears on a typical screen. If your site is not optimized (or responsive) for mobile devices, however, the differences can be extreme. If it isn't responsive, then instead of having the content fit or adapt to the screen of a mobile device, the site will look exactly as it does on a larger screen and appear small and hard to read.

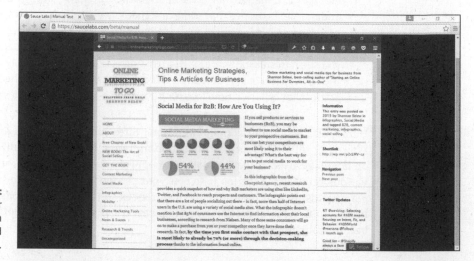

FIGURE 6-1:
Compare your site in more than one browser and device.

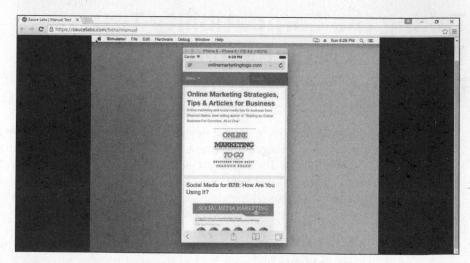

FIGURE 6-2:
When testing for mobile compatibility, don't forget to check both iPhone and Android displays.

WARNING

It's critical that your website is designed to be compatible on mobile devices. That's because in 2015, Google updated its search algorithm to focus on "mobile friendly" sites. Dubbed "mobilegeddon" within the search industry, Google made it clear that websites should be easily viewable on mobile devices, such as smartphones. Those who didn't comply would see their website rankings drop if a site didn't meet Google's "mobile friendly" test. When your site is ready, make sure it complies with the mobile viewing standards. Take Google's "mobile friendly" test at www.google.com/webmasters/tools/mobile-friendly.

Checking it out

How do you check for browser discrepancies? The obvious answer is to install every possible browser (or at least the mainstream ones) on your computer and run a trial version of your site on each one. Because you can download browsers for free, the only cost to you is your time. However, you could spend weeks manually checking hundreds of different browser editions. Instead, use a testing tool. For a small fee, tools such as GhostLabs (www.vanamco.com/ghostlab) test for browser compatibility and other functionality important to the overall user experience, such as links, downloads and forms. Free tools, such as Browserling (www.browserling.com), also quickly test for browser compatibility.

No matter which tool you use, look for glaring inconsistencies that make your information difficult to read, prevent images from loading, or omit information completely.

Another issue to test for is screen resolution, or how your site looks in different resolution settings. (Don't confuse this term with the physical measurement of your monitor's screen.) By *resolution*, we mean the number of pixels (or miniscule dots) that make up an image on the computer screen. The current most commonly used resolution settings are 1366 x 768 and 1920 x 1080, but there are many more that must be considered. Within each resolution is a designated amount of viewable space, which can affect how your website looks on a computer. Computer users can choose which resolution to use on their computers.

REMEMBER

With the emphasis on mobile-friendly design and the need to meet viewer's preferences no matter what type or size of device they use, many websites now use *responsive* design. This involves a type of code that allows the website to automatically "respond" to the type of device it's being viewed in and essentially resize itself to fit the device. We discuss responsive design in more detail in Chapter 2 of this minibook.

Testing on Mac, Windows, or whatever

If checking for browser compatibility and screen resolution isn't enough already, another major element is involved in testing your site. You have to test your site on different operating systems. For example, you might wonder what your site looks like using Macintosh OS X when you designed it on a PC using Windows 10. And we haven't even mentioned Linux!

Keeping people in mind

Even if you know the basic information to test when you're launching your site, you always have to consider a growing list of issues. For instance, your site should be accessible for viewers with disabilities, according to the World Wide Web Consortium (W3C) Web Content Accessibility Guidelines (WCAG) and other government regulations. Complying with these guidelines involves using slightly different coding, color contrasts, and text options for images, for instance.

TIP

Web-based services, such as CynthiaSays (www.cynthiasays.com) or WAVE (http://wave.webaim.org), can quickly scan your site to confirm accessibility. Both services check the code behind your design as well as the viewable areas to check for proper functionality according to WCAG standards.

Although you might not want to hear this advice right now, you should routinely test your site for these and other issues, long after you pass the initial launch stage. Keeping your site current and easy to use for the largest possible number of people is standard in the world of online business.

Taking a Trial Run

When a major company releases a software program, game, or website, it often has a limited distribution in a beta version. *Beta* means that the work is in test mode and is subject to change. A beta test, or a product in *beta mode,* is typically released to a large segment of the general public. As for *your* site, we suggest showing a beta version to a limited group of users in a trial run.

REMEMBER

You can push your trial site *live* (make it available to the public) and not worry about lots of people finding it because it takes search engines a little bit of time to index the site. However, to be safe, you may prefer to keep the trial version a bit more private and difficult to find so that you can continue testing and making changes. Simply place all the HTML files for your site under a subfolder of your domain, such as www.mysitenamehere.com/testing/index.html. Google also provides some great tools and information on when and how to index your site and how to remove a URL from the search engine; check out Google Webmaster Tools at www.google.com/webmasters. Or try Bing Webmaster Tools at www.bing.com/toolbox/webmaster.

YOUR SITE LAUNCH CHECKLIST

Before you click that last button to make your website live, be sure to check off each box (as it applies to you) on this list:

❑ My site map (or the layout and structure of all my web pages) is complete.

❑ The site map matches my web pages — exactly.

❑ Each website page is displayed and is fully accessible.

❑ Each link works properly and takes me to the appropriate page.

❑ All graphics and photos are loaded quickly and completely, and the images are crisp and clean.

❑ My content is free of misspellings and grammatical errors.

❑ Pricing information and product or service descriptions are correct.

❑ Pages with online forms or registration information function when I click the Submit button, and the information is sent (in the specified format) to the designated point of contact.

❑ Text boxes or drop-down boxes on forms and other pages work correctly.

❑ Buttons for top-level menus function properly on every page.

❑ Special commands that are spelled out with coding language (HTML, CSS, or PHP, for example) show up properly when the site loads.

❑ My credit card processor or other payment service option is in place and working.

❑ All functions related to e-commerce, such as my shopping cart, operate correctly.

❑ I've included any appropriate membership icons, logos, or emblems (such as the ones used by members of the Better Business Bureau or Chamber of Commerce).

(continued)

(continued)

❑ I tested the site for browser compatibility and screen resolution.

❑ I tested the site using a broadband connection.

❑ My contact information (email address or phone number) is clearly displayed and easy to find.

❑ The copyright symbol and current year, as well as a link to my privacy policy and website terms, are prominently displayed at the bottom of every page.

These users include (ideally) friends, family members, and a few prospective customers who are willing to provide you with honest feedback. Upload the site and run a live trial version for a day or two. Everyone then has a chance to visit the site several times before you take it down again for final changes.

Your beta users should be on the lookout for common errors you might have missed, features or links that don't work correctly, videos and graphics that load improperly — or not at all — and the general appearance and overall ease of use of the site. (For instance, the site should be intuitive to visitors, and the names of the page links and buttons must make sense to other people, not just to you.)

Three, Two, One — Takeoff!

NASA used to launch its space shuttle missions at certain times of the day and under the most forgiving weather conditions. Although we guarantee that the weather outside isn't a concern for your launch, certain times are better than others for sending your site out on the Net.

Particularly when you're using a freelance website designer, you should have input about when your site launches. Because that person usually sends the files to the server on your behalf, request that your site be launched early in the week. That way, if a problem surfaces, you have plenty of time during the workweek to fix it. Frustration is quick to set in when you launch a site on Friday afternoon and shortly thereafter you discover a problem that you have to live with for the entire weekend.

REMEMBER

When you use an outside developer, you're asked to sign a waiver when the project is finished. The waiver says that your site is accurate and that all requested changes were made. You get a sense of finality when your site comes off a project-management list. Sign the waiver only when you're completely satisfied.

The web developer is then released from additional work after the site is launched. If your provider charges for maintenance (or changes) to the site, the signed waiver signals that the provider can switch you from the development stage to the web maintenance stage, which can cost you.

Avoid launching the day before a long holiday weekend, regardless of whether you or someone else designs your site. Of course, larger websites might find that launching a site over a holiday is advantageous. The slower period gives the company an extended shot at a trial run — and one more opportunity to correct errors. If a site has been well marketed, the opposite effect can occur: It can be a hit by a large amount of traffic because more people are home and spending time online. However, unless you spend a lot of money and effort investing in prelaunch publicity and advertising, high traffic flow shouldn't be an issue for you at the beginning — holiday or not.

REMEMBER

Nothing has to be forever on the web. If you discover a mistake after your website goes up, don't panic. You can easily make a correction. The web is certainly not static, so updates are usually a snap.

Plenty of excitement should accompany your site's sendoff to the web. This major accomplishment is the start of something potentially lucrative. Celebrate!

4

Online and Operating

Contents at a Glance

IN THIS CHAPTER

» **Acquiring and reselling tangible products**

» **Finding revenue-sharing opportunities with affiliate sites**

» **Selling your professional services**

» **Distributing information for profit**

» **Creating a mix of revenue streams**

Chapter **1**

Determining Your Revenue Model

F ace it: Whenever you start an online business, you must answer one question before you answer any others — how will you make money?

You can have the most brilliant, original, or quirky idea ever conceived, but the concept doesn't hold water if you don't have a viable plan to bring in dollars. The good news is that, as the web continues to mature, a number of viable ways to make money have emerged. In this chapter, we break down the various revenue models on which you can base your online business.

Selling Tangible Products

A natural choice for making money online is to sell some sort of product. You might already have a fantastic product, or you might need to search for a mix of products that you can buy and resell to others over the web. Either way, selling a tangible product over the Internet has proven to be a successful online earnings model ever since e-commerce began taking off in the early 1990s.

Projecting how you'll make a profit

When you deal in tangible goods and services, the question of how to make a profit often boils down to a simple four-word phrase: "Buy low, sell high." As entrepreneurs have always known, you have to sell something for more than you originally paid for it to make money. Even if you're able to catch fish from the sea and sell them to big food suppliers, or if you're able to create works of art with the fruit of your talent, you still incur business expenses. A fisherman has to pay for a boat, fuel, and equipment. An artist has to buy paint, brushes, and canvas. No matter what you sell, you have to project how much you're going to spend in acquiring or producing the product, and how much you can reasonably get for it in the marketplace. The difference is your profit.

Before you even spend your first penny buying or producing tangible products to sell, take a moment and ask yourself some basic questions that will help you project your potential revenue:

>> What does it cost to produce or purchase my product?

>> How much is my overhead: the cost for utilities, rent, salaries, and transportation, for example?

>> Can I price the product in such a way that it covers my overhead and purchasing costs and still remains competitive with similar products?

>> Will added shipping costs skew (or diminish) that competitive price point?

>> What volume of products do I need to sell each month to reach my desired profit margins?

>> How much traffic (how many visitors) must I drive to my site *and* convert to customers in order to reach those sales goals?

>> How much do I need to spend on marketing to attract that level of traffic?

Write all the projected expenses and income on a piece of paper or using your computer. Do some in-depth thinking about whether you can make your business plan (that's what this is, after all) work successfully. If your profit isn't enough to make a living or at least make enough for your immediate needs, make adjustments now. That might mean finding more products, raising prices, reducing expenses, or all these. Run the numbers past any experienced businesspeople among your family or friends who can serve as mentors.

REMEMBER

Knowing for certain whether a product-based revenue model will meet your financial needs is difficult — a lot depends on the product itself. In Chapter 6 of this minibook, we show you how to research and further test your product ideas — whether you created the item or are buying products for resale.

Manufacturing and selling your own goods

In terms of sheer profit margin, you can rarely do better than creating your own products for little money and selling them online. If you're creative and enterprising, you can sell your own work by using e-commerce sites, auction sites such as eBay, and social media channels such as Instagram. Websites set up to act as an online marketplace specifically for artisan wares are also available, such as Etsy (www.etsy.com) or Aftcra (www.aftcra.com), where artists and hobbyists can list their own handmade or vintage works for sale.

The kinds of items you can sell online is limited only by your imagination. You might sell delicately smocked dresses for children or funky, hand-strung beaded jewelry. Or maybe you want to develop an original board game or peddle custom-designed iPad covers. Rest assured that all these products have a place on the innovative Internet.

As you might expect, a few characteristics give your personal handiwork a leg up on the competition, including

- » **Quality:** Without exception, consumers expect a product that's worthy of its price tag. When you're creating your own products, you have total control over quality. Make sure your designs are finished and your workmanship is of a high level before you put items up for sale.

- » **Originality:** If your handmade product is a unique twist on a mass-marketed type of product, you can have rewards. Internet shoppers are always looking for products that are slightly different from the items available in most retail stores.

- » **Appeal:** Maybe your handmade product isn't unique but is part of a specialized, hard-to-find or popular group of products (such as personalized cellphone or Android phone cases). Narrowing your product's appeal by audience is a good way to increase revenue potential. We discuss niche markets more in depth in Book 10.

- » **Built-in customer base:** Perhaps your product is designed to appeal to a specific group of people, such as a religious group that makes woven altar cloths for churches. Having a clearly identifiable existing customer base that you can market to makes selling your product that much easier.

When you're making a product from scratch, the way in which you earn money can vary. If your product meets one or more of these descriptors, chances are good that you will do well. At least you're off to a good start!

Buying tangible goods and selling them online

Even if you don't have the creative ability to craft your own products, you still have plenty of options for making money online. The overwhelming majority of online entrepreneurs are people who buy tangible goods at low prices and sell them online for a profit. You can either sell directly from your own website or allow another website to market your products.

Selling directly online means that customers come directly to you (by way of your website) to buy an item. There's no middleman. The marketing, publicity, and fulfillment are up to you — in other words, it's a lot of work, but the rewards can be great. If you don't have any experience selling, it makes sense to allow other websites, such as eBay, to market your products. The website brings you customers and provides you with systems for creating sales descriptions and receiving payments. Your host website charges fees for its services, but you don't have to do all the work.

Whether you sell directly or sign up with another website to sell your goods, you have to find a source for your products. Three of the most popular options — finding your own merchandise, finding a wholesale supplier, and finding a drop shipper — are described in the sections that follow.

Finding your own merchandise

Many people who sell online begin at home or close to home. They clean out their closets, their garages, and their attics, and then sell the extra merchandise. Then they move on to the homes of their relatives.

Others scour flea markets, estate sales, garage sales, secondhand stores, dollar stores, and many other marketplaces, looking for treasures they can sell online at a profit. Sellers who are lucky enough to find a reliable source of desirable merchandise can make part or perhaps even all of their income. The problem is that the time spent searching, hauling, and bringing home the items to sell is considerable. Not only that, but there's the question of where to store all the products and the boxes used to ship them: You either have to delegate a room in your house for this purpose or rent warehouse space. It's hard to build up a sufficient inventory to make a living at selling online.

Buying wholesale

Owners of traditional retail stores are accustomed to buying their inventories wholesale or becoming distributors for particular products or brands. The same option is available for your online store. When you buy wholesale, you purchase products at a discounted price and then resell them to your customer base at a marked-up price. You're responsible for ensuring that these tasks are completed:

>> **Purchase inventory in bulk.** You can't buy just one hair dryer. You have to commit to an entire case (or several cases) to get a discount.

>> **Warehouse the inventory.** Wholesalers don't let you keep all those cases of products at their place. You're expected to store the inventory you purchase for your site, even if you have to keep it around for several months. You have to find space for it in your home or rent a warehouse, and because online merchants tend to buy higher quantities of merchandise at wholesale than they do scouring flea markets, this proposition can turn into an expensive one.

>> **Ship the products to your customers.** Because you keep the merchandise at your place of business, you have to handle packaging and shipping each item (unless you hire employees to help you). See Chapter 7 of this minibook to find out more about packaging and shipping your products.

>> **Handle returns and exchanges from customers.** If a customer is unhappy with a product or the item is damaged, it has to be shipped back to you to be dealt with accordingly.

The drawbacks for a small online business are probably obvious. Among the biggest is that your out-of-pocket cash commitment is hefty. If you're just starting out, you take a financial hit right off the bat.

Of course, you have to have a place to store all these products, too. A garage or spare bedroom might suffice for some, but others will eventually need to rent storage space. That overhead expense certainly eats into your profitability. Many online merchants find that the third option listed for sourcing merchandise to sell — drop shippers — enables them to market their products without having to deal with having to store and handle inventory.

REMEMBER

When you purchase merchandise from a wholesaler, you typically must provide some form of proof that you're a legitimate business (and that you're not buying for personal use). Wholesalers might ask you for a state-issued reseller's certificate or a federal tax ID number. And if the wholesaler doesn't require these items, you might not be paying truly wholesale prices.

Going inventory-free: Drop shipping

For many online entrepreneurs, the ideal setup is working with a *drop shipper*, a company that sells you merchandise at wholesale prices but only when you sell to a member of the public at a retail price you specify. You don't need to spend lots of money building inventory with a drop shipper; you're billed only when you make a sale. And the drop shipper stores the inventory for you and ships your products as you sell them. Drop shippers are ready to provide you with a steady stream of merchandise, and you don't even have to worry about warehouse space. When you use drop shipping, you can select products from other manufacturers, set a price for each item, and then turn around and offer the products for resale on your site. You're able to focus on presenting and marketing the products while the drop shipper handles fulfillment.

The factor that makes this model especially attractive is that you don't buy or hold any inventory. Instead, you wait until a customer places an order from your site. After the payment has cleared, you forward an order to your drop shipper and pay for the product. (You're charged a wholesale or discounted price, whereas your customer pays you full retail price.) The drop shipper then sends the product directly to your customer. You make money on the difference between your cost for buying the product from the drop shipper and the price you charge your customer. As far as your customer knows, the merchandise is coming directly from you. Other perceived benefits include being able to offer excellent customer service and concentrate on marketing, rather than on manufacturing, the product. You don't have to deal with the headaches of managing inventory and shipping products. You can focus on the front end — the sales process.

What's the downside? Lots of companies claim to be reputable drop shippers, but many aren't trustworthy. You have to scrutinize certain issues to create a realistic picture of your income potential:

>> **Lack of control:** When you work with a drop shipper, you don't control how the merchandise is packed or shipped or how quickly it arrives. Discuss with the drop shipper which shipping method should be used.

>> **Possible inventory problems:** You depend on your drop shipper to have the inventory in stock when someone purchases it. If it's not there, you have to explain delays to your customers.

>> **Return policies:** Make sure your drop shipper accepts returns. If the drop shipper doesn't, you'll be stuck with the bill when the customer expresses dissatisfaction and wants to send something back.

>> **Dealing with a lack of volume discounts:** Because you're not purchasing products in bulk, the discounted retail price is typically higher than when you buy wholesale. This price difference can translate to lower profit margins for you. If you sell consistently, you may be able to negotiate a lower price eventually, but at first your profit margin is less than if you purchase at wholesale and sell directly to the public.

>> **Handling less-competitive pricing:** To offset lower profit margins, you might be tempted to mark up the product's price significantly. The risk is that your product might not be price competitive in the marketplace. That's not a bad thing — as long as you can balance it with another value proposition (such as excellent customer service or a huge product selection).

>> **Balancing demand and value:** With profit margins a little tighter, you might search for drop-shipped products sold at the deepest discounts. Although your profit margin can rise because of this factor, the product won't sell if it doesn't have mass appeal.

>> **Driving traffic:** When you pay more for a product (in exchange for the convenience of on-demand ordering), your profit becomes a true numbers game. You have to attract a much larger number of visitors to your site and increase the rate of conversion to realize the same, or similar, profit margins as a site that's buying wholesale (see the preceding section) or selling custom products.

Identifying drop shippers and wholesalers is the first step when using this strategy to earn revenues online. Several reputable resources for product sourcing, or locating a drop shipper, are available — at a price. For access to a directory of drop shippers and wholesalers, you may pay a one-time fee or a monthly fee that also includes access to various support and marketing tools. Some drop-shipper resources also allow you to integrate with your eBay store, letting you push product descriptions and listings directly to the site. The same type of integration is sometimes available for e-commerce solution providers and storefronts, such as Shopify (www.shopify.com), 1ShoppingCart (www.1shoppingcart.com), and Big-Commerce (www.bigcommerce.com). You can learn more about using storefronts in Book 8. Here are a few good resources for finding suppliers that drop-ship products:

>> Doba (www.doba.com)

>> Inventory Source (www.inventorysource.com)

>> SaleHoo (www.salehoo.com)

>> Worldwide Brands (www.worldwidebrands.com)

Selling Your Professional Services

Sometimes the issue isn't which types of products you have to offer. Instead, you have to ask, "What can I *do* for you?" Another source for making money online is selling your services. There is a rising movement of using independent contractors or freelancers for a wide variety of jobs. Yes, freelancing, or selling professional services, is not a new concept, but it has never been as prolific or accepted as it has been in recent years. Sometimes called the "Gig Economy," this services-based market is growing at a phenomenal pace. In 2018, one in ten U.S. workers, or close to 10 percent of the population, were independent contractors, according to the U.S. Department of Labor. Research from multiple sources agree that number will expand to more than 40 percent in the next decade. Most online services fall into one of five key areas:

>> **Creative:** These products are delivered as a service. For example, you might be a graphic artist who develops logos, a writer who is paid to create ad copy, or an artist who paints portraits from photographs that customers upload to your website.

>> **Organizational:** If your site is an organization based on paid memberships, we consider it a service website. Typically, your members pay for access to a group of services in exchange for a renewable fee.

>> **Hospitality and labor:** You may rent out your apartment as part of the online marketplace for vacation rentals using sites such as Airbnb (www.airbnb.com). Or you may compete with cab companies and offer your services as an independent driver through mobile apps such as Uber (www.uber.com) or Lyft (www.lyft.com). These are examples of a continuously expanding segment of the gig economy and are considered part of the online services industry.

>> **Professional:** These folks are accountants, attorneys, public relations agents — you get the idea. Whatever the service, not only do you market it online, but your customers can purchase the service over the Internet.

>> **Software-based:** A variety of websites provide software online that their visitors can use with their web browsers. Sometimes called an application service provider (ASP) or software as a service (SaaS), it's almost a hybrid of a service and a product. A company uses a website to sell software or a process that's delivered or managed as a web-based service. Some examples are an online payroll-processing firm, a website hosting service, and a shopping cart program.

Whatever service you want to promote online, you need to have a clear picture of the benefits and downsides so that you can maximize your chances of success.

Understanding the pros and cons

You gain a distinct benefit, geographically speaking, from offering any type of service-driven revenue stream online. For example, if you're a graphic artist living in a small rural town, the number of people who regularly need your service is limited. By selling your services from a website, you can quickly broaden your prospective customer base.

Selling your professional services online has a downside, too. As you know, revenues from most service-based business are limited by the products you can produce — there are only so many hours in a day! Your final output (and income potential) is based on your, or your staff's, available billable hours. You can take the following actions to minimize this type of effect on your revenues:

>> Increase your hourly rate

>> Hire additional staff

>> Replicate your service as a web-based deliverable product

>> Add complementary sources of revenue (other services or products)

For many professionals, the added visibility that comes with a website outweighs the disadvantages. And these days, professionals need to be on the web just to keep up with the competition.

Building credibility

One of the most important issues for anyone who sells his services online is *credibility*. What experience or credentials do you have that help you stand out from the crowd? Although you can reach a larger number of prospective clients on the web, you're also up against more competitors. And when people purchase services over the Internet, they look for indications that you're legitimate and skilled.

Unlike meeting with a potential customer in your offline business, you don't always have the opportunity to establish a direct relationship with a prospective client. Your website serves as that introduction and relationship builder. If information about your service isn't available (or obvious), your potential customer will click through to a competitor's site. Similarly, there are more opportunities for customers to use online reviews to rate the quality of your service (and your attitude, timeliness, and other factors). Reviews and ratings are also visible within mobile apps. Before you have a chance to make an impression on a new customer, you can bet a previous customer has rated you. Customer reviews can boost up or bottom out your revenue-generating potential.

Establishing your credibility isn't difficult. Your website can feature any or all of these items, to help solidify your reputation and put potential customers at ease:

>> **Degrees or certifications:** Adding this information to your bio on the About Us page gives prospective customers a sense of security. If you have

certifications in niche areas, this information is especially effective for building credibility.

» **Company history:** The issue of the number of years you've been in business is especially important if your website services are new but you've been in business offline for quite some time.

» **Clients:** Even if you don't have any heavy-hitter clients on board, a short list of named clients illustrates your legitimacy (and the fact that people hire you).

» **Case studies:** Describing how your service was used to help solve a customer's problem is an effective way to communicate a success story. A case study demonstrates the different ways your services can benefit someone.

» **Testimonials:** Whenever you finish a project that has gone well, ask your client to provide a testimonial or online review. One or two sentences (or four or five stars flagged in a star rating system) are plenty to let others know that you did a good job.

TIP

When developing your own client testimonials and case studies, consider delivering the information by using videos, which continue to increase in popularity. The most effective videos are short (under 90 seconds) and easy to consume. Plus, you don't have to pay high production costs — with inexpensive equipment, you can easily make low-budget but professional videos.

» **Social media endorsements:** Sites such as LinkedIn offer the opportunity for clients and customers to recommend you. The process is simple and is much like a traditional testimonial that happens to be accessible online. Don't hesitate to ask for that recommendation. Similarly, use other social media sites, such as Twitter, Facebook, Google+, and YouTube, to spread the news of your successes. Or eavesdrop on these open communications and find people who are already saying good things about you.

» **Recognition:** Any awards or kudos you receive definitely build confidence in your capabilities.

» **Press clippings:** Don't be shy. If you appear in a newspaper or magazine article, shout it from the rooftop or from your home page. Links to this type of publicity serve as validation from a third party.

» **Reviews:** Unlike testimonials vetted by you and posted on your website, you can't control the public reviews left on third-party sites (such as Angie's List) and within mobile service apps (such as Uber). Don't let that stop you from encouraging happy customers to take a minute to leave a positive review on these sites. Often these external reviews show up in search engine rankings ahead of, or in line with, your website. These reviews often are considered to be more credible than those posted to your website or in your marketing materials because you haven't controlled them. For that reason, it is particularly important to have good reviews floating out in cyberspace, so don't hesitate to ask for a positive rating.

>> **Referrals:** Similarly, if other experts, service providers, or organizations tout your skills, let site visitors see that you're considered a leader in your field.

TIP

Add a link to your membership organizations at the bottom of your website's home page. Making these elements highly visible on your front page can encourage a new visitor to your site to hang around a little longer.

Adding the items in the preceding list to your site also helps you deal with another issue: When you run an online service company, you have to *market yourself*, just like you would market any product. Being hesitant about promoting your talent affects your earnings.

TIP

If you're not comfortable blowing your own horn or you just don't have time, hire a professional. Count it as part of your marketing expenses, as you would when you buy banner ads or Google AdWords.

Selling Thought Leadership

The Internet holds so much information that simply finding the data you need the most is a time-consuming process. Some of the most successful businesses on the web got their start by simply organizing the mountain of online content and making key information easier to find. The two most notable examples are Yahoo!, which developed one of the first indexes of websites, and Google, which created one of the most effective search engines ever. Both companies have been around for approximately two decades and continue to successfully use information and profit from it online — but in very different ways. Whereas Google has dominated the pay-per-click ad market (with Google Ads) and moved into video (purchasing YouTube), social media, voice services, and more, Yahoo! has been a news and media platform generating most of its revenue from ad sales. The point is that developing and profiting from information is still a viable online business moneymaker — and it's a matter of choosing which type of information provides the best opportunity for you.

When it comes to content, *almost anything* can be converted and packaged into some sellable format. Especially if you're already a subject matter expert, or you have a professional services business and you've already built up credibility, you have the opportunity to develop valuable content based on your expertise and insight. Some experts create exclusive membership-based organizations and charge a subscription fee for accessing some or all of their articles. It's possible to charge money for articles (such as white papers and how-to guides), research data, training programs, video how-to series, mobile applications, and, well, you name it.

The subject of providing saleable content online holds so much promise that we dedicate an entire chapter to it. If this area interests you, check out Chapter 3 of this minibook to find out how to transition your expertise into e-books, webinars, and other online content-based products. Whether you create a website that organizes information or you sell articles or other information online, developing marketable content requires only four initial steps:

1. **Originate.**

   In this step, you create the product. Converting and saving your words, music, or images to a media format is a fairly simple and straightforward process.

2. **Replicate.**

   After you have an information product, your next step is to package it for resale by converting the content into a type of downloadable file distributed over an Internet connection. The file might be a PDF document, an image file, or even a link to a password-protected website that contains the information.

3. **Disseminate.**

   After the content is stored in the preferred format, you're ready to put it up for sale. You have lots of ways to make the content available for download: You can use standard shopping carts that integrate with content products, or you can use web-based services that distribute content on your behalf. You may prefer to deliver your content through popular social media channels, such as Instagram, and profit not from the sale of the content itself, but from selling *sponsorships* of your content brand, or by becoming a social media influencer. (We discuss this idea further in Book 10, Chapter 2.)

4. **Update.**

   Making minor revisions or updating content is a matter of returning to the original document or file. After the corrections are made, you save the changes and then replace the old media with the most recent version.

Ease of production aside, you're probably curious about how much you truly can earn. That number is hard to pinpoint because you can charge in several ways and because getting consistent numbers for this new industry is challenging. That said, from year to year, analysts gauge a steady increase in revenues from paid content, with totals reaching several billion dollars. As Google's changing rules for online search results put more and more emphasis on quality content (in order to rank high in results), and as audiences worldwide can't seem to quench their thirst for online content (especially videos), there doesn't appear to be a ceiling for revenue generated from some form of content. There have been significant acquisitions and purchases of content-heavy sites that prove content is king! HuffPost, essentially a news-style blog site, was sold for $315 million. Re/Code, a website filled with content for technology enthusiasts and developers, was purchased by Vox (another online media conglomerate) in a deal valued at nearly $20 million. And LinkedIn spent $1.5 billion to buy Lynda.com, an online training resource, which continues its success as a leader in training content for individuals and corporations.

Companies such as YouTube, Apple, Netflix, and even traditional media sites for major networks have expanded the meaning of *content.* Apps, videos, and music have already skyrocketed into the arena of sought-after content. The new demand has caused a tug-of-war between two strategies: offering paid content versus offering free content subsidized by advertising. (We think paid content will continue to grow.) Prominent media organizations are leading the way and establishing a legitimate (and lucrative) market.

Perhaps responding to growing preferences, content distributors big and small are also offering content in single quantities. One of the best-known examples is the Apple iTunes Store, which struck a chord with fans when it started selling downloadable songs for 99 cents apiece. Online bookstores, such as Amazon and Barnes & Noble, also offer paid content that's immediately downloadable for use with their respective media or e-readers. Note that your price point and potential revenue for this model largely depend on three factors:

>> The type of content you're offering (and how it is traditionally packaged)

>> The popularity of your content

>> The way your content is being sold by your competitors

Getting Social (Media) for Profit

Although paid programming is undoubtedly expanding on the web, it's not the only game in town. Content is being used to sustain another rapidly expanding online business model: social commerce. The term *social commerce* refers to buying and selling products and services on or via social media platforms. Consider that in the first quarter of 2019, almost 30 percent of Internet users in the United States purchased something online after seeing it on social media, according to research from eMarketer. That number is expected to continue to climb as social media sites yield greater influence and get better at in-application buying opportunities, which means you don't even have to leave the social media platform to complete a purchase.

You don't have to be an established online retailer to benefit from social commerce. Social media sites, including Instagram, Facebook, and Pinterest, have proven to be viable platforms to enable or influence many types of revenue-generating opportunities. Here are a few ways you can use social media to bring in the dollars as part of your online revenue model:

>> **Become a social influencer.** Perhaps you follow certain people on Instagram or Snapchat who aren't celebrities or aren't even particularly well known outside of social media. Nonetheless, you like them because they have lots of interesting ideas and tips, are humorous, or just consistently share intriguing or fun images. You follow them on social media because they're either helpful or entertaining. Chances are, you've also seen these social media personalities talk about a particular brand or product, and even share images or videos of them using the product. Most likely, you've been following a social influencer, and he or she has gotten paid money to talk about, share, or generally promote that brand or product.

How much earning potential are we talking about? It's estimated that social influencers with less than 10,000 followers (called *nanoinfluencers*) earn more than $30,000 a year! Of course, the more followers you have, the greater your earning potential. Those influencers with more than 1 million followers can request as much as $100,000 per social media share or post! As you can see, there's a wide range of earning potential, but brands are increasingly dedicating advertising budget (real dollars!) to pay social influencers, just as they set money aside for traditional advertising. If you have a unique point of view, enjoy posting on social media, and are able to build followers, this is a viable revenue model.

>> **Engage in crowd sourcing.** Maybe you don't have the desire to be a social influencer, but you're good at identifying some of the up-and-coming influencers and interacting with them. You may consider using social media as a crowd-sourcing venue for companies. Think of this as being a middleman. Let's say a brand wants to try out a new product and get feedback on it from a range of prospective customers. What better way to do that than to sample it on social media with the brand's target customer base? That brand would come to you to help it identify smaller pockets of influencers (who aren't necessarily getting paid yet, but have a wide area of influence within their own social network — maybe they have only a few thousand followers). You get paid to identify these influencers and get them to share information on the brand's new product. Then you monitor and collect feedback (or social responses to the product) and report back to the brand.

This is a niche opportunity that makes sense if you already specialize in a certain industry or have particular expertise that exposes you to those pockets of influencers. For example, we know of a small media production company that expanded its revenues by being a crowd sourcer for music labels. When the label has a new artist or new song it wants to test out, the label uses this production company to distribute the music to influencers and gauge the reaction to the artist and song. If it's positive, the music label uses that as an indicator that it may have a viable hit on its hands! Lots of other types of businesses and products would benefit from crowd sourcing via social media.

>> **Build your brand.** In this chapter, we discuss the options of creating your own products to sell online. Perhaps you already have one or more unique or new products, but you haven't gained traction in selling them. Social media is the perfect vehicle for building a following (and customer base!) for your own brand. Think of it as being a social influencer for the sole purpose of promoting your products.

Instagram and YouTube are two of the best social media platforms for brand building, because you can share images and videos. The trick to brand building is that you have to put as much effort into creating content that shows you're an expert as you do simply peddling your product. In fact, your product is secondary to your expertise.

For example, a teenage girl may become well known for her video reviews of popular beauty products. Then she could end up creating her own line of beauty products. Because she has already built an audience that respects her opinion, it's not difficult to shift that endorsement to her own line. British beauty influencer Zoë Sugg did just that! She started on YouTube, sharing videos of her cosmetics purchases, and quickly built an impressive amount of followers (over 10 million at last count!) on Instagram. Not long ago she used that influence to launch her own cosmetics and lifestyle brand, called Zoella. That's how you use social influence to start and grow a business!

>> **Tackle direct sales.** Last, but certainly not least, is the most direct way to earn revenue through social media, and that's selling your product via social media channels. At the heart of social commerce is online retail sales. It's a big opportunity that shows no sign of slowing down. Of course, you don't need a retail business with hundreds of products to be successful. You may have a boutique offering of only a few products — maybe it's a line of handmade jewelry or hand-knitted scarves and sweaters. Instagram, Facebook, Pinterest, and even Snapchat offer lots of revenue opportunity for specialty products.

We understand there's lots more to creating or finding products to sell as an online retailer. Plus, there are plenty of other ways you can grow your business through social media (and traditional advertising methods on these channels). If you want to dig in deeper to these topics, we discuss other aspects of them in Book 7.

Analyzing Opportunities

The question you eventually want to ask is, where is my best opportunity to earn revenue online? To find the ballpark amount of what you can eventually earn, we recommend researching your closest competitors. Although this method is far from scientific, it's a start.

Begin by checking out your competitors' products, including pricing. It doesn't matter what type of product you're selling, this technique applies across almost all the areas we review in this chapter, from selling thought leadership content to selling handmade wares on social media. The goal is to look for companies or individuals that are having success online and determine what's contributing to their revenue models. Then, look at ways you can replicate a similar approach, or look for gaps in their offerings where you can become the leader in an area that your competitor is missing.

TIP

When researching competitors to analyze your best opportunities, look for or study competitor information, such as the following:

>> **Website or online shop:** What does the site look like and how easy is it to navigate or find products? Pay attention to special offers and other indicators of what's selling (or not!).

>> **Social media accounts:** Become a follower and monitor their activity and the types of information or products they promote. Also take note of comments and likes from their other followers to see what's getting positive feedback.

>> **Pricing and fees:** Whether you're selling tangible products or packaged content, it's usually important to be price competitive, so keep a record of similar offerings and what the viable price range seems to be for those items you want to sell.

>> **Reviews and customer feedback:** One of the best places to get competitor intel is from other customers! Read online reviews and comments in social media posts to better understand what a competitor is doing well or where they're stumbling. This is also a good place to collect feedback on specific products and get a feel for what interests your shared target market of customers and where there are opportunities for related product offerings.

When building an online revenue model, you shouldn't base *all* your decisions on what a competitor is or isn't doing. But it's a good data point as you're analyzing what is and isn't working in the marketplace. Especially if you're trying something for the first time and have limited experience or knowledge about the product or service you're developing, you can learn a lot from those with similar business models.

Choosing an Affiliate Advertising Program

One of the most effective ways to take advantage of online advertising to enhance your income online is to set up an affiliate program. An *affiliate* agreement enables other sites to refer traffic to your website, usually in exchange for a small commission on each sale that originates from its referral traffic. You can set up an affiliate program based on one of these methods:

>> **Pay per click:** You pay each time a link to your site or product is clicked.

>> **Pay by lead:** You pay whenever a referred customer completes an online form, for example.

>> **Pay by flat rate:** You pay a set fee as opposed to a percentage of each sale.

You might be interested in becoming an affiliate for others as a way to earn revenue, too. In Chapter 2 of this minibook, we show you how to start adding existing affiliate programs to your website.

A big benefit of establishing your own affiliate arrangement is that you maintain control over how your product is distributed to your customers. You're still the one handling and shipping the product, even though both you and your affiliate are likely to have contact with the customer. Another inherent benefit is that affiliate programs serve as a cost-effective marketing tool for building awareness about your product or website.

Setting up an affiliate program isn't complicated, although you're responsible for keeping up with some critical functions:

>> **Create and review affiliate guidelines.** You establish your terms and conditions as part of a legally binding affiliate agreement. You also must review affiliate sites to make sure that they comply with your guidelines for affiliates.

>> **Track affiliate sales.** Providing working links for routing and tracking affiliate traffic is an essential part of your offering. You also need to keep up with ongoing totals of affiliate sales.

>> **Report affiliate income.** In addition to providing regular earnings reports to your affiliates, you have to report their income for tax purposes. That process requires sending 1099 forms to affiliates each tax year and reporting their income to the IRS.

>> **Offer marketing materials.** An affiliate program is more effective when you provide your resellers with enthusiastic support, including everything from banner ads to electronic newsletters advertising special promotions.

>> **Keep in touch.** Affiliates are like any other type of customer: If you want them to keep doing business with you, you have to service them. Your job is to communicate with your affiliates to keep them interested in, and (you hope) successful in, your particular program.

Setting up and maintaining any one of the preceding items for your affiliates can appear daunting at first. Dozens of legitimate companies are available, however, to manage affiliate programs for you. These pay-for-performance marketing firms not only run your program but also actively solicit and qualify new affiliates on your behalf. Of course, they also take a cut of your sales in exchange for this service.

If you prefer to manage an affiliate program in-house, plenty of software programs can make your job quite easy. The affiliate-management software available from AffiliateWiz at `www.affiliatewiz.com` has lots of features, and installation support is included when you purchase the software license. Its software starts at $699.

TIP

If $699 is a little steep for you, consider an alternative, such as iDevAffiliate, available from `www.iDevDirect.com`. This company offers a hosted plan (run on its servers) for as little as $39 a month and a social media option for $49 a month. Or, you can self-host for a one-time fee of $199.

REMEMBER

You can set up an affiliate program for any type of product or service your website offers. As long as you can afford to offer a percentage of sales anytime a "buying" visitor is referred to your site, affiliate programs can be effective.

Putting It All Together: Multiple Revenue Streams

Who says that you have to choose only *one* source for earning the big bucks online? Merging different online business models is smart business. The catch is deciding when and how to add different revenue streams to the mix. In our experience, you start by striking the right balance between your core customer base and your primary earnings strategy. At the same time, remember not to bite off more than you can chew. Also focus on the sales strategies that you can handle comfortably so that you don't become overwhelmed.

Begin by identifying your *earnings anchor*. This primary moneymaker provides you with a steady source of income and is the type of business most closely linked to the identity of your site — and your target audience.

After you establish an anchor, you can look for *complementary* products or services. These items extend the value of your site and increase your earnings potential.

TIP

When you're determining what revenue streams to add to a site, and when, we recommend these two philosophies:

>> **Any added sources of income should complement, rather than take away from, your core business model.** Always remember your target audience, and make sure that you're appealing to their preferences or needs.

>> **Although a single earnings source might be necessary initially, it pays to diversify.** For example, try not to depend on one revenue stream (or product or service) for more than 60 percent of your total sales. If one of your sources suddenly takes a nosedive in its earnings potential, the rest of your revenue mix can compensate — at least temporarily.

Chapter **2**

Making Money with Affiliate Programs

Affiliate programs, or revenue-sharing plans, have been around for quite some time, both online and off. Online versions became more than a passing fad when companies such as Wal-Mart, Target, and Best Buy started offering them. A big-box retailer doesn't set up this type of program unless it has something to gain — usually, money. As online ads and paid searches became more competitive, the door for affiliate programs was opened even further. Affiliate programs, in a nutshell, pay you to send them customers. If a purchase is made by one of your referrals, you receive a small percentage of the profit or a one-time flat referral fee.

Brand-name retailers aside, some affiliate programs are good, some are (admittedly) a little cheesy, and others are an outright bust. In this chapter, we help you sort out the winners from the losers so that you can earn affiliate income from your own website.

Looking at How Affiliate Programs Work

Revenue-sharing programs are simple to set up and easy to run as a sideline to your existing website. No kidding: Earning money through an affiliate program boils down to five steps:

1. Find a program that offers a product or service you like.

2. Sign up online by completing the affiliate agreement.

3. Place links to the program on your existing website.

4. Actively promote the affiliate program through banners, newsletters, and other suggested online marketing tactics.

5. Collect revenue.

On the surface, these steps are exactly what's required of you. Revving up the revenue stream takes a little more of your time and energy, of course. The amount of effort is minimal, though, compared to other online moneymaking strategies you might try.

Affiliate marketing can also be more than an add-on revenue stream for an existing site. As with any type of website, your success as an affiliate marketer depends on your ability to drive traffic to your site. A serious affiliate marketer may build and maintain multiple sites. These sites are often product review sites with lots of product comparisons and reviews and affiliate ads or links to the products or product trials. Serious affiliate marketers also spend thousands of dollars on pay-per-click advertising (such as Google AdWords), but the return on the investment can be well worth it. As the popularity of the concept has grown, it's become a competitive (but still extremely profitable) industry.

Whether you want to be an aggressive affiliate marketer or just use affiliate marketing for a secondary revenue stream for an existing website, here are the secrets to building a lucrative affiliate-marketing program:

>> **Find a good match.** Think about your site's audience and the type of information they're looking for. Finding affiliate programs that offer products and services that appeal to your built-in customer base gives you a head start toward success. Similarly, if you plan to create a website around affiliate programs, match your marketing efforts to that prospective customer. If your site is marketed to business owners, an affiliate program for a toy store doesn't go over well with your customers. However, a site created to appeal to the demands of working mothers or home-based working moms is a much better fit with a toy store. Matching the products and services to your site is especially important because the type of content on your website is a tool for

driving traffic. The people searching for your content should be the same target customer for the affiliate products and services you choose to add to your site.

>> **Drive traffic.** One reason why the affiliate program creator offers the opportunity is to increase the number of potential customers who see its offering. How? By driving website traffic from one site (your site) to another (its site). For you, making money as an affiliate marketer depends on your ability to create large continual streams of qualified visitors to the affiliate link by using a variety of marketing activities.

REMEMBER

Notice that we didn't mention one word about finding a *quality* product or service. Sadly, that's because a lot of people have made good money with lowbrow programs. We're not saying that the programs were illegal or even deceptive. Rather, a few e-books weren't well written or were filled with old, outdated information. For a few software products, you could have found shareware equivalents and downloaded them for free. Still, all these items appeared to sell like hot cakes.

For whatever reason, quality isn't always a critical factor in the world of affiliate marketing. Or at least it's something that can be overlooked. That said, there are also thousands of legitimate, quality products and services that have strong affiliate programs and even depend on affiliate marketers for not only outright sales, but also leads. This is especially true in the business to business (B2B) market where it is highly competitive and expensive to generate quality online customer leads. For the record, we believe that finding an affiliate program with a product or service that you would personally buy is important. Selling something that you believe in is so much easier than selling something you don't like.

Understanding some affiliate terms

When you're shopping for affiliate programs, you run into words or phrases associated with the affiliate process. Some you may recognize, and others are probably new to you. Become familiar with these concepts so that you can understand what's involved in participating in a successful affiliate program:

>> **Advertiser:** A company or site that wants other sites (affiliates) to sell its merchandise

>> **Affiliate:** An individual, a company, or a site that's paid money to promote another company's products or services

>> **Affiliate network:** A single company that oversees affiliate programs for multiple vendors and then recruits and approves affiliates on behalf of the companies it represents

- >> **AutoRenew:** A feature that automatically renews an affiliate's account upon expiration of the original term or length of time

- >> **Cookies:** Technology used in coordination with web browsers to store information about a specific user

- >> **Cost per click (CPC):** An amount of money an advertiser pays a site each time a visitor responds to an ad (specifically, by clicking a link or an ad)

- >> **Creatives:** Advertising material (usually such items as banner ads, links, email content, and pop-up ads) that you, the affiliate, use to promote items to visitors

- >> **Merchant:** Another term for advertiser

- >> **Pay-for-performance:** The process of rewarding a company or website (usually with money) for driving traffic to another site

- >> **Publisher:** The company or site that wants to be an affiliate

- >> **Qualifying link:** An approved link given to an affiliate to place on a website to earn commissions

- >> **Required URL:** The specific website address where affiliate links must point to earn commissions for referred traffic, or visitors

- >> **Subaffiliate:** Another site that's managed under a single affiliate account; anything other than your primary website that's added to your account

- >> **Tracking tag (or tag):** A device, usually a link, given to an affiliate to keep up with the success of a campaign; allows visits to be tracked

- >> **Unique visitors:** A specific number of individuals who visit a site within a certain period, usually counted in a daily or monthly time frame

Types of affiliate payments

Not all affiliate income is equal. You can add different types of links or offers to your website, and each translates into a different level of payment. In other words, some actions are worth more money to advertisers. Here is a breakdown of the common affiliate payment types:

- >> **CPA (cost per action):** Just like it sounds, CPAs are determined by some sort of predetermined action that a visitor takes in relation to the affiliate promotions you offer on your website.

- >> **CPC (cost per click):** This payment is based on the amount of traffic you send to the advertiser's or merchant's website after the visitors clicked a link on your site.

>> **CPL (cost per lead):** Often associated with product trials, you are paid when someone completes a form and becomes a lead for the merchant. Leads are particularly important for B2B (business-to-business) companies and, depending on the type of offer, CPLs can have a high payout.

>> **CPS (cost per sale):** You are paid when someone purchases a product or service after clicking a link or an ad from your website. CPS payments are also usually higher because they result in a sale.

Finding an affiliate program

Affiliate–marketing programs are broken into three common sources, or places where they originate:

>> **Retail sites:** Plenty of traditional retailers offer bona fide affiliate programs. Among some of the bigger names are Target, The Container Store, Nordstrom's, and Lowe's. Of course, each one is using an affiliate program to drive sales of its *online* business, not its bricks-and-mortar version. One way to locate stores with affiliate programs is simply to make a list of your favorites and do the research. The process takes time, but it's worth it. Alternatively, you can search for your favorite retailers in an affiliate network (which manages affiliate programs for many different businesses). Most major retailers use an affiliate network to manage their program.

REMEMBER

A store with an affiliate program may identify the opportunity on its website. Look for the Affiliates tab on a site's home page, or sometimes on the About Us page. However, some large retailers may not publicly promote their affiliate program. For those, you'll have to depend on finding them listed in an affiliate network site — keep reading to learn more about these.

>> **Established online vendors:** Many branded names that are best known for delivering products through their Internet presence cater to affiliates. Topping the list are e-commerce giants Apple iTunes and Dell (computers).

>> **Pay-for-performance networks:** In addition to searching independent sites, all-in-one sites can save you time. Pay-for-performance networks have assembled hundreds or thousands of affiliate-marketing programs under one roof.

An advantage of using a network is that you can apply for multiple programs at one time, and you can manage an unlimited number of your affiliate accounts in one place. Because major retailers often use networks to handle their affiliate programs, you're privy to exclusive promotions reserved only for the networks' affiliates. Networks are also a good way to locate category-specific programs, such as security software or gardening supplies, or to find lesser known products and services, such as e-books targeted to small businesses or coupon offers for pregnant women.

The networks on this list offer affiliate programs for just about everything under the sun:

- *ClickBooth:* www.clickbooth.com
- *CJ Affiliate:* www.cj.com
- *Pepperjam:* www.pepperjam.com
- *Amazon Associates:* http://affiliate-program.amazon.com
- *Rakuten Marketing:* www.rakutenmarketing.com

TIP

When you're signing up as an affiliate, visit any community message boards set up for affiliates. Find out what tools other affiliates found successful. If you're assigned to an affiliate-marketing manager, don't hesitate to drop an email and ask for suggestions based on your site's core audience.

Signing Up for an Affiliate Network

After you locate a specific program or an affiliate network that appeals to you, you can sign up. The process typically takes less than 5 minutes. For example, follow these steps to sign up for the ClickBank program:

1. **Go to the site's home page at** www.pepperjam.com.

2. **Toward the bottom of the page, click the I'm A Publisher Or Influencer link.**

   You see information and resources helping you learn more about affiliate marketing.

3. **Near the bottom of the page, click the Become a Partner link.**

   You see a page with a form to set up an account.

4. **Fill in your company and personal and payment information, and complete the required information about promotional methods and social media accounts.**

   The form contains standard questions, such as name, address, and website name. You must create a password, and you'll need a PayPal account to receive future payments. You're also asked to read the affiliate agreement, ensure that you agree with the terms, and check the box to accept the contract.

5. **Click the Submit button.**

6. **Watch for an email message from the company and follow its instructions.**

   The email also contains information about your new affiliate account.

SCOURING FOR DETAILS

When you're perusing an affiliate-marketing program that interests you, note the following before signing up to participate.

- **Commission structure:** Review the payout system for the program. Commission is usually calculated as a percentage of sales or as a flat dollar rate. However, the amounts may be based on minimum sales levels, which isn't a best-case scenario. Alternatively, programs that reward you with larger commissions as your volume increases are beneficial. Or if a product requires a recurring fee (such as a monthly subscription), you may receive a one-time payment rather than residuals. Knowing the payout rates comes in handy for comparing programs.

- **Method for payment:** You may get to choose how and when to receive payment. Look for details, including the currency used for payment; a set dollar amount accumulated before being paid (often, a $25 minimum); monthly or quarterly distributions; and the option for direct deposit into your account.

- **Refunds:** Find the program's policy for handling customer returns or refunds. Understand how and when that money is taken out of your account.

- **Recordkeeping:** Established affiliate programs typically offer a simple but sophisticated accounting system. You can view your complete commission history in addition to what's in your account. Always confirm that the program provides this type of account review, and find out how frequently it's updated (in real time, daily, or only at month's end).

- **Tracking:** One frustration occurs when an affiliate program doesn't provide an effective way to track statistics for your affiliate link. The best programs make it easy to understand how many click-throughs you get in addition to final purchases.

- **Cookies:** For well-known sites that receive plenty of traffic on their own, having a cookie tracker in place for affiliates is important. You know that someone will inevitably go to a site after clicking your affiliate link and then leave without buying anything. The following week, that person might be ready to go back and make a purchase. With affiliate link cookies in place, the site can monitor the visits and offer credit for your original referral. Most cookies are good for 10 to 14 days.

- **Limits or exclusions:** Larger programs may have restrictions on what products or services are included in an affiliate program. Or you may have to follow strict guidelines for promoting certain products or using product images. Always read the fine print so that you're not caught off guard.

- **Penalties:** Even an unintentional violation can lead to a slap on the wrist (such as a small monetary fine or a scathing letter) or to having your account turned off. Read the terms and conditions document carefully to understand how and when you may be penalized.

(continued)

Making Money with
Affiliate Programs

(continued)

- **Restrictive marketing strategies:** Affiliate marketers commonly specify how affiliates can and cannot market their programs. Most restrictions refer to emailing strategies that can lead to trouble for the affiliates as violations of antispam laws. Companies are cracking down on this issue because they're the ones being held responsible (legally) for your (the affiliate's) actions. To avoid having your account closed over a simple mistake, look closely at which marketing strategies are prohibited or considered offensive.

- **Logos, banners, and content:** Affiliate programs want you to do well, so they typically provide you with marketing tools. Before signing up for a program, peruse the marketing collateral that's at your disposal. Is it enough? Is there a variety? Are they quality pieces? Would you, or could you, really use them? This issue is important because you may be restricted from creating your own marketing materials and have to use theirs.

TIP

Your approval for participating in an affiliate program may not come quickly because every legitimate program has criteria for eligibility, although some are more lenient than others. For example, many affiliate programs don't process your application unless you have an active, or live, site. Other programs also require a minimum number of unique visitors. Completing an application also doesn't guarantee you'll be accepted into the program. Plan to apply to more than one affiliate program.

Some affiliates review your site in detail and may take several days before approving your application. Other programs provide immediate electronic approval as long as you meet basic requirements, such as

- » An active website

- » A valid Social Security number or employer identification number

- » Verification that your site doesn't violate any of the network's terms and conditions

After your approval with an affiliate network is confirmed, it's easy to apply for as many individual programs as you like. Typically, the merchants are separated by categories. After you select the boxes of the programs that interest you, your application is submitted automatically. You then receive notification of acceptance (or not) in your email.

REMEMBER

You can join multiple affiliate programs as well as programs run by different affiliate networks.

Avoiding Scams and Questionable Content

As you now know, even something as popular as online poker can come with serious legal strings attached. After you join an affiliate program for something like that, you're at risk of paying the price if things aren't on the up-and-up. Last time we checked, claiming ignorance doesn't get you a Get Out of Jail Free card.

Illegal affiliations

Participation in any illegal affiliate programs is limited by the governing laws of your home state or country. You must know the law and then abide by it. To avoid becoming an outlaw, follow these safety tips:

>> **Always read the terms and conditions of the affiliate agreement.** Affiliate programs might disclose legal caveats to you in easy-to-find warnings on their sites, but more than likely you find them in the fine print. Read agreements carefully to determine your potential liabilities for participating.

>> **Look for clues to the country of origin.** Affiliate programs run from foreign countries, or without a U.S. base of operations, may be a sign that the activity isn't permitted stateside. Or when you sign up for an affiliate program, you may be asked to enter your country of origin. After doing so, watch for a message or special instruction that serves as a disclaimer about doing business in particular countries.

>> **Conduct a search.** Although this tip isn't foolproof, you can start verifying the legitimacy of a program by doing a simple search. Enter in a search engine the name of the company you want to do business with or the type of program (online games, for example). Especially if it's a hot topic, you quickly find any red flags.

>> **Investigate the company.** Although some specific products or subjects may be off-limits, sometimes you run into blacklisted companies. Participating in an affiliate program with one of these companies can label you as "aiding and abetting." If something seems questionable, don't hesitate to check out the company further. Start with the Better Business Bureau Online at www.bbbonline.org.

>> **Check with authorities.** The U.S. Department of Justice has information on a handful of questionable Internet activities, including online gambling and selling prescription medication online. Visit the site at www.usdoj.gov. The Federal Trade Commission is another source for validating illegal affiliate operations. You can access it at www.ftc.gov.

Questionable affiliations

Affiliate programs that are technically legal but considered somewhat shady or distasteful are a sore spot. The "shady or distasteful" part of that description may sound like a line from the *Leave It to Beaver* generation, but it holds true.

These affiliate-marketing programs aren't completely on the up-and-up because of the validity of their offerings or their operational practices. For example, if a program has a long list of complaints registered by unhappy customers and affiliates, this company is skirting disaster. Or maybe the program is connected to obscene or pornographic products and there's a question about how the material is being distributed.

For lots of reasons, think twice before affiliating with these types of organizations. Be aware that your site's name and reputation become linked with any program you promote. With that advice in mind, here's a list of red flags to watch for when you review affiliate programs:

>> **No money-back guarantee is offered.** Be wary of programs that don't provide product guarantees or some form of money-back guarantee to customers. As a prospective affiliate, this one definitely presents a red flag. You can get stuck holding the bag and taking the blame when your referred customers get burned.

>> **Returning a product is especially complicated.** Nobody likes to deal with returns, but reputable companies offer return policies. Usually, you don't need an act of Congress to make the exchange!

>> **Corporate information isn't readily available or verifiable.** Legitimate companies place contact information prominently on their websites. You can also cross-reference and verify company information by using domain-registration services and other affiliations.

>> **Affiliates or customers are unhappy.** Monitor the parent site's message boards, or other community message boards, for tales of broken promises and disastrous customer service.

>> **No support is offered.** The purpose of an affiliate program is to use other sites to drive more traffic and customers to your product. A company with that goal in mind provides resources and support to help affiliates be successful. Newsletters, contact information for technical support, links, banner ads, and other marketing materials are the norm in legitimate affiliate programs. If these items aren't mentioned, trouble might lay ahead.

WARNING

>> **A sign-up fee is required.** Signing up for most affiliate programs is free. If you have to pay to join or have your application "screened," run!

>> **Scam associations are obvious.** You may find a company with no complaints that promotes the type of material that is often labeled as a scam or shows up on consumer watchdog lists. Work-at-home programs and business opportunities are often among the list of top offenders (although plenty of legitimate ones exist, too).

>> **Legal proceedings have been initiated.** Although you might not have any concrete information, check for lawsuits that have been filed against a company or any pending legal proceedings that might point to fraud in the making. You can check with the Better Business Bureau online or call your state's attorney general's office. This information might also show up in an Internet search.

Another source of telling information is a company's affiliate agreement, along with its policy for accepting affiliate marketers.

Look for affiliate programs that adhere to strict guidelines. A legitimate program typically turns down approval of a site or cancels an affiliate agreement that has any of these characteristics:

>> **Inactive URL:** Because your site cannot be verified, the domain may not match what you entered or your site may be under construction.

>> **Trademark infringement:** You have references to registered names or logos on your site.

>> **Mismatched information:** The information you provide doesn't match your tax information, business license registration, or domain registration from other, legitimate resources.

>> **Questionable content:** Your site contains pornography or obscene information; contains hate-oriented information; distributes or links to illegal substances; promotes gambling activities; or is otherwise deemed questionable.

>> **Questionable recruiting:** Affiliates who plan to market a program by using aggressive email campaigns can violate anti-spamming laws.

WARNING

Based on your state of residence, you may not be eligible to participate in an affiliate program. California and other states passed a law requiring the collection of taxes on all online sales, regardless of whether you have a physical location in the state — and they extended this law to cover affiliates. For that reason, major online retailers (such as Amazon) have pulled eligibility of affiliate participation to businesses and individuals residing in these states, which also includes Connecticut, Rhode Island, Colorado, Illinois, Arkansas, and North Carolina. Doing this helps Amazon avoid penalties for tax collection oversights and the creation of complicated tax collection procedures to cover all its affiliates.

IN THIS CHAPTER

» Creating an information product

» Finding hot topics to write about

» Writing, formatting, and distributing an e-book

» Earning revenue from informational videos on YouTube

» Developing and promoting a webinar

Chapter **3**

Turning Information into Profit: From E-Books to Webinars

Many people think that online sales involve physical products, where you put something in a box and ship it off to Jane Smith in Iowa, who ordered your product online. These eager sellers sometimes overlook the most valuable "product" they can offer the buying community: their knowledge. The adage goes "Knowledge is power." Well, if power leads to wealth, knowledge also leads to wealth. Thanks to many of the technological advances of computers and the Internet, it's now much easier to build a system and earn money by sharing your information, knowledge, and techniques with people who desperately want to learn.

Information products are becoming one of the hottest categories of products you can find on the Internet. Unlike a physical product that has material costs (such as the cost of the paper for a book or the cost of microchips and a metal case for a computer), an information product can have zero physical costs. Unlike a television or car that has to roll off an assembly line and requires a certain amount of labor to produce one unit, you can make infinite copies of an information product — instantaneously — and meet whatever demand you have for your product. In the past, information products required printing, postage, transportation, and other fees to distribute information. Now you can send an electronic version of your information product anywhere in the world through an email message or with a URL web link.

In this chapter, we talk about the world of information products and how you can create, benefit, and profit from them. We show you how to create your information product, research and refine your topic, and lay out the information in a clear and concise format. Then we show you how to make your information available to customers by putting it into an *electronic book* (or *e-book*), an online video for websites such as YouTube, or a web seminar *(webinar)*.

Creating Your Own Information Product

The best example of an information product is something you probably have (or used to have) in your car: a map. A map is simply a physical representation of highways, streets, intersections, and landmarks that tells you about a detailed but specific topic: how the roads in a certain area are laid out and intersect with each other. You then read and interpret the map to solve a specific problem — namely, how to move from point A to point B. Your information products should work in a similar manner. You simply organize a specific, complete set of information about a given topic, present it in a clear fashion, and collect money for distributing the information.

Finding hot topics

Which information should you sell? The answer varies, depending on your knowledge, experience, and goals. The topic of your information product is essential, so ask yourself a few questions to get started:

>> **What am I good at?** Suppose you're at a party or get-together and a friend or an acquaintance hears about your job and life story and asks, "Hey, how did you do such-and-such?" or "What did you need to know to get that opportunity?" That's a source for your information product.

If your life experience has trained you to excel at a difficult topic, such as assembling a complicated piece of equipment or laying out an interior design for a new home, you can capture and record that experience to help others and profit from the experience. People pay for experience all the time — if they didn't, every consultant in the world would be out of a job!

>> **What are people having problems with?** If you notice that a number of people are having the same problem in one area, an information product to help solve that problem can be quite profitable.

Sometimes, the information is out there but it's hard to find, it's packaged poorly, or it isn't explained well. For example, someone who had attended driving school for a traffic violation found out how to legally challenge traffic tickets in court, exploit the most common loopholes that cause tickets to be dismissed, and inform drivers of all their legal rights when investigating and disputing traffic tickets. He wasn't a born expert, but he learned what he needed to know and made money by presenting that information in an organized and clear fashion.

>> **What areas of service does my business provide?** Sometimes, the best way to explain what your business does is to transfer some key functions or knowledge areas of your business into an information product, and use it to introduce clients to your business or get noticed in your community.

Real estate agents commonly package small information packets describing the top 10 things that new homeowners should look for in new homes. By distributing this packet, an agent can provide instant value to a potential client, show experience in an area, and, hopefully, gain some business beyond what the packet explains.

TIP

Put together a focus group consisting of your family members and friends. Ask them which books they bought recently, which magazines they subscribe to, and which television programs they watch. It doesn't hurt to expand your reach by talking to your customers or people in your field and asking them similar questions. Understanding your market is critical for any product, including information products.

Researching the information

After you know what area you want your information product to focus on, you have to research the information. In some cases, even though you may know everything you want to say, that doesn't mean you're done with this step. You should always start by making a list of everything you need to complete this product, even if the only thing you need is your experience.

As you prepare your list, you may want to start by creating the outline of your information product and matching up your research with sections of the product. For example, if you know that part of your product will include a contact list of professionals, one research item should be "Compile list of professionals." Every section of your product should have at least one research task, even if that task is "Think about it and write it down."

Before you finish your list, make sure that you cover the three Cs:

REMEMBER

>> **Current:** Make sure that your information is current. Even if you're an expert in a certain area, the rules may have changed since you last looked into it. If you're writing a guide for self-employed people doing their own taxes, for example, brush up on the new tax laws. If you're writing a guide to hot travel sites, revisit those sites and make some phone calls to make sure that everything is still open and accessible. Add a task to your research list to do follow-up, or *fact checking,* as they call it in the media.

>> **Competition:** See what else is out there, and read up on other information products in your area. Find out what areas are covered, the length of the product (in pages), how much is being charged, and the means of distribution to sell it.

Don't copy other people's paragraphs word for word. Just get an idea of the scope that they cover, and make sure that your product is competitive with (and, you hope, better than) those other products.

>> **Content:** What's the meat of your information product? What's the substance of the information you will charge for? Sure, you might copy some background information, some examples, and some information from a third-party source (such as the address, phone number, and mission statement of a business that someone needs to call as part of your product), but the specialized information you're adding is the reason that people are buying your product. Sometimes, the value of a product consists of the random pieces of information gathered into one document; at other times, the value lies in a streamlined set of instructions that nobody else has provided.

Organizing your thoughts

Even if you know your topic backward and forward, can you convey this information so that anyone can understand it? Some of the most brilliant people in the world may specialize in their areas but cannot commit that information to words and pictures to explain it to others. Explain the process or product in a clear and straightforward manner.

TIP

The best way to organize all your information into a product is to imagine that you're the customer for this item. Determine which information you would need to see first. Think about what state your customers are in when they start reading your product. If you have any assumptions about what your customers have done before they start reading, make those assumptions clear from the beginning. For example, if your information product is only for people who have already signed up with a particular web host, make sure that you state up front: "Do not read any further until you select your web host and sign up for an account."

Many people organize their information by using this structure:

1. Explain the problem.

Summarize why people bought this product, the situation they're in, and what this product provides. "Still on the lookout for a great apartment near your work? If you're ready to find that perfect apartment, this 10-page guide walks you through all the steps and puts you on the right track."

2. Lay out the solution.

Start to give the "meat" of the product as you lay out the core of your information.

3. Give examples.

As you're explaining the situation, be sure to give lots of examples and hypothetical situations of how your information is used in practice.

4. Summarize with a conclusion.

Give a concise overview of what you just presented, remind readers of the most important points you brought up, and give them an action item showing what they can do after they read your product.

TIP

Use figures and illustrations to make your point. People respond to visual cues better than they do to words, so be sure to include illustrations in your information product to drive home your point. You can use computer screenshots, drawings or blueprints, or photos relating to your topic.

As you lay out your document, make sure that the sections make sense in the order you present them so that readers can logically understand the points being made. Research has shown that people respond well to a story format, with these three parts:

>> **Beginning:** Explain the problem.

>> **Middle:** Describe your solution.

>> **End:** Give examples of using your information.

TIP

Use appendixes, glossaries, and indexes to help people find specific facts quickly. This way, people can use your product as a reference guide after they initially read it.

Providing E-Books

One common way to capture and present an information product is in an electronic book, or e-book. Unlike a physical book you hold in your hands, an *e-book* is simply an electronic version of a book that you read on a computer screen, a specialized reader device (Amazon and Rakuten make multiple models), or your favorite mobile device (iPad, tablet computer, smartphone). Because the content of an e-book is stored in an electronic file, you have several options for storing it.

The great thing about an e-book is that you, as the creator, can choose a style for setting it up:

» Use chapters such as the ones you find in a physical book, with a beginning, a middle, and an end.

» Style your e-book as an academic term paper composed of page after page of prose, with examples, figures, and appendices.

» Use a long table with rows and columns of information in a directory-style format.

As you put together an e-book, its structure depends on the information you're presenting. Some e-books read like miniature books, with their own tables of contents, indexes, and chapter headings. If your e-book is long, consider breaking the content into clear, easy to-find headings. If your e-book is shorter than a typical chapter, an introductory paragraph is usually sufficient to explain its flow and structure.

Creating the document

Because most people use computer programs such as Microsoft Word to write their documents, creating an e-book is easy. You can simply convert your document file into an e-book in a few steps. Then again, if you write everything using pen and paper, the first thing you'll need to do is enter all that information into a word processor, such as Microsoft Word.

One format for an e-book is Portable Document Format, or PDF. This technology was developed by Adobe so that people could exchange documents without losing their style and formatting. Adobe has provided free software, the Adobe Reader, which allows anyone to read a document by using the PDF standard. Businesses around the world have adopted PDF as their standard for reading and exchanging documents. One great thing about PDF is that you can lock your PDF file so your customers can't change or edit the document. After the text is created, it's locked into place and your formatting decisions don't get lost or changed. Every customer sees the same page layout.

PDF refers to a specific kind of computer file that stores formatting information along with text and graphics. When you send the file to other people, it appears the same way to them when they view or print the file.

You have different ways to create a PDF file. Microsoft Word has a built-in feature that will convert your document to PDF. You can also find software on the Internet whose only function is to convert different kinds of documents into PDF files or to print your files as PDF output instead of sending the files to the printer.

If you plan on creating a steady stream of PDF files, check out Adobe PDF Pack, an Internet-based utility at www.acrobat.com/createpdf. You can pay for a monthly or yearly subscription that allows you to create unlimited PDF conversions. If you use a Mac, PDF creation is included inside many of your applications.

You can store your e-book in formats other than PDF. Most computers, smartphones, tablets, and most e-book readers (such as the Sony eReader) support the ePub format, which allows authors to protect their digital rights. Some people use scanners to take pictures of the pages in their e-books and save each page as its own image file. The most common picture formats are JPG, GIF, and BMP. By using image files, you (the creator) can lock in the text and formatting, just like in a PDF file.

Distributing your e-book on e-shelves

You created your e-book; now you might wonder how to hand it to your customers. In most cases, you also want to collect payment before you send the e-book to them. You can use one of these methods to distribute your e-book:

>> Sell it directly on your website.

>> List it on Amazon.com, BarnesandNoble.com, or Apple's iTunes Store as a product.

>> Offer print-on-demand physical copies of your e-book with the Lulu xPress app as part of your Shopify store. You can learn more at http://ecommerce.lulu.com.

>> Find a partner business that reaches the same customers as your target audience.

After the payment is collected, you can offer your customers several options for delivering the e-book to them:

>> **Download:** Store your e-book on an Internet web server and tie it into a web page on your server or a third-party server. When people use a web browser to go to the web page and click a special link, the browser asks whether they want to open the file or save it to their computers. The main copy of the e-book always remains on the server; each time a customer clicks the link, however, a new copy is created and sent from your web server to your customer's computer.

>> **Email:** Most email programs allow you to attach an e-book file to an email message. After you collect payment, you create a message to send to your customer, attach a copy of your e-book, and send off the message. Just like in the download method, your original, or *master*, copy of the e-book never leaves you. Instead, a new copy is made and attached to the email sent to your customer.

>> **Flash/USB drive:** Even though you're dealing with an electronic product that requires no physical media, you'll find that certain customers still want to buy something they can hold in their hands, or perhaps you want to bundle your e-book with other physical products as a larger sale. Some e-book creators copy their e-books to Flash/USB drives and then sell those drives with the e-books on them. This method can be especially effective if you're selling a large e-book that requires a long download time over the Internet. As mentioned earlier, you can package your e-book with other documents or holders, to add some weight to your product.

Creating Informational Videos for Profit

Nowadays, when people want to learn more about a topic, they might type their question in a search engine such as Google and read up on the topic. Others learn better by having someone explain that topic in a lecture or demonstration format, such as a live tutorial or a PowerPoint slide presentation. With the explosion in popularity for video websites such as YouTube, many people who want to see someone explain a topic look for short informational videos on these sites.

Many entrepreneurs are taking advantage of this medium and creating special content for sites such as YouTube and profiting in several ways:

>> **Embedded advertising:** YouTube has a program in which it will insert an advertisement that viewers have to watch to see the video. YouTube shares the revenue from this ad with the creator of the video in a 70/30 split (70 percent for the creator, 30 percent for YouTube). In addition, YouTube Partner Program can allow you to earn money through channel memberships, merchandise sales on your watch pages, highlight customer chats on your stream, and even earn part of a YouTube Premium member's subscription fee if they watch your content. For more information, check out YouTube's Partner Program website at `https://support.google.com/youtube/topic/14965`.

>> **Website referral:** Many online videos have an embedded URL that points viewers to the speaker's website. Sometimes, the video is a simple commercial or preview for a more expensive information product on the person's website; other times the video is meant to explain the usage of a product for sale on someone's website.

>> **Affiliate and Google ads:** You can use videos to promote affiliate products and make money when someone clicks your video to go directly to that affiliate to buy that product. Also, you can incorporate Google advertising inside or beside your video when it plays.

>> **Educational revenue:** People who like to learn by watching longer web videos can subscribe to sites such as Udemy or LinkedIn Learning (formerly Lynda.com) and pay one monthly fee to watch any video from their catalog. Teachers who are chosen to create classes for these sites earn a percentage of the revenue collected each month, depending on the number of views of their class compared to the total monthly viewership of that site's customer base.

Putting Together a Webinar

Although e-books and short videos can be effective in teaching people valuable information, sometimes customers require a detailed explanation of a more complex topic, with live voices or slides or drawings to complement the information. Thus, the multibillion-dollar seminar business was formed. With technology now making it easier to transmit audio, video, and text all at once, education and technology have melded into the *webinar*, or web seminar.

Think of a webinar as watching a seminar on your computer or other Internet-connected device. During the seminar, you might

>> Watch an audio feed of the instructor talking.

>> View Microsoft PowerPoint slides on your screen.

>> Read an outline of the presentation.

>> Write some text notes.

>> Use a chat window to ask the instructor some questions (or talk to your fellow seminar attendees) at the end of the presentation.

This technology is possible on a large scale because of the number of people who have broadband connections to the Internet using high-speed data connections through their home Internet or smartphone's data provider. These connections allow that information — the audio, video, and text — to be carried to someone's computer or other Internet-connected device live, in real time as the presenter is giving the seminar. After the presenter has recorded the information, the webinar can be viewed any time, instead of requiring a live real-time connection, so the same seminar can be sold and viewed by an unlimited number of customers.

The easiest way to decide whether to create a webinar is to ask yourself whether the video and audio add value to the presentation and whether the entire presentation is necessary to teach the subject matter, rather than one video or a series of short videos. Does the presence of video add to the value you're giving your customer? Does your point come across better if people can see you or a live demonstration of what you're trying to do? For example, if you're selling an information product about how to assemble a motorcycle, a live video demonstration of the bike being assembled can demonstrate the process better than any book can.

REMEMBER

In case you're not sure whether a webinar is the right choice, take a look at your competition in that area. If everyone else is presenting webinars, you need to create one to compete. Conversely, if no one is creating webinars and no videos are readily available in that topic area, you can stand out by creating one. Whoever first invests the time and resources in this newer technology will be rewarded.

Your recording session

If you've taught a class or presented a lecture or seminar, you have the ingredients for creating your own webinar. You can simply have someone record you as you give your next seminar and then edit the video and audio to create your webinar file. If you make your own PowerPoint slides, you can simply record yourself explaining the information and then add the PowerPoint slides to the audio file to create a basic webinar. In this situation, you simply indicate when during the audio file to move ahead with a new slide.

Several companies can help you develop your webinar by providing the tools and assistance to combine your video recording, audio recording, and slides to create your webinar. Some of those sites include

>> **Cisco WebEx:** www.webex.com

>> **GoToWebinar:** www.gotowebinar.com

>> **Zoom:** www.zoom.us

For example, WebEx employees can also help you create a webinar to deliver information live from your laptop to an eager audience. Your customers then can connect to you by using WebEx and watch the proceedings from their Internet-connected device. You can find more information by going to www.webex.com/training-online.html, scrolling down and reviewing the Training features.

Finding your audience

You have two main ways to reach your customers with a webinar:

>> Customers can watch you deliver the webinar live.

>> You can record the webinar so that customers can download it and view it later.

Based on how you present your information, you need a specific strategy for finding the right audience for your webinar.

If you're presenting a webinar live, recruiting customers is similar to finding students for a live class. Choose a date and start advertising it weeks in advance. Then plan a day and time that's conducive to the audience you're reaching. If it's a business crowd, target sometime during the week and during the workday, perhaps a lunch seminar or an afternoon meeting. If you're targeting a consumer audience, a weeknight after dinner or a weekend might be more appropriate. You charge admission to your webinar just like you do for a class, but rather than give out a conference room number, you provide an Internet link that customers can use to connect to your webinar.

Even if you present the information live, you should always record it to sell to students down the road. Selling a recorded webinar is like selling an e-book. The date of purchase isn't as critical, and all the necessary information is available at the time of purchase, so focus on the immediate sale. At the moment of payment, the buyer should receive access to the special Internet link to start downloading the webinar. The recorded webinar gives customers immediate gratification, although they don't get to ask questions while they're watching it.

IN THIS CHAPTER

» **Taking credit cards**

» **Obtaining a merchant account**

» **Setting up your gateway and payment processor**

» **Offering payment options beyond credit cards**

» **Avoiding fraudulent charges and other online credit risks**

Chapter **4**

Paying with the Right Payment Options

O ne indisputable fact about running an online business is that you can't very well sell products over the Internet if you don't have a way to accept money from customers. Fortunately, you have a bevy of options.

One common solution is to accept credit cards, just as any bricks-and-mortar store does. With credit and debit cards most commonly used for online shopping, customers expect to be able to pay this way. Fortunately, the acceptance and growth of e-commerce have simplified the process for online merchants. In less than a week (and sometimes within 48 hours), you can be ready to accept your first online credit card order.

Then again, not all customers have credit cards ready at their fingertips. Or perhaps they don't want to use credit cards online for security reasons. As an e-commerce merchant, you should provide those customers with an alternative payment solution.

In this chapter, we tell you about all the payment options available to your online business, and we show you how to start setting them up on your site.

Accepting Credit Card Payments

Enabling a website to accept credit cards is one of the most misunderstood functions of e-commerce. A shopper understands that she has to type her credit card number into a box on her computer screen and then click the Purchase button. And she knows that, after a few seconds, she receives an approval (or not) for her purchase. Although everything that happens between these two points comes across as a mystical unknown occurrence, not a drop of magic is involved in this simple process (see Figure 4-1).

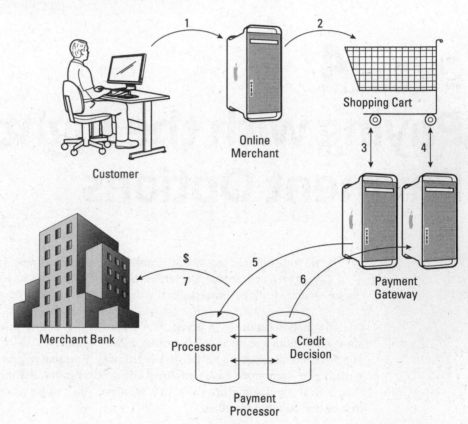

FIGURE 4-1:
Processing credit cards online.

Here's how it works:

1. A customer goes shopping on your site and puts products into a virtual cart.

Shopping cart software that you add to your site allows customers to select products for purchase. When customers are ready to check out, the shopping cart starts the process of ringing up the sale.

2. The customer pays for the product by using a credit card.

   Your shopping cart program should provide an online form for the customer to complete, including personal information, shipping details, and a credit card number with expiration date and, possibly, a verification code from the back of the card. (An expedited checkout process may be used for returning customers.)

3. Your site sends that credit card information to a payment gateway.

   The *gateway* is a virtual gate through which information is transmitted, or passed between your site and a credit card processing site. The gateway, like the little box you use to swipe your card when you're shopping in a traditional store, is a tool for communicating information between the store and the credit card company.

4. A payment processor receives and verifies your customer's information.

   The processor's job is to talk with the company or bank that issues the credit card. The processor ensures that the card is valid and that it has enough credit to cover the purchase.

5. The processor sends a credit decision back to the gateway.

   The processor finds out whether your customer is approved or declined for the purchase and transmits that data right back to the payment gateway.

6. Your gateway passes along the approval decision (approval or denial) to your shopping cart and finalizes the shopping transaction.

   Your customer sees a final message saying that the purchase is approved (or not). From there, your shopping cart program can provide a receipt, shipping details, and an invitation to shop again.

   Steps 2–6 take only a few seconds, and then your customer's purchase is complete.

7. While your customer is receiving an approval message, the processor is sending the money to your bank account.

   After the credit card issuer says that credit is available, the processor makes sure that money is sent to your bank and deposited into your merchant account.

REMEMBER

Although this process is happening within milliseconds of the approval process, you might not see the money in your account for two to three business days.

Securing a merchant account

Now that you better understand the process, you're ready to get it set up on your site. The first step is to secure a merchant account. You can choose from several resources:

>> **Bank:** You can turn to your local bank to set up a merchant account. After all, your business checking account resides there. Most banks now offer e-commerce merchant services as part of their standard small-business service packages. However, be aware of a few issues. Banks often

- Have a more rigid approval process for online businesses because they're still considered high-risk ventures

- Pass your application to a third-party company for approval (as opposed to processing and managing it internally)

- Increase your costs for a merchant account because the bank is essentially a middleman and receives a commission on the referral of your account

>> **Direct provider:** You can access many of the same direct merchant account providers that your local bank might use. By going directly to a processor to set up a merchant account, you can cut out some of the initial costs. You can set up a merchant account with one of these processors:

- *Chase Merchant Services:* https://merchantservices.chase.com

- *Flagship Merchant Services:* www.flagshipmerchantservices.com

- *National Bankcard:* www.nationalbankcard.com

- *TSYS Genius Checkout:* www.tsys.com/solutions/products-services/merchant/genius/genius-checkout

>> **Third-party processor:** This type of company or independent agent offers the following types of merchant account services:

- *Broker:* This person is usually an independent sales rep who makes a commission from brokering or signing up new customers. A broker who represents more than one company can help you compare and find the best rates available. (Brokers are not as common as they once were, given the increased access to so many online options.)

- *Online service:* Companies that once offered a primary service, such as a shopping cart program, are now including bundled access to multiple companion services. Setting up merchant accounts is among those services. Network Solutions, originally best known as a domain registrar, is an example of an online company expanding its e-commerce service offerings to include merchant services (www.networksolutions.com). Similarly, storefronts or e-commerce solutions, such as Shopify (www.shopify.com), act as a third-party processor for their customers, so all your back-end operational and processing functions are tied with your online store — in one place.

Online specialist: Possibly considered an online service provider, PayPal (www.paypal.com) is slightly different because the company specializes in online payments. Through its PayPal Payments Pro program, it offers e-retailers a complete solution that includes a merchant account and payment gateway for a low monthly fee, plus credit card transaction fees. Alternative or nontraditional services include Square (www.squareup.com) and Stripe (www.stripe.com). These hybrid online specialists are similar to PayPal, but the setup to start accepting credit card payments takes just minutes and does not require the setup of a separate merchant account. Stripe is unusual, in that it bypasses the payment gateway — to accept payments with Stripe, all you need is a Stripe account. These alternative online specialists also allow you to accept credit card transactions on mobile devices. Stripe also allows you to accept other payment options including Bitcoin (the Internet currency), Apple Pay, Android Pay (mobile phone payments), and Alipay (from China).

TIP

If you deal with one of the larger online services or online specialists, you can take advantage of their economies of scale and find a better deal on some items. For example, these sites may have inexpensive flat monthly service fees and no set-up fees or application fees. They also tend to have lower rates as well as higher approval and acceptance rates for online businesses because they target that customer base.

REMEMBER

If you reside outside the United States or you expect to have a larger international customer base, make sure the merchant account can meet your needs. European countries in particular have different regulatory concerns than the United States, and your merchant account provider should understand and meet those requirements.

Choosing a payment gateway

As soon as you receive the go-ahead to accept credit cards, your next action is typically to choose a payment gateway, unless you're using an alternative online specialist that doesn't require a gateway.

REMEMBER

The gateway talks to the credit card companies, your banks, and your website. Needless to say, the gateway plays an important role in your e-commerce equation.

If you're receiving bundled services from one source, your merchant account provider might already have a designated gateway for you to use. That's good news because it indicates that a relationship is already established. Both ends know how to successfully come together in the middle, so to speak. Alternatively, the provider might have partnerships set up with several gateways. They simply let you select the one you want to use. Or you might be left to search for a payment gateway on your own.

You can choose from hundreds of payment gateways, and hooking up with the wrong one can bring your sales to a halt (sometimes before they get started). Don't worry, though: You should have no trouble finding the right match. Look for a payment gateway that has these characteristics:

>> **Diversity:** To be effective, your gateway needs to work with all major credit cards, including MasterCard, Visa, and American Express.

>> **Compatibility:** One of the most important requirements is that the gateway integrates with your shopping cart software. Although major gateways are already set up to talk with the majority of off-the-shelf shopping carts, it never hurts to verify that your gateway is compatible.

If your shopping cart is custom designed or is a lesser-known software, you might have to do a little programming to make your gateway communicate with your site.

>> **Timely payments:** Each gateway has its own rules for when and how to make payment to your bank. Choose a gateway that deposits your money within a few days at most (as opposed to once a month or so).

>> **Support:** As with any service provider, make sure that your payment gateway has customer service support, including tech support available at any time of the day or night.

>> **Accessibility:** You should be able to view the status of your transactions in an online report, along with other management tools.

>> **Feature-rich:** Payment gateways have a surprising number of features you can use (or add for a fee). Allowing for recurring billing and additional payment options on your customer accounts and fraud-protection tools for you are desirable features. Even though these options might not be a big deal now, you want them available as your site grows.

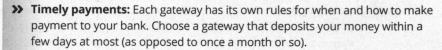

With the increasing demand for mobile payments, look for payment gateways that offer secure payment processing from mobile devices.

TIP

Today, you can choose from dozens, if not hundreds, of payment gateways. When you're ready to get started, here's a list of some better-known payment gateways you can contact:

>> **Authorize:** www.authorize.net

>> **Cardstream:** www.cardstream.com (based in the United Kingdom)

>> **Chase Paymentech:** www.chasepaymentech.com

>> **2Checkout:** www.2checkout.com

TIP

When you're comparing the cost of payment gateways, be sure to look at gateway resellers, too. Some offer a limited number of transactions for free when you sign up. In some cases, you don't have to pay additional fees on your first 1,000 transactions.

Reading the fine print: Fees

When you're applying to become an authorized credit card merchant, be sure to compare service providers. Although base rates might remain similar, other unexpected fees could swing the pendulum in favor of one over another. To compare apples to apples, you need to understand the different types of fees you might encounter:

>> **Application:** Some agents charge a nominal fee for processing your application. Expect to pay at least $100.

>> **Setup:** This fee covers the cost of establishing your merchant account and can range from $200 to $1,000 or more. A typical fee is $200 or $300.

>> **Discount rate:** Each time one of your customers make a purchase with a credit card, your merchant account provider takes a cut of the sale. The amount varies based on the type of card that's used but is usually between 2 and 4 percent.

REMEMBER

Your account should specify Internet, mail order, or telephone sales. Because you can't swipe an actual credit card, rates for these types of transactions are typically higher (sometimes by as much as a full point) than those for offline retailers.

>> **Terminal cost:** When you're swiping credit cards or manually punching in account numbers, you need a small electric terminal or box. You might have to lease or purchase this equipment, which can add several hundred dollars to your annual costs. For e-commerce sales, a terminal usually isn't required. In some cases, you can use a phone app to swipe credit cards.

>> **Statement:** This monthly fee covers the merchant account provider's cost of compiling, printing, and mailing a monthly statement of your account. The fee can be several dollars.

TIP

You might be able to eliminate this fee by choosing to access your reports online rather than on paper statements you receive by postal mail. When you ask your provider whether you have this option, also confirm how long online statements are available for viewing. (You print your own copies to serve as a permanent record, if needed.)

>> **Transaction:** You pay a small processing fee for each credit card transaction. This nominal amount is usually less than 25 cents per transaction. And yes, it's in addition to your discount rate.

>> **Monthly minimum:** If you expect to have a limited number of sales (maybe your business is new or you just don't expect a lot of traffic early on), your merchant account provider might establish a minimum charge level. If your sales, number of transactions, or combined discount rate and transaction fees don't exceed that minimum, the company tacks on an additional charge. In other words, the company is counting on you to process lots of orders so that it makes more money. You pay for it either way, though.

>> **Charge back:** Whenever a customer disputes a purchase with the credit card company, the dollar amount of that purchase is taken from your bank account. Your merchant account provider might also charge you an additional fee for processing this transaction. Online orders that don't require signatures (or the physical cards to process) are especially susceptible to charge backs.

>> **Termination:** Whether you're switching merchant providers or closing up shop, your original contract might contain a termination fee. Sometimes this fee can be as much as $1,000 or more.

TIP

Before signing any agreement, seek out the clause that details the steps you have to take to cancel the agreement. If early termination is expensive, make sure that a companion clause specifies that you can upgrade when new features are released. Today's version of the latest and greatest feature can be quickly usurped in a few months. You don't want to get stuck paying big bucks for features that don't keep pace with your growing business. Some competitive providers don't lock you into long-term contracts, so take the time to compare the pros and cons of each provider.

Offering Alternative Payment Options

You might think that credit cards have a hold on the online shopping market. Indeed, the majority of customers prefer paying that way. Yet online security concerns and the demand for flexibility are driving the need for alternative options.

You receive a definite benefit when you expand your customers' payment choices. Online stores that offer only credit cards as a payment source can still get a substantial number of their visitors to purchase something. But by adding PayPal or e-checks (or electronic checks), you can sometimes boost that conversion rate by nearly 25 percent, according to research by PayPal.

Gaining more customers by being flexible is a no-brainer, as they say. As luck would have it, you can offer customers more than a handful of alternative payment solutions:

>> **PayPal:** One of the most popular alternatives is allowing customers to pay by using a PayPal account. As we mentioned when discussing merchant accounts, PayPal specializes in online payment processing. It offers many options, is a one-stop shop for all your e-commerce payment needs, and is widely recognized. To start using this option, go to www.paypal.com.

>> **Electronic checks:** This service, also called *Automated Clearing House (ACH) processing,* allows a customer to use funds taken directly from a personal or business bank account. The funds are then deposited directly into your bank account. For you, this service represents lower processing fees per transaction than with credit cards. Fees can range from 30 cents per transaction to more than a dollar for each check. Increasingly, payment gateways are making electronic check processing available for your website. Or you can use a third-party e-check provider, such as

- *iChex:* www.ichex.com

- *Forte:* www.forte.net/all-in-one-payment-solution

- *PaySimple:* www.paysimple.com

>> **Gift cards:** Offering gift certificates or gift cards on your site is an easy way to extend payment options while increasing your sales.

>> **Instant credit:** If your customers could buy now and pay later, don't you think that it would help prevent shopping cart abandonment? Well, companies are now providing online retailers a way to do just that. At the time of checkout, your customer essentially receives approval for the dollar amount of the purchase. This process usually takes no more than 15 seconds. Then the customer has a

set amount of time to make the payment. Don't worry: You receive the funds immediately, as you would with any other type of payment. A third-party company handles everything for you. Check out PayPal Credit (www.paypalcredit.com).

» **Offline payments:** An option that's sometimes overlooked is allowing customers to send in payments by using a less technically advanced method. Although only a small percentage of shoppers are likely to use these options, it could be worthwhile. After all, it's certainly not cost prohibitive to extend these options:

- Send payment through Western Union.

- Mail checks through the U.S. Postal Service.

- Pay by phone (requires a credit card, but some customers feel safer this way).

Managing the Payment Process to Protect Your Income

Believe it or not, one day you will receive a fraudulent charge back from a customer. You lose the money, plus handling fees charged by the credit card company. Of course, a charge back is only one type of online fraud you have to worry about. Dealing with stolen credit cards is another common headache.

Don't despair yet. Credit card companies, payment gateways, and processors are working diligently to help protect your online business from thieves. All you have to do is choose to implement their protective services. To help minimize your risks, search out these standard security features from your payment gateway provider:

» **Address verification service (AVS):** Each time an order is placed, the physical street address on file with the credit card issuer is compared to the billing address the customer gives you with an order.

» **Card code verification (CCV):** Customers must enter both a credit card account number and a special three- or four-digit code called the CCV. The code is usually on the back of the credit card.

» **Filtering:** You can use several security filtering tools. One type allows you to set a monetary limit for additional security checks on orders that exceed that amount. Other filters screen for suspicious orders and identify IP addresses that have excessive amounts of purchases within a short period.

>> **Address blocking:** By using this tool, you can block IP addresses from your site. In this case, the addresses are known sources of earlier fraudulent orders.

>> **Authorized AIM IP:** When you submit Advanced Integration Method (AIM) transactions, you can designate a server's specific IP addresses that are allowed to transmit transactions.

REMEMBER

As a smaller online business (generating less than $5 million in annual sales), you typically have a lower fraud rate than large online retailers. That's because smaller businesses process fewer transactions, validate orders manually (usually), and fight charge backs by calling customers personally.

Chapter **5**

Putting the (Shopping) Cart before the Horse

o you absolutely need a shopping cart? No. If you sell only a few items, you can easily get by with using an online order form. Customers making a purchase can print the form and then fax it to you (yes, some people still do that). Or, after customers fill out designated boxes on the online form and click Send, the results arrive in your inbox for manual order processing.

With that in mind, here's the real question: Do you *want* a shopping cart for your website? Absolutely — especially if you sell more than a handful of items. We encourage you to use a shopping cart regardless of how many products you plan to sell.

Assuming that you're serious about making money online and growing a viable e-commerce business, a shopping cart is an essential tool. For starters, it speaks to the credibility and security of your website. From a customer's point of view, using an antiquated, form-based process on a website can give the impression that the site is a small, mom-and-pop type of business. A lack of a fully functioning shopping cart may also cause concerns about the site's security. If customers think their credit card information won't be handled properly, you could lose sales.

Additionally, a good shopping cart makes doing business with you easier — and makes managing and growing your online business easier as well. In other words . . . a shopping cart is an absolute necessity for your online e-commerce business! This chapter helps you sort through all the latest options so that you can start selling like a real pro.

Not All Carts Are Created Equal

Today's sophisticated applications have grown into more than simple shopping baskets for online customers. You can also incorporate quite a few tools into your shopping cart program. Your job is to figure out which features you need most, right now — and which features will serve you best in the long run. Before you can do either, you have to understand what's out there and what's important to use. Changes in shopping behavior and the e-commerce market make this knowledge critical to your business success.

A shopping cart with mobile commerce enabled, for example, is now more than a nice-to-have marketing feature. According to a report from eMarketer (www.emarketer.com), mobile commerce (or m-commerce), accounts for nearly 35 percent of all U.S. e-commerce sales, adding up to $204 billion in 2019. For smartphone owners, the average spend is expected to exceed $1,700 per year. M-commerce sales in Asia, Europe, and Latin America continue outpacing growth in the United States. Regardless of location, there's no sign that mobile purchases are slowing, so a mobile-ready shopping cart is a must. Speaking of international online shoppers, global sales are increasingly responsible for driving a great deal of business for all types of e-commerce sites. If you plan to sell internationally, choosing a shopping cart that handles multiple currencies and integrates with payment gateways from countries beyond North American borders is critical.

As you can see, you have a lot to consider about the necessary functionality and features of a shopping cart. To make this process easier, we divide the most sought-after features into four standard categories:

>> Back-end management

>> Customer-centric elements

>> Integration and maintenance

>> Promotion and marketing

Back-end management

Each shopping cart program has a set of administration tools. Although the specifics vary among types of software, ultimately these tools give you control of your shopping cart. Here's a list of features to look for in admin tools:

TIP

» **Administrative functions:** Passwords, pricing changes, and options such as font size or number of items to display on a page are examples of the most basic settings that an administrator controls. Other admin functions should allow for easy management of order processing, inventory, shipping, returns, and more.

   If you're not the type to be tethered to a desk, or you travel a good deal and don't have staff to stay behind and manage your business, look for shopping carts that can be managed from mobile devices. You may need an app for your iPhone, iPad, or Android device that gives you mobile-ready access to the administrative features in your shopping cart.

» **Customization:** Choices, choices — this factor is important when you're using a shopping cart program. The more you can change colors and fonts, for example, the more likely you are to create a shopping cart that melds with the rest of your site. Some shopping carts offer ready-to-use templates for simplicity, but you still want the capability to make small changes.

» **Exporting:** Always confirm that you can export your products from the shopping cart. This feature is critical if you end up using a different shopping cart down the road and need to transfer your inventory.

» **Importing:** Having to enter your products into a shopping cart one by one is the last thing you want to do. If you have dozens of product numbers (similar to bar codes), you would be typing at your keyboard for several days. Look for programs that allow you to import your products from an Excel spreadsheet (or a similar method).

» **Inventory:** If your shopping cart feature is integrated with your inventory system (if you already have one), you can easily manage your offline stock from your website.

» **Taxes:** A critical component of an e-commerce business is proper tax calculation on orders. The shopping cart needs to be easily configured to calculate local and state taxes.

» **Currencies:** Can the shopping cart handle more than one or two currencies? If you're selling internationally, you want to make to be able to accept money in multiple currencies.

>> **Shipping:** You'll probably use more than one type of carrier, such as UPS and FedEx, for your shipping needs. The shopping cart should not only integrate with multiple shipping carriers but also give you flexibility in determining and calculating shipping rates. For example, you may want to offer flat-rate shipping for some items but tiered or location-based shipping rates for others. Some shopping carts can also get automated shipping rates calculated directly from the shipping carriers.

>> **Recurring billing:** Do you sell web-based services in the B2B (business-to-business) market that are charged monthly? Or perhaps you offer membership-based product sales, such as a cheese of the month club, in the B2C (business-to-consumer) market? If you offer a subscription-based service, you may need a shopping cart that can handle *recurring billing,* or the capability to process payments more than once over a period of time. Look for shopping carts with a recurring feature that allows you to set time intervals (such as every month) and terms for billing your customers.

>> **Payment gateways:** Hundreds of payment gateways exist, so make sure that your shopping cart integrates with and supports the gateway you selected to process credit cards. This capability can be especially important if you're selling internationally. If a list of supported payment gateways is not readily available for the shopping cart you're considering, talk with a salesperson and get written confirmation of the gateways supported.

>> **Wizards:** Use these tools to customize your shopping cart and integrate it with your website. The wizard walks you step by step through the entire process. You may also see a wizard referred to as an easy or simple GUI (graphical user interface).

Customer-centric elements

Which features are most important to your customers? When you're test-driving a shopping cart demo, try to view the experience from the eyes of your shoppers. Does the cart help your customers process their orders quickly? Or does it leave them frustrated and stick your site with a bad case of shopping cart abandonment? Here are some additional elements or features you can include that can benefit your customers (sometimes these features are considered add-on features or widgets and you must pay more to have them included in your shopping cart):

>> **Product views:** Customers can't touch or feel your products when they're shopping online. The only qualities on which customers can base their purchasing decisions are the images and descriptions you give them. Be sure to use a shopping cart that allows you to upload multiple images for one product.

...

TIP

The use of 3D and virtual reality tools is likely to become an important option for e-commerce retailers to show products. Online retail sites are starting to experiment with virtual reality technology that gives users more realistic views of products and product placement in their homes. The technology may start out clunky, but we think 3D product views will become more sought after by consumers, so keep your eyes open for these customer-centric viewing options in the near future.

>> **Save settings:** Can your customers save products in their shopping carts and then return later to make purchases? The capability to save these settings and others makes the shopping experience more pleasant.

>> **Store data:** Does the cart give your customers the option to store their data? This feature prevents returning customers from having to reenter account information repeatedly. Having the option to save the data (especially credit card information) is equally important, however. Some customers would rather not sacrifice possible security risks in favor of convenience.

>> **Wish list:** Some customers like to be able to designate products of interest that they're not ready to buy. Try to find a shopping cart that lets customers save favorite products to wish lists that can be shared with friends and family.

>> **View order:** Your customers should be able to view complete orders as they shop or when they check out. Having to view a series of pages before they can see their total shipping costs, for example, is particularly frustrating.

Integration and maintenance

For your shopping cart to work optimally, it has to become a seamless part of your overall site. If it doesn't work, you need to be able to get help. Along these lines, you have to consider several critical integration and maintenance factors:

>> **Access to support:** When and how is support available if you have trouble with your shopping cart? The best-case scenario is to have access to live support seven days a week. If you have to wait to get help, *your customers* also have to wait, and they aren't fond of waiting. Don't forget to ask whether you pay an extra fee for all that technical support.

>> **Accommodation of other customer accounts:** Your shopping cart should have the flexibility to handle all types of orders — from wholesale orders to affiliates. Even if you don't need the flexibility today, you want to know that it's already built into your cart for use as you grow.

>> **Communication with shipping and handling:** In addition to integrating your shopping cart with major shipping providers (such as UPS), you have to look closely at how orders are relayed for shipping and handling. Can you customize how and where the order requests are sent? For example, each time an order request is forwarded to your shipping department, can you have a duplicate copy emailed to another department?

>> **Integration with third-party applications:** Your shopping cart needs to fully integrate with the other components of your business, including accounting- and inventory-management systems and your CRM (customer relationship management) software. One of the stickiest points of integrating any type of third-party business system with your shopping cart software is how well your shopping cart can relay information to the other system. If these two programs can't function together (or integrate with each other), your workload doubles.

TIP

Some shopping carts may offer an API (application programming interface) or a set of APIs that allow you access to the shopping cart for further customization or integration. Keep in mind that using APIs may require hiring or contracting with a software developer (or someone with development or coding skills).

Promotion and marketing

Of all the benefits a shopping cart can offer, the area of promotion and marketing usually receives the least amount of scrutiny before the purchase. Your first inclination is probably to look at how many products a shopping cart holds. Then you find out how much it will cost you. Marketing is one of the last items you consider, perhaps because you don't realize a shopping cart can offer that feature.

Think again! The following list of marketing and promotion functions is a small sample of how your shopping cart can help you increase sales. See how many features are built into your shopping cart of choice:

>> **Bundled products or services:** Based on a customer's buying preferences, put together groups of products offered at a slight discount from what your customer would spend to purchase each item separately.

>> **Shopping cart abandonment deterrence:** Customers often add products to a shopping cart only to leave the site before finalizing their purchase. Many reasons exist for this behavior — everything from a complicated checkout process that frustrates the customer to the customer simply changing her mind and leaving the site. Look for shopping cart abandonment features that not only capture the data of the lost sale but also let you easily send automated or customized email to try and reengage the customer.

>> **Coupons:** Set up coupon codes to be entered by customers at the time of purchase.

>> **Cross selling:** Suggest similar or complementary products that customers might like when they view certain products or check out.

>> **Data feeds:** Your shopping cart should communicate your product information with other comparison shopping sites, including Google Product Search, Shopping.com, Shopzilla, Shop.com, and Yahoo! Shopping.

>> **Discounts:** Set up different types of customer groups (such as wholesale or frequent buyer) to give a discount based on buying behavior. Or offer limited-time discounts by product.

>> **Email communications:** Send newsletters or specials to your customers by email. You would do this in addition to emails used as a result of shopping cart abandonment.

>> **Featured products or specials:** Highlight certain products or limited-time offers throughout your website.

>> **Free-shipping option:** Offer free shipping as a marketing special. This feature can be an important competitive advantage during busy shopping seasons.

>> **Gift certificates:** A helpful seasonal (or year-round) tool is to offer the option of purchasing and using gift certificates, or virtual gift cards.

>> **On-site search capability:** A good search tool helps customers easily find products based on several search criteria, such as brand name, category, or generic product name.

>> **Product reviews and ratings:** Feature additional information on product pages to increase credibility and boost the potential for purchase.

>> **Search-engine friendliness:** Use the shopping cart built-in features to better market your products in major search engines. A shopping cart might offer `<TITLE>` and `<META>` tags for every product page or `<ALT>` tags with keywords.

>> **Social commerce:** Integrate with social networking sites such as Twitter, Facebook, Instagram, and Pinterest. This type of feature provides a way to promote specials, coupon offers, and other discounts; to share customers' purchases with their friends; and to spread positive reviews of your products and customer service.

>> **Survey tools:** Find out what customers are thinking by displaying a brief survey before checkout or whenever a customer abandons a shopping cart.

>> **Tell-a-friend functionality:** Enable customers to pass along product pages to friends and family members.

>> **Upselling:** Offer an incentive to purchase more products by upselling — for example, "Buy one, get one at half price" or "Buy two and get one free."

You don't have to use all these marketing tools. They might even feel overwhelming at first. Don't worry: That's perfectly natural. However, we recommend using a shopping cart that has a variety of promotional features. Then, as you become more comfortable, start testing the waters and increasing your sales.

Shopping Around for the Best Hosted Solution

Marketing features and administrative tools aren't the only features that can sway your decision in selecting a cart. You can make your decision based on how the cart is delivered to you (or set up for use). For instance, one easy alternative is to use a *hosted* solution. The shopping cart is stored on someone else's server and you pay to have access to it. A cloud-based solution is by far the most common option today.

Hosted shopping carts have four specific advantages:

>> **Cost:** A hosted solution is a more affordable option, especially for a first e-commerce endeavor. For a small monthly fee (sometimes for less than 10 bucks), you gain access to an extensive set of shopping cart features.

>> **Simplicity:** Because most shopping carts easily integrate into existing websites, theoretically they should be easy to get up and running.

>> **Support:** You get access to customer and technical support, usually around the clock. When your learning curve is still steep, it's nice to know that you have a place to turn for help, any time of the night or day.

>> **Flexibility:** When you use a hosted solution, you don't have to make a long-term commitment. Try it and see whether you like it. If you're on a monthly plan, you can terminate the agreement fairly easily. As long as the shopping cart has a good exporting feature, you can move your products to another solution if your current one isn't working.

As we mentioned, most people go with a hosted shopping cart (probably without even thinking about it as an option) because it is the prevailing method for delivering most e-commerce services. Start-up online retailers find it easy to turn to a single hosted vendor for everything from their domain name and hosting to a shopping cart and payment gateway. In this section, we describe a few popular shopping carts to start you on your search for the perfect hosted shopping cart solution.

You might instead decide to use a *storefront*, an all-in-one e-commerce solution. If you do, a hosted shopping cart is included with your storefront as part of the complete package. If you go this route, remember that each storefront has its own shopping cart with different features. We include a popular storefront shopping cart in this section, too, to give you an idea of what to consider. If you want to know more about using storefronts, you can discover all the details in Book 8, Chapter 1.

1ShoppingCart

The 1ShoppingCart (www.1shoppingcart.com) shopping cart has been around for a long time and has a large fan base. The company has moved beyond operating as only a hosted shopping cart and now offers marketing automation (email marketing and contact management) and other promotional services. We like 1ShoppingCart because its shopping cart functionality remains a powerhouse in the e-commerce industry. You can choose from three plans, which all include the company's email marketing tools, and post-sale upselling services as part of the package. The basic plan, called Plus, is $34 per month for a single user (but promotions are sometimes available). You can also choose from the Premium plan for $119 per month for five users, or the Ultimate plan for $249 per month, also for five users. Besides the number of user licenses, the biggest difference between the monthly plans is the amount of storage space and variance in transaction fees for credit card payments; the Premium plan also includes a free domain name and a SSL security certificate.

1ShoppingCart has an extensive set of shopping cart features, with great flexibility and choice. For example, 1ShoppingCart supports up to six shipping methods, in addition to international shipping, and provides a variety of ways to calculate shipping (including the option for free customer shipping). It also has a robust recurring billing feature and an impressive set of upsell features customized to the buyer's shopping history.

TIP

You can get one month of free service of the 1ShoppingCart shopping cart, but you must go ahead and sign up as a customer, which means providing credit card information. If you know this is the right shopping cart solution for you, it doesn't hurt to have that extra month of free service as you're learning the solution and setting up your online store. Or, you can cancel the account prior to the free trial ending.

Foxy

Foxy (www.foxy.io) is a true hosted shopping cart, but several things make this solution unique. For starters, Foxy began as a secure e-commerce platform — *not* a jack of all trades or a turnkey solution.

Unlike many typical shopping cart solutions, Foxy does not attempt to include other back-end functionality, such as accounting, CRM (customer relationship management), or affiliate marketing. However, it has made its Hypermedia application programming interface (API) so that the Foxy e-commerce functionality can be integrated with almost any platform or application. Although we usually suggest that start-up online retailers choose a shopping cart with more functionality, Foxy is an exception. It is set up as a solution for developers to use on behalf of online retailers. Yes, this means you need to work with a developer if you do not have certain programming skills. Again, this seems contrary to our typical advice, but in certain circumstances, Foxy makes it worthwhile to pay someone.

If you need a fully customizable shopping cart and the ease of a hosted product once customization is complete, Foxy is the ideal fit. It is fully customizable and can integrate with just about any third-party software, from QuickBooks to Salesforce; or it can integrate with your own custom store or community using the Hypermedia API. The shopping cart features one-page checkout, guest checkout, coupons and discounts, international shipping, tax calculations, and unlimited shipping options, including multi-shipping (shipping to multiple addresses from a single order), free in-store pickup, and free ground shipping. Foxy also supports integration with nearly 100 payment gateways and allows for alternative payment methods (including Bitcoin). The most important take-away when considering choosing Foxy for your shopping cart is remembering that it is a fully customizable, hosted solution.

How much does it cost? This is where it gets even more interesting. Foxy starts out free, for as long as you need it — with a catch. Think of it as an unlimited free trial that gives you plenty of time to set up, customize, and learn to use the software, without needing a credit card to sign up for the trial. You pay for the service only when you are ready to launch your store live. This is beneficial because it doesn't mean you're throwing away money for monthly service fees while your store is still in development. When it comes time to pay up, Foxy uses a combination of monthly and per-transaction fees. The standard plan is $15 per month, plus a transaction fee of .5 percent (up to a maximum of 15 cents) with the first 100 transactions free. A custom SLL certificate costs $100 annually. The advanced plan is $250 per month with the same .5 percent transaction fee (up to a maximum of 5 cents), with the first 1,000 transactions free. The advanced plan does not charge for a custom SSL certificate. If your needs are particularly extensive, Foxy offers an Enterprise plan for $2,000 per month.

REMEMBER

SLL stands for Secure Sockets Layer, and an SSL certificate is a means of authenticating a website and encrypting sensitive information (like credit card numbers) that passes between the site and a user. You can learn more about SSL certificates in Book 3, Chapter 4.

You may be scratching your head and again asking, "How much does it cost?" Here's an example to help explain its pricing model. On the standard plan, if your average order is $25 and you have 200 transactions a month, you would pay approximately $28 per month. If you sell less than 100 items in a month, you only pay $15. This pricing model is beneficial if you stay under the maximum allowed number of free monthly transactions, or if your number of transactions fluctuate based on seasonality, for example. In that case, you are not locked into paying a high monthly fee just because you have a peak selling season each year.

Shopify

Shopify (www.shopify.com) is not only a hosted shopping cart but also a complete e-commerce solution that has received rave reviews since launching in 2006. With Shopify, you get access to a long list of shopping cart features at a price ranging from $29 to $299 per month. In addition to the number of user accounts you get, the biggest difference between monthly plans comes down to some important shopping cart features. Abandoned cart recovery, gift cards, and real-time carrier shipping calculations (from UPS, FedEx, and USPS) are available only in the two more expensive monthly plans. In addition, some key administrative-tracking and -reporting capabilities are available only in the most expensive monthly plan.

If your e-commerce needs don't fit the standard mold, Shopify has designed two other unique pricing plans. A super basic version is available if you want to sell only on Facebook. Dubbed Shopify Lite, it costs only $9 per month. You can find more information on this option by clicking a link found on the Pricing page. The other option is an Enterprise package that includes lots of bells and whistles, no transaction fees, and allows you to sell on social media sites such as Facebook and Pinterest. Pricing varies for this option so you'll need to get on the phone and talk with a Shopify salesperson. (Although most e-commerce start-ups don't need to even think about this level of service, we still like to mention the availability of enterprise plans for existing, large e-tailers who are considering different back-end options for their online stores.)

Also good to know, Shopify's shopping cart integrates with over 100 payment gateways, including several popular European payment gateways. If you're selling internationally, Shopify's shopping cart is particularly useful because it supports website checkout in more than 50 different languages. It also handles multiple currencies and automatically calculates major county and state tax rates.

A mobile version of the shopping cart is included free with all monthly Shopify plans, which means your customers can buy products from any mobile device. Shopify also provides an app that enables you to manage orders from your mobile phone. Because Shopify is a complete e-commerce solution, it offers lots of free and low-cost templates for your online store, including some that are *responsive* (mobile-ready), helping to ensure that your complete site (including your shopping cart) is displayed properly on every mobile device. Customers are more likely to not only browse products from their phones but also drop items into the shopping cart and complete the purchase. For a complete list of features included with the Shopify shopping cart, visit www.shopify.com/online/ecommerce-solutions.

Finding Stand-Alone Shopping Cart Software

Before so many hosted shopping carts flooded the market, stand-alone or off-the-shelf software was your best bet for a quick, inexpensive solution. The software was available from an Internet service provider (ISP), or you could license the product yourself. A stand-alone shopping cart allows you to add the software to your own server. Many web developers pursue this option and then become resellers of their particular shopping cart programs.

When you use this type of shopping cart, one big advantage is that you aren't tied to a specific web host. In theory, that feature makes managing your store easier if you switch service providers. However, with importing and exporting functions now a common tool in most shopping carts, where your site is hosted is less of a concern. Other advantages include control and price. For larger stores, the price issue is particularly important. Whereas you might pay $250 to $2,500 per month (or more) for a hosted shopping cart that supports an unlimited number of products with complex back-end and feature requirements, you might find that paying a little more up-front makes it easier on you as your company grows.

In general, we recommend stand-alone shopping carts for larger retailers who have an existing website. If you're just starting out or are a small online retailer, it's hard to beat the convenience, support, and savings of either a hosted or an all-in-one e-commerce solution. In fact, many stand-alone shopping cart software providers are now hosted or storefront solutions.

If you want to get your hands on one of the remaining stand-alone shopping carts, you can approach it in two ways:

>> **Purchase:** You can buy software outright. Depending on the shopping cart, the price can range anywhere from $499 for a basic program to more than $2,000 for a more dynamic software product.

>> **License:** More often than not, software vendors require that you license the use of their products. The process is like leasing a car: You pay a monthly or an annual fee for the right to use the software, but you don't own it.

When you're purchasing or licensing a shopping cart, technical support may or may not be included in the price. You might have to purchase a separate technical support package, which adds to your overall cost for the product.

Here are two remaining providers:

>> **ShopFactory** (www.shopfactory.com): Provides the capability to create ready-to-go storefronts with shopping cart systems included (or sold separately).

>> **X-Cart** (www.x-cart.com): A PHP e-commerce software that you can buy and download, it includes many standard shopping cart features, is mobile-ready, and can be customized. A free version is available for new or small e-commerce stores.

If you run your website using WordPress, the popular (and free) blogging software, you can use a free WordPress plug-in to add a simple shopping cart to your site. Simply search the WordPress plug-in directory, at http://wordpress.org/extend/plugins, using the term *shopping cart*.

Before purchasing an off-the-shelf shopping cart, find out whether your preferred payment gateway is supported by the shopping cart. Conversely, after you buy the software, know which gateways are compatible before selecting one for your store. If you happen to choose one that's not supported, extra programming might be required.

Designing a Custom Cart

Custom cart development takes place when you program (or someone you hire programs) a shopping cart unique to your needs. You are truly building a shopping cart from the ground up!

On the bright side, you can get a program that meets your specifications in every way. And if you know how to program or have someone willing to donate the time (or give you a steal on the price), this option can be less expensive than an off-the-shelf, or hosted, solution.

Then again, hiring someone can get expensive fast, especially if you require a good amount of customization. (Remember too that you can get an incredibly robust hosted shopping cart for less than a few hundred dollars per year.) Another problem is that a customized solution can be difficult to integrate with payment gateways or will involve at least some additional coding. Perhaps the biggest drawbacks are the limitations on support and ease of scalability. Every time you hit a snag, you have to go back to the developer for help. If your needs change or you discover a feature you want to incorporate, you're again dependent on your developer, which can get expensive.

If you do hire someone to build a custom solution, you'll have a wide variety of options. With access to developers around the world, you may find some good deals by outsourcing the work to firms in other countries, such as India. The cost of a custom project can vary widely (as can the level of skill or customer service you get from contractors), so shop around for the best option. Be sure to compare the details between multiple quotes for your project, so that you understand what is or is not included in the bid. Also ask for a few customer references. If you have a large enterprise, these issues might be small deterrents. For a small online business, your money and time might be better spent elsewhere.

If you decide to delve into the custom route, you will need to take the following actions:

>> **Get bids and quotes.** Gather at least three bids before selecting a developer. Then ask for a final quote delivered in writing before you begin the project.

To ensure that you can compare apples to apples, provide each prospective programmer with the same list of specifications. Ask each company to develop a bid from *your* list.

>> **Define support.** Discuss what types of setup and ongoing support are available, including when support is available and how soon a support issue will be addressed. (Support might be available only during weekdays, for example, and processing your request might take three business days.) The cost of the support should also be included in the final quote.

>> **Determine the timeline.** Be specific about the length of time involved for any type of software development project. Set a series of targets or objectives that should be completed by a certain date. This guidepost ensures that the project stays on track.

>> **Get the details.** The more nitty-gritty specifics you can nail down, the better. Find out how many programmers typically work on a project. More programmers can result in faster delivery of your system but can also add to its overall cost.

Lots of reasonably priced hosted and off-the-shelf shopping cart solutions are available, with impressive lists of features. With so many options at hand, consider whether custom features or unique needs are really worth the delay in time and the amount of out-of-pocket cash necessary to implement a custom cart.

Chapter **6**

Taking Inventory

Y ou probably know someone who is a fantastic salesperson. Usually, this person is described as being capable of "selling anything to anyone." Well, the Internet is similar to that top-notch salesperson. It can sell just about anything to almost anyone around the world — with your help, of course. As any good salesperson understands, however, you have to know a few tricks of the trade. The same statement holds true for selling online: To do well, you have to know a few tricks. In the case of choosing inventory, you simply need some additional information to give your business a boost.

REMEMBER

How do you decide what to stock up on to give your business a leg up? To create the ideal inventory for your online business, always keep in mind these three points:

» **Product:** The goods or services you sell should be readily available for you to purchase and stock and reflect items of interest to your customers.

» **Pricing:** The amount you charge for your product must make it attractive to customers while providing you with a reasonable profit. Or, your products must be unique or truly upscale to warrant a higher price. We discuss the advantages of a niche market in Book 10, Chapter 1.

» **Selection:** The range of products you offer your customers is more than a matter of quantity. Offer variations of the same product so that your customers can choose from alternative sizes, colors, and styles.

Fortunately, deciding which type of product to promote — and at which price — isn't complicated. In fact, several useful tools and methods can help you determine potential sales chart-toppers.

Finding Out What's Popular

One thing is certain, the world loves data — and there's plenty of it to be had. You may have heard terms such as *business intelligence (BI)* and *big data*. Both involve tracking, collecting, and analyzing all sorts of metrics or data points to form a more detailed picture about what's happening in a particular area, such as what items are selling well during a specified time period. You can access this type of information from various sources, and sometimes it's free. One place to turn for high-level sales data on a wide range of product types is Amazon. The mega online retailer moves a lot of products and readily shares which ones are selling best at any given time. (The Amazon Best Sellers list is updated hourly!) Using Amazon Best Sellers, you can explore any of its product categories to see which individual products are climbing up or down the chain of most-wanted items. Although you can't access specific sales figures, you can see the following information:

>> Numeric ranking of 1 to 100 in the top sellers list

>> Product rating by customers

>> Sales rank and recent movement up or down the list by percentage

Within each product category, you can also access a list of top 100 sellers based on subcategories. For example, looking at the Amazon Best Sellers list of Games, in the Toys and Games category, you can sort by the top 100 products. Within the category, you could drill down to something even more specific in this category, such as New Releases or Most Wished For.

Although this view has limitations, you can still get a good sense of what people are buying because of the amount and diversity of products sold. Part of what makes Amazon a terrific resource for this information is that the mega retailer has more than three dozen product categories from appliances and jewelry to pet supplies and beauty. Within each main category there is also a detailed breakdown of subcategories. This allows you to be specific in your research. And if you dig into the buyer reviews for the top sellers, you can possibly get more granular product detail and why people bought the product or why they like it. Granted, it takes a good bit of time to read product reviews, but the task is worthwhile when you're building an inventory of online products for your business.

HOT TIPS FOR CHOOSING THE RIGHT PRODUCTS

When you're deciding which products to offer for sale online, ask yourself these questions:

- Will shipping the product be difficult? Large, bulky products can add to your shipping woes.

- Will larger products, which are expensive to ship, deter customers from making a purchase online?

- Are you selling perishable food products? If so, do they meet federal food handling, storage, and shipping guidelines?

- Is the product fragile, and does it require special handling?

- How much product does a supplier require you to buy at one time to receive the best price?

- Where will you keep the inventory? Do you have suitable storage facilities, or do you have to pay for (rent) additional space?

- If you have to store the inventory, is it important to you that smaller products, flat products, and information products take up less room?

- If you're making custom products by hand, how long do you spend fulfilling an order? Can you keep up with demand?

- Are you familiar with the product?

Two other popular websites can provide a glimpse of the types of products that are selling well. Etsy (www.etsy.com), an online marketplace for handmade and vintage items and craft supplies, and eBay (www.ebay.com), the online auction site, attract lots of buyers for a variety of products. Both sites are good sources for helping you decide what types of products should be in your inventory.

A third-party site called Craftcount (www.craftcount.com) uses an application programming interface (API) from Etsy to track top Etsy sellers daily, and top products by category and country. Stores with more than 1,000 sales are tracked, and the information is updated every 24 hours. If you think information about handmade items couldn't possibly help drive your own inventory decisions, consider this: Large retailers have started turning to Etsy to look for popular products to stock in their own stores. Big-box retailers often work directly with top-selling

Etsy store owners to reproduce their handmade bestsellers. If you happen to sell similar types of goods — from apparel to home goods — this type of report could prove to be a good source for beefing up your store inventory.

To research a much wider variety of products, you can turn to eBay. To access the sales data, however, you need to invest in a tool called Terapeak (www.terapeak.com). This tool provides a detailed view into the most popular products selling on eBay over a given period of time as well as which listings are resulting in sales. The tool provides data from the past three years of purchases. You can also access pricing recommendations and search for keyword recommendations (based on what words buyers are using to search for products). Although Terapeak is designed for current eBay sellers, it is also a source of insightful data for building a sought-after inventory of products for your online store. Terapeak pricing plans start at approximately $20 per month, but you can access a free trial, which may be enough to give you helpful information. Starting in 2019, Terapeak is a free tool included with some eBay store subscriptions! As a bonus, once you identify top-selling products, Terapeak helps you source the same or similar products on Alibaba (www.alibaba.com), which is a company that connects you with products and suppliers. Terapeak is a one-stop resource for research and products!

Putting Together All Your Research

When you're starting a new business, it's comforting to be able to validate your decisions. That's exactly what market research allows you to do. If your searches show that a potential product or service is in high demand, it's a signal that you're on the right track. Or if you're having trouble selecting products to stock your web inventory, the popularity listings in your research can spur your imagination.

Some established companies specialize in market research. Their background work is summarized in concise reports that forecast trends and buying behaviors. For the best results, search each company's data bank of reports for titles or topics such as e-commerce, online retailing, and e-business. Although some resources provide free information, others are paid services. Reports can range from several hundred dollars to more than a thousand dollars. For that reason, take extra care to read the descriptions and the date of the report to make sure they have the most accurate and current information for your purpose.

The following companies specialize in market research:

>> **eMarketer** (www.emarketer.com): Specializes in providing data and analysis on trends in e-business, online marketing, and emerging technologies. The site also offers free articles for limited periods, so check it frequently.

>> **Forrester** (www.forrester.com): Offers information specifically about technology and business. Product areas and services include data and research reports, consulting services, and community programs.

>> **Digital Commerce 360** (www.digitalcommerce360.com): Provides a series of Top 500 guides for e-retailers, including the top 500 sites based on annual sales and the top 500 up-and-coming sites based on sales. These are pay-to-access and usually start at $299 per report. Digital Commerce 360 also offers free articles detailing online trends and news, as well as access to detailed research and reports with premium memberships.

Pricing Your Products

After you decide which products or services you're most interested in selling, it's time to price your merchandise. Having delved into the results of your research, you probably have a good idea of which items have the best chance of selling. However, no matter how trendy or in demand your products are, setting the wrong prices might leave you with unsold inventory. In this section, we take a look at some pricing strategies and considerations to make sure that you move the merchandise directly into your buyers' hands.

REMEMBER

When you're tagging your merchandise, the following factors are the most probable *price influencers*, or factors that affect your sticker price:

>> **Demand:** Whether customers are seeking out your product because it either meets a need or is thought to be a desirable or trendy item.

>> **Competition:** Not only who, but also *how many,* competitors you have, and what *prices* they have established for the same or similar products you're selling.

>> **Market position:** How you want your business to be perceived by customers in the marketplace. For example, an upscale store with high-end products might influence pricing strategies in one direction while a larger, warehouse-type of image might warrant a more competitive pricing strategy.

>> **Cost:** How much you pay (your expense) to create or purchase the product before reselling it to your customer.

>> **Profitability:** How much money you want to make each time an item is sold, after you've considered all expenses or costs associated with selling the item.

Product pricing is one of the most critical business decisions you make. Researching all the advice and pricing models offered in textbooks or by economists, however, can leave your head spinning. Keep it simple. The basic number for you to grasp is the product's cost, which incorporates every expense associated with your item, including the wholesale price you paid (the raw costs of materials to make the product); overhead costs ranging from utilities to Internet service fees; commissions; and packaging and shipping costs to deliver the product to your customer.

REMEMBER

Costs or expenses that don't fluctuate are *fixed costs* and are often considered overhead (such as rent). Expenses that might change periodically are *variable expenses*. The price of your product should cover all variable expenses and help contribute toward your fixed costs.

After you understand the cost of what you're selling, you can begin making pricing decisions. Use one of the following common pricing strategies:

>> **Cost-plus:** This method requires you to total the costs of your expenses associated with the product and then add an amount you want to make as profit. The resulting dollar amount represents the pricing *floor,* or the lowest price you should charge.

>> **Value-based:** With this strategy, you're setting a price that reflects the highest amount you believe your customers are willing to pay for the product. Unlike the cost-plus method, this one considers market conditions, such as demand, competition, and the perceived benefits (or value) of your product's features.

For example, if your cost for selling a coffee mug is $4.50, should you turn around and try to sell it for that same price? No, you have to make a respectable profit. That amount depends on how much you want — within reason, of course. If you decide that you have to clear $5.50 on every mug, for example, your price is set at $10.00 per item (cost-plus pricing).

By using value-based pricing, you might be able to set a higher price based on consideration of other factors. For example, how much are customers *willing* to pay for a coffee mug? In other words, what cost does the market bear? Perhaps, in the case of an Elvis mug, its perceived value is much greater than the perceived value of other styles of mugs. You might be able to sell each mug for $15.00 or more. Of course, even if your customers are willing to pay that much, they might find a better deal elsewhere. Your next consideration is to find out how much your competitors are charging for the same or similar products. If $9.99 is the top price on other sites, it might be unreasonable for you to expect to set a much higher price.

Now that you have the basic information needed to determine a baseline price for your product or service, you have to consider one more factor: your inventory.

Building Your Inventory

Choosing the best products and prices for your online business is certainly an important factor in starting your new business. You have to consider another issue too: Exactly how much inventory you should keep on hand, or how many different products you should have available for sale. The answer depends on not only the type of products you're selling but also the type of business strategy you want to execute.

REMEMBER

Savvy online shoppers are accustomed to an endless array of choices because they can easily jump from one website to another. These customers are quick to make a decision about whether your site's inventory meets their expectations.

REMEMBER

To keep the attention of most online shoppers, have a clear strategy for the type and amount of product you choose to offer.

We don't mean that you have to carry hundreds, or even thousands, of products to find success online. But you can follow a few distinct strategies for building an appropriate online inventory. Each one comes with its own advantages and disadvantages, as discussed in the following sections.

Stocking up as a low-price leader

Competing based on price can be a tricky situation, although it's certainly one option for an inventory strategy. If price is the primary decision-making factor in whether your customers buy, keep this advice in mind:

>> **Provide many choices.** Offer lots of choices. Your customers are looking for good deals, and might not even have a specific item in mind when they're shopping. You have to stock up.

>> **Change products often.** Another consideration with this type of inventory is how often you need to change out products. Even if your site doesn't see large volumes of traffic, returning customers expect a revolving inventory. If they discover that your inventory stays pretty much the same after several return visits, they'll stop coming back.

REMEMBER

To help avoid the *click-through syndrome* (customers quickly view all your products without stopping to make a purchase), make sure your site offers a large variety of products that are rotated or switched out often.

Becoming all things to all people with trial-and-error inventory

This strategy is a category that swallows up many first-time online entrepreneurs. You don't truly have a strategy. Instead, you end up offering a little bit of everything, until you can form a better idea of what sells. This trial-and-error method, often referred to as offering a *chaotic* variety of products, can be cumbersome but necessary. To reduce stress and quickly try to find the best products to keep in stock, consider these tips:

>> **Showcase a variety of products but in limited supply.** Nothing is wrong with offering a large variety of products. To keep expenses and storage issues to a minimum, maintain a relatively low level of inventory on all products.

>> **Rotate featured products often.** Because you're testing the waters with customer preferences, highlight different products daily or weekly. Featuring or spotlighting select items helps you quickly narrow which products your customers respond to most.

>> **Track your results to find out inventory needs.** You want to see which types of products your customers respond to most, so maintain thorough sales records. After you have more information about your visitors' buying habits, you can begin scaling down the number of products and adjusting your inventory to provide a better selection.

Specializing with limited inventory

Specializing in a field usually leads to the best inventory strategy. And doing so provides the most likely chance for success when you're building your online business. You might decide to deal exclusively in English teapots or maintenance supply parts for the army. Artists and craftspeople are usually in this category, too. They typically work in only one medium, such as black-and-white photography or high-grade wood carvings. If specializing sounds like your cup of tea, consider the following advice when building your inventory:

>> **Offer a select number of products.** Focus on the quality or uniqueness of the products rather than on mass quantity. You can afford to keep relatively low levels of inventory, as long as you're always searching for new items to replenish your stock.

>> **Position yourself as an expert.** Because you deal in a narrow type of product, visitors are more likely to seek you out for your expertise. You can keep inventory levels low and charge a finder's fee or consulting fee to help customers locate similar products on request.

TIP

Keep inventories low and establish an active network with others for quickly locating similar products. Being able to direct customers to other resources, or locate special pieces in a timely manner, provides a valuable service that can also keep customers returning to your website.

TIP

If you're an artist selling handmade goods or crafts, you can test market conditions by first selling on Etsy. With this strategy, you don't have to invest in your own full-scale e-commerce website with lots of inventory. Or you can maintain an Etsy shop in addition to your full website, and test new inventory on Etsy.

Taking Inventory

IN THIS CHAPTER

» **Planning the logistics of your operation**

» **Setting up an in-house fulfillment system**

» **Outsourcing your shipping area to someone else**

» **Learning the rules of shipping and handling**

» **Maintaining your information as you pack up and ship out**

Chapter **7**

Fulfilling Expectations and Orders

S etting up your online business can be full of excitement and milestones. The true payoff, though, is best realized when that first payment rolls in for something you sold. Seeing a paper check or an electronic deposit right in front of you helps cement the idea of what you're doing and provides validation of the business you created. Even though you may feel satisfied when you see the money, don't think you're done.

After the order is completed and the payment has cleared, you still need to handle one area of the sale. *Fulfillment,* or filling the order, is simply the practice of delivering the product to the buyer after payment has been received. In a retail store, fulfillment is easy: You hand your customers a shopping bag with the purchase and the sales receipt, and they walk out the door. In an online business, you need to perform a few steps to make order fulfillment happen. Thankfully, with all the advances in Internet technology and shipping services, achieving this goal is easier than ever.

Of course, planning for order fulfillment doesn't start when the money comes through your door. In this chapter, we talk about the elements that can affect fulfillment, starting with how you set up your business. We talk about strategies you can implement to handle your product storage and organization, and how to pack and ship your items. In some cases, the best step you can take is to turn shipping over to another company and pay it to deliver your products to the right customers.

REMEMBER

The moment you receive that payment, the clock is ticking and your customer is eagerly awaiting the item. A customer who experiences a bad fulfillment process will remember nothing else about your business, even if your website is well designed and the ordering process was easy to complete.

Figuring Out the Logistics of Shipping

How do you set up the entire flow of your business? Start by thinking about the operations and daily tasks that make your business work. Then lay out everything and decide how the business can best operate. To help you plan all these tasks, ask yourself these questions:

>> Does my online business operate from my home or a dedicated office space?

>> Should I buy products for resale or have someone else ship the goods?

>> Does a physical store or presence have to work with my online business?

>> How many employees need access to the merchandise and system?

Track the flow of one of your items for sale from beginning to end:

>> Receive the product from your supplier.

>> Prepare the product for sale.

>> Store the product while it's up for sale.

>> Pack the product after it's sold.

>> Ship the product after it's packaged.

Think about when and where these events take place, so you can plan the logistics of your business. *Logistics* simply refers to how you manage the operations of your business. You might need to dedicate a room in your house, or you might need to coordinate products and shipments through a warehouse that has different vendors and manufacturers.

The key is to set up a model that fits your business. You have no reason to buy an expensive software inventory program if you sell 10 or 20 items per month. Likewise, don't expect to run a multimillion-dollar venture with a pencil and pad of paper. Choose a system that lets you know at any given time where your inventory is in the process, whether it's receiving, photographing, listing, packing, or shipping.

Developing an In-House Fulfillment Model

Many small businesses take care of their own fulfillment, which means that they pack and ship their own products and send them out the door. Doing so allows these businesses to control the quality of their shipments so that they know that their customers are being served. Typically, doing so makes sense: Because the inventory is on-site, orders can be packed at the source and sent out rather than relayed to some far-flung warehouse.

Setting up an in-house fulfillment model requires first having enough inventory on hand and available at your location. In the beginning, you need to estimate orders and decide how many different products to carry in your store. Be sure to have enough on hand to fill initial orders. After you're in business a while, you'll know from your average order level how much inventory to have. After you know how much inventory you need to have in stock, you can plan for the space required to hold this inventory.

REMEMBER

Don't let a lack of available space be the reason that you don't carry more inventory. Different fulfillment models, both in-house and outsourced, allow you to hold more products than your current available space allows.

Your relationships with your vendors help determine the amount of space that's required. If you receive shipments in batches, make sure that you have enough space available to take in a shipment and hold it until sales for that order come in. If you have a responsive vendor that can ship items in a just-in-time approach, your space requirement can be much lower.

TECHNICAL STUFF

In *just-in-time* inventory management, vendors deliver their products to you just before you need them for listing or shipping out. If you're receiving shipments just in time, you don't need to have a big warehouse to store upcoming orders. However, if your just-in-time vendor is late with a shipment, you have nothing to sell or send out to your customers.

If the space you require is more than the available space at your location, either look at temporary storage, such as a storage locker, or rent dedicated industrial or warehouse space for your inventory. If you acquire additional storage away from your location, make sure that you keep at least one sample of each product close at hand, so you can take photographs, write descriptions for your website, and refer to the item when necessary to answer customers' questions.

TIP

If you rent a storage locker to hold inventory, ask the management team whether it can accept packages for you and place them in your unit. This way, you don't have to be present when your shipments come in or worry about sending them to storage from your home.

After your space requirement is resolved, think about labor: Who will pack and ship your products? The number of orders to be packed and shipped can help determine the number of fulfillment workers required. If you're packing only a few orders a day, you or one of your employees might handle the task. As the number of orders continues to grow, consider hiring a dedicated employee to perform the fulfillment or reassign someone to focus only on fulfillment.

Deciding to Outsource Fulfillment

Most people have a passion for the businesses they want to create. Whether someone is turning her knowledge of, and experience with, a hobby into a business or solving a need and providing a product that people want, a business owner dreams of turning a business idea into a reality. A business owner usually doesn't dream, however, of a massive shipping-and-warehouse operation (unless that person is in charge of UPS or FedEx). Therefore, many business owners choose to outsource their fulfillment operations to someone else so that they can focus on the most important element: their businesses. After all, just because you're good at selling widgets doesn't mean that you're good at packing and shipping them.

Contrary to popular belief, you don't need to have a Fortune 500 corporation to outsource fulfillment. Small businesses around the world outsource this process. This action not only reduces the amount of space you require but also frees you and your employees to work on other aspects of your business.

Enter the *fulfillment house*, a business whose sole job is to handle the packing and shipping of other people's goods. By grouping multiple clients' shipping operations, a fulfillment house can employ fewer people to handle the volume of goods than individual companies who hire their own staffs. These fulfillment companies create state-of-the-art, computerized inventory-management systems and train their employees to be efficient in this process.

Outsourcing companies also offer specialized and enhanced service in these other areas that affect your business:

>> **Customer service:** Every time a customer calls to ask a question about an order, make a special request, or have a product returned, someone has to handle the call. Fulfillment houses typically employ their own customer

service teams to manage these calls. The houses worry about hiring, training, and maintaining the calls and about handling the request so that you don't have to.

>> **Reporting:** As your business grows, you need to keep track of how many orders go out for each product line and then analyze that data. Most fulfillment houses have some sort of tracking and reporting capability built into their systems so that they can deliver reports and let you know what's going on, to help you plan for your next phase.

>> **Scalability:** Suppose that you operate a seasonal business, such as stocking Christmas gift items, and you have to quickly grow and expand your inventory space to meet demand. Doing it yourself means worrying about reserving temporary space in September that you need to give up in early January. If you use a fulfillment service, you can draw on its resources and let it worry about finding the space. If your business grows quickly, a good fulfillment partner accommodates that growth easily.

Finding an outsourcing partner

When you're ready to outsource the fulfillment process, you're probably wondering what the first step is. Your first inclination may be to open a Google search window and type in "outsourcing," but then what do you do when you see millions of search results? Every business magazine and talk show discusses the effect of outsourcing for bigger corporations, but what about small businesses? Some outsourcing companies are targeted to small-business accounts, especially online businesses.

OUTSOURCE SOME AND KEEP THE REST

Many online business owners dive into the fulfillment outsourcing question by giving up only a part of the fulfillment process and keeping the rest in-house. After all, their business reputations are on the line. Start with a test situation (one small function), and see how your outsourcing partner handles it.

Consider hiring a college student to help you a few times a week to pack and ship orders. It's a quick way to bring on some additional help and free up some of your time. If things work out with the student, you can bring him onboard for more hours per week. Additionally, you can hire more students or part-time help and soon have your own shipping department filled with extra help.

After all, these companies know that if they can pool several inventories of small businesses, they can manage those accounts with a smaller team of trained personnel and one warehouse. In other cases, your outsourcing partner can be a similar business that has its fulfillment process down to a science and has decided to use that expertise to make money for other companies by solving their fulfillment headaches.

As you look for a fulfillment partner, keep a few guidelines in mind:

>> **Know your budget.** Some companies can complete a part of your fulfillment process, and others assume control of your entire shipping department. Know how much you can afford to spend, to guide yourself to a partner that's right for you. Understand that you're saving employee labor time and salary when you're outsourcing your fulfillment, so factor those into your budget.

>> **Shop around.** Just like shopping for any other type of service professional for your business, get two or three estimates. Develop a feel for the service levels each offers, and see whether one company is willing to match another's price.

>> **Factor in all the costs.** You can easily see a price quote from a company and think that it shows the total cost. Before you sign anything, make sure that you understand all the requirements you will have to provide to the fulfillment partner and factor in all the costs. One quote might be cheaper because your company is still handling part of the fulfillment process, for example.

When you're ready to look for a partner, start by asking around: Ask your vendors, manufacturing partners, and even fellow business owners in places such as Chamber of Commerce get-togethers, small-business workshops, and online forums. Internet searches on Google and Yahoo! will turn up lots of leads, so do your research. See what other business owners say on message boards and in forums.

Here are some Internet companies to get you started:

>> **eFulfillment Service:** www.efulfillmentservice.com

>> **Rakuten Super Logistics:** www.rakutensl.com

>> **ShipBob:** www.shipbob.com

>> **Strategic Fulfillment Group (SFG):** http://www.sfgnetwork.com/business-solutions/ecommerce-fulfillment

Look for a company that specializes in your area (such as ShipBob for e-commerce) or provides the reporting features you need, such as eFulfillment Services' Fulfillment Control Panel system.

TIP

You can even turn your shipping company into your outsourcing partner. UPS Contract Logistics, for example, helps businesses around the world coordinate their supplies, orders, and product flow. The company's range of supply chain services and business technology services help take care of your fulfillment headaches. Go to www.ups-scs.com/logistics for more information.

Establishing your outsourcing relationship

After you find the outsourcing partner you want, it's time to create an agreement and determine the terms of your relationship. You have to agree on terms such as service level and the rate of customer response. You need to know how quickly the company ships your products, what materials it uses to pack them, and how quickly it responds to customer requests.

Here are the factors in this relationship that should concern you:

>> **Reputation and service level:** Even though the outsourcing company is doing the work, *your* name and reputation are on the line with your customers. If something goes wrong, guess who gets blamed? Yep, you do! Make sure that your partner is willing to commit to a service level that doesn't embarrass you or annoy your customers.

>> **Scalability:** As you grow, your outsourcing partner must be able to grow with you. After all, you're turning to your partner to smoothly handle a part of your business so that you can expand the operation. If the company is struggling to keep up the pace of your business, you run the risk of your whole operation falling apart.

>> **Experience:** Your outsourcing partner's management team needs to have the right experience in the right areas to lead that company. You're paying for experience, so make sure that team members are well versed in controlling

- Back-end computer systems

- Customer service

- Inventory management

- Logistics

>> **Subject matter knowledge:** A product is a product is a product. It helps, though, to find a partner that can understand your specific product line, whether it's computer chips or dried fruit. See whether this partner has ever handled an account similar to yours and understands some of the nuances of your product line, to better anticipate any problems or questions that might arise.

Operating with an outsourced fulfillment house

When you're ready to start working with a fulfillment house, don't just sign the lowest-price contract and begin transferring inventory to it. You need to talk about how your relationship will work, what expectations you have for the company, and — believe it or not — what expectations it has of you. After all, even though you might have hired the fulfillment house to do "all the work," you, as the client, still need to provide these items:

>> **Inventory:** Most fulfillment houses take on your inventory and warehouse it at their locations. Decide how much inventory to transfer, when to do it, and when and how replacement inventory should funnel in. Make sure that you carefully assess your inventory before it leaves your business, and double-check the inventory list when it arrives. Some fulfillment companies provide the trucks and labor to move inventory; others need you to make the arrangements.

>> **Order information:** When orders come in, find a reliable and automated way to move that order information over to your fulfillment house. Depending on how you capture orders and which computer systems your fulfillment house uses, you can transfer orders as they occur or as a group of orders every day (in a *daily batch*). In some cases, you can have the fulfillment company operate the order-collection part of your business so that the order goes directly from the customers' computer screens to the company's databases.

If the fulfillment house is taking your orders, make sure that you receive a detailed report containing all customer data and order information. After all, customer orders are the building blocks for a customer list that helps your business thrive.

>> **Payment:** Fulfillment houses don't pack and ship your orders out of the goodness of their hearts, so they need to get paid. You have several options for handling this cost:

- Build the extra cost into the shipping amount of your orders, and have that money transferred each time the company fills an order.

- Instead of transferring money each time an order is filled, have the company invoice you for a couple of months' worth of orders as a reserve or retainer. (You may be required to pay a reserve amount anyway to cover initial orders.) As you see the costs accumulate, you should begin to estimate the monthly cost better and can arrange payments that better fit the cash flow of your company.

- If the company is taking your orders and payment, it can keep its portion of the shipping amount and pay you for the goods it ships out.

After a certain length of time, you should receive a report detailing the activity your fulfillment house has performed. Never just file the report without looking it over. This report gives you a revealing look at the flow of your business and shows you how products are moving out the door. If you're concerned about the quality of the fulfillment house's work, compare the ship dates of those orders to the times you received them, and calculate how quickly this company is processing your business orders.

As your inventory level goes down at the fulfillment house, you need to have an event that triggers the transfer of more inventory. This *inventory replenishment level* is the point at which the inventory on hand is projected to drop to zero before the next delivery from your business would usually occur. Many fulfillment houses can help you calculate this number because they use sophisticated computer tracking systems that monitor shipment levels and predict how long it takes to ship all inventory in their possession. They usually factor in some time to cover unexpected delays in inventory transfers or unusual bumps in your orders. When you negotiate this cushion of products with your fulfillment house, choose a level that keeps orders flowing but doesn't back up the warehouse.

TIP

If your fulfillment provider is far away from the location of your products, calculate the cost of transferring inventory versus storing that inventory at the warehouse. Reducing a long, expensive inventory transfer by one per year can save you more money than the storage fees you pay at a warehouse.

Assessing the quality of the fulfillment work

When you get a sense of the quantity of work that your fulfillment partner is performing, look at the quality of its work also. Most important, determine whether your customers are happy with the packages they receive. Were the items well packed? Did packaging materials withstand the pressures of being shipped cross-country? Did your customers receive their orders in a reasonable amount of time?

The easiest way to find this information is to provide a phone number that your customers can call to report any problems. In some cases, the fulfillment house can also be your customer service partner. This way, if a problem with a customer's order occurs, a fulfillment person can go into your inventory on-site, pull a replacement set of products, ship it immediately, and let the customer know that the replacement is on its way. Make sure that you receive a monthly report of any customer service calls, and see whether that number goes up or down.

You can also go one step further: Rather than wait to hear whether a problem has occurred, reach out and ask your customers in the form of a survey. You don't want to bother them too much, but sometimes a simple survey packaged into each order can elicit some helpful feedback. Give prizes (such as gift certificates) or guaranteed discounts (such as free shipping on future orders) to customers who respond. You can partner with a company such as BizRate Insights (www.bizrateinsights.com) that coordinates online surveys of customers and gives you the results. This way, you can uncover any problems before they get out of control.

If you notice a problem, talk to your fulfillment partner. Be direct, not confrontational. Find out the cause of the problem, see whether it can be fixed, and inquire about how your partner will ensure that it doesn't happen again. You can never prevent all problems, but you can help make sure that they don't happen as often.

Shaping Up and Shipping Out

The immediate gratification that customers feel when they order something from your business applies also to the fulfillment of those orders. Customers want to hold a product in their hands as soon as possible, and some customers are willing to pay even more to receive their order faster. Customers often have a favorite shipping carrier, or a carrier that they don't want you to use.

When those same people hear the term *shipping and handling,* they usually envision you performing these basic steps:

1. Pull an item off the shelf.

2. Put that item and a packing slip or invoice in the box.

3. Add packing material to fill up any empty space in the box.

4. Seal the box with tape.

5. Put the customer's name and address and your business return address on top of the box.

6. Ship the box.

Even though these steps demonstrate the basic flow of the shipping process, you can make it happen in many ways. If you're handling the shipment of your business orders, you can take advantage of some existing systems to make your life easier.

Giving your customers shipping options

In the end, the best way to satisfy both your business goals and the customer's shopping goals is to offer multiple shipping options to your customers.

Giving customers options can mean that you offer a variety in

>> **Shipping carriers:** You're willing to ship something by using FedEx, UPS, or the U.S. Postal Service.

>> **Shipping methods:** If your only carrier is FedEx, for example, customers can pay for Next Day Air, 2-Day Air, or Ground (with an average delivery time of one or two weeks).

>> **Order mixing:** A customer who orders multiple items can choose which items get which type of shipping. For example, a customer who orders a heavy computer system and a light book about computers can have the book delivered to start reading the next day, and have the heavy computer system delivered by ground in two weeks.

When you offer customers these options, you (as either an in-house or outsourced business) have to be ready to use each service whenever it's needed. You have to know the common rates and link to their websites to find updated pricing quotes based on different weights and sizes. You also have to update your shopping cart with these different options so that customers can pick and choose.

REMEMBER

The rewards of these efforts are best expressed in terms of customer satisfaction. Giving your customers shipping choices is like giving them product choices; they feel more in control of the shopping experience and that your business is willing to cater to them. Often, an online business charges a flat fee for the lowest shipping rate and slowest delivery service. Although that strategy might work for some customers, you're missing the customers who need items immediately or by a guaranteed date.

The best example of the power of multiple shipping options is Amazon. To spur sales, it offers free shipping if you spend at least $25 on an order, and it ships items with its own fleet of delivery options. However, customers can specify all or part of their orders to be sent a certain way, and they can pay the appropriate rate for faster shipping, such as Next Day Air or 2nd Day Air.

Setting up accounts with carriers

Two truths apply to shipping companies:

>> They always seem to break even the most carefully packed items.

>> They're always competing for your business.

The amount of gross revenue generated by shipping online orders has become a primary means of producing revenue. Therefore, carriers are fighting to keep customers by virtue of their service — and adding new features and adjusting prices whenever necessary to succeed.

Because the shipping companies' goal is to maximize revenue, they cater to higher-volume customers. They're usually online businesses, like yours, that have a number of orders to be shipped each day, week, or month. Online businesses that are setting up accounts with one or more carriers are finding, therefore, that they have some negotiating power for better rates or more services.

To sign up for a business account, choose one of these methods:

>> Contact the company by phone and work with a sales representative to set up your account.

>> Go to a shipping company's website and look for a Business Accounts link for the appropriate forms to fill out.

>> Go directly to a shipping company's office and ask to speak to a representative to set up an account.

When you start to talk to these companies, they ask you a number of questions to gauge your level of shipping. Determine your answers to the following questions before you start calling:

>> How many packages do you expect to ship in a month? How many do you send in an average week? What are your high and low numbers for a week?

>> What size and weight are the packages you typically send?

>> Are your customers mostly in the United States, or do you send a mix of domestic and international packages?

>> What percentage of orders do you ship by using an air option, such as Next Day, 2nd Day, or 3 Day? What percentage do you send by ground?

REMEMBER

If you're setting up your shipping system from scratch, be sure to tell the company that you're providing estimates based on your initial research and by talking to fellow business owners in your field. Although you aren't bound by these numbers, the company needs an estimate to be able to set up your account.

When you start reviewing these details with the company, ask about rates and price breaks for certain shipping levels. Find out whether your current level is close to a certain price tier for shipping, and see whether you can raise your order shipments to meet that new level to save money for your business. Meeting a goal is easier if you can aim for a measurable number.

An account with a shipping company is typically free of monthly charges, unless you add a special service. The company keeps a payment method on file so that you can accrue shipping charges and make one monthly payment. That way, you're not always paying out when you want to ship a package. Your shipping department then runs much more smoothly and you qualify for corporate rates.

TIP

After you sign up for an account with a shipping carrier, always remember to review your monthly bill. Never assume that the carrier automatically screens your bill or lets you know when you've been overcharged.

Creating online postage and labels

One of the best developments in Internet technology over the years (especially if you're in the fulfillment field) is being able to print postage from your computer and create your own shipping labels. Although you can still stand in line at the post office, now you can prepare packages at home or at your business and drop off addressed packages with your carrier.

If you need to buy postage for various sizes of letters or packages, you can print postage by the package or join a service such as Endicia and pay a monthly fee to print all the postage you need. You sign up for an account and provide a credit card number. When you print postage, these services charge your account and send to your printer a special coded label that acts as your stamp. Every month, you pay for only the stamps you print.

Here are some of these services:

>> **Endicia:** www.endicia.com

>> **Pitney Bowes:** www.pitneybowes.com

>> **ShipWire:** www.shipwire.com/w/support/parcel-service

>> **USPS Click-N-Ship:** cns.usps.com/labelInformation.shtml

For example, rather than print the stamps for a customer's order, you print a pre-paid label that has all the customer's address information, your return address, and the postage paid. You stick this label at the top of the package and hand off the package to the shipping company. Every month, your account is charged for the shipping costs of all the labels you prepared.

Virtually every big shipping company can now generate these shipping labels from their websites, including FedEx, UPS, and the U.S. Postal Service. You simply log in to a company's website with your account number and then start specifying customer addresses and the weights and dimensions of each order.

TIP

If you're using these online shipping tools to create labels, invest in an accurate scale that measures as close to the ounce as possible. Make sure that the scale's capacity can accommodate a large order. If you're selling only light items, such as stamps and coins, a scale that measures by the ounce, up to 25 pounds, is fine. If you sell electronics and computers, buy a scale that can measure up to 150 to 300 pounds instead.

Having items picked up for delivery

After you do all the work to prepare your packages, they still have to move from you to your shipping company. In the past, you had to load your car or company van, drive down to the shipping company's office, fight for parking, and then stand in line to unload your vehicle.

Almost all the big shipping companies now come to you to get your items:

>> **U.S. Postal Service:** If you print your shipping labels in advance and pay for your postage online, a postal employee can pick up the item on her normal route. When you schedule a pickup, someone picks up all your Express Mail and Priority Mail packages in a 2-hour period that you specify.

>> **Other carriers:** Carriers such as UPS and FedEx work more on demand. If you're receiving a package from one of these carriers, you can hand off your completed packages when the driver arrives, but you have to know that the shipment is coming. For business accounts, these carriers typically offer weekly or daily pickup, based on the needs of your business. If you have a low-volume account, you're charged for this feature, and the rates vary. Depending on how many orders per month you can guarantee, however, one item you can request during your account setup is a free daily pickup. Ask your shipping company for more details.

TIP

If you're printing labels online for a given company, you can usually ask for a pickup when you create the label.

Shipping international orders

Customers around the world are communicating with each other instantaneously by using the Internet, cellular data networks, and smartphones. These methods have allowed online businesses to reach millions of new potential customers. Shipping companies have responded by beefing up their international shipping options, which gives you more options for servicing your customers.

The only shipper that reaches most countries in the world is the U.S. Postal Service. The U.S. Postal Service offers air-mail service, which can take at least a week to reach its destination country. Although the USPS offers insurance for packages to most countries, it typically doesn't provide any tracking capability. The only service it offers that guarantees a tracking number and insurance is its Priority Mail Express International service, which is expensive.

TIP

To see a list of countries and services that the USPS delivers to internationally, go to pe.usps.com/text/imm/immctry.htm.

If you want to use UPS, FedEx, or other carriers to ship packages, you have to send them by some form of air mail, which can be quite expensive for heavy items. Although these services automatically issue tracking numbers, in some cases their tracking capabilities end when the packages enter their destination countries. Each country also places specific limits on package weight and dimensions. Consult each company's website for specific information about country-specific limits.

In all cases, you're required to fill out a customs form to document the following information about an item:

>> The country of origin

>> The quantity

>> An item description

>> The value of each product in the package

Shippers such as UPS and FedEx incorporate the customs form information into the label-creation process so that when you create your label, the appropriate shipping documents are created alongside it. The USPS uses two customs forms:

>> **CN 22/Form 2976:** For First Class, small Priority Mail, or Priority Mail Express International packages that are worth less than $400 and have no insurance

>> **Form 2976-A:** For larger Priority Mail International or Priority Mail Express International packages that are worth more than $400 and have insurance

TIP

You can fill out USPS customs forms online by starting at www.usps.com/international/customs-forms.htm.

In some cases, the destination country requires you to complete a certificate of origin or a signed affidavit that certifies the origin country of an exported item. Some countries also require that you

>> Have your goods inspected by an independent, third-party organization

>> Include a certificate of inspection with your label and customs forms

For more detailed information on how to send large shipments overseas, consult the International Chamber of Commerce website (www.iccwbo.org).

For smaller shipments that you send directly to customers, you typically need to classify your shipment in one of four categories:

>> **Commercial sample:** Samples or free product trials

>> **Documents:** Catalogs and paperwork

>> **Gift:** Products that customers didn't pay for

>> **Other:** Most other types of shipments

WARNING

An international customer might ask you to classify a package as a gift and specify a lower amount for the value. Be aware that you can insure a package for only the value you state and that falsifying a customs document can result in fines and penalties levied against you and your customer.

Maintaining the Back End

As you expand your business, keep track of how your fulfillment operation works so that it can grow with your business. Investing in good recordkeeping enables you to not only provide customers with tracking numbers and copies of invoices but also see what's working and what's not so that you can make necessary improvements.

Deciding on a database

You have several choices for storing your business information. Many online businesses create one or more databases to store these types of data:

>> Customer information

>> Order information

>> Payment information

>> Product information

Sometimes a business owner chooses a database solely because it can "talk to" the shopping cart or website software that the business uses. At other times, the database was installed first and the business owner wants to ensure that all other products can communicate with it. Other small-business owners organize their information by using spreadsheets in a financial program such as Microsoft Excel.

The key for you is that your database — in whatever form — needs to be accessible and searchable. You and your employees need to be able to see your data easily. You use your database to answer questions about your business (such as "How many customers do we have?" or "Which orders are ready for shipment?" or "Who still owes us money?") and to store information about how your business is doing financially.

REMEMBER

Your order-information database should list not only the products that someone ordered but also these items:

>> Carrier name

>> Internet link, if possible, to monitor the shipment

>> Invoice number

>> Order-packing date

>> Shipment date

>> Tracking number

As you're setting up your business, here are some questions to help you determine which database program to use:

>> Is a database program in your budget?

>> Which programs work well with your other software systems, such as your web server or electronic shopping cart?

>> How many people need access to the database? Are all the people in one building (or on one internal computer network), or are they spread out around the world?

>> Which software programs do you have access to?

Using handheld scanners and bar codes

Inventory tracking is a process that even a small online business can afford to implement. You don't have to be Wal-Mart or Home Depot to use technology to help organize your inventory. You just have to spend some time setting up the equipment and codes to make it work. You can use handheld scanners (or newer smartphones that support the RedLaser app, such as the Apple iPhone) to read bar codes identified on your products to help keep track of your overall product inventory.

Here's how inventory tracking works:

1. **Make sure that each individual product for resale has some sort of bar code on its box.**

   The bar code can be either the Universal Product Code (UPC) that comes with the product or one you provide by using an inventory-management program.

2. **Decide where in your warehouse or inventory area you want to store the product.**

3. **Scan a special bar code that represents the shelf or rack number.**

   Use a handheld scanner (like the ones used in grocery stores or by delivery personnel) or a smartphone equipped with the RedLaser app and an inventory app.

4. **Scan the bar code of the product.**

5. **Sync your scanner and inventory-management software.**

Syncing occurs when two sources of information "talk" to each other electronically to ensure that both sources have the same up-to-date information.

Developing a shelving inventory system

Many online businesses buy industrial-strength racks and shelving systems for organizing their products. You can find these systems at most hardware stores, such as Home Depot and Lowes, for a couple of hundred dollars apiece (with some assembly required). After you buy and set up these racks, label each shelf properly and start storing your products on these shelves. Then, whenever you need a product, you can just walk over to your shelves and look to find the product you need. If you keep similar items together, locating and retrieving the product you need is that much easier.

Some popular ways of organizing your shelves involve grouping items by category, size, or color on one shelf or in one area. Keep different items that look similar far away from each other so that you don't mistakenly grab the wrong item for order fulfillment.

Feeding orders into the shipping department

You might think that when you receive an online order, red lights should start flashing and sirens should sound to announce its arrival. Although that level of drama isn't necessary, you need to make sure that your orders are being properly funneled to your shipping area so that they're packaged and sent in a reasonable length of time. You can

>> **Print orders from a printer automatically.** Then, whoever is in charge of fulfillment can grab the printout and start pulling the inventory.

>> **Print manifests or invoices (known as *pick-and-pull sheets*) from the preceding day's orders.** Items are picked off the shelves in your warehouse area and pulled into the packing area.

If you're outsourcing your fulfillment operation, you can specify that customers receive an email every time they place an order. A duplicate of that email is sent to a specific email account for new orders at the fulfillment house, and the employees monitor and print an order every time an email is received or print a batch of email at certain times during the day.

After an order is prepared and packed, the last pieces of information to capture on the back end are the package shipment date and tracking number. If you're using online postage creation tools, that information is already captured. If you're creating your own postage and labels, be sure to keep a copy of every tracking number and shipping date and then feed that information into your order database.

5

Managing
Security Risks

Contents at a Glance

Chapter **1**

Understanding Security and Your Risks

I nternet-related fraud cost consumers and businesses $2.7 billion in financial losses in 2018, as reported by the Internet Crime Complaint Center (IC3), which is a joint effort between the Federal Bureau of Investigations (FBI) and the National White Collar Crime Center, established to track cybercrime. Founded in 2000, the government-based organization receives more than 350,000 complaints from U.S. consumers each year, or approximately 900 complaints every day. These complaints represent only 15 percent of actual incidents, as most go unreported, according to the IC3.

As both a consumer and an e-commerce merchant, you are vulnerable to becoming a victim of cybercrime. Each year the IC3 receives a large number of complaints involving identity theft and nondelivery of payment or merchandise, including credit card chargebacks. Complaints from both buyers and sellers continue to grow. Technology has advanced to help protect against fraud, and both consumers and merchants are doing more than ever before to combat fraud. Unfortunately, e-commerce continues to breed opportunities for online thieves in areas that include credit card fraud, phishing scams, personal and business email scams, identity theft, and personal data breaches.

In recent years, it has become almost common place to hear news of large-scale security attacks and data breaches from all types of businesses and organizations, including retailers such as Target, credit card companies such as Capital One, and even from financial and credit monitoring companies, such as Equifax. Even the IRS has fallen victim to a major security breach that exposed the personal data of millions of U.S. taxpayers. In each case, some type of malware or intentional online breach was suspected in the compromise of customers' credit card data, Social Security numbers, and other valuable, personally identifiable information that translate into estimated financial losses in the billions for each incident. In fact, the 2017 Equifax breach is considered one of the largest in the United States, affecting more than 150 million people. In 2019, the company finally settled investigations from federal and state agencies and agreed to pay nearly $700 million in claims to those consumers impacted (with some eligible for as much as $20,000 each). It's not only the "big guys" that have to pay the price of a data breach. Any type and size of merchant (and its customers) is susceptible to cyber-related crime. The burden *always* falls on you, the online business owner, to provide a safe, secure shopping environment for your customers while protecting both your customers and yourself from potential financial losses.

In this chapter, we talk about what you can do to keep your customers as safe as possible so that they continue shopping with you.

Legal Responsibility: The Merchant and the Customer

As the owner of your business, you're responsible for protecting not only your data but that of your customers as well. With identity theft and fraud continuing to rise at alarming rates, credit card companies and regulatory agencies are saddling e-commerce merchants with the bill (including shipping fees and the costs of the goods). You can prevent your customers from being victims of identity theft and fraud — and stay in business yourself — by being vigilant about the credit card payments you accept and keeping your customers' information as private as possible.

Avoiding chargebacks

Most of the time, fraud comes in the form of *chargebacks.* Customers using credit cards and other online forms of payments (that access credit cards and bank accounts) can request that charges be removed. The Fair Credit Billing Act (FCBA) allows consumers to dispute purchases.

A customer can request that a charge be removed for two reasons:

>> The card is stolen or otherwise used without the legal cardholder's permission.

>> The customer doesn't believe that you fulfilled your obligation in delivering the product. (You either didn't deliver it or delivered a different product from what you promised.) Mistakenly delivering an incorrect product isn't a true case of fraud, but it does lead to chargebacks. It becomes fraud if you did indeed ship the correct product but the customer insists that you did not. Often referred to as "friendly fraud," the purposefully deceitful act represents the largest portion of e-commerce chargebacks.

Chargebacks happen frequently, and proving a customer wrong is difficult — and expensive — for an online business. LexisNexis reports that online retailers lost, on average, close to 2 percent in revenue to fraud in 2018. Online fraud is rising nearly 30 percent year over year. For example, for each dollar in fraud, online retailers actually lose $3.29 in actual revenue in 2018, compared to less than $2.50 in 2017, according to LexisNexis. The cost of fraud is due in part to chargebacks and their related fees and costs. Because you simply don't have the same ability to authenticate or verify a cardholder's identification as you do in a bricks-and-mortar environment, you get stuck with the cost of the merchandise, the shipping fees (possibly), and the processing fee that your credit card vendor charges for every transaction. Those amounts, as estimated by LexisNexis, add up quickly. Another concern lies in the fact that fraud prevention is advancing in traditional retail stores with the increased use of EMV or "chip" technology in credit cards and debit cards. Many industry analysts anticipate these renewed efforts to protect offline theft will drive fraud attempts away from bricks-and-mortar stores and toward online stores.

It may seem like a gloomy time for the e-commerce landscape, but don't despair! Being educated about online fraud is the best way to fight it. Fortunately, you can minimize your risk of excessive chargebacks. To avoid them, use some basic security strategies for your site:

>> **Verify the cardholder's address.** Credit card merchants offer an address verification service (AVS) that compares the billing address a customer provides with the cardholder's name. You're notified immediately if the billing address and name don't match the information associated with the account. You can also make this comparison manually if AVS protection isn't included with your online merchant account.

>> **Get the card verification value.** When you're completing an order from a customer, make sure to ask for the card verification value (CVV2). Because this set of numbers appears only on the customer's credit card, the customer

must have physical access to the card to see the numbers. This set of numbers appears as four digits on the front of an American Express card or as three digits on the back of a Visa, MasterCard, or Discover card.

» **Use 3D Secure.** The 3D verification process is just as it sounds. It uses multiple sources to help identify the validity of the payment method for an online transaction. Online merchants have hesitated to use this approach in the past because it requires the consumer to leave the merchant's website for a moment and validate the payment on a third-party site, such as that of the credit card issuer (Visa or MasterCard). This interruption to the purchase process is thought to contribute to shopping cart abandonment. However, improvements have been made to the verification process, making it less cumbersome to the buyer when checking out.

» **Process only approved transactions.** If a card is declined for any reason, don't process it. Although this advice seems obvious, you might be tempted to believe that the message is a mistake and try to process the order anyway.

» **Scrutinize email addresses.** Always ask for a customer's email address at the time of purchase. If the address looks suspicious, don't hesitate to call the customer and verify the order.

» **Be wary of excessive orders.** Buyers using stolen or compromised credit cards sometimes purchase extremely large orders or purchase several units of the same item. Call the number on the billing address to verify unusual orders.

» **Maintain good records.** Keep copies of an online order transaction, verification emails, and records of any other communication you might have with the customer.

» **Keep your end of the bargain.** If you experience a delay in shipping the product or the product is out of stock, notify the customer immediately and do not make any charges until the product ships.

» **Clearly post your return policy.** Preventing or fighting a chargeback is tough if you're not clear about your return and shipping policies. Having this information readily available to customers makes it difficult for customers to use the lack of information or lack of a formal policy as a reason to decline a payment to you.

» **Follow merchant-issued policies.** Whether you use PayPal or a credit card vendor to process customer transactions, be aware of its chargeback policy. The newer chargeback policies from many credit card vendors often limit what types of charges are protected (for example, excluding charges to crowdfunding sites because of an increased risk). If you deal in those types of transactions, you are excluded from protection. Always make sure you're following the vendor's recommendations for the prevention and dispute of chargebacks.

You can dispute any chargeback by contacting your credit card vendor directly. Before calling, be prepared to show how you complied with verifying the card's authenticity at the time of purchase. Hang in there because you might have to wait several months for a claim to be settled.

The Federal Trade Commission and other agencies offer information to help your business comply with e-commerce policies. You can access the information from its website at www.ftc.gov.

Other private organizations are dedicated to helping protect you and your customers from all types of online fraud. You can join a membership-based group, such as the Merchant Risk Council (www.merchantriskcouncil.org). It provides access to articles, tools, and vendors that help you secure your site.

Protecting privacy: GDPR and growing compliance concerns

When you're tackling security concerns, you have two goals as an online merchant: Do everything possible to make your site secure and safe for both you and your customers, and promote buyer confidence by letting visitors know that you take all necessary precautions to keep the online shopping experience safe. Your data compliance efforts must also confirm to legal requirements issues by regulatory agencies, which have expanding oversight into how companies use consumers' personal data. One of the most wide-sweeping policies is the General Data Protection Regulation (GDPR) policy that went into effect in May 2018.

GDPR is a law that originated in and most impacts consumers in the European Union (EU), because it's designed to protect the personal data of EU citizens. However, companies around the world, including the United States, are required to follow the policy and violators can expect steep financial penalties. What is the policy? Basically, it outlines a standard for how companies can use and store an individual's personal data, including identity information (such as name, address, birth date, and so on) and online tracking data (such as location, IP address, and website data captured by online cookies). The list of personal data included in the registration is much longer, but these two buckets of personal data are often what most concerns your online business.

How do you comply with GDPR? First, it's important to understand that GDPR is a complex policy with a lot of latitude in how it should be interpreted, so it's important to seek clarity from legal professionals. But we're going to give you a general overview of what you must do to be in GDPR compliance. You must be aware of your website visitors and online customers that are EU citizens (including those who live or work in countries outside the EU) and clearly communicate when and how you use their personal data; and you must ensure that they have agreed to receive your marketing and communications efforts. One common example of this is with email. EU citizens must opt in or choose to receive almost all types of email communications, especially those that are promotional. And you must track and monitor the data you collect, even when they opt in, and keep records on this information. As part of GDPR, at any time a EU citizen has the right to request a full report from your online business of what personal data you have of that person and how it has been used and stored. And you must be able to provide this information!

You may be thinking, "I don't plan to sell products to people outside the United States, so this doesn't concern me." We're here to tell you that it *does* concern you, for two important reasons:

>> You may have customers living in or visiting the United States but who are still EU citizens, so you must adhere to the policy.

>> It's widely expected that GDPR, or something very similar to it, will soon be adopted by other countries, including the United States. In fact, Brazil has already announced its GDPR policy, which goes into effect in 2020.

Again, it's still very early to tell how strictly GDPR will be enforced and how much organizations may be penalized, but it's critical that your online business understand GDPR and make it part of your compliance efforts.

TIP

To start understanding GDPR and get more information and guidance on what it is, how to maintain compliance, and what to expect in penalties and fines, you can check out the site www.gdpr.eu. While on the site, you can also view its online "GDPR checklist for data controllers" to get a better idea of how to prepare for GDPR compliance.

Of course, compliance doesn't end with GDPR. One of the best ways to stay ahead of the security game in general is by being clear about your online policies. Other regulatory agencies, not just those in the EU, usually want confirmation that you're looking out for your customers' best interests. Here are two types of policies you can institute:

>> **Security:** A security policy should explain what protection is in place when you're processing customers' orders. You want to educate visitors on how information is collected, stored, and protected.

>> **Privacy:** This type of policy was once best known for letting customers know whether their email addresses were shared with or sold to third parties. Similar to GDPR, privacy policies are now much more inclusive: They include details on which information is collected and why; how customers can update,

change, or delete stored information; and how they can notify you if they believe that their information has been breached. When you develop your policy, consider these three categories, which can be areas of concern:

- *Personally identifiable:* Information that connects your customer to your site

- *Sensitive:* Information that's private to customers, such as transaction histories or email addresses

- *Legally protected:* Information protected by law, including credit card numbers, financial accounts, medical records, and even education-related details

Privacy and security policies are the two types most prevalent to your site. Don't forget that online fraud and chargebacks are always at issue, too. You need to include or refer to other types of policies, especially when a customer makes a purchase. Don't hesitate to direct buyers to policies that spell out conditions relating to shipping, back orders, returns, and even customer disputes. (Book 1, Chapter 5 covers these policies in depth.)

Keeping Your Website Secure

No matter how much online security and privacy policies are heightened, buyers are still uncertain about their online security and privacy. Research shows that people are hesitant to give out personal information or credit card numbers to websites, even though e-commerce has become accepted as a viable alternative to storefront shopping. The risk of online fraud and identity theft are two big factors that make consumers skeptical, but lots of other issues keep online shoppers frustrated. The Federal Trade Commission (FTC) tracks top complaints of online shoppers. You probably aren't surprised to know these complaints include things such as never receiving merchandise, not having refunds honored, and other misrepresentations by online merchants.

The FTC also keeps track of which online products or industries warrant the most complaints. Shop-at-a-home or catalog sales account for close to a fifth of the complaints each year, while Internet auctions typically comprise only a small percentage of the complaints. Although these complaints don't seem to keep people from buying online, they provide another reason to go out of your way to make your site secure. One of the easiest and, possibly, most expected ways to do this is by using *Secure Sockets Layer* (SSL) certificates.

SSL is a protocol, or method of communication, for scrambling information as it travels across the Internet. Any type of data, whether it's a medical record or credit card number, can be encoded so that only the authorized sender and receiver can view it. Without this protocol, the sending process would be similar to stuffing all your private information into a clear plastic bag, sealing it, and passing it around a crowded room. Even though the bag is tightly closed, anyone who has access to it can see everything inside.

Having an SSL certificate for your website lets customers know that their confidential information is protected when they send it over the Internet for you to process.

Using SSL is just a matter of licensing the right to use the protocol through an approved vendor and having it installed on your server. You can get a certificate directly from a private company, such as Symantec (now part of Broadcom), or (usually) from your web hosting or domain registration company. Some e-commerce and shopping cart providers now offer basic SSL certificates for free as part of their monthly or annual service plans. If buying one directly, prices vary greatly. Some are advertised for less than $10, but a more typical range is $300 to more than $2,000 annually. The difference in price depends on the type of certificate you choose and the level of validation attached to it. For instance, the SSL certificate on the low end of the range may validate only your site's domain name. The more expensive certificates often provide financial warranties of varying amounts and validate these factors:

>> Domain name registration

>> Business owner's identity

>> Company identity and address (possibly requiring copies of business licenses and incorporation documents)

The more expensive SSL certificates also claim to provide a higher level of encryption. The industry standard is 128-bit encryption, and an advanced 256-bit version is available. A higher level of encryption just makes compromising (or hacking) data a little more difficult.

TIP

If you're not certain what level of encryption you need for your SSL certificate, or how those levels may affect your customers when they visit your site, check out the great resource page on the Symantec website that discusses SSL certificates and more: www.websecurity.digicert.com/ssl-certificate.

After you purchase your SSL certificate, you're given instructions on how to activate it on your site's server. However, in many cases, your web hosting company or a professional website developer can install the encryption certificate for you.

If you use an e-commerce–enabled server that's shared by others, or use a third-party merchant like PayPal, you might not have to purchase an individual SSL certificate. Some companies provide encryption service to all their customers by using a single server.

Displaying Seals of Approval

When most people shop at a store online, they look for signs that the business is legitimate — particularly if it's new or located in a different city or if they're just not familiar with it. Offline, people look for a valid business license hanging behind the counter or a local Chamber of Commerce sign.

The online equivalent of the local Chamber of Commerce is a seal of approval from one or more third-party organizations. Customers feel safer shopping online with you when you post a seal of approval on your site. Table 1-1 lists organizations that provide seals. Although these seals aren't requirements, they definitely boost buyer confidence.

TABLE 1-1 **Organizations Providing Reliability and Privacy Seals**

Organization	Seal Type	Reliability	Fees
BBB (www.bbb.org)	BBB Accredited, Dynamic	Member of Better Business Bureau; in business one year	Membership fee; licensing fee based on size of company
McAfee SECURE (www.mcafeesecure.com/for-websites)	McAfee SECURE Certification	Site information submitted for review	Monthly fee starting at $299
TRUSTe Privacy Certifications (www.trustarc.com)	TRUSTe certifications from TrustArc for websites, apps, cloud, downloads, and more	Pass site audit	Annual fee

You can apply for the following types of seals:

>> **Reliability:** Posting this type of seal on your site confirms that its sponsoring companies have verified information about your business. Additionally, it confirms that you agree to abide by certain online advertising and operating standards and dispute-resolution guidelines. Often, part of the qualifying process for the seal requires that you be in business for a certain length of time (usually, a minimum of a year).

>> **Privacy:** You're eligible to display a privacy seal on your site if you meet stringent guidelines. You usually have to create, post, and adhere to a privacy policy, along with other industry standard recommendations. The organization issuing the seal is likely to conduct a security and privacy assessment on your site before giving you the seal.

>> **Kids' privacy:** The Children's Online Privacy Protection Act (COPPA) hands out a seal of its own. Check out Book 1, Chapter 5 for more information.

Because application and licensing fees can range from slightly less than a hundred dollars to several hundred dollars for each seal, you might not be prepared to apply for them when you're just starting your business.

Chapter **2**

Developing a Plan: Security and Business Continuity

E ach year, businesses suffer millions of dollars in loss due to unexpected events ranging from security breaches to natural disasters. The first step in protecting your business from a costly computer invasion or minimizing the impact from a catastrophe is developing a plan. Your plan doesn't have to be complicated or expensive. However, you do need to give your business continuity plan (how you respond after disaster strikes) and security strategy (how you prevent issues from occurring) more than a passing thought. In fact, put your plan on paper so that you and your employees have a written plan of action.

As an online business, it makes sense to invest time into protecting you and your customers from hackers and cybercrooks with topnotch online security. Equally important, even if you don't have a bricks-and-mortar location, is preparing for events that can compromise your network infrastructure, disrupt product deliveries, destroy inventory, and more. Trust us, there is a lot that can go wrong (think blizzards, earthquakes, and fire). The fun of doomsday daydreaming doesn't stop here, though. After all, what good is a plan if you don't implement it? You also have to invest in a decent online security system (or two) and maybe even bring in a few professionals to ensure that you're properly prepared. If these upfront considerations are ones you've thought about — but haven't gotten around to accomplishing — this chapter has your name on it.

Making a Plan

Coming up with a plan is easier than you might think. It really comes down to making a few lists and checking them twice. Where do you start? Whether you rework an old plan or build one from scratch, the six major components to an effective business continuity and security plan are

>> Policies and procedures

>> Inventory and skills assessments

>> Risk analysis

>> Existing security measures

>> Action plan and backup alternatives

>> People, resources, and follow-up communications

In the following sections, we guide you through the details to include in each of these components for your plan.

Policies and procedures

If you're part of a larger online business, you might already have a book of policies and procedures carefully spelled out, tightly bound, and neatly filed away in every employee's desk. The reality for a smaller online company, though, is that you probably haven't had time to think about formal procedures. If you're working solo, you might still be skeptical about needing to write these types of policies.

REMEMBER

As an online business owner, the purpose of your business continuity and security plan is to protect both you and your customers. By establishing and implementing written policies, especially a detailed security policy, you reduce the risk of overlooking holes or flaws in the plan.

Honestly, the amount of information that has been published about how to write a security policy could fill a small room. No wonder the task of writing one has become cumbersome. However, in a smaller company, you can concentrate on the basics.

Here's a baseline rule for establishing your security policies: The magnitude of how much policy you need should fit the breadth of your organization and the depth of the risk factor you want to protect.

In other words, IBM might require several hundred policies whereas you might need only five policies. At the end of the day, if either you or IBM suffers a sub-stantial security breach because a policy wasn't effectively in place, you're both in the same boat. And we don't mean in a good way.

With that in mind, follow these steps to create your own policies (however many you might need):

1. Write your overall goals or objectives for your security policy.

Break down the big-picture goal of protecting your online business into a few smaller chunks of information or goals. Maybe you're more concerned with outside threats or establishing guidelines for employees. Or you might be most interested in protecting yourself legally and need written policies in place to set precedents.

2. Create a list of areas in your organization that require protection.

After each item, make a notation of which ones are better served by the implementation of a formal policy. Use the checklist in Table 2-1 as a guide to the areas that are open to possible security risks.

TABLE 2-1   Security Coverage Checklist

Security Risk	Currently Secured	Requires Formal Policy
Desktop computers	❑ Yes ❑ No	❑ Yes ❑ No
Laptop computers	❑ Yes ❑ No	❑ Yes ❑ No
Employee devices	❑ Yes ❑ No	❑ Yes ❑ No
Mobile devices	❑ Yes ❑ No	❑ Yes ❑ No
Email	❑ Yes ❑ No	❑ Yes ❑ No
Bank or financial information	❑ Yes ❑ No	❑ Yes ❑ No
Server	❑ Yes ❑ No	❑ Yes ❑ No
Wireless network	❑ Yes ❑ No	❑ Yes ❑ No
Firewall	❑ Yes ❑ No	❑ Yes ❑ No
Internet provider	❑ Yes ❑ No	❑ Yes ❑ No
Software subscription services	❑ Yes ❑ No	❑ Yes ❑ No

(continued)

TABLE 2-1 *(continued)*

Security Risk	Currently Secured	Requires Formal Policy
Customer data and credit card numbers	❏ Yes ❏ No	❏ Yes ❏ No
Social media accounts	❏ Yes ❏ No	❏ Yes ❏ No
Passwords	❏ Yes ❏ No	❏ Yes ❏ No
Database	❏ Yes ❏ No	❏ Yes ❏ No
Cloud-based applications and services	❏ Yes ❏ No	❏ Yes ❏ No
Inventory	❏ Yes ❏ No	❏ Yes ❏ No
Products	❏ Yes ❏ No	❏ Yes ❏ No
Back-end system	❏ Yes ❏ No	❏ Yes ❏ No
Offices or other facilities	❏ Yes ❏ No	❏ Yes ❏ No
Other physical properties or facilities	❏ Yes ❏ No	❏ Yes ❏ No
Files or other miscellaneous	❏ Yes ❏ No	❏ Yes ❏ No
Intellectual property	❏ Yes ❏ No	❏ Yes ❏ No

3. Determine the *scope* (number of policies) that is legitimately warranted for the size and need of your organization.

In reviewing your list of goals in Step 2, you might find that it makes sense to combine several components into a single policy. Conversely, other areas might produce larger or more frequent risks and require a stand-alone policy.

4. Starting with your first policy, write its purpose and provide an overview of its importance to the organization.

For instance, you might create a policy about who can access your primary email account. Your goal might be to restrict usage to only designated personnel — and doing so is important so that confidential communications aren't compromised.

5. Detail the scope of your policy.

Specify which employees or level of employees the policy applies to. Also indicate which locations, systems, and data are affected by the policy. Refer to your list in Step 2 to make sure that you include all areas that might be affected.

6. Write the operational guidelines of the policy.

The guidelines are the cold, hard facts. Be specific about which actions and behaviors can and cannot happen under the policy.

7. **After the guidelines are in place, write a paragraph about how the policy should be implemented.**

In this part of the policy, provide information such as how employees are to be notified of the policy as well as specific penalties for not enforcing the rules.

8. **Document the date when the policy was created.**

Every time you update the policy, add the next revision date. Leave the earlier version dates so that you have a running history of the document.

9. **(Optional) Add details to the policy.**

You might include a glossary of terms or cross-reference additional procedures and policies that might also intertwine with this one.

10. **Repeat Steps 4–9 for each policy.**

After you finish writing all your security policies, you're ready to place them in the front section of your written business continuity and security plan.

Inventory and skills assessments

One helpful component for your overall plan is to create a catalog, or *inventory*, of your equipment and the information that you're protecting. Table 2-2 serves as an inventory assessment guide, and we tell you in this section how to fill it in.

TABLE 2-2   **Equipment Inventory Assessment Guide**

	Description or MAC Address of Computer	Registration	Username	Travels Off-Site? Y or N	Security Risk: High or Low	Other Information
Hardware						
Software						
Peripheral components						
Servers						
Cloud-based applications						
Documents						

When you're filling in the guide, your final inventory list should capture the following information:

>> **Hardware:** Record a complete list of your laptops and desktops, including supplemental information, such as their serial numbers and the names of people who use each machine. Also list any warranty information per machine. Denote which systems have DVD and other components. For laptops, note whether the equipment is carried off-site.

>> **Software:** Log an inventory of your company's software. Include details such as user registration information, licensing restrictions (single or multiple user), and registration numbers. If possible, note which software is loaded on the computers.

>> **Peripheral components:** This list might include data drives; printers; scanners; tablets, iPhone, Android, and other smartphones and mobile devices; handheld devices; portable memory storage devices; extra monitors or keyboards; networking equipment; and even plain old cellphones.

REMEMBER

Employees frequently want to use their own smartphones and mobile devices for both personal and business use, which is referred to as the bring your own device (BYOD) trend. You should include BYOD policies and procedures as part of your overall risk analysis and planning.

TIP

Break out your inventory by each individual piece of equipment or software program. That way, you can compile serial numbers and registration numbers or other unique identifying factors for each piece. This is an important part of business continuity planning and may be required by insurance companies when filing claims for damage or loss.

>> **Cloud-based applications:** Make an inventory of any cloud- or web-enabled programs and services that your business uses, whether for delivering customer surveys, printing online postage, managing customer relationships, or providing business phone service. Detail which computers maintain licenses for each application or have access to web-based solutions. Make a note of any cloud-based applications or licenses that do *not* include automatic renewals or version upgrades, so you know to track required upgrades and security patches, for example.

WARNING

When creating an inventory of applications delivered over the Internet, don't overlook instant-messaging programs and music or video-related applications. You might not use them, but your employees probably have them installed. Increasingly, these programs are becoming an easy delivery method for viruses, worms, and other malicious activity. You want these programs accounted for in your inventory so that proper security measures can be applied.

>> **Social media:** Although social media is not a tangible or hard asset, we recommend including a detailed log of all your business social media accounts as part of your inventory list. Social media accounts have increasingly proven

to be vulnerable to security threats, especially if passwords are used across multiple accounts. As part of your inventory assessment, keep track of which platforms you use, associated passwords, and those in your organization who have access to the accounts.

>> **Documents:** This group includes not only critical files but also your intellectual property, promotional materials stored on your computer, financial data, customer data (contracts and invoices), and current and archived email messages.

After you complete this equipment assessment, turn your attention to a skills inventory. (You can add it to the bottom of your inventory assessment.) Compose a paragraph or a complete list of the security expertise that you and your employees have. You can include certifications or other applicable training, too. By conducting a skills assessment, you can see when you need to call in outside security consultants — or how much of that expertise you might need.

TIP

A skills inventory can further help you determine points of educational training needed for you and your staff so that you can develop more internal expertise.

Risk analysis

One of the most important pieces of your plan is the *risk analysis* portion, in which you identify possible threats, determine your greatest vulnerabilities, and calculate the potential impact should your business not be able to function for a period of time. This important exercise forces you to evaluate the factors that hold the most potential for harming your online business. Your first action is to make a list of all potential threats that can compromise your security and your ability to operate. Classify these security occurrences, or disruptive *events*, under the following categories:

>> **External threats:** Include any risk that originates outside your business. You typically have no control over these events (other than being prepared to combat them if they occur):

- *Viruses and worms:* Also group Trojan horses and other harmful programs in this category.

- *Malware:* Include any type of malicious software that can be unknowingly installed on your computer from an outside source, such as spam, adware, and spyware.

- *Phishing:* Add this popular method of tricking and defrauding employees to your analysis. A phishing scam is an email that looks like it comes from a legitimate source but is from a fake company. This type of scam can add up to lots of lost dollars if an employee reveals sensitive data (credit card number, password, and more) to an online scammer.

- *Malicious intruders:* Consider any type of activity originating from another individual that's meant to harm you. Include hackers, former employees, competitors, and thieves. Don't forget that theft can occur on-site (at your place of business) or off-site (such as at airports and coffeehouses). Comparatively, hackers steal intellectual property and data by way of an Internet connection. Hackers can also do damage by shutting down your network or your website.

- *Outages:* Power outages, or any type of disruption to water or utility services, is a serious consideration when operating an online business. Network outages from cloud-based service vendors (from your hosted phone service and website server to your online accounting software and inventory program) can also wreak havoc to your operations for a few minutes to several hours (or longer).

- *Weather:* It may not qualify as a complete disaster, but think about weather-related incidents that impede normal operations to you or your customers. For instance, a snowstorm may cause delays to already time-sensitive holiday delivery schedules. Or, extreme heat in the summer may interfere with storage and delivery of perishable food items you sell online.

- *Disasters:* Address floods, tornadoes, hurricanes, and fire as possible external risks. As part of business continuity planning, you should also consider the risks if one of these events happens not only to your business location, but to that of a key vendor. If your primary vendor is hit with disaster, is it still able to provide you with products or services? If not, do you have a backup vendor?

REMEMBER

A critical part of business continuity planning is to consider any and all potential threats to your business, both onsite and offsite. Vendors, delivery services, and online service providers are all critical parts of your chain of operations that could disrupt your online business should their businesses experience a disaster. You cannot prevent these events from occurring, but you can control how you respond to them by having a plan B in place and ready to go in order to minimize the damage.

>> **Internal threats:** Although not always intentional, these incidents occur from within your own operations. Internal threats can do serious damage as well as expose your vulnerabilities:

- *Malicious intent:* Employees or other people might have somewhat unlimited access to your assets. Unfortunately, not everyone is as nice or honest as you want to believe. Consider the possibility that a serious — and intentional — breach of security can occur right under your nose.

- *Accidents and user error:* Think of any accidents or human errors that can occur. Coffee spills on laptop computers, accidentally deleted data, dropped monitors — the list is endless.

- *Failures:* Specifically, these failures are system failures. Whether your computer crashes, your software bombs, or your Internet connection or server goes down, these failures are all part of an unwanted security risk.

After you put on your doomsday hat and identify all possible threats that can take you down, go one step further and prioritize each one according to its level of risk. You can do this by using a hierarchical ranking system. Or you might prefer to assign a low, medium, or high risk value for each of your items.

REMEMBER

Ranking your risks is a subjective process that requires you to be open-minded and honest in evaluating the security of your business. If you don't feel that you can be objective, consider bringing in outside help.

If you find that a risk analysis shows your business to be at a medium- to high-level risk for attacks, accidents, or failures, consider inviting a paid technology or business consultant to evaluate your business and offer solutions. The costs of improving your security and beefing up your disaster-recovery plans will be paid back in the long run by reducing the odds of your losing data, damaging your reputation, putting customer information at risk, and shutting down your ability to operate.

Existing security measures

Unless you're in the planning phases for a new business, you probably already implemented some level of security. Here's the appropriate place in the plan to specify which actions to take.

You want to describe firewalls, antivirus software, and other basic security measures that provide some level of protection. However, you can add any routine security-related systems or functions you conduct. For example, you should plan to

» Change passwords regularly (some apps and subscription software services require you to do this on a regular basis).

» Back up your data regularly.

» Perform routine system maintenance and software updates.

» Implement physical security measures, such as alarm systems or fireproof safes.

» Minimize access to servers and business-critical computers by storing them in a secure location, such as a controlled server room or lockable closet.

REMEMBER

No matter what, be honest. If the last time you backed up data was several months ago, don't include it as a security measure that you can check off your list.

Action plan and backup alternatives

To some degree, you can consider the action plan the meat of your document. After all the assessments, inventories, and analysis, you're ready for a true plan of action.

The first part of an action plan is creating a communications tree. No, we're not talking about a tree with leaves, but rather a phone tree! It's a diagram that has branches (or lists) of critical people to call or communicate with in case of disaster or other critical business disruption. A communications tree should start with you, as the business owner, and may include a list of the most important employees, public relations contact (if it requires external or public notice), vendor contacts, legal contacts, insurance agent . . . the list can be as extensive or brief as required. The important part of communications is just that — you need to be able to quickly communicate important information to the people in your organization and make sure the appropriate information is also communicated to customers. Be sure you have back-up phone numbers, email, and emergency contact information for your employees.

Once your communications tree is in place, you can turn your attention to the rest of your action plan. Based on the information you collected (see the earlier sections of this chapter), you can readily spot your strengths and weaknesses in the realm of security and business continuity. And now you can focus on what we like to refer to as your *points for improvement (PfI)*, or the specific areas where you find weaknesses that should be corrected.

By concentrating on your PfI, you can create a step-by-step plan of action to beef up your security and business operations. In each step, be specific. Here are examples of some of the steps that you might include in your own plan of action:

>> Purchase and install external security locks for all laptops.

>> Turn on the Automatic Update feature on all desktop computers to activate a fixed schedule for installing all new software updates.

>> Purchase a password generator and choose quarterly dates for changing passwords.

>> Implement redundancy (or backup) for service and system failures that occur onsite or offsite.

>> Identify secondary sources for key products and services offered by primary vendors.

>> Create a scheduled backup, specifically for customer data such as order histories.

Find an online service for an additional backup so that your data is stored off-site yet still readily accessible if your on-site files and backups are destroyed.

Your plan of action might include a couple dozen steps or only a few. You have a thorough action plan when all your PfI are accounted for and the security holes are plugged.

TIP

Compare your action steps with the security policies and procedures you already created. Your plan of action for security should take into account those policies and contribute to each one being effectively implemented.

People, resources, and follow-up communications

The final component of your security and business continuity plan addresses the resources (and budget) that are required to put your plan into action. Make a list that identifies all the purchases you need to make to fulfill your plan, especially the security component of your plan. Include a price estimate for each item. If your total is hefty, prioritize which ones fall under the must-have category as well as which ones can wait.

In addition to the resources that require cash, you should include all other resources used in your plan. For instance, budget the time for yourself or employees to attend an Internet security class. Even if a vendor offers this type of training session for free, attendance still requires a small investment in human resources capital.

The last piece of this section should include a timeline for change. Assign both a reasonable date for completion and a person who's responsible for each action item. Schedule a recurring date for reviewing the progress of your plan's implementation, too.

REMEMBER

No matter how many action items you develop or how many pages your security plan turns out to be, its true worth is measured in one way: Does it work? If your plan is thorough and realistic, your answer should be a resounding "Yes!"

Creating a Budget for Your Plan

Developing a written security document is an investment in itself. If nothing else, it bears the cost of your time. But as the resources and follow-up section of your security and business continuity plan indicates, that step is only the beginning when it comes to paying the price for peace of mind and preparedness. You probably already put down a fair chunk of change but haven't tallied your investment. The typical places in which you probably already spent money include business insurance for your computer, office equipment and other material structures, antivirus software, a good firewall for your network, and other backup and redundancy services.

Determining how much more you need to spend depends on your circumstances. As an online business, the bulk of your budget is likely to go toward security. The ongoing threat of cyber-related crime, in addition to the number and magnitude of actual incidents, has kept businesses spending an expanding portion of their IT budgets on security. Spending on security information products and services is expected to hit an all-time high, exceeding $124 billion (globally) in 2019, according to Gartner (www.gartner.com).

To come up with a reasonable and effective budget for your business, take another look at your resources list from your security plan and determine the total value of the resources you're protecting.

Figure out how much a security breach can cost if you *don't* make that investment. Roughly calculate the value of your equipment: all your hardware, software — everything. Then assign a value to the intellectual property you need to protect. It's probably a whopping number. For e-commerce sites, another financial factor is identity theft. You have to consider the potential dollar value of your loss if a hacker gains access to your customer information. Lawsuits and insurance aside, consider it from another perspective: If your site has a major compromise of customer data, those customers must be notified. That situation can be a public relations nightmare — and can result in the loss of future orders.

REMEMBER

When determining your security budget, be sure to include the cost of compliance. As the owner of an online business, you may be required to implement and maintain additional security procedures to protect customer data as part of government regulations or private industry standards. Examples of these compliance issues include the Health Insurance Portability and Accountability Act (HIPAA) and the Payment Card Industry Data Security Standard (PCI DSS).

No one can tell you how much you need to spend, or should be willing to spend, on security. When deciding how much to invest for security, ask yourself these two questions:

>> What's the value of the assets I'm protecting?

>> Is that amount worth the cost of security?

TIP

After you list the value of your assets, give this detailed inventory list to your insurance company to verify that you have the proper type and amount of coverage for your business. Don't forget to save a copy of this list for yourself in case disaster strikes.

Finding Security Resources

After you commit to your security budget, you can find plenty of outside resources that are happy to assist you in spending it. And you have lots of do-it-yourself opportunities, too. You have to decide when — and whether — an outside source is warranted for both security resources and business continuity consultants. Then you should determine which resource is the best one for you to use.

When searching for help with security issues and business continuity planning, you have many choices. More than likely, they fall into one of these categories:

>> **Consultants:** Often specializing in a particular area of security or business planning, a consultant can be hired to offer an initial assessment or to assist with the complete solution. Most consultants bill in one of two ways:

- *Hourly:* Some consultants charge by the hour, which typically ranges from $80 to $300 (or more) per hour, depending on your geographic location and on the consultant's specialty.

- *Flat fee:* A consultant can also bill you a flat fee based on the scope of the project. As a general rule, the more complicated your issue — or the more specialized the expertise of the consultant — the more you can expect to pay.

>> **Experts:** Experts can be individuals who work in a technical-support environment or who have full-time jobs in a related subject area (and advise informally or on a part-time basis). You can find experts in your vendor relationships or in community service programs for businesses (such as Service Corps of Retired Executives, or SCORE). The cost of an expert's time varies widely but usually is on the lower end of a consultant's fee. You might even find volunteers.

REMEMBER

When paying for an expert or hiring a consultant, check out the person's certifications and ask for references. You should ask even if you're getting help for free (although it's more difficult to be selective if you aren't paying someone).

>> **Training programs:** Call them seminars, training programs, or webinars, these resources provide information from a classroom perspective. Rather than provide individual support, these types of programs are targeted for a large group of people. Cost for this type of instruction varies. A one-day seminar might cost $300 or $400; a webcast or an online class might be free.

TIP

When attending a vendor-sponsored training program or seminar, the solutions that are offered tend to focus on that particular vendor's products. If you want unbiased guidance, make sure that someone other than a vendor or distributor teaches the session.

» **Self-help:** As in a training program, you can go the self-help route to seek out the knowledge base you need to educate yourself. The cost ultimately is a result of your time and any resources you purchase.

You have to decide which solution is right for you, and knowing when to go somewhere else is usually pretty clear. It's determined by these four key factors:

» **Budget:** You might have the money to spend on outside assistance, or you might be particularly budget conscious. As with the issue of time, hiring someone else and spending your labor dollars on other projects might make more sense.

» **Expertise:** Either you have the knowledge to resolve the issue or you don't. If you don't have the expertise, you must have the ability and the time to learn.

» **Scope:** Determine how serious the problem is and whether it's limited to your immediate network or reaches outside it.

» **Time:** If the issue is critical or you're reacting to a problem that already occurred, you probably want immediate action. Or you might be taking preventive measures. If so, time is on your side. Even if you have the time, consider whether it's best spent somewhere else. You might prefer to call in the experts.

IN THIS CHAPTER

» **Shutting down your site**

» **Breaking through security barriers**

» **Spreading Internet illnesses**

» **No phishing allowed**

» **Putting the brakes on mobile scammers**

Chapter **3**

Spotting and Thwarting Hackers and Net-Thieves

I n 2019, nearly 5 billion people, or approximately 58 percent of the world's population, used the Internet worldwide. More than half of those users accessed the Internet using a smartphone or other mobile device. (Mobile devices continue to be the preferred way people are accessing the Internet, even over desktop computers!) And there are more than 118 million smart speaker devices (such as Amazon's Alexa device) in the United States alone, increasing the use of voice search to access the Internet. In 2020, half of all online searches are expected to be via voice search. With so many people and businesses online today, especially using Wi-Fi with smart devices, the Internet has provided a unique opportunity for cybercriminals, or what we refer to as the *Net-thief*. Global losses from cyber-related crimes surpassed the $2 trillion mark in 2019, according to Juniper Research. And there's no sign of it slowing down. Online thieves continue to find new and sneaky ways to rob you of money, data, and a sense of personal security.

Given that figure, if you haven't been on the receiving end of an online security threat, consider yourself lucky. As an online business owner, your vulnerability to cyberattacks increases. Studies show that companies suffer from multiple security incidents per year from hackers, viruses, worms, spyware, and other malicious efforts. And when companies are suffering from Internet-related attacks, they can lose an average of a few hundred dollars per attack in small incidents, and potentially millions, or even billions, of dollars in revenue in larger, more severe attacks.

As an online business owner, you need to minimize the opportunity for any type of security interference that threatens your success. Before you can defend yourself and your computer, though, you need to know what to expect. In this chapter, we review the security threats that are most likely to take a bite out of your business if you let your guard down.

Fending Off Attacks

Companies of all sizes, online and off, are vulnerable to lots of types of cyber-crime. Approximately 60 percent of businesses have been victim to attacks that include Denial of Service (DoS), phishing, and social engineering, according to Cybint. As an online small business, you have to be extra vigilant against cyber threats, especially malware intrusions, DoS attacks, and phishing scams. If you're not familiar with these types of vulnerabilities, don't worry — we explain them in this chapter and help you understand how to keep your online business safe.

Let's start with DoS attacks, and the more harmful DDoS attack. Any time an Internet thief, or Net-thief, can prevent you or your customers from accessing websites and other online information or applications, it's a *denial-of-service (DoS)* attack. Not to get too technical, but it's important to understand how this works. A DoS attack comes from a single source of origin (a server) to send requests to a single server, essentially overwhelming the server so that it isn't able to allow any more web traffic to access it. That means your site appears shut down or offline! Now, consider a distributed DoS (DDoS), which ups the impact considerably because it comes from multiple sources or devices (at the same time), all working together to attack the same victim — you! DDoS attacks are now more common and, as you may imagine, much more effective in bringing down a website. Okay, maybe you don't think that your website is large enough or popular enough to interest someone in disrupting it. Think again! According to Juniper Research, almost half of all cybercrime is targeted specifically on small businesses! And DDoS attacks are considered one of the top Internet security threats. Why should savvy cyber criminals be interested in a small online business like yours? Some research indicates that your small business is a target because you typically have less sophisticated online security and are easier to breach.

Even if your site is fairly secure, consider this: What if the company your business uses for online payment transactions is attacked? Or maybe your online banking site is hit? Worse, what if the company that hosts your website falls prey to a DDoS attack? You and hundreds of other small sites can be wiped out for several hours — or an entire day or more. Each of these is a real possibility and is an example of how easily a DDoS attack can prevent you from being productive or possibly even hurt your company financially.

Plus, DDoS attack–launching tools are now fairly cheap and easy to come by, so instigating an attack has become easier. An intruder can divert legitimate traffic away from your site and drive it to other sites. The attacker may be paid every time your customers visit the rogue site, whether or not they intended to go there. With lots of dollars at stake, you can understand why the frequency of DDoS attacks has spiked.

Fending off either a DoS or DDoS episode isn't easy. After you're under attack, your choice of responses is limited. However, you can take certain steps to reduce the chances of an attack occurring and to minimize the damage that can be done if your site suffers from any DoS attack:

- » **Know your host.** When selecting a hosting company for your website, understand which security measures it has in place. Ask how your host would work with you if your site experienced a DoS or DDoS attack as well as whether security experts are part of its support staff. The more prevention at the network level, the better.

- » **Update the basics.** Individual users and their computers are also responsible for creating security holes. The best defense is to continually update antivirus and spyware programs as well as download the most recent patches (or fixes) for your computer systems. Keep your browsers updated, too — especially Internet Explorer, which has proven to be quite susceptible.

- » **Report attacks.** If your site comes under a DDoS attack, report it to the FBI. A special division of the FBI, the Internet Crime Complaint Center (IC3), was created to address these concerns. You can access the division at www.ic3. gov. Additionally, the U.S. Computer Emergency Readiness Team (US CERT), which is part of the U.S. Department of Homeland Security, monitors, tracks, and responds to cyberthreats. You can report attacks on the US CERT website at https://complaint.ic3.gov.

- » **Block traffic.** You can work with your host company to block traffic coming from suspicious or malicious IP addresses. Although you run the risk of also blocking legitimate users, this choice might be your best option.

- » **Be aware.** As DDoS attacks increase in frequency and type, you must stay up-to-date on security issues. Your best defense against any attack is to be aware and knowledgeable of current threats and recommended preventive measures.

TIP

To stay ahead of potential cyberthreats, get tips to keep your business secure by visiting the tip site from US CERT at www.us-cert.gov/ncas.

Deterring Hackers

Behind every DoS or DDoS attack or any other harmful Internet-related threat is usually a single person or group of people (or *hackers*) responsible for starting the malicious activity. These hackers are generally anyone not authorized or given permission to intrude on or gain access to your information systems. It's not easy discovering the identity of these electronic thieves. Consider that most hacking incidents originate from outside the United States (which is responsible for less than 2 percent of known attacks).

For most online businesses, the threat of hackers is simply based on the possibility of making money from your site. The "rewards" for this type of action can be enormous for a hacker. There have been several notorious hacking incidents that have targeted retailers and restaurants, including Capital One, Target, T.J. Maxx, and Wendy's. In each case, the hackers obtained customers' personal data, including online passwords, and credit and debit card information stored by the businesses and stole millions of dollars from unsuspecting customers. Similarly, when Sony's online game network, PlayStation, was breached a few years ago, hackers obtained access to the credit card numbers and passwords of millions of Sony customers. The network was shut down for 23 days and for a staggering financial loss of more than $171 million. Again, big or small, online companies have a lot to lose to a hacker.

Among the most popular methods of hacking-for-pay are stealing these elements:

>> **Keystrokes:** This kind of attack might not seem like a big deal, but even inexperienced hackers can monitor and record the keystrokes on your computer. By using a keystroke logger tool, hackers capture your data, making it a snap to gain access to your system.

>> **Sales:** Hackers divert your traffic to a rogue site (which might even look like yours), where customers spend money, in the belief that the site is legitimate.

>> **Data:** By obtaining passwords to your or your customer's secure data, hackers can build a lucrative business. With passwords, hackers gain access to pertinent information, such as bank accounts, birthdates, and Social Security numbers.

>> **Credit card numbers:** Hackers relish the chance to obtain your customers' stored credit card numbers. These days, those numbers can easily be resold for cash — and before anyone realizes that the accounts have been compromised.

As we've shown, your data is worth a lot of money to a Net-thief. Sites that fall prey to this type of hacker are vulnerable because they're easy targets. Think of this type of breach in terms of your home's security: Although locks and alarms don't always stop thieves, they deter them. Given the choice, most bad guys break into places that are easier to get into and out of without being noticed.

If a hacker sees that you're sloppy with security, he doesn't waste any time taking advantage of you. These days, computer programs allow a hacker to scan the Internet and look for vulnerable sites.

Implementing firewalls and antivirus software certainly helps deter a hacker. You can take some additional measures to irritate a cybercrook:

>> **Use uncommon passwords.** Yes, using uncommon passwords is good ol' common sense, yet most people choose passwords that are easy to remember or have special meanings, such as birthdates and anniversaries. Many people also use a simple string of numbers, such as *1234*, or other combinations that are easy for a cybercriminal to decipher. Instead, use a nonsensical or complex mixture of words and numbers. Be sure to create a different password for each application or program that you access.

REMEMBER

For added security, you can get help creating unique passwords by using a *password generator.* This software creates random passwords for you. Free password-generator programs are available, or you can purchase programs, usually for less than $100, depending on whether it's for personal or business use.

>> **Change passwords frequently.** Merely creating good passwords isn't enough. You have to create them repeatedly. Generate new passwords every 3 months (depending on the sensitivity of the information being accessed) for applications you use all the time. Change other passwords annually for low security-risk applications or websites.

TIP

Remembering unique and constantly changing passwords is difficult. And keeping written records of your passwords defeats the purpose of changing them. Now you can get help remembering passwords by using a password manager. KeePass is a free, open-source application that keeps all your passwords locked away, so to speak, in a secure database with only one master key, or key file. You can get started creating a secure password manager by visiting www.keepass.info.

>> **Keep data out of site.** Hackers can originate close to home. Whether you're working from home or an office surrounded by employees, get into the habit of protecting your information. Don't leave account numbers, passwords, and other pertinent data out in the open. Thieves lurk everywhere.

>> **Shut down your computers.** In this 24/7 world of the Internet, you're always open for business. It's tempting to leave your computers on around the clock, too. A better idea is to shut them off at the end of day to limit the possibility of unwelcome access to your system. This advice is especially good if you have a home-based business and use cable modems to access the Internet. The shared bandwidth makes you much more vulnerable.

TIP

If you use computers with built-in cameras, shutting down your computer also prevents hackers from infiltrating your camera and gaining visual access to your home or office.

>> **Update your computer system automatically.** Configure your computer for automatic updates to your operating system.

Avoiding Viruses, Malware, and Other Threats

According to the McAfee security firm, hundreds of thousands of active virus threats are invading computers right now. Named for the germlike nature of an illness that rapidly spreads, viruses were originally a nuisance more than anything else. Similar to thwarting hacking, programmers face the challenge of preventing the spread of irritants from one computer to another.

A *virus* is a program or piece of programming code and is usually spread by way of email attachments. The attachments can be Word documents, photos, games, or other types of applications. By opening the attachment, you unknowingly unleash the virus onto your computer and possibly help spread it to others. Viruses are almost impossible for you to detect without using some type of antivirus software.

The capability to hide a virus combined with its ease of distribution makes these attacks increasingly more threatening to the health of your computer and your online business. Some computer experts now refer to viruses as a part of *malware*, short for *mal*icious soft*ware*. Malware activity had a year-over-year increase of nearly 70 percent in 2019, according to the Center for Internet Security. Some of the top threats include the following:

>> **Emotet:** Emotet, which downloads a banking trojan, is the top offender. It can spread through malicious links or file attachments.

>> **WannaCry:** WannaCry is considered ransomware because it stops the encryption process and locks down your computer. Then the hacker demands ransom money, or payment, to grant you access again to your computer and all the files stored on it. If you don't pay, you lose all your files!

>> **Kovter:** Kovter is also tricky because it's difficult to detect and its purpose is to block or disrupt antivirus programs on your computer.

As you see, there are lots of concerns when it comes to malware and what it can do to you, and hackers continue to design new ways to cause chaos online.

Here are some other types of malware, viruses, and annoyances to be aware of:

>> **Worms:** Unlike most viruses, worms don't need your help to spread. You don't have to open an attachment or accidentally launch a harmful program. A *worm* simply replicates itself and then spreads to other computers over a shared network. Worms have been known to go after specific computer hardware, such as routers. After compromising the router, it scans for other vulnerable devices on the network and replicates itself to infect those devices. Other well-known worms have caused havoc (and major inconvenience to users) by continuously shutting down infected computers.

Worms have also been used to infect mobile phones, and other smart devices, including smart speakers, such as Alexa. Worms are not only infectious but also potentially costly because they can be used to capture personal data and credit card numbers.

>> **Trojans:** A computer Trojan employs the same type of subterfuge as the Greek Trojan horse. Delivered in a seemingly harmless package (usually by email), it sneaks onto your computer system. Then, without your permission, it opens and performs some type of unwanted activity, such as shutting down your computer. Unlike some other threats, Trojans do not replicate themselves.

>> **Ransomware:** This type of malware, such as WannaCry, is used by hackers to access your computer files and hold the data hostage. Imagine opening your computer to find a hostage note appear on the screen. You cannot get to anything on your computer; the note instructs you to deposit money into an account within a certain amount of time or lose all your files, photos, tax documents, invoices — whatever you have stored on your computer! This is ransomware and it's a popular form of malware used by hackers and cybercriminals.

>> **Adware:** This phenomenon started out as annoying pop-up windows that disrupted your computer surfing with unwanted ads. Adware has been around for a long time, but it continues to be big business. Someone makes money every time this advertising software displays ads.

>> **Spyware:** Much like adware, spyware is a type of malicious software that plants itself deep into your computer system, posing as a legitimate program. It wants to stay around as long as possible so that it can collect information about you. Spyware can redirect you to certain websites or track and record your personal information and send it back to the spyware's originator — without your knowledge.

>> **Botnets:** When your computer is infected with malware, it can also become the unknown host that helps spread malicious software to other computers. Essentially, your computer becomes part of a robot network called a *botnet,* which is made up of thousands of controlled computers that instruct

your computer (and other vulnerable computers now in their network) to send out infected emails, without your permission.

>> **Hoaxes:** It isn't unusual for rumors about false virus threats to circulate around the Internet. Although these little pranks don't infect your computer, they waste your time. You can tell whether a threat is real or a hoax by noting these characteristics:

- *Source:* If an email alert came from your antivirus software provider or another trusted source, it's probably real. If it's part of a chain of emails being circulated by friends and family, it's more likely to be a fake.

- *Participation:* An email alerting you to this latest threat and prompting you to send it to everyone you know to spread the news is a classic sign of a hoax.

- *Authority:* If the email contains a link to a recognized antivirus software vendor or a legitimate Internet security source, it's probably real. If not, you might be participating in a virus hoax.

Keeping Your Domain Name Safe

Ever since the Internet started gaining in popularity, devious minds with a creative bent have found ways to cause problems. In addition to the other methods that hijackers use to derail your sales and your business — such as virus and DDoS attacks — a determined Net-thief has one more trick: stealing your domain.

Domain slamming occurs when you're tricked into moving your registered domain from one registrar to another. In this scenario, you receive an email saying that it's time to renew your domain. It even appears to be from your legitimate registrar. Unfortunately, a competing registrar has gained your information and is waiting to collect a domain renewal fee from you. Although domain slamming might be more economically detrimental to your originating domain registrar (they lose your business), it's still a hassle for you, too.

Somewhat more disturbing is the opportunity for a hacker to take over your domain by using the registration process. When a thief takes possession of your domain, you can spend years trying to get it back. Some documented cases show that small e-commerce companies never recover ownership. Whether your domain is hijacked for a day or an eternity, here are some common problems that occur when your name is stolen out from under you:

>> **Reselling:** Your domain name can be resold to an unsuspecting third party. Popular names can fetch millions of dollars, making domain hijacking a lucrative career for a thief.

>> **Lost sales:** If you have an active e-commerce site that's taken over, you lose sales during the time it takes to regain ownership. Some companies have lost thousands of dollars in sales, not to mention the legal expenses involved in recovering the domain name.

>> **Damaged reputation:** Even if you regain your site domain, you might be stuck convincing customers that it's safe to shop with you again. In some cases, stolen domains are used to redirect visitors to sites that download adware or spyware onto computers. Unsuspecting customers might be hard-pressed to return to your site.

Here's how domain stealing happens: If hackers can find enough personal information about your account, they can transfer your registered domain into their name and basically take ownership of your domain in a few short hours. Most of the information needed to achieve this process can be found by simply viewing the public records of the WHOIS directory.

TIP

To prevent having personal or business information readily available for public viewing, choose to make your contact information private. The WHOIS directory then shows a third-party vendor — a *proxy* — as the point of contact and lists its information rather than yours. Your domain registrar offers the private registration service for a small annual fee.

Here are some other tips you can follow to minimize the risk of domain hijacking:

>> **Lock down:** Registrars offer the simple and free service of *locking down* (restricting others from changing) your URL. When registering your domain, select the check box indicating that you want to lock the domain name. If you have an active domain name, you can change its lockdown status by using account-management tools or sending a lockdown request by email (or phone) to customer support.

>> **24/7 support:** Use domain registrars that offer 24-hour support or give you access to support after business hours. This strategy is important so that if you discover that your domain has been hijacked, you can start the investigative and recovery process immediately.

>> **Standard notification:** Choose domain registration services that state standard methods of contacting you for changes or that will agree to contact you by using multiple methods (such as by both phone and email).

>> **Review status:** Frequently check the WHOIS directory to ensure that you're still listed as the owner of the domain and that your contact information is current and correct.

GLOSSARY OF SECURITY THREATS

Do you recognize all the threats that can pose a hazard to your computer and your business? Test your security knowledge by checking out this list:

- **Adware:** This type of software displays ads and pop-up windows on your computer. More than just annoying, adware includes code that tracks your personal information and shares it with third parties without your knowledge.

- **Blended threat:** Just like it sounds, this attack incorporates several types of threats to maximize the damage in one shot. For example, a virus might be distributed by email while a Trojan horse hides in an attached file to cause further damage to your computer.

- **Botnet:** This form of malware is unknowingly placed on your computer, which then becomes part of an army of thousands of computers that are controlled and instructed when and where to send infected emails to other computers, without your permission or knowledge.

- **Data-driven attack:** Seemingly harmless, this threat is encoded with data that you, the user, unknowingly execute to launch an attack. This type is dangerous because it can sneak through your firewall.

- **DNS spoofing:** This process happens when a hacker assumes the DNS (Domain Name System) name of another system but redirects you to an unauthorized site. The domain name of the legitimate site appears just as it should, but you're now on a different site.

- **Flooding:** Flooding happens when a large amount of information is directed to a particular system, contributing to a denial-of-service (DoS) attack.

- **Identity theft:** In this method, a Net-thief uses any number of security threats to gain access to your personal information, or that of your customers, for his or her own financial gain. Most commonly, the type of information consists of bank records, credit card numbers, Social Security numbers, and any other data that would allow someone else to assume your identity for financial gain.

- **Pharming:** This strategy tries to obtain personal data, such as credit card numbers, by using domain spoofing. Pharming poisons your DNS server by infusing false information that then redirects your customers elsewhere. As far as the customers know, they're still on your website because the domain doesn't change. Any information they provide during the visit is pharmed by the attacker.

- **Phishing:** In this ploy, you receive what looks like a legitimate email from a large, recognizable site, but the email is actually from unknown sources. The hope is that you respond to their request to update and verify personal and financial information.

- **Smurfing:** This type of software mounts a DoS attack by broadcasting large amounts of data.

- **Spyware:** Any software that uses your Internet connection without your knowledge or permission is spyware. It's usually distributed by using free or unknown programs that you download from the Internet. After the spyware is installed, it watches your activity on the Internet and transmits that information to other Bad Guys.

To discover more security-related terms and find information on protecting your computer, visit the National Cyber Security Alliance at its website, www.staysafeonline.org.

Staying Away from Email Scams

You should be familiar with two schemes that affect the way you handle email and keep your business safe: phishing ("fishing") and pharming ("farming"). Both methods use unscrupulous means to find personal or private account information about you and then use it for a hacker's personal gain. While both scams have been around for a long time, they are simple and easy for the Net-thief to deploy. Email scams remain a popular method for tricking people into giving up lots and lots of money! Two of the most common types of email threats are phishing and pharming.

Phishing

Phishing occurs when you receive an email that seems to be from a legitimate source, such as PayPal, Amazon, or even your bank. The email usually requests that you immediately update your account information because it has been compromised or needs to be verified for other reasons. When you click the link (included in your email notice), a bogus site opens that captures your personal information as you "update" the account. Legitimate companies have done a good job of alerting users to potential phishing scams and making it easier for you to spot emails that don't originate with the company.

Generally, you should be aware of these details:

>> **Account verification:** Most legitimate emails from a member-based company or financial institution now include the last three or four digits of your account number. If the email doesn't have any highly personalized or account-specific information, it might be a fake.

>> **Contact information:** Check whether the contact information at the bottom of an email matches the source that it's supposedly sent from. Email contact information should come from the company's primary URL, such as support@paypal.com — not support@paypalsecurity.com, for example.

>> **Collecting data:** A legitimate request should not ask you to submit, update, or verify private and confidential information by completing an email-based form or replying to that email. You should be able to visit the company's website (without using a link in the email) to update account information.

>> **Notice of urgency:** Most phishing scams insist that you reply right away or act immediately. Bogus emails scare you into the thinking your information is being compromised and that you must act right now.

>> **Contact customer support:** If an email looks legitimate but you're still not certain, play it safe and call the toll-free number listed on the back of your credit card or the one listed on the company's website.

Pharming

You also have to worry about pharming (pronounced like "farming"). Suppose that you visit a favorite shopping site. You type the domain name, and the site pops up momentarily on your screen. You log in using your password, enter your credit card information to buy products, and perhaps fork over some personal information as part of an online giveaway. Everything seems normal. What you don't realize is that a hacker has rerouted you to a website that looks like the one you intended to visit, but this one is bogus. In the meantime, all the passwords and personal information you entered into the site are *pharmed* out and the data is used for malicious purposes.

The best protection against pharming attacks as an individual user is to

>> Keep your firewall updated

>> Keep antivirus software current

>> Install patches and updates to your browser

In your Internet business, protecting your site from becoming a victim of pharming is much more difficult. In fact, no sure way to avoid it exists. The best defense is to talk with the company that hosts your site, to ensure that its servers are running the latest updates of DNS software and that all patches are installed. If you have an in-house server, you or your IT manager should be responsible for the same thing.

Mobile Security Risks

The continuing popularity of mobile devices, from smartphones to smart speakers, has only increased the appeal of the wireless world to not only users, but also to opportunist cybercriminals. Many e-commerce applications and solutions used to manage all areas of your online business now come with the capability of using the app or service via a mobile device. That means you can run your online business from almost anywhere.

Freedom of that nature comes with a price, of course — *security risks.* Like it or not, if you're using a wireless connection, you're vulnerable. The increase of mobile applications is undeniably at the center of many wireless security concerns. Whether you use an iPhone, an iPad, or an Android device, you are at risk to data breaches that can occur right under your nose.

Another business and consumer trend that is raising the bar on mobile security risks is the growing popularity of cloud-based computing. Also referred to software as a service (SaaS), cloud solutions are essentially the use of subscription-based or pay-for-use service over the Internet in real-time. This type of computing has become an affordable way for businesses of all sizes to expand their capabilities. For example, a business can host its phone system in the cloud and use cloud-based shopping carts. Most business services can be delivered from and managed in the cloud. Although cloud computing isn't strictly wireless, this "outside the network" approach to conducting online business introduces the opportunity for increased security risks.

Still another pervasive trend is called IoT, or the Internet of Things. IoT, in simple terms, allows a collection of unrelated devices to communicate to one another — this is a network of devices that each use unique identifiers to help transmit data without the need for people to be involved. For example, you may recall seeing a commercial for a new refrigerator that can send information directly to your smartphone about what items you need replenished. IoT is also enabling lots of other "shortcuts" in the home and office, but the wireless transmission opens up the opportunity for interference by the Net-thief or simple mischief makers.

With mobile usage skyrocketing and technology advances allowing more services to be consumed *in the cloud,* it's important to understand as much as you can about wireless security.

Understanding How a Wireless LAN Works

Before you can protect against a security breach of any kind, consider how a wireless network operates. In short, a *wireless local area network* (WLAN) provides access to the Internet without the need for cables or other wires hooking directly into your computer. Instead, an access point (AP) connects other wireless devices to your local area network (LAN). Then high-frequency radio waves transmit the signal from the LAN to your mobile computer. Figure 3-1 shows you an overview of this process.

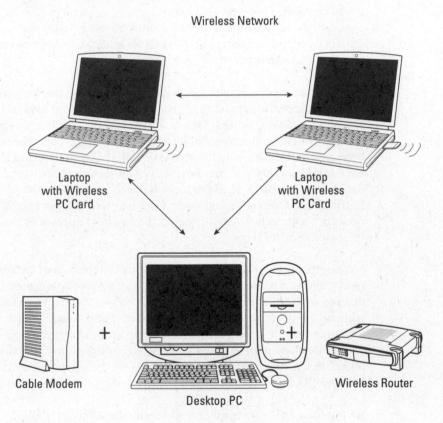

Wireless Network

Laptop with Wireless PC Card

Laptop with Wireless PC Card

Cable Modem

Desktop PC

Wireless Router

FIGURE 3-1: Overview of a wireless network.

Keep in mind that whether the wireless LAN is set up in your home, in a hotel, or at a city park, the result is the same: You share a signal that's broadcast over public airwaves. Why does this matter to you? Think about your house as it sits in the middle of your neighborhood. Now imagine that your house has no walls. If you don't mind neighbors — or perfect strangers, for that matter — being able to walk through your house and root around in your drawers and file cabinets, you don't have a problem. However, if you have things you would rather not share (such as credit card numbers, passwords, and other sensitive data), being exposed to that degree can be harmful.

REMEMBER

This might seem like a far-fetched example. However, someone using a laptop or any other wireless device (portable gaming devices come to mind) can pick up and use your wireless signal from outside your home or office — without your even knowing it.

Any type of security measure is only a deterrent. If someone really wants access to your network, he or she will find a way. In most cases, though, online thieves and hackers take a more random approach. They look for someone who is careless or naive and then take advantage of that opportunity to intrude.

Unfortunately, wireless networks can leave plenty of doors unlocked to usher in a roaming thief. Check out some of the threats that leave your wireless network exposed:

>> **Sniffing:** Hackers use software programs called *sniffers* that scan the activity (or traffic) on a network. When a sniffer detects a vulnerability, it grabs data that's being sent across the wireless network connection.

>> **Sidejacking:** Using a program called Firesheep, essentially anyone can use an open Wi-Fi connection in a public facility to take advantage of another user in that same Wi-Fi environment. In this case, the unsuspecting user logs into a website, such as Amazon, and upon the verification of the user's name and password, a cookie is created for that and subsequent sessions. When sidejackers use Firesheep, they intercept the session cookie, basically snagging it as their own, and can then proceed to assume the identity of the original user and buy things under that name or account. In our example, the sidejacker now has the cookie and Amazon can't tell whether or not the legal member is using it.

>> **Wardriving:** Using a wireless device, such as a laptop or smartphone, a person literally drives around picking up unprotected wireless signals from homes and businesses. The wireless identification information (service set identifier, or SSID) is documented along with your physical address. Your information is put into an online database that lets curious thieves know that your wireless network is accessible.

>> **Evil twin:** In this scenario, your access to a legitimate wireless access point is blocked or jammed. Then you're redirected to a second access point that's managed by a hacker. At that point, all the information you transmit is vulnerable, and thieves can even capture keystrokes to find passwords. This type of threat most often occurs in public Wi-Fi spots such as airports and coffee shops.

>> **WiPhishing:** Similar to the evil twin threat, thieves basically lure you to what looks like a safe access point. By using common SSIDs of public hotspots, your computer connects to a hacker's network. Again, your information becomes readily viewable; in some cases, viruses and Trojans are unknowingly sent to your system.

>> **Snoopy:** With this threat, mobile phones and any other wireless devices with Wi-Fi enabled are at risk of being compromised by drones. It sounds like something out of a spy novel, but drones armed with computers programmed to track and profile wireless devices and intercept or spoof a network can capture your data. The attacker gains access to all types of data (such as passwords and credit card numbers) shared between the mobile device and the intended network.

Obviously, the real problem with these and other wireless network threats is that your bottom line is at risk. For online thieves, it's not a harmless hobby: It represents money in their pocket and out of yours. That's why investing in precautionary security measures is worthwhile.

Establishing Barriers

When protecting your wireless network, you can choose from a range of services, applications, and common procedures that can lower the risk of being compromised.

Following your common sense

Here are some basic rules you can follow to minimize your risk:

>> **Shut down.** As silly as this method might sound, simply turning off your laptop when you're not using it reduces the chance for intrusion on your network. This technique also includes cutting the power to your cable or DSL.

>> **Limit sharing.** Allow your networked computers to have shared access to only limited files or directories rather than to hard drives. In fact, you might want to disable file and print sharing.

>> **Add a personal firewall.** A personal firewall installed on your laptop or on other individual computers provides another layer of protection between you and the wireless world.

>> **Configure WPA2.** Ensure that all devices on your network are configured or set up to use WPA2, the enhanced version of wireless encryption. If not, the less protective WEP wireless encryption becomes the default.

>> **Disable broadcast.** You can turn off the broadcast SSID feature that automatically searches for and logs on to a wireless connection. In other words, don't leave the Wi-Fi setting of your wireless device always turned on.

>> **Change the SSID.** Wireless network devices that you buy are supplied with a preset SSID, which makes access convenient for thieves. Because this preset SSID identifies your network, you should immediately create a new SSID after installation of the wireless device. Create your SSID by following suggested guidelines for creating any password:

- *Characters:* Combine letters and numbers.

- *Length:* Use the number of characters allowed. (If the limit is 12, for example, use all 12 characters.)

- *Uniqueness:* Your SSID should be different from any of your other passwords.

- *Updates:* Change your SSID every three to four months.

REMEMBER

To change your SSID, disable the broadcast feature, or configure devices for WPA, refer to the owner's manual supplied with your particular wireless router or access point.

>> **Update your OS and apps.** Make sure you always install OS (operating system) updates, as well as any updates to applications you use, as soon as the updates are available. The updates frequently include patches or fixes to security flaws.

REMEMBER

The increased use of social media networks, virtual games, cloud-based services, and other apps on wireless devices provides plenty of opportunity for security vulnerabilities. One of the best ways to fight it is to install the most recent updates, as soon as they are available.

>> **Use two-factor authentication.** This security process requires two methods of identification, usually a password (something you know) and a physical token (something you have), such as your mobile phone. If Net-thieves get your password over a wireless network, they must still have the physical token before they can gain access to your online data.

Many websites provide two-factor authentication, and taking the time to enable it is worthwhile. Some of the most important sites where you should consider using it are Gmail, PayPal, Amazon Web Services, Apple, Dropbox, Microsoft, and WordPress. Because social media sites are increasingly vulnerable to security attacks, two-factor authentication is recommended for LinkedIn, Twitter, and Facebook. Keep in mind that if a site such as Twitter

Spotting and Thwarting Hackers and Net-Thieves

gets hacked and passwords are stolen (which has happened several times recently), the stolen passwords are run through programs to find matches to other sites that use the same password. If you use the same password for multiple sites (a real no-no!), you could have a serious data breach on your hands. Similarly, more sites allow you to sign in by using a *social login*. This means you let other websites use your social media profiles (access passwords and login information) from Facebook or other popular sites. If you stay logged into the social networks then this type of login is a time-saving shortcut, but it leaves you more vulnerable to thieves. We recommend avoiding social logins if at all possible.

Setting up a virtual private network

When you use a *virtual private network* (VPN), you create a protective tunnel around your wireless connection. The VPN keeps your transmission secure and also keeps out anyone not specifically granted access. To set up a VPN for your home office or small business, you can purchase a wireless VPN firewall from companies such as Netgear (`www.netgear.com`).

If you plan to work frequently at hotspots, consider signing up for a subscription-based VPN service. As we mentioned, one of the biggest threats when working from free Wi-Fi hotspots is Firesheep. Because Firesheep is so easy to access and use, the chances of becoming a victim of this threat are super high. So far, one of the best protections against a Firesheep attack is having a VPN. You can connect to a VPN for added protection in restaurants, hotels, airports, or any other Wi-Fi hotspot. Check out providers such as Private Internet Access (`www.privateinternetaccess.com`), which costs as little as $10 per month. TorGuard (`www.torguard.net`) offers a few options for VPN services, starting at $6 per month.

Keeping an eye on your connection

No single method is best for protecting against wireless crimes. Instead, use a combination of security measures and common sense. You can never be too secure — the more the more measures you take, the better off you are.

Chapter **4**

Locking Down Your Site and Your Business

I f you've spent any time on a computer, you know most of the security drills about spam, viruses, and other unwanted intruders. (If not, turn to Chapter 2 of this minibook to create a top-notch security plan for fending off online predators.)

As an online business owner, your responsibility to run a secure site is now increased in magnitude. In addition to watching out for your best interests, you must realize that your customers depend on you to take the appropriate precautions. In this chapter, we show you good security measures and provide information and tools so that you can increase protection for yourself and your customers.

Protecting against Personal Data Loss and Credit Card Fraud

Operating an Internet business means that you're likely collecting, processing, and storing (or safeguarding) credit card data regularly. Additionally, you are a gatekeeper for lots of personal data, from passwords to Social Security numbers. You therefore have to look at data breaches and potential credit card fraud from two points of view: yours and the customer's.

Minimizing your financial losses

E-commerce sites lose billions of dollars to online credit card fraud every year. Worldwide, credit card fraud reached nearly $25 billion in 2018, according to The Nilson Report (www.nilsonreport.com). The United States topped the charts, responsible for more than 39 percent of the reported fraud. Identity theft and fraud cases also hit a record high of three million complaints in 2018, according to the U.S. Federal Trade Commission (FTC). Although 50 percent of those complaints involved credit card fraud, approximately 27 percent of all complaints were specific to online shopping! The losses don't stop there. Data breaches caused by hackers or malicious intent cost businesses $3.92 million (on average) *per breach* worldwide in 2019, according to the annual data breach report from IBM. However, that cost nearly doubles in the United States where the average cost per individual breach is $8.19 million. Included in that financial loss is the actual cost of the lost data, recovery and mediation costs, and the estimated cost to the company's reputation.

As an online business, your vulnerability to these types of losses is real. We don't say this to scare you, but to illustrate how quickly costs add up from what might seem like a minor, one-time security slip. And consider that while protection against credit card fraud is tightening offline, with the required use of new data chip credit and debit cards, fraud experts anticipate this will only drive up fraud attempts online. Shoppers may be more willing to buy online than ever before, but security concerns over credit card and personal data loss still worry consumers. The fear of identity theft and credit card fraud make 68 percent of consumers hesitant to buy online, according to a study from Bizrate Insights (https://bizrateinsights.com). All these statistics add up to potentially less revenue for your online business.

You want to be aware of potential security problems so you can combat them and protect your prospective revenue. Here are just a few of the ways that your online business can get hit with fraudulent transactions — and end up losing merchandise and money:

>> Customers buy a product but then claim that they didn't order it (or file a similar complaint), and the credit card company deletes the charge.

>> You unknowingly process stolen credit cards.

>> You process invalid credit cards or cards that you should have declined.

Although you might think that the big online retailers are most at risk, smaller sites are often more likely targets because smaller sites usually have less sophisticated resources for detecting fraud. Fraudulent credit card orders increasingly account for a larger percentage of all processed online orders. Although the percentage is still relatively small (less than 10 percent), that doesn't help if you're the one suffering a loss.

Protecting against online crime means that you have to stay alert, cautious, and informed. As with any security concern, seek ways to reduce your risk:

>> **Validate credit cards.** Whether you process manually or in real-time, confirm that the credit card is approved. If a card is declined or shows up with a questionable item, resist the urge to process it anyway.

>> **Verify suspicious orders.** Don't hesitate to contact a customer by email or phone to confirm an order to validate a card number. If everything is okay, your customer will be impressed that you take this degree of precaution.

>> **Fight excessive charge backs.** Even if a card is valid, a customer can steal from you by refusing to pay for the product or service after receiving it. If the customer gives a valid reason (such as the product was damaged or appears to have been used or refurbished), the credit card company removes the charge. Because you have no signature on file for an online transaction, you're stuck paying the bill — plus a chargeback fee from your credit card company. You can challenge the claim by responding to the chargeback complaint that the credit card company sends you. You need diligence and patience to fight this type of complaint, and you won't win them all. Still, you can recover some losses, making your time invested worthwhile. (For more information on fighting chargebacks, see Chapter 1 of this minibook.)

TIP

If you suspect a problem or perhaps an honest mistake, call your customer directly to work it out. Keeping good records and documenting follow-up calls go a long way toward fighting chargebacks.

>> **Add fraud protection.** Online payment processors sometimes offer fraud protection programs for e-commerce sites. These services add screening features as well as links to fraud alerts to minimize the acceptance of bad orders. This service is considered an add-on, so expect to pay a monthly fee, plus a small transaction fee on every order.

>> **Use card codes.** As part of your ordering process, ask for the credit card verification code, which usually appears as a three-digit number on the back of a Visa or MasterCard credit card, or a four-digit number on the front of an American Express card. Asking for this information requires that the user has the physical card in hand (or at least knows the number).

>> **Accept online checks.** You can choose to accept electronic checks or Internet checks to provide another payment alternative with fewer fraud risks. On the flip side, restricting your payment options can hurt your sales. Limiting customers to only one form of payment (such as online checks) likely can turn off many customers.

TIP

Work directly with your online payment processor to see how to further protect yourself. When selling on eBay or other third–party sites, always read the fraud policies to understand your rights as a merchant — before a sale goes wrong.

Protecting customers' privacy and financial data

Luckily, only a small percentage of customers — if any — turn out to be thieves. A bigger challenge is protecting your customers' data from online crooks and potential carelessness. One of these violations can land your customers' data in the wrong hands — and also land you in a lot of hot water:

» **Online security breach:** A lone successful hacking attempt can leave your online database of records as open game. Names, addresses, passwords, and credit card numbers — some of the most sought-after information — is easily left at risk.

» **Offline theft:** Someone can break into your office and access customer files filled with personal financial data. Don't discount *internal theft,* where the thief is someone you knowingly invite into your office space.

» **Sloppy disposal:** Okay, maybe you have extra copies of customer data or you decide that the statute of IRS limitations has passed and you can now get rid of old files. How you dispose of this information can leave customer records vulnerable.

» **Vendor carelessness:** Your security and data storage practices aren't the only factors that can lead to a mishap. Any vendor that you partner with — and who has access to your customer data — can cause a security mishap. (Think about scandals in which credit card companies and delivery services have mishandled or lost customer information.) How they handle — or mishandle — data can affect your site's reputation.

The preceding list gives you some good ideas about how easily a problem can occur. Now all you have to do is make sure it doesn't. Take these precautions to minimize your risk:

» **Store data properly.** You probably have two basic methods of keeping data — hard copy files and online databases. Make sure that each one is tightly secured:

- *Hard copy:* Paperwork and hard copies of backup files that contain sensitive customer information must be kept in locked file cabinets or in rooms and storage facilities with locks and limited access.

- *Online:* Online information should be password protected and have the added protection of a firewall.

» **Dump your data properly.** When it's time to get rid of hard copy documents, these files must be thoroughly shredded. You can even hire a professional document disposal service that will come to your location to shred documents. How convenient is that?

TIP

Before getting rid of old computers or disposing of any electronic files, erase or overwrite the machine or files (as opposed to simply deleting individual files). You can use a free, downloadable program from Active@ KillDisk at www.killdisk.com. Or try guaranteed erasure and hard drive destruction services from companies such as Shred-it (www.shredit.com) or Ontrack (www.ontrack.com). It's also worthwhile to completely remove the hard drive from the computer before disposing of or selling the equipment.

» **Add layers of security.** Be sure to protect any type of company information, not just customer data. Showing that you have multiple layers of security processes is important. Having only one type or layer of security can become a compliance issue if your data is compromised. Include these items in your layers, as shown in Figure 4-1:

- *Antivirus:* Keep antivirus software updated.

- *Backups:* Back up data regularly.

- *Checks:* Conduct regular security checks.

- *Encryption:* Use encryption tools to code information in case your data is compromised. Encryption lets you hide your data from hackers and other unwanted eyes. Only someone with the proper password can decrypt the information for proper viewing.

- *Firewalls:* Maintain active firewalls on your computers and servers.

- *Inventory:* Keep an inventory of your files.

- *Offline security:* Lock up data that's stored offline.

- *Security policy:* Write an official security policy to ensure that you cover your bases (see Chapter 2 of this minibook).

- *VPN:* Use a virtual private network (VPN) when sending information over a wireless connection.

» **Institute a notification policy.** Taking preventive measures also involves planning for the worst. Follow up your privacy policy with an internal policy describing how you will handle a security breach as well as the process for notifying authorities and customers.

WARNING

You might be a one-person show when you're starting your online business, but the stakes for messing up are the same as they are for the big guys. Mishandling, losing, or compromising customer information can cost you thousands of dollars in fines, possible jail time, and untold damage to your image as a reputable online store.

```
┌─────────────────────────────────────────────┐
│                                               │
│              LAYERS OF SECURITY               │
│                                               │
│                                               │
│                  Proactive                    │
│                 ─────────                      │
│             Utilize Encryption Tools          │
│                      ↑                         │
│          Enable VPN on Wireless Network       │
│                      ↑                         │
│              Use Password Generator           │
│                                               │
│                                               │
│                  Preventive                   │
│                 ──────────                     │
│            Activate Antivirus Software        │
│                      ↑                         │
│    Install Antispyware & Adware-Blocking Software │
│                      ↑                         │
│               Enable Firewalls                 │
│                      ↑                         │
│          Secure Office Data & Hardware         │
│                                               │
│                                               │
│                 Maintenance                    │
│                ────────────                    │
│            Establish Security Policy           │
│                      ↑                         │
│  Conduct Regular Security Checks & System Updates │
│                      ↑                         │
│            Maintain Inventory of Files         │
│                      ↑                         │
│             Back Up Data Regularly             │
│                                               │
└─────────────────────────────────────────────┘
```

FIGURE 4-1:
Layers of security.

Backing Up Your Data

Stop. Take a moment and think about the information you store on your computer. Consider the amount of time you spend creating, updating, and maintaining your website. Now imagine that all that information disappears in a blink of the eye. Yikes!

Most of us go through our business day assuming that nothing really bad will ever happen. That's followed by the assumption that the contents of your website and your computer files are perfectly safe and always at your disposal. Guess again. You can lose data through human error (coffee splashed on your laptop, for example) or natural disasters, such as hurricanes.

You can prevent disasters from becoming cataclysmic by properly backing up and storing your data. Try these methods:

>> **Store data on a removable storage device.** A common way to back up data is to save it to an external hard drive. You can also use a flash drive, as long as it has enough memory.

One goal of backing up data is to have your information available in case of a disaster, such as hurricanes, tornadoes, and flooding — which we've seen plenty of in the last few years. If your computer is stolen or destroyed in a fire, having data backed up on a hard drive doesn't do much good. You can make a duplicate copy that's not backed up as often but is saved to disk and stored in a fireproof safe or in a safe-deposit box. Or you can keep your information backed up in a cloud solution for a few dollars a month.

>> **Use a cloud-based or remote backup service.** One advantage of using a hosted or cloud-based backup service is that your data is stored off-site. If anything calamitous happens at your location, you can retrieve a copy from your backup provider and immediately restore your data. Backup services can cost as little as $10 per month and increase to several hundred dollars per month depending on the features you want and the amount of storage space required. Shop around for the best deal.

>> **Back up your operating system.** If you operate Windows, Microsoft includes a few options to back up files and recover your PC, depending on which version of Windows you operate. You can find out about your options at `https://support.microsoft.com`.

If you're using an Apple Macintosh, Mac OS X includes Time Machine for free, which allows you to automatically back up your system. You can get the details, along with other options, at `http://support.apple.com`.

Microsoft's security updates for Windows 7 ended as of January 2020. It's critical to stay up to date on any security and support notices for software you use, whether that's version updates or End of Life (EOL) notices for the software and support of the software.

In addition to the data you keep on your computer, make sure that the web pages stored on your server are also backed up. Check with your hosting service to determine how and when backups are made and also what you must do to access them.

Adding Firewalls

One of the best lines of defense against viruses and intruders is having a firewall installed on your computer. Think of a *firewall* as a security guard standing watch at all the doors and windows of your computer. The firewall monitors the traffic, decides what's safe, and then gives permission to enter. If the firewall detects a threat, it shuts the door and blocks the intruder.

Firewalls are particularly important because hackers are aggressive creatures. They actively search for networks that are unprotected or have disabled firewalls. To a Net-thief, that situation is the equivalent of having an open invitation to browse through all the files on your computer. The lack of firewalls also makes it easy to install harmful programs that infect or shut down your computer or — worse — scoop up and send out to the hacker pertinent information (such as passwords and bank account numbers) without your knowledge.

WARNING

If a pesky virus manages to break through your front lines of defense, a firewall cannot remove or quarantine infected files. You still need to run antivirus software in addition to installing a firewall.

For added security, we recommend that you do the following:

>> **Enable individual firewalls.** When your computer is part of a local area network (LAN), most routers have a firewall installed. For the best defense, though, enable a personal firewall on each computer.

>> **Add an enhanced firewall.** Install a second dynamic firewall to gain protection from both incoming and outgoing traffic and to provide an additional layer of security. You can buy firewall software, often combined with antivirus software or other security tools, for $40 and up. One popular product is ZoneAlarm, which offers free and paid versions of its firewall solution at www.zonealarm.com.

6

Online Marketing Basics

Contents at a Glance

IN THIS CHAPTER

» **Knowing what it takes to succeed in digital marketing**

» **Breaking down the online buyer's journey**

» **Calculating the visitors-to-sales ratio at your site**

» **Discovering your high-volume traffic periods**

» **Marketing your site to drive traffic through the roof**

» **Getting customers to make the decision to buy**

Chapter **1**

Jump-Starting Traffic and Driving Sales

You've probably heard the old saying "Build it and they will come." And you probably know by now that this particular theory doesn't necessarily apply to your website. Instead, your site is competing for visitors with hundreds of thousands (if not millions) of other sites. If that's not intimidating enough, consider that you have to not only figure out how to get people to come to your website, but also entice them to stay long enough to explore your site, and then convince them to buy something from you.

These challenges are common to all online businesses. An effective digital marketing strategy can help drive interest and traffic to your site, while a solid content strategy should keep your website visitors engaged longer. Then, it all boils down to your conversion rate — how many browsers become buyers. In this chapter, we introduce you to the concepts you need to know to attract and engage visitors, then we show you why your site's conversion rate matters and describe some strategies for increasing it, even for those visitors who aren't quite ready to buy yet. After you master the basics in this chapter, you're prepared to take a closer look at specific online marketing tactics to boost traffic and convert visitors to buyers as discussed in the rest of the chapters in this minibook. Let's get started with the basics!

Defining Key Elements for Digital Marketing Success

Now that you have an online business, you'll need a cohesive digital marketing strategy to find and win over prospective customers. What is digital marketing? It's really no different from traditional marketing — except that all the channels you use are, well, digital! Instead of a printed newsletter that you mail to prospects, you have blog articles and e-newsletters that you send out in an email. Instead of placing an ad in a magazine, you create online ads that are distributed through Google Ads or other online ad networks.

The *strategy* part of digital marketing is simply putting all the individual components together into a cohesive plan and then monitoring and measuring the results. As part of your long-term digital marketing strategy, you'll develop short-term online marketing campaigns with specific goals in mind. For example, one goal may be to increase sales of a new product line you're offering. Once you create an offer to entice prospects, you'll use content and promotional offers (coupons, for instance) to advertise through multiple digital channels.

To determine whether the campaign is a success, and whether you need to tweak your overall strategy, you track the campaign metrics (how many people saw your offer online, how many visitors flowed through to a specific page on your website, and how many people took advantage of the offer and actually became leads, or customers). Then you do it all over again with a new campaign — according to your strategy! Here are the basic channels and components that go into a digital marketing strategy:

>> **Website:** Okay, this one may seem obvious because you have an online business, but all your website properties (main site, micro-sites, landing pages, e-commerce store, and blogs) should all be considered under this category. You want to think about the role each site plays (along with specific, individual pages) in your digital strategy and online marketing campaigns. Each page of your site has a specific purpose, and you should identify the goals and conversion points for each page.

>> **SEO:** Search engine optimization encompasses all the activities you do to promote organic traffic. Sometimes referred to as *natural search*, it's basically the "free" traffic you get as a result of showing up in search engine results on Google, Yahoo!, and other search engine sites. There are certain actions, or optimization efforts, you can take to improve your rankings. (We discuss this in more detail in Chapter 6 of this minibook.)

>> **SEM:** Search engine marketing includes all your paid activities. SEM includes PPC (pay-per-click) ads, display, and retargeting ads. This term also encompasses any paid ads you run in social media. (You learn more about SEM, including Google Ads, in Chapter 3 of this minibook.)

>> **Social Media:** Facebook, Twitter, LinkedIn, Snapchat, Instagram . . . one or all of these social media platforms is likely to have a role in your digital marketing. You use these channels to share content, find and interact with potential buyers, and identify industry influencers. Want to know more about social media marketing? We cover it in detail in Chapter 3 of this minibook.

>> **Marketing automation:** This is a fancy term for your email marketing solution. It's the system that lets you create and send email communications to your visitors and customers. You can also build landing pages and track important metrics tied to your email campaigns. There are easy solutions designed specifically for small businesses, like MailChimp (www.mailchimp.com), HubSpot (www.hubspot.com), and Pardot (www.pardot.com). Or, for more complex needs, you might consider Marketo (www.marketo.com) or Eloqua (www.oracle.com/marketingcloud/products/marketing-automation).

>> **Mobile:** We cannot express enough the growing importance of mobile devices in driving traffic and sales for your online business. When it comes to digital marketing, mobile phones and tablets are critical channels for all types of communications and ads (and as a traffic source).

>> **Metrics:** A big advantage of digital marketing over traditional marketing is that there are lots of ways to track all types of success indicators, from website traffic sources and bounce rates to email click-through rates and CTA (call to action) conversions. The trick with digital marketing is remembering to step back and look at the complete story that data provides you, and not get stuck on one single piece of the data pie — which can be misleading. We give you more information on metrics in Chapter 5 of this minibook, and show you how to clearly define what constitutes success of an online campaign so you can track those success indicators from start to finish.

>> **Video:** Once thought to be a piece of your content strategy that was nice to have, video has become an integral part of a smart digital strategy. One reason is because customers like a quick way to consume content, especially on social media platforms. Another reason is because YouTube has become the second-largest search engine behind Google! Yes, that means that your prospective

customers are going to YouTube and searching for information, just as they do on Google. Having video that can be found in YouTube, and then drive traffic to your site, is now a must.

>> **Content:** What's the common denominator across all digital marketing tactics and campaigns? Content, of course! Just about every piece of written content and visual media gets grouped into the category of content — from website copy and white papers to videos and graphics. In digital marketing, content is what helps drive traffic and convinces visitors to buy your products and services.

Getting to Know Your Buyers — Really Well

You may not realize it, but online buyers know a *lot* about you before you even realize they exist. In B2B (business-to-business) companies, approximately 70 percent of online buyers have already made a buying decision before they reach out to your sales team. In business-to-consumer (B2C), as much as 90 percent of online buyers have decided upon the product or service they want to buy before they finally hit the Buy Now button on your website. That's because buyers invest a good amount of time in researching competing products and services, and even your online business.

Where are they getting all the information? Online shoppers do thorough searches on Google and YouTube, read online reviews, visit online communities and social media sites to ask others for opinions, watch video demos, and look to independent third-party sites and articles for information. This is all part of the *online buyer's journey* — or the actions buyers take before they make a final buying decision. How do you reach these buyers before they go to your competitors? You need to know who they are, what motivates them, and provide them with the right information (at the right time) to guide them through their journey and to your Buy Now button! The following sections tell you what you need to know about your buyers to provide them with the best possible content.

Developing buyer personas

A *persona* is a detailed description of a buyer. It describes who the person is, what problem that person wants to solve (that would bring him or her to your website), and gives details on what makes this person tick. Your online business likely has several different types of buyers, so you want to create a different persona for each one of those buyers. For example, if you're selling specialty cakes online, you may have a buyer persona of a bride (or groom) who wants a wedding cake; a woman who buys special-occasion cakes; an administrative assistant who buys birthday cakes for quarterly employee celebrations; and a business owner who sends gourmet cakes as thank-you gifts to special customers.

Each of these personas has a story that includes who they are, what they do for a living, what they do in their free time, what they like (their interests), and so on. The more details you have available for a persona, the more you understand what makes them a good match for your product. In our specialty bakery example, each persona also has very different reasons for why he or she would buy a gourmet cake and when he or she needs it. The more you know about these personas, or prospective buyers, the better you understand how to talk to them and convince them to buy from you instead of other online specialty bakers. Where do you get this information? You research and talk to your existing customers! Create personas based on your actual customers and let them help you fill in the details for your fictional personas.

Defining buying stages

Once you have created buyer personas, you should know more about when each type of persona is likely to look for your products, and then you can create content and offers that are most likely to interest them and attract them to your site. But there's one other piece of information you need to understand — the various stages of the buying process. As we mentioned, online buying is a journey that has different stages. Each stage represents a general time period based on the buyer's level of interest and knowledge. Here are the three primary buyer stages:

>> **Awareness:** In this early stage, a buyer may not yet fully realize she has a problem or a need to solve. She is just beginning to realize that she isn't as productive as she could be at work, for example. But she doesn't realize that there are technology products or services that could make her more efficient. In this stage, she is researching very general problems or symptoms, but is not yet aware of a specific brand and how it resolves the problem. She's reading blog posts and online articles and participating in group chats on social media and online forums commiserating with other people who are having the same problems.

>> **Consideration:** Once a buyer knows he has a problem, he wants to find a solution. But he's not yet made up his mind as to which solution is best. For example, maybe this is a young professional, a millennial, who needs a better razor, but doesn't want to pay a lot or have the inconvenience of going into stores. This buyer already knows he wants to buy his razors online, but isn't sure what type is best. He also knows he might be interested in buying from a subscription-based online buyers club, but he doesn't know which one is best or cheapest. In this stage of the buying process, he's doing a lot of detailed

research about specific products and vendors, reading online reviews, watching product videos, and comparing one type of razor to another.

>> **Decision:** In the final stage of the buyer's journey, your prospect has decided what she wants to buy and has narrowed the decision of where or from whom she wants to buy. In this case, she's spending a lot of time on your website watching branded webinars or product tutorials, comparing prices, and trying to understand the specifics of your product or service. She has a need, but is still dependent upon getting the right information from you to convince her she's making the best decision.

If you can match the best content or offer to the buying stage, you are more likely to keep prospective customers interested. Then you can guide them all the way to that final decision to buy.

Calculating Your Site's Conversion Rate

In any retail business, the goal is to *convert* a window shopper to a real buyer. And now that you understand who your buyers are, what's important to them, and where they are in the buyer's journey, well, it's much easier to convince them to take an action and convert! For e-commerce businesses, there are many different types of conversion rates you care about, but for now let's look at a simple formula to determine generally how successful you are at converting shoppers to buyers. The basic formula, called your *conversion rate*, is the number of visitors who come to your site and then buy from you for a given period of time. For example, suppose that on one day, 15 people buy something from your website and you get a total of 1,500 unique visits to your site that same day. You calculate your conversion rate by dividing 15 by 1,500, for a 1 percent conversion rate for the day. That's simple enough. The concept becomes complicated, though, when you try to pin down exactly which number represents a good conversion rate.

Before we try to identify a healthy conversion rate, recall that we said that many types of conversion rates are worth tracking, and lots of factors influence the final number. For starters, in this book we often talk about conversion rates in terms of e-commerce, or B2C sites, but B2B sites must consider conversion rates, too. What's the difference? In B2C, the ultimate conversion is visitor-to-checkout (completing the online purchase of the product you're selling). You probably want to know the visitor-to-cart conversion rate (visitors who put products in their shopping carts but didn't complete the purchase). The difference between visitor-to-cart and visitor-to-checkout conversion rates reveals shopping cart abandonment rates. Whereas in B2B, you may have a more involved sales process where customers buy from a salesperson, instead of online. In that case, your conversion rates may track your online lead generation (submitting a web form or downloading a white paper, for example). Similarly, nonprofits may also measure different conversion rates — percentage of people registering for a fundraising event, clicking to make a donation, signing up to become a volunteer, or sharing a promotional video. Whether you're a nonprofit, an online retailer selling B2C, or you have a B2B website that needs to generate leads, here are some other conversion rates that may matter to you:

>> **Format:** An action, or conversion, occurs not only in a shopping cart but also on a non-e-commerce web page, on a landing page (that may reside off your primary website), or in an email. You'd need to monitor conversion rates for all these types of pages or conversion points in an online buying journey.

>> **Device:** Conversions and what they mean or how they are made may differ by the type of device from which they originate, such as a desktop computer, a tablet, or a mobile device (smartphone). Note that the mobile device category may include both smartphones and tablets. Smart-home devices, like Alexa from Amazon, are expanding the places (or devices) where conversions are happening. Although this is still new, it's an areas that continues to grow and deserves close monitoring because it influences how customers buy online.

>> **Visitor or source:** You may have one ideal conversion rate for North American website traffic and a separate rate for international traffic. Depending on your data's *granularity*, or the level of detail you have available about your website traffic, you might be able to track conversion rates in more specific ways. For example, you might have a conversion rate by customer type (new customer or returning customer), or by visitor type (new site visitor or returning visitor), or by industry, or even by referral source (affiliate sites, social media sites, Google ads, organic search, other third-party websites), or by promotion.

Understanding that a one-size-fits-all conversion rate does not exist is important — and necessary when evaluating how to improve that rate! When you dig deeper, the details or data behind a single conversion rate number can reveal very different information.

Experts cite different acceptable conversion rate percentages. You often hear an average conversion rate of 2 to 4 percent for e-commerce sites. We've seen everything from .05 percent to nearly 8 percent, depending on the type of site and time of year. For established, larger online brands, a conversion rate of 20 percent or more is not unusual. With B2B sites, conversion rates are often cited as being even higher, sometimes close to 30 percent for some conversion types.

Before benchmarking any of these conversion rates against your site, make sure you know exactly what those percentages represent. Is the percentage an across-site average or does it apply only to shopping cart conversions or to a particular type of offer? Is the percentage for a particular day, for one event, or across a year? For example, a popular e-commerce conversion rate for researchers to track surrounds Cyber Monday (the Monday following Thanksgiving), which is typically thought to be the busiest online shopping day of the year. In the past, for this one day, conversion rates for new customers have tracked close to 5 percent for online retailers, but these numbers don't always reflect Cyber Monday conversion rates for small online retailers with less than a million dollars in revenue.

When researching conversion rates, use industry data that most closely matches your type of online business and know exactly what type of conversion is being tracked. For our purposes, let's consider 2 percent a good conversion rate for first-time visitors to your e-commerce site throughout the calendar year.

What if your site has 500 visitors per day? At a 2 percent conversion rate, that's about 10 sales (500 × .02) per day. That number seems a little depressing — unless you have some incredibly high profit margins! Based on this equation, one way to drive up sales is to drive more traffic to your site.

To figure out how many visitors you need for a healthy 2 percent conversion rate, follow these steps:

1. **Determine the number of sales you need per day to stay in business.**

2. **Divide the number of sales by .02 (the 2 percent conversion rate).**

    This number becomes your targeted goal. For example, if you want 100 sales per day, your target goal is 5,000 visitors per day.

Before you get too comfortable, keep in mind the following factors that influence your true conversion rate:

>> **Qualified traffic:** If you're shooting in the dark for traffic, that conversion rate becomes a sliding scale. However, by identifying visitors who are most likely to become buyers (a higher quality of site visitor), you can put your efforts into targeting this demographic. Theoretically, you attract fewer visitors, but more of them buy.

>> **Site construction:** Everything from the layout and navigation of your home page to your search feature and shopping cart affect the probability that your visitors will be converted to buyers. The more intuitive, attractive, and useful your site, the better your likely conversion rates.

>> **Quality product or service:** If you have a product or service that nobody wants, the number of visitors you can attract to your site doesn't matter. The conversion rate will be zero!

- » **Content:** Your website pages may be designed to attract visitors but not designed to immediately convert buyers. A blog, for example, may be written to gain exposure for your brand or website, but you don't expect first-time visitors to your blog to become buyers. A sitewide conversion rate (based on total number of visitors) can be misleading; tracking conversion rates for specific pages may be preferable.

- » **Price point:** You can drive up conversion rates by using pricing strategies. Unless you can maintain price-based leverage in the marketplace, however, consider these rates falsely inflated.

Considering all these factors, another method for increasing sales is to increase your site's rate of conversion. We address that topic in a moment. First, let's look at what you can do to increase your traffic.

Figuring Out When You Get the Most Traffic

In addition to increasing the sheer volume of traffic, you have to look at the whole picture to increase your sales numbers. Part of navigating that landscape involves figuring out what time of day you're driving the bulk of your traffic to your site.

The average day is divided into several important time segments, called *dayparts*. This concept is important if you happen to own a business — even an online business that's open 24 hours a day, every day.

For example, a restaurant typically receives the majority of its sales at three specific times during the day: breakfast, lunch, and dinner. It works in a similar way with the Internet, but there are typically five dayparts that represent typical patterns of online traffic:

- » **Early morning (6 a.m. to 8 a.m.):** Fewer people shop during these hours. Research indicates online retail buying drops by half in most cases.

  If you sell to an international audience, you may have customers who are buying during a daypart that is considered slow for your location. Typically, this customer segment or daypart should be a very small percentage of your overall site visitors.

- » **Daytime (8 a.m. to 5 p.m.):** This period is one of the busiest online times for 25- to 54-year-old professionals. Conversion rates for online retailers often peak between 10 a.m. and 1 p.m. That's right: Your customers typically spend

REMEMBER

their lunch hours checking out your site. Not only that — they're also willing to make a purchase.

>> **Evening (5 p.m. to 11 p.m.):** Between the time folks arrive home from work and the time they go to bed, they apparently have enough downtime to do a little more online shopping.

>> **Late night (11 p.m. to 6 a.m.):** This period isn't a busy one. Sure, some night owls are still looking for deals, but they're in the minority.

>> **Weekend:** Yes, Saturday and Sunday get their own daypart! The conversion rates vary for the weekend daypart, but you can count on the peak periods being somewhat similar to weekday buying habits.

Does all this mean that you should close shop during the wee hours of the dayparts? Of course not! This data may not reflect daypart activity and buying patterns for your particular site. Plus, the Internet is always open and you can potentially have customers during any daypart. To make the most of marketing to your prime dayparts, here are some strategies you can explore:

>> **Balanced ad spending:** If you know when your customers are most receptive to your ads, that's when you want to spend the largest amount of money to get your ads shown. Similarly, you may want to decrease spending amounts during downtimes.

>> **Increased ad revenue:** Alternatively, if you sell advertising, you may be able to make more money per impression during busy dayparts.

>> **Targeted specials:** Don't just run more ads during your slow periods. Create offers and time-sensitive pricing specials targeted to the frenzied shoppers from your busiest dayparts, too. With the right offer, you may be able to bump an already strong conversion rate into an outstanding conversion rate. You can also use a retargeting strategy to target ads to site visitors no matter what time of day they visit your site. Retargeting is a way of continuing to show ads to visitors even after they leave your website (tracking capabilities allow the ads to follow your visitors to other sites and be displayed on those sites).

You should also think about your specific site and to whom it appeals most. If the majority of customers are teens, for example, the likelihood that they will buy from you during the weekday lunch hour drops. Evening and weekend dayparts may be busier for you because your customers aren't in school during these periods. However, lunchtime may present an opportunity to reach out to their parents (or to other secondary customers). Consider promoting your site's gift cards to this customer.

Balance the daypart information with what you already know about your customers. Always ask these questions:

>> Who are my primary customers?

>> Based on their lifestyles, when will my customers most likely visit my site?

>> How can I serve my customers better during the specific dayparts when they're most likely to be ready to shop?

>> What new, or secondary, customer base can I reach by taking advantage of peak dayparts?

>> What type of offer or incentive can I create to attract new customers?

>> How can I better serve my customers during the least-busy dayparts?

>> What can I do to improve traffic and buying during nonpeak dayparts?

REMEMBER

While breaking out daypart activity might provide some interesting information, it's only one data point for consideration. There might be other factors that are stronger indications of buying behaviors or other areas where you have more ability to influence. When analyzing data, remember to take a step back and try to see the entire picture, and don't base your marketing decisions on a single slice of the data pie.

Leading Customers to the Right Web Pages

Getting prospective customers to stand up and take note of your website isn't difficult, but you have to be consistent, thorough, and unrelenting. First, take a multipronged approach that includes both online and offline marketing efforts. Second, consider the best place, or specific page on your website to drive traffic. You can get started by using the following techniques to generally increase traffic and bump up conversion rates:

>> **Keyword searches:** Paid keywords, such as Google Ads, can be a cost-effective method of driving targeted traffic to your site, if you budget wisely and target the right kinds of keywords. Although the cost-per-click (CPC) rate has gone up significantly in the past few years for popular search terms, plenty of keyword search phrases are still affordable — especially long-tail keyword phrases. For example, the term *flower pots* is a broader term and may therefore be more expensive than *container gardening with terracotta flower pots*. (Check out Chapter 6 of this minibook to find out more about paid keywords.)

TIP

Google offers lots of resources to help you learn everything from the basics of using Ads to mastering advanced user strategies and tips. These resources are available in the Google Ads overview at https://ads.google.com.

» **Organic search:** Considering web shoppers' dependency on Google, Yahoo!, and others for getting your site to rank high remains an important way to drive traffic. Search engine optimization is a critical strategy when driving *organic* (non-paid) search results. To gain organic traffic, you must optimize your site with the right content and appropriate keywords. We show you how to reach that all-important rank in Chapter 6 of this minibook.

» **External links:** Increasing the number of sites that link to your site is usually a safe bet for attracting qualified visitors. Similarly, getting link referrals from online custom reviews and blogs can greatly increase traffic to your site.

» **Affiliate traffic:** Setting up an affiliate program can also help direct traffic your way. (Of course, you may not want to take on this task until your site is more established.) See Book 4, Chapter 2, where we discuss affiliates in more detail.

» **Advertising:** Paid banner advertising, display ads, retargeting (showing ads in other websites or social media sites to people who have already visited one of your web pages or landing pages but did not convert), and even direct-mail campaigns can generate just enough interest to make a visit worthwhile.

» **Offline efforts:** Everything you do doesn't have to take place online. Promoting your site offline (such as on business cards and by networking) can help drive traffic, too.

» **Content:** Building content on your site gives customers a reason to check out your site and then hang around long enough to buy something. Content is also a critical part of driving organic search traffic to your site. We cover the different content that you can provide (such as reviews) in Book 3, Chapter 5.

» **E-newsletters:** Whatever the method you use to reach customers, the idea is to connect with them. After they form a relationship with you or define a need that you can answer, they will follow your lead — right back to your site. See Book 4, Chapter 3 to find out how to put together an e-newsletter.

As we discuss throughout this book, it's not just about *how* you drive traffic to your site, but *where* you drive traffic. Not every page on your site serves the same purpose. And as mentioned in this chapter, depending on your buyer persona and what stage the buyer is in the buying process, you want to send them to the right spot to match their intent.

Consider our example of the specialty bakery and the buyer persona of the administrative assistant. Let's call him Adam. You know that Adam is responsible for buying cakes on special occasions such as employee birthdays and promotions.

An upcoming event is National Boss's Day, and Adam is likely looking for a way for the team to recognize their boss. In this case, you know the persona, the reason he wants to buy, and that he needs to make a purchasing decision (in this case, place an order for a cake!) by a specific date.

Let's say you run a Facebook ad campaign for National Boss's Day. Where is the best place on your website to send Adam (or drive visitors similar to Adam) from the ad? You could send him to your bakery's home page, but that's very general. It tells a lot about the bakery and different types of cakes you offer, but it may take him a while to click through to the right page to place an order for the cake, or he may get sidetracked looking at other types of cakes and never follow through with an order for the boss's cake. A better option is to send him directly to a landing page that's all about celebrating National Boss's Day with a cake designed specifically for his boss and offers an incentive or discount for calling to place a custom order. Or, you could send Adam to a product page on your website that showcases different types of designs for National Boss's Day and allows Adam to immediately click an order button to buy one of the standard cakes.

By matching the buyer's intent (stage) and persona to a specific page that has a clear goal, you're more likely to get the designated conversion you want, whether that means the buyer orders a product or watches a product demonstration.

Enticing Customers to Convert

Driving traffic is certainly one approach to increasing your rate of success. After all, if converting visitors to buyers is indeed a numbers game, the more site visitors, the more buyers you *potentially* will convert. Your actual conversion rate may remain the same, but if you now have 4,000 visitors per day (instead of the 500 we used in our earlier example), your 2 percent conversion rate should bring in 80 sales. Right?

Statistically, your odds for gaining more sales should increase with a greater number of visitors. But consider the cost of increasing those odds. Using paid keyword searches and online advertising, you could end up spending thousands of dollars (or more!) for that increased traffic count. A different approach is to increase your rate of conversion by getting more of your visitors to buy. For example, by increasing your conversion rate to 4 percent with your existing website traffic, you essentially double your sales, without spending the money required to double your traffic.

How do you get people to click that Buy button more frequently? One part of the answer requires attracting more of the right type of visitors to your website — those visitors who have signaled they are more interested in buying based on the personas and stages of the buyer's journey. The second part of the answer is focusing on site functionality that may deter conversions. According to research, the following factors influence the conversion of browsers to buyers:

>> **Your site's security:** Buyers prefer to make a purchase from the site that is most secure. This means keeping your SSL certificate updated and clearly displaying privacy policies and recognizable trust seals, such as those from the Better Business Bureau.

>> **Multiple options for payments:** Customers want and need choices when it comes to making a purchase. These options include credit cards, debit cards, PayPal, and extended payment option programs.

In addition, increasing conversion rates may also be a matter of making buying easier:

>> **Decrease clicks.** Reduce the number of clicks required to get from your home page to a product page, or from the product page to completing the purchase transaction.

>> **Minimize buying headaches.** Some research shows the rate of shopping cart abandonment at 60 percent to 75 percent! You can reduce that percentage by requiring only a few steps to complete a purchase, or by increasing the functionality of your shopping cart.

>> **Incentivize buying now.** Offer reasons for a customer to buy on the spot, such as a small discount, a freebie that comes with the purchase, or free shipping — but only if the customer makes a purchase on that day's visit to your site.

>> **Add online chat.** Include the opportunity for guests to receive real-time support using online chat. Having the ability to get product questions answered immediately can speed up a customer's decision to buy.

>> **Guarantee it.** Whether you offer a money-back guarantee or the manufacturer of a product offers a full or limited warranty, make this information readily available to your shoppers. Also include a link to your store's return policy. These pieces of information can put customers at ease and make them more willing to purchase an item from you.

>> **Display customer reviews.** It's no secret that as consumers, almost all of us are influenced by others' experiences and opinions, which is one reason why product reviews by customers are so popular. Your online customers may be more inclined to make a purchasing decision if they can see that other customers were satisfied with the product.

In addition, you should think like a customer. When making changes to your site, consider what factors influence your own decision to buy when shopping with an online retailer. Chances are, the things that encourage or discourage your buying behaviors are the same as for your customers. And addressing these concerns is the first step to boosting your site's conversion rate. Understanding how site design and functionality influence buying behaviors is part of designing for user experience (also referred to as UX). We discuss how to improve UX design of your website in Book 3.

Purchasing right now: The instant customer

The best scenario for any online business is having every single visitor who stops by your website make a purchase. Not only would you have a phenomenal conversion rate, but hitting your desired revenue goals would also be a slam dunk! Given that we've already shared the fact that conversion rates are often on the lower side, a 100 percent conversion is probably unlikely.

You can increase the likelihood that a visitor becomes a buyer by using some of the strategies in this chapter, but there are also some visitors who are more likely to buy sooner, rather than later. How do you know if they're ready to buy right away? It goes back to understanding your buyer personas and defining what makes them tick, or in this case, buy.

Here are some of the most frequent types of instant buyers. We're betting you'll have few of these that frequent your website, or can be convinced to stop by and spend money, today!

>> **Repeat customers:** As an existing online business, you're sitting on a gold mine of data, including customers who keep coming back to buy more. Figure out how often they buy, when they buy (time of year, time of day, and so on), and why they buy or what prompts a purchase (such as a special offer or discount coupon). These are the buyers who it makes sense to invest time and dollars to target with ads and email or anything that brings them to your site.

>> **Spontaneous buyers:** There's a reason that grocery stores and traditional retailers put a lot of effort into displaying merchandise at or near the checkout register. These areas are often stocked with splurge items, or treats that don't always make it on a shopping list. That's because it pays to tempt shoppers with one more quick purchase while they wait in line to pay. The same goes for your online buyers. Some types of buyers are likely to make a quick decision based on a tempting offer. In e-commerce, social media is an ideal place to target these spontaneous buyers. For those visitors who make it to your website and have already made a purchase, you can increase the average purchase by offering a price discount to add a complementary

product to their shopping cart, or offer free shipping if they buy another $25 worth of product.

>> **Engaged buyers:** Some visitors to your website give off buying signals, or strong indicators that they're ready to make a purchase. Perhaps they have visited a specific, typically high-converting landing page, or visited lots of pages on your site over a short period of time. Or, maybe they've initiated online chats and asked detailed questions about a product. Equally engaging is that they've responded to an email or social media ad with a time-sensitive offer. These are all signals that this visitor is highly likely to buy, soon.

>> **Occasion-driven buyers:** As in the examples we use in this chapter, there are some buyers who have a specific timeline, or deadline, for buying — like the administrative assistant who needs a cake for National Boss's Day. There are lots of types of occasions or events that may force an online buying decision. Think in terms of holidays, weddings, proms, graduation, or anything that has a hard end date associated with it. Even B2B buyers have similar deadline-driven occasions, especially around the end of the quarter or end of the year when a buyer may be in a crunch to show progress on a goal or meeting budget and spending deadlines for new tools. Attracting these buyers to your site at the time they need to make a purchasing decision often results in a shorter sales cycle than is typical.

Nurturing the indecisive (or not-yet-ready to convert) site visitor

Not all site visitors are as easily convinced to make a purchase but that doesn't mean you give up on them. You never know, these more cautious shoppers may just become some of your most loyal customers. After all, they've taken a lot of time to get to know you, research your products, and read online reviews. In fact, these seemingly indecisive visitors have probably decided they *want* to buy from you, or at least they're seriously considering it — they just need a little more convincing. This is the perfect type of website visitor for you to spend time nurturing, or giving them a bit of TLC (and a lot more information) to lead them to a final purchase. Here are two ways to reach and nurture this hesitant buyer.

>> **Email:** This is when it pays to have a good marketing automation platform, like HubSpot. When you can identify your site visitors (you know their email addresses and they give permission for you to send them emails), add them to an email marketing campaign. Usually, this means emailing them on a regular schedule over a certain period of time. For B2C, this cadence may be once every two weeks for six months. For B2B, it may mean emailing once a month for a full year. The idea is to stay in touch and send emails that contain

interesting or helpful information to nudge them a little further down the buyer's journey. They may need to see videos showing ways to use the product, or maybe they want more customer testimonials. As they respond to the emails and engage with the content, this provides information back to you as to what additional content or information they need to finally pull the lever and make a purchase.

>> **Retarget:** Another way to stay in front of indecisive buyers and make sure they're getting helpful content is to use paid media (such as Google Ads and social media ads) to retarget your site visitors. *Retargeting* is basically following would-be buyers after they leave your site and showing them ads in the places they visit next. For example, maybe you have a visitor who looked at one of your product pages for waffle irons but left before buying one. Then he went to Facebook to check out his news feed. You can retarget him or show him more ads about your waffle iron. You may even prompt a sponsored video to show up that takes a humorous approach to why waffles are better than pancakes. The point is that you keep your product and your website in front of him after he leaves your site.

The goal of nurturing visitors who don't make an instant buying decision is to simply keep top-of-mind awareness about your website and the products or services you offer. Sometimes, these buyers need more education on why it makes sense to buy from you, and email is the perfect vehicle for this. Other times, you may need to just keep popping up in front of the site visitor and give a little nudge to encourage a purchase, which is where social media ads and retargeting come into play. Want to learn more about this approach to online marketing? We discuss using social media and Google Ads in Chapter 3 of this minibook.

Chapter **2**

Your Own Public Relations for the Web

Although *PR* stands for *press release,* you don't always have to draw attention to your business in the form of a press release. Publicity can come in many forms, and by using the Internet, you can differentiate yourself and your company to attract customers in lots of ways. You've probably heard the phrase "There's no such thing as bad publicity." Well, if your customers are unhappy and advise everyone they know to avoid your business, we're sure that it won't help your bottom line.

You must be out among the community you depend on to build a relationship for customers to connect and use your business. You not only gain a sense of what customers want and need in their lives, but also connect with the community to help sell the story of you and your business. Consider the time you spend online reaching out to your community as an investment. You're building intangible relations, the goodwill that a positive company can generate, and the reason why these customers should shop with you and not someone else.

In this chapter, we focus on the publicity that revolves more around you and your product knowledge. We explore different ways in which you can indirectly promote your company while demonstrating your expertise and competence in your product's subject area. If you establish yourself as a leader or expert, customers will consider your business.

Every time you give, you receive in return. When you contribute information, opinions, reviews, or specific knowledge, people see that it's coming from the owner of Business X, not just from an individual. They believe that they can get to know both you and, through you, your business. Customers are looking for a connection, a bond, a reason to go with a particular business. Give it to them.

Writing Reviews

Most shoppers are used to seeing positive and glowing comments about a product clearly printed on the product box. They more highly value third-party independent reviews, however. After all, what company would slap the label *Worst Product Ever* on its product packaging? However, if thousands or millions of people are rallying because they're not happy with a product, consumers will give that action much more weight than a company's endorsements.

The independent testing organization Consumer Reports (www.consumerreports.org) rates everything from automobiles to computers to garden equipment. It has more than 4 million subscribers to its magazine and an estimated 2 million people to its subscription website, where thousands of reviews, statistical test data, and evaluations are available for members to see. When customers are shopping online, they don't have the option to ask their local shopkeeper what he or she thinks about an item or to hear about how that shopkeeper helped a customer with an item that worked well (or not so well) at home. Customers turn then to reviews written online about the product, which is where you can make your entrance.

As someone with access to these products, and a history with them, you likely know more than the average person about some of the products you sell. Although you might not have used everything you sell, you have a better idea about how to evaluate a product or you gathered enough customer comments to form an opinion based on a fact.

When you write reviews, readers typically can access your profile and find out more about you. You might be surprised at the number of people who take the time to do so. Maybe they were impressed or intrigued by your comments about a product and want to learn more. Or maybe they're impressed by your depth of knowledge and want to know what else you approve or disapprove of. After customers identify you as knowledgeable, your opinion takes on greater weight, and so does your business.

In this section, we show you how to put those thoughts together and write some reviews of the products you sell.

Finding the best places to post reviews

The most valuable place your reviews can be posted is on your own website. After all, you're contributing this value to help your online business succeed and empower your customers to make better decisions. Therefore, you should incorporate any reviews you write to appear alongside the products you're selling on your own website.

After that, you want to spread the word about your knowledge and demonstrate to the larger community your experience with, and the professionalism of, a given product, to raise your profile as a product expert and expose new potential customers to your company. Start by doing some investigating online, and look for websites that offer reviews of products you carry.

These major online sites offer reviews:

>> **YouTube (www.youtube.com):** We're currently living in the era of video, where people use their smartphones to record quick, sometimes amusing, mostly helpful reviews of things they use and love. (There's a whole industry of people recording their efforts to unbox products!) You can search on YouTube to find the best or most relevant reviews based on the products or specifics you want, and learn from other people's analysis and recommendations on what to buy, in categories that range the entire spectrum.

>> **Amazon (www.amazon.com):** The world's largest online retailer offers a wealth of reviews for its growing catalog of items. These reviews and comments are some of the drawing points for customers to this site.

>> **Yelp (www.yelp.com):** The world's largest review-centric site focuses more on the service industry, but when people want to use a specific vendor or try a specific business, odds are, they're going to Yelp to see what other people say about the business. Encourage your customers and partners to provide reviews, but be careful not to explicitly bribe or coerce any reviews from them. You want natural, organic reviews from happy customers to encourage future business.

>> **CNet Reviews (www.cnet.com/reviews):** This online technology news site has amassed a growing array of product reviews for computers and consumer electronics and even services such as web hosting. Below the editor's reviews is a section where all user reviews are grouped and averaged per product.

>> **Facebook (www.facebook.com):** Every page that you can like, whether it's for a local business, brand, event, or almost any organization, has a Reviews section where its users can input their reviews, as shown in Figure 2-1. These reviews are summarized on the main page, but you can click through and read what other users think of the business or brand behind their Facebook page.

FIGURE 2-1:
Read reviews
about businesses
and brands on
Facebook.

Other places cater to different niches, such as Growing a Green Family's Product Reviews (www.growingagreenfamily.com/green-product-reviews) for ecofriendly products and *PC Magazine* (www.pcmag.com/reviews) for computer components. If necessary, ask some of your customers where they do their research before they buy. For truly unfiltered reviews, check out Reddit (www.reddit.com) and see if there is a subchannel for your product. Lots of different consumers create threads on a daily basis about everything.

REMEMBER

Every once in a while, you should check up on your product reviews to see what other readers are saying in response. Reader feedback can provide invaluable advice about whether your reviews are hitting the mark or are too confusing. Keep an open mind about their comments, and treat this strategy as another learning exercise.

In the end, you should be persistent and not overbearing. Allocate a specific amount of time per week to contribute reviews so that you don't spend all your time filling up page after page. Stay current, and approach new avenues as you have time. If you deal in new products, make sure that you're one of the first people to review a product. That way, you lend greater authority to your opinion and provide your own helpful early warning if you review an item you sell that customers have a frustrating time using properly.

Writing the review, section by section

After you know where to post your review, it's time to write one! You don't need an English degree to write reviews, and you don't have to carefully research, document, and stamp each one for approval. Most people are looking for honest, candid, easy-to-understand information that breaks down the essentials about a product. The best way we have heard someone describe how to write a review is this: "If friends asked you what you thought about product X, you could hand them your review as the answer."

TIP

Have the product in front of you when you start writing. Being able to hold up the product, scan its box, read its specifications, and experiment with the product can trigger thoughts and confirm suspicions when you're writing a review.

When you're ready to write a review, make sure that it has these basic sections:

REMEMBER

>> **Initial impressions:** Start by writing your initial impressions of the product. What were your initial thoughts the first time you saw the product? What did you think about the first time you used the product? What were you hoping the product would provide, and what did you expect it to be?

Don't worry about immediately assigning a product a number between 1 and 10 or coming up with a title. These issues should be the last ones you write about, because writing the rest of the review can lead you to the ultimate ranking answer.

Your initial impressions should provide a quick summary of the product, your impressions, and a sense of whether you favor it. Someone reading only your first paragraph should see all the basic information and know whether you approve or disapprove.

>> **Pros:** Write the reasons you like the product, no matter how big or small the issue. Include the ways that this product is better than similar products on the market, and describe its best features.

>> **Cons:** Write the reasons you dislike the product. Think of the features you're not happy with or that you wish could be changed. Note whether the problem prevents you from using the product correctly or just bothers you individually. Obviously, rank the problems that affect your usage higher than your personal opinion.

>> **Experience with the product:** Regardless of whether you love the product or hate it, does it do what it's supposed to do? If it's a digital camera, for example, does it take high-quality photos? Even if the camera is hard to use and its battery life is low, does it perform its main functions? Most products have a purpose or a use, and people want to know how this product can help them. A great-looking item might be completely useless, or an item that solves a big problem might be difficult to use.

TIP

Talk about your experience with your product in a positive, non-confrontational way. Don't say that you love it because it sells well. Say that you love it because the product is so solid that your customers love it and that's why it sells well.

» **Recommendations:** Would you buy your product? Would you recommend it to someone? Would you recommend it only for a specialized need or a certain kind of user?

After you complete all these areas, you should have a good idea of how you would rank the product on a scale from 1 to 10. You might be asked to rank certain individual characteristics on some websites, so consider them last too, after you think about the good, the bad, and the ugly.

The title of your review should be a one-sentence summary that captures the essence of what you're saying. The easiest titles to write are for products you absolutely love ("This product is the best thing since sliced bread!") or absolutely hate ("Don't buy this product, even if they're giving it away!"). For most reviews that lie between these two ends of the spectrum, choose a good point and a bad point, and emphasize the one you most agree with. For example, say something like "Good product for the money, but don't expect full features!" or "Product X: Adequate but in need of improvement."

TIP

Make sure that your reviews are sincere and honest. Don't rave about a product just because you sell it and hope that a good review will boost sales. Readers will see through an insincere review, and your plan could backfire because they will go online and warn other consumers not to trust you or your reviews, opinions, or business.

After you have completed your written review, you can also turn it into a video review. Record yourself in front of a computer webcam, a handheld video recorder or tablet device (such as an Apple iPad), or even certain smartphones, and then upload the product review to popular video-sharing sites such as YouTube. Don't forget to brand your review by embedding a link to your website. Video allows you to visually demonstrate a physical product, which will only add to your review's effect. If and when you do a number of video reviews, you can set up your own YouTube channel where people can subscribe to you and see your most recent postings.

Becoming an Online Influencer

Building a business is not only time-consuming, but also rewarding and educational. Your work, however, doesn't end with your own website. Interaction with the community is essential for any business, whether you hang a shingle or code a web page. On the Internet, you have ways to participate as a business owner that lend credibility and raise the collective energy of your community, who will remember those qualities when it's time to buy. Your expertise can help you become an *influencer,* sharing your knowledge with others in the hopes of gaining a following that will listen to you and perhaps check out your business.

Speaking out with video

In the past, you could make connections with potential customers by agreeing to speak at their Rotary Club or Chamber of Commerce meetings about your chosen subject area. The Internet and high technology have combined to create different ways for you to deliver that same information — without the rubber chicken and the echo from the borrowed sound system. The two most popular ways to communicate online are through graphics and videos, and Instagram and YouTube are the top sites to post and communicate this information.

The old adage is that a picture speaks a thousand words. Today, online culture values the use of pictures so much that a site like Instagram was born, simply to post and display images that matter to you (and hopefully other people), whether it's on a personal or professional level. Other Instagram users decide who they want to follow, and those people's pictures make up a person's Instagram feed, which most Instagram users monitor on a daily (or more frequent) basis.

TIP

Because your "followers" are choosing to follow you, the pictures you post need to convey a certain purpose. If all you do is post one boring product picture after another, with very little information in the caption/comment section, you won't gain many followers. Instead, focus on the newest and greatest products that hit your inventory, sale images of specific promotions, behind-the-scenes photos of what's going on within your business, or how customers or employees are actually using the products you sell. You want to offer a careful balance of information and entertainment through Instagram. We recommend looking at existing Instagram accounts from your competitors or people in your product space to see what the prevalent strategies are that matter to your industry. And check out *Instagram For Business For Dummies,* by Jennifer Herman, Eric Butow, and Corey Walker (Wiley), for tips and trick.

When you prepare and deliver a webinar, you control the message, the delivery of that message, and all the accompanying information that goes with the message. The formatting of your presentation is always the same with a webinar, and your presence cannot be deleted, because your image, voice, and slides drive the presentation. One leading service that produces webinars is WebEx Event Center. You can read about WebEx Event Center services and prices by going to `www.webex.com/products/webinars-and-online-events.html`.

In the past, many people learned through in-person seminars or web seminars (known as *webinars*), but today many people learn through shorter videos, and one of the leading websites that hosts and promotes this content is YouTube, which is owned by Google. YouTube is considered the second most popular search engine based on number of requests, as people now type their queries into YouTube to get an answer delivered to them with video, not just with plain words with Google.

Whether you use your smartphone, laptop webcam, or professional video equipment to record your videos, the key is to focus on a clear delivery of information, something that can take a few minutes (on average) to illustrate. As you record more and more videos, you may want to consider getting your own YouTube channel so that all your videos are accessible in one spot to all your current and potential customers.

Given the volume of educational videos on YouTube, YouTube organized this information into a dedicated YouTube channel called Creator Academy (https:// creatoracademy.youtube.com/page/education). Your focused educational videos can be a part of this system and help potential customers learn more about areas where you can offer useful information.

TIP

Given the shorter time frame with a YouTube video, organize your thoughts for a video like you're delivering one precise lesson, not an entire classroom lecture.

Book 4, Chapter 3 provides more information about how you can turn video into its own profit center rather than just a mechanism for raising your profile.

Billing yourself as an expert

Given the immense amount of information and options for consumers, the easiest way for them to cut through all the noise and presentations of the high-tech world to find what they're looking for is to rely on the low-tech, time-tested tradition known as *word of mouth*. Most customers make their decisions based on recommendations from family members and friends. In the absence of a friend or family member, however, online consumers look for an expert in that area. That's where you come in.

Expertise isn't a degree that a university can confer on you; it's the real-world experience you build up in a given subject area or product category. It's up to you to share that information in a constructive way so that customers see you as the expert. After customers start asking you for advice, they also find out about your business. When it's time for them to buy a product, they're much more likely to choose someone they consider an expert over a nameless, faceless website with a slightly lower price.

To become an expert, spend some time in the places where your potential customers congregate and ask questions about your area of expertise. Four of the most popular places to frequent are Twitter, LinkedIn, discussion groups, and mailing lists. Follow these general steps:

1. **Identify the discussion groups, LinkedIn Groups, Facebook groups, or Twitter topics that pertain to your area.**

Dig around, do some research, and use search engines or your favorite websites to see where people are gathering online to discuss topics.

2. **Join the designated groups, and find out how to participate correctly.**

Take the time to complete the registration processes at each of these sites, and choose usernames that advertise you, not your business. If people see that a corporate name is contributing information, they might see it as an invasion for sales only. (For Twitter, see what topic names, or *hashtags,* are used consistently, and be sure to use the relevant hashtag in your reply.)

3. **Set up your profile and signature file.**

Make sure that your business and website address are clearly mentioned at the bottom of your signature file and Twitter Profile Bio field, so that people can follow up if they're interested.

TIP

In your profile and signature page, always reference one landing page, or a web page that will consistently reference all your online posts, websites, and online references.

4. **Start looking for discussions and questions that you can contribute to easily.**

Start by monitoring conversations to develop a sense for the tone that people use in their responses. Don't feel that you have to dive in right away. Start by providing a comment here and there, and take some time in the beginning to observe the atmosphere and get to know the major contributors.

WARNING

Don't use these places for blatant self-promotion. Participate in a healthy manner, and make sure that your signature file contains a line or two about your web business.

5. **Set up a regular schedule to contribute to one or more discussions.**

Include this process in your weekly routine so that you don't forget about it as time goes on. Maybe you spend a half-hour each Tuesday logging in to see the most active discussions. You can spend a few minutes each day and look for the most relevant discussions for your area. Find something that fits your schedule so that you have the time to participate without feeling rushed.

TIP

Make sure that each posting is free of any obvious spelling and grammatical errors. Use a word processing program, such as Microsoft Word, to write your post so that you can easily check and correct mistakes. Then copy and paste your words into the listing.

Writing Articles

When people share information, they don't limit themselves to just one or two channels. Countless sites are set up to satisfy people's need for more information, organized around every imaginable subject, discipline, passion, hobby, and criteria. Although these sites are good at organization and attracting traffic, they all usually want help with one particular area: content.

People who contribute content gain lots of exposure by sharing their information. The exposure comes from one simple requirement that you tie in to your free articles: Your name, as the author, contains a profile that links to your website. You allow anyone to publish, reprint, or distribute your article, as long as your profile information is attached. That way, everyone who reads these articles knows that you're the source of that information and is inclined to check out your company's website to see what else is out there.

Free distribution of your articles has other important benefits. As more and more websites pick up your article and publish it, more search engines pick up the link in your profile. Many search engines, especially Google, now rank search results based partially on how many people make references to a given web page. Your articles create more references on the web, and ultimately raise your ranking, so you naturally appear in a user's search results and don't have to pay as much in search engine advertising. (See Book 6, Chapter 3 for more information on search engine advertising.)

Tailoring your article topics

When you were told to write a paper in school, you probably didn't have much choice about the topic. Now you have complete control, so be sure to write articles that appeal to your customer base. You can easily fall into the trap of writing only what you know, even if that topic is nowhere near what your customers would be reading.

REMEMBER

Writing what you know about works in the beginning, if you need some motivation to start writing articles.

As a business owner, you're already looking to stay ahead of the curve to see where your market is heading. Now you get to use that knowledge to help tell customers what to expect. You can choose from a variety of angles for your article, including these:

>> Provide straightforward, concise explanations and examples of a new technology.

>> Provide "the personal touch" by describing how you got through a certain situation and what you learned from it.

>> List four or five nonobvious ways that a product or service can be beneficial.

>> Create a step-by-step guide for accomplishing a specific task.

>> Describe how to improve a (popular) way of doing something.

>> Specify what not to do in a given area.

>> Create a case study showing someone's right and wrong actions, and then explain why.

You can also use existing data to help you develop the articles that should appeal to your customer base. Websites like NinjaOutreach (www.ninjaoutreach.com) crawl social media sites in your industry to help you understand who you're trying to reach and which current influencers are doing the best job, so you can learn from their output. When writing your articles, be sure to integrate the keywords that your customers are using to find you. Don't use so many keywords that it feels like spam, but use the right keywords when appropriate.

One point to consider is the length of your article because that may influence the topic. If you're looking for a "quick hit," then a popular type of article is the *listicle*, which is basically a step list or top-ten list that can be easily scanned. If you want to write a longform post about a bigger topic, make sure it's something that you can write about at length and not something you have to struggle to complete. Many Internet users are interested in both types of articles, and everything in between, to the point that sites like Facebook now help estimate how many minutes it'll take to read a linked article.

The best topics, sometimes, are about issues you just faced with your business or your personal online adventures. Think about how you handled a given situation. Did you learn a new trick or two along the way? Did the recommended solution pan out? Did an unorthodox method (or even the tried-and-true method) produce measurable results? If so, ask yourself this question: "Would other people benefit from what I just learned?" If so, and if you're not revealing a competitive advantage, start making notes to turn into an article.

Putting together your article

Don't be afraid to brainstorm and jot down ideas to revisit later. Your articles have to capture readers' attention, even if it's just for the first paragraph, so it has to be relevant, useful, and interesting. Most people — whether they're reading newspaper stories, magazine features, or online write-ups — see a headline, read (maybe) the first paragraph, and then move on. That's why articles have to grab you in the first paragraph.

Put together your articles in this fashion:

TIP

>> **The first paragraph** presents the overall picture. You need to accurately and vividly describe the situation you address in your article. If the article is about a solution to a problem, first discuss the problem. Remind readers about how much of a headache this problem can cause, and detail the pain, so to speak. If you're writing a step-by-step guide, use the first paragraph to talk about the problem this guide will solve. Then make sure that you end the first paragraph by telling readers what you will say in the rest of the article.

>> **Middle paragraphs** contain the "meat," or the essence, of the article — namely, the information that readers want to read. Stay away from technical jargon or low-level details or specifics, and provide an overview in plain English of what readers should do, look into, or implement themselves. Let them do the additional research of finding the specifics. Your article should identify the solution path and give readers enough information to continue investigating.

Nowadays, people are using interviews as part of their articles, so don't be afraid to interview others and sprinkle their responses as they relate to the article topic. In addition, some articles are just "guest posts" from other people, like your partners, customers, or colleagues.

>> **The last paragraph** wraps up your article with a summary of what you presented, and shares either a success story or a result that readers can expect afterward. If readers need to take action after reading your article, you want to leave them with an important reason to get started, even if it's an obvious reason.

The average length of an article is about 300 to 600 words, or one or two double-spaced pages in a word processor. If you're direct and to the point, don't worry about sending out a 280-word article. Conversely, if your article continues page after page, it had better be useful and not repetitive or fluffy.

Even though you're not being graded on your work, be sure to check for any spelling or grammatical errors before you send it out. Mistakes detract from the professional image you want to convey in your article, which would defeat the purpose.

If you're curious about whether your article is ready for distribution, use a small group of friends, employees, or customers as your test market by sending them a copy and asking for honest feedback. Don't expect them to correct any mistakes — just listen to their feedback and consider their comments. A peer review usually makes a piece stronger, and a stronger article is more effective.

Spreading your (article) knowledge

After you write and prepare your article with the correct profile and web link, you need to distribute the goods. The easiest way to start is to use the channels easily available to you — specifically, your social media pages, a blog (if you have one), or information/content for your online business website. Many articles make great blog posts or new items for your Facebook business page or Twitter stream. You gain publicity and reinforce the image you're presenting to your audience. Every reference to a new article shows how you're working to keep the community informed and gives you a great reason for a new, current blog entry.

After those initial steps, see if your customers, employees, or network at large would be willing or interested in sharing it with their own communities. Good information is valued over a simple sales pitch all the time, and as long as you're clearly credited as the author of the article, with at least one link back to your website or profile, the spread of information will only enhance your ability to be an influencer and to help your online business.

If you're already a member of niche news sites, you could check into submitting your article directly to them. Look for an email address of the editorial director or a reporter in the About Us section of that website, and send an introductory letter along with your article. You might be offered a column or contributor status, or you can serve, at the least, as a good source to find quotes for the site's upcoming articles in your area of expertise. The effort of sharing these articles all goes back to raising your exposure and achieving expert status. After all, you never know who might read your article next.

IN THIS CHAPTER

» Implementing a total marketing strategy

» Creating a long-term conversation with customers by using social media

» Offering newsletters to lure in potential customers

» Advertising through a pay-per-click strategy

» Marketing your business in nonelectric ways

Chapter 3

Web Marketing at Work

Regardless of how big your online business is or will become, the power of the web is a far-reaching and low-cost way to effectively turn people on to what you provide. One reason for the effectiveness of web marketing is the power of *one-to-one marketing*. Rather than create TV ads that speak to tens of millions of people during a popular sitcom, for example, web marketing speaks directly to your interested customers and builds a one-to-one connection between a potential customer and your business. These first-time buyers can become repeat customers who spread the word about your company to new customers; your business continues to grow with each wave. Online sites such as Craigslist grew in popularity because people came together not just to buy and sell stuff but also to find jobs, apartments, romance, and events in their geographical areas.

Many people believe that web marketing works for only the big companies that can rent banner ads and host lavish websites with large email distribution lists. The truth is that small businesses and entrepreneurs, just like you, can benefit from the same techniques that the larger companies employ, by investing time and effort along with dollars. In this chapter, we show you how to use these marketing techniques to reach potential customers.

Developing a Marketing Strategy

In the early days of the Internet, you could build a website, get mentioned in the right places, and instantly receive a stream of customers, whether you sold sweaters or homemade apple butter. You didn't have much competition, and a hungry audience would soak up whatever they could find. Now, websites and online commerce companies sell everything that's legal (and a few things that aren't), and competition is fierce and ever-present. The days of building a website and receiving instant traffic are mostly over. In this section, we show you how to use branding and a targeted advertising strategy to spread the word about your business.

REMEMBER

Hit the right concept at the right time, however, and you might find early success. When people heard of Google, a search engine that provided relevant results, they started using it more and more. When anyone could create a video file and share that video on the Internet with other users, who could rate and comment on those videos, YouTube jumped to the top of the charts of the social networking trend.

Devising your brand

To get your business noticed, you need to come up with a basic, all-encompassing strategy. This strategy defines and drives your marketing efforts. Always send the right message from the start so that you don't confuse your customers and waste your money.

The first part of your strategy is to create your brand image. Your *brand image* is the message that your company portrays in everything you do, from telling people about your business to treating its customers a certain way to providing value through your products and services. It's not one piece, but rather the overall sense that customers and your general audience get when they think of your business. Your brand is shaped by the successful combination of a memorable logo, a catchy slogan, a distinctive color scheme, and more. These elements all influence how your customers view your business, but individually, these elements are not your brand. Your brand is the impression your customers have of your business, and that impression is triggered by seeing the memorable logo, catchy slogan, distinctive color scheme, and more.

What should your brand be? Consider these points to get you started as you devise your brand:

>> **Competitive prices:** Because you have an online business, you're not paying for expensive retail space and a carpet for customers to trip on as they walk through the front door. You can therefore offer lower prices than your offline competitors.

>> **Convenience:** Your customers can interact with the business even when they're wearing pajamas.

>> **Customize requests:** You can provide each customer's specific request or match people with similar interests.

Although we could give you more examples, the lesson here is that you have options. Choose the brand that fits with your company.

Working the brand

After you have an idea for an appropriate brand, it's time to share it with the world. Because your business operates online, you can easily promote your business online. Billions of dollars are spent each year on web advertising (just look at Google's numbers), and the numbers increase each quarter.

Rather than pay for a billboard that you hope people see on their way to work, make your web advertising stare customers in the face — literally. You're speaking to a captive audience because the advertising is part of the screen, built into the web page in a variety of ways. In addition, you have a better chance of having the right ad reach the right customer because you can better target who receives which ad.

Because many companies offer advertising opportunities, you want to find the markets that best push your brand. Think about whom you want to reach with your brand. If your brand involves power tools and improving the home, maybe a website that offers cooking tips isn't the right place for you to advertise. If your company appeals to the teenage consumer, YouTube, chat applications like WhatsApp, and social media websites are good places to start.

You can reach out through the web and advertise your brand and company in many ways:

>> **Paid advertising:** Many sites offer options, such as banner ads, center ads, and paid-placement spots where you can rent space based on how many people click through to your website. This way, you can track the *click ratio* to see how effective certain sites are to your brand, and pay only when someone who wants to find out more clicks your link.

TECHNICAL STUFF

Click ratio refers to the percentage of people who click a specific ad based on the total population who saw that ad. You calculate the click ratio by dividing the number of times someone clicked an ad by the number of times the ad was displayed. On average, click ratios can range from 0.5 or 1 percent to 5 or 10 percent on specialized sites.

>> **Social media:** Businesses of all sizes are using social media websites, such as Facebook, Twitter, Instagram, Pinterest, and Tumblr, to reach out where their customers are hanging out. These businesses use the sites to stay relevant, broadcast important information, and create a long-term connection with potential and existing customers instead of just trying to sell one product. With social media, you're selling the customer on your business, not a particular product.

>> **Partnerships:** Rather than pay outright to be on someone's website, come up with a partnership deal in which you and another company promote each other to your users. You can make

- *A simple deal:* You and the other company put each other's banner ads on your own site.

- *A complex deal:* You and the other company create joint promotions and provide links back and forth.

>> **Classified advertising:** Rather than place banner ads that advertise your company, you can take out classified ads that market a specific product or sale item. Many sites allow you to post free ads, such as Craigslist (`www.craigslist.org`), LetGo (`www.letgo.com`), OfferUp (`www.offerup.com`), and even some local community social network online classifieds sections.

>> **Product placement:** In this form of advertising, you arrange to get your products mentioned and your website referenced by someone else. You can do it through a blog, or someone can feature a review of your product on a website after you send a sample.

>> **Keyword searches:** Search engines offer advertising that can appear on the same web page as search results. You can bid on the right to have your ad appear for a given keyword that someone types. See the "Searching for Traffic with Search Engine Advertising" section, later in this chapter, for more information.

Big advertising campaigns don't necessarily mean big budgets. You need to think about every move that you make online, and the best campaigns start at home. Your own website needs to reflect the brand that you want to present to your customers. Every email you send should mention your business and website address. When you contribute to any online discussions, chat rooms, or groups, make sure that your business and website are carefully displayed at the bottom of any posting you make. Small actions like these can lead to name recognition, which can lead to customer recognition and acquisition.

Gaining a Following with Social Media

Someone once said, "Go where your customers are." When people started using social media websites such as Facebook to keep in touch with each other and share updates, businesses quickly followed, building their own presences and business pages where fans of that business could stay in touch with that business; hear about contests, promotions, and sales; and have direct communication when there was something they liked (or disliked) about the business.

Today, websites use social media for various purposes. Some websites maintain Facebook and Twitter accounts simply to broadcast upcoming sales, specials, and Facebook-only or Twitter-only discounts or deals. As mentioned earlier in this chapter, other websites have an expanded presence that includes social media sites such as Google+, Instagram, Pinterest, and Tumblr, where they share photos and new content, host unique contests, gather feedback on new products, and handle customer service inquiries immediately to prevent a backlash when something goes wrong. Some businesses go one step further and create original content for their social media presence or partner with other companies via social media to promote nonprofit causes or to create media events.

Using social media properly

A common mistake many businesses make with social media is to sign up for an account with these websites, set up some basic information initially, and then ignore or forget to use or update these accounts on a regular basis. Social media requires a long-term commitment, not a short-term promotion window. The most successful social media presences for businesses are updated regularly and contain useful, interesting, and helpful information not necessarily tied to the specific products or services of that business.

The other big mistake that businesses make with social media is to treat this avenue like other forms of advertising (such as search engine paid advertising) and try to make sales immediately from their social media audience. These companies talk only about products and specific sales on specific SKUs, and answer every question with "Well, we recommend the XJ9000 for that, because . . ."

When businesses understand that their social media presence needs to be a long-term, non-sales-focused, ongoing discussion between them and their customers, they begin to see the following benefits:

>> **Build trust and connections.** People like to shop with companies they know and trust. As your social media users interact with you on an ongoing basis, they get a feel for your company, see updates from your company, and begin

to include your company in their daily activities. They gain a higher sense of trust because they know you're a real company with real people instead of some "faceless" website that treats them like a number.

>> **Put some humanity in your posts.** Although you are a business, your customers will want to see the "human" side of the business, whether it's through showing a sense of humor, sharing employee pictures and likes/dislikes, or describing life at the company behind the scenes. Keep the content product-free, and you increase the likelihood of new and current customers increasing their bond with your company.

>> **Learn about problems before they explode.** Social media is immediate, so customers can write on Facebook or tweet about your product as soon as they receive it. When you have an ongoing presence, your customers can contact you immediately or you can monitor discussions regarding your brand. If some dissatisfaction or trouble is brewing online, you can respond right away and try to resolve open issues before letters are written and angry mobs show up on your doorstep.

>> **Turn customers into ambassadors.** The real power of social media comes from people passing along links, pictures, and information to their own networks immediately. When you announce something through your Facebook, Twitter, Google+, or other accounts, your current users can send the announcement to their own networks, so their friends see your updates as well. Information can be rebroadcast multiple times on multiple networks — suddenly, your update can go viral and gain exposure to thousands or even millions of potential customers overnight, mainly because the update came from a friend, not from some anonymous business.

Social media has other benefits as well, but we hope the core message is clear: Social media allows you to create an ongoing, one-on-one connection with your customers so that they can interact with you whether or not they're shopping, which leads to greater loyalty and more frequent purchases. As we discussed, the best way to proceed is to first do some planning, which we discuss in the next section.

TIP

If you want a guide for a detailed social media marketing strategy, check out *Social Media Marketing All-in-One For Dummies*, 4th Edition, by Jan Zimmerman and Deborah Ng (Wiley).

Determine who will administer your social media accounts

When you decide to use social media for your business, your first job is to determine who will administer the social media accounts for your business: perhaps someone in marketing, sales, public relations, IT, or a dedicated social media coordinator. You want to be consistent, so rotating the responsibility to different staff members is probably a bad idea.

When trying to decide who will administer the accounts, you should keep a few things in mind:

>> **Technical ability:** You will want someone comfortable with using technology, even for things as simple as writing and posting a Facebook update. As you grow your portfolio of social media accounts, you'll want someone who can handle video uploads, social media management software, and the ability to learn new social media sites.

>> **Consistency:** Whoever is managing the accounts needs to be able to give some time to this on a daily basis. If you pick someone who can only log on 1 hour a week, you miss out on the timeliness of social media and risk not responding to problems that could explode in your face.

>> **Writing ability:** While some social media sites, such as Twitter, don't require a lot of language skills to craft a lengthy message, other sites, such as Facebook, require someone who can write an appropriate post and answer questions in a clear and responsible fashion. This person will be "representing" the company online, so pick someone who can craft a message quickly, as you won't always have time to proofread everything this person posts online.

>> **Access to different divisions:** To represent all elements of your business, you want a social media coordinator who can, at minimum, get information from the different departments of your company.

Once you determine who will monitor your social media accounts, setting up a Facebook business page is easy. Here are the steps:

1. **Go to the Facebook home page at** www.facebook.com.

    The screen shown in Figure 3-1 appears.

2. **Click the Create a Page for a Celebrity, Band, or Business link (refer to Figure 3-1).**

    The Create a Page screen appears, as shown in Figure 3-2.

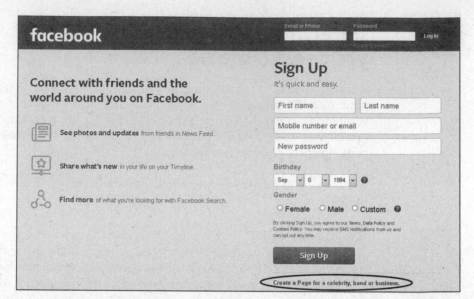

FIGURE 3-1:
Click the link to
create a business
page.

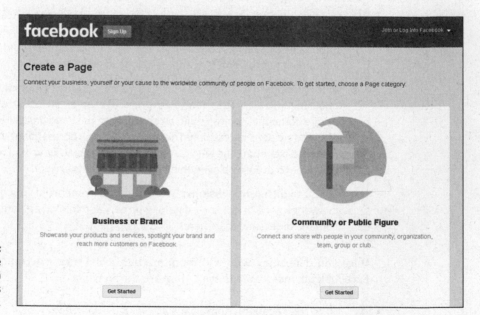

FIGURE 3-2:
Choose the type
of organization
that best matches
your business.

3. **Select a page option.**

Facebook has streamlined the options into two main categories: Business or
Brand, and Community or Public Figure. If your business revolves around a
specific public figure, you could pick Community or Public Figure, but most
people will probably pick Business or Brand here.

4. **Click the Get Started button under your page option.**

   Facebook wants to know whether to tie this new business page with an existing Facebook user account.

5. **Provide Facebook user account information for your business page:**

   - *If you already have a Facebook account,* log in and associate your user account with this new business account.

     Don't worry, your personal info will not show up on the business page. This information lets Facebook know who will be the administrator of the business page.

   - *If you don't have a Facebook account,* provide an email address and password that you'll use to log in as your business.

6. **Follow the prompts to start customizing your Facebook page.**

   Facebook begins with a step-by-step setup process. Simply fill out the prompts (like page name and category) and click Next in each section to add elements such as your profile photo and cover photo. When you're done, you'll see your newly created Facebook page. From here, you can continue to add content before promoting it to the world.

After you build your Facebook page, add a link to it from your website. Many companies use a clickable Facebook button to signify their Facebook page link. If you're using other social media sites, such as Twitter, don't forget to tweet your new Facebook page URL. Use any other means of communication with your customers — a newsletter, email marketing, marketing literature, or a sign in your store — to let them know about your Facebook page.

Reeling in Customers with Newsletters

You enticed someone to visit your site and maybe even buy something. What you really want, though, is a repeat customer. Studies have shown that getting an existing customer to return to your site is as much as six times more effective than getting a brand-new customer. You have to give people reasons to come back, and a newsletter gives them an added benefit of shopping with you and a reason for them to consider your business for their next purchase.

Newsletters are quickly becoming one of the most popular ways to promote a business. Customers are relying on regular communication, like newsletters, to keep companies at the top of their mind on a constant basis. Most newsletters are a combination of articles and information, with definite *plugs* for, or mentions of, specific products, sales events, or company news.

A regular newsletter to which people can subscribe has many benefits. You can

>> **Communicate with your customers.** Newsletters give you the opportunity to share why you're in business and what you can offer your customers. Although most people have trained themselves to skip pure advertisements, reading stories or tips can break down customer defenses so that they listen and find out more.

>> **Share information.** The products you sell have a specific use, so helping customers use the products more effectively gives your business an added value. If you sell cooking supplies, provide recipes and describe how your products help make different foods, for example. If you sell books in a specific genre, post customer reviews of the newest releases so that customers can decide whether they want to buy the latest Stephen King horror novel or "ripped from the headlines" legal thriller. Add pictures from your Instagram account, plus links to video clips to expand your multimedia capabilities.

WARNING

Don't just fill a newsletter with product announcements, sales offers, and discounts because then you have a flyer, not a newsletter. Carefully balance the content and promotion that goes into each newsletter. Although some people recommend a specific balance, such as 30 percent sales and 70 percent information, the key is to provide enough good information to make the newsletter worthwhile to the customer. In addition, don't load your newsletter with too many large files, like embedded video files.

>> **Build a connection.** If consumers become accustomed to receiving from you a regular newsletter that they find helpful, they build a connection in their minds that you're now a trusted source and will consider your business more carefully. They might think, "Oh, yeah, that's the company that sends out the Top 10 Tips that I read every week. Those people know what they're talking about, so I'll use them to order my next batch of supplies." In addition, by tying in customer stories or feedback that they shared via social media, in the newsletter, you create another bond by featuring the customer and giving your business a human face.

Creating your newsletter doesn't have to be a large and complex project full of deadlines and drama where you yell "Stop the presses!" whenever a new idea comes in. You do, however, have to do some planning, be consistent, and follow some guidelines. In the following sections, we discuss the planning you need to do.

TIP

You can also check out the excellent *E-Mail Marketing For Dummies*, 2nd Edition, by John Arnold for more information on developing and distributing your newsletter.

Decide who will write your newsletter

Many business owners think that their job is to create each newsletter and come up with all its fabulous content. If you have a staff, that shouldn't be the case. As the owner, you might want to have your own newsletter column or introduction to which you sign your name, and then have different people contribute different parts of the newsletter. Decide in advance who will produce which section because it's better to have that system in place than to scramble every time a newsletter needs to be created.

REMEMBER

Don't forget about your customers. They can help you write your newsletter. You can include a Letters section, where customers get to share their experiences, ask questions (that you can answer in the newsletter), or be honored by you, the business owner, for reaching a certain milestone. Customers love to see themselves in print, and it shows potential customers that real people use your business. As mentioned earlier, perhaps look through your social media channels for customer feedback and see if it's appropriate to feature in your newsletter.

Decide what your newsletter will cover

You need to provide different, fresh, and relevant content every time. Stay current on the issues affecting your industry by reading industry-relevant news websites, niche magazines, and social media feeds in your subject area to help generate ideas.

WARNING

Don't include any stories from other sources in your newsletters without their express consent. If you or someone on your staff creates the content, you can refer to quotes or statistics from articles, as long as you cite the source in your content.

Decide when to issue your newsletter

You need to decide at the beginning how frequently your newsletter is released: once or more per week, monthly, or quarterly. Make sure you publish the newsletter on a consistent schedule. Readers lose interest with late or varied schedules, so choose a publishing time that you and your business can handle without much stress. You can publish on a less frequent schedule as long as you're reliable. Come up with an editorial schedule for your newsletters, keeping in mind that you can always schedule "special editions" to coincide with special campaigns and product launches, for example.

You also need to decide on which day of the week you will publish. Some companies target the day of new product releases to send out their newsletters. A movie and book seller might choose Tuesdays for its newsletter release because new movies and books hit stores that day. Another site might choose a weekend day so that its newsletter can serve as a weekly summary of events and readers can follow up when they're not at work.

Decide on a format for your newsletter

You can use a number of different computer programs to create a newsletter, although you can present it in only two main formats:

>> **Plain text** has words and web links but few to no graphics. Although plain-text newsletters can be read by anyone, typically avoid the junk/spam folders on various email clients better than HTML, and are quick to send and receive, they can look plain, which necessitates the need for a well-crafted font.

>> **HTML** has words, graphics, and design formatting to look exactly like a web page. HTML newsletters can look cool and sophisticated but can't be interpreted by every email system and can take a long time to show up onscreen.

TIP

You can create two different versions and ask your readers during the sign-up process which version they want to receive. If you want to be safe, create just a clean, plain-text format, which everyone can enjoy.

Decide how to distribute your newsletter

After you create your newsletter, you have to get it to your readers. After your customer list grows beyond a few people, you can't just open an email window, insert your newsletter, and send it to thousands of people at one time. You need to talk to your Internet service provider (ISP) to make sure that you can distribute the same newsletter to hundreds or thousands of people. By notifying your ISP, you ensure that it doesn't just shut down your newsletter when someone suddenly sees the increased traffic.

WARNING

Send your newsletter only to people who specifically request it. Don't just spam everyone you've done business with in the past.

If you have trouble sending the newsletter through your normal ISP, you can contract a company to manage the newsletter distribution for you. This way, its computer systems handle the mailing of your newsletter and can coordinate the automatic subscriptions of new readers or the *unsubscriptions* (removals) of customers when they want to stop receiving the newsletter. Table 3-1 lists a few of these companies.

TABLE 3-1   **Email Newsletter Distribution Services**

Name	URL
Constant Contact	`www.constantcontact.com`
HubSpot	`www.hubspot.com`
MailChimp	`www.mailchimp.com`
Marketo Engage	`www.marketo.com/marketo-engage`

TIP

On your website, maintain an archive of all past newsletters, which simply adds more content for your customers. Not only can new and existing customers read your newsletter online, instead of relying on an email program, but the search engines scan your newsletters, which can lead to more customers finding your website. Just make sure the archive is easy to find on your website.

Automating Routine Tasks

How many times in the past had you tried to reach a company through a toll-free hotline only to be put on hold or made to listen to an endless array of recorded messages? Had you pressed a number on the keypad so many times that the number has now rubbed off the button? If you're like us, you hung up and never did business with that company again.

Guard against this situation when customers interact with your online business. If they can't quickly add or delete themselves from your newsletter mailing list or respond to an email or banner offer, they get frustrated and leave. They might never come back, no matter how many offers and deals you throw their way.

Enter automation. By setting up automatic processes, your marketing campaign can go 24/7. And with automation handling routine tasks, you're free to handle more business deals (such as finding the right merchandise, analyzing your sales numbers, or hiring the right staff to increase your business).

Here are some tools you can use to automate parts of the process:

>> **Autoresponders:** This tool automatically generates an email response based on an incoming request, such as when someone joins your newsletter mailing list. An autoresponder can add that person's name to the database and send him or her a welcome message (full of information about your company) and maybe even an introductory newsletter issue.

WARNING

Don't abuse the autoresponder with every process you have in customer interaction. The last thing customers want is form letters every time they send you email, especially if the form letter response has nothing to do with their original question. Reserve the autoresponder for situations that have only one expected response, such as addition to or deletion from a mailing list.

>> **Ticklers:** Send out *ticklers* (automatic reminders or updates) every few weeks by using contact managers such as Hubspot CRM or Salesforce. Include a variety of offers in your tickler to slowly but surely encourage these contacts to try out your company and your products.

>> **Archived information:** Sometimes, the best way you can help your customers is to enable them to help themselves. Dedicate a portion of your website to hold all your marketing collateral and information. Put the most frequently asked questions (FAQs) in this help section, and make sure that it's accessible from any page of your website.

TIP

Try putting your marketing material in different formats to appeal to different customers. You can turn a brochure into a short YouTube demonstration video, a PowerPoint presentation into a Pinterest board, or a meeting into a downloadable webinar, for example. Each new format serves as a hook to a portion of your audience. See Book 4, Chapter 3 for more information on creating different products.

Searching for Traffic with Search Engine Advertising

If you were building a gas station, would you have it on a rural country road or a freeway off-ramp? The answer is simple: You want to position your business where your customers are located. The best businesses in the world can't succeed if their customers can't find them. That's why location and access are so important, even for an online business.

You want to position yourself where the traffic is, and nowadays most people find websites through search engines. Therefore, set up shop right on a search engine page with advertising, and benefit from that "drive-by" traffic.

After all, one big benefit of search engine advertising is that you know in advance what the target consumer is looking for. Search engine advertising works like this: You tie your products or website to specific keywords. When someone types those keywords in the search page, your ad is displayed. Suppose that a potential customer is doing a search on Google for a certain brand of golf clubs. If your business sells that brand, your ad can appear at the top of the search results, as shown in Figure 3-3. Because the ad is targeted only to people who demonstrate that interest, your rate of return is higher than in a generic ad.

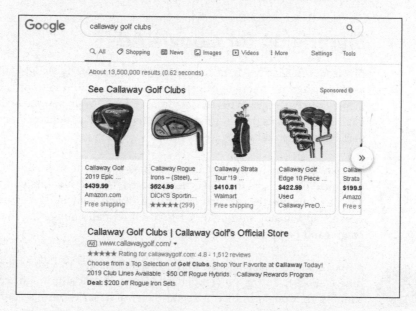

FIGURE 3-3: Google displays ads alongside its search results.

Google and Yahoo! are the two biggest companies in the area of search engine advertising, but they are by no means the only games in town. Table 3-2 lists the major companies that offer search engine advertising, which include social media sites like YouTube, which many people consider the second most popular search engine after Google. We show you in the following section how to sign up for Google Ads.

TABLE 3-2 **Search Engine Advertising Companies**

Company	Service	URL
Google	Google Ads	https://ads.google.com
Microsoft	Microsoft Advertising	http://about.ads.microsoft.com
Verizon	Verizon Media Advertising	www.verizonmedia.com/advertising
YouTube	YouTube Advertising	www.youtube.com/ads

If your products appeal to a certain niche audience, check to see whether news or portal sites that cater to that industry also accept search advertising on their sites. Although some of these websites have outsourced their advertising to companies such as Google or Verizon Media, the sites still control the ads that are displayed and are usually open to a partnership or paid arrangement.

Signing up for Google Ads

The leader in search engine ads is Google Ads, formerly Google AdWords. You can use this program to create your own ads and to bid on keywords that trigger the display of those ads. When a Google user types your keywords during a search, your ad appears as part of the results screen, with a Sponsored or Ad identifier as part of the ad (refer to Figure 3-3).

You pay only for the times your ad is clicked, not the number of times your ad is displayed on the screen. Like other services, Google Ads lets you set a budget, so you pay only for the ads you can afford. When your budget is used up, your ad doesn't appear any more. You even specify a daily budget so that your ad campaign can't be spent in the first day.

A Google Ads *campaign* doesn't refer to a politician's run for office; it means running a specific ad for a given budget. Your ad campaign might consist of one ad running on Google until you spend $100, or a series of ads running for several weeks to promote a new product.

Your customization of the campaign isn't limited to just the keyword. Using Google Ads, you can choose your target area (a city, territory, or country), and Google targets where the search user is from, whether it's from the search itself, the specific IP address of the computer, or the preferences that the user has set up. By using this targeting, you can show different ads to different territories, offer specific ads and promotions to specific areas, or even create your own test markets where only a specific group of computer users is presented with a given ad.

We discuss Google Ads because it's popular and easy to use. All the services work similarly, so just choose the one that works best for you.

Setting up a Google campaign

If you're interested in setting up your own Google Ads campaign, type your keywords and look at the ads that already appear on Google for your targeted subject area. Get an idea of the ads that you're competing against and the words they use to craft their ads. This strategy should give you some ideas for your ad.

REMEMBER

Write your ad copy and have two or three people proofread it before building your campaign. Also take the time to think of the right keywords to use in advance so that you're not guessing when it's time to build the campaign.

When you're ready to build a Google Ads campaign, just follow these steps:

1. Go to `http://ads.google.com` **and click the Start Now button.**

2. **Tie your Google Ads account to an existing Google account or create an account. Then click Continue.**

To create a Google account, enter an email address and a password plus some key personal data.

3. **Tell Google Ads about your advertising goals so it can help build your first ad campaign. Then click Next and provide basic business information.**

First, click the advertising goal that best aligns with what you're trying to do, then click Next. Google asks for information about your business, as shown in Figure 3-4. Provide your business name and website URL in the boxes provided. Click Next to set the audience you'd like to reach with this campaign.

FIGURE 3-4:
Tell Google Ads some info about your business.

4. **On the Audience screen, start setting up the parameters for your campaign:**

a. *Decide on the locations for your ad.*

b. *Select the networks that can display your ad.*

5. **After selecting your audience network, click Next.**

6. **In the window that appears, specify the keywords that will trigger your ad (see Figure 3-5), and then click Next.**

   Specify one or more keywords related to the product you want to advertise. Google Ads will fill in some of the more popular keyword phrases related to the website category that Google thinks best matches your website, and offer you additional choices, along with potential audience size. You can remove any of its choices and add your own keyword phrases to the list.

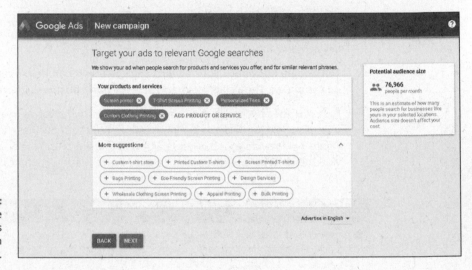

FIGURE 3-5:
Choose the keyword phrases to associate with your ad.

7. **Set your bids.**

8. **Compose your ad:**

   a. *Scroll down and click the Write Your Ad link.*

   b. *In the Headline 1 box, enter up to 30 characters.*

   c. *In the Headline 2 box, enter up to an additional 30 characters.*

      You do not have to enter a display URL, as Google will use the beginning of your Landing Page URL to display in the ad.

   d. *In the Description box, enter up to 90 characters.*

   e. *In the Clicks on Your Ad Go To box, enter the URL that will take your new customer to your website.*

      Make sure you put any promo codes or tracking words in your landing page URL.

   f. *Click the Next button.*

TIP

You don't have to link your ad to your home page. Instead, you can specify a web page on your website that presents a special offer to only those people who click your ad. In this way, you can track the number of people who view that page.

9. **On the Budget and Review screen, shown in Figure 3-6, set up the daily budget parameters for your campaign:**

   a. *Google will offer you three potential daily budgets. You can click any of those links if you're okay with setting the budget to one of the suggestions.*

   b. *You can also scroll down and click Enter Your Own Budget and set your bid price manually.*

   c. *Click the Save button.*

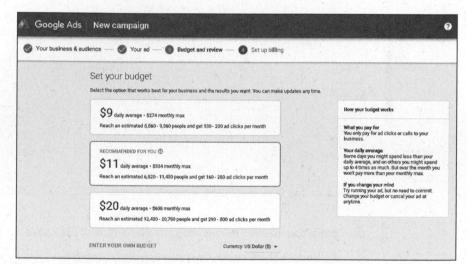

FIGURE 3-6:
Set your daily ad budget here.

10. **Review your campaign settings, and then provide your billing information.**

    Enter your billing country, account type, and payment information.

11. **(Optional) Read the terms of the Google Ads program, by clicking the appropriate link above the Submit button.**

12. **Review everything you've entered and then click Submit.**

Your ad begins to appear on Google almost instantly. Go to the main Google page and perform a few searches to see where your ad ends up on the results page.

Determining the right amount per click

After you set up your account, you want to know where your pricing is positioning you on the page. Follow these steps to check on your pay-per-click rate:

1. **Go to** www.google.com, **type your keyword phrase, and click the Google Search button.**

   On the results screen, look for your ad in the list just below the Search box. If it doesn't even appear, you're not paying enough to appear on the first screen; you have to click the See More Sponsored Links link to see your ad.

2. **Log in to your Google Ads account, and click to the specific campaign.**

   Look for your campaign name among the list of campaigns (see Figure 3-7).

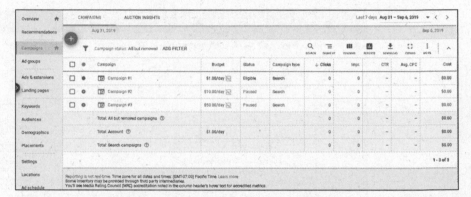

FIGURE 3-7: Access your Google Ads campaigns.

3. **Raise the maximum amount you're paying, and click Save.**

4. **Go back to the Google results screen and refresh it.**

   You can refresh screens in most web browsers by pressing F5. See what position your ad moves to on the page. If you see a jump in the placement of your ad, you have an idea of what your competitors have spent to get their positions, and what it will take to keep this new position. If your position hasn't jumped, your competitors are paying even more than your new amount to keep their top spots.

5. **Repeat Steps 3 and 4 to fine-tune the position of your ad on the page.**

   The top spot is the costliest to own, so consider whether a healthy positioning on the first results screen — albeit a few spots down — is the best economical solution for you.

REMEMBER

When you fine-tune your campaign, don't expect those price levels to be in effect forever. Your competitors are fine-tuning their campaigns, too, so be sure to revisit your campaign from time to time to achieve maximum effectiveness.

Deciding when to use pay-per-click

Search engine advertising is one popular way that you can drive traffic to your storefront, although it's not necessarily the right way for every business. You need to consider a few elements of your business that will affect your advertising efforts:

>> **Your marketing budget:** If you have an unlimited marketing budget, pay-per-click is an ideal solution to generate subscribers and sales. If your budget is small, you might be better off sticking to other marketing techniques and adding pay-per-click ads to your strategy as your budget increases.

TIP

Dedicate a small portion of your budget to experiment with pay-per-click, and be ready to analyze the results after your test to see whether the results justify the cost. See the nearby sidebar, "Doing the math on pay-per-click," to figure out how to interpret the results.

>> **Your product:** Are the products you're selling in demand and hard to find? Or are they steady products with a limited audience? If your products sell well to anybody who can find you, pay-per-click is the way to go. If the awareness of your company is already high, however, pay-per-click might be effective only during limited promotional periods in which the combination of a pay-per-click ad sending a user to your website and a special sale greeting can result in customers who place an order.

>> **Your product margin:** If your product sales are slower but with a high profit margin, a pay-per-click ad can be effective as long as you get a decent conversion of browsers to buyers. Basically, if you make enough money from the sale of a product, you can afford to go find 10 leads, for example, if one of those 10 decides to buy. If you're operating on a razor-thin profit margin, however, you need quantity, not quality, and a targeted approach such as pay-per-click might cost too much in the long run.

>> **Your competitors:** Keep an eye on your competition, and see how they're attracting customers. If your customer base is more of a niche than a mass market, you definitely have to adopt similar marketing techniques to divert those customers to your website rather than to someone else's. If your competitors are using pay-per-click, you might find that outbidding them is worth the price to convert a potential customer.

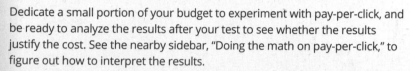

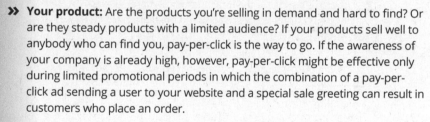

Web Marketing at Work

DOING THE MATH ON PAY-PER-CLICK

One way to determine whether a pay-per-click ad campaign will be effective is to study certain numbers related to how your online business now operates. You need to know three numbers:

- **Your average profit margin per sale:** The difference between the price the customer paid for a product and the price you paid to obtain the product.

- **Your site's *conversion ratio:*** The percentage of people who order something from you, based on your site's total number of visitors.

- **Your site's *click-through ratio:*** The percentage of people who have clicked a link to get to your website, based on the total number of people who saw that link.

Suppose that your average profit margin is $20, your conversion ratio is 5 percent, and your click-through ratio is 4 percent. If 20 people click through from an ad, one person should order and generate $20 in profit. Each click-through visitor is then worth $1 to you (or $20 × 5 percent); if you can achieve that click-through rate for $1 or less, you should have a profitable campaign.

If you're paying for the total number of ads displayed, you can calculate the value of getting 1,000 impressions (a common measurement for these types of ads) by using these numbers again:

- 1,000 impressions * 4 percent click-through ratio = 40 visitors

- 40 visitors * 5 percent conversion ratio = 2 paying customers

- 2 paying customers × $20 profit margin = $40 profit

- $40 profit / 1,000 impressions = $40 CPM (cost per thousand — M for the Roman equivalent of a thousand)

These results demonstrate why you need to know how your online business is performing before the ad campaign, and why monitoring the results after the campaign tells you whether to continue doing campaigns.

Marketing Your Company Offline

Even though you're running an online business, you don't have to do all your marketing online, too. Any communication that you do on behalf of your business should feature your online store and web address. Here are some offline media you can use to advertise and spread the word about your online business:

» **Business cards:** Add your website address, email address, and website slogan to each of your business cards along with your name, address, and phone number. You never know who might learn about your website from seeing your business card.

» **Business flyers and brochures:** Whenever you hand out any form of paper that explains your business, you should include not only your website address but also a description of what the website adds to your business. Even if you're just reminding people that your website acts as a support site after a customer buys your product, the inclusion of your website in the brochure reinforces the website's importance.

» **Catalogs:** Something about a printed catalog encourages customers to browse and shop. Even some of the most recognizable e-commerce companies, such as Amazon, will send out printed catalogs to remind people of the goods at their online sites. Although a catalog reinforces the product line, your website should always be mentioned in any catalog as another easy way to order from you.

» **Invoices and purchase orders:** Putting your website address and a mention of your site features on your invoices and purchase orders can remind your suppliers and vendors to check out your website and maybe even recommend ways that they can transact with you online.

» **Voice-mail greetings:** As customers call to ask questions or place orders, part of your on-hold message or initial greeting can gently remind them that they can find more information on your website.

» **Company vehicles:** If you have company trucks or vans making deliveries for your company, why not use that big space to remind passersby that your business is now online? You might be surprised at the potential for orders to come in with the comment "I saw your website when your truck drove past me."

» **Boxes:** One way that Amazon distinguishes itself is by plastering the Amazon logo on its customized boxes and mailers. Not only do customers know instantly that their orders have arrived, but anyone around them is also gently reminded of the Amazon brand. Other retailers have followed suit, such as Walmart with its `www.walmart.com` web address clearly marked on its blue boxes.

Chapter **4**

Converting Browsers to Buyers

P eople measure online businesses by using different statistics (such as total revenue, total profit, and total number of customers). Another measurement, however, exists in the online world that doesn't exist in a bricks-and-mortar business: *Stickiness* indicates how many minutes a user stays at a certain website.

Stickiness is measured from the moment online users first load your website on their screen to the moment they either move on to another website or close the web browser, including the time spent browsing around the site and deciding what to do there. The longer the average time, the stickier the web business. The more time that people spend on your website, the greater the chance that they will purchase one or more of your products or interact with other customers.

REMEMBER

Some online businesses are stickier because of their purpose. Compare businesses such as YouTube or Facebook to a business such as Google Maps. Facebook and YouTube offer lots of reasons for users to browse around, but Google Maps offers only a couple of reasons (maps and driving directions).

Strive to make your website as sticky as possible. Customers who keep coming back are more likely to buy your products — which is, of course, important to your bottom line. In this chapter, we show you how to keep your website fresh and buyer friendly, and how to make your customers feel important so that you can convert browsers to buyers.

Giving Customers a Reason to Stay on Your Site

To increase your website's stickiness, give customers a reason to hang around, come back, or participate more in your business. Here are some ways you can make your online business stickier:

TIP

>> **Provide original content.** This information can come in the form of videos, tips and tricks, reviews, opinions, or social media stories. You can write about the hottest new product, list 10 ways a customer can use a product, or share stories about how customers use your products. In today's multimedia age, you should include videos and podcasts on your website as well as on sites such as YouTube, which then point people to your website.

Two ways to reuse your original content are to put that information into newsletters to keep your customers informed and to repeat the information on your social media outlets, such as your Facebook business page, Twitter feed, YouTube channel, and Instagram channels.

>> **Create social media pages for your business.** In this day and age, the best way to allow customers to talk to each other is through social media. When customers interact with you via social media, they can ask questions and receive answers about your product line and get to know each other and your staff. You're no longer an impersonal company, as you become more relatable and "real" to your customer base. Then, add Share buttons on your website so your customers can share your content with their friends on their favorite social media networks.

>> **Keep your content up-to-date.** You can create a blog, maintained by either yourself or one of your employees, to provide in-depth, always changing content for your customers. Insert sections of your Facebook page onto your website, so customers who are Facebook users can see their friends' likes and comments. Stay active on different social media sites such as Twitter, Instagram, Google+, Tumblr, and Pinterest.

>> **Encourage your customers to provide content.** Ask loyal customers to write reviews, guides, and anecdotes that you post on your website or they post on your Facebook or Yelp page. Some businesses even have contests where the contributor of the best story every month gets a gift certificate, for example.

>> **Publish help and product support.** If these elements apply to the products you are selling on your website, you can make items such as the following available on your website:

- A FAQs (frequently asked questions) section

- Support documents

- Articles and schematics that describe how to install, assemble, or fix problems with your products

Providing your own content on your site

Regardless of what kind of business you're running, you should offer content to the buyer. Buyers want original information that they can't get anywhere else. It's like visiting a local store and persuading the owner, an expert in the field, to tell you all about products for sale and how to use them. One reason that Amazon is so successful is that it provides tons of customer and editor reviews, how-to guides, and bestseller lists.

Providing information can lead to more sales and happier customers. Start with information or entertainment that matters to your customers. If you sell books, have your employees provide their "picks" or short reviews of their favorite new releases for the month, or write the reviews yourself. If you sell consumer electronics, perhaps you can create and promote an unboxing of the product, or talk about shopping for the best digital camera and then compare some of the top brands and discuss their features, either through video or via a web page.

REMEMBER

When you provide content for your website, don't forget to include links and references to the products you sell. Avoid flashing banners and loud sounds; instead, post a thumbnail picture of the product you're discussing, set up so that the customer can click the thumbnail and go straight to that product page.

You can also go above and beyond by providing information that anyone would want, not just your core customers. Provide links and sources to general news stories or local city guides, for example. You can specialize in an area and become the ultimate authority on it, in the hope that when people come to your site to read your content, they will stay and check out your product selection. Some financial websites are popular and ranked highly on search engines, for example, because they provide interactive tools such as rate calculators, which enable people to calculate the lowest interest payments necessary on a loan or a mortgage.

Getting other people to provide your content

As the person maintaining your business, you might think that you have to provide all your content, although that might not be the case. Some of the biggest online businesses rely on others for the content their users depend on every day! Tap into that global community, and encourage these people to contribute to your business:

>> **Customers:** Besides you, who knows more about your products than your customers? Encourage them to provide stories, reviews, and opinions regarding products you sell and similar products in your area. You gain the content, the authenticity of a real customer, and the support of that customer, who feels even more invested in your business.

TIP

If you have a well-known or experienced customer, see whether he or she would be willing to create a regular column or video series for your website. Promise a featured spot on your site and maybe some credit toward purchases, and give customers a fun reason to come back regularly to your business.

If you run online contests or have discussions with your customers and fans on a social media site, such as a Facebook business page, a Twitter account, or an Instagram account, include that content on your website or add a link to your website. Companies big and small are running photo or anecdote contests that gather tons of interaction from their customers. For example, the Pilot pen company held a contest in which it asked customers to write a handwritten note, take a photo of it, and post the photo on Instagram with the #PowerToThePen hashtag. This contest was tied in to the Pilot website and its social media channels.

>> **Suppliers:** The manufacturers, distributors, and suppliers you work with are usually trying to build their brands, too, so involve them in your online business. Let your customers know the newest and greatest things coming from your manufacturer, even if it's just links to its website and announcements about contests, promotions, or events your customers can participate in.

>> **Social media sources:** You can include widgets on your website that feed in content from your social media channels, as well as social media buttons on every web page, where customers and fans can access your various social media presences.

Anticipating Customer Needs

Veteran business owners can tell you that to succeed, your goal should be to not just meet your customers' expectations but to also anticipate and respond to those expectations. Online retailers are no different: You need to read buyers' minds and figure out what they want so that you have the products to meet their demand — rather than watch your competition make off with your customers and your revenue.

You have a few ways to figure out what your customers want:

>> **Take a look at your sales data.** Watch the purchases made through your business to see who's buying what and how much customers are spending per order.

>> **Monitor your customers' questions and comments.** Whether customers communicate by email, phone, Facebook or Twitter posts, or a web form, if they're starting to ask for similar products, investigate!

>> **Check out your competition.** See what other sites are providing, putting on sale, raising prices on, and carrying in their stores.

>> **Look at other resources that talk about your product lines.** See what websites are promoting or hyping as "the next great thing." Read online news and discussion groups, magazines, books, and newspapers, and watch TV shows about your product areas, to see what people are talking about, preparing for, and predicting for that industry.

>> **Go to trade groups, conventions, or organizations.** Attend trade shows for your product area, whether it's Electronic Entertainment Expo (E3) for video games, Consumer Electronics Show for general consumer electronics, or American Toy Fair for the newest action figures, to get an idea of what your buyers want next. Subscribe to these organizations' newsletters to get up-to-date information. You should always order catalogs from manufacturers that belong to these groups and ask to be on their mailing lists.

Using web analytics tools

Customer orders aren't the only evidence of what customers want from your business. Because you're online, you can keep track of the different web pages that customers view. Web analytic tools gather information about particular pages your customers are looking at and analyze everything from the path a customer takes in your store, to the length of time she spent on every page, to the *conversion rate* (the percentage of people who placed an order out of all visitors). Every time a customer moves through your website, the analytics tools gather more useful information. You can start these tools and see reports and analysis.

TECHNICAL STUFF

Web analytics tools are technical programs that crunch data that your website provider automatically creates and maintains for you. That data keeps track of all the web page requests your customers ask for when they browse your website.

When you're using a web analytics tool, ask yourself these questions:

» What pages are looked at the most? The least?

» How many pages does the average customer look at?

» What's the last page that customers look at before they leave? Is it an order confirmation page, or did they give up before ordering?

» Are customers following the same flow through your site? That is, do they typically look at the same web pages in the same order as everyone else?

» Are customers viewing the newest web pages you provide? Are they sticking to the same core pages regardless of whether those pages are updated?

After you know this information, you can update your website by deleting the pages (or content) that no one is looking at. By streamlining the buying process this way, you continue to meet your customers' expectations and keep them returning.

Predicting future purchases

Mutual fund companies are notorious for this disclaimer: "Past performance is not an indicator of future returns." In the e-commerce world, however, past purchases are an excellent indicator of what customers will buy next — so much so that a company such as Amazon tracks every single activity (not just purchases) performed by customers on its website. Your customer logs are good indicators of what your customers are looking at, but you should also look at what they're buying.

One benefit you enjoy in an online business is not being limited by physical shelf space and, in some cases, the cost of carrying the products before purchase. So, you hopefully offer an expansive array of products. After your orders come in, though, you want to see which products customers are ordering the most. Are these products concentrated in one or two subcategories, or are they spread out among your catalog of goods?

REMEMBER

Obviously, if a product line is flying off the virtual shelf, you should restock it as soon as possible. If the product is a fad item, however, such as the Rainbow Loom (a crafting kit to help kids make rubber band bracelets) or the Shake Weight, you don't want to get stuck with a warehouse full of that item after the fad ends.

To choose future products to stock and to anticipate your customers' wants, look at what they're willing to buy from you today. As you examine past purchases, consider these dimensions:

>> **Average price per sold item:** At what price levels are your highest-selling products? This price gives you an idea of whether limited, high-priced items or mass-quantity, low-priced items would work better for your business. After all, if your customers are used to buying the hottest computer accessories for less than $50, selling a $2,000 laptop might be out of their reach.

>> **Average order size:** The average amount of money spent per order doesn't necessarily correspond to the average price per item. Although your customers might love your site for inexpensive items, they could be willing to purchase multiple items, resulting in a big order. They might be occasional buyers who buy expensive items. Find products that fit into your customers' average order and get them to exceed this number. Offer free shipping on a larger order, for example, to help increase your average order size. (This is a technique made famous by Amazon.com.)

If you increase your customers' average order amount, you're increasing their value to your business. Consider new products that meet or exceed your current average order size. You want this number to go up, not down.

>> **Luxury or necessity:** Are your customers buying entertainment products with their disposable income, or are they purchasing everyday items that they need continually? Look beyond the fad or trend, and figure out what part of their budget you're reaching. Continue to stock products that are so cool, so cheap, or so easy to use that customers *have* to have them, or stock products that customers need or see as automatic buys. Then they will continue to buy from you rather than look around for someplace better.

>> **Technology items:** If you're selling items with lots of technology built in (even if they're kitchen appliances), always have an eye on the next model, iteration, or version. Keep enough on hand to satisfy current demand and also acquire newer models so that customers can stay ahead of the curve or stay where they are until they're ready to buy the new model.

>> **The 80-20 rule:** Are 80 percent of your orders coming from 20 percent of your customers? Chances are, 80 percent of the products sold come from 20 percent of the category areas. The way to make the biggest effect on your business is to increase the 80 percent of sales, so be ready to continue serving the customers of that 80 percent group.

Organizing a Buyer-Friendly Site

For a regular business, being friendly to buyers means saying "Hello" when they walk through the door, shaking their hands, and smiling at them. For an online business, friendly means creating a buyer-friendly site that makes sense to buyers and makes their lives easier. After all, they're coming to you partially because they don't want to get in their cars, fight traffic, battle for parking spots at the mall, and navigate their way through the sea of humanity just to get a new pair of jeans.

When buyers come to your website, provide them with a few basic pieces of information right off the bat, or else they will click their way to the next business. Go to your home page, and make sure that it answers these basic questions:

» What is your business?

» What's the primary focus of your business?

» What does your business offer consumers?

» What makes your business good enough to earn a customer's trust and, therefore, an order?

» Is this clear to understand when using a mobile device to view your site?

» How would a customer start shopping on your site?

If your opening page can't answer these questions, your website isn't buyer friendly. You want to be straightforward and direct with your buyers because, in essence, your business reason for existence is to help a customer with a specific need. In this section, we talk about what you can do to spiff up your website to offer customers a satisfying shopping experience.

Streamlining the shopping process

All-night convenience stores can charge two to three times the grocery store price for items for a good reason. People want convenience, especially online, so being able to grab an item and leave is crucial.

An example of an easy-in-easy-out website is the Amazon 1-Click system. For returning customers, Amazon fills in all their information ahead of time so that they can choose their items, make an immediate purchase with the click of a single button, and leave. Customers return to Amazon because they know that Amazon's 1-Click system works right every time and they don't have to retype their credit card number, shipping address, and other information. Their accounts are already created, so they can pop in and get what they need. That's great service. (Add to that the Amazon Prime membership, where members get free two-day shipping on any size order from Amazon, and it makes Amazon's shopping process even easier and more convenient.)

On your website, make sure that your shoppers can always

>> **Reach their shopping carts and accounts:** No matter where on your website shoppers might be, they should always be able to look in their shopping carts or check their accounts. We recommend including links to these two functions along the top of every web page so that they're always just a click away.

>> **Understand the total costs of their order:** If customers can't figure out what the shipping cost will be for their order before having to enter credit card and full address information, many will abandon their shopping cart. The same concept goes for customers who get hit with taxes or extra fees on the final screens of the order process instead of before payment information is required.

>> **Access any product specials you offer from the home page:** The less hunting buyers have to do, the quicker they can add your specials to their carts and continue shopping or check out.

TIP

When you're designing the page flow of your website, reduce as many in-between steps as possible. If the majority of your shoppers pay by credit card, don't ask customers how they will pay. Display a page where customers can either fill in their credit card information or choose other forms of payment.

>> **Search for a specific item:** Your customers can use the search function to interact with your business by telling you exactly what they want to buy. Add to your navigation section a search box or link that appears on every page of your website.

Check whether the software or web host you're using to create your website offers a search function. Make sure that the search offers customers a focused set of results or the most relevant product.

>> **See the content on a page at a glance:** We can't stress enough the importance of clear headings and labels. Your customers are drawn to the biggest type on the page. Every page on your website should have a clear and relevant heading at the top, and subheadings throughout the page if you're presenting a long list of products or options.

REMEMBER

As simple as it sounds, make sure that headings or categories correspond to what customers are seeing on the page. If a category talks about clearance items and you're displaying new, full-priced goods, you'll lose your customers fast as their trust in you starts to evaporate.

Keeping Your Shopping Cart Simple

Most studies about online shopping include the percentage of online e-commerce shopping carts that are left abandoned by their users. Some statistics state that customers abandon anywhere from 45 to 90 percent of all shopping carts, for a variety of reasons:

>> They're turned off by the high cost of either the item or the shipping and handling.

>> They can't find all the information or functionality that they need to finish.

>> They're uncomfortable registering or handing over credit card data online.

>> They're unsure how to completely check out with their items and pay for their purchases.

>> They're afraid to place their final orders.

TIP

For these reasons, keep in mind some helpful tips and avoid the common traps of having shopping carts on your e-commerce site:

>> **Make the shopping cart easy to find.** Sometimes, the only way for customers to even access their shopping carts is to click a link that's available on only certain web pages. At other times, they see their shopping carts only after adding items. Put the shopping cart link at or near the top of every web page. Create a second browser window that's small or always minimized, and put the shopping cart information on that screen.

>> **Make the shopping cart updatable.** Your customers should be able to add, update, and delete products in their orders at any time. When they make changes, they probably want to see their updated totals. If customers change shipping options or choose an out-of-state address, they want to see any total changes. Make sure that any change to an order triggers your software program to recalculate the order amount and display the revised order with a revised total.

>> **Require no upfront information to use the shopping cart.** If your customers can't easily add items to their shopping cart first and give personal information later, you might scare them off by forcing them to register or type lots of data first. Enable them to shop, and then require the other information before they place orders.

REMEMBER

At some point before an order is complete, don't forget to ask "How did you hear about this site?" Provide a box for the referral name, email address, or promotion code so that you can better track your marketing efforts.

» **Provide help from the shopping cart page.** Always have available on the shopping cart screen at least one web link to a list of frequently asked questions (FAQs) about how to use the shopping cart. Nothing is worse for customers than getting stuck when they try to add something to their shopping carts and can't find any help. Don't leave customers wandering around your store aimlessly; throw them the virtual rope in advance.

TIP

You can also offer live help with chat technology. When buyers click the chat link, they can chat with your customer service representatives (or you, depending on the size of your business) and have their questions answered on the spot. Several companies offer software that augments your website with chat technology, such as

- LiveChat (`www.livechatinc.com`)

- ProvideSupport (`www.providesupport.com`)

- UserLike (`www.userlike.com`)

» **Allow customers to easily add or remove items.** Customers make multiple decisions, usually when they're deciding what to order. They need the flexibility to update, add, or delete any single line item in the shopping cart without affecting the rest of the order. Customers who have to delete everything and start over are likely to just "walk out."

» **Protect customers' information.** When you collect sensitive information — such as credit card numbers, birthdates, or bank account information — make sure that your shopping cart is using a safe technology, such as Secure Socket Layers (SSL). A customer should see a URL starting with `https://` (depending on the web browser the customer is using, he may also see a closed-lock icon in the address bar of the web browser) to indicate that data can be safely entered on the page. If the URL doesn't start with https://, entering data isn't 100 percent safe on that page. Pages containing data about your products don't have to use SSL; when in doubt, though, secure the page. (See Book 5 for more information about security.)

REMEMBER

Don't just secure customers' information; tell them about it! Create a special window or web page detailing how you're protecting their vital information. When you reassure customers that you're looking out for them in the beginning, they're more likely to buy.

Avoiding Assumptions about Your Customers

You have to make plenty of decisions every day, and you can easily fall into the trap that you have to know everything to make your business work. You don't have to know everything, although you do have to know whom to ask or where to look.

When you're wondering whether the actions you're taking in your business are truly converting browsers to buyers, step back a moment to see what's going on. Pull up your website and click through the pages yourself. Just because the pages and offers grab *you* doesn't necessarily mean that customers will react the same way. It's a good start, though. In this section, we show you ways to see your site from the customers' perspective so that you can provide them with exactly what they need.

Asking customers for feedback

Many times, your buyers know what they want — sometimes before you do. They're the ones using your products, talking to each other on your discussion board, and looking for the next great product. You should always provide a way for your customers to give you general or specific feedback using a feedback form.

TIP

One of the best ways to encourage regular, ongoing feedback is to participate in social media sites such as Facebook or Twitter. Encourage customers to become followers so they can share experiences, ask questions, or learn more about your business.

Most websites used to incorporate some sort of feedback form, whether as part of a help system or a contact system or even as part of a guest book, but nowadays, many companies rely on social media interaction or enable customers to email them from the website.

If your most loyal customers are asking for a particular product, consider stocking it so that you don't lose them to your competition.

REMEMBER

If shoppers want a fad item, especially one that requires a large investment, stock only what you feel that you can definitely sell. If the shelf life of a product could become very short, you don't want to blindly act on your customers' inquiries. (Just ask the businesses that are sitting on a warehouse full of Neopets.)

Make sure that customer inquiries and feedback are fed into the inventory acquisition phase as quickly as possible. You have no excuse for not considering a new product line if your customers have given you notice about the item. Some items sell more quickly than others, and you need some time to find the right distributor or manufacturer and set up an account.

TIP

Test a new product line on a subset of customers before investing too much of your inventory budget on one item. Buy enough of the product to get it in stock quickly and serve a subset of customers. Send a targeted email or direct-mail piece to assess the response for the test audience. If the numbers are good, reorder more and repeat the test, or integrate the new product into your catalog.

Encourage customers to help keep you on the cutting edge by rewarding them for their feedback. Include surveys, links to social media outlets such as Facebook or Twitter, toll-free hotline numbers, or follow-up email in your communications with buyers. Make contacting you as easy as possible for them, and use giveaways, promotions, or incentives to push these customers into giving you their valuable advice.

TIP

Create a buyer council or a volunteer group of buyers that you can poll regularly to find out what customers know about a product area. Choose some steady customers with whom you've built relationships, and ask whether they're interested in joining. Most will accept to get a feeling of ownership and to get their opinions heard.

Remembering your customers

Many online business owners get started in areas they know well and are passionate about. Then they fall into the trap of assuming that they're the perfect target audience for their own online stores, and their own preferences get in the way of doing business. If this happens to you, your bottom line — and the future flow of customers to your site — could be harmed.

When you decide which products to carry in your store, ask yourself "Am I choosing these items because I like them — or because I think that my buyers will like them?" Put your customers' needs and desires ahead of your own. Even if you're putting yourself in the role of a potential buyer, you carry certain biases that your customers might not carry.

REMEMBER

Put your buyers' interests ahead of your own. You're not selling to yourself — you're selling to your customers! Offer products that they want to buy, at prices they're willing to pay. See the section "Anticipating Customer Needs," earlier in this chapter, for tips on finding out what people are buying.

Be open to what your customers, and the orders they place, are telling you. We have met enough business owners who were too afraid or too ignorant about venturing outside their known worlds to try new product lines. Those folks usually lost great opportunities to expand their business.

REMEMBER

If you don't have the items buyers want, they will go somewhere else to find them. And chances are good that they won't come back to you. Buyers remember who serves them best. Respond accordingly.

Encouraging Viewers to Buy

Being available to your customers is important for people who stumble across your site while searching for something. To generate sales, however, you need to encourage those people to take action and buy something from your site. You can build a clean and robust website, full of exciting products, and then wonder why you aren't making sales. In the world of e-commerce, building your website isn't enough. You have to close the deal. Encourage buyers to place your products in their shopping carts and then commit to placing orders. You created your website to give them the means to do so, and now you have to give them a little nudge. In this section, we describe two techniques to convert browsers to buyers: Give them a time-limited offer, and then reinforce that offer when they're leaving your website.

Offering deals and promotions

Special deals and promotions are the most common way to ask for the sale because you're giving buyers a specific buying proposition. You're offering something to sweeten the deal, whether it's a discount, a free additional item, or an extra service. Usually, though, a successful deal or promotion has that all-critical time limit. You can limit these elements:

>> **The length of time that an offer is available:** "Good for only the next 24 hours."

>> **The number of people who can take advantage of the offer:** "Only the next 25 customers can act on this deal."

>> **The specific outlet you use to make your offer:** "Like us on Facebook to qualify for an exclusive offer."

>> **The supply of the product:** "Order now — supplies are limited."

A time limit spurs customers to act. Otherwise, if an offer is always out there, it's a regular deal, not a special offer.

You can choose from a number of events that can trigger a special deal or promotion:

>> A customer registers for the first time.

>> A customer adds a second, fifth, or tenth item to the shopping cart.

>> A specified length of time (15 or 30 minutes, for example) has elapsed and the customer still hasn't added anything to the shopping cart.

>> The customer visits your website by using a special web address.

Pushing to make a sale works: It forces a buyer to make a decision, and if the customer is getting a good deal, the impulse to buy can kick in and seal the deal. Although you don't necessarily want to be overly aggressive, you can't just believe the line from *Field of Dreams:* "If you build it, he will come." Customers might come, but they might not shop. You have to encourage the sale.

Using pop-up and modal windows effectively

It's very easy to think of a web browser window as the only visible space where you can interact with customers. However, thanks to advancing technology, you can have more than one window while a customer is browsing or buying from you. The most popular form of "extra" windows is called a *pop-up window;* here, you can create a new web browser window to open on a customer's computer screen. Pop-up windows are most commonly recognized as advertisements (intentional or unintentional) that appear while readers are using different media sites, for example. But pop-up windows can be used by e-commerce websites to highlight special deals, offer chat windows to provide more direct support to the customer, or show more information about a product without the main window disappearing on them.

WARNING

Don't rely too much on or have too many pop-up windows interrupting the shopping experience. That can detract from sales.

Speaking of going for the sale, many shop owners never think of the one instance in which they can ask for the sale: when a customer is leaving a website and moving to something else. Some special web programming language commands in the customer's web browser kick into gear when the customer chooses a different website or closes the web browser window. Instead of a pop-up window, you can create a *modal window,* which opens inside the current web page and must be interacted with before the user can access any content that's obscured by the modal window.

Some business owners think, "Well, if they're leaving my store, they definitely don't want anything." Your customers might not be able to find the deal they're looking for. Or they might want to comparison-shop before making the purchase. Maybe they just got bored because nothing unusual popped up or happened while they were shopping at your store.

The moment customers leave your site, you know a few things about them:

> **They just spent some time in your online business.** They browsed, looked at some products, and read some pages. Your business is now on their mind and they have at least considered your offerings.

> **They had some specific interest in browsing your site.** Maybe they were looking for a product, an ad caught their eye, or they were a referral. These buyers are interested.

> **They're leaving your website, so you have little left to lose.** After all, if you present them with something more and they don't want it, what are they going to do? Leave? They already made the decision to leave, so what does it hurt to give them one final offer?

Your browsing customers are knowledgeable about, and interested in, your business and your products, and they're motivated and ready to leave. It's a perfect time to make a final offer. Call it your goodbye offer or your before-you-go offer. Display a pop-up or modal window that encourages your viewer to consider a new offer or discount. Now is your last opportunity to make an impression (during this particular shopping session), so make it count.

REMEMBER

Pop-up and modal ads are annoying, so use them sparingly on your website. You can reserve the use of these types of ads for goodbye offers. This way, you're not annoying customers while they shop; you're just offering one last reminder as they're going out the door.

If your browsing customers are dead set against shopping, they will close this offer window just as fast as they left your site. If they were tempted to buy but remained on the fence, this goodbye offer might be enough to swing them back your way. Remember the adage: You never know until you try. The same concept holds true when you're asking for the sale.

TIP

When you implement this offer, make sure that it appears only if the browsing customer hasn't purchased anything. You don't want happy buyers to suddenly realize that they could have saved money if they had just tried to leave your site first. In this case, your goodbye offer should be a chance to add to an order or receive faster shipping for a lower price.

When your goodbye offer is in place, you can study your website statistics to find out if your offer is effective by comparing your success rate with your normal customer conversion rate. Just like with any other deal or promotion, you can make changes or even remove this offer based on customer results.

IN THIS CHAPTER

» Monitoring your website traffic

» Interpreting the records gathered by your web server

» Using software like Google Analytics to assemble reports on website usage

» Implementing techniques to gain more information from your visitors

» Asking your customers the right questions

» Updating your website to correct or improve performance

Chapter **5**

Analyzing and Monitoring Your Customers

After you build your website, your next step is to ask, "How can I make my site better?" Your initial version is rarely your current version. You create your site, watch how users interact with you, make changes, watch how users react to those changes, make more changes, watch some more, and then repeat the process. This process is ongoing as you evolve your site to meet the changing needs of your customers.

Analyzing your website can tell you a lot about your business that other metrics (measurements) — such as sales volume, average order amount, and repeat customers — cannot tell you. You can figure out exactly which web pages on your site are the most and least popular. You can see how many people start with your home page, and then calculate the average number of pages a user sees before leaving. You can even find out where users come from when they arrive at your website and determine the last thing they see before they leave.

In this chapter, we look at the field of website analysis, from traffic monitoring to gathering customer feedback. We help you break down the massive amount of raw data you have on your site and turn it into useful statistics that can change your business — mainly with sophisticated but easy-to-use software. You find out which pieces of information are more important than others and how to focus your analysis to study individual user behavior. You can then use this data to make useful updates to your website and study the immediate and lasting effect of your changes.

REMEMBER

The best changes that come from website analysis are gradual, or *evolutionary,* changes. Look at how sites such as Amazon and Facebook handle changes. Their interfaces don't radically change every week, although subtle and gradual changes are always being introduced, to respond to customers and enhance the experience.

Tracking Trends

If you sit at an outdoor café and watch traffic drive by, you begin to get a sense of patterns. You can estimate the number of cars that drive by; determine the most popular makes, models, and colors; establish whether the cars are zooming past or crawling by; and ascertain whether they're coming in groups or as a continuous stream.

You can apply the same techniques to monitoring your website traffic. If you want to understand the behaviors of the traffic, you need to know basic information and understand the trends that are occurring:

>> The number of visitors coming to your website

>> The number of *unique* visitors coming to your site

>> Which websites are referring viewers to your site

>> Which web pages are the most frequently viewed and the least frequently viewed

>> The number of web pages that the average visitor sees in one visit

You can track this usage without monitoring direct website traffic, although this method mainly involves direct customer interaction. You can contact a research group to find sample visitors and perform *usability testing,* where the research group introduces visitors to your website, asks them to interact with it, and then studies their activities to see whether they can intuitively find their way around your website, place an order, and perform basic functions. Based on these user interactions, the research group makes recommendations to you about changes you should make to your website to make it more user friendly or easier to use.

You can also solicit direct customer feedback through surveys, follow-up phone calls, or email response forms. Many websites gather this feedback by contacting past customers or people who have just ordered something from the website, and then getting their opinions about a variety of issues. This method is useful for identifying issues that need correcting or promoting, or to add insight or qualitative information to the level of your website's usefulness, beyond what the quantitative information is telling you through trend analysis. Find out more about adding qualitative information in the section "Getting to Know Your Customer," later in this chapter.

Measuring Website Traffic

Every time your web server receives a request from a visitor and displays a web page for that visitor, it creates an entry for the request in a log file on the web server. The log file records all the activity your website experiences. The server captures a lot of information in this file that you can then use to get a better idea of how your website is being used and operated by visitors and customers.

Thankfully, instead of reading log files to gain this information, there is website software that will read this information and present it to you in an easier-to-follow format, as well as provide reports and charts to give you an idea of trends, highlights, and important information that require your action. Called *traffic analysis* software, these software programs build a summary of your website traffic criteria and can

>> Break apart each log file entry

>> Group together similar entries

>> Factor out known entries, such as search engine bot programs

>> Calculate totals and averages

While there are different traffic analysis software options to choose from, we are using Google Analytics in this chapter. Consult with your technical staff or web administrator to see if your particular website comes with analytics software you can use.

When you study website traffic, statistics can help you improve your online business in at least three key areas. Google Analytics summarizes these three areas in an easy-to-follow ABC fashion:

>> **Acquisition:** How do you acquire or get people to your website?

>> **Behavior:** What are your users doing on your website after you acquire them?

>> **Conversion:** How are you turning the casual viewer into someone who buys something (or does a direct action on your site like joining a newsletter)?

In Google Analytics, the Audience Overview section gives you a clear idea of the traffic you are receiving to your website (see Figure 5-1). The Audience Overview looks at a number of statistics, which you can study in an hourly, daily, weekly, or monthly rate (just click the appropriate square in the top-right corner of the report).

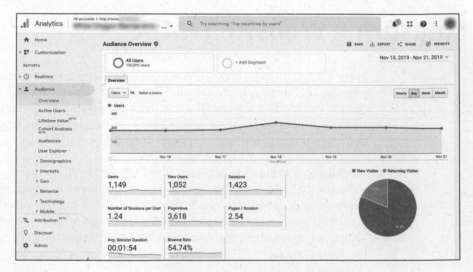

FIGURE 5-1:
Your analytics reports shows you all the visitors and what they looked at.

Your Audience Overview tells you a lot about your website:

>> The average length and number of pages visited on your site

>> The "stickiness" of your site, or how long people stay to look around

>> The demographic types of visitors who come to your site

>> The capability of your site to present your web pages effectively

Defining the terms of traffic analysis

Your website measures a *hit* whenever a piece of your website, whether it's a web page or a graphics file or another object, is sent over the Internet to someone's web browser. You might hear this activity described as "My website got a million hits last month." That statement is saying that your website handled a million different requests for everything from text to images to audio tracks.

Although some people think of hits purely as visitors, a web page might have nine different graphics and generate ten hits every time it's accessed. Why? When a visitor wants to view the web page, the web server sends out the HTML code of the page as the first request, and then the server sends nine separate graphics files, one by one, and records each of those transmissions as a separate hit.

This process is the reason that measuring hits isn't as important as other metrics, although it does give you a good baseline to understand the level of demand. When you're talking to advertisers, finding funding, or planning a marketing campaign, a high hit count doesn't spell success on its own.

A *page view*, on the other hand, happens when a visitor views a particular page. This number, which is independent of the number of elements that might be present on a web page, usually correlates to the number of visits to a particular page, especially on your home page.

Because most websites have multiple pages, you should be more concerned with the unique number of visits, or *unique visitors*, to your site. Your analytic software will look at the log files for some identifying information, such as an IP address, and correlate that information to your page views. If the software sees the same IP address viewing multiple pages, it will get an idea of the average number of pages viewed per user.

TECHNICAL STUFF

An *IP address*, or *Internet Protocol address*, is a series of four sets of numbers (in a range from 0 to 256) defining a computer's location on the Internet. An example of an IP address is 99.84.168.103 (which belongs to Dummies.com). Each IP address is unique to one computer at a time. Many users are assigned an IP address *dynamically*, which means that they're assigned a unique set of numbers the moment they sign on to the Internet, and they lose the right to those numbers when they're done. Some people, like those using cable modems or university computers, have the same IP address, or *static IP address*, all the time.

Most investors, suppliers, and employees, including you, are interested in knowing the number of unique visitors to your website. One of the easiest ways to figure out that number is when your website software implements a system where it places a text file (a cookie) on each visitor's computer. Turn to the later section "Storing data using cookies" to find out how to use cookies.

PUBLIC COMPUTERS SKEW THE DATA

Shared (or public) computers, like those you find at public libraries, Internet cafés, schools, and even some workplaces, are always on and always connected to the Internet, and they always use the same IP address to access the Internet. For this reason, your website log file shows every request coming from a shared computer as the same user. If you see 50 page views coming from the same IP address, you don't necessarily know, therefore, whether the page request is coming from 1 person or 10 people.

As a result, your analytics software has to look at other elements, such as the length of time a page is served, to figure out the average number of page views per visitor. Typically, these software programs take into account some calculated averages, and then they can break apart a heavily used IP address to represent an average number of users. For example, if the software can see that an average visitor to your site views, on average, 5 web pages, and the software sees 50 page views from one IP, it assumes the IP address represents 10 unique visitors.

Referring to your user acquisitions

In some cases, a separate file on your web server (sometimes known as a *referrer file*) contains the sources of all your web page requests. In Google Analytics, this area is called Audience Acquisition, or how you are getting your incoming users. You can see an example of an acquisition report in Figure 5-2. The sources you see are mostly other websites that link to you or search engine links where a visitor has typed certain keywords and found your site as one of the results.

FIGURE 5-2:
See where your website visitors are coming from.

For example, organic search means that someone typed keywords into a search engine such as Google and then clicked a link from the search results screen (not an advertisement on that screen, but a link inside the main section of the results screen) to arrive at your website. The beauty of organic search is that, sometimes, the referrer file will capture a link that contains the keywords the visitor typed to eventually end up on your site. This information alone can be invaluable when you're planning web-marketing campaigns. (See Chapter 3 of this minibook for more information on conducting a web advertising campaign.) If you see specific keywords or phrases in your reports for organic search results, you know that those words are powerful terms that bring people to your site.

TIP

If you're running a web-marketing campaign, you should distinguish search result referrals from sponsored ad referrals. If you include a keyword at the end of the link you provide for the sponsored ad, the keyword shows up correctly in the referrer file. For example, if you're linking to your home page and creating a Google Ads campaign, you can add the link `www.yourwebsite.com?GoogleAd11` to help interpret your results.

You might also see "direct" as a source of traffic, which could be links that come from your website where you're linking people from one page to another page on your website.

Direct traffic can also mean that users just typed your URL directly into their web browsers or have your website set up as a bookmark in their browsers so that they can go directly to your site. This entry is a good thing to see because it indicates that people are being drawn naturally to your website without having to find it from another website.

Examining viewer behavior

Getting viewers to your website is step 1. Once they arrive to your website, the next question is how they are using the site or which web pages (and how many) they are viewing before they leave the website.

One key metric that you will see with analysis software is something called the *bounce rate.* The bounce rate (for any given "entry" or starting page on your website) is the percentage of viewers who, after arriving at that given page, leave the website (or "bounce") without viewing any other pages within that website. This rate is used by many website owners to gauge the effectiveness of their website. After all, if people arrive and immediately go somewhere else without clicking in deeper, that's a lot of "wasted traffic" that isn't earning the owner any sales or loyalty from the user.

Bounce rates are not just important for your website's direct success. Search engines study bounce rates as well, and theorize that, if people arrive at that page and then immediately leave, then the web page isn't a useful result and will then lower that web page's ranking within the search results.

Your analysis software, in conjunction with your website software, should be able to track the path that users take when navigating your website. (For example, a path could be when a user arrives at your home page, then clicks on a product page, then clicks on a Buy button, then completes the buy screen and clicks on Order, and then sees the summary/receipt page and clicks away from the website.) If you get an overall view of everyone's path or "user flow" from page to page, you can begin to detect patterns of viewer usage. More important, you will see where in the path that users leave or bounce from your website, which could indicate to you an area that needs to be revised or improve in order to increase retention and eventually sales.

Google Analytics provides a Behavior Flow report that shows an overall view of people's paths through your website, as shown in Figure 5-3. One area of interest in these reports is the color extension to the right of a page entry. If you hover your mouse over that area, you'll see the number of drop-offs (or people leaving) from that page, and the corresponding percentage of those drop-offs to overall traffic.

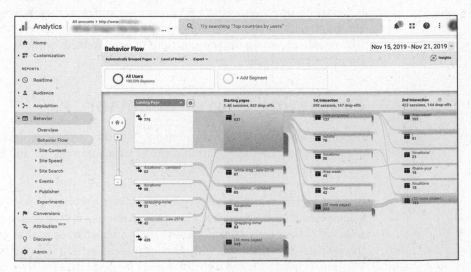

FIGURE 5-3:
See how your viewers are navigating your website.

Other statistics to monitor when studying user behavior include:

WARNING

>> **Popular landing pages:** Are your visitors starting on your home page, or a specific page within your website? By studying the popular landing pages, you can gain an idea about which pages to optimize and make sure those pages load quickly, are optimized with the right content, and have the correct links to help you generate sales.

You should also be aware of your most popular *exit* pages, which represent the point in a customer's path when the person gives up and goes somewhere else. Sometimes, it's the final order confirmation screen, which is what you want to see. Most times, however, you see another page, which should encourage you to investigate why that's the case. Maybe that page gives a negative impression of your website. Perhaps you're encouraging your customer to check out another website and he or she is following that link rather than continuing with you. A page on your site might contain invalid, outdated, or useless information and links. The report shows you the *where*, and you need to determine *why* it's an exit page.

>> **Site speed:** It's not always whether the web page is correct, but also how fast it loads for the user. In the era of fast connections to the Internet and instant gratification, users want their pages to load and display quickly or they could move onto a competitor. Analytics software helps show you how quickly users got their web pages and how quickly they navigated through the site. If you are noticing a particular web page that is loading more slowly than others (perhaps due to too many images, too many website or database queries, or special technology like Flash or video files), you may consider optimizing or fixing that page to improve loading time.

>> **Site search:** No website should be complete without an internal search engine, and keeping track of what keywords your viewers are typing into your own search engine will tell you what products or pages need to be front and center and easily accessible.

Checking abandoned shopping cart logs

Typically, an e-commerce shopping cart creates a file that contains a customer order. As the customer makes changes to that order, the shopping cart program adds or deletes from the file. When the customer checks out and pays for the order, the shopping cart converts the file into something else and deletes it from memory.

However, numerous studies indicate that website visitors abandon their shopping carts as much as 90 percent of the time. By looking at the shopping cart files that don't get ordered, you get an idea of how many people start the process but don't finish. You can compare this number to the number of orders you receive to calculate the percentage of potential customers that complete an order. This is the biggest statistic to help you gauge and improve *conversions,* or the number of viewers who end up becoming buyers.

Suppose you receive 50 orders for products in a month and then search for your shopping cart files and find 150 that were never processed. Your result means that 200 customers started the process, but only 50 finished, which is a 25 percent completion ratio for your visitors. When you know your ratio, you can start to take steps to improve it; we show you how in the section "Using Your Data to Understand Your Business," near the end of this chapter.

You can also find out which products are more popular by counting which ones get added to the carts. If someone took the time to physically add a product to his or her shopping cart, there is intent and demand for the item. You can use this information to help guide future product orders.

Measuring traffic against activity

Your website traffic data shows you a lot of information. To give these numbers some perspective so that you can make higher-level decisions, especially when it comes to conversions, you have to match the traffic with other indicators of activity on your website:

>> Number of orders

>> Average order size

>> Number of registered customers (if you offer registration)

>> Total sales volume

>> Average number of products per order

>> Most common search terms (if you have your own site search engine)

The reason to compare these numbers is to give you an idea of how much your traffic is influencing your sales. Suppose that your website gets 1,000 unique visitors one month and you see that you're getting 250 orders from 200 unique customers that month. Theoretically, if you can double the number of visitors you receive in a month, you should see a similar increase in your orders and unique customers. Perhaps it doesn't double, but if you can estimate the benefit of bringing in more people, you can estimate the amount of money you can spend to increase traffic.

Putting together all this information gives you a complete picture of how your business is operating. Knowing these factors helps you make dozens of decisions that affect your entire business.

Analyzing Your Traffic Analysis Software

As we mention earlier in this chapter, it's not recommended that you attempt to manually analyze your website information (from areas like your log files) to get your website statistics. Therefore, we highly recommend using traffic analysis software such as Google Analytics, which you can find at `www.google.com/analytics`. However, there are varying levels of software available in the marketplace. You can choose from different versions and levels of traffic analysis software: basic, detailed, and enterprise or big business.

Basic analysis software

When you're using a basic analysis tool, you're looking for a program to create summaries of traffic information for a given period. Some tools, such as Angelfish Digital Analytics software (`http://analytics.angelfishstats.com`), run on your self-hosted server. Others, such as Clicky (`www.clicky.com`), Google Marketing Platform (which includes Google Analytics; `www.google.com/analytics`), or Hotjar (`www.hotjar.com`), present data in both columnar and graphical formats for easy viewing.

Here are some statistics that every program should produce or estimate:

>> Total number of visitors and unique visitors

>> Average number of daily visitors

>> Total and average number of page views

>> Total and average number of hits

>> Average length of a visit (in minutes or number of page views)

Although the software you use might produce additional results, you can usually count on these categories being calculated. As an example, if you're using a free tool that creates a text summary and you requested a summary for your October 2019 traffic data, you might see results like this:

```
Period: Tue-1-Oct-2019 12:00 to Thu-31-Oct-2019 23:59 (31 days).
Total successful requests: 2,221
Average successful requests per day: 72
```

```
Total successful requests for pages: 948
Total failed requests: 75
Total redirected requests: 349
Number of distinct files requested: 42
Number of distinct hosts served: 618
Number of new hosts served in last 7 days: 72
Total data transferred: 25,349 kbytes
Average data transferred per day: 844,967 bytes
```

This data gives you some important numbers for future demand. By looking at the total and average amount of data being transferred, you get an idea of the bandwidth you need to purchase for your website. You can see how many different web pages are being looked at on your site. In this example, 42 different web pages were requested. If your website has only 50 or 60 total pages, your customers are using a wide range of your site. If you have 200 or 300 pages, you need to see which pages are being loaded and figure out what to do with the rest.

You can also see more detailed information with Google Analytics (see Figure 5-4). Google Analytics provides line graphs and summary tables to draw a detailed picture of your website's usage statistics, broken down by month and arranged by different criteria.

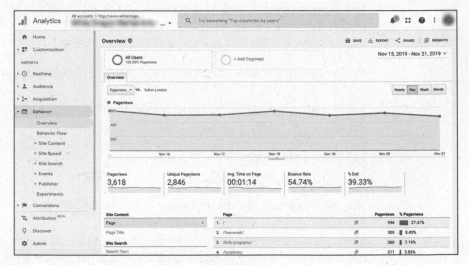

FIGURE 5-4:
Look at your website traffic numbers month by month.

Detailed analysis software

At some point, you want to see more advanced information about how your website operates so that you can make targeted changes and updates to improve performance. At this stage, you should look into buying a tool such as WebTrends (www.webtrends.com) or SmarterStats (www.smartertools.com/smarterstats) to analyze your log files and provide more defined criteria, such as

>> A detailed breakdown of page views

>> The most common referral links used by your visitors

>> The pages from which users are most often exiting your site

>> The number or percentage of return visitors

>> The most popular web browsers used by your visitors

>> The most popular search engines that deliver your traffic

>> The amount of nonhuman traffic (such as search engine programs)

>> The busiest and slowest parts of the day for your web traffic

These tools come with a number of predefined reports that help you understand your visitors' and customers' sophisticated interaction with your website. As you change the dates of the period you want to analyze, the graphs are updated automatically. This way, you can compare traffic levels for different weeks, months, or even seasons.

TIP

Upload your log files or grant access for these analysis software programs to read your log files automatically. You might have to install these programs on your web server to get them to work properly. Follow the setup instructions and talk to your web-hosting provider if you need specific path or filename details.

Enterprise or big business

As your business grows, you might want to move up to an enterprise-level solution, such as one of these programs:

>> **Adobe Analytics:** www.adobe.com/analytics/adobe-analytics.html

>> **Zap:** www.zapbi.com

>> **IBMCognos Analytics:** www.ibm.com/products/cognos-analytics

In this case, you want to install the service on your web host. The key to using these programs is being able to write your own queries to the database, which means that you come up with your own specific requests for summary data.

WARNING

Some programs require that you know a specific computer language, such as SQL, to create your own reports. If someone in your business is focused on information technology, have that person help you develop the language necessary to build these reports.

Collecting the Correct Information

After people start taking advantage of website traffic analysis, they sometimes fall into the trap of believing that the software does all the work of collecting the right data. You have to realize that although your web server collects some types of information, you can collect other types yourself. In this section, we discuss how you can use your website to reach out and collect more specific information without your customers having to cough up their Social Security numbers.

Storing data using cookies

Any web server can create a standard file on a visitor's computer, to keep track of that visitor's activity and interaction with the web server. That file is known as a *cookie* because it leaves "crumbs" of information that the web server can access when the user visits that website. A cookie is a website owner's friend in many respects because it can show him or her what an individual user is doing on the site. You can track individual behavior and calculate unique visitors and session length much more precisely than by using log files. You can focus on one user for any length of time, from a few days to a few months, to see what the user does on every visit. You can see which web pages the user looks at and the order of those pages and then correlate that information to the user's orders and sign-up activity.

Cookies help move your focus from a site-specific level to a customer level. When you add cookies to your server log files, you can gauge the efficiency of your marketing campaigns with precision. You can judge for yourself how effective your campaigns are so that you're not relying solely on your advertiser reports.

To turn on the use of cookies, ask your web-hosting provider to enable them for your web server. After you do that, tell your provider which basic fields you want to use and capture in your cookies, such as

>> The visitor's IP address

>> The visitor's username or account name

>> The date and time of the visits

Because of newer laws like the EU's General Data Protection Regulation (GDPR), websites are required to get the consent of their users before storing a cookie on their computers. You must provide a pop-up (as shown in Figure 5-5) or built-in message on your website home page informing any users that you use cookies to collect data, and they must click an Accept button to allow you to store a cookie on their computers.

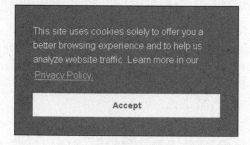

FIGURE 5-5:
Ask your customers to agree to your placing cookies on their computers.

REMEMBER

Your customers can refuse to have cookies stored on their computers, or they might use public computers, so their cookies won't be consistent. Even if you don't get a 100 percent view of your traffic, using cookies is much more precise than just analyzing your log files.

After you enable cookies on your web server, your last step is to ensure that your traffic analysis software can access the cookies that your web server leaves. That way, the software can incorporate that information into its reports and update its figures accordingly.

Adding information to your links

When you're looking at your log files, you see keywords in the string that represent a referral URL. Sometimes, these keywords are search terms used by visitors when they're using search engines. At other times, however, those specific terms were created for the purpose of communicating information.

You can *tag*, or add special keywords referred to as *UTM codes*, to your URL to track the success of a marketing campaign. For example, you can tag your URL with different UTM codes specifically for your Facebook post, a specific tweet, an email newsletter, and other marketing materials, which can help you judge the efficiency and reach of each announcement separately. Add the UTM code after

Analyzing and Monitoring Your Customers

the name of the HTML file by typing a question mark (?) and then the UTM code, like this:

```
<a href="http://www.yourwebsite.com/index.html?GoogleAd1">
```

This way, when someone uses your targeted URL, the traffic analysis software can determine the number of times the UTM code (GoogleAd1, in this example) was sent in the URL as a percentage of the total number of requests and then calculate a percentage.

If you continue to include this UTM code throughout the ordering process, your analysis software can determine the conversion rate of browsers to buyers by studying how many buyers used a UTM code as a percentage of the number of the browsers who came to your website.

Studying the path analysis

Your customers eventually follow a path of specific web pages that take them from start to finish on your site. Although individual customers might check out different parts of your website along the way, they need to visit a minimum number of web pages to go from a browsing customer to a paid customer. This minimum number of pages is sometimes called the *critical path* of your website.

Suppose that your website targets different levels of customers and has a special section for small-business customers. Your critical path might look like this:

> Home page → Small-business home page → Small-business catalog page → Order review page → Order checkout page

When you identify the critical path for your customers, you can combine this knowledge with the traffic analysis you already completed to determine when and where people are dropping out of the order process. If you improve this process for your users, you should see an increased number of completed orders and a decreased number of abandoned shopping carts.

Suppose that you're studying the order checkout path. Here are some ways you can integrate all your research:

>> If your report of the most common exit pages shows the order review page as a common exit page, something in the order review process might be confusing or counterintuitive to your users.

» If your referrer report indicates that a number of people are jumping to your frequently asked questions (FAQs) page or privacy policy page from your order review page, your customers most likely need or want more information before they check out. When they jump out of the critical path, a percentage of them never come back to the review or checkout phase. Therefore, you can integrate some of this content into your order review page and see whether fewer people exit before completing the review page.

» An order checkout page that involves multiple steps and shows people linking back and forth to the same pages could indicate that users are caught in a loop and can't break out to finish their orders. You might need to combine certain steps on one page or provide more clearly labeled links to convince customers to move forward.

Besides keeping your customers from dropping out of the order process, the other reason for studying your paths is to help you decide to redesign your website. Your customers eventually make their own path through your website, despite any warnings or guidelines you post. You can either continue to try to steer those customers or study their paths and incorporate that information into your site design so that the most common paths are recognized and supported by your website links and structure.

REMEMBER

Just as a river cuts its own path through the countryside, your customers will cut their own path through your website. You should always support that path and optimize your site around it rather than fight it and prevent customers from moving around the way they want.

Getting to Know Your Customer

If you've ever walked into a store to buy batteries, you know that sometimes, the store wants to know a lot about you. The clerk might ask for your zip code, and sometimes your address, even if you're paying cash. The people who run the company do this so that they can get an understanding of the customers who walk through their door and how those customers shop. Although you may find this process annoying or off-putting, you probably accommodate the request. The store can then accurately predict, for example, which customers from which zip codes will order the most batteries.

Gathering customer information is a delicate but ultimately profitable venture because analyzing that information gives you razorlike focus on how your customers interact with you. Just like supermarkets that encourage their customers to use loyalty cards when they shop, websites are now gathering information on a customer level, independent of the traffic information that their web browser leaves with your website. Because the customer is now signed in to the website, every activity is recorded and assigned to a customer account, which can be analyzed and aggregated without worrying about issues such as IP addresses and cookies.

As you understand your individual customers better, you move the focus of your data from your overall website statistics to your customers, where the common factor isn't your entire website but rather the average customer and what he or she does on your website. Begin by having your traffic analysis program identify a unique visitor and then summarize information, such as average length of a visit or session.

Your goal is to find customer-specific patterns, not overall site trends. Collect data from your customer interactions that allow you to gain insight into customers' browsing and buying behavior. At this point, you should add tags or information on pages that matter to your customers, whether it's the order process screen or customer login screen.

Your existing customers have already told you a lot about themselves, including their

>> Names

>> Mailing address(es)

>> Credit card information

>> Order lists of products

At some point, consider signing up users when they arrive at your website or when they want to learn more or do more on your website. Then tie that information into both the traffic and order statistics, to give yourself a true customer focus on your website activity.

When a customer has to log in to your website to use it, you can track every movement and tie those movements to a specific user ID number. Typically, users need some sort of incentive to reveal their personal information and complete a sign-up process. Some websites offer their members exclusive, premium content that casual browsing customers cannot access. Other sites require accounts to be created before products can be added to their shopping carts. You need to determine which special features you want to give to people who sign up with you.

TIP

When you use a sign-up process, you lose a certain percentage of browsers who could have become buyers. If you see a big drop-off in activity after instituting a sign-up process, consider assigning a guest account to your procedures. A user who wants to shop can convert a guest account to a permanent account.

Most websites ask for basic information whenever someone signs up for an account:

>> User's name

>> Address

>> City, state, zip code

>> Phone number

>> Email address

However, if you think beyond these basic fields, you can ask users additional questions to draw a better picture of your customers, and even to gather ideas that can influence your website, such as these examples:

>> **Demographic information:** Gender, ethnicity, age, marital status, kids

>> **Psychographic information:** Likes, brand recognition, purchase reasons

>> **Lifestyle information:** Income, housing status, types of cars

>> **Interests and preferences:** Favorite subjects, products, and people

Use the data to better understand what customers want and to customize content to them. You can use analytics software like Hotjar to help you create the survey, as shown in Figure 5-6, to ask the right questions for existing customers.

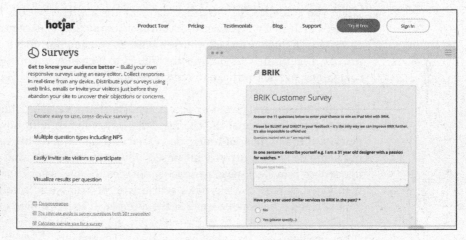

FIGURE 5-6:
Ask customers what they like to buy and use that information.

The options you present can be limited if your customers don't contribute information; if you make it required, however, you can lose a substantial number of potential and actual customers. Make this information-gathering process optional so that customers who don't want to reveal their information aren't blocked from using your website.

Using Your Data to Understand Your Business

Collecting your website traffic and usage data is important for understanding your business. The true value of all this collection and analysis becomes evident when you act on the data and implement changes to your site. After all, what good is learning about a problem if you don't correct it?

Watching trends to find out average behavior

After you set up and collect your data, you have to monitor the activity levels to see trends and behavior so that you have a benchmark for comparison when you're ready to make changes. After all, if you don't know the average behavior of your website, you don't know where it has room for improvement.

When you study traffic and usage patterns for a longer period, look for any big changes in the data. If you see that your traffic suddenly experienced a big increase or suffered a huge drop, ask yourself what is causing big spikes or drops in your activity. Determine whether they're related to a change you made (such as an ad campaign), overall traffic, or a random event.

To fully investigate, create or access reports that give you detailed information from around the time of the change. This way, you can hunt down big problems quickly. If the number of orders decreased and the number of errors about pages not being delivered correctly increased, you know that your web server or Internet service provider was experiencing outages. If your website was unexpectedly mentioned as part of a big news article, you probably saw a spike in visitors to your site and (you hope) a spike in the number of orders placed on your site.

Other problems are less obvious to identify. Diagnosing these situations involves looking at web page activity and seeing which statistics have been affected by the change in activity. As you look at your site, be aware of any changes you made to the web pages, however big or small, and see whether the dates of those changes match up with the change in usage. Sometimes, a simple change disrupts an otherwise stable process and causes unexpected problems. If you watch trends, however, you can spot problems early and then fix them.

Identifying areas of improvement

You have many ways to know when something needs updating. When your car bounces over a pothole and says "ka-thunk," you know that it's time to repave the road. On your website, a report might indicate that traffic took a nosedive. Your email account might be filled with customers screaming IN ALL CAPS that you can't keep operating a certain way.

You can also look at the data you're collecting to start making predictions before problems get out of hand. Find out which web pages your users

>> Gravitate to

>> Avoid

>> View most often and least often

Sometimes, the problem is a factor that your data can only partially identify. Suppose that your traffic report indicates that people check your website every morning. In addition to having traffic data, you know that your product catalog is updated only at the end of the business day, when you hear back from your suppliers. Put together those two pieces of information, and you have a timing problem because your site isn't as current as possible when visitors check it out. They might move on if they see you as unresponsive. In this example, you have to figure out a way to update your inventory each morning.

Put yourself in the role of your customer. Start at your home page and try to place an order. Use your traffic and usage data to back up your assumptions about how to proceed. If you find a page frustrating to use and it shows up on your most common exit pages, you've identified an area to improve.

REMEMBER

Don't overlook the importance of direct customer feedback for website improvements. Encourage regular dialogue, use follow-up surveys, and stay in contact with a portion of your customers at all times. They're usually up front about what can be improved and what has to be changed. After they identify a concern, you can research your data to choose your next step.

Deciding on a change

As you look at all your data and trends, identify an area that can be improved. Look at all factors that can influence its poor performance, and choose an element to change on your website that mimics a part of the site that performs well. Look at competitors' websites to see whether they handle the process differently. Ask customers for feedback on how you should handle the process.

When you're ready to update a part of your website, follow these steps:

1. **Make sure that you have a beginning set of statistics before you implement the change.**

   You need a set of data specifying how your website operated before the change, to use for later comparison.

2. **Make the change on your website.**

   Many sites post notices about maintenance periods, where their sites are temporarily unavailable while new updates are posted. Typically, these updates take place during the night for U.S. customers so that the updates have the least effect on traffic. Use the maintenance period to send new versions of your web pages to your web server.

3. **Gather your traffic statistics after the change is posted to your website.**

Watch the usage data after the new version is available, and notice whether traffic went up, as predicted, or down. Notice also whether other parts of your website were affected and whether orders increased.

Following up

Any change to your website can affect all your other processes. Therefore, you must follow up any change you make to your website, to make sure that you haven't disrupted anything else. You also have to study customer reaction to your changes and make sure that they benefit from them as much as possible.

Sometimes, you need to *roll back* the change (remove the update or go back to the old process). Although the techniques discussed in this chapter give you lots of insight into customer behavior, traffic analysis doesn't predict events with 100 percent accuracy. That's why you must stay flexible and judge whether any updates still provide value after they're implemented.

Chapter **6**

Mastering Search Engines, Optimization, and Rankings

I f you earn prominent placement for your business where traffic is flowing, customers are more likely to stop by, look around, and buy something before they leave. Now, with the ever-growing and ever-changing nature of the Internet, many people are using search engines as their on ramp, or premier starting point for web browsing. After all, if potential customers think that they are going to end up at a search engine to find something, why wouldn't they start there? As a consequence, search results are becoming the gateway to the web, which is exactly where you want to be, offering your products.

In Chapter 3 of this minibook, we talk about marketing yourself in the sponsored ads that are part of the standard search results page. In this chapter, we put the more valuable real estate — the search results themselves — front and center and show you how to improve the quality of your search engine placements.

We also discuss the inner workings of the biggest search engines and then show you how you can influence those engines in your favor. Nothing about these tricks is illegal — you're just increasing your presence in the right areas to get noticed more easily. We also show you how to stay near the top and describe more direct ways to "wave people down" in those search engine results.

Navigating the Ins and Outs of Major Search Engines

When you open a search engine web page and type some words in the search box, do you ever wonder how the search engine produces your search results? Do you imagine a blindfolded person tossing darts at newspapers spread over a wall? Maybe a chicken is let loose to peck its way to a few sites that are then transmitted to you. Although the true answer isn't as comical, search engines use different procedures and methods to compare information against similar sites to come up with the all-important rankings.

Companies that figure out these procedures are the ones that continually find themselves near the top of the rankings. Other businesses, which might have well-designed websites that are chock-full of information, could get buried on page 10 or page 20 of the results. A few years ago, human intervention could elevate worthy sites to the top and give them featured placement. Now, however, the placement process is almost all computerized — and because computers follow rules, logic dictates that if you follow the rules, the computers will follow you.

REMEMBER

The full set of rules that search engines use to order all their results are tightly guarded secrets because those rules, known as *algorithms*, set companies apart in this area. Google, in particular, uses complex rules.

These rules do change, but there's a core set of rules we focus on in this chapter that will help you the most as you work to improve your search engine results position:

>> You need to make sure the important **keywords** (for your website) are found on the pages within your website, with importance assigned to their placement, frequency, and association with web links.

>> You want as many **incoming links** to your website as possible. Your ranking is assessed by both the quantity and quality (Google PageRank or equivalent "trusted website" gauge) of those incoming links.

>> The more **useful content** found within your website, the better. Sometimes, there is a favorable bonus given to frequently updated content such as a blog or social media.

>> In the end, your content needs to be **"human-friendly,"** which means it should be readable to a human being and not engineered to impress a search engine computer, easy to find within your website, and marked with the correct HTML tags to tell the search engine what the content represents.

We cover each of these points throughout the chapter, so let's start with keywords. The words you enter into a search engine typically aren't ordinary words. They're *keywords*, or specific words tied to a particular subject you're interested in. When you go to a search engine, you should give that engine the keywords, or most targeted words, that describe your search.

Search engines work like this:

1. You go to your favorite search engine, type a search term (a keyword) in the text box, and click Search to see the results.

2. Your search engine matches your search term against its database to look for relevant mentions of that keyword and relevant pages that are interpreted as the best "answers" for your search terms.

The database is made up of countless entries of different web pages that were gathered by either computer programs (known as *bots* or *spiders* in the technical world) or human editors.

The search engine doesn't analyze entire web pages by scanning every word in a page against the keyword you specified. Instead, the search engine looks through *notes*, or a shorthand representation of that page. These notes (which summarize the page) are taken from such elements as

>> The name of the website and particular web page

>> Words used in the *title* (or *head*) of the web page

>> Words used in the *name* of the web page (keyword.html for example)

>> The first paragraph or two of the web page

>> Words assigned by the web page to represent the title and description (by using the ‹META› tag, which we discuss in the section "Creating META tags," later in this chapter)

>> Internet web links present on the web page

>> Words used by other web pages that offer a link to the web page

In fact, the first page of the search results lists web pages that contain your search term. We discuss how to insert your keywords into these various places on your web pages later in this chapter, in the section "Placing Keywords in Key Spots on Your Website."

REMEMBER

You're not limited to a single keyword. You can have multiple keywords or even phrases of keywords. However, you have a better chance of promoting a handful of keywords or phrases than trying to be the website that offers everything to everyone. Think about the most important or valuable phrases that your customers will use when they search for the products you sell.

Getting Your Website Noticed by Search Engines

Whether people are waving their hands in front of a crowd or smiling for TV cameras, they like to be noticed. To succeed in business, you're always told, "Stand out from the rest and be noticed." As business owners struggle with the notion of getting noticed on a finite budget, creative measures come into play.

As we discuss in the preceding section, increasing your website's visibility on search engines involves knowing the rules they use and ensuring that your site follows those rules. Search engines don't solely base their rankings on keywords. If they did, a web page that mentions the same word a thousand times would be at the top of their rankings. Instead, search engines look primarily at incoming links and amount of content.

Incoming links, or *references*, are simply how many other websites offer a link to a given web page on your website. The more links that point to a particular page, the higher that page appears on the search engine rankings, especially on Google. The generic reasoning by the search engine algorithms is that, if other websites are pointing their visitors to a particular page, that page must have more relevant content than other, nonlinked pages. Think of an incoming link as some other website "vouching" for the usefulness of your website.

Having other websites link to your web page is the next step in search engine optimization (SEO). Greater weight is given to a web page whose referring links use the main keywords for that page in the text for that link. Suppose that you're trying to promote a web page for Arctic Technology Solutions. You have the best URL you can get for the keywords in your company name, `www.arctictechnologysolutions.com`, and leading IT consultants link to your website. Now, tell these consultants to build the link this way:

```
<a href=https://www.arctictechnologysolutions.com> Talk to
    Arctic Technology Solutions! </a>
```

Notice that the clickable text that points to your website contains the same keywords as your URL. The search engines receive a double message that your website contains the text *Arctic Technology Solutions* because its computer programs read the keywords in both the HTML command and the clickable words.

Search engines look not just at the link itself but also at the website from where the incoming link is originating. Therefore, here are a few additional issues to keep in mind:

>> **The more reputable the website, the higher value the link brings you.** Search engines typically assign a higher value to links from websites that are highly respected. Therefore, an incoming link from Google, Yahoo!, or one of the top 10 sites on the Internet helps your search engine rankings much more than a link from your friend's toy review website. Aim for known websites, educational institutions, if possible, or even government agencies when applicable.

>> **Reprioritize new content whenever possible.** As your business progresses, and you continue to generate new content, whether it's for the website, blog, or social media channels, you need to make sure that new content is easily available on your website and receives the highest priority. Search engines are giving a higher priority to new content, so make sure any new content is highlighted and focused on when optimizing your website.

>> **Make sure that the referring website is relevant to your business.** Getting reputable websites to link to you is important, but search engines also look for relevance. Does it make sense for them to link to you? Do your sites have something in common or something complementary? For example, having a technology review site link to your organic garden business may not be relevant, but having *Better Homes and Gardens* magazine link to your garden business is relevant.

>> **The age of the website name may be a factor.** Search engines check for a website's age by looking at the date the domain name was created in the main domain name database. For example, a website created in the late 1990s has obviously been in the database longer than a website whose domain name was first registered two weeks ago. Therefore, aim for incoming links from websites with some history. Check WHOIS (`www.whois.com`) to find the age of a website.

>> **The best links are incoming only, not reciprocal.** When two websites link to each other in the hope of raising each other's search engine ranking, the links are *reciprocal*. However, reciprocal links carry a lower ranking weight than incoming only links. If several websites create a looping chain of links, where Site A links to Site B, Site B links to Site X, and Site X links back to Site A, Google will lower the weight of all those links. If a website links to you without a link back to it, that incoming link helps your ranking a lot more.

More and more, search engines are evaluating your search engine ranking by the amount of useful content, or how much quality information, you offer on your website. Websites with more content — articles, blog entries, calculators, reviews and guides, or plain text — are more useful to someone searching for information and are typically given higher search result rankings than sites with little content. That content, however, should be unique to your website, not just reprinted from other sites.

Some people have a goal of writing an article a day for their sites. In a year, you can turn 10 or 15 minutes of writing into 365 articles! Or you could hire someone to create content for you. Just make sure the content is readable and not simply packed with the keywords you think you need on your site. Search engines penalize sites that are overloaded with keywords, also known as *keyword stuffing*.

As mentioned before, search engines look for "fresh" or recently added content to your website, and one of the best ways to ensure a steady stream of new content is by linking your social media channels and blogs (Facebook, Twitter, Pinterest, Tumblr, Instagram, and others) to your website, so that information will count toward your website's overall standing in search engine rankings. As an example, if you search for a specific person (instead of a product or service), many times the first page of search engine results will contain the person's profile on social media networks like Facebook, LinkedIn, or Twitter.

Placing Keywords in Key Spots on Your Website

Content is important, but people also search the Internet with words, so understanding and using keywords is still an important part of preparing your website for search engine traffic, especially the placement of those words and information that makes it useful to search engines but also readable by human beings. You can use different methods to incorporate on your web pages the keywords that will be viewed as the most relevant and important words that represent your page and still preserve the "readability" and usefulness of the content. The keywords must appear in multiple locations so that the search engine bots know that those keywords represent the content of your page.

The most important factor is, as they say in real estate, location, location, location. Sure, you can write a web page about the hundred greatest uses for a ball-peen hammer and use the words *ball-peen hammer* repeatedly in the body of the web page. But you can find better locations than the body of the web page to attract the attention of search engine bots more reliably and consistently. Some locations are invisible to the web browser, and others are hiding in plain sight.

Keywords that are invisible

Web pages are built in *HyperText Markup Language,* or *HTML.* Commands aplenty identify the information contained in a web page. For keyword purposes, the most important tag to use in your web page is ‹META›. It defines the name, purpose, author, and date of a web page. Search engines read this tag to catalog web pages more efficiently.

Because of this command's purpose, search engine bots are interested in knowing what information is assigned to ‹META› tags. They take that information with a grain of salt, however, because they know that the ‹META› tag info is being written by a biased source — the author of the page. Nevertheless, the ‹META› tag information is added to the formula for reading and interpreting web pages.

REMEMBER

If you're having someone design your web pages, be sure to ask specifically whether he's defining ‹META› tags for every single web page on your site. These optional tags are commonly forgotten because they don't affect the performance of the web page on the server.

The ‹META› tag is specific to only the individual web page where the tag resides. Therefore, the information in the ‹META› tag for your home page is (and should be) completely or significantly different from an interior web page that focuses on one product line.

Creating META tags

For each web page, insert at least two ‹META› tags into the HTML for the page. More options are available, such as defining the author of the page or the last revision date of the web page. Although you might want to define these fields for other reasons, they're not as helpful for targeting search engines.

REMEMBER

Include these ‹META› tags as part of the head of each web page, not the body section.

Mastering Search Engines, Optimization, and Rankings

META TAGS CAN SPEAK FOREIGN LANGUAGES

In this global era of the Internet, your audience is no longer restricted to one region or country. Similarly, your keywords are no longer restricted to one language. The ‹META› tag has the capability to assign keywords to a particular language set, so you can have a different tag for Americans who speak English, Britons who speak English, and almost everyone in Central or South America and in Spain who speaks Spanish.

You can define an attribute of the ‹META› tag known as lang (short for *language*). The search engines implement a filter if they see the lang attribute defined and then assign the correct keywords to the specified language in the web surfer's preferences.

If you sell soccer jerseys and sweaters, for example, your ‹META› tags might look like this:

```
<META name="keywords" lang="en-us" content="soccer, jersey,
    sweater">
<META name="keywords" lang="en" content="football, jersey,
    jumper">
<META name="keywords" lang="es" content="futbol, Jersey,
    sueter">
```

The syntax of a ‹META› tag works in two parts: You define which type of ‹META› tag you want to use by assigning a name to it, and then you assign the content for that ‹META› tag. For example, if you want to assign the keywords *Arctic*, *Technology*, and *Solutions*, your ‹META› tag would look like this:

```
<META name="keywords" content="Arctic, Technology,
    Solutions">
```

Unlike in other HTML commands, a closing tag isn't necessary. This line of code is sufficient. You need a separate ‹META› tag, however, for each type of information you want to define. Figure 6-1 shows how to separate the definition from the keywords by using two ‹META› tags.

The two ‹META› tags you need to include are keywords and description. For added effect, some people repeat their keywords as part of their descriptions. The search engines, though, are reading the ‹META› description and looking for context. A laundry list of keywords in the ‹META› description tag, therefore, doesn't improve your results. A creative integration can help your efforts, though.

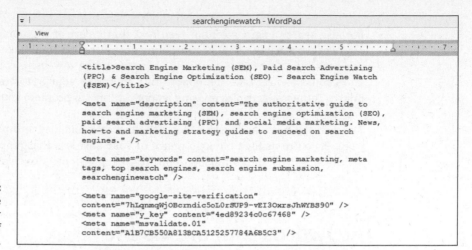

FIGURE 6-1:
Use separate
<META> tags for
different types of
information.

If you're selling gourmet artichoke sauces, your <META> tags might look like this:

```
<META name="keywords" content="Gourmet, Artichoke, Sauces">
<META name="description" content="Our gourmet chefs have picked
    the freshest artichokes to create gourmet artichoke sauces
    sure to liven up any artichoke recipe!">
```

Note the repeated use of the targeted keywords as part of the context of a readable, legible sentence. Although the <META> description tag doesn't have a hard limit, using more than one or two sentences dilutes any meaning you hope to get from using the tag in the first place. Simply put, if you overload the description tag, you water down your results to the point that the search engines don't know any more what's particularly meaningful. Moreover, search engines can *lower* your search ranking result if they think that you are *keyword stuffing*, or putting too many instances of the keywords on your web page.

Adding ALT attributes

A valuable addition to the HTML image tag is the ALT attribute. This attribute is assigned to image files loaded onto a web page. The ALT attribute is a description of the graphical image that's displayed on the web page if the web browser cannot load the image properly on the screen. Additionally, in web browsers such as Internet Explorer and Netscape's Mozilla, a user can hover the cursor over the image to see the information assigned to the ALT attribute.

REMEMBER

If you're using the basic Firefox web browser, don't expect to see any ALT text when you hover your cursor over the image. This program treats the ALT information as originally intended, and it's displayed only if the image doesn't load properly.

Because search engines cannot read text that's part of a graphical image, they read the ALT attribute, if it's defined, and give it some weight. Like the ‹META› tag, the optional ALT attribute is easily forgotten when a website is being designed. You should always take the opportunity to define your ALT attributes for your images; otherwise, you're missing an opportunity to promote your keywords.

The ALT attribute is added to the ‹IMG› tag that includes an image on the web page. If you're using a big logo image of your business that represents gourmet artichoke sauces, the command to insert the image looks like this:

```
<IMG SRC="logo.jpg" ALT="Gourmet Artichoke Sauces Logo">
```

Keywords that are visible

Although search engines rely on HTML commands such as the ‹META› tag to gain an understanding of the purpose of a web page, their computer programs are more interested in divining the "natural" meaning of a web page, by interpreting the text visible on the page and understanding what the page itself is trying to convey to users. Therefore, make sure that the keywords that best identify your web page are clearly used in some visible — but not obvious — locations:

>> **Page name:** Every web page is simply a file containing HTML commands and text, and each file has to have a name. The last three or four letters of the filename after the period must be htm or html because of web standards. Everything in front of the period in the filename is up to you. If you set up a page to sell tennis equipment, for example, don't use an abstract name, such as order.html. Instead, name this special page tennis.html or tennis-equipment.html.

TIP

If you're designing your website for optimal search engine recognition and one web page offers two or more categories of products, divide the product line and dedicate a single page for each one. This way, you can gear everything on each page toward the specific product the page represents.

>> **Page title:** Every web page on your website should have a title, regardless of the purpose of the page. Search engines pick up this valuable space.

REMEMBER

The worst thing you can do is leave an empty title. The second-worst thing you can do is use a vague or meaningless title, such as "Welcome to my website!" or "Stuff for you." Make sure that each title has the important keywords for that page.

>> **Page headings:** Human eyes pick up headlines quicker than any other text on the page. Computer programs read headlines and assign a greater weight to them than to the text on the page. You can be more specific in the headings than in the title — just focus the headings on the page content, not on your overall site.

» **First sentence:** The first sentence on the page is typically a summary or an overview of what the page offers. Because some search engines don't index an entire page of text, make sure that the first sentence draws a clear picture of your intentions for the page.

» **Text inside links:** Search engine bots are hungry for web links, so make sure that any clickable text contains the right keywords for that link. The bots assign weight to those keywords because they're being referenced by the link.

In addition to adding keywords in these locations, you should still fine-tune your pages to mention your keywords throughout the text, as shown in Figure 6-2. Work these keywords into the flow of the text in a way that isn't jarring to readers. Don't just offer strings of keywords that don't form complete sentences. Search engine bots pick up on context, so they flag as nonessential any out-of-place lists of keywords they find.

FIGURE 6-2: See how important keywords are used throughout the page.

WARNING

Don't display any valuable keywords as graphics files on your web page. Search engine bots can scan only the text in the HTML file (or the ALT attribute for an image) — not the contents of a graphics file. If you have to use graphics, for a navigation menu or header, for example, complement that menu with a text menu at the bottom of the page. This way, you're using the keywords as text and the keywords are clickable text, which improves your site's ranking.

Arranging Your Pages Strategically

Your website is simply the collection of various web pages that make up your overall business. Therefore, you want every web page in your business to be well defined and serve a specific purpose. You don't want to create web pages whose only goal is to attract search engines with keywords and defined tags. Instead, you want pages that make sense to users and search engine bots.

Keep the following rules in mind when you're constructing the web pages in your business:

>> **One page, one focus.** If one web page contains two or more product lines, consider breaking up that page so that each line has its own page. You can still have a category index page, which you can optimize with your overall business mission, and each product page can then be a launching pad for that subset of your business.

>> **Define your page.** Make sure that all your definitions, tags, and keyword mentions are at the top of your HTML source code for your web page. Some search engines limit the number of characters per page they take, and you don't want to lose out because you added a lot of comments or JavaScript code first.

>> **Think about keyword density.** Focus each web page to target a select group of keywords and phrases. This technique increases the weight of each of these phrases more than when you try to use every keyword in every page (a practice known as *keyword density*). When the same words are used repeatedly, search engines see this density of words and assign greater weight to the few words that are used than does an average website that tries to be popular for every popular keyword.

>> **Put away the bells and whistles.** If your web page excessively uses elements such as graphics, animation, and video or audio files on the same page as valuable product information, separate the extra features into their own section of the website or create two versions — one with just text and basic graphics and one with all the extras. The search engine bots give up on loading a page if it takes too long, and so will your customers.

Submitting Your Site to Search Engines

Don't wait for other people to reference your website. The most straightforward way to make search engines notice your site is for you to tell them directly. Years ago, in the search engine submission process, website owners could file reports containing information about their sites and the URLs and content used on their sites. Although most of this information gathering is now done by the search engines' automatic programs, called *spiders* (because they crawl around the Internet looking for information), some search engines still allow you to submit information about your site on top of their automatic gathering methods.

Signing up with Google

Google sends its own programs, known as *Googlebots*, around the web looking for new sites to add to its index. However, if you don't want to wait around and hope that a Googlebot will magically land on your website, especially when you're just starting out, then you can take an extra step.

Google has a Search Console tool that allows you to either submit a sitemap of your website for its programs to crawl or to identify your site by having Google fetch a site that you're the owner of and request indexing of that website.

You can submit a sitemap of your website to Google using *one* of the following methods (whichever method is most convenient for you):

>> Go to www.google.com/webmasters/tools/submit-url. Google asks you to log in and redirects you to the Search Console page. Follow the instructions to send Google your URL information.

>> Open up your robots.txt file that exists on your web server, and add the following line of text to it:

Sitemap: http://www.yourwebsitename.com/sitemap_location.xml

Google will find this change when it crawls, and it go to your sitemap and scan your entire site.

>> Use the Google Ping function to tell Google about your sitemap. In a new web browser window, type the following URL, and press Enter:

http://www.google.com/ping?sitemap=https://www.yourwebsitename.com/sitemap.xml

Google will register this ping request and show you a confirmation screen.

WARNING

Google does not guarantee that any new URL will be added to its index and it cannot promise a specific turnaround time for considering or indexing your sitemap.

TIP

You can submit more targeted content to Google besides just your website. Check out the article from Google at `https://support.google.com/webmasters/answer/6259634` for more information.

Submitting to other search engines

You may think that submitting your site and having it picked up by Google is all you need to do. After all, who uses the other, smaller search engines? The answer is that search engines such as Google do. By increasing your mention in all the smaller search engines, you get more referrals to your website, which leads to higher rankings on Google.

TIP

If you know from studying your website analytics that customers are using a particular search engine, you should definitely do whatever is necessary to be indexed by that search engine. See Chapter 5 of this minibook for more information on how to analyze your website data.

Following are some smaller but active search engines with free submittal pages:

>> **Beamed:** `www.beamed.com/search/AddURL.html`

>> **ExactSeek:** `www.exactseek.com/add.html`

>> **WhatUSeek:** `www.whatuseek.com/addurl.shtml`

Many small to medium-size search engines — such as Ask.com and Lycos — have their own ways of accepting submissions (mainly by paid inclusion), and others no longer have a manual submission process. Search engines rise and fall in popularity, just like the results they display, so do your homework and follow up with any up-and-coming search programs.

WARNING

Many businesses offer, for a price, guaranteed submissions to hundreds, or even thousands, of search engines. Many links that are offered are no longer valid because companies are absorbed or go bust. Do your research before signing up with a company that makes big promises about search engine inclusion.

Watching Your Rankings

Although website pages might last forever in a search engine's database, the website's importance or relevancy doesn't carry over. As website owners try to figure out ways to improve their positions in search engine results, search engines update their systems and algorithms to reduce the effect of specific popular tricks.

One such practice is *keyword spamming.* Website owners used to hide paragraphs of targeted keywords by matching the color of the keyword's text with the color of the web page background. For example, the owner of a website using a white background could have put in a block of keywords using white text. These keywords are invisible to customers browsing the website because the white text doesn't show up on a white background. The spiders that download the information from the web page can see the keywords, however, and they assign weight to those keywords regardless of whether they're relevant. Search engines now compare the colors being used and eliminate those keywords, even if the colors being used are slight variations of each other. This practice isn't as common nowadays, but it's important to advise against it in case someone recommends you try it.

As a business owner, you need to stay informed of the changes the search engines make to their programs, and then update your website accordingly to take advantage of whatever the new rules enforce. The last thing you want is to optimize your website based on one set of rules and then have your website ignored because the rules changed and you didn't update your site.

A variety of websites provide news, updates, columns, and information about major and secondary search engines. If you want to stay up to date with search engine techniques, follow some of these sites:

» **Search Engine Watch:** This site calls itself the "Source for Search Engine Marketing," and many users agree. The company uses a variety of mechanisms — such as news articles, blogs, discussion boards, and a marketplace for vendors of search engine optimization (SEO) products — to spread the word about search engine marketing. It offers a wide variety of free content and a reserved Members section (which has premium articles written by experts), an extensive archive of information, and a private newsletter. It even sponsors the Search Engine Strategies Conference and Expo, in different cities around the world, to promote the same concepts as the site. Visit www.searchenginewatch.com.

» **Seochat:** If you're looking for a particular discussion area that covers either a general search engine (such as Google, Yahoo!, or MSN) or a discussion about a particular topic (such as link building), Seochat (www.seochat.com) is the place for you. It has a number of discussion boards — including a section dedicated to e-commerce development — that provide help and discussion for online-store professionals or the graphic design or database work that your website requires.

» **Search Engine Journal:** What better way to find out what search engine optimization professionals are thinking than to keep up with their journal? Search Engine Journal provides in-depth guides by subject, reports breaking news, and has expert guest contributors review and comment on the newest and most popular events in the SEO space. It even provides perspectives targeted to entrepreneurs, ad agency professionals, content marketing professionals, and more. Visit its site or subscribe to its newsletter at www.searchenginejournal.com.

Moving Up in the Rankings

The key isn't always to be in the top spot. Considering the enormous amount of new information that becomes indexed every day — not to mention the continual updating of search engine algorithms — you can waste a lot of time trying to stay on top by retaining the top search engine result for your important keywords.

You should have two goals for your ranking in the search engine results:

» A position that's high enough on the list before a potential customer sees your competitors.

» A position among the first page or two. (Keep in mind that a person using a smartphone to conduct a search will have fewer results per page, making a high placement even more important.)

Most people who are presented with multiple pages of search engine results typically skim the first page and try a few links. A few of them then go to the second page and try more links. After the second or even third page of results, however, if the destination sites aren't close to what the user is looking for, that person typically enters a new string of keywords, sees a different set of results, and tries again.

You can earn a prominent spot by using keywords in the right spots or partnering with a business to link to your website. If you're interested in staying ahead of your competition, though, read these next few sections. We show you how to find your rankings and then how to keep an eye on your competition.

Knowing where you stand

You can't know where you're going unless you know where you are. Your first job is to understand what the search engines know about your website. Search engines provide a growing number of tools that can open a window into their databases and show you what they know about you.

Internet company Moz offers the Link Explorer tool, which shows you all the information it can find about a specific website. Some information this tool provides is available by creating a free account, but you can get more information by subscribing to Moz's services, such as its Moz Pro program. Follow these steps to use Link Explorer:

1. **Go to** http://opensiteexplorer.org.

    The opening page for Link Explorer appears.

2. **In the text box, enter the URL of the website you want to analyze, and then click the Search button.**

    You don't need to enter the http:// part of the URL.

    After you enter the domain, click the button, and create a free account to use the website, the results screen is displayed.

REMEMBER

3. **Click the Inbound Links section to view all the inbound links for that website, displayed in their natural search order.**

    After we entered www.dummies.com in Step 2, we saw a page similar to the one shown in Figure 6-3, where you can review the general summary of statistics for your chosen website. (The website adds the http:// part when the screen is displayed.) When you click the Inbound Links section, you get a new page where the results include the first 50 links of the1.2 million links from 54,500 root domains (or unique websites) that link to Dummies.com. You can click the title and URL of the linking page to see the page where the link exists.

FIGURE 6-3:
See the overall statistics of a website.

4. **Click the Top Pages menu item from the left navigation bar of options to see which pages on your site are the highest-ranked pages for your specified domain.**

   The Top Pages view shows you which web pages in the specified domain have the highest ranking, based on a combination of factors, including inbound links, the amount of linking domains, and content on that page.

Seeing what your competition is doing

No analysis of your website is complete without looking at your competition. If your website is the only one in your given area, this step is unnecessary. Chances are, however, that you have more than one competitor and you're trying to figure out how to steer customers to your site and away from the others. You have to recognize the difference between these two types of competitors:

» **Direct:** These businesses are the same size as yours and offer a similar (or almost identical) product mix to your target set of customers.

» **Indirect:** This type of competitor happens to sell some of the same products you sell (divisions of a big retailer, for example).

You can learn about your competitors by visiting their websites to see their web page design and find out what they offer to customers. Also ask yourself these questions about your competition:

» Which keywords are they using in their website names?

» Which keywords are showing up in their web page titles and headings?

» Which <META> keywords and descriptions are they using? (In your web browser, choose View⇨ Source to see the HTML source code.)

» How many other links point back to their websites?

» Where does their content (website, social media sites, blogs, and so on) appear?

WARNING

Don't cut and paste any info from a competitor's website. That site has an automatic implied copyright the minute it's created and posted on the Internet. Although you can observe and apply techniques or concepts, you cannot plagiarize the text or reuse a site's graphics or photos without permission.

As you're reviewing your competitors' websites, note the techniques they use that you don't implement. Then compare their search engine results to your results on multiple search engines. Concepts that work well on one engine might not be picked up on another site. Find out what works, and avoid what doesn't.

Creating your own referrals

Some website owners have decided that if they can't get other websites to offer a link to them, why not build their own links? The sole purpose of some websites is to serve as part of a newly built network to promote a central site. When you go to these referral sites, it's obvious in some cases that they're built for only one reason. As search engines have adapted their rules, they ignore sites whose only purpose is to link to someone else.

The right way to achieve your own network is to build a series of targeted, focused content sites, each of which feeds into your main e-commerce business. Suppose that you sell pet supplies. Rather than add original content solely to your e-commerce site, you can set up targeted websites about dogs, cats, birds, fish, gerbils, and hamsters. You can then focus on building up these websites by becoming an authority or expert in these areas. After you have fellow enthusiasts hooked on your information, you can refer those people to your e-commerce site when they're ready to buy something.

Getting another website to cross-promote with you is easier when you're exchanging links with a content site, not with an obvious potential competitor. You can always offer excerpts of your content on the e-commerce site, in case your repeat customers come straight back and want to read something first.

TIP

You can promote your products on sale at places such as Facebook, Twitter, Instagram, Tumblr, Pinterest, and other social networking, blog, or profile web pages. Each third-party website has its own restrictions, so you may want to check the terms and conditions for these websites if you launch something with a questionable link.

7
Retail to E-Tail

Contents at a Glance

IN THIS CHAPTER

» Deciding whether a website can help your business

» Perfecting your timing when you're launching a site

» Building on your store's existing identity

» Mapping out the details for your online move

» Putting your inventory on the web

Chapter **1**

Expanding Online to Keep and Grow Customers

I f you're reading this chapter, it's probably safe to assume you are an existing retailer who hasn't opened up shop online, or hasn't made the most of your web presence. You're not alone. Only 25 percent of small businesses currently have a website enabled for e-commerce or conducting sales, according to a 2019 Small Business Scorecard report from SurePayroll. And 28 percent of those surveyed still have no website at all! That's unfortunate, because there's a lot of opportunity (revenue!) that is earned, driven, and influenced online. In fact, your customers most likely assume that they can just as easily shop online with you as they can shop from your retail location. After all, in a time when you can buy everything from wine to Windex online and have it shipped to your door, why wouldn't you also be able to buy from your favorite local retailer's website? The great news is that there truly hasn't been a better time than now to expand your retail footprint online.

Traditional retailers, once thought to be at a disadvantage for having to compete with pure-play e-commerce sites, are now in an enviable position of easily having the best of both worlds. If you don't believe us, consider the continuing "clicks to bricks" trend in which online-only e-tailers are opening up bricks-and-mortar locations! Dominant e-commerce players, such as Amazon and Google are early adopters of the trend of expanding to offline stores. Why do these mega online brands want a physical storefront, too? They've learned *webrooming* (or online browsing) drives offline sales and *showrooming* (or in-store browsing) drives online sales. Smaller online stores, especially in the fashion industry, are also taking notice of the trend and sometimes test the offline storefront using *pop-up* (temporary) retail locations. Large or small, the takeaway for retailers is the same: There's opportunity in having both an online and a traditional storefront.

The modern customer navigates back and forth between the two shopping experiences of online and offline buying. When a brand has only one experience (or destination), it risks losing a sale. You've possibly seen the same happen when a customer comes into your store to "check out" a product in person, only to purchase from an online competitor because of perceived price differences, product availability, or other reasons. A traditional storefront is the ultimate showroom, providing a much-needed tactile experience, allowing customers to touch, taste, and smell products — something the web has yet to enable shoppers. Beyond the try-before-you-buy syndrome, online brands also realize a physical presence is important for building a relationship with the customer and serving as a vehicle for marketing to them.

Consider that e-commerce sales in the United States are projected to reach more than $530 billion in 2020, according to Forrester Research. Those numbers get even larger when you factor in the power of influence your web store has over traditional retail store sales. Forrester Research found that a larger amount of offline sales are driven or influenced by customers doing online research. By 2021, more than half of retail sales will be influenced by "digital touchpoints," either in direct online purchases or indirect web-influenced sales.

What does this mean for you? Simply put, when moving your store online, you not only add new web sales to your revenue stream, but also probably improve or influence your in-store sales, too. What are you waiting for? Let's start helping you move your store online today. In this chapter, we explain what you need to do to make the transition from your bricks-and-mortar store to an online store.

Making the Decision to Move Your Store Online

While you're thinking of taking your business online, ask yourself this basic question: Why do I want to move my business online? Even with all the encouraging statistics we shared with you, if you're making the move only because it's expected or because everyone else is doing it, you might want to think about it a little more. Having an online presence is essential, but you shouldn't rush into it without a plan and without the proper resources. You should make the move for the right reasons — and be prepared.

You're ready to get serious about building an online site when that site can help you reach a specific goal that makes your business stronger. Typically, these reasons include

>> **To expand:** Going online opens another channel for selling your products. If your site is executed properly, it helps increase your revenue and profit potentials online and off — a standard goal for any business.

>> **To control the cost of growth:** Expanding onto the Internet can be much less expensive than opening another physical location. Additionally, an online store potentially reaches a national or an international customer base rather than confines you to a limited geographic area. You reach more customers for less money. That's smart business.

>> **To create awareness:** Your site is an extension of your marketing efforts. It becomes a permanent, online advertisement for your bricks-and-mortar store. Sometimes, you might have a site solely to support your other marketing or PR activities. If you're already getting a lot of exposure through your current marketing methods, you need a place to direct prospective customers for more information. Either way, customers won't easily forget about your store when you're continually communicating with them, both online and offline.

>> **To better compete:** Competition no longer comes from only the store around the corner, but from all types of online stores, too. The "me too" approach to moving online shouldn't be the only reason to make the decision. But it's becoming more difficult to maintain sales, let alone grow sales, if you can't compete both offline and online.

>> **To drive traffic:** No matter how much, or how little, inventory you offer for sale online, you're ultimately building foot traffic to your store, too — those web-influenced sales we mentioned. Your site is an interactive marketing tool. For example, to attract new customers, you can use paid and *localized* (targeted to your local market) keyword searches and search engine optimization (refer to Book 6, Chapter 6). And online coupons, emails, and e-newsletters become incentives to purchase (online and off). You decide where you want to direct the traffic.

Ultimately, your reason for starting an online store must make sense as part of your business strategy. As with any other decision, this choice deserves your deliberate and considerable attention.

Unfortunately, some offline entrepreneurs haven't thought through their online strategies. In fact, they don't have strategies. This type of storeowner is chastised by customers for not having a website. Eventually, the storeowner gives in and decides to buy a domain name and throws something up there just so that he can say, "I have a site!" Ultimately, this approach further frustrates the customer and the storeowner.

You may be wondering if there's ever a legitimate reason to avoid e-commerce expansion. Here are the four scenarios in which we advise delaying moving your company online:

>> **You lack appropriate resources.** Sometimes, employees and other well-meaning friends or family are willing to create an e-commerce–enabled site for you. Maybe they truly want to help, or perhaps they want the opportunity to expand their own skill set. If they truly have the capability, that's a boon. If not, a hastily or poorly developed website won't appease your customers. Before moving online, it's important to have the necessary knowledge and talent to dedicate to the project. If you trust this task to someone else, then make sure to ask for samples of that person's work and for references. If you don't have access to the appropriate resources or enough of them (whether paid or volunteers), then push the pause button on your online expansion.

>> **You're unable to maintain the site.** Just as you need the resources to launch your e-commerce store, you need time and people to keep up the online store. E-commerce does not thrive with a set-it-and-forget-it mentality. Similar to your physical store, e-commerce requires someone to work and manage it every day.

>> **You lack the budget.** It's true that building a website or adding an e-commerce component to a site is no longer cost-prohibitive. However, it still requires an investment. For example, if you don't have the ability or time to create the website (including taking pictures of products and writing descriptions), you'll need to pay someone to do that for you. There's also the monthly expense of your shopping cart, which can range from a few dollars for a few products, to several hundred dollars for a larger inventory (which is the most likely scenario for an existing retailer). If e-commerce is an important part of your strategy, you can find the necessary money to fund it; but without a realistic budget in place your growth plan could be jeopardized.

>> **Your business is failing.** If your retail sales are way down and you're on the brink of closure, you might think that moving your store online is the only answer. However, having a website isn't a cure-all for what ails your business. Instead, e-commerce is only an element within your business. Therefore, if your offline store is already flailing, your online version is likely to face equal — if not greater — struggles.

Use this list to guide the planning, strategy, and timing of your online store, not as a permanent roadblock. Having a fully functioning e-commerce site to mirror your offline retail store is almost a necessity today. Done correctly, it's also a game changer for your business, fueling sales and widening your customer base — provided you think about the timing of your decision and take control.

Finding the Right Time

To find the right time to make the move online, you have to step back and analyze the situation as objectively as possible. Does creating an online store truly fit into your business plan right now? In what ways would an online store contribute to your short-term and long-term goals? Is there a better time to move your business online?

In addition to your internal store goals, you have to consider external factors. The presence of an online store doesn't mean customers will flock to it and spend, spend, spend! You have to market your online store just as you do your offline location — and external conditions can play a big role in your success. What are the current market conditions for your industry? In what general direction is the national economy heading? If your customers aren't spending right now, you might want to conserve the money that you originally budgeted for your site development. On the flip side, if market factors are pushing the demand for your type of products, you might want to bump up the development of your site by a few months.

Make time to track industry trends, both online and off. Regularly check out the issues by reading trade magazines and following industry-related research. Start with research from Gartner (www.gartner.com) and Forrester Research (www.forrester.com).

Taking into account seasonal latitude

As a retailer, you probably have a particularly busy season, when you earn the majority of your revenues. Your busy season might be the end of the year when most holiday shopping drives sales. Or, if you sell recreational items, such as bikes or swimming pool accessories, the summer is probably when you gear up for brisk business.

Your products are most in demand during this period, which can affect your plans for starting a site in two ways:

>> **Development time:** Building a site takes time. Even if you're outsourcing the work, you're intricately involved in the process. Creating your first online endeavor during your store's most hectic time of year is a bad idea. If you're already loaded with work, you're likely to make hasty site-related decisions or drop the project altogether out of sheer frustration. You can offset this potential for disaster by planning around your store's busy time.

Start working on your site right after your busy season ends. Although you might anticipate a development timeline of only a few months, many events and circumstances can delay or extend that deadline. Even adding e-commerce to an existing site can take more time than expected, with all those pictures to take and descriptions to write. Beginning site construction (or expansion) at the close of your business's high point gives you plenty of cushion before that busy time rolls around again.

>> **Launch time:** Planning to launch a site during your seasonal high point isn't a grand idea. You need time to test the site to see how it works and to find and correct errors. Sure, you and your developer test most of these items before you take the site *live* (the point at which you put it on the Internet), but plenty of minor glitches go unnoticed by everyone but your customers. If you launch the site before your busy season begins, you have more time to respond to these customer issues and resolve them. And because fewer customers are likely to be affected by the problems, you can keep the issues contained.

Don't be shy about letting your customers know that your site is new. Make a point to ask for feedback and suggestions for improvement or to be notified of trouble spots. Reward customers who send you information. You can give them coupons or other small gifts to thank them for their time.

Timing your launch around an event

Similar to seasonal timing, other events can influence when you decide to launch your site, such as an annual event that your store participates in. You might think that an event where all your potential customers are gathered is the perfect time to unveil your site. Keep in mind, though, that perfect timing isn't always as perfect as it seems.

If you insist on coordinating your site's debut with an event-driven date, keep in mind the following points:

>> Double the amount of time that you think you need for your site's development.

>> Add another six to eight weeks to that date for testing and customer feedback.

>> Don't commit to using your site for event-related promotions (just in case).

>> Avoid using event-specific merchandise in the launch of your site.

If your store's online premiere is tied to an immovable date, hope for the best — and plan for the worst.

TIP

Instead of launching your new site in sync with an in-store event, consider using the event to promote the future online store's debut. Collect email addresses to send a notification when the site is live and offer a coupon or other special incentive for them to visit your new online store.

Dedicating manpower

You need to find the time for a project the size of a website launch. Regardless of what else you have going on in your business (and your life), at the end of the day you have to dedicate your time to the cause.

Although you can hire out the bulk of the development work for your site, you need to be involved in a long string of commitments during the process, including these tasks:

>> Find and hire a website designer (two to three weeks).

>> Define the scope of the project (eight to ten hours).

>> Decide on the site design (one to two weeks).

>> Choose a shopping cart solution or e-commerce platform (one to two weeks).

- » Coordinate payment-processing options (three to five days).
- » Select initial inventory to stock your online store (two to three weeks).
- » Review, edit, and approve content and images (one to two weeks, at least).
- » Create a site launch campaign (one week).

You get the idea — you're going to be busy!

Take a look at your average day and then tack on a minimum of another two to three hours for managing site-related tasks. The time that you devote to your site includes meetings with your design team and your staff as well as the time you need for decision-making. Block off at least half a day on the weekends for site work, too. You probably need to use this schedule for about three to six months.

Bridging Your Offline Store with Your Online Store

All too often, a retailer is eager to have an e-commerce alternative and then takes a somewhat haphazard approach. Most traditional entrepreneurs who are unfamiliar with the Internet tend to view the physical store and the online store as two separate, different entities. When you treat your bricks-and-mortar store and your online store differently, customers have two different experiences with your company — and become confused about which experience truly represents your brand.

Seamlessly bridge your bricks-and-mortar store (your company's history) with your online store (your brand's future). With this approach, you can provide a single, cohesive user experience. Focus on these three critical areas: identity, image, and integration.

In this section, we show you how one company — Williams-Sonoma — does an outstanding job of meeting these three objectives. Williams-Sonoma remains one of our favorite examples of how an established retailer keeps its website's design and functionality current while staying true to its brand's in-store image for a cohesive customer experience. Customers and industry analysts agree that this brand gets its online strategy right. In 2018, Williams-Sonoma consistently ranked as one of the top 25 e-commerce retailers in North America. As of 2019, the e-commerce portion accounts for 50 percent of the brand's total sales, according to analysis by Zach's Equity Research. Let's take a closer look at how it makes it work and how you can emulate.

Finding your identity

Identity incorporates all the physical characteristics that your customers associate with your store. It's your logo, color palettes, store layout, and any other details that contribute to your store's distinctiveness.

When you visit the bricks-and-mortar Williams-Sonoma, you see a lot of natural, muted, neutral colors as a backdrop on the walls. The color scheme is simple and understated with crisp whites and a clean, tailored appearance outside and inside. The occasional pop of color springs from the products themselves, neatly arranged as part of the in-store displays. The online version of the store (`www.williams-sonoma.com`) has the same feel to it: A bright white background provides a neutral palate that lets featured products grab the spotlight. Product images are crisp and bright and reflect the way the company's high-end products shine in its stores.

Creating an image

Image incorporates not only the physical appearance of your store but also how customers perceive it. Is your store considered a high-end retail store with select but pricey items? Or is your store an eclectic mix of trendy yet unique gifts? Are you known for exceptional customer service? Or do customers enjoy browsing in a low-key environment? All these details contribute to your store's image, and you want that image to carry over to your online store.

One thing that sets apart Williams-Sonoma is the helpful information it provides, often in the form of in-store product demonstrations, cooking classes, and personalized shopping services. The store has created an image of being a solution provider for upscale kitchen products. It carried that image online by including recipes that incorporate cooking ingredients or products for sale on the site (and in-store). The website also makes it easy to find in-store events and seasonal cooking classes.

Further keeping with its image of being helpful, the Williams-Sonoma website makes personal recommendations for other products and services you might like, based on your online browsing experience and matched to what customers with similar tastes have also viewed and purchased. The site also features seasonal cooking and entertaining tips, meal ideas, and highlights special products. It's all part of the brand's image of being your source for cooking needs — whether you shop online or in the store.

Integrating your shopping cart

Less visible to the customer is the functionality of your site on the back end. In particular, you need to consider how your online inventory is managed. Your goal is to integrate the back end to work alongside your offline inventory system. For example, if a customer orders a product from your site, that product should be in stock. If it's not, you want that information to be available to the customer at the time of the order.

REMEMBER

The technology choices you make (such as which inventory-management solutions and shopping carts you use) ultimately determine the types of buying experiences your customers have on your site. (For more information about shopping carts and inventory management, refer to Book 4, Chapters 5 and 6, respectively.)

We really can't tell you how or whether the Williams-Sonoma online shopping cart is tied into a particular store's inventory or whether it's integrated with a shipping warehouse. Frankly, as a customer, you don't need those details, but you do want the shopping experience to be seamless. This is one area where many national, e-commerce retailers have made progress in enabling inventory tracking at the store level. In other words, if you are researching products online but want to buy locally, many online stores will show whether that item is in stock at your local stores. Plus, they allow you to purchase items online with same-day pick up in your local store. This is a good example of integrating the online and offline buying experience to help increase sales and foot traffic. Williams-Sonoma is among the e-commerce retail leaders that have made this a staple of online shopping today. When it comes to shipping options, Williams-Sonoma also makes options very clear for customers. You can find out whether you need to expedite shipping for a holiday-themed item to arrive by a particular date or how long a product on back order might take to arrive. If you have an account, you have an express checkout option. Or if you don't want to take the time to register, you can check out quickly as a guest. These examples of making the buying experience as helpful and frictionless as possible are part of the many reasons we appreciate this brand's online store.

Making a Flawless Transition

Granted, a national retail chain has a much larger budget for a website than you do. Even so, your smaller store can embrace the same concepts that the big boys use for a smooth, effective online transition. The best way to make this transition is to plan.

Adding an e-commerce component to your store is similar to planning a big party or a major event. Part of your plan is already in place: You have an approximate time frame for making your project a reality. To make that timetable more manageable, break it into three smaller chunks, or *stages:* orientation, implementation, and evaluation. For each stage, create a checklist of activities that should occur during that stage.

Stage 1: Orientation

When you're talking about moving your store online, the orientation stage includes everything from conducting initial research to evaluating and choosing the best vendors and software applications.

Following are some of the tasks that you should accomplish in the orientation stage:

» **Identify and research your competitors.** Check out the competition's sites, and even purchase items to get a feel for how their shopping carts work. Put together a list of products and price points (refer to Book 4, Chapter 6). See the "Building an Inventory" section, later in this chapter, for more information about this step.

» **Set up your website.** Research a hosting solution, choose a domain, and set up your server. (To find out about these tasks, refer to Book 3.) Then you're ready to begin integrating your existing back-end solution with your online processes.

» **Decide on payment options.** Determine which forms of payment (credit cards, PayPal, or gift certificates, for example) you want to accept on your website. Contact your bank provider and ask about its options for online transactions. Or choose from the options provided with your e-commerce platform.

» **Evaluate shopping vendors and other customer service options.** Decide whether you're going to provide live or email-based support, for example.

Take a look at Table 1-1 to get an idea of how to start a checklist of the tasks you need to accomplish during this stage.

TABLE 1-1   **Orientation Checklist**

Action Item	Result/Resources	Decision	Notes
Identify all competitors			
Research competitors			
Study their sites			
Purchase their products online			
Test their customer service functions			
Return a product to check the process			
Maintain list of similar products and price points offered by competitors			
Review industry trends			
Check for domain availability			
Determine options for hosting solutions			
Compare third-party hosting versus internal servers			
Locate top three shopping cart products or e-commerce platforms			
Compare prices			
List capabilities			
Note limitations			

Stage 2: Implementation

In the implementation stage, you move from just thinking about your website to making it happen. You're building the site, integrating your back-end systems, and creating offline and online marketing tools to use.

Take a look at all the research you compiled in the orientation stage, and start making some decisions:

>> **Set a budget and a schedule.** Create these items to keep track of your money and your time.

>> **Approve the site design.** Create the *copy* (text) for the site and gather any content from other people, such as reviews and testimonials.

>> **Go live with the site and create a site map for search engines.** Start making your URL visible to the public.

Table 1-2 shows how to set up a checklist to keep you on track while implementing your site.

TABLE 1-2 ### Implementation Checklist

Action Item	Status	Implementation Date	Completed?
Set budget			
Create development schedule			
Develop marketing plan			
Register domain			
Contract with SEO specialist (if applicable)			
Approve site design			
Approve site map			
Obtain web hosting service			
Purchase additional hardware (if applicable)			
Initiate vendor agreements (payment processors, fulfillment, and so on)			
Select shopping cart software			
Create product list for initial launch			
Set prices			
Complete product details			
Choose product images			
Add image tags			
Write product descriptions			
Upload products to shopping cart			
Create all web copy			
Develop FAQs			

Stage 3: Evaluation

Technically, after your site is up, the evaluation stage never ends. You need to continuously test, review, and revise your site to maintain its functionality and appeal.

Here are some elements that you want to keep your eye on after your site goes live:

» **Site performance:** Check how long individual pages take to load, how many page views you're getting (refer to Book 6, Chapter 5), and whether all your links are working.

» **Shopping cart:** See whether the cart is working as it should.

» **Shipping and handling:** Make sure that orders are being fulfilled in a timely manner and that customers are happy with your service.

Table 1-3 gives you an idea of how to start a checklist for this stage.

TABLE 1-3 **Evaluation Checklist**

Function/Area	Last Update	Status	Problems or Concerns	Corrective Action	Complete By
Site performance					
Load times					
Page view					
24/7 access (no downtime)					
All apps work					
Internal links work					
External links work					
Home page					
Info is correct					
Graphics load properly					
Policies current					
Individual product pages					
Product images					
Product descriptions					
Customer reviews					
Supporting content					

Building an Inventory

A big part of planning for a successful transition online involves selecting the right inventory from the start.

The pressure of choosing the best products to sell on the Internet might seem like a daunting task. Unlike other e-commerce sites that are starting from scratch, however, you have a distinct advantage: product mastery. You not only have an existing inventory but also know it intimately. You understand exactly what sells and what doesn't, and you have an established sales history with actual data to prove it.

Consider the number of conversations you've had with customers over the years. Because of that feedback, you have a firm grasp on why your customers like a product and what they might need to know about it before making their final purchasing decisions. That's exactly the information you need to move those same products online without missing a beat.

Follow these steps to begin building your online inventory:

1. **Pull together a list of your current inventory.**

    We hope that you have this list already. If not, you need to create an up-to-date and complete inventory list.

2. **Separate your current inventory into categories.**

    For example, you can group products according to which areas will help or hinder how well they sell online. These categories include

    - *Top sellers:* Items at the top of your moneymaking list.

    - *Exclusive items:* Unique, hard to find, or handcrafted items.

REMEMBER

    If you're an approved reseller or licensed dealer for a particular product or brand, check your agreement for any conditions or terms on how or where you can sell.

    - *Shipping weight:* Heavier or bulkier items that are more expensive to ship.

TIP

    You don't have to eliminate items that might be too bulky, and thus too expensive, to ship. Instead, make those items special orders and have customers email or call for quotes that include shipping. Or make the products available only for in-store pickup.

    - *Availability:* Items that are in stock or readily accessible from the manufacturer or supplier.

    - *Drop-ship capability:* Items that can be shipped directly from the manufacturer or supplier, which saves your inventory space.

3. **Rank your inventory.**

    List items in order from those most suitable for selling online to those least suitable. Suitable items are easy to ship, not unusual in size or shape, and nonperishable. Food items and products such as flowers that are perishable are still suitable for online sales, but do require additional planning for the best packing and shipping options to maintain freshness.

REMEMBER

    When selling food and other perishable items, including plants, in the United States, check for shipping restrictions or limitations with individual states. Some states do not allow certain products to be mailed or shipped from out of state.

4. **Go online and find as many websites as you can that sell items similar to those in your inventory (starting with the products at the top of your list).**

    Make a record of these sites so that you can watch them as you prepare to build your store. Study the sites and determine how they compare to your store and future site. How are the competing sites branded? Are they easy to find in the search engines? Do they ship globally? What advantages and disadvantages does your store have in comparison to these stores? What do you like or dislike about how they promote the products?

5. **Compare the sticker prices of the actual products. Mark on your inventory list the products that are price competitive.**

    When you're comparing prices, factor in all the pricing considerations, including sales tax and shipping and handling fees.

6. **Review your inventory list and reprioritize, if you need to.**

    Move or drop those items for which you don't have a strong competitive advantage. Bump to the top of your list the products that make your store shine.

TIP

    Keep this data because it not only helps you decide which items are ideal for your online inventory but can also help guide you in promoting your products later.

7. **Determine the number of products you want to sell online.**

    Revisit your strategy. If the purpose of your site is to sell merchandise, the more products, the better. If you're just promoting your brand, starting with a smaller number of products might work fine. Or you might be limited in the number of products that your shopping cart program allows (without investing more money in a shopping cart).

REMEMBER

    Rather than delete items, consider adding ones that aren't part of your current store inventory. Nothing is wrong with adding to the list, if it makes sense and especially if vendors can *drop-ship* (pack and mail the product directly to your customer).

8. **Apply the *customer factor* (any customer-related information that can influence an online purchase).**

Here's where your years of customer interaction come in handy. Evaluate the products through the eyes of your customers. Which items are difficult to sell because customers need additional information? Can you present that information in an online product description? (Or maybe the product sells even better online because you can give the customer additional product detail.) If the customer might see some aspect of your product in a negative way, now is the time to delete an item from your online inventory.

9. **Delete any products based on their image — or, rather, lack of one.**

Sort through your inventory and figure out which products have photos available from a vendor or manufacturer. The quality of the product images on your website directly reflects the image of your store. If a high-resolution quality photo doesn't exist, you have two choices:

- Drop the product from your online inventory.

- Spend the money to hire a professional photographer.

Although amateur pictures taken with a digital camera might work on eBay, customers expect higher quality from a retail store. You can get away with using amateur photos, of course, but statistics do support the philosophy that the better the quality of the product images, the more likely they will sell. Hiring a professional photographer is worth the investment.

TIP

Ask your vendor whether any marketing program incentives are available that could help offset the cost of a photo shoot. For example, you might agree to feature certain products on the home page of your site or use them in your store's offline marketing materials. In return, you might be eligible to participate in a vendor's marketing reimbursement program (which can equal several hundred dollars for a small retailer).

REMEMBER

You need to take pictures that feature several different angles of the product. Most products sell better if a customer can see multiple views of the item; if the site offers the option to show a product being used or positioned in a setting; and if a customer can zoom in on the picture for a more detailed view. You must have permission to use photos that are not your own, unless you've paid a fee to license the image. When it comes to product photos, your vendor or supplier may provide you with the right to use various images.

Chapter **2**

Managing the Differences between In-Store and Online Commerce

I t wasn't that long ago that we treated online shoppers as if they came from an entirely different planet from that of in-store buyers. And it was true that each group was often put into a marketing silo based on certain characteristics and behaviors. Fast forward just a few years and we realize that these two types of customers are actually the *same* customer who simply has different preferences based on when, how, and where he or she buys. Today, when preparing how to handle the different types of buying destinations (from a website, from inside a retail store, from a social media application, or from a mobile device), it's important to focus on customer experience — or the expectations a customer has for each retail location (whether physical or virtual).

Are there still differences between the online and offline customer that you need to consider? The short answer is yes! Your job is to entice customers to buy. To do that, you have to get to know your customers — and understand their expectations for all types of shopping destinations. In this chapter, we cover what your customers really want for both offline and online shopping and how you can accommodate these customers' buying needs.

Comparing Online and Offline Customers

When you launch an online store, your ultimate goal is to accommodate the way your customers want to shop in order to grow your retail sales. Whether that means finding new customers via your online brand or getting existing customers to buy more or buy more often, you're hoping that your online store becomes an extension of your physical retail presence and provides the incentive to buy, buy, buy.

There remains an interesting difference between customers who prefer to shop online and those who visit your retail store, and that's how much and how often they spend. A 2019 survey from *Marketing Insider* revealed that 58 percent of customers spend more money online than inside a retail store. Less than 35 percent claim to spend more money when visiting a store. In addition to where customers are spending the most, data also shows that online repeat customers are increasingly valuable to retailers. While only 15 percent of online customers have spent with you before, these repeat shoppers account for nearly one-third of your total online revenue, according to an annual "State of e-Commerce" report from Yotpo (www.yotpo.com). Investing in online customer retention really pays off, especially considering they spend three times as much as a one-time customer. As you can see, spending time growing your online business is worthwhile. But before you can change your customers' behaviors and get that high-dollar repeat business, you have to understand them, especially in the area of e-commerce.

Once accidental or happenstance, most online shopping is now quite purposeful. Your customers are making a conscientious decision each time they make a purchase online. To better understand their decisions, compare some of the reasons why your customers might choose to shop in your store as opposed to shopping online.

Customers showing up in your bricks-and-mortar store expect these features:

» **Security:** Your customers may think that shopping in your store is more secure than giving out credit card information on your website.

» **Guaranteed delivery:** Sometimes, purchasing a product is a time-sensitive issue. If customers need an item in their hands by a certain time or date, shopping online may become an afterthought. This need-it-now mentality is especially true during a holiday rush.

TIP

>> **Instant gratification:** Waiting for a product to ship isn't everyone's idea of shopping. Sometimes, customers need or want an item immediately, and shopping in a store gives that instantaneous gratification.

Offering same-day pickup inside your store when ordering customer orders online is another way to convert online browsers to buyers. Offering the convenience of shopping online with the instant gratification of buying in-store is profitable compromise.

>> **Loyalty:** Customers who are familiar with your store feel a connection. They often translate that into a perceived relationship with you and your employees. These customers are loyal and expect loyalty from you in return. The opportunity to build loyal relationships is one of the reasons online-only businesses, such as Amazon, are now expanding to physical storefronts.

>> **Service:** Having access to personalized service is a big plus for many traditional shoppers. These customers typically believe that shopping in a store is the only way to find that level of assistance, and they don't realize (or believe) that they can find quality sales support online.

>> **Only option:** Some customers simply don't consider other buying alternatives. They may think that in-store shopping is the only option because they aren't comfortable or familiar with the Internet, don't have online access, or aren't aware that they can shop online with your store.

>> **Try it before you buy it:** This is also known as the *tactile effect*. Some customers need to see, touch, smell, or try products before making a buying decision. In this case, shopping over the Internet doesn't do the trick.

>> **Avoid extra charges:** Shipping cost is the main factor working against online shopping. Many customers decide to shop offline simply to avoid additional shipping and handling fees tacked on to their purchases. While many large e-tailers now offer free shipping year-round, smaller retailers can't always absorb that cost, putting them at a particular disadvantage when it comes to buying online.

TIP

Online shoppers who do not want to pay shipping costs are more likely to buy offline, from your local store, if you offer price matching to the online store's price. Price matching can give your store a competitive advantage, if you can afford to discount some or all of your merchandise. If you decide to promote price matching in your store, make sure you clarify any exceptions of products or brands you cannot discount.

Virtual customers have the following expectations from your online store:

>> **Research material:** Shopping online provides the opportunity for detailed research before making a final purchasing decision. Shoppers can find product reviews, read customer feedback, compare brands and prices, and then make a purchase — all in a matter of minutes. Research shows that male customers are especially prone to do a little digging before they start buying online. Some mobile-savvy customers now stand in a store and use their smartphone to compare prices and styles or to check availability of products online. (This type of behavior can work for or against you.) However, data shows that 65 percent of online customers read online reviews before making a purchase.

>> **Hard-to-find items:** An item may be out of stock in a store or may not even be available locally. Shopping online provides access to products that aren't otherwise readily available.

>> **Niche or specialty items:** Customers are frequently drawn to online stores because those stores provide access to specialty items, including vintage goods, collector's items, or any other type of exclusive or niche product.

>> **Convenient store hours:** Round-the-clock shopping is tough to beat. These customers enjoy the flexibility that comes with virtual shopping — and knowing that the store is never closed.

>> **A better value:** Although shipping costs may be of concern to an in-store shopper, an online buyer may factor in the cost of gas and time. In this scenario, convenience also becomes a cost-savings factor.

>> **The best price:** Comparing prices and finding the best deal online is a snap these days. That ability to get the lowdown on a price for any given product is the reason that many buyers head straight to the Internet to shop.

>> **Extended inventory:** Retail stores traditionally have limited shelf space, but a website can house a lot more virtual inventory. (And products can often be *drop shipped* — ordered and shipped directly from a manufacturer or a supplier.) Because many web shoppers believe that they have access to a wider product selection online, e-commerce stores are often their first stop for shopping.

What Your Online Customers Expect from You

Customers shop online for many reasons (see the preceding section to read about some of those reasons). But you need to recognize another underlying difference between online and in–store shoppers: Online customers have great expectations for your online retail location. Sure, all customers are particular and — dare we say — demanding, but the Internet has raised the bar. It's up to you to make sure that your online store performs. In the following sections, we talk about what online customers expect of you.

Round-the-clock hours

Most customers expect your store to be open 24 hours a day, 7 days a week. Granted, meeting this need seems like a cinch. After all, after you put your site out on the web, it's . . . there. Right? Unfortunately, running a store 24/7 involves a little bit more work. Your customers are used to having 100 percent access to online stores, whether it's midnight or midmorning. Here are a couple of site-related tasks that you may want to consider:

>> **Customer support:** Can your customers contact you in the middle of the night and expect to receive an answer? Is there web-based "chat" with a virtual customer service representative to answer questions? Or will prospective buyers receive help only during normal business hours? Ultimately, that's your call. But you have to decide the rules up front and then let your customers know.

>> **Routine maintenance:** Maintenance includes any factor from your server going down (and your store being temporarily offline) to a glitch in your payment gateway provider that may prevent credit cards from being processed. When you're open for business around the clock, it helps to have a backup plan for all the things that could go wrong when you're not at the helm. For example, while shopping on a niche retail site one weekend, a glitch in the shopping cart prompted it to ask for a password before finishing the checkout process — even though we didn't have one, and it didn't provide an option to create one as a first-time shopper. Weekend assistance was unavailable, so the online retailer lost our sale — and countless others that weekend. It's just as easy for customers to sail over to a competitor's site to find what they want when they need it.

A variety of payment methods

Accepting multiple forms of payment is a necessity online. Customers may be more forgiving when they shop in your retail location, because they can whip out a checkbook or cash. In the world of web retail, customers simply leave your store and surf to a competitor. See Book 4, Chapter 4 about the wealth of payment options you can make available to your customers.

Everything a customer could want, plus the kitchen sink

Virtual inventory is a big component in e-commerce. It doesn't matter whether you store all your products in a warehouse behind your retail location or have orders drop-shipped from a supplier. Customers want you to provide a large selection of choices, including everything you have available in your retail location. In addition, customers expect your store to be well stocked — at all times. Increasingly, online browsers want the option to see if an item is in-stock in your retail location. Having a backend management system that integrates your e-commerce inventory with your store inventory (in real time!) is a worthwhile feature that can help boost sales.

REMEMBER

If a product is on back order or temporarily out of stock, your customers expect to be notified before they start the checkout process and preferably when they try to add the product to their shopping cart.

TIP

Some shopping cart programs have a feature that displays a message when a product is running low, such as "Only 2 Left." If your software can't display such a message, manually add the disclaimer "Almost Out" to your product description when inventory of your best sellers gets low.

Have it your way: The seamless shopping experience

If there's one word that is gaining importance in the retail world it's this one: *omnichannel*. You may be familiar with the term when it comes to using many or all (from the word *omnis*) channels to market to your customers. You probably have a marketing strategy to target customers through multiple channels, including social media, television ads, online ads, and so on. That's based on you reaching out to the customer. Lately, omnichannel retail strategy refers to understanding how the customer chooses to shop with you and providing an uninterrupted shopping experience between your retail destinations (in-store, on the website, through mobile devices and apps, from social media platforms, and so on).

Instead of putting customers into a bucket of being either online customers or offline customers, when it comes to omnichannel, it's better to think of them all as *digital* customers. These are the new type of retail customers we mention at the beginning of this chapter. These customers are technology savvy and want to buy from your website, from inside your store, or from a mobile app — or from all three, at the same time! For example, this customer is likely standing in your retail store looking at a product on your shelf while simultaneously checking your website from her smartphone to see if you have it in a different color, while also using a mobile app to compare prices with other retailers.

Meeting this customer's needs through an omnichannel approach really comes down to having the right technology in place to enable it, and a strategy in place to execute it well. Offering customers a true omnichannel shopping experience starts with the following three requirements:

>> **Brand consistency:** The image of your store, how it looks and feels, should be the same on your website and your social media channels. Whether customers are shopping from a shared pin on Pinterest or opening a mobile app, your retail brand needs to be recognizable across channels.

>> **Backend management integration:** As mentioned, you want an inventory system that tracks data from inside your store, as well as on your website. You want loyalty programs to recognize buyers in the store just as easily as they do online. In other words, you want your backend systems to talk to each other and share from the same pool of information.

>> **In-store customer aptitude:** Part of offering an easy, integrated shopping experience requires that you have the proper in-store resources. This includes technology, such as an iPad for every sales person, to the proper training of employees so they understand how to use that iPad to help customers. If a customer wants a shirt in a color that's out of stock in the store, the employee should be able to go the customer with the iPad in-hand and verify availability of the shirt color online or in another retail location, and be able to let the customer purchase that item in-store and choose whether to have it delivered to the customer or available for pickup at the store of choice. Both the technology and sales mentality need to be in place to deliver on this experience.

REMEMBER

When you are in the early stages of transitioning from a traditional retail store to an e-commerce store, we recognize that having an omnichannel strategy is an advanced approach with a higher difficulty level. Because inventory systems and other backend technology solutions are required for omnichannel, if you can *plan now* for that strategy, it will reduce future headaches. By investing today in the solutions with the most flexibility, it's a lot easier than trying to add-on modules or completely change technologies down the road.

Details, details, details

Speaking of giving customers everything they want, when and how they want it, savvy digital shoppers are spoiled by the amount of information they can find with the stroke of a key. But too much information can overwhelm customers and distract them from purchasing. Thus, your challenge is to anticipate which information a shopper really needs (and wants) to know about a product and then provide that info (and only that info) in a succinct and accessible manner. The fol-lowing list gives you some of the most sought-after product information:

>> **Product descriptions:** Listing the color and style of a coffee table is helpful, but if you leave out its dimensions, customers will hesitate to make a pur-chase. You need to make all the details of a product available to your cus-tomer. The trick is to offer the information in layers. In other words, give a brief description of the product, along with a photo, but then give customers the option to click a link for more details or additional photos.

>> **Visual information:** You can't try on different sizes or styles of clothing in an online store. Even the best photos may make it difficult to see other details that make a product special. Increasingly, online retailers are turning to the power of video to give that almost-in-person experience. Videos that demon-strate the product in use or display it on a real person provide a better view of the product and may prompt a purchase.

>> **Reviews:** Customer reviews came into vogue after Amazon made them popular on its site. Providing easy access to reviews by experts or other credible sources (such as magazines) is also a hot demand from online customers.

>> **Delivery options:** Customers want to understand, at the absolute least, the different methods of delivery your site offers. This information includes the provider of the service (U.S. Postal Service, UPS, FedEx, or some other shipping company), the delivery options (for example, Express or Ground), and the cost. In addition, customers want to have access to a shipping number and a direct link to track the delivery status of their packages.

TIP

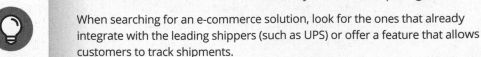

When searching for an e-commerce solution, look for the ones that already integrate with the leading shippers (such as UPS) or offer a feature that allows customers to track shipments.

>> **Contact information:** Make sure that customers can easily find your phone number and email address. (And then make sure that you respond when a customer contacts you.)

>> **Return policies:** Online shoppers want to know return and exchange policies before they make that final purchase. Especially when buying clothing or perishable items, your customers want to be reassured that they can get a fair deal if something goes wrong when they receive the product. Keeping your return policies clearly posted on your site not only helps make the sale but also reduces confusion later.

Methods for coping with the holiday rush

Having your return policy clearly accessible is certainly a plus during a busy holiday season. But that's the bare minimum. Keep in mind that customer expectations peak during holidays and high-demand seasonal periods. Whenever your rush occurs, you can prepare for it in the following ways:

>> **Offer rush deliveries:** Your delivery company may not have a problem with rush delivery, but you need to make sure that you can get the items packed and out the door to meet the hectic pace. Several online stores, such as Amazon, help customers know exactly when they can expect their order to arrive based on when they place it. For example, a message appears that says if you order by a specific date, you will receive your order by a specific date. This message helps customers decide what type of shipping option they should choose.

>> **Extend delivery times:** Again, you just need to handle those last-minute orders that arrive the day before (or the day of) the major holiday. Whether or not you can extend your delivery times often depends on whether you have enough help behind the scenes to keep filling those orders.

>> **Prepare for backups:** Even if everything goes smoothly on your side, the delivery company might drop the ball. We saw this happen during the now infamous 2013 holiday season when extreme weather conditions, along with a surge of online sales, prevented major delivery companies from making deliveries promised by online retailers to show up in time for Christmas. Since that catastrophic online shopping season, e-tailers learned the hard way that you can't always predict this type of widespread delivery failure, but you can prepare for it. Make sure your policies clearly state how failed deliveries will be handled, even if they're not your fault. Sometimes, reimbursements or offering a special discount on the next purchase can go a long way in creating goodwill.

>> **Stock up on inventory:** Nothing is worse than running out of a hot item and finding out that you can't get more in until after the holiday. You may want to go a little heavy on your inventory or alert your suppliers to the potential of increased demand.

>> **Bulk up on service representatives:** Customers don't hesitate to ask for help when it comes to holiday shopping.

REMEMBER

Although the busiest retail season is typically November and December, other holiday periods also drive sales. According to recent research, online sales also heat up during Valentine's Day, Easter, and Mother's Day (for example).

Superior customer service

At the heart of the difference in shopping online, as opposed to in a store, is the customer service. The level of support that you provide your online customers is one of the single most influential factors in whether those customers return to your site to buy again. You probably don't doubt that superior service is important in your store. But a high level of service is even more important online because customers are limited in their ability to interact with your products. Customers depend on you to provide as much information about a product as you can so that they can make an immediate buying decision. They can't pick up a product and examine it up close. If you don't have enough detail on your website or a customer has an unusual question, you want that customer to be able to reach you.

Fortunately, offering exceptional customer service from your site has become pretty darn easy. The technology is readily available, and implementing it doesn't cost you an arm and a leg. Here are a few of the ways you can reach out to your customers:

>> **Email:** One of the easiest ways to provide customers with information about your products is by letting them contact you by email. You can make shopping easy by posting a customer service email address throughout your site. Remember to respond in a timely manner. Just a few years ago, it was acceptable to respond to email within a 24-hour period, but customers now expect much faster response times — usually within a few hours.

TIP

Use an automated responder to automatically generate a return email that notifies your customer that you received the email he or she sent. Acknowledge customers' requests while providing a time for when you will contact them. Also give them alternative options for reaching you faster.

>> **Phone:** Clearly posting a direct phone number so that shoppers can access customer support is an absolute must. If you can swing it, get yourself a toll-free number. If you don't have a 24-hour support line, be sure to post the normal operating hours of customer service.

>> **Social media:** Customer service no longer originates only from your website. The proliferation of social gives customers another way to get the attention of online retailers, especially if customers think they are being ignored or are not getting help quickly enough. Many online retailers are frustrated because social media has become another place where they have to service customers — and those customers expect a response in minutes, rather than hours. In addition, customer service through social media occurs in an open forum that exposes problems to the public. However, for online businesses that embrace customer service and do it well, social media has proven to be a terrific way to turn unhappy customers into loyal brand advocates. As a small-business owner, be prepared to monitor social media for customer concerns and address them as quickly as possible.

>> **Live chat:** Although some online shoppers like the anonymity that the Internet provides, many more demand instantaneous support, such as they might find in your bricks-and-mortar store. To answer that need, consider offering standby customer support representatives through live-chat technology. This tool helps customers immediately connect to a person who can answer their questions (through either an instant-messenger-style format or audio over the computer). Some companies tout that live chat has increased online sales significantly, increased average order values, and decreased customer support costs. If you decide to use live chat, look for software that enables integration with mobile devices and social media.

TIP

Most live-chat software providers offer a free trial, and in some cases, you can get started with the service for as little as $49 a month. Check out live-chat services from LivePerson (`www.liveperson.com`), which offers pricing based on your website's traffic (a great feature for smaller sites), and Bold360 (`www.bold360.com`), which offers a range of pricing plans based on the type of chat interactions and features you need.

Establishing Patterns

Getting customers to buy from you (at any location) comes down to establishing buying patterns. You take part in forming your customers' buying patterns by helping them develop the habit of coming to *you* as opposed to a competitor. After you understand your customers and what they want, you're in a position to start creating that pattern. To establish a buying pattern with your customers, you need to provide three things as an online retailer:

>> **Information:** Your site is a place to shop, but it's also a resource for product information. After you establish yourself as an authority on your product lines, customers begin making a conscious decision to go to you first.

>> **Buying opportunities:** Experienced web shoppers aren't looking strictly for information. They want a reason to buy, too. You can give them access to regular specials or limited-time-only offers, exclusive sales, and select or new merchandise to convince them to buy.

>> **Reliability:** In addition to providing a good inventory and terrific customer service, the entire buying process at your site has to pass muster — from the time your customers pull up your home page to when the purchased product is delivered to their doorstep. When you have the opportunity to prove yourself as a reliable retailer (and use that opportunity), customers get used to coming to you to shop.

Chapter **3**

Window Dressing for the Online Display

As a bricks-and-mortar retailer, you probably gave a great deal of attention and thought to your store's appearance — the selection of paint colors, the placement of shelving, and even the way each product is positioned. You probably agonized for days, if not weeks, over each decision — and for good reason, too.

Major retailers spend a substantial amount of time and money sorting through the same details. And when they find that perfect look, it becomes a blueprint for every store that follows.

Why go to all this trouble? Your goal in creating a positive shopping environment is to increase sales. That process begins with the look of your store. The way products are arranged contributes to an overall feeling or mood. Customers will buy more if they're comfortable shopping in your store, can find what they need, and are treated well. Retail merchandizing experts have shown that careful attention to in-store displays can have a direct (positive) effect on your sales.

The same concept holds true for your online store. In one e-commerce case study, a global online retailer experimented with how they featured a group of lighting fixtures on their website. They claimed to see an increase of 30 percent in their online sales for one particular product grouping. Similarly, other functions or features of your online store can make a difference in sales. For example, adding video or enabling additional product views and providing the capability to zoom in on product images for a closer look contribute to sales increases of more than 15 percent, according to industry research.

The result is clear: The way you position or feature your products online could mean earning several hundred dollars (or more) a day in online retail sales. That's worth it, in our opinion. With that result in mind, in this chapter, we show you how to map your very own online-store blueprint.

Creating the Right Look for Your Online Store

Imagine for a moment that one of your customers is blindfolded and brought into your offline store (without knowing where she is being taken). After the blindfold is removed, the customer should be able to tell that she's in your store. For example, do you carry specialty products or a line of signature items? Do you use bright, unconventional colors on the walls?

Transferring your physical image, or *identity*, to your online store is a major part of creating the right look for your site. Plus, you want to convey a consistent brand experience wherever your products are being sold. When it comes to the design of your online presence, we recommend starting the process by choosing a single element that you believe customers most readily identify with your store. The main factor that makes your store special may be one of these features:

>> **Architectural element:** Maybe the shape of your store's building makes it stand out. Or perhaps you designed the interior with special features, such as high vaulted ceilings, curved walls, or dramatic windows. Sometimes, the physical appearance of your location leaves a lasting impression.

>> **Color scheme:** The interior and exterior of your store may be filled with soft, muted tones or wild, bright, eye-popping colors. Either way, these telling color combinations may provide your customers with a strong association with your store.

>> **Logo:** Your physical store's brand or identity often originates from your business logo. The logo design, colors, fonts, and overall personality often lend themselves to the best place to start with your online store's design.

>> **Location:** Some stores take their images directly from their surroundings. For example, you may be located in a trendy, upscale part of your city. Or maybe you're part of an eclectic revitalization of a downtown area. Then again, your customers may know you best as "that shop by the beach." Your store may be associated with a vacation hot spot or a well-known tourist destination.

>> **Theme:** Your store may be created around a particular theme, such as birthday parties or business travel.

>> **Event or activity:** Perhaps you hold an annual event closely tied to the image of your store. Or maybe you have certain ongoing activities that draw attention.

>> **People:** Every once in a while, a store is less about the products it sells and more identifiable with the person who owns it. So maybe you're a pseudo-celebrity — or an outright famous person. Either way, if that's the case, your personal image may be most closely tied to the image of your store.

>> **Selection:** Superstore retailers are known for offering a wide variety of products. Although you may not compete at that level, you may be best known for your extensive selection of a particular brand or type of product.

>> **Price:** Ah, price. You may be on the super-exclusive high end or the rock-bottom low end.

>> **Customer service:** During a time when many stores compete on price alone, retailers (particularly smaller ones) that focus on customer service receive lots of attention. If customer service is your forte, that may be what customers remember most about you.

>> **Niche:** Maybe you specialize in Mexican pottery, collectible Disney products, or nostalgic items from the 1950s. If you have a streamlined product base that appeals to a highly targeted customer audience, you can bet that this specialization makes up your total image.

Your offline store identity gives you a starting point for your website design. As you build your site, this element gives you a clear place to return if you get off-track from the image you want to project. Your store identity is a guideline.

REMEMBER

Similarly, after you begin promoting your online store, having a single element related to your image gives you a useful tie-in for advertisements, promotions, and marketing materials. And even though this identifier is what you're best known for in your local (offline) market, it can become a unique selling point in a crowded online marketplace.

Creating the Perfect Shopping Experience

The right image is just the beginning. The look of an online store can be nearly flawless, but after you open the door (or enter the website), you may find a different story. Regardless of your store's image on the outside, if customers have difficulties with the actual shopping experience inside, you can quickly lose those customers.

As a shopkeeper, you have to make great strides to carry your complete image from the outside in. For an online store, that inside image is all about organization.

For example, any large bookseller probably has thousands and thousands of books packing the shelves and tables of its store. Yet every book has its place. Each one is neatly categorized according to subject matter, release dates, clearance items, sales, or even product type (books, magazines, greeting cards, and gifts, for example). With all this managed chaos, the store still has room for wide aisles, chairs and sofas, and an entire coffee shop.

When you visit the online version of the bookstore, you should find the same strategy at play. The navigation should provide clear choices that mimic the categories you find in the store.

To achieve this level of detail online, start by taking a tour of your bricks-and-mortar location. Think about all the ways that you categorize products to make shopping (and inventory management) easy. These categories often include

>> **Brand name:** People shop by designer labels and other recognized brands.

>> **Product type or style:** These distinctions can even be product categories within categories. For example, a drugstore might carry makeup, books, and school supplies. You can divide the categories further by lipsticks and eye shadows, bestsellers and bargain books, and pens and notebooks.

>> **Price:** Although it may be more difficult to do in your offline store, you can allow online customers to sort products based on price (from high to low or from low to high).

>> **Sale or clearance items:** Everybody likes a bargain. Your customers are no different, and they appreciate when a bargain is easy to spot.

>> **Discontinued items:** These products won't be produced any more, and especially with collectibles, customers want to know that they won't be able to find these items on the shelves (real or virtual) any more.

>> **New release (or just in):** Books and DVDs aren't the only items that are classified this way. Products are continually being updated, or new items are introduced in a product line. Even if an item isn't hot off the press for the manufacturer, it may be the first time you have it in your store.

>> **Solution:** Increasingly, products are categorized by the problem they help customers solve. In books, for example, you can find an entire section of self-help categories. You can probably categorize your products in a similar fashion (for example, kitchen tools and bathroom cleaners).

Organizing your products in categories

However you categorize products, carrying your retail store's organization through to your online store isn't difficult. It just takes some, well . . . organization.

You may not realize (or may have forgotten) how and why you placed your products the way you have in your bricks-and-mortar store. Follow these steps to refresh your memory and come up with a plan to organize your online store:

1. **Draw a diagram of the inside of your retail store.**

Your diagram doesn't have to be drawn to scale. But the drawing should clearly show the layout of your store, including shelving units, display cases, and doorways.

2. **On a separate piece of paper, make a corresponding list of all the items you have displayed.**

This step helps you make an inventory of everything that's placed out on the floor (where customers shop) and detail where it's displayed. Label shelves and tables in your store diagram with numbers or letters. The corresponding list should indicate which products are stored where; note why you organize them that way.

3. **Create a list of top-selling items.**

Pull this list from your store's inventory and sales reports. When you have your list, look to see where those top-selling items are located in your store. Do you see any noticeable patterns?

4. **Identify your merchandising hot spots.**

Your *merchandising hot spots* are the places that receive the most attention because of their physical location in the store. Items next to your cash register, in your front window (if you have one), and near the front door where customers can see them when they walk into the store are all examples of merchandising hot spots.

5. **Group products into categories that you want to use online.**

Take your preferred product groupings and incorporate them into your website's site map. Basically, you're merchandising your online store by using the identifiable trends from your offline location.

REMEMBER

One product can appear in several categories. Your shopping cart software should allow you to easily cross-reference items in multiple categories.

Offering a search function

In addition to creating a plan for the layout of your online store, you can offer customers another critical organizational function: a web-based search tool.

You're probably familiar with using Google or Yahoo! to search the Internet for keywords. Well, online stores have found that the same kind of tool is a true boon to business. Think about search tools in comparison to your store: A customer can come in and ask a sales associate where something is located in your store. Online shoppers, however, have to depend on using the clues on your site's menu bar. Including a search function on your home page eliminates customers having to guess in which category they can find a certain product.

WARNING

Not all search functions are created equal, especially when your online store deals with thousands of products. Make sure that customers can search by using the smallest detail (such as a brief product description, a brand name, or even color) and still find what they want.

Look for a search tool that

>> **Searches by a specific keyword term:** If you type a keyword such as *shelves,* the search returns all similar items.

>> **Sorts the results:** Customers should be able to further sort their search terms. For example, Macy's online store at www.macys.com allows customers to further search or filter by such things as price, brand, color, customer product reviews and ratings, and even special discounts or offers. The additional sorting function prevents a large number of results from overwhelming customers.

>> **Displays similar or complementary items:** When customers click a product, they should see a list of items that they might be interested in buying, based on the original search term.

>> **Allows exclusions:** Site searches that allow customers to specify certain words or terms that should not be included in search results are helpful for returning more accurate results.

>> **Shows customers specific ads or promotions:** Customers should see ads targeted to them, based on the results of their keyword searches. Targeted ads can convert visitors to buyers.

Beyond Window Shopping: Designs and Functions That Lure Traffic

A good site design makes attracting buyers to your site much easier. The aesthetics of your site matter, but you also need functionality. These elements can keep your site's traffic flowing (and, you hope, convert that traffic to sales):

>> **General appearance:** Research indicates that shoppers are more likely to purchase from a site that has a professional and trustworthy appearance. Although nothing's wrong with fun and wacky (if it fits your product), just make sure that you also show that you're responsible. For example, clearly display your terms of agreement, return policies, and contact information, and make sure that you have a reliable shopping cart program.

>> **Uncluttered appearance:** Resist the urge to pack your site's pages full of information, promotions, and product choices. When a site has too much going on, customers become overwhelmed. Rather than buy, they flee.

>> **Simplicity:** Keep both the graphical design of your site and the information you provide simple. A popular design trend for making e-commerce sites more appealing is a simplified color scheme. The phrase "less is more" is one to take to heart when selling online.

REMEMBER

Even if your offline brand is funky and full of color, you can still make online design decisions that keep visitors from feeling overwhelmed when they first visit your site. A good example of this approach is the online niche retailer, Caron's Beach House. Specializing in coastal home décor, the site is filled with beach-inspired products. It would be easy for the large amount of bright and colorful products to overwhelm the site design, but the company found an aesthetically pleasing point of compromise for the e-commerce site (www.caronsbeachhouse.com). As you see in Figure 3-1, the site has a neutral white background to balance the vibrant product photos. The site is still true to the colorful beach theme, but it doesn't overwhelm visitors or interfere with the online customer experience.

FIGURE 3-1:
A vibrant, colorful offline brand can have a clean, uncluttered online design for a better customer experience.

>> **Good navigation:** A sure way to convert visitors to buyers is with your site's ease of navigation. Shoppers should be able to move from one place to another on your site relatively easily. And your navigation system should be intuitive so that a customer clearly understands how your site is structured.

>> **Special landing pages:** A unique landing page attracts buyers and increases your odds for a sale. A *landing page* is usually focused on one product or service and is used as a stand-alone web page, or as an entry page to your website. You might promote a link to that particular page or use that link in an online ad — and instead of new visitors coming to your home page, they "land" on this specific page first. (This type of page is also referred to as an *entrance page* because visitors enter your site from this special page instead of your home page.) If you want to promote a new high-end tent on your outdoors site, for example, you can create a page that's only about that tent. Visitors don't waste time sorting through your entire inventory when all they really want is a tent, increasing the likelihood that they will make a quick purchase.

>> **Links:** Set up your site so that customers don't have to click many links to reach their destination.

>> **Layered information:** You may want to give customers the option to go deeper into the site to find more detailed information. Simply provide the details in layers. Usually, you see layering when a product is displayed with a photo and a general description. If customers want to know the item's dimensions or see alternative views of the product, they can do so by clicking the next link (or layer) of product detail.

» **Cash register:** From an easy checkout process to the opportunity to *suggestive sell* (offer similar products or useful items, such as batteries), the function of the cash register — or shopping cart — program is one of the most important elements of good design.

» **Product display:** Provide customers with simple headlines, good images, and detailed information. The basic information, such as an item's price and how to purchase it, should be clearly displayed.

» **Special promotions:** Offering discounts or limited-time offers is a good way to convert buyers. But these specials don't do you any good if a person can't find those offers or the offers aren't in line with what a person is buying (or shopping for). Carefully place targeted promotions in your site to make them effective.

Having good design and the right image for your website isn't that different from what you already do in your bricks-and-mortar store.

IN THIS CHAPTER

» Understanding mobile commerce for retailers

» Texting and mobile alerts to trigger buying

» Targeting local customers online

» Attracting business with social media ads

» Using alternative marketing strategies

Chapter **4**

Revving Up with Mobile Marketing, Social Media, and More

L eading retailers agree that e-commerce is a necessity and that online sales consistently show more growth than in-store sales. With more stores coming online and shoppers becoming increasingly savvy, cost-conscious buyers, it's undeniable that online retailing is highly competitive. As a retailer, you have to make every possible effort to reach customers and convince them to buy from you. For storefront locations, you need to not only reach out from your website but also draw local online shoppers to your location. Mobile commerce, or *m-commerce*, offers unique advantages to both online and traditional retailers looking to extend their brands online.

For the most part, m-commerce refers to the way companies use smartphones and other mobile devices, such as tablets, to market and sell to customers. If you own a smartphone, especially an Android or iPhone, chances are good that you've already experienced mobile commerce. For example, have you

>> Paid a bill by entering a specific code into your smartphone?

>> Used a mobile app to order dinner from your favorite restaurant?

>> Voted for a contestant on a reality show by texting a short numerical message?

>> Entered a contest or giveaway?

>> Sent a short text (to request information)?

>> Checked into an event, concert, or a restaurant through social media and received a perk in exchange for promoting the event or business in real-time to your friends?

>> Paid for gas, groceries, or a cup of your favorite java using a payment app on your smartphone?

>> Made a donation to the Red Cross or other charitable organization by sending a short text from your phone?

>> Received a text message from a favorite store, alerting you to an exclusive, limited-time bargain?

All these examples demonstrate m-commerce, and more applications are on the way. Mobile commerce for retailers in the United States hit $208 billion in 2018, and should represent the majority of ecommerce spending by 2021, according to eMarketer. Retail isn't the only industry seeing growth. In the world of finance alone, the growth of m-commerce (mobile commerce) and related activities is taking hold at a phenomenal rate, from paying bills through your smartphone to depositing a check with your smartphone or tablet. These mobile banking activities are anticipated to expand, as more than 2 billion users (globally) were using mobile banking in 2018, according to Juniper Research.

As a traditional retailer, even if you don't actively participate in m-commerce, your business most likely benefits from it. That's because consumers actively use location search functionality in a mobile device to find a business, product, service, or event. Google reports that 40% of all mobile searches have "local intent," which means people search with the purpose of taking action within the specific geographic region of the search. Other reports estimate that anywhere from one-third to one-half (or more) of mobile searches result in a purchase from a local business — sometimes within an hour of searching!

One reason for these impressive statistics and staggering predictions is technology. Many smartphones can access the Internet and make transactions with speeds and functionality similar to those of a desktop computer. Plus, screen sizes of mobile phones have increased and mobile search capabilities (and accuracy) have improved to provide a better customer experience.

You can find more about mobile commerce from the Mobile Marketing Association at www.mmaglobal.com.

In this chapter, we offer you a glimpse of how m-commerce is poised to change the way customers buy. We also explain how mobile interacts with social media and other localized marketing opportunities in a way that allows you to capitalize on mobile shoppers to increase sales.

Distinguishing between Different Types of Mobile Commerce

The growth of m-commerce has exceeded expectations. Consider that years ago, mobile conversion rates were typically small, averaging .6 percent for smartphones and 1.5 percent for tablets, and 56 percent of mobile purchases were less than $50. Today, m-commerce accounts for 40 percent of online-only ecommerce sales and nearly 3 percent of in-store retail sales. Although shopping from tablets was previously accountable for most m-commerce sales, the current growth in m-commerce sales is coming from smartphones. By 2019, 34 percent of all U.S. e-commerce sales will originate from smartphones, and by 2021, eMarketer anticipates that m-commerce sales globally will account for more than half of all e-commerce sales.

Why does it matter what type of mobile device shoppers use? The main reason is because the use of smartphones typically indicates that your customers are truly mobile at the moment of search, compared to tablets, which are still most likely to be used from a stationary location (such as a home). That means smartphone shoppers may already be nearby or en route to your store when searching, or may start a search from within your retail location. Research shows that when customers search in-store on their smartphones for product information, they typically make a purchase, even if it's not the same product the customer originally intended to buy.

Consider that consumers shopping locally or in-store are quite comfortable using their mobile phones for the following retail-related activities:

>> View emails for promotions from online retailers

>> Get information about retailers (such as directions, business hours, and contact information)

>> Research products and compare prices

>> Receive texts with codes for special offers

>> Redeem coupon codes

The last two items on that list are especially good news for retailers online and offline because using m-commerce to deliver special offers and coupons helps drive revenue for your business. With that in mind, here are some ways you can now use mobile commerce, all of which we discuss in greater detail in the following sections:

>> **SMS alerts:** Companies use SMS (Short Message Service) to send short text messages to their customers' smartphones. For example, Redbox, the video vending-machine company, sends daily or weekly messages about new video releases, movie trivia, and more to subscribers who have chosen to receive text alerts. The goal is to drive subscribers to the Redbox website, to keep them actively engaged, and to entice customers to go to a vending machine and check out a movie.

>> **Text-to-buy:** Some savvy marketing companies are using an instant gratification type of application for mobile commerce. With text-to-buy, companies place traditional advertisements for a specific product on billboards, in television or radio commercials, in print ads, and online in social network sites. Included in the ad is a special numerical code (usually a short string of numbers or letters). The consumer enters the code into a smartphone and buys the product.

REMEMBER

Text-to-buy ads are an effective way to strike while the iron is hot, or to get a customer to buy while he's thinking about the product he just saw in an ad.

>> **Mobile coupons:** Some customers may still be reluctant to make a purchase by using a smartphone, but you can still reach out to them by sending them mobile coupons (m-coupons) by smartphone. Customers can then go online or to your physical location, provide the coupon code, and make a purchase. Just like that, the customer gets a good deal and you get a bump in sales.

>> **QR codes:** These small graphic icons are about the size of a postage stamp. You see them printed in magazine ads and in books, on in-store displays, and online on websites. They allow your customer to use a smartphone to snap a

picture of the image and reveal something of interest — from a coupon code to a how-to manual. QR (Quick Response) codes have dipped in popularity, but because they offer a way to quickly access additional product information (from a store shelf, for example), they can be used to boost mobile browsing and encourage more buying. For that reason, we wouldn't count them out as an effective m-commerce tool just yet.

>> **Check-in specials:** Retailers can offer coupons or other specials to customers who use social media (such as Facebook) to *check in,* or publicly announce that they are on-site at your location. The customer should be able to redeem your offer on the spot (not on a future visit). This reward seems counterintuitive because the idea of a coupon is to bring people to you who otherwise wouldn't be shopping with you. However, this on-the-spot reward is important because it encourages existing customers to let their friends and followers know that they are at your location — think of it as nearly free advertising.

>> **Mobile pay:** A common point of frustration for in-store buyers is long lines at checkout or slow checkout. As part of m-commerce, mobile could eliminate the "counter-top" purchase in-store. Instead, customers can use a retailer's app via smartphones to check out in-store or buy ahead from outside the store and then pick-up in the store. Restaurants are already seeing success with this approach. As of 2018, Mobile Order and Pay now accounts for 13 percent of all Starbucks transactions in the United States. Similarly, Domino's mobile order-ahead app has not only surpassed tens of millions of downloads, but the company has seen average purchase amounts increase by 17 percent per order.

You may not want to use *all* these examples for your online store. But you can expect that customers will demand more options when doing business with your store through m–commerce, so you don't want to ignore this important industry trend, either.

Sending text alerts

Sending short text messages (called SMS messages) over a smartphone is an easy and affordable way to communicate with customers. It works especially well for these tasks:

>> Sending reminders about an event, a product, or a service

>> Creating immediate awareness

>> Sending maintenance notices or appointment reminders for services

>> Providing notice that products are available for in-store pickup

>> Hosting a contest, or sending information related to contests

>> Sending special offers

REMEMBER

Customers must opt-in, or choose, to receive text alerts. Similar to email marketing, certain rules apply regarding how and when you can send messages via mobile phones to customers. Do not send unsolicited texts. Especially because customers can be charged a per-text fee by their cellular service provider, a business can get in trouble if it doesn't ask permission to advertise or market to a customer using SMS alerts. You must also give customers the ability to opt-out or choose to stop receiving text alerts.

TIP

Encourage customers to opt-in to receive text alerts by offering a special incentive or one-time perk, such as a discount off the next purchase. The mega-retailer Kohl's actively promotes its text-based "mobile sales alerts" on its website and offers customers a 15 percent discount. The company also clearly states approximately how many alerts per week a customer may receive, in order to help set expectations.

REMEMBER

When you use any type of mobile campaign to promote your store, you should follow a few rules. Make sure that your mobile message recipient always opts-in to the campaign. Additionally, ask customers to submit a keyword or short code to signal their desire to participate. And, of course, never sell your mobile contact list to other retailers.

Distributing mobile coupons

It's hard to say what's driving the demand for mobile coupons, which were once thought to be a disruptive nuisance. Perhaps Americans are becoming more cost-conscious and are on the lookout for a deal. Or maybe they are simply curious as to how mobile coupons work. Whatever the reason, billions of mobile coupons are being distributed each year. According to research from Ipsos OTX, 70 percent of people surveyed said that receiving coupons or discounts is the top reason they stay connected to their favorite brands, and that percentage continues to grow as more people realize the benefits of mobile coupons.

More consumers are enjoying the delivery of mobile coupons to get discounts and perks while they are near a particular store, for example. Retailers (both online and offline) are finding that mobile coupons are spurring a type of spontaneous buying, ultimately driving more sales and greater revenue for their stores. Even so, other research reveals that a large percentage of mobile coupons go unused — but even if not used, they are influencing future buying decisions. The fact that so many mobile coupons are being distributed is a good indicator that the demand for them is likely to continue growing as they become more mainstream.

What's the big deal about having coupons sent to your phone? For starters, they are coupons sent to your phone! Seriously, as a traditional or online retailer, mobile coupons have been shown to

>> Generate better engagement and response rates with customers

>> Increase customer loyalty

>> Cost less than traditional advertising

>> Reach customers when they are near your location

>> Be easier to administer than other advertising

A growing number of companies offer SMS and mobile coupon services, along with other mobile marketing services and tools. Try one of the following:

>> **Simple Texting** (www.simpletexting.com): Offers a number of marketing options for SMS services. Service is available to a large number of companies outside the United States. In some cases, a minimum purchase may be required.

>> **EzTexting** (www.eztexting.com): With a host of different plans for businesses, EzTexting costs as little as a few cents per text (not exceeding 5 cents) in a true pay-as-you-go format. They also offer monthly plans, based on usage, that range from approximately $30 to $150 per month.

>> **Vibes** (www.vibes.com): This company has a range of mobile marketing and SMS services as part of its mobile engagement platform, especially after its acquisition of Red Fish Media. As m-commerce has become more popular, this company has expanded its offerings and now helps brands with all parts of mobile marketing.

>> **Avid Mobile** (www.avidmobile.com): Boasting an all-in-one application that integrates SMS, mobile coupons and email, Avid Mobile also provides enhanced reporting and simplified developer tools. The company's app provides users with an easy way to build custom mobile websites, apps and landing pages. A free trial is available that does not require a credit card.

>> **Trumpia** (www.trumpia.com): This full-service SMS software lets you do automated mass texting, as well as individual texting with enhanced targeting capabilities. Pricing is available by company size, including standard ($195 per month), professional ($495), and small-enterprise ($995 per month). Additional plans are available for mid to large enterprises and custom projects.

Omnichannel

An important consideration when discussing online and offline sales is referred to as *omnichannel,* or *cross-channel.* This phrase takes into account the way that shopping is distributed, or spread across, multiple platforms and how retailers must have a cohesive strategy to not only market to all these channels, but enable shopping across and between various channels. Just as shoppers like to have a choice of whether to shop in your physical retail location or online, consumers now want even more choices for the way they shop and buy online, including mobile devices (both smartphones and tablets) and social media websites (from Instagram to Pinterest). Just as we discussed the capability to market to consumers through these platforms, you also want to offer the capability to shop, or buy, directly from the same platforms with the least amount of interference or disruption to the buying process.

Several companies are offering mobile shopping platforms that integrate with your online store or your social media profiles, such as Facebook and Twitter. If you're using platforms like Shopify (www.shopify.com) or Squarespace (www.squarespace.com), they will be able to offer an optimized mobile store that's integrated with your existing website to offer a truly mobile shopping experience. As you include more mobile and social media buying experiences with your store, look for other service providers and technologies that help integrate the shopping experience across multiple channels.

Localizing with Ads

As you saw with some of the targeted mobile coupons and ads, one advantage that mobile commerce offers is the capability to reach customers in a specific geographic region. The concept of *localization,* or local advertising, isn't restricted to mobile applications. If you're an online retailer who also has a bricks-and-mortar location, local search can mean big business for you. As competition and market conditions tighten, local paid search is expected to grow as an important advertising strategy for retailers. As targeting continues to improve and as mobile usage increases, localized search is expected to keep rising. In the next few years, an estimated 30 percent of all searches will be local, and more than 80 percent of all local searches will be on smartphones.

In this process, also referred to as *geotargeting,* your business ads appear as part of search results that are based on a geographic location. The concept of local marketing is used by plenty of sites, such as Craigslist and Angie's List. However, in the area of paid local search, Google remains the industry giant, accounting for more than 84 percent of paid searches. Google uses a geotargeting program that provides paid search results based on a user's computer IP address, which can be associated with a specific physical location. While search engines have previously dominated localized advertising opportunities, social media is quickly shaking up the mix with Facebook proving to be a worthy contender against Google. The message is clear that consumers are responding to localized, mobile marketing, and as a retailer, it's important you consider emerging options.

Google Ads

Using Google Ads is comparable to placing an ad in your local newspaper. You purchase a specific amount of space (or ad size) for a set dollar amount to entice customers to come into your store. You can even specify a section of the paper in which your ad should appear. For example, if you have a sporting goods store, your ad might appear in the sports section of the newspaper. Google works almost the same way.

In this case, your ad is displayed in the search engine based on a prospective customer's search results (called SERP). Suppose that someone uses Google to search for soccer balls. Your text ad, typically a few sentences long, shows up either on the top of the screen with other sponsored ads, or at the bottom of the search results as shown in Figure 4-1.

FIGURE 4-1:
Drive local traffic with Google Ads.

Unlike with traditional print ads, with Google Ads you choose the keywords that trigger your ad to appear and you decide how much you want to pay for the ad space. When you use Ads, you aren't paying for a certain ad size but, rather, for a certain number of hits on your ad. In this process, known as *cost per click*, or *CPC*, you pay only when prospective customers click your text link. (Another common industry term for this type of marketing or advertising is PPC, or *pay per click*.)

Geotargeting takes CPC one step further. You also might decide that you want your ad to appear *only* when the prospective customer is searching from a specific location, such as a country or city. For example, if your sports store is based in Raleigh, North Carolina, and someone in that area searches for soccer balls, your ad appears. If the person clicks your ad, you're charged the amount that you agreed to pay. You can pay as little as a few pennies up to several dollars or more for each click. Google is also driving similar types of localized or geographically based results in all their organic (non-paid) search results.

If you set the price, or CPC, that you're willing to pay (as we just mentioned), you may be wondering why you would ever agree to pay a high dollar amount. It's simple: Because you're basically bidding on the price of the ad, or in this case, the CPC, your price correlates with the popularity of the keyword on which you're bidding. The more popular your keyword or your keywords, the more people are willing to pay for them, which drives up the price and the competition for your *ad position*, or where it gets placed within search results. You might still choose to bid a smaller amount for your CPC, but that means your ad will appear fewer times or in a lower position on the page. To be competitive, you may have to pay a higher CPC.

TIP

You can limit the cost of your keywords by bidding on specific words or phrases, as opposed to choosing more general terms. Rather than bid on *soccer balls*, for example, bid on a specific type or name-brand soccer ball. Or use a phrase such as *soccer balls for kids* or *youth soccer balls*. You see fewer results, but they should also lead to a more qualified buyer for a smaller ad price.

Registration for Google Ads is free, except for a minimal setup fee, and requires no contracts or minimum spending requirements. You're charged only when someone clicks your text ad. With Google Ads, you can

>> Create campaigns for multiple products or websites, using multiple sets of keywords

>> Target multiple locations at once (instead of only one zip code, or city, for example)

>> Use images, video, and audio with the ad, as opposed to only text

>> Gain access to various advanced planning and budgeting tools

>> Set daily budget limits (for greater control) versus monthly budget limits

TIP

You can extend the value of organic (not paid for) localized search results by taking advantage of Google's free local search placement, part of an overall initiative to support local businesses, called Google My Business. Registering with Google My Business helps make sure that your business shows up (map and all) when a search for a local place or term is searched. To register, visit www.google.com/business. Did we mention this service is free?

We show you how to sign up for Google Ads in Book 6, Chapter 3.

No matter which type of advertising program you choose to use, you can bet that spending money smartly on locally targeted ads is a good move. Increasingly, your local customers expect deals, discounts, and special incentives for choosing to shop with you — and they want to access these offers on the spot. You don't have to go overboard with localized or mobile promotions, but expect these types of advertising options to continue to grow in popularity.

Social media ads

One of the most popular activities for consumers to do on their mobile phones is spend time perusing social media sites, including Facebook, Twitter, Instagram, Snapchat, and others. Not only are your customers engaging with friends online, but they're also shopping from within the social media platforms — and often they don't even have to go to the retailer's website to complete a purchase. As an e-tailer with a local store, social media offers another way for you to target and influence buyers based on specific information, such as interests, keywords, and, yes, location. Most important, social media advertising is incredibly affordable, and usually much more cost-effective than Google Ads. Facebook and Twitter are perhaps the easiest ways to get started with social media ads.

REMEMBER

You can offer sponsored content (or ads) in Instagram, which is managed through Facebook (as Facebook owns Instagram). To get started, you first need to connect your Instagram feed to your Facebook page. You can only connect one account, so choose wisely if you, for some reason, maintain multiple Instagram profiles.

Facebook promotes local retail

If you've been on Facebook at all, you're used to the types of ads you can see within your news feed, especially from a mobile phone. The ads look like posts that a friend may have shared, with photos or video and a little bit of text. The difference with ads is that they have headlines to help grab someone's attention, and, in tiny print, the posts contain the word "sponsored," so people understand that it is an ad. As a retailer, Facebook ads are incredibly simple to put together, they are cheap, and they allow you to target who sees the ads based on gender, interests, likes, and location. These factors make Facebook a pretty good investment for retail advertising.

Facebook has enhanced its focus on local store marketing with a new advertising option called Dynamic Ads for retailers. It lets retailers show Facebook users ads that feature products that are available in stores closest to them. For example, if you've been searching for a new Weber grill, you may see an ad for Home Depot that features the exact grill you want to buy, and, even better, it is currently in stock at a Home Depot location just half a mile from you! The ads are integrated with the retailer's product catalog, and the ad can dynamically change based on location and availability. This new ad program is being tested by some of the larger retailers, but we're betting smaller, local retailers will soon be using these in-store traffic-driving ads.

In the meantime, follow these steps to get started with a simple location-based ad for your Facebook page:

1. **After you are logged into your Facebook page, go to your Settings page by selecting the down arrow in the top-right corner of the screen and selecting Settings.**

    You see a new screen with options to edit various controls for the page and a navigation menu on the left with additional options. (To advertise in Instagram, select Instagram Ads in the left navigation pane.)

2. **At the bottom of the Settings page, click Create Ad.**

    The Facebook Ads Manager screen appears. This program contains an intuitive guide to help you create an ad based on your goals, which Facebook calls *Objectives*. This includes options such as increasing conversions on your website, improving attendance at an event you're hosting, or promoting your page. For this purpose, you want to reach people who are nearby your store.

3. **Select Quick Creation for your ad campaign creation.**

    A new image shows up at the bottom of the screen that says Local Awareness. It has a form field for you to input the name of your ad campaign. You can make up any name you want for the campaign, but it's always advisable to use a descriptive name so that you remember what the campaign was promoting (such as "Summer Clearance Local Shoppers").

4. **Enter a campaign name in the space provided.**

5. **Scroll down to Campaign Objective and select Store Traffic under the Conversions group.**

6. **Next, set the specific ad parameters, including location, budget, and placements.**

If you manage more than one Facebook page, you'll first select which page this ad campaign is for. Then, you see a map that shows the general vicinity of your business. It is here where you choose who sees the ad. This is called setting the Audience.

7. **To set the Audience, enter your business street address (if not already entered), and then use the drop-down menu next to the address form field to choose the radius around your store for showing the ad.**

You can choose pre-set options ranging from 1 mile to 50 miles, or you can set a custom radius. If you choose a 5-mile radius, and someone is 3 miles away from your store, that person will be shown your ad.

8. **Next, select the age range and gender of those whom you want to see your Facebook ad.**

As you choose the radius, ages, and gender, Facebook will show you the potential reach, or total number of people who are likely to see your ad. Facebook also breaks this number out to an estimated daily reach, and automatically shows you the numbers for both Facebook and Instagram.

9. **Continue to scroll down the page to complete the rest of your ad setup, including placement and budget.**

Facebook auto-fills the option for Automatic Placement, which determines when the ad is shown to the designated audience. You can customize placement, but we recommend letting Facebook proceed with the automatic option to make things easy for you.

10. **Set your budget and your ad schedule.**

Choose how much money you want to spend on your ad. You can set a daily spend ($5 each day) or a lifetime campaign spend ($50), and the ad runs until that total amount is used up, whether it takes an hour, a day, or a week to go through the budget.

In this same section, you also choose what period of time you want the ad to run. Facebook gives you the option of running Continuously (until the budget runs out), or you can set a specific date range using the calendar settings Facebook provides.

You also have the option here to name the specific ad (earlier you named the whole campaign, which may end up having several individual ads in it). You can name the ad set based on some descriptor, like whom the ad targets or what date range it's running.

11. **Click Continue to set up the ads.**

You see a new page with different style of ad layouts. Choose Carousel for multiple images, Single Image, Single Video, or Slideshow for a looping video style ad with multiple images.

12. **Select your image and upload it to the ad.**

Once you choose an ad layout, Facebook guides you on how to select and upload the appropriate image or video. If you don't have your own images, you can choose from a small photo stock library provided by Facebook.

When using your own images, follow the recommended image specs. Facebook shows this information to you in the right sidebar, next to the ad layout page.

13. **Scroll down the page once you have finished adding your images or video, and add your text for the ad, the destination, and the call to action.**

You see a small box or form field labeled "Text."

14. **Enter the text that you want to appear with your ad.**

It's usually best to keep it brief and limit the number of characters to fewer than 75.

15. **In the next small box, enter the Headline for your ad.**

The headline should be short, just a few words, and catchy or interesting enough to get people's attention.

TIP

On the right side of the page, Facebook shows you a real-time view of the ad you are creating.

16. **Choose a destination and call to action for your ad.**

When people click on the ad, you have the option to send them directly to your Facebook page or to a specific URL (a page on your website, for example).

Scroll down to select the call to action from the drop-down list of options. You can choose a call to action such as, Get Directions or Call Now. There are also advanced options if you want to use more detailed information for the destination and call to action, but we recommend keeping it simple to start.

17. **Click the Place Order button to complete your ad set up.**

You can choose to Review your order and see a pop-up box that shows everything you've selected for your ad (from audience to budget).

18. **Once you are happy with your ad, select the Place Order button.**

If not already set up, Facebook will have you complete credit card information to pay for the ad before it starts running.

REMEMBER

You can always pause a live campaign, edit a campaign, or stop a campaign even before your budget runs out.

Twitter provides targeted ad options

Another popular way of combining the power of social media and mobile commerce is via Twitter (www.twitter.com). This social media platform emerged as an industry heavyweight after quickly rocketing into the spotlight as a way for individuals and companies to hold and follow short conversations via text style of messages of 280 characters or fewer. Unlike having a conversation with just a single person, Twitter allows an unlimited number of people to follow your conversation and lets you follow or track dozens or hundreds (or more) of conversations by others.

As an online or traditional retailer, your customers can follow frequent updates from your company on the status of a release of a hot new product, such as a video game. Or you might be opening a new store or hosting a special event (online or offline), and customers can learn about it or follow updates about it by using Twitter.

Twitter has been introducing additional ways to use the social platform for in-network shopping. Through Twitter Cards (a form of Twitter advertising), online retailers can expand their typical short tweets by using images, additional information, detailed lead generators (a call to action, such as downloading your app), or a buying incentive (such as a discounted price). The process is like adding a small virtual card or display area to your standard tweet. These advertising cards launch the buying process for your store. You can also use Promoted Tweets, another form of in-platform advertising, to target segments of Twitter users with special offers.

Amazon initiated a direct buy option from within Twitter by using the hashtag #AmazonCart with promoted products. Consumers respond to product promotions and have the featured item placed directly in their Amazon shopping carts for later checkout. The buying option has been going strong for a couple of years and other major retailers have experimented with this in-platform shopping option, too. As this form of *social selling*, or selling through social media, develops, look for innovative new ways to turn occasional customers into a community of loyal followers for your brand.

To find out who might be looking for information about your store or site, use the Twitter search function to track conversations by inserting keywords. For example, if your online store is MyPlace.com, just enter that name in the search box; Twitter pulls all current and archived conversations in which your site's name is mentioned. This feature is not only a helpful way to find out what customers are saying about you and your products, but also it can help shape the type of ads or promotions you use in Twitter. You can also create a list within Twitter that is made up of people who have mentioned your brand in tweets, and you can create an ad targeted to this list of people.

REMEMBER

Twitter is also a popular way for customers to voice dissatisfaction. Tweets from unhappy customers can attract negative attention to your brand, and can sometimes add up to a bevy of complaints about your product or service if other people start responding to or sharing the original tweeted complaint. Mobile phones make it even easier for customers to complain on social media, anytime and from anywhere. You need to pay careful attention to negative tweets about your business and respond to them quickly, or they can detract from the paid investment you've made for advertising in the platform.

Alternative Ways to Boost Localized Spending

As we have said repeatedly, online e-commerce, in-store shopping, and mobile buying have come together as a trifecta of retail. Traditional retailers are increasingly looking for interesting new ways to advantage of today's customers' multi-pronged approach to buying. Here are some other buying options to consider offering your customers to help boost your revenue online and off.

Subscription services

Innovative e-commerce retailers started the subscription service trend several years ago, and it has proven to have staying power. If you're not familiar with this sales approach, it allows customers to sign up and pre-pay for monthly (or biweekly) product deliveries. Customers can now get a wide variety of products including a week's worth of ready-to-cook meals (boxes packed with fresh produce, proteins, and recipe cards) thanks to online stores like Hello Fresh and Blue Apron; a monthly stash of pet supplies, foods, and treats from Chewy.com and Barkbox.com; and a host of different types of personal products such as makeup (www.birchbox.com) and razors (www.harrys.com).

As the success of this industry has increased, traditional retailers are offering similar programs. Why? Consider that traffic to subscription box websites has risen 3,000 percent in recent years compared to a 168 percent increase in traffic to the top 500 online retail sites, according to research from Hitwise (http:// connexity.com). For established retailers, subscription box services offer a way to increase repeat business (and potentially higher average sales) from already loyal customers. As this marketing opportunity matures, the trick to subscription boxes is ensuring that there is real value there for the customer, and it's not only about convenience. Making it worthwhile for your customer to commit to an ongoing delivery of products may mean offering other incentives, such as a standing 15 to 20 percent discount on every box, or providing free sample products with each delivery. The upside for you is a consistent stream of revenue, especially if you require customers to commit to a minimum monthly plan verses a month-by-month option.

REMEMBER

Setting up a subscription box service may require a one-time investment in additional technologies or apps for your website in order to maintain the program. You also want to provide customers with a simple online management tool (as part of their customer profile) that allows them to pause the subscription service or opt out of it.

In-store pickup

Target, Kohl's, and Wal-Mart are among the many major retailers that have discovered the customer's affinity toward pay-ahead convenience. Customers can purchase products online, from mobile devices or the desktop, and skip the hassle of maneuvering through aisles and waiting in line to checkout. Instead, the retailer has the customer's purchases waiting for her (usually at a customer service counter). Or, in the case of Wal-Mart, customers don't even have to leave their cars; instead, employees deliver the goods right to the customers' cars. If not scheduling a specific pickup time, customers can opt to receive a text alert on their smartphones when the order is packed and ready to pick up.

The concept continues to grow in popularity, and over one-third of the top 500 retailers in the United States now offer some type of in-store pickup option. Target has seen its program grow 60 percent year over year in the 2018 holiday season, and for 2018, it helped the retailer boost digital sales 25 percent, marking the fifth year of growth in its digital sales. The downside for all retailers using this tactic is that consumers' expectations for pickup services are constantly increasing. A recent survey indicated that more than 50 percent of customers expect products to be ready for pickup within 2 hours, and in some cases the goal is under 20 minutes.

When implementing a buy online, pick up in-store program, there are several important items to consider, especially if you are a smaller retailer with limited resources:

>> **Staffing:** Not only do you need to have employees available to "shop" the inventory from your store and pack it, but it also puts additional strain on your check-out lines, especially if you don't have a designated customer service area. That means customers who ordered online to avoid long in-store lines could get exasperated because they end up having to wait anyway. Plan carefully how to restructure in-store check-out areas to accommodate for online orders.

>> **Mobile alerts:** You'll need the capability to send text alerts to customers' mobile phones to let them know items are ready for pickup.

>> **Backend inventory management:** As we mentioned when discussing omnichannel retail, it's critical that you have real-time insight into all your inventory, and that your online system talk to or communicate this information with your offline system. There's nothing worse than a customer ordering an item online for in-store pickup, only to find out that it's actually out of stock at the store.

>> **Shopping cart localization features:** Similar to having your inventory system inline, your website's shopping cart should ideally have the ability to show item availability by store location (if you have more than one location), and provide a view into payments from your in-store Point of Sale (POS) system.

>> **Holidays:** Even the most well-oiled in-store pickup machine can run amuck during a particularly busy time, such as the holidays. You'll want to have a plan for increased staffing levels, and improved in-store customer flow for those buying online.

Trying new ways to increase revenue is a necessity, but that doesn't mean you can take shortcuts to more sales, especially where mobile is concerned. Plan to make regular investments in technology, from mobile apps to e-commerce solutions, in order to help your store compete with everyone from big-box retailers to online start-ups.

Chapter 5

Troubleshooting the Transition to Online Retail

As you move your retail store online, you can always hope that things will go perfectly. In reality, you can expect a few minor bumps along the way. This chapter talks about navigating over the bumps and avoiding the big potholes after your site goes live.

The good news is that your customers probably won't even notice most of the small issues that are to be expected when an e-commerce site launches. The secret to surviving is planning now for those situations most likely to cause you stress.

Handling Returns in the Store from Online Sales

Suppose that you have store policies already in place, but it's now time to update your return or exchange policy. Given today's high rate of fraudulent activity, you're probably already wary (if not suspicious) of customers who hightail it back to your store with merchandise in hand.

Now you have to add the return of online orders to the mix. After your online store is up and running, someone will certainly make a purchase on your website, and the purchase might be the wrong size, or damaged, or in a style that the customer doesn't like.

Before you can decide how to handle the return, you have to ask yourself how you want to respond to it. If your goal is to work with your customers and make them happy, you want to develop a customer-friendly policy. One of the leading online retailers best known for its customer-centric approach is Zappos (www. zappos.com). It strives to exceed customer expectations is in its shipping and return policy. The online shoe retailer ships all products free and allows you to return products (up to 365 days later) — for free! (Of course, the merchandise can't be worn.) Zappos makes sure the return process is simple for customers, giving several options to easily send back products. For its elite Rewards members, it also offers an instant refund (as opposed to waiting one to two weeks). Not every online retailer, especially small start-up sites, can absorb shipping and return costs to this degree. However, as an established retailer with an existing bricks-and-mortar location, you have a competitive advantage to online-only e-commerce businesses. You can offer free returns to your stores! This way, you don't have to pay shipping and handling fees, and it provides an opportunity to get your customer back into your store.

Customer service may not be your first priority. Perhaps you are most interested in protecting your bottom line. In that case, you can approach the online return policy in a way that's most convenient for you. Don't worry. Lots of online retailers still require customers to pay their share of return costs and put strict policies in place for managing returns. Just be aware that your return policy can be strategically used as a competitive advantage, as it is with Zappos, or it can be a status quo policy designed to protect your cash flow.

Here are some decisions that you need to make about return policies:

» **Customer-friendly policy:** If you're taking this route, your policy might stipulate that you

- Pay for return shipping (or reimburse the customer for it) if a purchase is sent back by mail because the item is damaged or doesn't fit, for example

- Accept the return with no questions asked

- Give a complete refund or exchange the item

- Offer in-store credit for the same amount of the purchase (instead of a cash refund)

- Request (but not demand) a copy of the original receipt

» **Bottom-line policy:** When cutting corners is your biggest concern, protect yourself with these rules of return:

- No returns are made without an original receipt

- Limit the time for which returns are accepted (within 30 days from date of purchase, for example)

- Do not accept returns on sale, clearance, or discontinued items

- Returns must be made from the location where they were purchased (no in-store returns for online purchases)

REMEMBER

You get to decide the terms of your policies based on what makes the most sense for your business. The preceding suggestions are just that — suggestions. You may want to use all of them or a blend of the two approaches.

TIP

When sending items to your customers, pack a return/item exchange request form inside the box. Make sure that the form provides complete instructions for returning an item and states your return policy. Customers wanting to return an item can use this form to provide basic information (such as name and address) and a reason why they're returning the product. Or you may want to allow the customer to complete this process online, through their customer account, if your back-end technologies allow this type of feature.

Merging Existing Back-End Systems with Online Requirements

By the time you launch your website, you typically already have a lengthy history. You have established customers, extensive sales data, an inventory-management system, in-store policies, point-of-sale systems, ordering guidelines, and a host of vendors and suppliers at your beck and call.

Having that much structure and information definitely plays in your favor because you're not starting from scratch when you move into e-commerce. But integrating all these systems and procedures to an online business can present a few challenges to your back end.

Plenty of successful bricks-and-mortar stores launch basic e-commerce sites, each with a nice look but a fairly standard back-end shopping cart solution. The simplified approach to e-commerce can be beneficial because it's often easier to manage. If you enable fewer bells and whistles on a back-end solution, that may make the initial transition online achievable in a shorter timeframe. However, as an online site grows more popular, it requires a more significant investment in both site design and a new back-end solution. We've seen this happen with many small retailers that find success online, and it's simply part of the growing pains (and not a bad one at that).

There are several important take-aways to consider. First, a website isn't static. You have to continually update content on that your visitors see (just as you do an in-store display each season), as well as update back-end functionality as your needs and priorities change. Second, just because you transition a bricks-and-mortar store online, it doesn't mean that the site and the inventory you offer must be extensive. Again, your inventory management and back-end processes take time and care. You may need to scale up or back down to something more manageable for you. Bigger isn't always better.

Your online store may have different goals and require more complex back-end functionality. A bricks-and-mortar furniture store that took a different approach to online is Goedeker's (www.goedekers.com). The retailer launched an online version of its furniture store in an effort to compete with big-box retailers that were eating away at its local business.

The online store started with over 2,000 products — and today offers over 200,000 products! The online store grew to account for more than 90 percent of its sales, and it now ships to 48 states in the United States. The site's e-commerce solution is as dynamic as any national chain's, and the investment in a more advanced back-end system was necessary to handle the large inventory and huge customer base.

Managing inventory

One of the biggest headaches for an online retailer is handling inventory levels in a way that's least disruptive to both you and your online customer. At the heart of the matter, you need to make sure that your online store can communicate with your existing inventory system.

Here's an example of what typically happens when you have a kink in your inventory management. A customer goes to your site, places an order, pays for the order, and then expects it to be delivered according to your shipping policy. You receive the order and start filling it, only to find that the item is out of stock. Now you have to communicate with your customer to tell him or her that the product is on back order. As you know, this situation isn't ideal. For a better alternative, implement a system that communicates inventory levels with all your primary points of operations, including

>> Point-of-sale system (your retail location)

>> Online shopping cart

>> Call center

>> Warehouse

When investigating these different operations, make sure to determine whether each one can work with your inventory-management system. The best solution allows any (and possibly all) of these operations to communicate directly with your software inventory-management system to allow for a real-time updated tracking system of what you have in stock and what you need to reorder.

Fulfilling and shipping your orders

Chances are good that your store has already encountered the need to package an order and ship it somewhere. Depending on what type of store you have, you may do these tasks regularly (with catalog or telephone orders, for example) or only occasionally. But imagine that you suddenly have to ship out anywhere from 10 to 100 different packages every day. How does that affect your already hectic schedule? Do you have employees who can be dedicated to handling the process? Or does the idea of shipping orders evoke the image of you staying up late at night, digging for boxes, printing labels from your computer, and trying to meet last-minute pickup schedules?

Another concern with an increased number of shipments is space. Think about your existing location. Do you have dedicated space for packaging? If so, can in-store customers see the space or is it in a separate offsite warehouse? Regardless of where you ship the product from, how do you confirm that an order has gone out? Does computer software display that information, or are you keeping a manual checklist?

As you can see, you have a lot of questions to consider for what seems to be a simple process. Placing one of your products into a box and shipping it out to a customer isn't difficult but is more time consuming than you probably think.

One solution is to outsource the shipping-and-handling portion of the operation. Another option is to have many of your items drop-shipped to customers from your suppliers. However, you can also keep this function in-house, if you want. Check out Book 4, Chapter 7 to find out more about your shipping options.

Tracking your orders

You may already have internal systems for tracking customer orders. But now that you're selling online, you need to provide your customers with direct access to the status of their orders, particularly after those orders ship. You can minimize the number of calls and emails that you receive from customers by allowing them to directly check on a delivery. Anything that helps reduce your workload is a good thing! The truly good news is that the major shipping companies provide free online order-tracking tools for you to incorporate into your site (and many e-commerce solutions come with advanced shipping functionality already integrated and ready to go!). Here are the main shipping companies you'll want to work with for order delivery and tracking:

>> **DHL** (www.dhl.com): As a registered customer, you can use the DHL tracking tools and send automated email messages to customers. The messages include information so that customers can track the status of their orders. DHL also offers a complete e-fulfillment solution for multichannel (online) retailers. You can get the scoop on all its e-commerce services www.logistics.dhl/us-en/home/our-divisions/ecommerce.html.

>> **FedEx** (www.fedex.com/insight): Use the FedEx InSight tool to track shipments. You can see all your inbound and outbound shipments and get real-time updates of any potential delays. To let your customers track and manage their orders, encourage them to sign up for FedEx Delivery Manager. You can access other tools and resources at the FedEx Small Business Center at www.fedex.com/en-us/small-business, which includes a section for e-commerce.

>> **UPS** (www.ups.com): UPS also offers online-tracking tools for your customers. The delivery company has developed a set of applications that you can integrate directly into your website. By using UPS, you don't need to send

customers email messages with directions on order tracking or direct them to another site for tracking. Customers can check the status right on your site. You can check the list of approved vendors, such as Amazon, eBay, and GoDaddy, as part of the UPS Ready Program. You can also learn more about its e-commerce tools and solutions in the UPS MarketPlace Providers list. Find all these resources (and more) at www.ups.com/smallbusiness.

TIP

During the 2013 holiday buying season, extreme weather conditions across the United States wreaked havoc on shipping companies and prevented many online retailers, including mega ones such as Amazon, from making good on the standard holiday delivery promise, "Guaranteed to arrive by Christmas Eve" (when ordered by a certain day and time). Customers without gifts under their trees were furious, to say the least — but it was a problem outside everyone's control. Since then, the increasingly busy holiday seasons for online retailers have seen their fair share of weather woes to varying degrees. To address the concern of blizzards and extreme weather conditions that bring even UPS to a halt, e-tailers have updated their shipping and delivery policies. During the holiday rush updated polices are clearly displayed across their websites to note that they are not responsible for problems causing delayed deliveries that may occur on the shipper's end. We advise you to follow suit and add similar caveats to your shipping and delivery policies.

Maintaining site performance

Before you decide to sell your inventory online, you may already have some type of website. Sure, it's probably more of a basic site that shows off your logo and maybe a photo of your retail location and offers prospective customers a map to help them find your store. Perhaps there are even a few photos of sample inventory, but no way to actually buy it online. If that's the case, your site probably doesn't see a whole lot of traffic. And even you probably don't look at it that often. Well, after you enter the world of e-commerce, that situation is likely to change.

Now that you're an official online retailer, you need to understand your site's performance capabilities. For example, how much traffic can the site handle? If you exceed a particular limit of bandwidth usage, does your monthly hosting fee increase? What about the site design? Is it optimized for the best viewing in varying screen resolutions? Can a customer using a slower Internet connection shop your site as easily as a customer with a broadband connection? How well do product images load? These questions are just a sampling of the site performance issues that can surface as you begin selling online.

Deciding How to Handle Integration

Even if you're a smaller store, site-performance, inventory-management, and order-tracking solutions suddenly become major elements within your new business model. Even so, you probably start off needing to make only minor changes to your current way of doing business. That way, you have a chance to see what works and what doesn't, and you can then figure out what you need to change. This trial-by-error process is common.

However, if you already have sophisticated back-end processes or you're more of a midsize retailer, you may want to plan. In fact, you may find it worthwhile to hire a consultant to help you survey your systems and find the best hardware and software match to smoothly integrate your online operations.

No matter the size of your site, you can get a jump-start on the installation and integration of your hardware and software by using these four checkpoints:

>> **Review:** Make a list of all areas of your store operations, from your cash register (or point of sale) to your inventory system. Take a close look at how you currently handle each of these operations.

>> **Analyze:** You can begin deciding how, if at all, your current systems will translate to an online process. Can you use the software programs that you already have with your e-commerce site? Or is your software designed only for a traditional retail store? If you use manual programs, those programs can quickly get bogged down after your site experiences its first phase of growth.

>> **Decide:** After you have an idea of how well your existing procedures may or may not hold up, you have decisions to make. For example, are you ready to invest in new systems? Where will you get the money for upgrades? Are you comfortable managing your online retail operations in-house, or do you need to bring in the professionals?

>> **Investigate:** If you decide that you need a new software program or want to outsource some of your operations, start looking at your options. Begin familiarizing yourself with current terminology, leading technology vendors, and the typical price ranges for various back-end solutions.

One thing is certain: You won't find a shortage of experienced vendors ready to help you transition into the world of multichannel retailing. The systems in the following list are worth looking into to help integrate your offline location with your online store:

>> **CORESense** (www.coresense.com): CORESense offers multiple products that range from real-time inventory management to fulfillment and marketing.

>> **Epicor** (www.epicor.com): Epicor retail solutions include a cross-channel order-management system, which helps you provide real-time inventory management between your store's inventory, website, catalog, and even kiosk. It can link your site and in-store point-of-sale (POS) system to a call center.

>> **Celerant Technology Corp.** (www.celerant.com): Considered a multiretail channel solution, Celerant Command Retail software integrates multiple key e-commerce and retail functions into one database that gives you a detailed, real-time overview of your business operations. It offers solutions for e-commerce starting at $125 per month.

>> **NetSuite** (www.netsuite.com): Using the SuiteCommerce cloud-based solution (owned by Oracle), you can combine all your e-commerce, in-store POS (point of sale), and order management with your back-end systems. SuiteCommerce is one of several products and services offered specifically for e-commerce businesses of all sizes.

REMEMBER

Depending on the size of your business, you may be able to use an off-the-shelf, or web-based, e-commerce storefront solution, such as the ones we discuss in Book 8, Chapter 1. These solutions are very powerful and sometimes more affordable.

TIP

A current trend with vendors is to offer an *omni-channel* retail solution, which takes cross-channel or multi-channel solutions a step further by seamlessly integrating or connecting nearly every component of the customer experience, including mobility. When shopping for solutions, make sure you understand exactly what areas of your business can be managed or integrated and how that integration is achieved because products described as being multi-channel or omni-channel are often two very different types of solutions.

Extending Payment Options to Virtual Customers

The goal of providing a variety of payments is to take away an obstacle that may prevent customers from buying from you. However, the increasing competition for online sales is forcing online retailers such as yourself to always be on the lookout for new payment options.

TIP

For a list of vendors for your online business needs, check out the Internet Retailer vendor list, from Digital Commerce 360, which includes many payment processing vendors, along with other valuable resource categories. You can check it out using the Find a Vendor link at the bottom of its website at www.digitalcommerce360.com.

Whether customers purchase from your store or website or by email or phone, the future of online retailing comes down to two principles:

- ➤➤ Continually connect with your customers.
- ➤➤ Always give your customers options.

Buy now, pay later

Extended payment terms, deferred terms, or instant credit — call it what you like, this payment option is a popular alternative online payment solution. This type of credit basically allows customers to delay paying cash out of their pocket at the time of purchase. E-tailers offering flexible payment terms have seen as much as a 17 percent increase in sales, according to some retail industry reports. A 2018 global survey by BigCommerce revealed that 48 percent of online consumers said having the deferred payment solution influenced their purchasing decision, and 31 percent said they would not have made a purchase at all without the option for installment payments.

Deferred billing is the same as the offline promotion of "90 days same as cash." Allowing customers to take advantage of this type of payment can truly help your business if you sell higher-end items or want to increase your per-customer average sale. Customers often seek out this option during the holiday season, when they're already in a cash crunch. To set up a deferred billing arrangement, start by talking with your bank or merchant provider.

Another option that's exceeding expectations for online retailers is the deferred payment program offered by vendors such as FuturePay and PayPal Credit. These programs act as a fast and secure way to buy online but customers pay in the future. Plus, customers can take advantage of special financing options to spread out payments without penalty or interest. Your customer gets approved for a certain credit limit and then receives a billing statement. You receive the full payment amount in the short-term, regardless of the customer's payment plan. Customers like this approach for the following reasons:

- » **Speed:** At the time of purchase, your customers are usually asked for a few items, such as their date of birth and the last four digits of their Social Security number. (The vendor's banking partner uses this information to make a quick credit check.) Approval is returned in a matter of seconds, in most cases. Customers may also apply directly on the vendors' websites before shopping with you. In that case, they come to your website, preapproved to spend.

- » **Security:** Because PayPal Credit and FuturePay don't require giving out extensive information or using credit cards, some customers view it as a safer way to make a purchase.

- » **Linked to PayPal:** With PayPal Credit, customers can link their deferred payment account with their PayPal account, giving them a hassle-free, alternative form of payment during checkout at your site. It also doesn't hurt to have the name recognition of PayPal to instill confidence in your customers so they are comfortable using this alternative payment arrangement.

As an online retailer, you're bound to like this alternative payment solution for these reasons:

- » **No risk:** PayPal and FuturePay accept all the risk when extending credit to your customers, so you don't have to worry about losing anything if a customer doesn't pay.

- » **Affordable:** When we last checked, the processing fee was still slightly less than for most credit cards.

- » **Sales boost:** Online merchants are experiencing both higher ticket averages (customers spending more per visit) and increased repeat purchases from existing customers using the service.

TIP

Consider offering additional payment options, such as Visa Checkout (`https://usa.visa.com/run-your-business/small-business-tools/payment-technology/visa-checkout.html`), established by Visa. Although it doesn't offer a line of credit separate from the credit already extended through Visa, it is a fast, secure way to pay. Visa Checkout allows customers to link any other credit or debit cards to Visa — again, as a means to provide quick and secure online shopping options.

Check and cash alternatives

Millennials make up the largest generation since the Baby Boomers, and they are influencing almost every part of society, including online shopping. Born after 1980, these 20- and 30-somethings are very different from previous generations. Why does this matter when it comes to offering alternative payments in your online store? According to recent industry research, each millennial owns an average of 2.3 credit cards, and many millennials prefer to not have any credit cards at all. Even though this generation is at ease shopping online, even through mobile devices, they prefer not to pay with a credit card. That adds up to a lot of potential customers who may not be able to buy from you online if you accept only the standard credit card options for purchasing.

To get around the no credit card dilemma, another payment method involves your site accepting various forms of checks, or even money orders. With Internet checks, you work through an independent processor that accepts money from a customer's bank account and then deposits it into your merchant account, usually in fewer than 15 days. You can check with your payment processor to find out whether it offers this type of service. An even easier check solution is offering Automated Clearing House (ACH) processing that transfers money directly from a customer's checking account to your merchant account, usually within 48 hours. Many vendors offer eChecks, or ACH processing services, for your e-commerce site. Most charge a monthly fee, plus a small transaction fee each time a customer uses the service (similar to but often much lower than a credit card processing fee). Check out various monthly plans for ACH transactions from vendors such as Forte (www.forte.net) and VeriCheck (www.vericheck.com).

An alternative payment solution that popped up as a payment alternative (to standard currency) in the online world is Bitcoin. This Internet-based currency is, in general, an alternative to cash. Bitcoins are stored in virtual wallets — the equivalent to online banks. Where do they come from? Without getting too technical, bitcoins are virtually mined (like you might mine for coal, but using a sophisticated computer program). You can also buy bitcoins (using real dollars) on an open market, similar to the stock exchange market.

Because bitcoin is a digital currency, it is not backed by the Federal Reserve or any other institution. Bitcoins were designed to increase in value over time because a limited number are available, and they get more difficult to obtain after time. In other words, you need more computing power to mine for bitcoins as time passes. Why are we bothering to tell you all this? Bitcoins have become a recognized form of online payment, even by large online retailers such as Overstock. That said, bitcoins remain a novelty and the risks of accepting them as an alternative form of payment are different from accepting eChecks and delayed billing options such as FuturePay. For these reasons, we don't recommend adding bitcoins to your list of alternative online payments, just yet. But we do think it's worthwhile to be aware of how this virtual currency progresses in the world of e-commerce.

8

E-Commerce Fundamentals

Contents at a Glance

Chapter **1**

Starting Up with E-Commerce Functionality

O ne of the easiest ways to get started selling your products online is through an e-commerce solution. This type of online storefront, or e-commerce-in-a-box, provides all the components necessary to build, manage, and promote your store in one convenient location.

Selling products online has increasingly become the norm for all types of businesses, both new and established. As a result, e-commerce solutions have become more diverse, offer increased functionality and are much less expensive. You might ask, "How does e-commerce differ from other ways I might sell online? What's special about it?"

Think of an online storefront as a shortcut to selling online because you can use one e-commerce solution for almost all your online selling needs. For example, you may have an existing website and you want to add a shopping cart solution so you can sell items from the site. There's no point in redesigning your entire site; you are simply adding functionality.

However, if you are starting from scratch and don't already have a website, there are e-commerce solution providers that help you build your site, host your site, add or create products, accept payments and sell the products, ship the products, track inventory, market your products . . . Whew! You get the idea — an e-commerce solution is truly a *one-stop shop* for everything you need to put a business online and start selling. This chapter explains the most popular — and most necessary — features available in e-commerce solutions and helps you make a decision about which all-in-one storefront would work best for your online business goals.

REMEMBER

Some e-commerce solutions have recognizable names. In this minibook, we cover Amazon in Chapter 2, Shopify in Chapter 3, and eBay in Chapter 4.

Knowing What You Want: Features

When choosing your online store, make sure that the following three essential elements are included. Together, these functions help qualify the storefront as a true all-in-one solution:

>> **Shopping cart:** This back-end feature allows customers to browse for, select, and purchase products. (If you want to know more, Book 4, Chapter 5 compares specific shopping cart features.)

>> **Payment processor:** This feature is a virtual cash register. Of course, customers need a way to pay you during checkout for the products they want. A storefront solution should give customers multiple options.

>> **Hosting solution:** You need a place to host your actual store. Your hosted shopping cart, however, doesn't have to share the service you use for your primary website. But one of the benefits of a storefront is that hosting is included in the deal, eliminating additional website hosting fees.

These bare necessities are just the tip of the iceberg when you're selecting features for your storefront. Most e-commerce solutions provide a long list of additional features and functionality. These features typically fall in three areas: performance; product merchandizing and marketing; and administration. All three are described in the following sections.

Performance

Unfortunately, performance is the area of a storefront that you don't always think about until something goes wrong or isn't what you expected, but it is truly the backbone of your operations. Paying special attention to these performance-related issues when selecting your storefront is ultimately worth your time:

TIP

» **Speed:** A lot of factors contribute to the speed of a storefront, and determining how the site's functionality will fare isn't always easy. The best way to find out is to visit some of your storefront's featured sites and see for yourself whether a lag in processing time occurs.

You can also sort through a storefront's community forum section to see whether other storeowners have complained about the storefront's *processing speed,* or the load time for pages.

» **Storage:** You want adequate disk space and bandwidth transfer available for your site. Even if your storefront starts small, you need room to grow without being immediately penalized with a higher rate. At a minimum, you should start with 1GB or 5GB capacity. Increasingly, the leading e-commerce solutions are offering unlimited storage and bandwidth in some, or all, pricing plans.

» **Security:** Proper security is an essential part of e-commerce. Before purchasing your storefront, understand what type of services or protections are offered to guard your store, and check for issues related to PCI (Payment Card Industry) compliance (we discuss these issues in detail in Book 2, Chapter 1).

» **Product quantity:** Some e-commerce solutions still place limits on the number of products you can sell under certain pricing plans. Which storefront you choose may turn into a price-based decision. The good news is that even with limitations on quantity, your monthly fee typically supports a substantial number of product listings (usually 50 to 100 products at the least expensive plan). Even better news, more e-commerce solutions are moving away from this type of pricing plan. Unless you are an enterprise (or very large business) with thousands of products, you can have hundreds of products across all plan options. The difference in pricing plans is instead based on differences in features, functionality, and support options.

» **E-product delivery:** If your storefront supports electronic products (e-books, for example), they can be delivered by way of customer-initiated downloads. You can also sell *membership* (a service with recurring fees) electronically. The capability to download some products in digital format (such as PDF files, music files, or video) or access digital services is growing, and you should definitely consider offering these kinds of products because they require no warehouse space and can offer substantial profit margins. See Book 4, Chapter 3 for more about selling e-products.

» **Import and export tools:** This feature lets you transfer large numbers of products into or out of the storefront. E-commerce solutions with this feature commonly let you dump products into the storefront from an Excel spreadsheet, for example. This feature can be a timesaver if you have a lot of inventory.

>> **Third-party integration:** Your online business will most likely use a number of different tools or software, from accounting to customer relationship management (CRM) solutions. Ideally, you want many of these tools to integrate, or work with one another, to maximize results. In particular, your storefront should work with as many of your other business tools as possible. In addition, many APIs (application programming interfaces) can provide access and integration to even more features and tools. When choosing an e-commerce solution, be sure to check which third-party solutions it supports as well as the diversity or expansiveness of its library of APIs.

>> **Support:** Having access to the e-commerce solution provider's technical support team can be your only lifeline at times. In the best possible situation, full tech support is available 24 hours a day, 7 days a week. As we mentioned previously, some pricing plans vary based on the level of support you want or need. Paying an additional $20 or $30 per month to get increased support may be worthwhile, especially if you're a small-business owner with limited tech support knowledge or resources.

>> **Templates:** One benefit of turning to an e-commerce solution is that you have access to templates for building out pages of the site. If you aren't a savvy web developer, predesigned web page templates are supposed to make it easy to open your store. To truly be of value, the e-commerce solution needs to offer an extensive array of template styles to choose from and should also allow for some level of customization. You may find templates set up by categories or industries, such as sports or clothing store themes. This approach takes into consideration current design and color trends specific to that business type, so getting started is even easier.

When reviewing website templates, be sure to confirm there are options for mobile-ready templates. If your storefront cannot be built so that it's easily viewable and searchable on mobile devices, like smartphones and tablets, that's problematic. In fact, Google will penalize your website in the search engine rankings if your site doesn't pass its mobile-friendly requirements.

>> **Wizards:** The e-commerce solution should offer a Setup Wizard to guide you through the process of building and customizing your storefront. Ideally, the wizard takes your store setup from start to finish without any major headaches. A non-intuitive wizard or one that is difficult to work with negates one of the biggest advantages of using a storefront — simplicity!

Spend time on the storefront's demo section and tinker with the wizard before making your final decision. If the demo isn't fully functioning, contact a sales representative. Ask the person to give you live access to the store-building tools for a week or so. This access gives you a chance to test-drive the real wizard.

Product merchandizing and marketing

A stellar storefront solution should provide a host of tools that assist you in promoting products (offering ideas based on past purchase histories, for example), and marketing them (by offering promotion codes, for example) to your customer base. After all, these features ultimately help you move more products and bump up your sales revenue:

» **Product images:** Ideally, customers should be able to view multiple images of a product, including an up close or enhanced view, before making a purchase. To make several images of a product available on your site, the store's product gallery has to allow for more than one image to be uploaded and viewed per product listing.

» **Customization component:** One major online trend is letting customers customize products. You can customize a product by adding a monogram, engraving a message, or modifying a color or style, for example. Because customizing is potentially a persuasive purchasing feature, your storefront's shopping-cart program should allow customers to add customizing instructions.

» **Cross-selling (or upselling):** This feature allows you to promote similar products on a single page. In other words, when customers add one product to the cart, you can then recommend or suggest another product. Also referred to as *suggestive selling,* cross-selling occurs during the checkout process, where you recommend additional products or services to the customer, based on the existing purchase. Cross-selling is a standard technique to raise the amount a customer spends in one visit to your store.

» **Discount pricing:** You may want to be able to set up special groups that can be assigned different prices. For example, you may want to offer a 10 percent discount in February to active military members and their families. Or you may want to allow certain resellers to receive a different price than your public customers. This feature lets you distinguish among types of customers and charge them different prices.

» **Promotions:** Coupon codes, gift certificates, loyalty and reward programs, and any other special offers can be set up as incentives for your customers. The complexities of this feature vary, so take a close look at what each storefront solution can and can't do. As an example, some storefronts allow you to deduct only a certain percentage rate or a flat dollar amount. Other programs allow promotions such buy-one-get-one-free (or half price).

» **Email marketing:** Staying in touch with your customer base is a surefire way to drive up sales. E-commerce solution providers offer wide variations of this feature. Some solutions may offer their own email function, while others may integrate with a third-party solution, such as MailChimp or iContact.

>> **Search engine friendly:** Search engine optimization (SEO) is being continuously integrated into e-commerce features. Having your individual product pages (or the images) tagged or optimized with special meta descriptions is an increasingly important element to helping your pages show up in search engine results. See Book 6, Chapter 6 to find out more about search engine optimization.

>> **Shopping feeds:** Similar to search engine marketing, your e-commerce store needs a way to hook into Google Shopping (formerly known as *Product Search*, Google's shopping comparison site) and other popular shopping sites. You use something called an *XML-data feed* to pull results from these types of sites into your own in the blink of an eye.

>> **Mobile commerce ready:** Increasingly, online customers want to shop for and buy your products by using a smartphone or tablet, so your storefront should be accessible by mobile devices and *optimized* for (easily viewed on) an iPhone, an Android phone, and any type of tablet. This functionality is growing in popularity, but not all e-commerce solutions offer this level of functionality — or it may cost more for you to have access to this type of feature. We discuss the benefits of mobile commerce in Book 7, Chapter 4.

>> **Social marketing:** Facebook, Pinterest, Instagram, Snapchat, YouTube, Twitter, and LinkedIn are among some of the popular social media sites today. Your customers want to interact with your brand using these sites; but how they do this is rapidly changing. Online customers now use social media to communicate with and about your business, receive special promotions and coupons, make purchases from your business, and even help sell your products to friends in their networks. Often customers want the opportunity to "like" companies on Facebook, tweet with them on Twitter, or follow them in Instagram. An e-commerce solution should offer the functionality necessary to make most, if not all, these interactions possible. The types of social media sites and the ways in which they're used to reach different customers constantly evolve.

Administration features

To do your job properly, you have to manage some behind-the-curtain activity. Access to administrative tools lets you oversee these processes. The following list shows the most common features that you'll be grateful to have included with (or added to) your storefront:

>> **Inventory management:** You need, at the very least, to keep track of your inventory levels and ensure that your existing inventory systems work cohesively with your storefront. Ideally, you should use real-time inventory tracking.

- » **Accounting system integration:** Look for e-commerce solutions that can sufficiently communicate data between your storefront and your accounting package. If this option is available, it's typically set up to integrate specifically with QuickBooks (a financial software package).

- » **Reporting functions:** Ah, the sales reports — and more. Your e-commerce solution should be able to track sales, returns, invoices, and more to provide you with the most *insight,* or business intelligence, possible.

- » **Payment system:** Not only do you need a payment gateway, but perhaps equally important, a good e-commerce solution should also offer a range of payment gateways, including everything from PayPal to Stripe (and international gateways, if you require it). Make sure the gateway you choose accepts multiple forms of payment because payment options can combat *shopping-cart abandonment,* the phenomenon that occurs when visitors leave your site without purchasing the items they placed in their carts (virtually abandoning their shopping carts).

- » **Tax calculation and reporting:** Like it or not, you probably have to deal with taxes online. Taxes can be a complicated issue because amounts vary by county and state. By identifying e-commerce solutions that are already set up to add taxes when required, you can save yourself much trouble.

- » **Multiple currencies:** You can use a feature that allows customers to make purchases with any type of currency. If you are selling internationally, this functionality is a must-have for your storefront.

- » **Integrated shipping tools:** UPS, FedEx, and DHL are among the most popular U.S. delivery systems for packages. And to get your customer's product delivered, you need to ensure that your storefront can talk to one or more of these organizations. Your storefront doesn't have to integrate with all these shipping options, but it should work with at least the one your site uses most.

- » **Analytics software:** Along with other tracking and reporting functions, your e-commerce solution should offer tools to help identify your traffic patterns and data on how your customers use the pages of your site. A good analytics program built in to the storefront can give you many of those answers.

Realizing What You Can Have: Cost

Most e-commerce solutions claim that the sky is the limit on functionality and scalability. They're not far off. But as you probably realize, your budget ultimately becomes either the enabler or the deterrent.

Figure out what you can afford. After you do that, you have to decide which elements you can't live without. As you consider what's most important, keep in mind the way that storefront solutions are typically priced:

>> **Monthly fee:** Most often, you're provided a monthly price for using the service, which should include your monthly hosting cost, too. You can cancel most monthly agreements at any time, as long as you follow the store's termination procedures.

>> **Annual fee:** You have the option of prepaying for a year or more of service. You usually receive a slight discount for paying annually rather than monthly.

WARNING

When you sign up for an e-commerce solution's annual account, you're typically prepaying for a year of service in advance. You can always cancel your agreement before the 12 months end. But in most cases, none of your money is refunded, so you lose the money that you prepaid for the remaining months.

>> **Tiered pricing:** Storefronts typically use a tiered pricing structure to suit all levels of need. They group benefits and features into different types of pricing plans. For example, if you need fewer features, or are fine with basic support, choose a basic plan for a lower monthly fee. But if you want the whole shebang, choose the more expensive plan (often called a gold or premium plan).

>> **Product capacity pricing:** Similar to tiered pricing, some e-commerce solutions still set pricing plans based on the number of products you want to support. If you have a smaller inventory, you may be able to get the benefit of all features in every plan and pay only according to the number of product listings.

>> **Activation fee:** You may have to pay for some sort of setup or activation fee when you sign up for the service. Nowadays, this fee is not as common but check the fine print to be sure.

TIP

Activation and other service fees may be waived when you sign up for an annual account or premium account. In addition, you can sometimes convince someone to waive these fees by signing up over the phone rather than online. Let the customer service rep know that you're willing to sign today if he or she can drop some of the upfront fees. It never hurts to ask!

When deciding how much you can afford to pay (and the way you want to pay for it), determine what you need. Start by considering how many products you want to sell and the amount of disk space you may need. After that, choose the features that are most important to you.

You can also break down the numbers another way. Look at how many products you have to sell on a monthly basis to cover the cost of the e-commerce solution. For example, suppose you choose a mid-level plan that costs $149 per month, includes an extensive list of features, and supports as many as 10,000 products. You have only 75 products, and your average amount of profit for each one is around $9. That means you have to sell at least 17 products per month just to cover the cost of your storefront.

On the flip side, you might choose an entry-level plan that some providers offer to help get you started. These plans often support less than 25 products and have fewer features, but may cost only $5 to $10 per month. Using the same profit margins, you now have to sell only three products each month to cover your e-commerce costs.

So, if you're just starting out in e-commerce and don't have any built-in traffic, the lower fee means fewer monetary risks. Choosing the right e-commerce solution (and the appropriate plan) is often a matter of figuring out what's most important to you.

Shopping for E-Commerce Solutions

After you know which features you want and figure out what you want to pay, you're ready to find a storefront solution. Here are some possibilities to look into:

>> **Online Store:** You might not know it from its name, but Online Store is a complete e-commerce solution from GoDaddy. This all-in-one solution is $25 per month (billed annually), including hosting and no caps on bandwidth, and it supports an unlimited number of products and includes 24/7 technical support. Mobile-optimized storefronts are included, too. The Online Store is a good deal for the price, but it doesn't have as many features as other solutions. Get the full scoop by visiting www.godaddy.com/websites/online-store.

>> **Volusion:** This e-commerce solution offers four pricing plans, ranging from $26 per month for unlimited products and storage to $269 per month for unlimited products and storage, plus access to priority support and consultation services. All prices include hosting, mobile responsive templates, and no transaction fees. All plans also include mobile commerce and social media tools. As for support, the two lower plan tiers offer only online support. You can check out this solution and the range of specific features offered across price plans at www.volusion.com.

>> **Shopify:** Launched in 2006, Shopify has proven itself to be a solid contender in the world of e-commerce solution providers. Shopify offers three primary pricing plans ranging from $29 to $299 per month. Each plan supports an unlimited number of products and provides 24/7 live support and mobile commerce functionality. If you use the Shopify payment gateway, there are no transaction fees on any of the three plans. Another interesting feature is Shopify POS, an Apple iPad point-of-sale system for your retail location. The list of features is too long to include here, but rest assured that plenty of impressive functionality and lots of marketing tools are included. The exception to this rule is a starter plan (called Shopify Lite) that costs $9 per month and enables you to sell on Facebook only. Shopify offers a free, two-week trial with no credit card required. To sign up for the trial or explore all the options offered by this e-commerce solution, visit www.shopify.com.

>> **BigCommerce:** BigCommerce is an industry leader, with a reputation for being a simple, powerful solution with an impressive list of features for the money. Its list of customers include many mega brand e-commerce retailers. It has recently added the BigCommerce Essentials brand to focus on small business solutions. Plans range from $29.95 to $249.95 per month and all plans include an unlimited number of products, unlimited storage and bandwidth, no transaction fees, no limit on the number of staff (or user) accounts, and 24/7 "live agent" technical support. The list of features that apply across plans is impressive, including social media tools, real-time shipping quotes, built-in blog and SEO, lots of payment options (including some international), and coupon and discount functions. The advanced plans include cart abandonment features, and provide a higher level of security features. Given the competitive pricing with so much advanced functionality across plans, it is clear that BigCommerce wants to be a market leader of e-commerce solutions for all sizes of online businesses. See the full list of features and pricing at www.bigcommerce.com.

>> **WordPress e-commerce plug-in:** If you use WordPress, the free blog software, for your site, you may also choose to use a plug-in for your e-commerce solution, such as WooCommerce, WP e-Commerce, and MarketPress. Did we mention these are often free (or super cheap)? The downside of using a WordPress plug-in is that it may have fewer features and payment gateway options than the non-free solutions and may require more work on your part for setup or customization (with limited, if any, technical support available). The best way to explore your options for a plug-in solution is to do a search for *ecommerce* in the WordPress Plugin Directory at http://wordpress.org/extend/plugins.

Chapter 2

Mastering the Amazon

I t may be a jungle out there, but Amazon has strategically cleared a path for the willing online entrepreneur. That wasn't always the case. You might recall the days when Amazon was launched and the idea of putting an entire bookstore online to make a (substantial) profit garnered its fair share of skepticism. The only thing about the site that got any attention back then was the big, wooden door that the company's founder, Jeff Bezos, used as a desk! Well, a few things have changed.

Consider that Amazon earned almost $233 billion in sales in 2018. That's not too shabby for a guy who didn't have a "real" desk. What's more exciting is that the site has continued to create business opportunities for people like you by selling products on Amazon. Having a slice of that billion-dollar pie probably sounds good!

Amazon has established multiple selling strategies for you to use: Marketplace, Professional Seller plan, and Fulfillment by Amazon, to name a few. In this chapter, we show you how to choose a sales model and follow the instructions that Amazon has carefully laid out for you.

Joining the Marketplace

Selling in the Amazon Marketplace as an individual seller is by far the quickest way to make some cash on Amazon. Considering its fee structure and setup, the Marketplace is a basic selling opportunity that will suit you if you want to sell only a few items. This clear-cut process has no start-up costs, which is an ideal way to get your feet wet if you haven't sold on Amazon previously.

After you register in the Marketplace, you can post a new or used item for sale. Your item is then listed alongside the same brand-new product sold on Amazon. Figure 2-1 shows an example of how used items appear on the same page as the new version of that item.

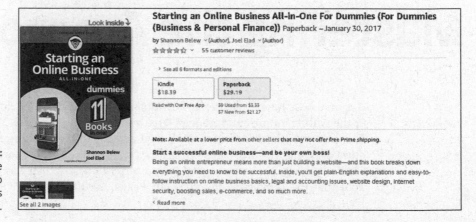

FIGURE 2-1: Marketplace items show up on Amazon's product pages.

Customers can choose to buy the item from Amazon or you (or someone else). When a customer decides to purchase from you, the customer adds the product to his or her shopping cart and pays for it on Amazon (like a normal purchase). Amazon then sends you (the seller) the customer's order information and you're responsible for shipping the product. Your Amazon seller's account is credited for the purchase amount, and then you receive a direct deposit from Amazon for the items that sold. (Although total amounts show up in your account immediately, deposits are distributed every 14 days.) That's it!

Amazon doesn't charge you any money to list an item. But you pay a fee when the item sells. Here's a list of the fees that Amazon deducts from your sales price:

>> **Referral fees:** Amazon bases referral fee (or commission) costs on the category in which your item is listed. (In many cases, there is a $1 minimum Referral Fee per item.) The commission percentages break down like this:

- *Books*: 15 percent

- *Cameras and photos:* 8 percent

- *Unlocked smartphones:* 8 percent

- *Computers:* 6 percent

- *Consumer electronics* (such as printers, video game consoles, and scanners): 8 percent

- *Electronic accessories and major appliances:* A sliding scale depending on the item price, starting at 15 percent and going down to 8 percent for higher-priced merchandise

- *Home & Garden and Kitchen*: 15 percent

- *Music & Musical instruments:* 15 percent

- *Sports, Toys & Games, and Video & DVD*: 15 percent

- *Tools and hardware:* 12 percent to 15 percent

- *Most other product lines:* 15 percent

There are also other categories that require approval from Amazon before you can sell in those categories. Those referral fee percentages are as follows:

- *Automotive parts and accessories:* 12 percent

- *Beauty, Grocery, and Gourmet Food, & Health products*: 8 percent to 15 percent

- *Clothing & Accessories*: 17 percent

- *Industrial & Scientific Equipment*: 12 percent

- *Jewelry:* A sliding scale depending on price, starting at 20 percent and going down to 5 percent for higher-priced items

- *Shoes, Handbags, and Sunglasses*: 15 percent to 18 percent

- *Watches:* 15 percent

>> **Transaction fee:** Amazon charges a flat fee of 99 cents for each item sold. (This fee is waived under the Professional Seller plan.)

>> **Variable closing fee:** This fee is the Amazon equivalent of a handling charge. For media items (books, music, video, DVDs, computer games, and software), the closing fee is $1.80 for standard or expedited shipping.

The advantage of shopping in the Marketplace is obvious for your customers: They receive the same product (used or new) at a discounted price. For you, the benefit is the ease of the selling process.

To get started with the Marketplace, first decide whether you want to start with a low volume (as an individual seller) or a high volume (as a Professional Seller). If you want to be a Professional Seller, see the next section for more information. Individual sellers should follow these steps:

1. **Go to Amazon at** www.amazon.com.

2. **Scroll down to the bottom of the home page and click the Sell on Amazon link, which is under the Make Money with Us header in the middle.**

   An overview page appears that briefly describes the options you can use when selling on Amazon.

3. **Scroll down until you see the option, "Just have a few items to sell?" and click the Sign Up to Become an Individual Seller link (see Figure 2-2).**

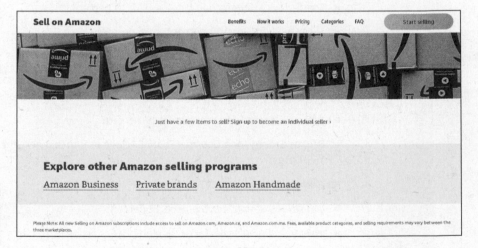

FIGURE 2-2: Amazon explains how you can sell items on its site.

4. **Log in to your Amazon account.**

   If you don't have an account, click the I Do Not Have an Amazon.com Password button and follow the instructions for creating one. You will also have to agree to Amazon's terms and conditions. You have to supply a valid credit card number, a U.S. bank account number, a U.S. phone number where Amazon can reach you directly, and your billing address.

If you're already an Amazon customer, your customer account information is automatically used for the registration process, speeding up the process significantly. But you always have the option to change or update your information.

To complete the registration process, you must be available to receive a verification phone call from Amazon. You enter the phone number where you can be reached, and then you respond to the automated prompts when called. Completing the verification process takes about 30 seconds.

When the registration process is complete, you will see the Amazon Seller Central overview page appear, as shown in Figure 2-3.

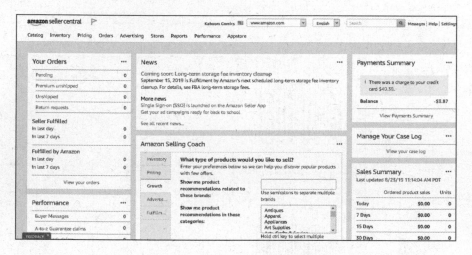

FIGURE 2-3:
Manage your sales at Amazon Seller Central.

5. **Roll your cursor over the Inventory link at the top of the screen, and then click the Add a Product link.**

   You can sell only products that Amazon sells. The screen shown in Figure 2-4 appears.

6. **Search for the product you want to sell by entering one of the following in the List It on Amazon text box:**

   - *Title or keyword:* Enter the title of your product or one or more keywords describing it.

   - *ISBN, UPC, or ASIN:* Enter an identifying code. You can find the International Standard Book Number (ISBN) or Universal Product Code (UPC) on the back of your product. Look for the Amazon Standard Identification Number (ASIN) on the item's product information page (see Figure 2-5).

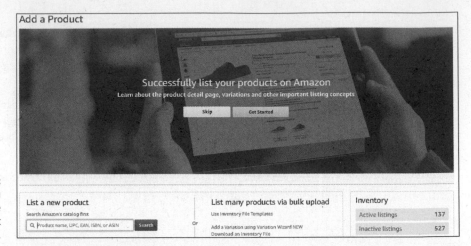

FIGURE 2-4:
Amazon asks you to search for the items you want to sell.

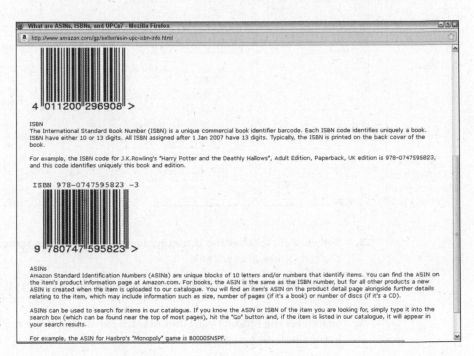

FIGURE 2-5:
Find the ISBN, UPC, or ASIN for your product.

7. **Click the Search button.**

   A results page appears that lists Amazon products that contain the title or search term you used.

8. **Identify the correct product in the list and then click the Sell Yours button to the right of the product.**

9. **Double-check to ensure that you have the right product.**

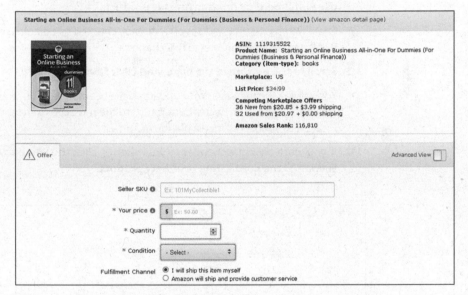

REMEMBER

Amazon requires that you sell the exact match to the product being sold on its website. For example, you should make sure to match items by the correct edition (for a book) or color (for a product).

10. **In the Your Price box, enter the price for your item.**

For comparison, Amazon shows you its current price and other Marketplace prices for this item in the Competing Marketplace Offers section of the Product Summary box, at the top right of the page (see Figure 2-6). You can also click the Match Low Price button, above the Your Price box, and Amazon will automatically fill in the lowest price.

Starting an Online Business All-in-One For Dummies (For Dummies (Business & Personal Finance)) (View amazon detail page)

ASIN: 1119315522
Product Name: Starting an Online Business All-in-One For Dummies (For Dummies (Business & Personal Finance))
Category (item-type): books

Marketplace: US

List Price: $34.99

Competing Marketplace Offers
36 New from $20.85 + $3.99 shipping
32 Used from $20.97 + $0.00 shipping

Amazon Sales Rank: 116,810

⚠ Offer   Advanced View ▢

Seller SKU ⓘ   Ex: 101MyCollectible1

* Your price ⓘ $ Ex: 50.00

* Quantity   [▾]

* Condition   - Select -   ▾

Fulfillment Channel   ◉ I will ship this item myself
                      ○ Amazon will ship and provide customer service

FIGURE 2-6:
Set the price,
quantity, and the
item's condition.

11. **Enter in the Quantity box the quantity of the item you're selling.**

12. **In the Condition drop-down list, select your item's condition.**

Your choices include terms such as New; Used — Like New; and Used — Very Good.

At this point, you can click the Save and Finish button to send your listing to Amazon. Or you can also toggle to Advanced View and input more criteria about your sale.

13. **(Optional) If you want to add more information to your listing, like a note about the book's condition, click the Advanced View button at the bottom right of the screen. More fields will appear to you, as shown in Figure 2-7. In the Condition Note text box, enter a few comments about the condition of your product.**

You can enter as many as 2,000 characters. Use this opportunity to further describe your product. In addition, you can indicate things like a Collectible edition or the condition of a dust jacket, if the book has one.

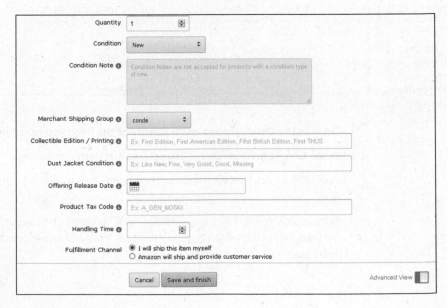

TIP

Adding more information about your product can increase sales.

14. **Under Fulfillment Channel, select either "I will ship this myself" or "Amazon will ship and provide customer service" if you are planning to use Fulfillment by Amazon for this product.**

The "I will ship this myself" option is already checked by default. We discuss Fulfillment by Amazon later in this chapter.

15. **Scroll to the bottom of the page, and click Save and Finish.**

You will see the message "Your updates have been submitted." You can also click the Facebook or Twitter button next to the message to share this new listing with your social media platforms.

16. **If you want to make changes to your listing, click the Edit button in the section of the page listing your new product.**

Quantity	1
Condition	New
Condition Note	Condition Notes are not accepted for products with a condition type of new.
Merchant Shipping Group	conde
Collectible Edition / Printing	Ex: First Edition, First American Edition, First British Edition, First THUS
Dust Jacket Condition	Ex: Like New, Fine, Very Good, Good, Missing
Offering Release Date	
Product Tax Code	Ex: A_GEN_NOTAX
Handling Time	
Fulfillment Channel	⦿ I will ship this item myself ◯ Amazon will ship and provide customer service

Cancel   Save and finish   Advanced View

FIGURE 2-7: Toggle to Advanced View to set other product sales information.

Amazon sends you a confirmation of your listing to your designated email address. Then you simply wait for the item to be sold. After 60 days, if the item doesn't sell, Amazon removes it from your listings. You don't pay any fees if your item doesn't sell.

TIP

If you have a Professional Seller account (see the next section), you can leave the listing on Amazon until you choose to remove it.

If you have a large volume of similar items that you want to sell on Amazon, but you don't have the fulfillment capabilities to handle shipping your orders, you can request enrollment in the Fulfillment by Amazon program. You ship your items to Amazon, it stores the items in its warehouse, and it ships the item directly to the customer when he or she orders that item from you. One of the biggest appeals of this program is that products that are fulfilled by Amazon qualify for free standard shipping (if the order is $35 or more) or free two-day shipping (if the customer subscribes to the Amazon Prime program). In addition, Amazon handles all customer service and return issues regarding these orders.

You can learn more by going to the Amazon Fulfillment Services home page at `http://services.amazon.com/fulfillment-by-amazon/benefits.html`. There are videos on the Benefits page that explain the process and how to register. We discuss Fulfillment by Amazon later in this chapter.

Achieving Professional Seller Status

Realizing that you might want to increase your sales potential by using Amazon, the site established the Professional Seller plan. You're a primary candidate for this type of account if you sell more than 40 orders per month. As a Professional seller, you're still selling in the Marketplace: The way your listings look, the options for where the listings appear, and the way you post your items for sale are the same (see the preceding section "Joining the Marketplace," for details about selling in the Marketplace).

When you become a Professional seller, you gain a few definite advantages:

>> **Reduced fees:** The 99-cent transaction fee is automatically waived for all Professional Seller accounts. All other commissions and fees remain, however.

>> **Bulk listing capabilities:** Designed for sellers of large inventory, the Professional Seller account provides tools that make it easier to load and manage multiple listings. Included among the tools are

- *Inventory File Templates:* Modify, delete, and upload thousands of products at one time.

- *Book Loader:* Match and upload books considered to have pre-ISBNs. Rare, collectible, or out-of-print books are in this category.

>> **Continuous listings:** Your listings never expire. You keep them posted until an item sells or you decide to remove them.

>> **Management functions:** You gain access to various reports that show the status of your account at any given time. These reports allow you to view all account activity (including items that shipped) during the past 15, 30, or 60 days.

>> **Fraud protection:** Amazon offers a payment fraud protection program to help eliminate fraudulent products. It also offers an A-to-Z Guarantee program that protects both the customers and you, in case something goes wrong with an order.

Unlike your basic Marketplace listing, opening a Professional Seller account comes at a price. Amazon charges $39.99 per month for a Professional Seller account (although it sometimes offers limited-time-only discounts for the first few months of service). Only Professional sellers are allowed to sell in the beauty products, grocery and gourmet food, and health and personal care categories. Additionally, several categories require special approval from Amazon before you can begin selling. These categories include automotive parts, cellphones and accessories, clothing and accessories, jewelry, motorcycles, ATV and protective gear, shoes, and watches. If you're selling in the toys and games category, note that Amazon doesn't accept new sellers in that category during the holiday season, which usually starts around late October and runs through early January.

Opening a Professional Seller account can truly pay off. You have access to several types of sales and business reports, including the following:

>> **Sales Dashboard:** Here, you can see a Sales Snapshot (total orders, total units ordered, sales amounts, average units per order, and average sales per order), as well as a Compare Sales graph that allows you to compare sales over a specific time period.

>> **Business Reports by Date:** Here, you can study your sales and traffic numbers by date range, see details on specific sales, and gauge your Seller Performance.

» **Business Reports by ASIN:** These reports focus more on sales based on the inventory you've input into the system that's available for sale. They allow you to gauge how specific categories of products are doing, as you can see how many Sessions, Page Views, and Buy Box placements you got for each inventory item, as well as the percentages of those items that sold in the specified date range of the report.

» **Sales and Orders by Month:** You can see up to two years of past sales, month by month, showing totals for orders, units, shipments, sales, and a graph charting your monthly sales, so you can detect trends or gauge the health of your overall sales activity.

To sign up for a Professional Seller account, click the Start Selling button on the Sell on Amazon page (refer to Figure 2-2).

REMEMBER

Although Amazon handles the payment process between you and your customer, you're responsible for any returns or refunds. If a seller requests a refund, he or she has to ship the item back to you, and you absorb the cost of shipping. All refunds can be handled directly from your Amazon Professional seller account.

Taking Advantage of the Fulfillment by Amazon Service

Amazon has cleverly created another opportunity to make money using its existing warehouse network and technologies, coupled with your products. Truly, there's an opportunity for just about everyone. If you've got products to sell, but you don't have the storage or infrastructure capabilities to pack and ship your orders, you can let Amazon do the work in its Fulfillment by Amazon (FBA) service.

Fulfillment by Amazon lets you create your listings, and then send the actual inventory to Amazon to store in its warehouses. When that product sells, Amazon warehouse personnel will pack and ship the item, just as if someone bought an Amazon-owned item, and sent it to the customer, and then you get paid just like any regular sale you make on Amazon. Of course, there are additional fees to participate, but the cost savings you enjoy from avoiding the packing and shipping, coupled with the fact that all FBA products qualify for free shipping under Amazon's Standard or Amazon Prime accounts, can make this program very worthwhile.

Mastering the Amazon

Additionally, all products you sell through Fulfillment by Amazon come with other great benefits:

>> **Amazon Customer Service:** All orders sent through FBA are supported by Amazon's own Customer Service team. Therefore, if your buyer has a problem with a shipment, the buyer deals directly with Amazon's support team and you never have to get involved. You get Amazon's customer service support at no additional charge.

>> **Amazon Return Management process:** All orders sent through FBA qualify for customers to use Amazon's Online Returns Center to manage any potential returns they want to make. This way, the buyer gets the comfort of a professional return process, and you don't have to worry about the logistics. Amazon does charge you a returns processing fee when this occurs.

>> **Your own e-commerce fulfillment:** You can send your items to be fulfilled by Amazon, but the sale of those items don't have to occur on the Amazon platform itself. Your FBA items can be sold on your own e-commerce site, and Amazon will still handle the fulfillment of those orders, just as if it were sold on Amazon directly. This way, you can offer your customers multiple shipping options, like one-day, two-day, and standard delivery, without the backend headache of doing the fulfillment. *Note:* There is a separate fee chart for storing and processing items that are being sold on your own site versus Amazon's site, and as you can imagine, it's more expensive when it's not sold on Amazon. However, you're getting the support and management of a world-class e-commerce company when you use FBA.

Once you have your Seller account on Amazon, you simply add FBA to your account by going to your existing inventory, selecting the products in your inventory that you'd like to send to Amazon to fulfill, and selecting the option Change to Fulfilled by Amazon from the drop-down list next to the Edit button for each item. Amazon will prompt you with a confirmation screen and then give you instructions on how to send those items to its warehouse.

Of course, any true evaluation of whether you should adapt Fulfillment by Amazon will require you to take a look at the pricing for using the system. The Fulfillment by Amazon pricing page (https://services.amazon.com/fulfillment-by-amazon/pricing.html) lets you review all the individual price options for different inventory items.

TIP

If you're looking for the most up-to-date information and advice on how to sell on Amazon, check out Amazon's Seller Forums discussion boards by going to http://sellercentral.amazon.com/forums.

IN THIS CHAPTER

» Setting up a Shopify e-commerce store

» Adding products to your store catalog

» Comparing package solutions

» Calculating the fees for using Shopify

» Using marketing systems to bring in more customers

Chapter **3**

Web-ify Your Store with Shopify

O ne big advantage of using Shopify is how it enables you to easily create your own store. Shopify walks you through the steps necessary to create, design, fill, and maintain your own store. Over the years, smaller companies have folded or changed or were acquired by other companies, so customers of these companies aren't sure what to expect. With Shopify, though, you know that your website will be fully functional and available because Shopify's popularity ensures that Shopify professionals will provide the technical expertise to keep all its websites running smoothly.

In this chapter, we talk about the many features that Shopify e-commerce stores offer you, the basic platform of the small-business solution, and how you perform basic navigation and item creation. We cover the different packages and describe how Shopify makes its money with this service. Finally, you discover how you can make more money with your Shopify store through marketing, customer relationships, and data analysis.

Why Open a Shopify Store?

Although you can order different levels of solutions with Shopify, a powerful base platform comes with every solution. Here are ten functions that every Shopify store can enjoy:

>> **Built-in shopping cart:** You can put an unlimited number of products into your Shopify store. Its shopping-cart software presents those items to your customers and lets them add them to, or delete them from, their own shopping baskets. Then the software interfaces with shipping companies and tax tables to show customers their costs when they check out.

>> **Detailed sales reports:** Shopify provides a set of detailed reports so that you can see what's selling, what's being clicked, and what's being searched. You even see which websites send you the most traffic and which web pages on your site are the most viewed.

>> **Inventory tracking:** If you don't want to sell out of your hottest product or you need an alert when your available inventory gets too low, Shopify has you covered. It manages your inventory and automatically stops selling a product if inventory drops to zero.

>> **Unlimited space and bandwidth:** If you have large image files or audio or video, you can relax. You get an unlimited amount of storage with each account and an unlimited amount of bandwidth to send those massive files each time a customer comes a-knockin'.

>> **Mobile app and support:** Not only does Shopify ensure that your store is optimized for customers using a mobile device, but also its mobile app allows you to manage your store operations on the go, as all your data is synced between your store and your mobile device.

>> **Secure technology:** With Shopify, your customers can enter information safely because you can create secure web pages by way of Secure Sockets Layer (SSL) technology (with a free SSL certificate) that encrypts sensitive data (such as credit card numbers) when customers transmit that info to you. Shopify will make sure your store is Level-1 PCI–compliant, which will protect your customers' data.

>> **Search engine optimization tools:** Shopify lets your customers leave SEO-friendly product reviews on your website, as well as help you customize important SEO practices like your meta tags, titles, and headers.

>> **Social media integration:** Shopify gives you the ability to have your website integrate with your different social media channels, from Facebook and Twitter to Pinterest, Instagram, and Tumblr. Shopify provides options such as Facebook Buy buttons, where customers can buy products while staying on your Facebook page.

>> **Automatic backups of your website:** Shopify takes a snapshot of your website every day and lets you go back and forth between those versions. If you accidentally lose data, you can restore the last version quickly. Shopify makes the backups without even asking or reminding you.

Setting Up Shop

When you're ready to set up a Shopify store, follow these steps:

1. **Go to the Shopify home page at** www.shopify.com, **and click the Start Free Trial button.**

You can also click the Start Free Trial button in the top right of the screen, as shown in Figure 3-1.

FIGURE 3-1:
Shopify guides you to its online sales solutions.

Shopify prompts you for an email address, password, and the name of your store. Later on in the process, you will pick the plan that best suits your needs. (The standard and advanced Shopify plans are recommended for established e-commerce or offline businesses.) We discuss the prices and benefits of these packages later in this chapter, in the "Selecting a Plan" section.

REMEMBER

Shopify offers more packages than just its e-commerce solutions. If you want to have a Point of Sale system, simply put Buy buttons on your social media pages, or find other ways to have Shopify's technology help power your business. Find out more at www.shopify.com.

2. **Answer some additional questions about your business goals (see Figure 3-2) and then click Next.**

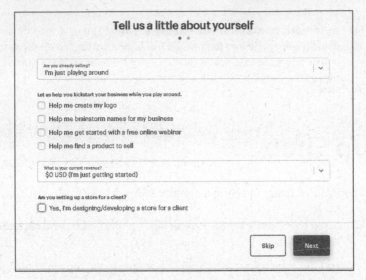

FIGURE 3-2:
Tell Shopify your
current business
status.

Shopify will want to know whether you're a new seller or an established store that's moving over to Shopify. It also wants to know your current revenue per year, and whether you are building a store for a client rather than for yourself.

Based on your answers, other options may show up, like the section "Let us help you kickstart your business while you play around." Based on the options you pick, Shopify will forward you videos and information to help you do online business tasks such as creating a logo or finding a product for sale. Take advantage of the library of help that Shopify has to offer.

3. **When Shopify prompts you for the address of your business, fill in the appropriate fields.**

   Shopify needs to know the location of your business in order to set the proper currency and tax rate for your store.

4. **Click the green Enter My Store button to finish initializing your account.**

   Shopify starts your free trial and takes you to your newly created Account page, as shown in Figure 3-3. The left menu contains all the major sections you will need to run your online store, so pay attention to all these options.

5. **Click the blue Select a Plan button to pick your Shopify plan.**

   You are taken to the page to select a plan for your store. You could also click Settings from the left menu and then click Account to get to the same plan page.

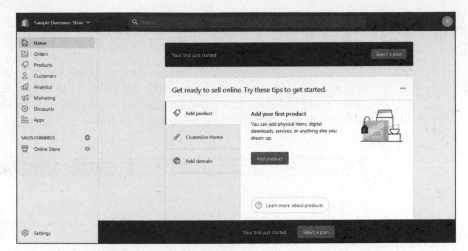

FIGURE 3-3:
Shopify creates
your trial account.

6. **Review your options (see Figure 3-4), and click the appropriate Choose This Plan button to sign up for that particular plan.**

   You are prompted to provide your billing information and leave a credit card on file for when your Shopify trial ends. Fill out the prompts as labeled and then pick a billing cycle (month by month, annual payment for 10 percent savings, or biennial payment for 20 percent savings).

7. **To finalize your order, scroll down to click the Start Plan button.**

   You need to select the check box to agree to Shopify's terms of service.

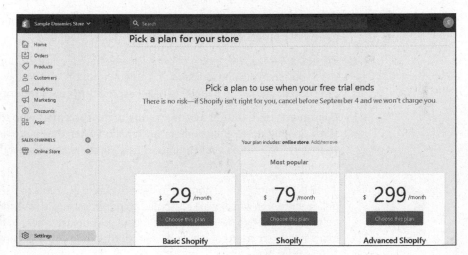

FIGURE 3-4:
Review the
Shopify plans
offered.

Managing Your Shopify Store

After you sign up with Shopify, you can control all aspects of your account. Go to www.shopify.com and click Log In at the top right of the screen. Enter your email address and password that you created when you signed up with Shopify, and that will bring you to your account home page, as shown in Figure 3-5.

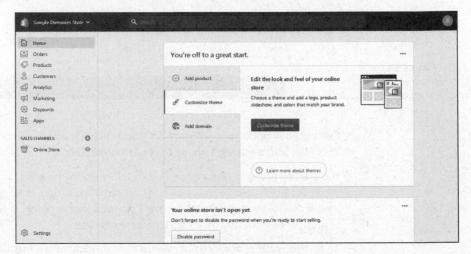

FIGURE 3-5:
Access all your account controls from one screen.

From the home page, you have access to the four main parts of your account:

>> **Orders:** Review all the orders your store has received, and use the tools to fulfill those orders with steps like printing shipping labels.

>> **Products:** Review the catalog of products you have for sale in your store. Here you can make updates, add and delete products, and review your inventory (if you set up Shopify to help keep track of your inventory count).

>> **Customers:** Here you get a better picture of the customers who shop at your store. Shopify stores all customers' information when they place an order with your store. You can also add or import existing customers into your Shopify customer records.

TIP

If you don't want your customers to have to create accounts to use your online store, you can disable customer accounts, making this section not that helpful. You need to decide whether you want your customers to take that extra step to create accounts, and whether they (and you) will benefit more or less from this.

» **Analytics:** From here, you can manage all the reporting features to see how your store is performing. The standard and advanced Shopify packages offer more robust analytics features, but those are designed for well-established stores that could benefit from deep customer analysis.

REMEMBER

The Settings page is at the bottom of the left menu and will be your most used section at the beginning as you configure many elements of your store during the entire setup process.

Constructing your catalog

Before we talk about designing your site, we want to focus on the core element of any vibrant e-commerce store, your "catalog" or list of products for sale. What's a store without products? Shopify has a central section entitled Products, which lets you enter your products for sale and also offers you the capability to track the inventory level as people place orders. You can update your inventory at any time, organize your inventory by different product data fields, and even import your entire product catalog at one time.

When you want to add a product to your store, follow these steps:

1. **From the Store home page, click the Products link.**

The main Products page is displayed. The first time you go to your Products page, you see the option to add your first product or set up an import of products, as shown in Figure 3-6. For this example, we go through the steps of adding a product directly.

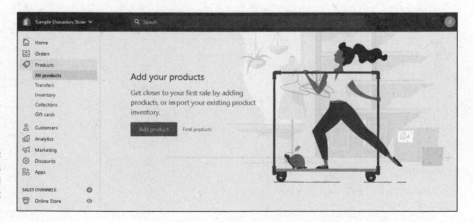

FIGURE 3-6:
Shopify wants to help you add your first product to your store.

2. **Click the Add Product button to get started.**

The one-page Add Product form appears.

3. **Complete the following information fields, as shown in Figure 3-7:**

- *Title:* Enter the name that you want your customers to see as the name of your product.

- *Description:* Enter the item description in this field. Write a description for your product that you want customers to see when they're looking at your item on your store page. Use the command buttons at the top of the text box (similar to Microsoft Word) to format your description so that it will show up on your store with specific font sizes, alignment, and so on.

- *Images:* Click the Upload Image link to specify the path where the digital image of your product is stored on your computer and upload it to your store.

- *Product type:* In this field, you select a category to assign to your product (for example, shirts, pants, socks, shoes).

- *Vendor:* Enter the manufacturer or brand name of the product in this field.

- (Optional) *Collections:* If you want to create a special collection (think custom category, for example) to assign your product to, this field is where you type in the collection name tied to the product. For example, you could create a Clearance collection, a New In Stock collection, or a themed collection like Movie Heroes.

- *Tags:* In this field, you can define tags, or "keywords," to be associated with your item for search capabilities. These tags won't be displayed to your shoppers on the product page.

FIGURE 3-7:
Enter key details about your product.

4. **Scroll to the pricing and shipping section and enter more details about your product (see Figure 3-8):**

- *Price:* Every product must have a numeric price.

- *Compare at price:* Think of this field as the "original retail price" and the price field as your sales price. When you use this field, your customers see both prices, with a line through the "Compare at price" number and the price highlighted.

- *Cost of item*: If you record your item cost in this field, later on the Analytics reporting will help you calculate profit, not just revenue, for your sales.

- *Stock Keeping Unit:* This is your ID field for the product, so create a unique identifier for each product. This is an internal measure so don't worry about the public having to decipher this field. You can enter letters, numbers, or both in this field.

- *Barcode (ISBN, UPC, GTIN, and so on):* This field should contain the identifier that came with the product, like a manufacturer's UPC number, ISBN number, or a GTIN (Global Trade Identification Number). If the product doesn't have one of these numbers, you can leave this field blank.

- *Inventory policy:* You can pick from a drop-down list of options. If you pick Track Inventory, a new field appears where you can assign the initial quantity of units for this product. (As orders are received, Shopify keeps track of the inventory level and decreases the quantity accordingly.) If you pick Do Not Track Inventory, no quantity information will be assigned to your product entry.

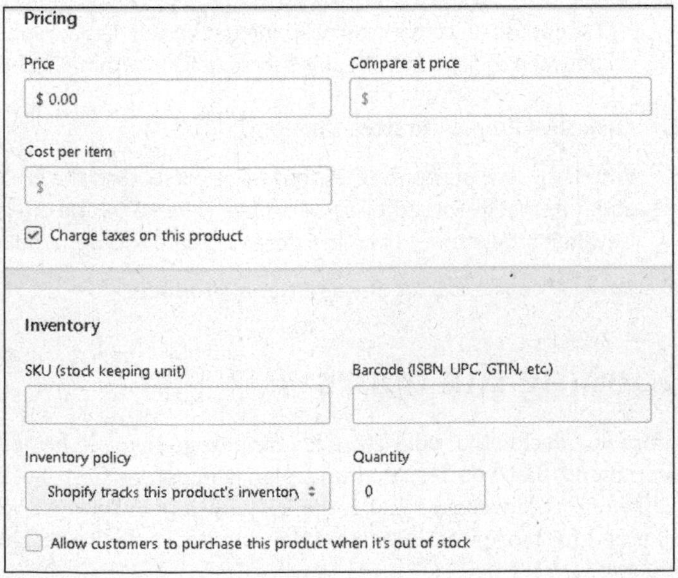

FIGURE 3-8: Complete the pricing and shipping information for your product.

- *"This is a physical item"*: Check the box if the product you're adding is a physical item. If you're selling a digital item, uncheck this box.

- *Weight:* Put the numeric weight of your item in this field. You can define the unit of measurement in the drop-down list next to this field.

- (Optional) *Country/Region of Origin:* If you ship overseas, you can assign the country that's the origin country for your product, and Shopify will include this when the customs paperwork is prepared.

- (Optional) *Harmonized system code:* If you ship overseas, you can assign an internationally recognized harmonized system code for your product, and Shopify will include this code when the customs paperwork is prepared.

- *Fulfillment service:* This option is mainly for the Advanced Shopify users, who have more real-time shipping options. For everybody else, the service is Manual as you fulfill your product sales. Make sure the "This product requires shipping" check box is selected for any product that's a physical product you have to mail out.

- *Variants:* If you offer the same product in different sizes or colors or other options, don't create individual product entries for each option. You simply click the Add Variant link and assign an option name and option values, one line at a time, like this:

Option name	Option values
Size	Small, Medium, Large
Color	Red, Blue, White, Black

TIP

Do not use any other internal punctuation, such as a colon or semicolon, between the options. Shopify is looking for a comma between each option.

5. **Click Save Product to store the item.**

   When you save the product, Shopify takes you back to the Products page, confirms that the product was saved (see Figure 3-9), and offers you links to view (the product) in your online store or create another product.

6. **Repeat Steps 2 to 5 for any additional products.**

Opening the doors

Before you decide that your store is going to go live and be open for business, we recommend that you research and plan your store first. See what you like and dislike on other websites and come up with a plan for your website. See Book 3, Chapter 3 for more information on developing a website design.

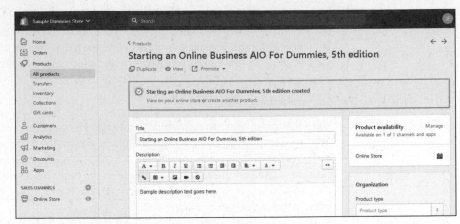

FIGURE 3-9:
Your product has
been added to
your store.

When you're ready to open your store for business, you should first think about the following steps:

1. **Design your store.**

You need to create the web pages that display your products. You can add pages and then define the navigation of your store by creating a main menu and organizing the pages you create into a simple navigation structure between a main menu and a footer menu at the bottom of the screen. Building the actual store requires some design work, and Shopify provides you with hundreds of free and premium web templates that you can use to build your pages. You can also hire a Shopify Expert to create a totally custom design. These Experts are preapproved professional designers, marketers, and developers who can help build your store.

2. **Add products.**

We cover adding products to your catalog in the previous section, "Constructing your catalog."

3. **Set up payment methods.**

You need to decide how you want to handle payment processing for your store. Shopify integrates with over 70 payment gateways around the world, from services like PayPal or iDEAL to systems like Bitcoin. Shopify also offers its own gateway, which offers competitive rates and allows you to accept credit cards. You can find more about payment processing in Book 4, Chapter 4.

4. **Set up tax rates.**

In today's age of Internet sales, you need to be aware of tax-collection policies. They vary from state to state, and new legislation is being considered as this book goes to press. Currently in most states, you need to collect sales tax from customers who live in the same state as your business. And in a growing number of cases, you may need to collect sales tax from customers outside your business state. Consult your local Chamber of Commerce, accountant, or state government's business office for specific information. At a minimum, you need to set up the tax rate for your local business area.

5. **Set up shipping rules.**

You need to define shipping methods and rates for your store. You can choose from vendors such as USPS, UPS, and FedEx. If you define shipping weights for each product in your store, Shopify can calculate shipping rates for each customer based on the weight of the items in the customer's shopping cart. You can also set flat shipping rates independent of the number or weight of items in the customer's shopping cart.

When you have gone through these five steps, you should also take a look at the other settings and capabilities Shopify offers you as a shop owner. You can set up notifications, custom domains, and even specific apps that your customers can download and use with your store. You can choose from 100 free and professional themes to make your store look great. You can add a fully functioning blog to help communicate and market to your customers. You can build a robust About Us page to let your customers know about your business and why you started this store, in order to help better connect with your customer base and distinguish yourself from the competition.

Selecting a Plan

Shopify offers different levels of its e-commerce service to coincide with the size and scope of your business. As your company grows, your plan can grow with it as you move up the scale to a more robust set of services.

With other services, you have to choose your features *à la carte* by cobbling together a plan. Shopify gives all its merchants a strong foundation, offering enhancements for its larger clients to fulfill the needs of a growing customer base. Shopify has years of experience in offering different tools — such as e-commerce, retail POS, even social media Buy buttons or pins for sites like Facebook, Twitter, or Pinterest — and those refined tools help make these packages that much more accessible.

Basic Shopify package: Starting out

Don't let the name fool you — the Basic Shopify package isn't a stripped-down, bargain-basement tool that holds only a few products. This package provides a rich set of features and is an excellent jumping-on point for new e-commerce retailers.

With the Basic package, you get the capability to build your own store, host any number of products, and design your site by using the Shopify tools. Some of the more advanced marketing and reporting techniques are reserved for more expensive packages, but most small businesses don't need them.

Shopify package: Moving up

The medium solution is the Shopify package, which contains all the features of the Basic Shopify package, but also offers more advanced features that bigger e-commerce stores need to run their enterprises.

Some of the benefits you receive in this standard package include

>> Five unique staff accounts (compared with two accounts with the Basic package)

>> Better shipping label discounts

>> The capability to view real-time advanced professional reporting tools

>> The capability to offer gift certificates/cards for your website

>> The capability to recover abandoned shopping carts

Advanced Shopify package: Building on solid ground

As e-commerce websites grew, Shopify needed a solution for its biggest customers. Although rich functions are important to bigger websites, you should care mostly about *scalability* — the capability to grow your website's capability to match an increased number of customers or demand. Therefore, Shopify created the Advanced Shopify package.

The Advanced Shopify package focuses on providing the right amount of capabilities to make sure that the customer's website brings in lots in sales just as smoothly as they were bringing in their first few orders. This is enhanced with an advanced report builder option and real-time carrier shipping options.

Breaking Down the Fees

With Shopify, you incur fees the moment you sign up and decide to use the system, after your free trial. Whereas some companies charge a one-time fee for creating an e-commerce site or provide free tools in exchange for ad placements or ownership, Shopify works on a subscription model with no setup fee. You pay every month that you use its solution. Your payment to Shopify consists of only two types of fees:

>> **Monthly fee:** Shopify charges a fixed monthly subscription fee for using its solution. You can save 10 percent on an annual plan, 20 percent on a biennial plan, or 25 percent on a three-year plan, if you pay for that term upfront. The month-by-month price varies by plans:

- *Basic Shopify:* $29 per month (10 percent discount when you sign up and pay for 12 months)

- *Shopify:* $79 per month (10 percent discount when you sign up and pay for 12 months)

- *Advanced Shopify:* $299 per month (10 percent discount when you sign up and pay for 12 months)

>> **Transaction fee:** Shopify offers you the choice of using its built-in Shopify Payments gateway system, or using an external payments gateway system to handle your online payments. There is no additional fee for using Shopify Payments, and its online credit card processing rates are reasonable. If you use an external payment gateway (such as Stripe or PayPal), Shopify charges you a transaction fee. The transaction fee is a percentage of your sales, depending on the package you select. As your sales go up, the percentage goes down:

- *Basic Shopify:* 2.0 percent

- *Shopify:* 1.0 percent

- *Advanced Shopify:* 0.5 percent

Shopify provides a number of functions with its e-commerce packages, but the company charges extra for some added services. Check out the various options at www.shopify.com to see if they make sense for the business you are planning to operate.

Growing with Your New Business Partner

After you use Shopify to build and run your web store, you're probably ready to expand and grow your business further. That's why Shopify offers you tools to help your online business grow.

Marketing programs

You can spread the message of your business in many ways through the Internet and in the physical world. Most people find that their biggest limitation is time because there are many more programs than there are hours in the day. That's where technology comes in. Shopify provides several ways to improve important merchandising features, such as the following:

» **Built-in search engine optimization:** Shopify provides total support for a lot of SEO best practices, like making sure your title and meta tags get filled in correctly for your website pages. They also update your sitemap.xml files so the search engines can detect any website updates automatically.

» **Discounts and coupons:** Shopify builds in functionality where you can provide specific discount codes as well as coupon codes to appeal to different customer bases and encourage repeat business.

» **Social media integration:** Shopify builds in buttons and functionality into its themes to allow your customers to share your products and store with their friend networks.

Customer-relationship management

You can build connections with your customers in lots of ways. The power of an online business is that you can reach your customers directly, one by one, rather than rely on a network of distributors, middlemen, and retailers to connect products with customers.

Shopify's Standard and Advanced packages allow you to offer features on your store such as gift certificates. You can also provide automatic discounts to your customers, whether it's a one-time promotion, a reward for their first purchase, or an incentive to come back for a new order. Shopify keeps track of the logistics so that you can provide a simple code to your customers that acts as a gift certificate or discount coupon and also update your customers' orders when needed.

After you get to know your customers, you can follow up with one of over 400 email marketing apps from the Shopify app store, like MailChimp (www.mailchimp.com), and they will help you build and execute an email marketing campaign. You can easily view your customer history with Shopify and organize customers into specific groups that you can market to directly. You can have the capability for customers to buy gift cards for your store to give to other people, and encourage those customers to write product reviews that would be stored and displayed on your store.

Some of these features are available only with the Standard and Advanced Shopify packages.

Sales reports

You must think that we love reports, the way we talk about them repeatedly in this book. We are fans of reports for one basic reason: You don't know where you can go if you don't understand where you've been. Shopify offers a number of sales reports to help you track what's succeeding and what isn't, so pay attention to these reports and make smart decisions about how to increase your business.

Simply click the Analytics link from the main Shopify menu to see the different reports under the Overview dashboard. Your sales reports give you a useful picture of how your website is doing overall. You can analyze sales by a number of factors, including time of day, customer, channel, and where the traffic is coming from. You can also analyze your visitors by location, landing page, or advertising campaign. You can use these reports if you subscribe to the Standard or Advanced Shopify subscription plan. You can even export that data to Microsoft Excel if you want to do further number crunching.

If you're interested in doing your own data analysis with Excel, check out *Excel Data Analysis For Dummies*, 4th Edition, by Paul McFedries.

After you see your customers' orders, you can then see how they found you in the first place. There is a report that analyzes sales based on the traffic referral source of the customer. For each visit, you see the *referring URL* of that customer, which is the web address your customer was viewing before coming to your website. Shopify even ties together the orders that came from these links so that you can see the revenue per visit. This information gives you an idea of how valuable a new customer can be — so that you know how much to spend to get that new customer to return.

TIP

If the referral URL is from a search engine, pay attention to the URL closely. You see the exact search terms the visitor typed in the search engine to find you. Knowing these words should definitely influence your SEO marketing campaigns.

Finally, let's talk about information you can learn that isn't actual sales or visits. Your customers can type search words and try to go directly to the product page they need. To track this type of customer, Shopify also shows the most frequent words in your own website's search engine. You see a ranked list of the top search terms your customers use every day to find your specific products. You can then compare this list with your inventory. Investigating the search terms used by customers can help you match the right product with the right customer. More important, you see a report of top search terms with no product results. This indicates a list of products your customers are looking for that you don't currently stock, which shows you what new products you should consider carrying in your store.

Chapter **4**

Making eBay THE Way

I n the past 25 years, eBay has grown from a quiet, small online bazaar into the most powerful consumer trading platform on Earth. Although other Internet companies grew overnight into sensations and burned out of existence just as quickly, eBay has remained profitable from the first month it started charging users.

eBay is an effective way to gain customers, establish cash flow, and turn over some inventory. The beautiful part of eBay is that it takes care of many routine tasks that you need to handle by using e-commerce: the trading platform, website, and software needed to transact the sale. The one thing that eBay can't provide on its own, however, is a guaranteed stream of customers or income. Building an eBay business requires some work and effort, combined with a number of strategies and tactics.

In this chapter, we show you how to get up and running on eBay with auctions and fixed-price sales. Then, when you have your feet wet, we detail how to advance to the big leagues with a dedicated eBay store.

REMEMBER

Running an eBay business doesn't require that you focus all your efforts on eBay. eBay can simply be one channel for selling goods and making money, or you can use eBay to start your business before you launch your own website. In this chapter, we present a plan for building steady, constant sales through this channel. You decide how you want to use eBay, based on your total online business strategy.

Understanding How eBay Works

Online sales usually involve four key elements: product, price, seller, and buyer. On eBay, buyers can pay a fixed price or compete with one another to win the item in a bidding system. If you've ever been to a live auction, you know that buyers raise their bid price until one bidder remains, and then that highest bidder pays the top price and receives the item. On eBay, members place a bid electronically rather than raise a paddle.

Here's the basic flow of an eBay transaction:

1. List an item for sale on eBay. See the "Setting Up an Item for Sale" section, later in this chapter.

2. If you list your item with a fixed price, a buyer who is interested in your item at that price will click the Buy It Now button to purchase the item, and eBay sends an email to you and the buyer.

3. If you list your item as an auction, a buyer places a bid on eBay for your item, indicating the highest price he or she is willing to pay. The buyer with the highest bid at the end of the auction's time period wins the item, and eBay sends an email to you and the highest bidder.

4. You send the buyer an invoice, indicating the total for the item sold, including shipping, handling, and sales tax (when applicable) and whether you accept PayPal or a credit card.

   If you need to set up your accepted forms of payment, see Book 4, Chapter 4.

5. The buyer sends you payment.

6. You mail the item to the buyer. See Book 4, Chapter 7 for info on shipping products to your buyers.

7. You and your bidder can leave comments about your transaction, known as *feedback,* on eBay. See the "Leaving feedback for your buyer" section, later in this chapter.

Getting Started on eBay

Signing up for eBay is easy and free. Your account can be used to browse, bid, and sell on eBay. The main requirement is that you have to be 18 years or older. Just fire up your Internet browser and go to www.ebay.com and follow these steps:

1. **Click the Register link in the top-left corner.**

   The Create an Account page appears, as shown in Figure 4-1.

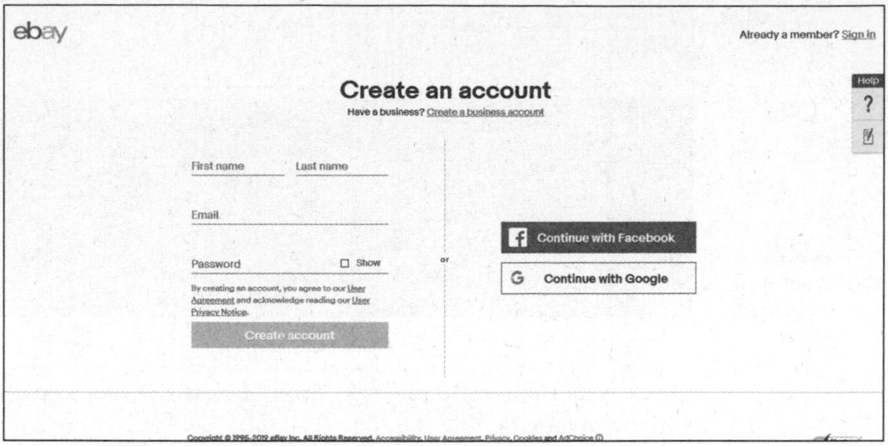

FIGURE 4-1:
Enter your
information here.

2. **Enter your personal information in the fields provided.**

You're required to give your full name and email address, which eBay keeps on file if it needs to communicate with you. Your password must be between 6 and 20 characters and must contain at least one letter and either a number or a symbol. Choose a password that no one can randomly guess.

Once you enter that information and click the Create account button, eBay will continue to prompt you for information like your mailing address, preferred categories, and, if you are registering a business account, your business information. Fill out the forms as presented, including how you plan to pay for your eBay fees (PayPal, bank account, or credit/debit card).

3. **Click the Submit button to continue.**

Your eBay account is created and eBay assigns you an initial unique user ID. The ID is the name you use to do business on eBay. It can be a variation of your own name (such as johndoe1), the name of your business (mybusiness. com), or the name of a category where you plan to sell (buddyselectronics).

You aren't stuck with your assigned choice. eBay allows you to change your user ID once every 30 days, which does not affect your user rating. Simply go into My eBay, click the Account tab, and then select Personal Information to change your ID.

TIP

4. **Click Continue.**

The eBay home page appears with a message ("Hi") and your first name in the upper-left corner of the screen, as shown in Figure 4-2. Your eBay account is now active.

FIGURE 4-2:
eBay creates your
account.

Check your email for a message from eBay with links to pages explaining what you can do next.

After you register on eBay, you have to perform some additional details before starting your first auction or opening a storefront:

>> **Sign up for PayPal.** PayPal, the eBay-owned division that handles online payment processing, lets you send or receive money based on your online sales, on or off eBay. You can maintain an account on PayPal for free — you pay only a transaction fee (typically 2.9 percent to 4.1 percent) when you receive a payment. Go to www.paypal.com to sign up.

REMEMBER

You can also sign up for a merchant account from your bank, where you can process credit cards directly. You must have either a PayPal or merchant account if you want to sell on eBay; PayPal is the recommended payment method. According to research from eBay, 90 percent of all eBay auctions offer PayPal as a payment method, and 80 percent of all transactions are paid for through PayPal.

>> **Set up a dedicated bank account.** Both eBay and PayPal require you to provide a credit card number and your bank account information to create an account. We recommend setting up a second bank account at a smaller bank and getting a Visa or MasterCard debit card through this account so that you can keep track of your eBay activity separately from your main banking transactions.

>> **Set up your profile page.** eBay allows you to have a profile description, photo, and cover photo to help advertise your own eBay store, talk about your online sales activities, and detail your reputation for doing business on the auction website. Your profile photo can be an image of your retail storefront, your company logo, or one of your products.

To edit your profile information, go to http://www.ebay.com/usr/ yourebayusername and click the Edit Profile button under your username to be able to update the description, profile, and cover photo (see Figure 4-3).

You can post a description up to 250 characters, attach a profile photo, and add a 1,200-x-1,200-pixel cover photo if you like. Simply click Done editing to save all your changes.

FIGURE 4-3:
Edit your eBay profile page.

>> **Research your competition.** You can find out how to price your items, see which items are selling well, and determine which ones to stay away from. In the Search box, which is at the top of every eBay page, type the words that describe the item you want to sell and click Search. To see past sales, select the Sold Listings or Completed Listings check box after you perform your first search. You can then sort these past sales by price, from highest to lowest, and see a snapshot of how your item has sold on eBay in the past couple of weeks. You can also sort by distance to see how nearby competitors are doing, or sort by oldest or newest listings to get a sense of price levels over time.

Research not only shows you what to expect as a price for your item but also gives you the following useful information:

- Which keywords to use in describing your item
- Which category on eBay to place your item in
- Which features you should mention about your item
- The current level of supply and demand for this item on eBay

Here are the main questions you should answer while doing research:

- Are the items I want to sell doing well on eBay?
- Are the prices the items are selling for enough for me to make a profit?

If the answer to either question is no, you may want to find other items to sell instead, before you invest time and money on a product line that's wrong for eBay.

TIP

You can take advantage of lots of other eBay features and options that we don't cover here. Check out *eBay Business All-in-One For Dummies*, 4th Edition, by Marsha Collier (Wiley), for an authoritative and complete reference to using eBay.

Setting Up an Item for Sale

Many sales on eBay are auctions. You know the kind: 1, 2, 3, *Sold to the highest bidder!* But rather than wave their hands enthusiastically, bidders place a bid on your auction by using their computers. On eBay, you have the choice of offering your item for sale as an auction or for a fixed price, so the buyer can click and buy immediately.

Either way, you set up an item listing by getting an item or a product you want to sell, writing a description of the product and taking photos of it, and creating a web page with all the basic information about that product.

When you're trying to decide whether to list your item as an auction or at a fixed price, here are some of the top reasons to consider an auction:

» **Auctions attract people's interest.** Shopping on eBay has become more than a matter of buying items. It's a form of entertainment, with bidding, competing, and winning. After people bid on an item, they're more likely to follow the auction to its completion and stay emotionally invested in acquiring the item.

» **Auctions move merchandise faster.** When you sell items on your own store or by using an eBay store, it can take days, weeks, or even months to find the right buyer. With an eBay auction, you can sell an item in five to ten days, on average, and find your high bidder, and some interested underbidders, more quickly. Think of the auction as a call to action, where the buyers decide to respond.

» **Auctions cost the seller only money per item, not per month.** When you operate an eBay store, you're paying a monthly fee regardless of how many items you sell. In an eBay auction, you pay a small fee to list the item for sale, as low as 10 cents, and another fee if the item sells.

» **Auctions let you test the water.** Rather than launch a full-blown store for your items, you can run a few eBay auctions and gauge the interest of the buying community. You can get an idea of success before investing in website design and programming.

Of course, auctions have some drawbacks. The fees involved in running auctions can add up if you're continually trying to sell something that receives no bids. Although the short time frame of the auction helps move inventory, it's also quickly forgotten in the minds of the buyer. You have to run a lot of auctions to build the constant presence needed to remind buyers of who you are. Without repeat buyers and the constant flow of goods, it's hard to build a sustainable flow of revenue by putting up random auctions every week. Still, auctions provide an excellent piece of the overall e-commerce business plan.

The easiest way to get started on eBay is to plunge ahead and set up an item for sale. Look around your business inventory for something that you want to sell and follow these steps:

1. **Click the Sign In link at** www.ebay.com.

2. **Enter your user ID and password, and then click the Sign In button.**

3. **Click the Sell link at the top right of any eBay page.**

   If you're a new seller, eBay may ask for additional information, such as your address, postal code, and phone number, before you can sell an item. You will be taken to the eBay Seller Hub page, specifically the Manage Active Listings page.

4. **Click the blue Create Listing button to start a new listing.**

   You will be prompted to choose between Single Listing or Multiple Listings. For the purposes of this example, I will assume you click Single Listing.

5. **Type a few words that describe your item, and then click Get Started.**

   After you click Get Started, eBay prompts you with a list of similar products from its catalog.

6. **If you see your item among the list that is presented, click the Select button next to that item.**

   Based on the words you entered, eBay searches its catalog and offers up the items that most likely match the words you entered. You can always click the See Details link next to the item to learn more before selecting it. If eBay doesn't offer any appropriate items, you can click Continue without selecting a product button at the bottom of the page.

7. **Click Continue.**

   You will be taken to the Create Your Listing page, and depending on whether you selected an item from eBay's catalog, you will see some of these fields already prefilled with information.

8. **Enter these elements:**

- *Title:* Incorporate the most frequently used keywords about your item so that buyers who search eBay's database for an item like yours can find it.

- *Category:* eBay organizes all its products under an extensive catalog system, so pick the category and subcategories that best fit where your product should reside.

- *Condition:* For most items, eBay now requires the seller to specify a specific condition, whether it's New, Like New, or whatever level of Used item applies to that category and type of item.

- *UPC code:* eBay is making a big effort to add an identifier to every listing on its site, when it is possible. Any item that contains a UPC code or ISBN number, for example, should have that information inputted in the UPC/ISBN field provided.

9. **Add photos to your auction as follows:**

a. *Scroll down the page to the Photos section and click the Add Photos link.*

A second window opens, asking you to identify where on your computer the pictures for the auction are located.

b. *Select the pictures.*

You can attach up to 12 photos per listing, so don't be afraid to show off every angle, defect, or unique quality of the item.

c. *Click the Upload button to send the pictures from your computer to eBay.*

eBay requires at least one photo per listing, with a minimum pixel size of 500 x 500 pixels. Make sure your main picture is large enough to use in your listing.

10. **Scroll down to the Item Specifics section and complete as many fields as you can.**

These fields allow you to assign specific details to your product listing depending on what you're selling. (For example, every shoe has a size, width, and color.) The more details you enter in the boxes provided, the more easily buyers can find your item because eBay allows buyers to search based on Item Specifics.

11. **Scroll down to the Item Description section and enter a description.**

Remember to add not only a description of the item but also all your policies about payment and shipping methods, as well as a return policy. Use the buttons that eBay provides above the Description window to add bold, italic, or underlined text as well as bulleted or numbered lists.

12. **Decide whether you want to sell your item in an auction or with a fixed price:**

a. *Scroll down to the next section, Selling Details, and, next to Format, click Auction or Fixed Price from the list provided.*

b. *Enter your starting bid or a fixed price.*

You can either enter the starting price of your auction (and assign a Reserve price or Buy It Now price or both) or click the drop-down arrow next to List As and select Fixed Price to sell your items for a fixed Buy It Now price. With a fixed price, you can choose to receive Best Offers, in which buyers can offer you a price below your fixed price and you choose whether to accept, counteroffer, or decline their offer.

c. *Set the duration and number of items in your lot.*

WARNING

If you want to sell more than one lot at a time, you must use the fixed-price listing. eBay does not allow multiple identical lots to be auctioned at the same time.

13. **Scroll down to the next section and choose your payment and return options, and then scroll down to choose your shipping options (see Figure 4-4).**

For shipping options, you can sell your item to customers only in the United States or around the world. If you don't want to ship something (such as a heavy or fragile item), choose the No Shipping: Local Pickup Only option.

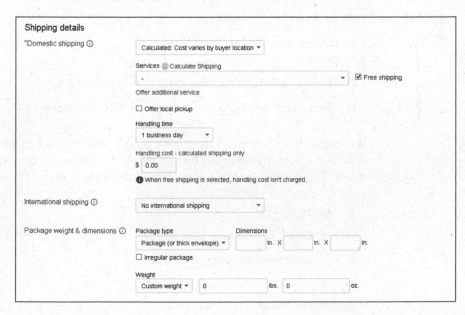

FIGURE 4-4:
You decide where in the world you're willing to ship your item.

TIP

You must enter a flat price for shipping or select Calculated from the drop-down list and let eBay calculate your postage costs based on the weight and the buyer's zip code.

14. **When everything looks good, scroll to the bottom of the page and click List Item.**

   Your listing goes live on the eBay site. If you want to fix something, go to your listing page and click Revise Your Item to return to the listing page and make corrections.

TIP

If you want to sell an additional similar item, you can click the Sell a Similar Item link to create a new auction, with all the information fields already filled in. You simply make the changes necessary for your second item and submit the new auction in a fraction of the time it took you to complete your first listing.

Maintaining your item listings

My eBay is your personal dashboard for monitoring your eBay buying and selling activity. You can get to that page by clicking the My eBay link, which appears at the top right of any eBay page. Instead of clicking that link, however, roll your cursor over it to view an expanded list of the various sections on the My eBay page, including Bids/Offers, Purchase History, and Selling. Click the Selling link to display the Seller Hub page and its distinct sections:

>> **Tasks:** Your to-do list showing what to complete

>> **Sales:** Your summary of sales

>> **Orders:** The status of all your current orders to fulfill and recent completed orders

>> **Listings:** Your items for sale, now or scheduled, on eBay

>> **Shortcuts:** Easy links to the most popular tasks for a seller

When you click the Active listings link (under the Listings header), you see a live snapshot of all items you have for sale on eBay: auction and fixed-price inventory items. This page shows you a lot of information about each item you're selling:

>> Current high bid

>> Number of bids that have been placed

>> Amount of time remaining in the auction

>> Number of people watching your item

>> Number of questions people have

When your item has completed the bidding stage, it appears on another page in My eBay's Seller Hub: Orders. This page provides a checklist of tasks you need to complete after the winning bidder has been determined. This way, you know what needs to be done for each item you sold.

Leaving feedback for your buyer

eBay buyers typically don't meet sellers, so these buyers require a level of trust to buy something sight unseen. eBay builds this trust by maintaining a feedback score, allowing the buyer to see the trading reputation of any eBay member instantly. Buying on eBay gives you a way to build a trading history and a positive reputation, which can help you as you start to sell on eBay.

SUCCESS ON eBay

Follow these guidelines to become successful on eBay:

- **Complete all fields to list your item on eBay.** Try to answer as many of the fields offered, from item specifics, to shipping and return policies, so eBay can properly display your item to all interested buyers. Select the condition of the item, the payment methods you accept, how you plan to ship the item, any return policies you offer, and any other item specifics you can provide. This improves the searchability of your item and increases the likelihood of a sale.

- **Write clear, concise descriptions.** Over half the shoppers on eBay are now using a mobile device to browse and buy, so a concise description is more key nowadays. Be sure to provide the key information your buyers want to know when they're making a decision about whether to buy your item. Therefore, use the Item Specifics fields to indicate the condition of the item (its functionality, make, manufacturer, brand name, and model number) and its physical characteristics (color, size, and weight), so your description doesn't have to repeat that information.

- **Define your shipping and return policies clearly.** eBay requires all sellers to specify defined shipping costs for all auctions, a defined handling time to process the auction, and a defined return policy for each auction. Therefore, think about your policies in advance, research the items your competitors are offering, and ensure that every auction you create has all its policies defined.

- **Add quality photos to your listings.** If a picture is worth a thousand words, it's worth even more on eBay because the buyer doesn't get to see the item until the bidding is over. Therefore, you want the best pictures you can produce: Blurry or dark photos just scare buyers away, and pictures that are too large take too long to appear can also turn buyers away.

For every transaction you participate in on eBay, whether you buy or sell, you're allowed to give feedback to the other party when the sale is completed. This feedback is aggregated into a numerical score for every eBay user, along with detailed seller ratings and a feedback record made up of comments from other users, as shown in Figure 4-5.

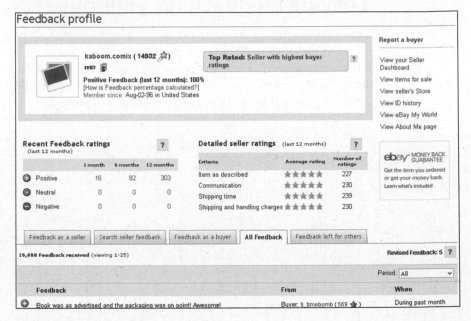

FIGURE 4-5: Feedback becomes your instant reputation on eBay.

As a buyer, you can leave three kinds of feedback for a seller:

>> **Positive:** Increases the feedback score by 1

>> **Neutral:** Doesn't affect the feedback score

>> **Negative:** Reduces the feedback score by 1

The seller is allowed to leave only positive feedback for the buyer or to report the buyer for not paying for the item. The feedback system is a way to report whether people complete transactions reasonably and fairly. It isn't supposed to be a complaint or vendetta forum, although some users see it that way. Positive feedback is left when the transaction was handled satisfactorily or if both parties worked out an agreement to resolve the transaction. Neutral or negative feedback should be reserved for only those transactions where sellers grossly misrepresent themselves and do absolutely nothing to correct the situation.

In addition, buyers can rate their sellers on four different dimensions of the transaction, using a scale from 1 to 5. These detailed seller ratings, or DSRs, are designed to weed out bad sellers and reward good sellers. The buyer can rate the seller based on these criteria:

>> **Item as described:** How closely does the item resemble its description in the auction? (A score of 5 means the same item, and 1 means grossly different.)

>> **Communication:** Did the seller communicate with you, as the buyer, sufficiently during the process? (A score of 5 means yes, and 1 means silence.)

>> **Shipping time:** How quickly from your payment (as the buyer) did the item arrive to you? (A score of 5 means a quick turnaround time, and 1 means that you waited a long time.)

>> **Shipping-and-handling charges:** Did the seller charge you a fair price to package and ship the item to you, based on the category average? (A score of 5 means that it was reasonable, and 1 means that it was outrageous.) If the seller offered free shipping, this option is not available to the buyer.

Every buyer's rating is then aggregated and shown on the seller's feedback page as a set of stars, from 1 to 5, as long as 10 buyers have responded in the past 3 or 12 months. Seller status and benefits are partially based on maintaining very high DSRs in all four dimensions.

WARNING

Feedback is rarely altered after it's given, so think carefully before giving feedback. If you're having a dispute with the other party, try to work out the situation before leaving feedback.

Every member's feedback score is represented next to his or her user ID, along with color-coded stars after the score reaches 10. Multiple feedback from the same person in the same week increases the score by only 1, so if Aunt Sally buys ten items from you at one time, it raises your score by only 1 point. If she buys one item per week, you receive multiple feedback credit for multiple sales, even if it's to the same buyer.

Opening an eBay Store

An eBay store is an interesting combination of eBay sales and your own e-commerce store. Think of owning an eBay store as owning a small shingle under eBay's massive marketplace.

With an eBay store, you benefit from these features:

>> **A dedicated e-commerce storefront:** You can direct your customers to one place, which you can advertise on any printed material you send to customers worldwide. Then you can see exactly which pages, which items, and which deals your customers looked at the most, so that you can see what's working and what's boring.

An eBay store can significantly increase your sales because it gives you another mechanism for reaching customers. Every time you sell an item on eBay, you can point the winner (and all your other bidders) to your eBay store to buy additional merchandise.

>> **The chance to sell many items on eBay with a lower fee structure:** You can list thousands of items in your eBay store at a lower insertion cost than listing each item without an eBay store. In addition, you're charged a lower sales fee (or final value fee) when an item sells in your store.

>> **Sales and marketing tools to sell your items:** If something doesn't sell right away, you can use a program called Markdown Manager to put an item (or an entire category of items) on sale by temporarily discounting the fixed price.

eBay Stores give you a place to sell your products online under a fixed address, but they also come with many other features to make your business more successful. Here's a look at five features that can assist you with running your eBay store:

>> **Sales reports:** On a month-by-month or three-month basis, review key numbers such as average sales price per item, sold items percentage, and repeat buyer percentage.

>> **Cross Promotion tool:** You can specify which of your items for sale is shown to potential customers when they're looking at one of your items. For example, if someone looks at a pair of your skis for sale, you can use the Cross Promotion tool to display boots, poles, and goggles.

>> **Advertising templates:** You can download these templates to create business cards, stationery, envelopes, flyers, and more.

>> **Coordinating active customer lists with email marketing:** The email newsletter function also helps you handle the mass email of marketing items, such as your monthly newsletter or sales announcements.

>> **Traffic reports:** Find out exactly which pages in your store receive the most traffic, which search words are used most often in store searches, and which inventory items are selling most quickly.

Have we sold you on running an eBay store? Well, before you do so, you need to know that you have to pay eBay some additional fees for the glory. Your very own eBay store ranges in price from $7.95 to $349.95 per month on average, depending on its functionality and placement. If you're running a small business, you can do quite well with the Starter or Basic package or the slightly more expensive Premium package, which includes bonus features for marketing and tracking your store. If you want to list thousands of items for sale at any time and want the lowest insertion fee structure, you may want to consider the (pricey) Anchor store plan. After you pay for a store subscription, you can add a set amount of items to your store for no insertion fee. (If you exceed your set amount, adding more items to your store costs 5 to 30 cents per listing per month that it's listed.) When the item sells, you pay a commission to eBay based on the category of the item.

Setting up shop

You retain a lot of control with your eBay store. Plus, you can study your customers' shopping habits. If you're ready to have your own eBay storefront, here's what you need to know.

REMEMBER

You have to have an active eBay seller's account with a minimum of 30 positive feedback comments, a credit card on file, and a PayPal Premier or Business account in good standing to open an eBay store. Try to build up your feedback score and gain some experience before opening an eBay store.

Before you open your store, make sure that you have these items lined up:

>> A good name chosen for your store; this name can be (and usually should be) different from your eBay user ID

>> A store inventory sufficient to make having a store worthwhile

>> The knowledge that you can handle the extra work of selling merchandise at any given time

When you're ready, go to stores.ebay.com, and follow these steps to open your store:

1. **On the Stores home page, click the Open a Store link.**

2. **Click the Subscribe Now button.**

3. **If necessary, log in with your user ID and password.**

   A Subscription Level page opens.

4. **Choose your subscription level.**

Your buyers won't know your store subscription level because all the core functionality comes with the Starter platform. Most sellers who are starting out choose the Starter ($7.95 per month) or Basic option ($27.95 per month) and later move up to the Premium level when they want to do more online marketing with their stores.

5. **Scroll down the page, and enter your store name in the box provided, and then click Continue.**

You can use as many as 35 characters for your store name, so choose wisely. Don't infringe on any copyrighted name, especially the word *eBay,* but make it memorable.

The Review and Submit page opens.

6. **Agree to the terms and click Subscribe.**

Your store is live!

Managing your store

After you sign up for an eBay store, it's time to get in there, spruce it up with some colors, logos, and products, and open it for business. At any time, you can manage your eBay store by clicking one of two links:

>> From your store's home page, scroll to the bottom of the page and click the Seller, Manage Store link.

>> From the eBay Stores home page, click the Manage My Store link.

The Manage My Store page opens, as shown in Figure 4-6. From here, you have access to the main features of your store, including but not limited to the ones in the following list:

>> **Store design:** Use the Display Settings option to choose from many preformatted templates that you can use for your eBay store design. You can define as many as 300 custom store categories, such as Top Picks of the Month or Gifts Under $10. If you want to add several pages to your store, such as a policies or shipping page, use the Custom Pages link.

>> **Store marketing:** You can control any email marketing campaigns you want to run for your eBay store. eBay helps coordinate any customer lists you build, coordinates the mass emailings of newsletters and special promotions, helps design flyers, and distributes product information. See Book 6, Chapter 3 for more general information about running an email marketing campaign.

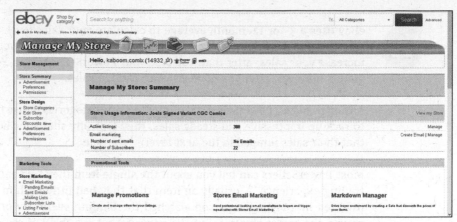

FIGURE 4-6:
The central hub
for updating your
eBay store.

>> **Item promotion:** When you link your items and set cross-promotion rules, this function controls it all. You can specify rules and preferences for how your items should be cross-promoted throughout your store, and set up favorites to appear as featured items on your store's home page.

>> **Logos and branding:** When you have a custom logo, use this function header to upload the logo to customized email messages that you use to communicate with your customers.

For a full, in-depth explanation of maximizing your eBay store experience, you can't go wrong with *Starting an eBay Business For Dummies,* 4th Edition, by Marsha Collier. This book is full of tips, tricks, and techniques that you can use to make your eBay store shine.

Becoming a PowerSeller

eBay has a special term for people who sell a steady amount of merchandise every month, earn a high amount of positive feedback, and comply with all eBay listing policies: *PowerSellers.* eBay has different levels of PowerSellers, starting with Bronze ($1,000 per month) and going all the way up to Titanium ($150,000 per month). Every PowerSeller has to maintain at least a 98 percent positive feedback rating with a minimum of 100 feedback comments earned on his or her account, and create at least four listings per month. When you qualify, eBay sends you an invitation to accept your PowerSeller status.

After you become a PowerSeller, eBay has another classification called Top Rated Seller, reserved for those PowerSellers with exceptional feedback and DSR scores. Top Rated Sellers qualify for special benefits, such as a discount on their sales (or final value) fees.

eBay uses a 3- or 12-month average to calculate your sales level. If your average sales level drops below the PowerSeller minimum, eBay gives you one month to increase your sales; after that, you lose your PowerSeller status. You can be reinstated, however, after you increase your average sales.

Although not all PowerSellers focus on the same categories or use the same means to rack up impressive and steady sales, they typically share one bond (the reason that their sales jumped to the next level): "the sale."

Most PowerSellers can tell you about the single item they sold early in their eBay trading experience — usually an item that they had little faith in or little money invested in. Maybe the person watched the bidding every day or every hour, or maybe she forgot about it. But she never forgot the thrill of seeing the high bid when the auction was over, and that's how she became hooked. She then invested the time and figured out the different techniques to work her way up to PowerSeller status.

After you achieve PowerSeller status, your focus is on every sale, not just a single memorable sale. To keep track of the growing number of sales and customers, many PowerSellers look into using a third-party tool. You might try a program such as SixBit (www.sixbit.com), which can help you manage listings and sales activities. If you carry a large volume, try an Enterprise solution from ChannelAdvisor (www.channeladvisor.com) to manage your sales across eBay and any other channels where you sell online, with every sale combined into easy-to-read reports.

For the ultimate source in third-party tools, check out eBay's Solutions Directory at http://solutions.ebay.com.

Chapter 5

Posting Pictures for Profit

A s social media has developed over the years, along with improved technology to support larger and larger flows of data (especially from smartphones and tablets), you've probably noticed the shift to more pictures and videos being shared instead of just words and web links. If the old adage is true — "A picture is worth a thousand words" — then the amount of communication has gone way up with the times. One of the most popular uses of social media was the sharing of photographs, and from that desire, a new social media website was developed. Instagram was developed specifically to allow people to easily share their favorite pictures with whomever is interested, at any time.

Today, Instagram is one of the most heavily trafficked social media sites out there. It helps users share photographs, videos, curated stories, and even live streaming. Every Instagram user has a feed that contains everything she posts to the site. When an Instagram user opens up the app, she can see a collection of posts from everyone that she's following on Instagram. (Because of the growth in usage, Instagram now uses an algorithm to decide which posts show up on a user's screen, so users can't see every post in chronological order like they did in the early days of Instagram.) Instagram became so popular that Facebook acquired it but had Instagram operate with its own identity and user base, separate from Facebook's main service. Mainly, users interact with Instagram strictly on their mobile devices (though some access from a laptop or desktop computer is possible).

Naturally, when businesses (of all sizes) see lots of potential customers getting together and communicating, they become interested in joining the conversation and either sharing information about their businesses or even making some money from direct product sales. Instagram understands that desire and has the capability for you to create a professional profile that comes with extra features geared for the needs of business owners, from extra contact options for customers, to increased analytic capabilities to improve business performance while on the service.

REMEMBER

If you want to get more in depth on the power of Instagram, you can always check out *Instagram For Business For Dummies*, by Jenn Herman, Corey Walker, and Eric Butow (Wiley).

In this chapter, we cover the basics of Instagram and what you need to know as an online business owner. Specifically, we cover building your profile, developing a community around your account, the different types of content you can post (from pictures to videos and more), and the direct commerce elements that could benefit your product sales.

Establishing Your Instagram Account

When you're ready to use Instagram, you'll need to have a mobile device handy, because the registration process needs to happen on that device, not a laptop or desktop computer. Setting up your account starts with a trip to either the iOS App Store (for Apple iOS devices) or Google Play Store (for Android users) to download the Instagram app. After you've downloaded the app, open it and follow the instructions to create a new account.

WARNING

You can log into Instagram using an existing Facebook account, but it's recommended that you create a new Instagram account so you can take full advantage of all the features that come with an Instagram account.

When you go to create your account, here are some tips to keep in mind when completing your Instagram profile:

>> **Your username should reflect your business's name, not your personal name.** Instagram will show your business name along with your username, but it's important that your username be relevant and memorable to people who are interacting with your business. The web address (officially known as a URL) of your new Instagram account is simply www.instagram.com/*yourusername*,

so you want to brand this URL for your business, not yourself. Like many other websites, your username has to be unique, so if someone else already took the name you wanted, you'll need to make your username unique. If you pick the same username as your Twitter handle, when your content is tagged and shared on Twitter, the username will link to your Twitter bio.

TIP

Because your Instagram username is just going to be one long string of characters, make sure that it's readable. If your business were named Joel's Comics, you could go with joelscomics, joels.comics, joels_comics, and so on, because you are allowed to incorporate periods, underscores, and numbers into your Instagram username.

>> **Have the web link in your bio go straight to your online business.** You're allowed to include one web address as part of the bio for your Instagram account. For an online store, point people directly to your store. Try to customize the link so you can later learn how much traffic is coming from Instagram to your main online store. (We discuss analytics more in Book 6, Chapter 5.)

TECHNICAL STUFF

You can use a website called a *link shortener* to create a unique URL for your Instagram bio. Two of the more popular choices are Google Link Shortener (`http://goo.gl`) and Bit.ly (`http://bit.ly`).

>> **Your personal and business Instagram accounts should be separate.** Your online store can (and should) have a personality and interact with people for fun, as well as commerce, but if you like to use Instagram personally, have a separate account for your personal use. The last thing you need is for a potential customer to be offended or confused by the personal photos and interactions that would show up on your personal feed.

Whether you're going to convert an existing personal account to a professional account, or you're signing up for Instagram for the first time, here are the steps to make sure you have a business account:

1. **Log into Instagram or, if you haven't created an account yet, follow the steps to create a new account until you get to your Welcome to Instagram home screen (shown in Figure 5-1).**

2. **Click the People icon in the lower-right corner of your screen to go to your Profile screen.**

3. **From the profile screen, click the three-lines icon in the upper-right corner to bring up a menu of options, as shown in Figure 5-2.**

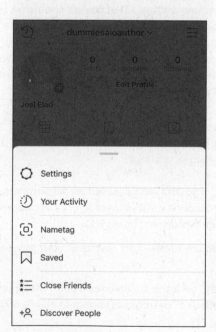

4. **Tap Settings.**

   The Settings menu appears.

5. **Tap Account.**

   You see a list of Account options, as shown in Figure 5-3.

base

FIGURE 5-3:
The Account
screen.

6. **Tap the Switch to Professional Account link.**

   Instagram asks if you're a Creator or Business.

7. **Tap Business and then tap Next.**

   Instagram informs you about the Insights functionality, and then, if it detects your Facebook account on the mobile device, it prompts you to connect your Facebook page, as shown in Figure 5-4

FIGURE 5-4:
Instagram is able
to connect your
business account
with your
Facebook page.

8. **If you're ready to connect your Facebook page, select the radio button next to the correct page (if you have more than one page) and tap Next to associate your Facebook page with your Instagram account.**

    Later in the chapter, we cover how to create Instagram Shoppable Posts. One of those requirements is an associated Facebook page.

    If you don't want to connect to Facebook, tap the Don't Connect to Facebook Now link to proceed.

9. **Provide your business contact information on the new screen that appears, as shown in Figure 5-5.**

    Instagram business accounts allow you to have a contact phone number, email address, and physical address for your Instagram followers to learn more about your business and reach out to you directly. Especially if you have a bricks-and-mortar store, it's advantageous to complete as much of this information as you feel comfortable providing.

10. **Tap Done to complete the process.**

Congratulations! You've now got an Instagram business account and you're ready to move forward. Be sure to complete your profile and bio, add a profile photo, and start following people before you really start posting on Instagram.

FIGURE 5-5:
Instagram can provide your contact info for customers to find on Instagram.

Enticing Customers to Your Instagram Offering

As you build it, it's not automatic that "the customers will come." You'll need to market and promote your efforts on Instagram, because you're competing with hundreds of millions of other users for people's attention. Thankfully, Instagram is one of the most popular sites and its visual nature creates an addictive way to stay "top of mind" with potential customers and buyers, so using the site correctly will help you reach your goals.

However, there are other steps you should consider as you build your account and grow your following on Instagram. Depending on the type of business and your specific goals, you won't have to follow every single tip, but any new or thriving Instagram account should keep the following in mind to gain success on the platform.

Publicizing your Instagram presence

Make a big deal about your presence on Instagram by showing off the name of your Instagram profile — and the web address of your Instagram profile — when you talk about your business. Adding a social media button for Instagram to your website, alongside your Facebook, Twitter, and any other social media accounts, is a natural first step. We're not saying that you have to draw 6-foot letters on the wall or plaster the windows with your Instagram address, but you should definitely incorporate your online store name and URL in all your store literature and promotional space.

This opportunity to promote your e-store includes items such as

>> **Business cards:** If you've got the space, consider adding the Instagram icon and your profile name or complete URL as part of the info on your business card. You could even include a business card in the box with every existing customer's purchase.

>> **Sales flyers:** Integrate your Instagram profile address into every flyer, usually along the bottom. Add a blurb on the flyer that says "Check us out on Instagram at. . . ." On the flyer, perhaps you can include any special "Instagram-only" discount codes that allow the customer to shop with you through Instagram at the same discount.

>> **Offline (in-person) counter displays and physical receipts:** If you have a bricks-and-mortar store alongside your online store, in addition to keeping your business cards or flyers prominently displayed next to the cash register or check-out area, put a sign on your cash register, and perhaps add a small counter display with a brochure or one-page flyer that someone can pick up and read while waiting to check out or take home.

>> **Invoices or receipts:** Customers may throw away your order boxes, your business cards, and your sales flyers, but they're likely to look at their invoice receipts again — at least once. Include your Instagram web address on the receipt.

>> **Live events:** When you set up at a convention, exhibition, or local event, your booth signage (along with dedicated literature handouts) can direct people to your Instagram presence as one way to connect to you.

>> **Print media:** Some people say that print is dead, but niche magazines and newspapers still cater to specific markets. Whether you run an advertisement in these media, write a guest article, or contribute to a "vendor directory" or other list, mentioning your Instagram address is another great way to move potential customers online.

Mentioning your Instagram profile's name isn't limited to including it on literature and promotional materials. Train your sales associates to casually mention your Instagram account when talking with customers. This reference can be a simple statement made to customers during checkout — for example, "Hey, you can also follow us on Instagram at *@YourInstagramName*." Or when a customer asks about an item, have your employees say, "You know, we just featured that item on our Instagram account with a special sale. You can go check it out at *@YourInstagramName*."

Displaying your online goods in your Instagram feed

Although promoting your Instagram presence is the first step, it surely isn't the last. One of the benefits you enjoy as an online store owner is that you've already got pictures of your online goods for your website, many of which can (possibly) be reused for your Instagram account! Given Instagram users' expectation of high-quality, eye-catching pictures, you may want to create new images or enhance current images to make them more appealing to this discerning audience, but with any luck, you won't have to start from scratch.

The most important thing to remember when adding photos to your Instagram account is this: You will *not* be simply adding product images, as is, on a regular basis and expect any measure of success. Some products may sell themselves, but there will need to be some level of customization or thought that goes into how you present yourself and get your customers excited about products you're promoting or selling through your Instagram account.

TIP

One of the best ways to get an idea of how you want to use photos on your Instagram account is to look for similar accounts that are already on Instagram and study how they position their products and get their customers excited or ready to buy through Instagram. Later in the chapter, in the section "Following the right people," we talk about studying other accounts for potential plans of action.

TIP

Before you post your first picture, come up with an overall strategy or purpose to your Instagram account. Look around, pretend you're a potential buyer, and see what your competition is doing. Then ask yourself whether you consider their actions appealing or unappealing. Decide on the tone and theme you want to take that will best fit with your business model and the products you're hoping to sell through Instagram.

TIP

Here are some specific ideas to keep in mind as far as what appeals to Instagram users interacting with businesses on the platform:

>> **Show them something they haven't seen, like behind the scenes content, sneak previews, or bonus information.** Any catalog can list the title, price, and stock image of a product. Instagram users are looking for more, specifically things they haven't seen before or can't see on a regular basis.

That's how you'll keep them hooked! By including them in the process, they're not just an average shopper — they're part of the process and more emotionally invested in your brand. They consider themselves "insiders" and build a relationship with your brand, which encourages purchases when they're ready to buy. Consider announcing sales or promotions on Instagram before your other social media channels or website, to give your Instagram users a sense of importance or priority.

>> **Use video or Instagram stories to make a product come to life for the viewer.** Previously, a static image of the product was the main way a product was "sold" to a potential buyer. Today, with the use of video clips and Instagram stories, you can demonstrate a product in use or a slideshow of images that tell the story much better than one or two static product images. We discuss video and Instagram stories in more depth in the later section "Providing Great Content and Community for Your Instagram Feed," later in this chapter.

>> **The visuals need to be striking, beautiful, or dynamic.** On Instagram, you're judged solely on the visual appeal of the pictures you post, so posting the highest-quality photo possible should pay off for you. Anything you can do to enhance the visual appeal is important, even if it means hiring a professional to either take or tweak the images you have to work with on Instagram. There are also filters and other tools available to enhance or differentiate your pictures before posting them to Instagram.

>> **Get your users involved.** Many companies feature customers using or wearing the products that the company is trying to sell, which comes across as more "authentic" to other users seeing this content — user-generated content is a positive endorsement for your brand. If other people are excited to use or wear your products, new buyers are more likely to try them.

TIP

One way of adding content to your Instagram feed is to repost any images from your Instagram followers. This practice, known as *regramming,* and it indicates that you're responsive to your audience and encourages those followers to continue to promote your brand to their followers. Just make sure you acknowledge credit of that image to the follower you're reposting images from first!

>> **Don't forget to include some form of a call to action.** It may be easier to focus on excitement and inclusion, but at the end of the day, you need to remind people of your goals by including some form of a call to action, whether it's reminding them to click the link in your bio for more information, including a promo code with information on how and where to buy an item, or asking for a reshare, like, or comment on the post. Not every post has to end with an actual sale, but the more engagement and promotion you can generate, the better your long-term future on Instagram.

Providing Great Content and Community for Your Instagram Feed

Now that you've thought about your strategy and prepped your Instagram account and list of users that you're following, it's time to start posting some content. In the subsequent sections, we cover the most popular types of content that you can post on Instagram, with some specific thoughts and tips for each category.

But in general, when posting content on Instagram, regardless of type, keep these points in mind:

» **Be consistent.** Many successful brands post once or twice per day, and that's it except for a rare special event or promotion. The key is to be consistent without flooding your users' feeds. You may experiment with the time of day you post to find an optimal time, but regular, consistent content posting is the way to win people over. It's quality over quantity, every time.

» **Your imagery needs to be uniform and match the color palette of your business.** Think about the color scheme of your logo, website, even the profile photo you use for your Instagram account, and the content you're posting. The actual photos or videos will change, but you want them to appear similar enough to match your branding effort. This creates a visual cue for your followers — when they see your color scheme, fonts, and so on, they'll instinctively know it's your brand, and not just some random post.

» **Set some goals or objectives.** In the beginning, your main goal will probably be learning the power of Instagram, building your initial following, and trying out different content. After a while, don't be afraid to set some specific goals, whether it's to increase followers, increase engagement on your posts, or some other metric that matters to your business. Trial and error will be a part of your plan, but random content posting, or throwing that proverbial spaghetti against the wall is not a good long-term strategy.

Focusing on pictures first

When Instagram started in 2010, it was a way for users to share pictures with each other, and that core mission hasn't disappeared. Instagram has about a billion users, and combined, they're posting billions of photos on a daily basis. According to Pew Research, over half of Instagram users check their account at least once a day, with 35 percent of accounts checking multiple times per day.

Many times, whether it's for minutes or hours, users are mindlessly scrolling through their feeds, checking out all the cool photos that people they follow have posted on Instagram. The visual element is more important than the caption or comments. Many users have to like or feel a connection to a particular photo to stop and interact with it.

Given the importance that photos have on Instagram, and users' desire to see cool, interesting, and beautiful things, there has been a growth in the use of specific tools to enhance and customize the photos for maximum attention. The most popular tool, called a *filter*, changes or enhances a photograph before it's posted on Instagram. Today, there are hundreds of filters, from the simple filters that auto-correct the zoom, brightness, shading, background color, and other image effects, to Snapchat filters that can add animal elements to your face, or animated effects that make your picture literally pop on the screen and become more playful, cute, and likely to be clicked!

Altering your photo doesn't have to stop with filters. There are lots of image-editing software options out there that you can use to help achieve that consistent branding we discuss earlier, and to make sure the photos are distinctive and eye-catching. Consult a graphic designer or photographer for more advice in this area, if needed. Because many of the photos you use will be captured on your mobile device and posted directly to Instagram, adding other photo-editing apps to your device, such as VSCO or Snapseed, could be a smart move.

Finally, based on your goals and the story you're deciding to tell, make sure the photos you post help tell that story, whether it's a designed infographic sharing some statistics, a posed photo of your product or employees, or reusing design elements like flyers, advertisements, or other graphics that are part of your online store or business.

Adding comments and hashtags

Words still matter on Instagram. People will hopefully be commenting on your posts. And you should be using hashtags to get your content noticed and help people find your content when they're searching for something interesting on Instagram.

You can only include letters, numbers, and emoji in a hashtag if you want it to work, so avoid any non-numerical characters, such as &, !, ?, _, and more.

As of this writing, Instagram allows up to 30 hashtags per post or comment. This way, you can include general hashtags and then add more specific hashtags when necessary. You don't have to use 30 hashtags every single time — many posts only require a few hashtags to communicate their relevance. If you flood every post with popular hashtags to gain visibility, you run the risk of getting attention for one picture that earn likes but won't lead to followers of your brand or product sales.

TIP

Some tips to keep in mind when creating hashtags:

>> **Brainstorm keywords and phrases** that are important to your brand and are most used by your customers and competition.

>> **Check your online store analytics** to see which search terms are the most popular when customers are looking for your online store, as those terms should carry over as relevant hashtags for your products.

>> **Use specific or niche hashtags** to draw a more focused, targeted, and relevant user base that will be more receptive to your content. (That said, a popular hashtag used sparingly on the most important posts shouldn't hurt you either.)

>> **Create unique hashtags when appropriate,** especially if you want to track specific campaigns or initiatives around a promotion, contest, or sale.

>> **Add the hashtags in the first comment of the post,** so it doesn't overpower your caption.

>> **Be consistent and use the same hashtags between your Instagram, Facebook, Twitter, and other social media accounts** to create a cross-platform synergy.

After you've tagged your photos with hashtags and posted your content with a caption, you're not necessarily done. When an item is posted, you can immediately start adding comments to the post, for a variety of reasons. As mentioned earlier, you might add the hashtags in the first comment, so it doesn't overpower the caption. Or, you may want to tag or highlight other Instagram users to see the post, or acknowledge their effort or contribution.

TIP

Make sure the other users get notified when you mention them, by making sure you include their @*username* in your response. That way, Instagram will notify them of your comment.

Following the right people

As you grow your Instagram following, it's important to recognize that it's just as important for you (and your business) to figure out who you plan to follow on Instagram yourself. Following the right people can help you do research and advance your own goals. Plus, it gets you out there with people who may follow you back and grow your following.

There are three core demographics you should follow on Instagram as you start out:

REMEMBER

» **Your closest competitors:** Odds are, you won't be the only business in your space to have an Instagram account. The good news is that you can follow your competitors and gain firsthand knowledge of what's working for them on the platform. Keep an eye on what kinds of content they're posting to Instagram, how often they post, and which of their posts receive the most likes and comments. It's good research that can pay off as you perfect your own content strategy and posting schedule.

When deciding on a potential competitor to follow, look at a number of factors — from its length of time on the site, to its total number of posts, regular posting schedule, and use of hashtags and captions with its content.

» **Potential customers:** Take a look at what Instagram users are posting and the hashtags they're using to mark their posts. See if there are potential customers who enjoy or use the products in your space, and follow their accounts. Similar to following your competition, following potential customers gives you an idea of what they like and comment on, and what they ignore or don't do. In addition, a number of Instagram followers will follow you back after you follow them, which just helps grow your own following with people already targeted to the interests you want in a following.

TIP

When you follow potential customers, don't forget to actually like and comment on their posts as well. Approach this interaction as trying to get to know them, not a hard sell. Comment on their recent posts, and especially their least active content to show you care. Positive interaction will help encourage them to check out your account and follow you back.

» **Influencers who could help promote you in the future:** *Influencers* (people with a large following who have a lot of sway, or influence, over what their audience likes and buys) can be a huge asset. Start by following them to get an idea of how they operate and the interactions they get from their following. Later, if you want to pursue some advertising or advanced strategies, and they're open to being hired, approach them for a potential marketing campaign for your business.

TIP

One other approach that a number of businesses have used for their Instagram accounts is to get other people to contribute to their content feed, which is normally referred as having *guest contributors*. Highlighting your current or potential user base is a great way to generate excitement amongst your followers. Having established experts or influencers contribute some content that somehow features your business or product line can provide a fresh alternative to the normal business content you're posting. As you build up your list of who to follow on Instagram, keep in mind which of these people might make a good guest contributor to your own business account.

Harnessing the power of video

If a picture is worth a thousand words, it stands to wonder what the worth is of a video file, which is, in essence, a sequential collection of individual photo stills that tell a story. With the growth of Instagram, YouTube, Facebook Live, and many other streaming options, along with better technology and advanced smartphones and tablets, video has quickly become a preferred format for communication. Therefore, Instagram allows you to share video content, as well as regular pictures, but there are some restrictions to keep in mind. As of this writing, Instagram will only stream the first 60 seconds of any video you post to your feed, so keep that in mind when creating and posting any video. If you add a video to your Instagram story, Instagram will only show the first 15 seconds of that video.

One option for posting videos to your Instagram feed is called Instagram Live, which is exactly what it sounds like: You post a live video file from your Instagram app in real time. You can't edit these files, and they're only available for 24 hours after you post the video, similar to Instagram Stories. However, because there's no editing, it's easy to implement: You just point, shoot, and record, and the file gets posted to your feed when you're done.

If you want to use longer video files up to 10 minutes, to promote your business or product sales, there is a feature that you can use to post these longer video files and gain attention: Instagram TV (IGTV). Although IGTV has its own app for viewing these videos, it's also embedded in the Instagram app for viewing as well. There are a number of marketing avenues you can use with IGTV, from hosting Q&A sessions about your business, to posting how-to demonstrations, to interacting with the people behind your products and brand, and much, much more. You can edit your video files in advance and include enhancements like embedded stickers, polls, and other interactive elements.

Creating Instagram stories for your business

There's a special kind of content that Instagram has created that can provide a lot of exposure for your business when followers go to their feed, and it's called Instagram stories. In essence, Instagram stories is a curated collection of photos and/or short video files (along with some creative captions and special overlays you can add) that you share to your story file, not the normal feed of content. You can share to your story at various times, or put it together all at once. It sits at the top of the screen and is only available to other Instagram users for 24 hours after you post content to the story.

This kind of ephemeral content is appealing to Instagram users for a number of reasons, including but not limited to the following:

>> Instagram stories show up at the top of user's feeds in a circle, so it's easy to access.

>> It's considered "fresh" because it's only temporary, so users may feel that it's urgent and want to check it out so they don't miss out.

>> You can share your Instagram story as a message to another user, which can increase the likelihood of that person not only viewing the story, but replying or responding to it, which drives up engagement.

>> You can time your Instagram story to promote an upcoming event, sales promotion, or breaking news that affects your industry.

REMEMBER

Although Instagram stories disappear 24 hours after you post them to your Instagram feed, you can store the files locally, and retool them for future use. You can also save them as Highlights on your Instagram profile, so people can view them later.

As of mid–2018, Instagram said that more than 400 million Instagram users were enjoying Instagram stories on a daily basis, making it one of the most popular features on their platform after only two years of implementation. When you add to your story, Instagram will add a purple circle around your profile photo, which is another signal to other Instagram users that you've added to your story and encourage them to check it out.

So, now that we've covered the popularity and usefulness of Instagram stories, the natural next question is what kind of content makes a good Instagram story? Although there is no one correct answer, here are some of the popular ways that other businesses have used Instagram stories:

>> **To provide product demonstrations or tutorials:** Because you can attach one or more video files that are 15 seconds in length, you can create step-by-step guides or show off the actual use or operation of a product you're selling. Many users enjoy watching videos of how a product works so they can learn how to properly use it.

>> **To run a contest or giveaway:** *Free* is a very powerful four-letter word for people. You can use an Instagram story to establish a contest or giveaway for your followers, by setting up the rules, showing off the prizes, and asking for engagement with various requirements (such as following your account or tagging their friends in the comments section) in order to participate in the contest or giveaway. If done correctly, a contest or giveaway can generate

engagement (which Instagram will favor when deciding what content to feature) and expand your list of followers.

>> **To promote limited-edition or timed sales:** Because Instagram stories are temporary, it's a perfect avenue for promoting a limited-time sale or product offering to your followers, which you can enhance with defined deadlines for the end of a sale. It can reinforce the need for your Instagram followers to pay attention to your stories for future specials and offers.

>> **To provide slice-of-life or in-the-moment videos that demonstrate the human side of your business:** Your Instagram feed should be more than just product sales and pure business. If you can capture a certain moment with a video or photo that shows customer interaction; something behind the scenes before, during, or after a special event; or even a day in the life of your employees, partners, or customers, you show something natural, organic, and exciting to attract attention and please your audience so they enjoy interacting with you on Instagram, which can lead to better engagement when you go for the sale.

Making Money through Product Sales on Instagram

Posting Pictures for Profit

Throughout this chapter, we cover a lot of basics and overall strategies about how to use Instagram to improve your business. In this section, we cover a specific topic that adds actual dollars and cents to your bottom line: direct product sales on your Instagram feed. When customers come to your online store, they view one or more pictures of a product, see a price, and have a method to commit to that purchase, mainly through a Buy or Add to Cart button. When customers look at your Instagram feed, they can have a similar experience.

The easiest and most "low-tech" way to accomplish this is by simply posting a picture of the product on your feed, and mentioning the price in the caption or first comment of the post. You can direct people to the URL in your bio to buy the item, or ask interested buyers to enter a comment indicating that they want to purchase that item. You could take it further by having an auction where buyers "outbid" each other by leaving comments of their current high bid until a predetermined end time, where the highest bid listed in a comment wins the item. When the sale is complete, you can send a direct message to the interested buyer with payment and invoice information on how to complete the sale.

There are apps that can help you with posting and managing product sales through your Instagram feed. Two of the more popular ones, as of this writing, are CommentSold (www.commentsold.com) and Inselly (www.inselly.com), and they work in conjunction with you to handle the mechanics of making sales happen on your Instagram feed. Some Instagram users create a special "Instagram-friendly" shoppable product page on their store that they use as their URL in their Instagram profile to direct interested buyers.

Instagram, in conjunction with its owner, Facebook, has created a program called Instagram Shoppable Posts where you're able to actually tag a product featured in your Instagram post that ties back to your catalog of products. Potential customers see a shopping bag icon embedded in the post, and they're able to tap that icon to reveal more information about the product and be directed to a URL where they can directly shop your online store and purchase the product.

As of this writing, there are a number of requirements that you need to meet in order to submit your account for approval into this program:

>> **You need an Instagram professional account,** not a personal account.

>> **You need to have a corresponding Facebook business page** to link to your Instagram business account.

>> **You need to connect your Instagram business account to a valid Facebook product catalog.** You can use Facebook Catalog Manager or Business Manager to create your catalog, or use platforms such as BigCommerce or Shopify that can provide you with a valid catalog.

>> **Your primary form of business has to be selling physical goods.** This may change in the future, but currently, your primary avenue of revenue needs to be the sale of physical products only.

>> **You must agree to Instagram's merchant agreement and commerce policies.** Instagram will prompt you with a link to review these items when you sign up.

After you've met the requirements, you can submit your Instagram account for approval to enable Instagram Shopping on your account. When you're ready, just follow these steps:

1. Open the Instagram app on your mobile device.

2. Tap the three-line icon on the home screen to bring up your options.

3. Tap the Settings icon (it looks like a gear wheel).

4. Tap Business.

5. Tap Shopping on Instagram.

Instagram goes through several steps to make sure your account is ready, and then you submit your account for review. Instagram will notify you whether your account is approved. If approved, you follow these steps:

1. Open the Instagram app on your mobile device.

2. Tap the three-line icon on the home screen to bring up your options.

3. Tap the Settings icon (it looks like a gear wheel).

4. Tap Business.

5. Tap Shopping on Instagram.

6. Select the product catalog that will be tied to your Instagram business account.

7. Tap Done.

Eventually, Instagram may be moving to a more direct system of integrating commerce into its business users' feeds. As of this writing, Instagram currently allows direct product sales for 20 of the biggest brands on the Internet through a preapproved program called Checkout on Instagram. However, depending on the success of this pilot program, there is hope that Instagram could expand it to include more businesses and more products.

TIP

If you've got a special product sale or event where you want to increase engagement or visibility, you can create an Instagram Ad and pay for further promotion of your content. Check out https://business.instagram.com/advertising for more information.

9

E-Business for Nonprofits

Contents at a Glance

Chapter **1**

Raining Donations: Fundamentals for Online Giving

Donations to nonprofits are seeing steady growth, but online and mobile giving are soaring. According to the annual Charitable Giving Report from Blackbaud (www.blackbaud.com), U.S. nonprofit organizations received nearly $32 billion in total donations in 2018, an average increase of nearly 2 percent over the previous year. The portion of online donations topped more than $2.7 billion.

The organization also found that online donations accounted for 8.5 percent of all giving for nonprofit organizations in 2018, and that has grown 9 percent since 2016. Small and medium-size nonprofit organizations saw the most growth in online donations, compared to large organizations. The average online donation in 2018 was $147. Even more encouraging is that new forms of online or digital giving, such as crowdfunding, peer-to-peer online giving, and social (media) giving continue to fuel more opportunities for giving for organizations of all sizes. And when it comes to how people want to give online, you cannot ignore the importance of mobile devices, where 24 percent of donations originate. This means that your website, along with all your online communications and campaigns (such as email) must be viewed just as easily from a smartphone or tablet as on a desktop computer.

One of the most successful and widespread (coordinated) online donation efforts originated on Twitter and has since become an annual social giving campaign for thousands of nonprofits. Using the #GivingTuesday hashtag, the campaign now stretches across almost all social media channels, encouraging people to make an online donation to their favorite charitable organization. In 2018, donors contributed a record-breaking $380 million in online contributions. That's a 39 percent increase from the previous year! It also resulted in 14.2 billion mentions on social media channels. You may be surprised to learn who is behind this generosity. Interestingly, women continue to be among the most active of the #GivingTuesday donors, and the median gift across all genders was $134. Does this sound like a donor demographic that your nonprofit might target? The point is that the people who participate in #GivingTuesday are not that different from donors offline. In fact, many nonprofits were able to use awareness with #GivingTuesday to garner offline donations, too. With donations made through social media continuing to rise, and overall online giving exceeding expectations — and even helping prompt more offline giving — one question remains: What are you waiting for?

Now is the time to bring your organization online, expand its web and social media presence — and its capability to capture the spirit of online giving. If you're unsure about how to accomplish these goals, we're here to help. In this chapter, we explain why online giving is appropriate for your cause and how to get everyone else in your organization on board.

Determining How Your Organization Can Benefit

Online giving, or *e-philanthropy,* refers to the concept of charitable organizations raising money from online donations. An evolving concept since it first came in vogue in 2000, online giving is no longer simply a means of asking for money over the Internet. Online donations are now a proven source for increasing fundraising dollars and expanding an organization's active donor base, beyond one-time giving events. One continued trend is event-prompted giving, where donations skyrocket following natural disasters in locations across the globe. Whether the catastrophe is an earthquake, a tsunami, or a tornado, the Internet has not only allowed organizations such as the Red Cross to collect much-needed donations but also served as a way to spread awareness and increase the generosity of giving offline, from clothing donations to blood drives.

A second trend is peer-to-peer online campaigns with viral (or quickly spreading) tendencies that build momentum through social media. Not only do these campaigns prompt one-time donations, but also they build widespread awareness of the cause. For example, the ALS Foundation was the beneficiary of one of the biggest viral giving campaigns that made a splash across the United States in 2014. Known as the "Ice Bucket Challenge," the campaign prompted people to challenge friends to dump a bucket of ice water on themselves and make a donation to the ALS Foundation. The friend in turn had to create a video of it, challenge a new friend, and share it on social media, such as Facebook and Twitter. In 30 days, the ALS Foundation raised more than $115 million, and people who had never heard of Lou Gehrig's disease were now knowledgeable about the fatal muscular degenerative illness. Other nonprofits have tried to mirror the viral campaign success of the ALS Foundation through similar "challenges." Although others haven't been as successful, this technique for online giving has still brought in millions in charitable donations and increased awareness for the causes. Whether prompted by friends, the result of a disaster, or the result of a well-planned campaign, online donations have a powerful effect and are accepted as a mainstream fundraising method.

For those reasons, online giving is now a recognized strategic tool that you can — and should — use for your nonprofit. This method of marketing touches all outreach initiatives and specifically encompasses these six areas in an organization:

» **Awareness building:** An effective online presence targets your internal (or existing) membership base *and* your external (or potential) audience. You can increase awareness for a specific campaign, event, or for your overall mission.

» **Donor development:** You're using the Internet to not only target one-time contributors but also build long-term donor relationships.

» **Membership retention:** The combination of targeted email communications, a useful website, and active social media accounts is a proven means of generating membership renewals for your nonprofit.

» **Volunteer and client recruitment:** Your organization thrives on financial contributions and the support of volunteers. Fortunately, your site can serve as a recruitment tool for both entities. Additionally, if your nonprofit is service based (such as debt-management or tax-preparation assistance for senior citizens), an online strategy can help you reach the audience most in need of your services.

» **Board outreach:** Although your board members are technically part of your volunteer base, you should consider board outreach and development to be a distinctive area in your organization. A fully integrated and well-maintained Internet initiative is an increasingly important method for keeping your board committed to your cause.

» **Grassroots activism:** The Internet is increasingly used as a way to elicit action at the basic level. From online petitions to email campaigns, response rates are rising among the masses, and the effort is paying off.

These are the key areas in which online initiatives should be regularly infiltrating your organization. Consider how each segment provides additional benefits to your cause, and then take a closer look at what your organization gains when it actively solicits online donors.

Savvy e-philanthropists have three characteristics in common:

» **Generosity:** Current research indicates that online donors are twice as likely to give to your cause, and they typically give twice as often as offline contributors.

» **Curiosity:** Online donors seek out information; they're eager to learn about your organization and its activities. Most important, these Net donors turn to the Internet for facts, figures, and general information before making their final giving decisions. In return, a donor who makes an informed decision takes the first step in forming a lasting bond with your organization versus a one-time random act of giving.

» **Loyalty:** The members of your nonprofit with whom you stay in touch over the Internet and social media are highly likely to not only stick around but also make more (and larger) donations over time. Therefore, if you're fostering the relationship, chances are good that your multiyear renewal rates will increase.

Convincing Your Board of Directors

After you're committed to using an online strategy to grow your donor base, the next step is convincing the rest of your organization that it's the right thing to do.

Persuading your board that online giving is a timely solution is easier than you think. You might just have to spend a little more time moving progressive ideas through the approval process. Consider the usual reasons that board members tend to reject or stall a new idea:

» They're fearful of the unknown — especially where technology is concerned.

» They've determined that it is too complicated, difficult, or time consuming to implement, and hiring an expert is cost-prohibitive.

» They're convinced that the costs outweigh the benefits.

» They've decided that someone else has a more compelling argument against it.

If you understand these four points, you can arm yourself with the power of persuasion. People engage in many spirited debates over the proposal of innovative concepts, yet plenty of fantastic ideas are eventually rolled into action because someone embraced a plan of persuasion and stuck with it.

Not every board fights the incorporation of an extensive Internet strategy. Heck, people might even line up to take turns making this idea a reality. You may be one of the lucky ones with a board member who knows that

>> Donating online is more widely accepted by donors.

>> Growing the next generation of donors, especially Millennials, requires an active online presence.

>> Security measures have made online giving a safer way to donate.

>> Average per donor contributions could rise.

However, if your board tends to scrutinize a plan before rubber-stamping it, you might find the information in this section especially helpful.

Tying the Internet strategy into your mission

One characteristic that all directors of nonprofits share is their belief in an organization's mission. Because the mission is usually the catalyst that prompts a member to get involved, use that synergy in your favor. With every point you make in support of e-philanthropy, tie that initiative directly into your mission statement.

Developing an online strategy

Many organizations still view the Internet as a one-time fundraising shot and continue to treat their sites as separate entities. That's not a good argument to convince a board to invest its organization's precious dollars. Instead, if you're ready to get your board of directors on board, make sure that you have a plan with a detailed and all-inclusive strategy.

Use the six points we outline earlier in "Determining How Your Organization Can Benefit," and feel free to add others that might pertain specifically to you. Create an Internet marketing plan that incorporates each one. From donor development to member retention, don't hesitate to use them all. Your proposal is illustrating that the Internet is more than a single action item and proving it to be a component of the bigger picture. With this strategy in hand, you're ahead of the game when the board gives your plan the green light.

Providing a budget-friendly proposal

When you present your proposal to your board members, expect them to search for the price tag for implementing your project. That final number is often a deal breaker for an organization with a limited budget. (What nonprofit does that statement *not* apply to?)

TIP

Be sure to take advantage of your organization's 501(c)3 status. Not doing so is the single biggest mistake that many organizations make when pricing technology.

Whether you're building or updating a website or purchasing back-end components to add to an existing site, follow these three simple rules:

REMEMBER

>> **Ask vendors for a discount or special pricing for nonprofit organizations.** Companies are usually willing to work with nonprofits, although it's not a price point that's typically advertised.

Always get multiple bids (from separate companies) for each service or technology, and use the same *specs*, or list of requirements. Then compare the prices, apples to apples, before making a final decision.

Never go with the first or only quote you receive. This may seem like commonsense advice, but we can't stress enough that shopping around can save you money.

>> **Use your board of directors as a resource.** Board members might have access to the services or technologies you need through a company they own or work for, or because of their own special skills. Services and equipment are often donated or sold at rock-bottom prices.

When a board member performs a service, such as updating your website, ask for a written contract. The contract should specify, as with any other vendor, start and finish dates, the scope of work and project details, and a review-and-approval process for signing off on the finished project. In case something goes wrong, the contract protects both sides. Even better, it can help avoid an uncomfortable situation with a board member.

>> **Check the Internet for organizations (both for-profit and not-for-profit) with technology programs specifically for nonprofits.** An untold number of resources offer free or discounted technology and related services to the nonprofit sector. In Chapter 2 of this minibook, we provide detailed information about several of these programs and the companies that sponsor them.

If you qualify for one of the technology programs, be sure to list your actual cost in the budget proposal. (Even if equipment is free, you might have to pay shipping or installation.) Then show a comparison of the bids you received from other commercial vendors. Board members appreciate seeing this type of cost savings. Just knowing that you found a good deal can sometimes sway the vote in your favor.

Offering case studies

Not everyone is a risk taker. In fact, most people tend to be conservative when they do new things. That's why boards especially love to hear other success stories before jumping into the unknown world of technology, and that's why we encourage you to find *case studies*, or examples of organizations, that benefitted from using an Internet strategy.

To increase the chances of your examples being well received, choose these types of case studies:

>> **Mirror images:** Feature organizations that are as similar as possible to yours in size, budget, mission, or donor profile.

>> **Matching projects:** Choose examples that use technology, or overall strategies, similar to what you're proposing.

>> **Multipurpose:** Case studies should demonstrate more than a single point of success. Ideally, the strategy should result in multiple benefits. Even better, the study should also tout recurring, or lasting, benefits for the organization.

TIP

You can find technology case studies in several ways. Talk with other organizations in your community, read a few national newsletters or magazines targeted to philanthropic organizations, or check out the websites of nonprofit consultants who frequently list detailed case studies for prospective clients to view. Network for Good provides access to case studies, white papers, and resources for online fundraising at www.networkforgood.com/non-profit-fundraising-resources.

Finding a champion for your cause

Plenty of experts specialize in both nonprofits and the design and implementation of Internet strategies. If you're uncertain about your own power of persuasion, consider inviting an expert to discuss the issue with your board. Even if you give an overview of the proposal, try to have a consultant on hand to answer likely questions.

REMEMBER

A consultant who offers to speak to your board for free usually hopes to eventually be hired. If you have no intention of engaging the consultant's services (even if the technology proposal is approved), be honest about it. Instead, negotiate a reasonable hourly fee to cover the consultant's time.

Garnering positive peer pressure

Hiring a professional isn't the only way to find support for your proposal. Other board members or staff members might be willing to jump on your bandwagon. Identify possible candidates, and find at least one other person to help champion your cause. Finding someone whose opinion is respected, or who has a knack for generating positive peer pressure, obviously helps.

Getting specific

You know that more than one board meeting might be necessary to make a decision about something that encompasses a large strategy. To help your cause, offer to assign ownership to another individual or to a committee that can gather additional information between meetings. This strategy also helps spread the burden of conducting the final research. Additionally, suggest that the plan be implemented over a designated period. If you split the project into specific stages, the overall goal appears more attainable.

Following is a sample timeline you can use for implementing a project:

February 1 (start date): Confirm project goals and estimated completion dates.

March 1 (decision date 1): Get board approval of budget.

May 1 (decision date 2): Accept technology vendor proposals.

September 5 (decision date 3): Get board approval of revised site and online giving campaign.

October 1 (implementation date): Site goes live and first online giving campaign kicks off.

Following are the action items targeted by week:

Week 1: Assign ad hoc committee.

Week 4: Verify or define goals for Internet strategy; identify needs for updated or new website; finalize budget.

Week 12: Research desired technology solutions; identify possible technology vendors; request and review proposals from web developers; select web developer and technology vendors.

Week 16: Select first online giving campaign using updated site and technology solutions.

Week 18: Review first draft of proposed site revision (aesthetic design with site map).

Week 24: Give all approved content, photos, and graphics to web designer.

Week 26: Finalize marketing plan for online campaign.

Week 30: Present new or revised site, along with initial online giving campaign, for board approval.

Week 31: Develop all elements of campaign, including social media elements, emails, and offline marketing support materials.

Week 32: Implement final changes and corrections to site.

Week 33: Prelaunch site internally (not for public access); test all features and make necessary changes; announce upcoming public launch of site and fundraising campaign kickoff.

Week 34: Launch new site and begin first online giving campaign.

As you know, starting and managing a project of this magnitude is not easy and requires the support of many people in your organization (as well as partners and solution providers outside your organization). Use this project list as a springboard to put your organization's project on the right track.

Chapter **2**

Adding Online Moneymakers to an Existing Site

The Internet has provided a platform for a wide variety of organizations, causes, and trends. Since the early dotcom days, entrepreneurs and companies have blazed a trail of innovation, pioneering sites such as eBay, Amazon, Travelocity, Facebook, and Twitter as well as smaller companies that have developed exciting and useful applications delivered online. At the same time, however, plenty of organizations have worked to simply keep up with current online technologies and trends, and others have, sadly, lagged well behind the rest. The laggards continue to resist current online solutions and resources — and it shows!

Unfortunately, this description also fits many of your nonprofit peers right now. An organization's online presence may suffer for many reasons. As with many important goals for a nonprofit, the lack of money and resources (staff) dictate when and how things get accomplished — even important things, such as the creation of a professional website. The good news is that you're committed to change. You're ready to bring your site into the next decade and fully embrace the opportunity of online fundraising. In this chapter, we arm you with information about your options and their costs so that you can make an informed decision and start raising funds and recruiting resources.

Determining Which Features Your Site Can Support

You probably have a basic website, with pages that explain your organization's mission, highlight a few of your annual fundraising events (along with some fuzzy photos), and list the names of your board of directors and officers. Then again, you might have developed a more detailed site structure and haven't yet implemented any type of online fundraising tools to go along with it.

Regardless, the first step in this process of adding money generators is to conduct a detailed analysis of all aspects of your technology, support resources, and site framework. Your primary objective is to realize current capabilities and address possible limitations.

TIP

If you've already implemented or designed a general technology plan, you can pull from it much of the information you need in this analysis. If you don't have this type of plan, the information you collect in this analysis can be transitioned into that document.

For this purpose, we recommend taking an inventory. Break down your situational analysis into the eight function areas shown in Figure 2-1.

Testing your backbone (connections)

Begin your technology analysis by taking a closer look at the power of your in-house computer connection. Are you still using dial-up to log on to the Internet? (We certainly hope that's not the case!) Or are you using a faster connection from a broadband-enabled service (typically, DSL, cable, or fiber)? Jot down the status of your current connection speed. If you're on a slower connection, note whether you can upgrade your connection.

Defining your technology requirements

When it comes to hardware and software, a couple of main theories exist:

>> **Buy only what you need and nothing else.** The idea is to buy items later when they become a necessity. You don't spend money on a larger display screen or a wireless mouse and keyboard, and you don't splurge for extra memory.

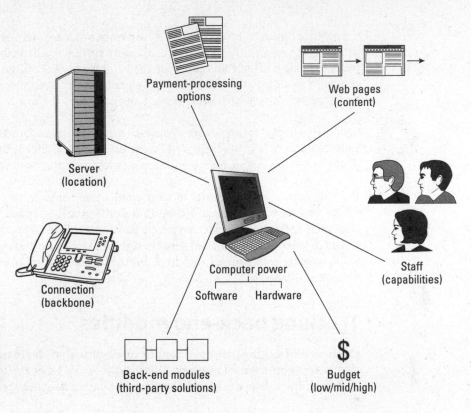

FIGURE 2-1:
Analyze your organization's eight function areas.

Payment-processing options

Web pages (content)

Server (location)

Staff (capabilities)

Connection (backbone)

Computer power

Software   Hardware

Back-end modules (third-party solutions)

Budget (low/mid/high)

>> **Buy as much as you can now rather than later.** In this theory, you get a better price by bundling all the components you need rather than buying them individually.

Both concepts are valid, and the one that you need to take into consideration depends on where you buy your hardware and software. Some vendors give discounts when you bundle printers, LCD screens, software, and other items with your basic purchase. Other vendors sell only bare-bones systems for extremely low prices, but these systems typically cannot be customized and are sold as is. Shop around with your list of requirements (divided into items you must have and the ones you can do without) and then do business with the vendor who can give you the best deal.

Processing payments

If you represent a nonprofit organization, you probably already accept donations. The issue for your technology analysis is *how* you accept them. If you accept only checks and cash, you should also have a merchant account with your bank or some other means of accepting credit card transactions. You might already accept debit and charge cards too, even if it's only offline. Well, your analysis is the place to spell it all out and put your cards (so to speak) on the table. Include a thorough description of the types of payments you accept, how they're collected and processed, and which company or bank processes them.

TIP

You may choose to add more robust e-commerce type functionality to your website. If so, when selecting a payment gateway, consider using a service that allows you to accept payments offline, too, such as Stripe, Square, or PayPal.

Use this part of your analysis to start conducting some research. For instance, maybe you have a merchant account but don't process payments online. Check with your merchant provider and your bank to explore what you have to do to collect payments through your website. If you're uncertain about which questions to ask or what your options are, check out the ins and outs of payment processing in Book 4, Chapter 4.

Tracking back-end modules

The module-tracking portion of your technology analysis is, more than any other part, a straightforward inventory. You need to know what types of applications and capabilities your site already has and whether to use these features.

In addition to considering the use of shopping carts, databases, and online form pages, think in broader terms to answer these types of questions:

>> Do you use a contact-management system to keep track of donors and volunteers?

>> Is a system in place for collecting and storing email addresses?

>> Is email now gathered from visitors to your website, or do you only collect addresses offline?

Try to compile a thorough list of all back-end applications. Note whether you use each particular feature, detail how you use it, and identify the name of the vendor you obtained it from (if applicable).

REMEMBER

One important reason for this part of your analysis is compatibility. As you add features, be sure not to replicate one that you already have.

Although we're specifically discussing the addition of online fundraising applications, a company might want to sell you, or encourage you to use, other services or features that are compatible with (or accessories to) the fundraising feature. Knowing what you already have helps prevent duplication and added costs. In addition, a vendor for one of your current applications might also offer fundraising applications. By checking with those providers first, you might be able to use those tools and receive a guarantee that they're compatible with some of your existing applications.

Mapping your site structure

Mapping your site structure is extremely easy. In fact, if you have a current site map of your website, this section of your technology analysis is partially complete.

Review your existing website page by page and create a site map of your pages, as shown in Figure 2-2. The map, similar in structure to an outline, uses hierarchical ranking to show how the site flows, or how subpages are linked to primary pages. Unless your site has hundreds of pages, this task isn't difficult.

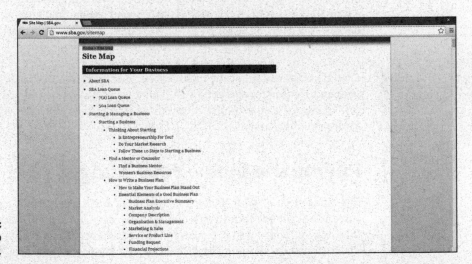

FIGURE 2-2:
Create a site map of your site.

TIP

Print a copy of each page of your site. The hard copy of your site is useful for reference and planning.

As you begin selecting online fundraising tools, use these pages to begin reconstructing your site to accommodate and promote the placement of those tools. Rather than completely reworking your site structure, you have to only identify the places where a visitor to your site is most likely to see and participate in the fundraising effort.

Determining staffing capabilities

Your staff members, board members, and volunteers are an important resource for your analysis. Not all organizations have a technical-support person on staff, so here's your chance to thoroughly analyze the strengths and weaknesses of your support base. Start this section of your analysis by making a list of your staff members and regular office volunteers. List each person's skills and educational background as they apply to technology. Although identifying people with highly technical skills, such as programming, web development, or IT maintenance is important, you should also reveal skill sets that are useful in today's online environment.

It's also worthwhile to take the same approach with your board of directors. Not all nonprofits have what's considered a "working" board; instead, they have advisors and fundraisers. Even if this is the case for your organization, identifying each board member's technical strength and professional background lets you know where to turn for knowledge resources when it comes to technology issues. As for staff and volunteers, look for those who understand and regularly use social networking sites or excel in graphic design, writing, and marketing. All these components will help support your online fundraising efforts.

REMEMBER

Even if you have a full-time technical-support position in-house, you should still take an inventory of everyone's skill sets. Seeing a defined list of everyone's skill sets is a terrific opportunity to tap in to hidden talent or uncover the need for a future training session.

Paying the piper: Your budget

The final piece of your analysis is probably the easiest to create. Identify your current budget for technology and website development. If you already have a line item in your annual report for this element, make a note of the number. Don't stop there, though: Detail whether this money is truly available for use. Is it already spent or earmarked for another project? Are there any restrictions on how the money can be spent? Be realistic about how much money is available or when it might be available.

If you don't have money already designated for technology upgrades in your budget, try to calculate a workable amount. Rather than use an actual dollar amount, assign a range. If you're broke, call it like you see it: Give it a low-end designation and assign it a range from zero to a few hundred dollars. A good midrange amount is usually from $1,500 to $5,000. Consider the high end to be anything over $5,000 and realistically capping out around $10,000. Depending on the size of your organization and any customizations, your numbers might be bumped up by several thousand dollars, especially if you are a larger, national nonprofit with more intricate site requirements. You get the idea.

TIP

When investing in software, there are lots of cloud-based technology solutions available today. Consider choosing a month-to-month price plan so that the technology is more budget-friendly (some plans, depending on the solution, can be as little as $15 per month). If offered, start out with a free trial to determine if the technology and its service provider are reliable and a good fit for your needs.

One reason that we prefer to assign a range for a budget analysis is that it makes a discussion with other people more palatable. If board members and other decision-makers know that you're looking in the low-end range of the scale, you're not immediately pinned down to a specific dollar amount. Likewise, when you're requesting price quotes from vendors, you feel less pressure to have to name the exact high-end dollar amount you can spend. Identifying a range that's budgeted for the project usually feels more comfortable.

Adding an Auction to Your Site

For individuals and businesses, online auctions continue to be a popular way to make money. (And as eBay has proven, there's no sign of these online auctions slowing down!) As an active part of the nonprofit sector, you probably know that onsite auctions have long been a staple of charity fundraising. Silent auctions are especially popular as stand-alone affairs or as add-ons to dinner galas and other live events. Thanks to the power of the Internet, the buck (literally) no longer stops there.

Your organization can increase the reach and earnings potential of your typical event-specific auction by putting it online. As with other fundraising tools, online auctions come in all shapes and sizes, so you can find the perfect fit for your organization. If you want to know more about eBay, turn to Book 8, Chapter 4.

Third-party auctions

From one point of view, a third-party auction — the "effortless" auction — is by far the easiest type for your organization to participate in. All you have to do is have your organization selected as a recipient charity. The auction itself is promoted and managed entirely from another company's website. These companies continually auction off items and then ration the proceeds to their approved nonprofits. Two examples are BiddingForGood and eBay.

The philanthropic auction service BiddingForGood is essentially an online community working for nonprofits. It promotes an ongoing auction of items that include furniture, clothing, collectibles, event tickets, and even celebrity items, which are sold from its website at www.biddingforgood.com. After the auction for each item ends, the proceeds go to the charity that provided the item or that was selected to receive the proceeds from the item. The site can host an entire auction for one charity or raise money from single auction items and donations. So far, the site has helped raise more than $462 million for schools, communities, and national charitable organizations.

eBay for Charity is open to any approved charitable organization. The program works with over 30,000 nonprofit organizations and raises millions of dollars every year from eBay auction items with 100% of the funds delivered to the non-profit. The program raised $84 million in 2017 alone! It teamed up with PayPal Giving — an independent 501(c)(3) — to handle auction-management services and screen and approve nonprofits that wish to participate. You must register and apply through PayPal Giving to be recognized as a legitimate charity. PayPal Giving reviews your mission statement and confirms your filing status with the U.S. Internal Revenue Service as part of the approval process. After you're in the system, eBay sellers can choose to donate anywhere from 10 to 100 percent of an item's winning bid to the charity of their choice. When a seller agrees to donate even a portion of the auction item's proceeds to your organization, a special ribbon icon is placed next to the item so that bidders know that the auction is part of a fundraiser or charitable donation.

As a bonus, any seller can choose to donate to your cause by selecting it from a list of certified charitable organizations and then designating it as a donation item after listing it on eBay.

TIP

You can encourage eBay shoppers to "follow" your organization on the site. According to eBay, shoppers that follow nonprofits on eBay spend 20 times more than other charitable donors. eBay offers other tips to help increase your success with eBay For Charity, which you can see by visiting `https://charity.ebay.com/for-nonprofits`.

You don't have to depend on the generosity of strangers. You can encourage your own members and longtime supporters to auction items on eBay and then donate the proceeds to your organization. Or you can become a direct seller and hold your own auction and list items for auction on your organization's eBay page. Becoming a direct seller also requires that you open a PayPal account first. You can check out all the requirements for becoming a direct seller for charity at `https://charity.ebay.com/help/charity-direct-seller`.

TIP

If hosting an online auction isn't in the cards for you, consider placing a Donate Now button on your nonprofit's page on eBay. You can allow cash donations of any amount, which are paid through PayPal. Or, donors can contribute to a charity of choice by giving when checking out. Enrolled nonprofits can participate in this option, too.

When an item is auctioned for an approved nonprofit, eBay issues a credit for any listing fees and final value fees when the total donation is between 10 and 100 percent of the winning bid. A nominal administration charge and a credit card processing fee may also apply. Although this simple process is a favorable alternative to managing your own online auction, you have to consider a few other pros and cons:

>> **Donation tracking:** eBay partners with PayPal Giving, which provides donor and donation reports, tax receipts, and other reporting options. Because not all auction websites offer a donation-reporting feature, though, decide whether it's a necessity for you.

>> **Delivering donations:** Every auction site has its own policy about when and how to deliver funds to your organization. For example, as a registered nonprofit and direct seller on eBay, donations get delivered to your PayPal account immediately. If you're receiving donations from other eBay sellers/buyers, eBay transfers funds to your bank account, but you usually don't see the donation for at least a month after the auction ends. Other auction websites send checks with final donation amounts, which are mailed either monthly or quarterly. Don't count online auction proceeds from third parties as immediate revenue.

>> **Confirm receipt:** In most cases, the website (or a partner organization) that's managing the auction takes responsibility for issuing tax receipts. However, always confirm that this is the case, and keep the site's contact information nearby. If benefactors have trouble getting a receipt, you'll know where to direct them for help.

>> **Promoting the auction:** As with any fundraiser, find out how auction items are promoted, and then ask whether the site offers other tools or resources to let your organization help promote the auction. Sometimes, you can do something as simple as add a logo to your website. Or perhaps email-based tools can be used to prompt bidding.

Direct auctions without the middleman — almost

In the *direct-selling* form of the online auction process, *you* are the seller *and* the recipient. (One example is offered through the eBay for Charity program.) You auction off your own items, such as excess inventory or old office equipment. On eBay for Charity, eBay provides the auction structure and reporting features, and you handle the rest.

Of course, you can take the direct path and fully manage your own online auction. You still need the support of a vendor, though, at least for the back-end technology. In exchange for your use of the technology and other accompanying services, you can expect to pay a setup fee, a one-time usage fee, and a percentage of sales from each auction item.

Another growing trend is having an auction-management site oversee and promote auctions for multiple nonprofits. Specifically, these auctions let people bid on access to celebrities or other high-value, luxury auction items. CharityBuzz (www.charitybuzz.com) is one of these sites. The benefit of working with CharityBuzz, or a site like this one, is that it can promote your unique auction items to a wider audience, one that is prepared and able to pay top dollar for a special item, such as dinner with a celebrity. The downside of this type of service is that you often have to be a larger national nonprofit to participate, or you have to come up with a star-studded auction item! CharityBuzz helps your organization brainstorm unique auction items and make them a reality, taking 20 percent of the auction total (with funds delivered in 30 days of the auction). Realize that working with this high-profile type of auction does take a serious commitment, but the payoff is potentially significant.

Of course, luxury auctions aren't for everyone. In fact, you may prefer to manage your auctions in-house. Fortunately, lots of other companies offer online auctionware and compatible services. The following companies can get you started:

>> **AuctionAnything.com:** www.auctionanything.com

>> **Auctria (formerly Charity Auction Organizer):** www.auctria.com

>> **Benefit Events:** www.benefitevents.com

>> **DoJiggy:** www.dojiggy.com

>> **Wild Apricot:** www.wildapricot.com/fundraising-software

Online fundraising doesn't have to have the same grand *scope,* or large scale, of an auction. But as anyone who has pulled off this type of event can tell you, online fundraising still requires lots of work.

Soliciting Donations on Your Site

Just as some sites manage auctions on behalf of different charities, other organizations solicit online donations for charities. Adding your nonprofit's name to the list takes only a few minutes.

Connecting with online giving sites

Online giving sites, or *charity portals,* typically work with thousands of types of charities. The portal actively solicits online donors, and then individuals choose which charities receive the donations. In some case, these sites also distribute their databases of nonprofits to larger entities, in an effort to increase giving potential.

A few of the largest and most widely recognized charity portals are

>> **CanadaHelps:** www.canadahelps.org

>> **JustGive:** www.justgiving.com/for-charities/international/new-charities

>> **Network for Good:** www.networkforgood.org

You pay no registration fee when you sign up with any of these three sites. However, they all deduct a small percentage of each donation (usually 3 percent) to cover their credit card processing fees. As for online reporting features and the transfer of donated funds to your organization, these items vary with each organization. You can check the FAQ section of each site to find more information on each organization's specific policies. Some of these sites also offer custom fundraising software and other tools, and there are monthly pricing plans for those.

Adding your nonprofit's name to each site's list of charities takes only a few minutes. When you're confirmed as a recognized charitable organization (typically within 48 hours), you're automatically listed on the site. You can also place on your website a link that directs your members to the charity portal. Then, when visitors to your site want to make a donation, they just click the appropriate link.

To be able to participate in any of these charity portals (and with many similar online programs for nonprofits), you first must register with GuideStar (www.guidestar.org), which is part of Philanthropic Research, Inc., a widely recognized nonprofit. Charity portals use GuideStar to certify nonprofits in good standing.

TIP

You gain other advantages by registering with GuideStar. Because sites such as Network for Good, Schwab Fund for Charitable Giving, and American Express also use the GuideStar database of charitable organizations to supplement their online databases for giving, you can be automatically listed on several charity portals. The GuideStar site alone attracts more than 20 million visitors each year and distributes billions to charities every year. That translates to a lot of potential donors (and dollars) for your cause.

Registering with GuideStar, or claiming your nonprofit's profile, is a two-part process: You set up an account and list your organization in the GuideStar system. When you're ready to get started, follow these steps to set up your account:

1. **Go to the GuideStar website at** www.guidestar.org.

2. **At the top right of the site's home page, click the Create Account link.**

   You see an online form on a new page that requests basic information to set up a free account. As you complete each section of the form, it takes you to another part of the form where you're asked to select your type of organization and your role. (This is where you can indicate that you work for, or with, a nonprofit.) Upon completion, an account is instantly created for you, and after receiving your confirmation email, you return to the home page and are already logged into your new account.

3. **While logged into your account, click the My Account link that appears in the drop-down box under your name at top of the home page.**

   You will see a new page with several links and options, including a link to nonprofit profiles. You may be required to request permission to update the report for your organization.

4. **Click the Manage Nonprofits Profiles link on your account page.**

   A search bar appears, asking you to enter the organization's Employer Identification Number (EIN).

5. **Enter the EIN or nonprofit name and choose the state located and then click the search icon (a magnifying glass).**

   A list of possible matches will appear and you must select the correct nonprofit. It will then verify your email address to grant permission. Permission is typically granted within 24 to 48 hours. Once approved, you proceed with the GuideStar Exchange registration.

6. **Set up your GuideStar Exchange account by providing the following information:**

   - *Email:* Enter the email address for your nonprofit.

   - *Contacts*: Enter the full name of the primary contact at the nonprofit and the name of the board chairman.

   - *Location:* Enter the geographic area served.

   - *Organization:* Specify which kind of nonprofit organization you are.

   - *Mission statement:* Provide your organization's official mission statement.

   - *Terms:* Accept all terms and conditions.

After completing the registration, you're an official bronze member with access to basic benefits. By completing more in-depth information about your organization, you become a silver or gold member, with access to additional benefits.

TIP

If your organization is an exempt nonprofit recognized by the IRS, you might already be listed on the GuideStar site. Although the basic listing is pulled from your IRS Form 990, it doesn't include full details about your organization. Update your report fully to ensure that as much information as possible is available about your organization.

Adding a Donate Now button

More than a dozen reputable sites provide you with the capability to accept online donations on your website without opening a merchant account for credit and debit cards. These sites work by providing you with a Donate Now button to place on your website. Visitors to your site click the button to contribute to your cause. The processing sites take care of the rest of the process on your behalf, by transferring donations into your account (in some cases, by mailing monthly or quarterly checks). Usually, these sites offer a range of online fundraising tools, and some sites make it easy to integrate a Donate Now button with your donor-management software for long-term tracking and nurturing.

Typically, the only fee for this service is a small percentage (usually no more than 6 percent), deducted from the donation total, to cover the processing fees charged by the credit card companies. Some sites may track these as two separate fees.

The types of additional fees charged by some Donate Now button services can include

» **A one-time setup charge:** Can be as much as $1,500

» **A monthly service fee:** Normally ranges from $15 to $25

» **A transaction fee to cover individual charges:** Might be a percentage of the donation or a flat fee

Shop and compare services. Some fees might include services that you don't need, so you're better off selecting another, lower-cost provider. Here's a sampling of the Donate Now button service providers you can explore:

» **Facebook (**www.facebook.com/business/help/694386777360892**):** This social media site offers a Donate Now button for nonprofits to use on their Facebook page so followers can make donations directly from the page.

>> **Blackbaud** (www.blackbaud.com): Designs software for nonprofit organizations and offers a range of services to help you increase giving amounts and manage donors.

>> **Network For Good** (www.networkforgood.org): One of the pioneer sites for digital giving, it offers donation pages to help you maximize online donations.

These types of sites often provide a range of services, products, and consulting help tailored to the needs of your nonprofit. Check out some of their other products while you're on their sites.

If you have access to some basic web development resources (a volunteer or board member with web development skills), it's now easy to add a call to action (CTA) button to your website with the text "Donate Now" and link that to a form on your site for collecting donations. In other words, you really don't have to depend on a third-party service for this feature anymore!

Revving up with mobile giving

A growing component of online fundraising is mobile giving, or the capability to make donations through smartphones or tablets. The use of mobile devices, particularly smartphones, continues to explode, so it's not surprising that mobile donations are rising, too. Mobile giving is now a necessary part of any nonprofit's fundraising strategy.

Mobile donations are effective, in part, because they are a convenient way to give. You don't have to write a check, mail an envelope, or attend a live event to make a donation. Mobile giving is as easy as tapping a few buttons! The ease of donating with a mobile device also encourages *impulse giving,* or that spur-of-the-moment decision to financially support a cause, even for an unfamiliar charitable organization. Mobile giving has also been an effective way to engage first-time donors and a younger generation of donors. Research shows that adults 18–34 years old are more likely to make a financial donation to a nonprofit if they can do so through a smartphone or even social media. Perhaps one reason why younger donors like mobile giving is because it often makes use of small or micro donations, in amounts as little as 50¢ or $1 and usually no more than $10 or $20. Mobile giving is a wonderful way to share your organization's cause with a new audience and help reach a broader base of potential donors.

How does mobile giving work? One method is the use of text messaging to send instant donations via wireless providers (such as AT&T and Verizon). This technique is popular following natural disasters, such as hurricanes and floods that strike communities. With this method, donors simply enter a designated code and text it to a special number to instantly donate a small, preset amount (usually $10) to the charitable organization. The donation is charged to the caller's smartphone bill. For example, you can make a $10 donation to the American Red Cross Disaster Relief Fund by using your mobile phone to text *REDCROSS* to 90999. The Red Cross promotes this mobile donation code on its website.

You may think this strategy works only for larger nonprofit organizations or is too difficult to set up or manage. However, local nonprofits as well as schools and churches can easily use text donations. Several online organizations make it easy to set up text-to-give campaigns. In addition to texting, plenty of mobile apps and websites encourage mobile giving. Some sites handle everything, including promotion. The nonprofit simply applies to get added to a list of qualifying charitable organizations. In other cases, your organization uses an app as an add-on to your website or live event; the app offers your existing donor base a more convenient way to give.

Check out some of these great mobile-giving tools, apps and websites:

>> **Mobile Giving** (www.mobilegiving.org): Individuals can donate to their charities of choice by texting from a mobile phone. The company is partnered with mobile service providers (like AT&T, Verizon, Sprint, T-Mobile, and others), and donations appear on the donor's mobile phone bill. Nonprofits can register with Mobile Giving to take part in a mobile giving strategy.

>> **OneToday** (https://onetoday.google.com): Using an app, Google sends messages to potential donors every day prompting them to make a small donation (usually less than $10) to one of the featured charitable organizations. The app makes giving suggestions based on the donor's interests, which helps increase the likelihood of a donation. Nonprofits register for free but must be an IRS-approved 501(c)(3).

>> **SimpleGive** (www.simplegive.com): Designed for churches and other nonprofits, this service helps increase fundraising and tithing through one-time and recurring mobile donations. Free and paid versions are available, but there are no setup fees or contracts.

>> **ZipGive** (www.zipgive.com): This full-service platform helps nonprofits raise money through text donations, mobile web forms, and recurring monthly mobile giving, and includes campaign- and donor-management tools. Fees start at $49.95 per year, plus a one-time setup fee.

Chapter **3**

Growing an Active Donor Base: Your Virtual Community

Wouldn't it be wonderful if you could put up your site, post your mission statement, and then watch as the generosity of strangers poured in for your cause? Well, it can happen — but not quite as easily as that! Getting people to donate to your cause takes effort on your part, mixed with a little bit of time and skill.

Creating a healthy online donor base is similar to organizing any other major fundraising campaign or event: It requires event planning, the ongoing help of volunteers and staff, a good marketing campaign, and (almost) flawless execution. The good news is that there is an entire online community of people who actively donate to causes on a regular basis. Tapping into this charitable community often means extending beyond your typical list of donors and volunteers. You not only raise more money from a new base of donors, but also you raise more broad-reaching awareness for your cause. In this chapter, we show you how to transfer those offline fundraising skills to your online efforts.

Building an Online Donor Base from Scratch

As with any commercial website, your online success depends on attracting customers. In this case, those customers are your donors, supporters, or constituents — or those potential donors that you aren't even aware exist yet. At the end of the day, your goal is to bring these qualified visitors to your site.

These people are actively interested in your mission and are prepared to invest money, time, and good will in your cause. To find and keep this online donor base, try these three actions, which we call the *G.E.E whiz factor*:

1. **G**et your site noticed.

2. **E**ngage passersby.

3. **E**stablish a relationship.

REMEMBER

It sounds simple. In truth, it *is* simple. The only difficult part is that many fantastic causes reach donors by way of the Internet, and, ultimately, your organization is competing with each one of them. That's why the ones that are the most successful in e-philanthropy are the ones that best communicate the G.E.E. whiz factor.

Get your site noticed

Develop a strategy to put your website on the map. This step requires actively promoting your site to existing members of your organization and introducing it to prospective donors based in local communities to those around the globe. The nonprofit animal rescue organization, A New Leash on Life (ANLOL), immediately shows visitors to its website (`http://anewleash.org`) all the ways they can get involved. From donating funds specifically to pay for vaccinations and surgery costs and giving time for fostering pets to volunteering to work in their retail donation stores and making donations to the stores. The site also makes it clear how visitors can follow and engage with the organization on various social media sites and help them spread the word (see Figure 3-1).

Similarly, the global nonprofit, International Fund for Animal Welfare (IFAW) uses every opportunity to get supporters to help spread the word. For example, this nonprofit not only consistently provides opportunities across its website to donate or become active in its cause, but also gets visitors to help drive more traffic (and potential donors) to its site. How? IFAW invites visitors to place an IFAW promotional banner on their own website or blog.

FIGURE 3-1:
Giving donors clear and simple options to get involved and spread the word helps your cause and increases traffic.

With ad banners, there are no forms to complete and no waiting periods for approval. Visitors simply choose the ad campaign and size of the banner they want to use and place it on their own website. It's that easy! In a matter of minutes, the IFAW can have its logo, name, and cause on someone else's site, all in an effort to help drive traffic and increase support. IFAW also has a Get Involved web page that shows a variety of ways to get involved, including everything from asking visitors to share the cause on social media sites to writing to U.S. senators to ask for help. As with the ad banners, the nonprofit makes it quick and simple to participate and help spread the word about its cause, while also attracting more visitors to its website! You can see for yourself at www.ifaw.org.

Engage passersby

Give visitors to your site a reason to be involved in your organization *right now*. Rather than simply post your mission statement, use the site's home page to highlight one of your success stories. Show how other donors have made a difference, and then list specific actions that visitors can take to help create another success story. Your home page is a natural location for providing information that inspires people. And placing action buttons and links nearby offers site visitors an easy way to get involved after your stories have worked their magic.

Use the home page to prominently show donation buttons for all the ways to give, whether that be money, time, or product. Instead of placing multiple Donate Now buttons on the home page, you can use a drop-down menu to show the various ways to help. This keeps your web page from looking cluttered or being difficult to navigate.

Establish a relationship

Getting people to take action once is a worthy goal; convincing them to become long-term donors is your real goal. To do that, use your website to keep people informed, to give them updates about how donations are being spent, and to expand their involvement into other areas of the organization.

The ALS Association, dedicated to fighting Lou Gehrig's disease, brings home the G.E.E. whiz factor by establishing a relationship with its donors. ALS generated global awareness through an accidental viral campaign called the Ice Bucket Challenge. The viral video challenge not only raised millions of dollars over a single summer, but also spread incredible awareness and education about a disease that previously had little name recognition. The nonprofit has built upon that campaign's success and promotes more ways to get to know the organization via its website. The site uses an image of an ice bucket in its main homepage banner — this immediately builds recognition with new followers who may have discovered the cause through the viral challenge. The site also invites donors to join its online community and shows specific ways to get involved from raising awareness to taking action.

Another G.E.E. whiz factor is that the site makes it clear how to get involved in a donor's own, local community and actively contribute to the cause. Donors can start an event in their community to raise awareness with dollars going to their local chapter of ALS, or start an online fund in memory or recognition of someone they know who suffers from the disease. The site also clearly promotes all its social media communities and encourages visitors to participate with the association there, as well. You can see the many ways the organization promotes involvement on its site in Figure 3-2.

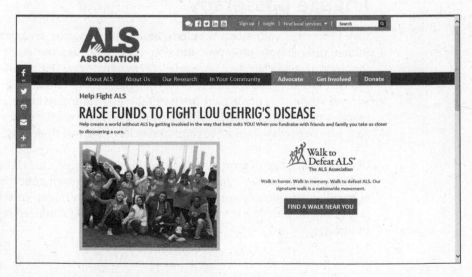

FIGURE 3-2:
Keep donors coming back by helping them feel involved by offering multiple ways to stay connected.

Putting Together a Plan to Reach Donors

After you have a good idea of what it takes to get your site noticed and to keep visitors coming back for more (see the preceding section), you can put together a plan for your own online efforts. Your plan should include these action items:

>> **Identify your prospective donors.** Whom do you want to target? Be specific — an "everyone" response doesn't count. What does your typical contributor look like? Include descriptors such as age, gender, marital status, personal interests, or any other factors that typically reflect your most faithful donors.

>> **Determine the desired donor actions.** What do you want people to do after they find your website? Are you interested solely in cash donations? Or are you soliciting in-kind donations and supplies? Perhaps you want to recruit volunteers, too.

TIP

When you determine all the possible actions, rank them in order of importance. Then you can decide how to place, or showcase, the opportunities on your site.

>> **Describe the rules of engagement.** How can you capture (and keep) the attention of your visitors? For example, consider the content you use on the site. Have people shared testimonials or success stories of how your organization has helped others? Use these stories to pique visitors' interest, and follow them with instructions on how to get involved.

REMEMBER

Visitor awareness building and education are probably expected at this point. In fact, now you want to use those objectives to help elicit a specific online action — whether that's making a contribution or having someone send your link to a friend.

>> **Define your donor pool.** Geographically, where are your prospective donors located? Does it matter to you? Your organization might have a national or an international appeal, or your mission might benefit a regionalized population. Even if your scope is limited, other people might be interested in your cause. What about people who move away from your city and still have ties to the area? What about others who are simply affected by your cause? Deciding where your donors are likely to come from, or how far out you want to go to reach them, is an important element of your online marketing efforts.

REMEMBER

The Internet readily allows you to localize your marketing efforts, if you choose. Or you can decide to cast your net far and wide. If this issue is important to you, use geographic descriptions in your <META> tags and page titles. That way, your organization is more likely to turn up in location-based results in search engines. Google also allows you to set an international geographic target for your website to improve location-specific search results (for more information, visit `https://support.google.com/webmasters/answer/62399?hl=en`). Because IP addresses are used to help determine the location from which a person is searching for information, it's important to take the steps needed to help your website appear in localized search results. The increasing use of mobile phones for conducting Internet searches makes local search results even more important for your business.

>> **Establish donor hangouts.** You want to create online marketing opportunities for your cause. To do that effectively, you need to know where your prospective donors are likely to hang out online. You can use these sites (social media sites or blogs, for example) to place banner ads, buy keyword advertising (paid searches), and post press releases.

>> **List giving partners.** Exchanging links with sites that complement yours is an effective way to expand your reach. You can also partner with other sites by offering to provide content, place informational links to research, or simply promote a fundraising event.

>> **Provide action opportunities.** Keep your donors involved by giving them lots of options to participate. Your plan should detail the ways in which people can not only donate money but also take action that makes them feel connected to your cause for the long haul.

>> **Specify follow-up.** Plan to stay in touch with your online donors. Email messages, electronic newsletters, podcasts, blogs, social networking sites — the list of ways to keep connecting is almost endless. You can use some or all forms of communication (online and offline) to stay in touch with donors and build lasting relationships.

Converting the Faithful

Although most online plans attack the issue of recruiting new donors, don't forget the ones who are already most familiar with you. Unless you have a recently launched nonprofit organization, you should have a fairly long list of existing supporters, which typically include

>> Previous donors

>> Full-fledged members or active donors

>> Participants in, or attendees of, earlier fundraiser events

>> Board members and volunteers (past and present)

>> Community supporters and sponsors

If you played your cards right, you collected the email addresses of these folks over the years. Even if you never had reason to use those addresses, you should still have them on file.

Your list of supporters and at least their current mailing addresses should be in a database. Regardless of whether you ever fully took advantage of this resource, you're now in a great position to do so. Obviously, these people represent a built-in group of followers. If nothing else, they're already aware of your organization and its mission. All you have to do is use your online initiative as a tool to step up their level of giving and involvement.

A great deal of recent e-philanthropy research indicates that people who give to charities over the Internet are likely to donate more — and do it more often. If you can convert a percentage of your offline contacts to online contributors, donations to your site might increase.

To see that happen, you have to reach out to everyone on your current list of names. Your objective is to get them active online.

REMEMBER

Despite the fact that online giving continues to prosper, not everyone on your list is up to speed in Internet giving. Some donors are always more comfortable sending donations by *snail mail* (sent by way of the U.S. Postal Service) or being involved face to face, so continue to provide those options.

How do you decide whether someone is willing to receive your message online? You have to ask, of course! To start converting your faithful followers, do the following:

>> **Send an electronic invite.** Use your data bank of existing email addresses and send a request for donors to visit your website. Making them aware of the site — and the ways they can stay involved online — is the first step in conversion.

>> **Reach out the old-fashioned way.** Send a postcard, make an announcement in your print newsletter, or write a letter. If all you have is a street address, reach out with traditional mailers and invite donors to check out your organization online — and include a postage-paid return envelope that makes it easy for donors to send a contribution back to you.

>> **Register constituents online.** For your next fundraising event, let folks register online. You then have the opportunity to collect updated email addresses and get them accustomed to communicating with you over the Internet.

A few issues are still at play here. What happens if that piece of snail mail sits in a pile unnoticed? Too bad you didn't have the recipient's email address! Then again, maybe your list of contacts contains old, outdated, or incorrect email addresses, which are useless.

One solution for these types of obstacles is to pay to obtain valid email addresses from your list of constituents. Several companies now offer services in which they match information about your existing list of donors with their current email addresses. You don't have to have existing email addresses to use the service — this type of company can cross-reference information from other email databases in order to find valid email addresses.

You're likely to find one of these three types of services helpful in your online business:

>> **Email appending:** You can cross-reference online databases to find someone's email address when all you have is a name, phone number, or street address.

   When you're choosing a company for email-appending services, make sure that its process complies with guidelines issued by the Data & Marketing Association (DMA) and the Association of Interactive Marketing (AIM).

>> **Email validating:** Your list of existing email addresses might be outdated or invalid due to errors (such as typos). Companies can now verify email addresses for you.

>> **Reverse appending:** If you're collecting email addresses online, the addresses might be all the information you have on prospective donors. A reverse appending service matches email addresses with valid street addresses.

Dozens of legitimate companies offer email appending and related services. Prices for these services vary; many charge based on the number of valid email addresses they find. Blackbaud (www.blackbaud.com), a company that specializes in assisting nonprofits, estimates that organizations usually convert 20 to 30 percent of their total donor lists to valid email addresses. DonorPerfect (www.donorperfect.com) and DonorWorks (www.donorworks.com) are also viable programs.

REMEMBER

After you get someone's valid email address, you still must obtain permission to send the recipient information about your organization (even if you already had the name in your records). The company performing the appending services should work with you to provide a final *opt-in,* or permission-based, list of valid email addresses. You must also be in compliance with all data privacy regulations, especially outside the United States. See more about the General Data Protection Regulation (GDPR) in Book 5, Chapter 1.

Reaching Out to People Surfing for Charities

Obtaining working email addresses is only one component of building an active base of online donors. Regardless of how many names you already have, you want to reach out to as many potential donors as possible.

Fortunately, a growing online trend is opening the door to millions of socially conscious Internet users. *Social networking* is a form of socializing through virtual communities. Some of the most recognizable social networking sites started with a focus toward entertainment, dating, and fostering friendships. Today, however, many social networking sites, such as LinkedIn, Facebook, Snapchat, Twitter, Instagram, Pinterest, and YouTube, have a much wider audience and are often used for business and nonprofit purposes. Even so, a derivative group of social networking sites is geared toward charitable giving and philanthropy in general. These sites connect individuals or large groups who share an interest in various causes. In addition to highlighting current nonprofit news and topics of interest, members can share their experiences in community message boards. Social networking sites also allow members to create their own personal pages (for free) to discuss the causes in which they're active, to create and circulate online petitions, to donate to featured organizations, and to learn about different types of nonprofits.

Check out the sites in this list:

>> **Care2:** With more than 36 million members, Care2 (www.Care2.com) is one of a growing number of sites that are proliferating social awareness online through online petitions and other outreach initiatives.

>> **Charity Navigator:** A special feature of this site (www.charitynavigator.org) is that it rates charitable organizations from its database of more than 8,000 organizations. Members can even track and compare charities on their own personalized web pages.

You must understand what makes outreach through social networking different from other types of outreach. At these sites, you don't plaster Donate Now buttons across personal pages or aggressively solicit for paid memberships to your organization. Instead, these sites provide a forum to educate the public about your cause by interacting with your prospective donors and volunteers. Think of that forum as a low-key grassroots type of marketing tool, and get creative!

You can get involved with these types of sites and spread your organization's mission in several ways:

>> **Sign up.** Become a member of the site. (Signing up is usually free.) Create your own personal page to discuss your cause, connect to similar groups, and send messages to friends in your online network.

>> **Actively contribute.** Join the discussions on the message boards. Find out what people are talking about and, when it's appropriate, let them know what your organization does and how they can get involved.

>> **Provide content.** Submit articles for the site's content, send press releases, and forward news briefs with information pertaining to your cause (such as the status of current legislation).

>> **Become a sponsor.** With millions of active and vocal members, your site's marketing dollars are likely to go far when you become a sponsor or paid advertiser on these types of sites.

>> **Submit your charity.** For sites that keep logs or reviews of nonprofit organizations, always send in the necessary information to keep your cause on the list.

REMEMBER

With the exception of paid advertising, nonprofit organizations can face limitations on how, when, or whether they can actively or directly solicit for membership or donations. Always read the FAQs (frequently asked questions) section of the sites, and review their terms and agreements to ensure that you follow the rules for promoting a specific cause.

Chapter **4**

Identifying Online Marketing Strategies That Fit the Cause

I n discussions of marketing strategies for nonprofit organizations, the term *marketing* can encompass many different activities, such as donor development, fundraising, education, awareness building, and public relations. For marketing purists, not all these items belong in a marketing discussion. Right or wrong, they all become part of a nonprofit's marketing mix.

In this chapter, we clarify what marketing means for nonprofit organizations, including taking advantage of opportunities that lead to growing your organization through online monetary donations and other contributions.

Asking for Donations

Online marketing provides more than one chance to ask directly for money (or whatever else your organization needs). You can even ask for donations repeatedly. The person on the other end won't even bat an eyelash. If you're uncomfortable asking people for money, the Internet removes that pressure of asking for donations face-to-face.

In fact, people checking out your website expect to be asked for donations. It's likely that they sought you out for the purpose of giving their time and money to your organization! It's time you become comfortable with the idea of using the Internet to ask people to give — over and over again. E-philanthropy provides a host of methods for doing so.

Multiplying donation buttons on your site

One of the most overlooked online marketing opportunities is the Donate Now button, which is typically a single button (or link) on the home page of a site. Clicking the button displays an online form page where a visitor can choose to contribute. The donation button has been a consistent and reliable tool for increasing online contribution dollars to nonprofits.

You can increase the potential for a donor response by increasing the number of places on your site that you ask for support. Note that we don't endorse randomly scattering Donate Now buttons throughout your site. Instead, take an integrated, thoughtful approach, and follow these pointers:

TIP

>> **Be position-savvy.** Visitors to your site view numerous pages. Make sure that donation buttons or links appear in as many spots as possible (without going overboard, of course). Visible areas of your site include

- The navigation bar

- The upper-right corner of each page

- The lower-center of the page

- The top or sides of the site's pages, for banner- or button-sized ads

>> **Ask in different ways.** Rather than repeat the phrase Donate Now on every page, use different terms that draw attention, such as these examples:

- Make a Difference

- Help Change a Life

- How to Contribute

- Ways You Can Help

- Get Involved Today

- Click to Contribute

>> **Latch on to content.** When you share a success story on your site or spotlight someone in need, ask for support. In addition to placing a button following the content, include links to donate within the article.

>> **Associate with a specific giving opportunity.** Consider the types of visitors your site attracts and why they're interested in learning about your cause. Someone might be more likely to give if your request is tied to a specific area of help. For example, you can link a request for a donation directly to research funding or to provide meals for a family in need. Be specific. You can also use donation buttons that specify different donation amounts as opposed to leaving the dollar amount blank. For example, use some donation buttons that say "Donate $5 Now" and others that ask for $25 or $100. By giving a range of prompted amounts you may get more response.

>> **Highlight alternatives.** Not everyone wants to, or can, donate money. You might offer information about how to participate in a fundraising event or write a member of Congress to speak out on an issue. The website for Surfrider Foundation, an organization dedicated to protecting oceans and beaches, has a variety of opportunities to help. For example, you can click a button to locate a chapter near you and get involved as a volunteer. In addition, there is a Take Action page on the site (see Figure 4-1) that clearly shows you how to take action by contacting various agencies or Congress and asking for support or change to particular programs. The organization does a good job of quickly providing you with options for getting involved and becoming a donor (via paid membership levels) by using clear calls to action and compelling images.

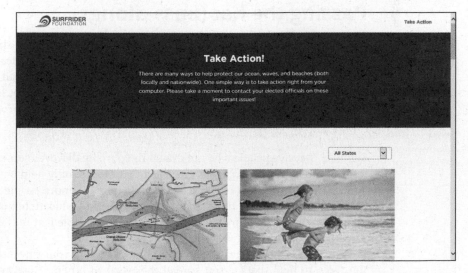

FIGURE 4-1: Provide clear calls to action and options to get involved.

>> **Encourage social connections.** One of the keys to building an active, loyal donor base is staying in touch. Social media and mobile interactions provide the perfect opportunity to keep awareness levels high and to ask for donations, long after someone leaves your website. Just make sure that you provide plenty of opportunities while people *are* visiting your site to like your Facebook page or follow your organization on Twitter or Instagram (or any other social media platform in which your nonprofit is active).

TIP

Use your Facebook page to host a Facebook Live video. The real-time video is shot through the camera on your mobile phone or computer desktop and it is shown live to all your followers. Plus, as they share or interact with you via video, it is shown on their friends' news feeds. Facebook Live is a great way to promote an upcoming fundraiser or other event, and to ask for a donation — in real time! You can also place a Donate Now button on your Facebook page.

>> **Make a final plea.** Before a visitor leaves your site, display a final request for help in a pop-up window. Rather than ask for a cash donation at this point, ask the person to register to receive additional information on supporting your organization. Collect only a name and an email address, to keep the process quick and unobtrusive. You can then automatically send email with specific requests for donations.

TIP

This type of follow-up email is the perfect time to spotlight a story about your cause and then ask prospective donors to sign up for your newsletter. Even if they don't donate directly from your email request, you can keep them informed and grow their activity level.

Passing the hat (pass-alongs)

As you might know from working with volunteers, sometimes these people are passionate about your cause. Because their enthusiasm and dedication are infectious, not long after they start working for your cause, they recruit plenty of their friends and family members. In the corporate world, this concept is referred to as creating *buzz*, or word-of-mouth marketing; people in the nonprofit world call it *pass-along* marketing.

Suppose that five people who are drawn to your site discover something useful or important about your organization. They want to not only help but also share the site with others. If each of those individuals tells ten more people they know and perhaps at least half of those people then choose to educate ten of their friends, your cause has been shared with several hundred people just in that short cycle!

If your cause can motivate just one person to act, your site can also provide the tools to help that person spread the word to others. Here are three simple techniques:

>> **Add a link or button on your site that asks visitors to send information to a friend.** A visitor who clicks the button can forward a message from you to a friend.

>> **Provide social sharing buttons that allows visitors to share information on your website by pushing it out on social media sites.** With the click of a button, it's easy to share an article, a tip, an event notice, or any other information with friends by posting it to Facebook, Twitter, Pinterest, or other sites. Your site can even encourage visitors to post automated messages to their social media accounts when making a donation or a pledge to help. Their friends see a message such as, "I just made a donation to Surfrider to help clean up the ocean. If you want to join the cause, visit Surfrider.com."

>> **Allow site visitors to start their own fundraising campaigns for your cause and invite their friends.** Peer-to-peer or friend-to-friend fundraising is a great way to let site visitors and loyal donors spread your organization's message. Organizations such as Charity: Water (`www.charitywater.org`) encourage visitors to engage their friends in fundraising through personal campaigns. The site makes it easy for visitors to set up their own fundraising pages and invite friends to donate or get involved. One example of a popular and easy campaign type that Charity: Water encourages is asking donors to make a pledge to raise donations on their birthday. It's an easy way to encourage giving!

TIP

If you're already using a nonprofit service provider, such as Blackbaud (`www.blackbaud.com`), for various fundraising tools, they often offer friend-to-friend campaign tools. Other providers that also include integration with social media platforms are Mighty Cause (`www.mightycause.com`) and CauseVox (`www.causevox.com`).

Building personalized pages for events

Expanding fundraising tools for volunteers and event participants is part of the friend-to-friend fundraising trend. In this case, the personalized donation pages are used with specific fundraising events and may even be integrated with event registration, as opposed to the general fundraising campaign we mention earlier. For example, the easiest way to help volunteers reach their donation goals for your organization is to offer personalized web pages to promote a specific fundraising event (such as a walk-a-thon).

Personalized pages are typically miniature websites that constituents can build themselves by using templates (or a selection of preformatted web pages). A page usually includes an organization's logo, information about its cause, event details, and the personal story of the fundraiser. Pictures and the real-time tracking of donation goals can also be added to the site.

FirstGiving (www.firstgiving.com) offers this type of service. In this case, your nonprofit can access the personal fundraising pages for an annual fee. Two charges are incurred when donations are made: a "performance" fee that ranges from 1.5 percent to 5 percent (based on type) on the actual donation and a standard credit card merchant fee. That means with a $50 donation, you still end up bringing in more than $45 to your nonprofit. There's also an annual account fee of $500. Even with the extra fees, if you use the services wisely and put time into managing it, there's no doubting the value of these services provided by FirstGiving:

>> Creates on-demand reports showing the funds that are raised

>> Collects donations and handles on-payment processing

>> Provides unlimited support

>> Manages online event registration

This unique solution helps supporters who are hesitant to fundraise in person.

TIP

Highlight your fundraisers' pages on your organization's main website, and provide prominent links directly to their personal sites. This way, you can easily offer prospective donors (visitors to your site) a specific, personalized way to give.

REMEMBER

Because these personal fundraiser pages often contain personal information (including email addresses), always get your volunteers' permission to post links from your site.

Circulating donation links offline

One way to increase the value of any type of volunteer effort (personalized fundraising pages or any other method) is to distribute your information by way of other established networks that your volunteers belong to, such as these examples:

>> Churches

>> Credit unions or banks

>> Employers

>> Member-based organizations or clubs

>> Professional associations

Although most organizations and almost all companies maintain no-solicitation policies, you can occasionally find loopholes. For example, employers tend to make exceptions if their employees are contributing to good causes. Similarly, if an employee or a spouse suffers from a health issue (such as diabetes or cancer), a company is often willing to promote the nonprofit organization associated with that person's problem. Coworkers and peers are also more likely to donate to your cause when they're supporting someone they know.

Here are a few ways to circulate news about your cause and increase visits (and donations) to your website:

>> **Create a newsletter.** Write a brief article about your volunteer and how that person is helping your organization. Your article can describe anything from raising money for a bike-a-thon to heading up a clothing drive. Include a web address where people can learn more and donate. If you create an electronic newsletter, provide an active link to your site.

>> **Use the company's internal communication sites.** For example, some companies may have an *intranet,* which is a private Internet site for the employer that's unavailable to the general public. Or, a company may use a wiki page, which is a website that allows collaboration and sharing of information among employees or company departments. In each case, employees access the shared site for news, general information, and critical updates. Provide a brief description (similar to a newsletter article) along with a button or link to your organization. You can then place the link in a prominent place on the shared site so that other employees or members can reach you and make donations.

>> **Get employees to like you on Facebook:** Social media provides another way to reach out to employees. If you have a Facebook page for your organization, you can encourage one or two employees who like your page to ask their coworkers to do the same. (You can also place donation buttons directly on your Facebook page to encourage giving right from the social media platform.) Getting people to join you on Facebook also gives you the opportunity to communicate with them frequently and provides a more direct way to share your organization's story. The same type of approach can be taken with other social media platforms (Snapchat and Instagram, for example) — anywhere you have prospective donors and can tell a good story through videos, pictures, or testimonials.

>> **Produce a member bulletin.** This regular email notification goes out to employees or members of an organization. Or you might produce a nonelectronic (printed) notice that's circulated in pay stubs or at meetings. Again, spread your message along with your website address to encourage others to get involved or make donations.

Cross-promoting

Not all donation requests have to originate from your site. You can take advantage of *cross-promotional marketing* strategies, too. In these programs, you work with another organization in a way that benefits both of you.

One type of charitable giving program, administered by major credit card companies, plays off the popular reward programs offered as incentives to cardholders. If you have a credit card, you know that many companies allow you to accumulate reward points based on a percentage of the dollar amount you charge to your card. For example, every $100 you spend may earn you 10 reward points. You could then redeem your points for a gift; for example, 2,500 points might qualify you for a $25 gift card to your favorite spa. Several companies now allow you to trade points for a charitable contribution of a specific dollar amount. What an idea!

Unlike formal partnerships with card companies, some programs simply require you to enroll or sign in to your American Express account. The American Express donation program, Just Giving, for card members is an example. When you're ready, visit `www.americanexpress.com/give`. After you've signed in to your account, you can redeem reward points to make donations by using the American Express card.

Making Donating Easy

With a little help from your friends (and their friends), your online fundraising efforts are bound to be a success. However, it's ultimately your job to make it easy for people to get involved. The key is to not only get the attention of would-be donors but also eliminate any barriers that might prevent them from contributing. Your website provides a backdrop for combining simplicity with donor-building strategies. Look into these features:

>> **Automated membership renewals:** When you're using your site to market for membership fees, do yourself and your new member a favor. Rather than ask for a one-time membership fee, give your donor other options, such as these:

- *A multiyear membership with an incentive:* Ask your potential donor to pay now to sign up for a three-year membership, and you'll give a bonus gift or discount.

- *Automatically membership renewal:* Gain permission for your organization to automatically renew the membership each year by charging the fee to a designated credit card.

>> **Recurring donations:** Donating by credit card is one of the simplest solutions you can ask for in online fundraising. Another option for incorporating this service is to set up the processing of recurring donations. This set dollar amount is then regularly (weekly, monthly, or even semiannually) charged to a credit card. Credit card companies sometimes offer this service directly from their websites, or you can manage the process internally.

WARNING

Recurring donations via credit cards are terrific options, but only if you make it clear to donors that they are choosing to continue contributions on a fixed, recurring schedule. If donors do not fully understand this option, they are likely to be surprised and angry when the next charge appears on their card statement. And that means you risk losing the donor, permanently!

>> **Simplified employee-matching programs:** When someone makes a contribution to your organization, doubling the donation can be a no-brainer. This option also serves as a strong incentive for people to give when they know their contribution is being doubled! All you have to do is

- Verify that the donor's employer has a matching program.

- Get the right form into the donor's hands.

- Make sure that the form is submitted.

- Ensure that the employer cuts a check to you.

Even if this process sounds simple, it can represent a lot of work that your supporters might not be willing to do. Or you might even overlook or forget the follow-up process. By implementing an automated donor-matching program on your website, you can immediately see your intake increase, in one of two ways:

- *Donor verification:* Provide a link from your site to an employee-matching database. The donor can verify that his employer participates, review the procedures for getting it approved, and review any conditions to the matching program.

- *Nonprofit verification:* Your organization verifies the participation of the donor's employer, *and* you use the information in the database to submit forms on behalf of the donor.

The DonorPerfect site (www.donorperfect.com) offers online software that enables you to track matching donations, pledges, grants, sponsorships, and even in-kind donations. You can choose from three versions, ranging in price from $159 to $479 per month (depending on the number of donor records you need to track and number of product features you want).

>> **An easing of the burden of making nonmonetary donations:** Does your organization accept clothing, food, toys, or even cars? These items aren't easily collected from a website! You can simplify the donation process, however, by partnering with a third-party collection center to pick up donated items. Allow your site's visitors to schedule a pickup online, or at least fill out an online form to start the process. You can also list drop-off spots that accept these donations for you. Better yet, consider allowing visitors to make online monetary donations that are then used to purchase items you need.

It might seem like you're doubling your efforts to simplify the process of making online donations, even when they have to be made offline. Before you think that it's not worth your effort, take a look at how one nonprofit turns nonmonetary items into a big treat — literally — for everyone! The Second Harvest Food Bank in Orange County, California, provides food of all types, whether it is donated, surplus, purchased, or grown by local farmers specifically for the cause. Since its founding, the organization has distributed more than 350 million pounds of donated and surplus food (the equivalent to 291 million meals!) to community residents in need. Through its website, the organization offers multiple ways to give that don't involve cash — including giving food. The site also highlights volunteer opportunities for kids, like helping harvest food directly from farms. The many different ways to give food items has served the organization's recipients well!

Chapter **5**

Legal Considerations for Nonprofit Organizations

pproximately 300,000 nonprofits lose their exempt status each year because they fail to file a report with the IRS for three consecutive years. This small omission brings big consequences. As the owner of a registered nonprofit organization, you're accustomed to the issue of compliance. Filling out annual reports for the IRS, issuing tax-deductible receipts to donors, and distributing legal waivers to volunteers are all a small part of your legal duties.

Fundraising over the Internet is no different. When you go online to seek donations, certain responsibilities come along with it, and overlooking even a few of those responsibilities can have a significant downside for your organization. Some of the issues we discuss in this chapter are internal compliance activities. Even if an action item isn't mandated by a government entity, it's still something you should do. Other issues mentioned in this chapter are legal requirements. If you're venturing into e-philanthropy for the first time, this chapter is required reading. Even if you know that you're up to speed with the latest online regulations, consider this chapter a review.

Designating Responsibility

You know who takes the legal heat when something goes wrong: Your board of directors is ultimately in charge of the well-being of your organization. Even so, responsibility follows an internal chain of command. Depending on the size of your nonprofit, that chain of command might include an executive director, an entire paid staff, or a group of directors and volunteers structured by committees.

Now that you're entering the realm of online donations, similar legal responsibilities and consequences apply. Although your board accepts these legal responsibilities, you should assign responsibility for your Internet initiative to a designated individual or committee in your organization. By incorporating this position, you're developing both internal expertise and an internal watchdog for your online operations.

We recommend having an internal watchdog, for two reasons:

>> **Branching out on the Internet is most likely new territory for you and your cause.** Initially, you might have to turn to outsiders for consultation and guidance. If you find good start-up assistance and develop a holistic Internet strategy, however, you find that online fundraising increasingly becomes a larger part of your overall revenues, resources, and image. Internet fundraising might grow from occupying 1 percent of your organization's pie chart to eventually meeting or exceeding the 50 percent mark. That amount is an extremely big piece of your pie to not have internal expertise assigned to it! Likewise, increasing contribution to that level takes a long time unless an insider is championing the initiative.

>> **Industry watchdogs, individuals, the media, and the federal government are increasingly scrutinizing online fundraising.** That scrutiny is a good thing — you want the playing field to be as fair and ethical as possible. Otherwise, as donors see more scams and corruption from supposedly legitimate charities, they decrease their online generosity. Scams will happen to some degree, no matter what, which is why you have to go out of your way to promote your organization's high standards and continue building long-term, trusting relationships with online givers. By keeping pace with external watchdogs, changing policies and procedures will not catch you unaware.

You can assign the responsibilities associated with being an internal watchdog to an individual staff member, a director, or an ad hoc committee (that you hope will become a permanent committee after your by-laws are adjusted). Although a larger, national organization might have the funds to hire staff members for this position, a smaller organization can still build this internal expertise by giving an employee the added responsibility.

When you're selecting the appropriate person, you don't have to look for someone with existing or extensive knowledge of the Internet. The person should be comfortable with the Internet and technology in general, though. The biggest factor, by far, is that the person you choose should be willing, able, and enthusiastic to learn.

TIP

Try to recruit a person who can — and will — assist your organization for a lengthy period, to cut down the amount of time you spend continually reeducate and retrain. Some organizations are successful in recruiting permanent volunteers when hiring extra staff members is out of the question. Usually, these retirees, home-based parents, and professionals don't have full-time paid positions.

The designated individual should focus on keeping policies and procedures in compliance with any local, state, or national guidelines. An Internet strategy liaison can further benefit your organization by serving in these added capacities:

>> **Point of contact (POC):** As the go-to person for questions regarding your online fundraisers, your designated POC should be responsible for overseeing or understanding all parts of your Internet strategy. The POC fills out the forms and updates any registrations on third-party sites, and assists your members, donors, and staff members with online fundraising issues.

>> **Trainer:** As your organization adds online fundraising tools and features or participates in online events, your Internet strategy liaison should be available to train other staff members, directors, and volunteers.

>> **Researcher and trend watcher:** In a quickly changing environment, having someone responsible for keeping up with the industry — from researching proposed policy changes to spotting innovative online tools for fundraising — is important.

>> **Advocate:** Just as you or others in your organization are championing the cause of bringing your nonprofit into the area of online fundraising, the need for that advocacy will always remain. Having someone who's knowledgeable and excited about the role of e-philanthropy helps further your cause in the long run.

Creating Online Policies

When you shop online, on many sites you probably notice links to the legal section. You often see online privacy policies, user agreements, return or exchange policies, and other protective verbiage. After you begin your online fundraising endeavors, you too need to create certain policies to display on your site and to provide some basic information to visitors.

Include these items:

- » **A privacy policy:** A privacy policy is a requirement. It's a statement that tells your visitors whether and how you collect information about them, such as email addresses, names, and physical addresses. It's also the place to let people know whether you're tracking their visits to your site through the use of cookies or other tools. If you're collecting information, tell them how you use it and state whether you share that information with others. A link to your privacy policy should be clearly displayed on the home page of your website.

- » **A security policy:** Similar to a privacy statement, your security policy lets visitors know how you store and protect their personal data. Although this policy is optional, you should use one if you collect donations online. In it, you explain how credit card data and other personal information are stored and protected. If you use a Donate Now button or an outside source to process online payments, let patrons know and then provide a link to that site's privacy and security policies.

- » **A COPPA statement:** If your nonprofit appeals to children or if you suspect that children might visit your site, you need to comply with the Children's Online Privacy Protection Act (COPPA). Regulated by the Federal Trade Commission (FTC), COPPA helps protect children and dictates how or whether a website can collect information about children, particularly those under the age of 13. The FTC provides guidelines for compliance and a children's online-privacy statement to post on your website. You can find details at the FTC website at www. business.ftc.gov/privacy-and-security/childrens-privacy.

- » **An explanation of funds:** Describe how donations are used in your organization and specify exactly where all the money goes. Online donors appreciate knowing that their charitable contributions are put to good use. If money can go toward separate endowments, lifetime giving opportunities, or other distinctive areas in your nonprofit, now is a good time to explain to donors. If donors can contribute in other ways (such as giving supplies, clothing, or food), break down those items into categories and display them so that donors readily understand their giving choices.

- » **Form 990:** You might want to create a policy allowing visitors to view your IRS Form 990 online. Although you're not required by law to provide this information, it assures prospective donors of the legitimacy of your site. If you don't want to post this information on your website, provide a link to GuideStar (now part of Candid), at www.guidestar.org, where visitors can view your form by searching the site's database.

>> **Contact information:** As the owner of a nonprofit, you must clearly provide contact information to your site's visitors. Providing an email address is helpful; offer a phone number and mailing address, too. Then prospective donors can reach you if they have more questions. Seeing your full contact information prominently displayed on your website is also reassuring.

Registering Your Charity

The most critical registration task you can do is to complete the individual state registration process. If you collect donations from people outside your organization's home state, you must register with the other states. This procedure is part of the individual states' solicitation laws, and compliance isn't optional. A few exceptions exist because only 40 states now require charities to register individually. (See www.irs.gov/charities to view more information about the state registration process.) Each state differs in how it requires registration, so we can't give you details on how to do so. Try an online search using your state name and the search terms *register, donations,* and *charity.*

Fortunately, a collaborative effort was created to make filing a little less burdensome for nonprofits. The National Association of State Charities Officials, in cooperation with the National Association of Attorneys General, created a unified registration statement (URS) to make multistate registration simple. The organization provides a registration kit in PDF format, which you can download from its site at www.multistatefiling.org. After you complete the information, you can submit the form to multiple states to register your organization.

WARNING

The unified registration statement kit isn't accepted by some states, including Colorado, Florida, and Oklahoma. If you use the URS kit, you aren't in compliance with these states and must register directly with each one. There are more than a dozen other states that accept the URS kit but require additional forms, and you will not be in compliance unless all forms are submitted.

REMEMBER

If you use a Donate Now button service, participate in an online charity portal or solicit donations through social media, you may still need to register with *all* 40 states. These methods for soliciting donations reach across the United States, in addition to Canada and other international locations, and may or may not be considered *passive* donations (which do not require multistate registration). If you don't register with all states, you can face serious penalties and stiff fines.

Legal Considerations for Nonprofit Organizations

If you need more information about what you have to do to collect donations, the IRS website for charitable organizations (www.irs.gov/Charities-&-Non-Profits/Charitable-Organizations) has information on various tax and compliance matters.

Gaining Seals of Approval

Another step you can take to maintain compliance is to sign up with entities that govern charities. We discuss two in this section: the Better Business Bureau and Charity Navigator.

Although these programs might cost you additional time and money, they're well worth the investment. As a respectable charity, you want prospective and existing donors to know that you have high standards and are in compliance with mandated regulations. Providing this level of assurance only helps to expand the success of your online fundraising initiatives.

In addition to national ranking and approval systems, some regional and statewide organizations keep up with the progress of your charity. For instance, Maryland Nonprofits offers a certification program for participating organizations. It awards a Standards for Excellence seal to area nonprofits that qualify under its peer approval process.

Better Business Bureau

The Better Business Bureau (BBB) is a nonprofit organization that works to monitor and improve the solicitation of funds. To assist with that goal, it developed the BBB Wise Giving Alliance (www.give.org). This online report and charity-evaluation system gives donors another reliable source for information about causes. The BBB offers the program to national organizations or organizations that solicit contributions in multiple states. If you're a smaller charity, you can still participate by way of your local BBB office. Register with the Wise Giving Alliance by clicking the "Starting the free accreditation process" link in the box titled "For Charities" toward the bottom right side of the page.

The organization's website maintains an up-to-date database of reports and financial information on select national organizations. You or your donors can scroll through the list of archived charities on the Wise Giving Alliance website. Simply look for the "National Charity Report List A–Z" link found under the "For Donors" section of the site.

An optional program you can participate in is the BBB Wise Giving Alliance Charity Seal Program. If you meet the approved accounting standards adopted by the program, you can post the Alliance's seal of approval on your website. The seal lets prospective donors know that you're in compliance with national giving standards. If you decide to apply for the seal, you must also sign a licensing agreement and pay a sliding-scale fee based on the amount of donations you took in during your last fiscal year. You can see the charities that participate by using the link called "National Charity Seal Participants," found in the bottom footer of the website.

REMEMBER

Even if you don't participate in the seal program, your organization might still show up in the BBB online database of charity reports.

Charity Navigator

Although Charity Navigator (www.charitynavigator.org) doesn't hand out a seal for websites, it doles out stars in its rating system of U.S. charities. It helps people and businesses evaluate the reputation and financial well-being of more than 7,000 charities and is itself a nonprofit but doesn't accept donations from any of the charities it monitors.

The information is pulled from an organization's IRS Form 990. The nonprofit organization uses an established set of criteria to weigh first the financial side of your organization and then the administrative side. In other words, it assigns values to your financial statements, fundraising efficiency, administration overhead, and ratio of working capital, to name a few. Your scores are then combined into a ranking system based on stars. As with hotel rating systems, the more stars you receive, the better. Your organization is likely to be ranked by Charity Navigator, whether you want it to be ranked or not. You can learn more about the types of charities that are evaluated and how the process works by clicking the "Methodologies" link at the top of the website's home page.

TIP

For nonprofit professionals, Charity Navigator offers a guide to help you understand and improve your organization's ranking. You can access and download the Nonprofit Outcomes Toolbox by clicking the FAQ for Charities link on the home page and then looking for the guide.

10

E-Commerce Trends and Market Opportunities

Contents at a Glance

Chapter **1**

Discovering Niche Markets

When you start an online business, the Internet offers plenty of untapped markets for you to explore. These markets are segments within existing industries that have a lot of potential because they haven't yet become saturated by sellers. You can certainly find this potential in *niche markets,* which are smaller, more defined segments of an existing market. In this chapter, we provide a few basic guidelines for working with a niche product and also show you how you can access these niche markets and sell to their loyal customers.

Deciding to Sell a Niche Product

When thinking about a niche market, imagine the market in terms of a pie. The whole pie represents an entire market — one that's usually well established. But cut out one piece of that pie, and that piece becomes a smaller market on its own. Instead of concentrating on selling the entire pie, you narrow your focus to that single slice.

The pet industry serves as a real-world example. More than 67 percent of U.S. homes own a pet — that's more than 70 million homes with at least one pet. As you might imagine, that number adds up to a lot of potential when it comes to pet-related expenditures. Pets do indeed represent a multibillion-dollar industry, with a record-breaking spend of more than $72.5 billion in 2018, according to the American Pet Products Association (APPA). That number was expected to top $75 billion in 2019! Of that amount, the largest subcategory is food, followed by vet care services. The subcategory of pet services, which includes everything from dog walking and pet sitting to grooming and training, is one of the fastest-growing areas — it has seen year over year growth of more than 10 percent.

Pet insurance continues to be a unique niche. Consider that dog owners alone spend more than $600 per year on veterinarian bills (which includes both routine services and surgical costs). Pet insurance premiums continue to rise sharply, in some cases at more than 15 times the normal inflation rate, often due to a vast amount of technological advancements in the vet industry. Even with the growing expense, insuring pets continues to be a big trend because the costs of surgeries and medicines are rising at an equally startling pace. However, fewer than 2 million pets, a very small percentage of the total pet population in the United States, are insured. These numbers show both a true demand and an opportunity for growth in this niche service offering.

To answer the demands of this customer base, websites such as Healthy Paws Pet Insurance (www.healthypawspetinsurance.com) and Petplan (www.gopetplan.com) offer online quotes and enrollment to pet owners. Pet insurance may be a relatively small piece of the industry, but for companies such as these, it also represents a significant amount of untapped potential. That's a niche market.

Another example of a niche market inside a larger industry is a product segment within the coffee industry, referred to as cold brew coffee. The slow brew process that it takes to create the liquid, caffeine-infused treat defines this ready-made beverage. The overall retail coffee industry in the United States is approximately $48 billion, with specialty coffee comprising 60 percent of that market. Although the overall coffee market has remained relatively flat in the past few years, some breakout brews are seeing consistent growth. Cold brew, originating in only the last decade, has quickly become a recognized contributor to the "specialty" category of coffees and is now recognized as an option by more than half of coffee drinkers. It continues to expand, and small brands like Jubilee Cold Brew (www.jubilee-cold-brew.myshopify.com) are among those companies capitalizing on the niche trend by selling their ready-made beverages offline and online. The company got into the market early, but is now competing with national brands, such as Starbucks and Dunkin' Donuts, that are also trying to jump into the cold brew market. We point this out to demonstrate that a niche market can be the equivalent of liquid gold for an enterprising online entrepreneur, but it can quickly become part of a highly competitive market.

As a small online business, you can enjoy the following advantages in a highly targeted market, especially if you identify the niche market opportunity early:

>> **Defined customer base:** If you do your homework, you usually have no trouble identifying your customers. And because you're dealing with a narrow focus, you can get to know your customers extremely well. You can respond to their needs and wants much more easily, thereby creating loyal customers.

>> **Customized messaging:** With a narrowly focused customer base and product or service type, creating highly customized content is easy. You can craft website articles, blog posts, videos, emails, and ads that have specific and highly relevant content matched to your audience or customer. Creating this type of customized content not only helps in marketing to potential customers but also can pay off with SEO (search engine optimization) because Google displays results with content specific to the search someone conducts. We explain this concept in more detail in Book 6, Chapter 6.

>> **Bigger bang for your buck:** Because you're selling to a target group of people, you can stretch your marketing dollars further. Rather than invest in mass advertising, you can place less expensive banner ads on smaller websites that attract your particular audience. You also pay less for Google AdWords because you can use specific key phrases that may be less costly than general keywords (for example, *expensive vet bills* versus *pets*). Reaching a specific group of people using social media ads on Facebook or Twitter is also easier and less costly. Targeted emails and podcasts are definitely budget-friendly for sites of all sizes.

>> **Pursued specialty:** When you provide products that are hard to come by, your customers often seek you out. In niche markets where there is less competition, the likelihood of people finding you online through organic searches increases. In other words, you can spend less in pay per click (PPC) advertising on search engines because your website may rank very high in search engine results.

>> **Positive word of mouth:** Word-of-mouth marketing (WOMM) is powerful, especially in a tight-knit community of customers. When these niche buyers find a quality provider of products or services, you can bet that they will talk to everyone else in their circle of like-minded friends.

Not to burst your bubble, but you should consider these few disadvantages, too:

>> **Limited customer base:** You're marketing to a much smaller group of potential customers. If the number of prospective buyers is too small, you can quickly reach market *saturation,* in which the pool of sellers is enough to satisfy the pool of buyers. Reaching market saturation levels is especially risky if you have a product or service that is likely to result in a one-time purchase.

>> **Restricted product expansion:** Finding new products to sell that complement your niche can be challenging. In a specialty market, you may find yourself stuck with the same product, even as sales begin to taper.

>> **Dreadful word of mouth:** Suppose that you make a few mistakes as you start growing your niche business. The same word-of-mouth marketing that could have been quite advantageous now becomes a killer. Because your customer base is small, negative comments can do a lot of damage to your site's sales. And the widespread use of blogs and community boards makes it especially easy to spread the negative online word to a connected community of buyers.

TIP

To offset bad word-of-mouth marketing, be even more aggressive in quickly resolving customer complaints. Follow up every order with a personalized email. Invite customers to share the results of their online shopping experience with you. Become active on social media and engage with and respond to followers to create positive (and public) customer interactions. If a customer has a problem, your attention to him or her (even after the fact) mitigates the damage, and this attention often redeems you in the eyes of your customers.

The disadvantages shouldn't deter your plans for a niche business. The benefits far outweigh any of the minor risks involved. But those risks give you all the more reason to be thorough in selecting the right niche to pursue. After all, if the interest hadn't been there, pet insurance could have bombed. Instead, the timing was right, and this niche has left animal lovers begging for more.

Finding Your Niche

Almost every established industry has a single piece of pie waiting to be divvied up. When searching out your online niche, here are some general guidelines to follow (to help you remember them, notice that the first letter in each term spells out the word *niche*):

>> **Notice:** All too often, niche markets are in plain sight — ripe for the picking. Some people see them, and others walk right by. So, stop and pay attention to your personal interests and those of your friends and family. After all, you're consumers. Take a look at which services or products you want or need that larger companies aren't providing. Watch for new trends, too. Find out what people are talking about, and determine what's hot and different right now. Trends are often predecessors to an emerging niche.

» **Investigate:** If you think you've hit on a great idea, it deserves an adequate level of attention. Research the larger market from which your niche originates, and determine whether it's a growing market. Check annual sales and identify top performers (the large companies) in that market. Find out what analysts and researchers are saying about possible spin-off segments of the market, and determine whether these industry experts have spotted the same niche that you noticed.

» **Competition and customers:** As with any other market, you have competitors in a niche. Do a little digging to uncover how many others are already servicing the market. If you have zero competition, you may want to reevaluate the demand.

Put your prospective customers under the microscope, too, and find out who they are. Be specific. Note whether they're single men with dogs, for example, or working mothers with young children. Figure out their preferences, current buying habits, and available income. The more you know about the people you're serving in this niche, the better chance you have of successfully marketing to them down the road.

TIP

Find out whether your competitors are catering to only that particular niche or whether it's just one more piece of their overall businesses. If your niche is only a piece of the competitors' pie, you have a possible advantage. You can specialize in the niche and become the expert.

» **Hypothesize:** Before you launch your niche-focused site, you need to test your theory. Maybe you developed the perfect product. It answers a definite need, and research shows that there's money to be made. To be sure, you have to test, test, test. Conduct small samples to find out whether people are truly interested. You have to know whether they're willing to pay for it, whether it answers their needs, and whether they're ready to buy from a new online resource.

» **Execute:** Create a solid plan for selling to your niche market. Sometimes, reaching this type of customer proves to be more difficult than marketing to a broader customer base. After all, you're talking about highly targeted and specific customers. Not only do you have to work harder to locate them, but one misstep in your marketing efforts can also destroy your credibility. An effective selling strategy clearly communicates how your product answers a specific or unique need for that niche customer.

REMEMBER

Niche customers are often quite knowledgeable and passionate about the niche that your product or service addresses. Can you speak their language? Talking the talk means being up to speed on current terminology, hot topics, and issues of importance.

TIP

Draw in your customers by providing timely, informative content on your website that supports the products and services you offer for that particular niche.

The Internet definitely provides an exciting opportunity to sell to a niche market, and often the opportunity is right under your nose. Many online entrepreneurs stumbled onto a niche market out of sheer necessity. In some cases, the market lacked a product that provided a much-needed solution. In other instances, a niche market started because an existing industry or market changed as the Internet matured. To stay ahead of the game, entrepreneurs identified smaller segments within their markets that weren't being served.

Tutor (www.tutor.com) is a shining example of how a need for a product can carve a healthy niche from a larger existing market. The e-learning, or online, self-paced learning market is expected to experience 18 percent year-over-year growth. Within that larger online learning market are lots of subcategories, including the kindergarten through 12th grade (K through 12) market. Both consumers and governments spend billions of dollars for products and services that focus on K through 12 students. And within that category is another emerging niche — online tutoring. Given the market size, the rising cost of college, and an increased emphasis on students obtaining academic scholarships to offset tuition, there are lots of reasons to be in this segment of the educational market. Tutor is a company taking advantage of that niche demand by providing online tutoring services for students. The website sells its online learning and tutoring services, in blocks of time, to parents and students all over the United States. Students aren't the only ones benefitting: Tutor has learned the value of launching an online business in a lucrative niche market!

How can you follow the example of companies like Tutor and Jubilee Cold Brew and identify early emerging market trends? The following companies offer e-newsletters and other online resources that track trends and future niches to help get you started carving a nook for yourself:

>> **Gartner Iconculture Consumer Insights:** www.iconoculture.com

>> **Pew Research Center:** www.pewresearch.org

>> **TrendHunter:** www.trendhunter.com

>> **Small Business Trends:** www.smallbiztrends.com

>> **TrendWatching:** www.trendwatching.com

IN THIS CHAPTER

» Connecting: The (virtual) reality of
social commerce

» Getting ready for your close-up with
video

» Selling through social

» Gathering, sharing, and making
a profit in communities

Chapter 2

Building Business via Social Commerce

Social networking and online communities continue to fuel opportunities in online niche markets. These social media platforms are no longer "only" another advertising channel for your online business. The surrounding niche opportunities that have sprouted up as a result of those first fertile sites have also proved lucrative, launching interesting new business models.

If you're naturally a social butterfly, or have already honed your offline networking skills, you may be surprised to discover how easy it is to transition those same attributes to a blooming social commerce endeavor. In this chapter, we introduce you to the most popular social networks and take a look at some of the money-making trends that have emerged from these platforms.

Setting the Virtual Stage for Success

It helps to understand the economics behind some of the biggest platforms, and which ones offer the best opportunity to fuel a niche business. There are four core social media platforms, or channels, that we consider responsible for helping prove social media is about more than sharing pictures of your last meal or sounding off with political rants. These include:

- >> **Facebook:** www.facebook.com
- >> **LinkedIn:** www.linkedin.com
- >> **Twitter:** www.twitter.com
- >> **YouTube:** www.youtube.com

Some of these are better suited for promoting a business as opposed to serving as a vehicle for the business, but all of them play a role in social commerce. In addition, to this core group of platforms, several others are also important, and we discuss them in more detail later in this chapter. For now, just know these platforms also have lots of social currency for a niche business:

- >> **Instagram:** www.instagram.com
- >> **Pinterest:** www.pinterest.com
- >> **Snapchat:** www.snapchat.com

You are likely familiar with Facebook, the granddaddy of all social media platforms. The public company is now worth billions. Since its founding, Facebook has bought other share-worthy social sites and applications, including Instagram (a photo-sharing app) for $1 billion, Oculus (a virtual reality company) for $2 billion, and WhatsApp (a mobile communications app) for $19 billion. Today, Instagram has moved beyond its filtered, photo sharing roots to serve as a launch pad for online "Insty" businesses, which we discuss later in this chapter.

Another of the core social media platforms, LinkedIn, has found great financial success, too. The career- and business-focused social networking platform was the first social media site to go public. Its stocks have performed consistently well, and Microsoft acquired it for over $26 billion! LinkedIn first became known as an advanced career site, a place to network and find new jobs. Because it is based on forming connections with existing contacts and then expanding your circle by asking for introductions to others, LinkedIn has a reputation as being a modern Rolodex for the social-savvy salesperson. You can also publish and share articles to your network and can participate in "groups" to share ideas and meet others as a way to expand your network. LinkedIn isn't the ideal social media platform to build a business from scratch, but it is an excellent platform to promote your business.

Next up on our list is Twitter, a popular platform that encourages you to follow people you may not know to expand your network (whereas Facebook and LinkedIn are more focused on connecting with people already in your personal or professional network). Based on the concept of openly sharing information (called "tweets") in 280 characters or less, Twitter is often the go-to social network for sharing current events, news, and opinions on celebrities, politics, pop culture, and sporting and entertainment events (such as the Super Bowl and the Oscars). Because tweets are shared openly in real-time, you can see trending topics nationwide, and even worldwide. Even though it's proven to be a popular platform, Twitter has had a more difficult time boosting new user growth and maintaining its financial worth. Following in the footsteps of its peers, the company went public in 2013, trading at per share highs of more than $70; but even recent stock prices remain reasonably strong at $30 per share. Twitter has had lows and highs in both stock prices and volume of tweets. Most recently, it has gotten a boost from celebrity and politically savvy tweeters, including the president of the United States. It has also led the way in altering advertising policies to exclude political ads. Although Twitter has taken a beating on occasion, it has remained a contender among the leading social media platforms and a valuable social commerce tool for any online business.

You may not consider YouTube as a social media platform, but it is truly a powerful social network, and one that has launched many Internet celebrities and online entrepreneurs. YouTube videos are seen by more people ages 18 to 49 years old than any cable television station in the United States. Owned by Google (the company paid $1.65 billion for it, less than a year after it launched), YouTube is a video-sharing network that is equally influential in search engine optimization (SEO). If done well, videos on YouTube can send a lot of organic traffic to your website!

By the way, almost all of these social media sites had humble beginnings. Facebook was founded by college kids living on campus, LinkedIn was started in someone's living room, and Twitter got its start in a small apartment. (Former PayPal executives developed YouTube, so it had a slight leg up as a social media start-up.) Like other (now) giant technology companies born out of garages, spare bedrooms, and college dorms, social networking sites and online communities are experiencing the same opportunities for growth.

We share these sites' journeys to financial successes to reinforce their credibility as legitimate businesses, and to point out that this is where you can find another option for pursuing your own success. So how do you generate income from these social networks? Let's take a closer look at these social media platforms and show you how online socializing can boost your social commerce earnings potential.

Using Online Socializing to Build Social Commerce

If you aren't familiar with the concept of online socializing, think of it in terms of attending a big networking event where hundreds or thousands of professionals might go to meet, mingle, build relationships, and drum up business. Lots of different types of online social networks exist, and they aren't always focused on business activities. Some communities are created solely for socializing, others are created for a specific group (such as business executives or hobbyists), and still others are developed as a support network for a particular group (such as moms). Because these types of online networks attract so many eyeballs (or visitors), you can use them to make money, either directly or indirectly.

Although online communities are often lumped into the social networking category, they are much more than a social site. Each offers something different and has its own pros and cons, especially when it comes to using them to grow an online business. Here's an overview of the top social media sites.

WARNING

In online communities, you interact with people from around the world, thus exposing yourself to virtual strangers. As a result, all these communities and social networking sites have had their share of problems. To reduce your risks, always read a site's policies, privacy statements, terms-and-conditions documents, and general member guidelines. Stay safe!

REMEMBER

You may also want to use social networks (or social media) as a way to promote your business. We discuss this process in more detail in Book 6 and illustrate how these sites help boost your business sales.

Facebook

Unless you've been hiding under a rock, you're familiar with the social networking giant Facebook, which was the first of its kind to carry social networking into the real world and get investors to see it as a business with potential. Facebook started with personal pages, which allow you and your (selected and approved) friends to view your profile and leave comments for you on your wall, but has expanded to include business pages. Companies are using these pages to extend their online presence into the social networking space.

What can businesses do with Facebook pages? Whether you have an e-commerce business or a bricks-and-mortar location, you want to create a profile of your business so that potential customers have an up-close look at what your business can do for them. In addition to the profile, fans of your business can leave a post or comment on your wall (or primary page), ask questions, seek out technical support, and share pictures of themselves using your product. Businesses use Facebook as a place to run contests, seek out information or research, and attract more customers by garnering more "likes." Facebook is also an ideal place to promote video content and other presentations in an effort to get your company in the face of those who count most — your customers. One effective way to use video on Facebook is to broadcast live using the Facebook Live feature. This feature allows you to live-stream video directly from your Facebook page. In fact, your followers are sent a notification that you are live in an effort to get fans to visit your page and watch in the moment. Perhaps our favorite part of Facebook Live is that the fans who are watching you can comment and ask questions while you are broadcasting — and you can answer your fans. Talk about a great way to interact with your potential customers and get them involved in your brand!

TIP

Use Facebook Live for product demonstrations, tips, or to conduct interesting interviews. Resist the urge to turn your video time into an "As Seen On TV"–style commercial broadcast from your Facebook page. Fans would much rather see something useful or entertaining than being hit in the face with an obvious sales pitch.

When you're ready to do some serious selling through Facebook, there are two main options. First, you can add CTAs (calls to actions) to your page and posts that allow people to get more information about a product or service. For example, you may want to promote an annual conference or fundraising event and would use a CTA button with the text "Register." Or, you might promote the use of a new mobile app your business created, and would use a CTA button with the text "Download App" or "Use App." This option is also helpful if you have a type of offering that requires more sales assistance than simply dropping a product into a shopping cart. For instance, you might offer a free trial and use a CTA button with the text "Try for Free," which takes the user to a page explaining the free trial. If you are taking a traditional e-commerce approach, you can set up a Facebook Store as one of your tabs from within your page. A Facebook Store lets fans buy products directly from your page. The only catch is that you need to connect your store to an online shopping cart or e-commerce provider, such as Shopify.

TIP

In addition to reading Book 6 to see how to buy and run an ad and other ways to use Facebook as a marketing tool, you might want to check out *Facebook Marketing All-in-One For Dummies*, 3rd Edition, by Andrea Vahl.

REMEMBER

Because deleting a Facebook page is extremely tedious, you should be prepared to always keep an eye on the posts. And should anything negative get posted on your wall, you want to be prepared with a policy or set of procedures in place to route and resolve bad comments. Otherwise, one or two negative comments that never get resolved could cost you lots of customers.

Twitter

Twitter exploded onto the social networking scene as a place to have real-time conversations. The object of Twitter is to build followers and have conversations — in 280 characters or less. After you sign up for this free web-based service, you can send as many (short) messages as you like.

Although it comes as a surprise to many, Twitter is a useful tool for business. For example, search functions make it easy to identify potential followers (and possible customers) based on your use of key search words. And, thanks to link-shortening tools, such as Bit.ly (www.bit.ly), it's easy to add a link back to your site to promote content such as blog posts, videos, and presentations, or to highlight your services and products. Using Twitter as a traffic-generating tool is one of the benefits it offers to your website. You can also use hash tags (the number or pound sign on your computer keyboard) to follow discussions on key phrases, promote key phrases, or allow others to discuss a topic relating to your business. Simply put the hash tag in front of the term you want to use and then tweet it. For example, #socialmedia will bring up all Twitter comments on that subject.

Like Facebook, Twitter offers promotional opportunities with paid advertising, including one option called *promoted tweets.* The ad program lets you target a particular audience on Twitter (segmented by keywords used in user profiles and in tweets, and by hash tags and popular trending topics, for example). Your promoted tweet is labeled as such at the bottom of the tweet and is then inserted into the top of your target audience's Twitter stream.

Twitter has also started offering another way to advertise by using Twitter cards. You add code to your website that allows images to be displayed with certain tweets. Or you can use a lead generation Twitter card, which lets you send tweets with images and allow a Twitter user to get a coupon or download an e-book directly from your tweet (without having to leave Twitter).

Does it work? For small businesses, advertising via Twitter is not only affordable but also apparently effective. According to Twitter, its users shop online nearly seven times a month, compared to four times a month for non-Twitter users. Not only that, but 60 percent of Twitter users purchase from small businesses. Similarly, Twitter says that over half of its users discovered a small business on Twitter for the first time. As a small online retailer, these stats are favorable, and they certainly make advertising on Twitter very appealing!

TIP

Unlike Facebook posts, which stay prominently featured on a page for a while, posts on Twitter rotate quickly through your followers' feeds. To ensure that as many followers as possible see your tweets, you want to post similar tweets several times or pin a tweet to the top of your profile so that it's the first tweet profile visitors see, even if the tweet was sent two days prior.

TIP

Twitter doesn't like you to tweet the exact message over and over again, so change your tweet message slightly each time you send it out.

LinkedIn

LinkedIn is one of the only (if not *the* only) social networking sites developed with businesses in mind. The site was also quick to develop a plan to earn money through advertising revenues and paid membership levels. It's also been successful at growing and maintaining sales.

Although these details are nice to know, you're probably more interested in how LinkedIn can help you. LinkedIn is like a virtual Rolodex (filled with your professional contacts) that's been moved online and expanded to include everything about you and your profession (everything from a résumé to your interests and most recent careers). Your first step in using the site is to create a user profile. (Your LinkedIn profile is scanned by all the major search engines.) Then you start building your network by adding people you know who are already on LinkedIn and inviting other people on LinkedIn who you would like to meet and add to your network.

If you're selling B2B (business to business), LinkedIn is an ideal social network for you. One of the advantages of LinkedIn as an advertising platform is that it allows you to target your ideal audience, whether by industry, profession, or geographic location. It's an effective social platform for lead generation in B2B because of its overall success rate in ad conversions. Most often you see a business offer a specific type of content (like a white paper or e-book) in exchange for a user's contact information. This equates to a legitimate B2B lead. The cost of LinkedIn advertising is typically higher than Twitter and Facebook, but the quality of the lead is considered much better. Included among the different advertising options on LinkedIn are the following:

>> Sponsored content

>> Sponsored InMail (ads delivered to a member's email inbox)

>> Text ads

>> Display and dynamic ads

LinkedIn heavily promotes *social selling,* which is essentially finding and selling to customers through social media. It is continually updating its platform and tools to make it easy for you to sell or prospect in the platform. With LinkedIn, you have the opportunity to

>> Expand your network through virtual introductions

>> Post updates on projects you're working on and events you're attending

>> Join groups with similar interests and participate in conversations

>> Use your profile to help get found in search engines

>> Use PDFs, PowerPoints, SlideShare presentations, and video to add to your profile information about your products or services

>> Publish content to its Pulse platform, which is shared across the social network

>> Promote events

Pinterest

Pinterest started out as just another social cataloging site (which we discuss at the end of this chapter). It's a collection of user-generated and user-shared images that members *pin*, or post, to personal boards — the virtual equivalent of posting something to a cork board. Pinterest has become one of the most popular image-sharing social networks. As a business or a blogger, your customers and readers can share images from your online store or blog directly to their Pinterest boards. In this way, your product images get shared across a huge network of Pinterest members. You can also add special tags, or *pins*, to your images that include product information (such as price) and link back to your website so that people who see the pin can then buy the product. These Shop the Look Pins are an easy way to allow Pinterest users to buy products directly from a shared image or post on Pinterest. You can learn more about Shop the Look Pins at https://business.pinterest.com/en/shop-the-look-pins. You can also advertise on Pinterest with promoted ads, videos, and apps.

TIP

Each of the social networks we discuss in this chapter can be connected directly to your website. How? Twitter and Facebook both have plug-ins or tools that let you post real-time feeds of your social networking accounts (or pages) on your site. For example, visitors can go to your main website and see a sidebar that contains the most recent comments posted on your Facebook wall and a real-time streaming Twitter feed. Look for instructions on Facebook and Twitter on how to grab some simple HTML code to place on your website to get things started. Most e-commerce solutions, blog platforms, and website builders provide the capability for you and customers to share information from your site to social media. Customers can share products, articles, reviews, videos, and just about anything else on your site.

Visual platforms

Similar to Pinterest, several other visual-based social media websites hold great potential as moneymakers. We provide more details on how to convert visual interest into currency, but first here's a quick overview of these picture-perfect social platforms:

>> **Instagram** (www.instagram.com): Instagram (now owned by Facebook) is a social media platform that lets you post photos and short (60-second) videos. You can then share your images across your other social media networks. The twist that makes Instagram special is that it allows you to add special filters to your images to give them a more creative look. In other words, you can take a picture on your smartphone, upload it to Instagram, and then add a fun filter on top of the picture to give it a faded look, or change it to black-and-white, or make it look like it was a Polaroid picture taken in the 1970s. You can do the same to short video clips. Creative and entertaining people can build a following of thousands of fans and generate revenue from the platform through brand sponsorships and Instagram shops. Instagram boutiques are especially popular with 18- to 34-year-old women who like the instant gratification of seeing and immediately buying trendy clothes, shoes, and jewelry from the social media platform.

TIP

Selling products from an Instagram boutique is much easier with the right tools. In addition to using hash tags that let users know products are for sale, there are lots of third-party resources available to help your buyers spot and purchase directly in Instagram, and to help you track sales. Get started with one of these tools: Have2HaveIt (https://have2have.it), Soldsie (www.soldsie.com), and Inselly (www.inselly.com).

>> **Snapchat** (www.snapchat.com): Snapchat popped onto the social media scene as a now you see it, now you don't app for sharing images. Images shared between friends on Snapchat disappear permanently in a few seconds. The non-permanency of shared content originally earned the social platform as a "sexting" service for teens (kids could share risqué images that disappeared quickly so there was seemingly little risk to the images showing up elsewhere). But the site overcame this image as a larger user base determined that those quickly disappearing messages actually made for a fun, entertaining experience. Today, Snapchat is a public company valued at almost $24 billion and has more than 200 million users every day. Its largest segment of users, which make up nearly 50 percent, are those between the ages of 18 and 24 years old. If you want to target millennials and younger generations for your niche business, this is the place to be! Of course, the exact process of how to sell to Snapchat users is still evolving. Currently, you can take advantage of ads, sponsorships, and geofilters (which let Snapchatters engage with you at a specific event or

location through these geographic specific filters). We're betting it won't be long before Snapchat figures out a creative way to let users share their stories and buy products in a snap!

TIP

Selling products in a visual social media platform is less about the product and more about showing off how the product looks on real people (from sellers to celebrities). Instagram and Snapchat users don't want to see a picture of a product on a white background with a description and price. That's boring! And, they can go to any online retailer and see the exact same image. Instead, these buyers want to see you wearing that cute coat while walking your adorable little dog; or they want to see how those dangly, shiny earrings catch the night light while you're on a date dancing the night away. In other words, you're selling a story, not just a product — but the story should be genuine and real. There's a fine line between looking like an awesome person with a trendy handbag people want to know about and being a model in a carefully manufactured ad.

WARNING

Depending on a single social media platform as a revenue generator is risky. This was demonstrated when Twitter abruptly announced the shuttering of Vine, its mobile video app. The decision left many content creators in a bind, but those making serious money from the social video stream really got hit hard. As with any type of business, it's critical to diversify your revenue streams.

Creating Your Own Video Channel

Statistically speaking, there's a good chance that you watch YouTube videos regularly — whether you see them in YouTube or when shared on another social media site such as Facebook. This online video site claims over two billion video views per day, with an average daily viewing time of around 15 minutes. Since it hit the Internet in 2005, YouTube has changed the way we use video in our everyday lives — we want to video everything in hopes of being the next online sensation, or we can't wait to see what other people do in their video to get everyone talking.

Basically, the online video pioneer has made it possible to monetize crazy, weird, funny, or even serious videos. You can make money from YouTube whether you are a professional filmmaker or hobbyist, or you just happen to have a video camera on your phone. The best way to explain these revenue-earning opportunities from YouTube is to look at a few examples.

Vloggers and video gamers

Vlogger is the term used to describe people who blog through video, rather than only writing articles. Just as traditional bloggers created a business out of producing steady content and catching the eye of brands willing to pay for the blogger's online influence, vloggers are following that same business model. And almost any topic is worthy of a vlog; from makeup and men's fashion to fishing lures and skateboards, there's probably an audience for it.

REMEMBER

In addition to YouTube, you can make and share videos on Instagram and Snapchat, and possibly make money purely from the video content created in those channels. Even if you don't use multiple social networks to create video, it's worth sharing your visual content across the board and building influence in all the networks. Cross-channel promotion goes a long way to increasing your reach and income-making potential.

If you need more than a quick video to get your point across, and you happen to enjoy playing video games, Twitch.tv might be your ticket to a niche video business. Think of Twitch.tv (www.twitch.tv) as a mix of YouTube and ESPN, the cable sports channel. It's similar to YouTube, in that Twitch is an online network that broadcasts video content, streamed live (you can prerecord, but that's not the preference), and is all about video games — playing them, watching others play them, and discussing them. So, it's sort of a sports network for the video game industry that includes the broadcast of e-sports (professional video gaming). One of the primary ways to make money on Twitch is through paid subscribers to your personal channel. Believe it or not, there are lots of eager fans who will pay recurring subscription fees to watch you play video games. The caveat is that you must either be really good at games and use the channel to show off your prowess and offer tips, or you must be entertaining (watching you play video games is fun or even comical). Twitch.tv launched in 2011, and it has more than 200 million broadcasters and more than 15 million daily users. Recognizing its huge potential, Amazon acquired Twitch in 2014, for $940 million in cash! Why not grab a (game) controller and get your cut of the earnings?

TIP

E-sports, along with amateur gaming, is a rapidly growing niche market, and Twitch.tv is the leader in the space. However, if you want an alternative, then consider trying YouTube Gaming (https://gaming.youtube.com), especially if you are already comfortable with YouTube as a video platform. The platform already boasts more than 83 million subscribers!

REMEMBER

As with any trend, the online video phenomenon has the possibility of diminishing. But that's no reason not to try it while it's still hot. And don't be afraid to use these trends as the basis for discovering the next big thing.

Instructional and premium content videos

YouTube has a lot of content. Although some of the most viral videos are usually quirky or funny, other types of video are doing well online. And when it comes to making a profit from videos, instructional videos are one way to fit the bill. Think of a how-to format that teaches someone how to do something, or a travel video that showcases popular vacation destinations and gives tips or suggestions when traveling. Corporate-style training videos, geared toward more professional endeavors, are also a good choice. If you prefer not to offer instructional or educational videos, but prefer to use your artistic eye to create short-form videos that show off locations, events, or other interesting imagery and graphics, there's a market for that, too!

Lots of companies need video segments, or premium video content, to use in their own ads or website, but don't have the in-house talent or budget to make their own videos. Instead, companies license the use of others' videos and this opens the door for another way to make money on your work. Or, you may develop a scripted video series or some other special style of video series that fans want to watch — and are willing to pay to watch via subscription fees! At the end of the day, video is still content. And if you offer quality content that people seek out, it's most likely content that sells.

TIP

Visual-based social media sites are extremely popular; and almost all social media sites encourage the use of images and videos in posts. The use of images can help a social media post get more engagement — the post is more likely not only to be seen but also to get liked, shared, or commented on by followers. This resulting need for visual content presents another moneymaking opportunity for you, not only with video, but also with any type of visual content, including original illustrations, images, photos, and even content that uses lots of graphics, such as infographics. If you can take good-quality photos or creative pictures, you can sell the rights for other companies and individuals to use those images. One place that promotes this service and connects amateur photographers with online buyers is Foap (www.foap.com). Check it out to see how you can trade your photos for dollars.

Although YouTube provides incredible traffic and moneymaking opportunities, getting your videos noticed can be tough with so much competition. However, you can use other video sites, such as the following sites that are quickly showing promise:

>> **Vimeo** (www.vimeo.com): Vimeo is a hosted video service provider that offers an extensive number of tools, promotional assistance, revenue share program, and advertising options. It also lets you offer multiple subscription offers for streaming your videos to customers or fans. These revenue-making

tools are available only through its Vimeo Pro account, which costs approximately $240 a year. It also offers a basic version for less than $85 per year. Learn more about its On Demand program and see examples at www.vimeo.com/ondemand/startselling.

>> **DailyMotion** (www.dailymotion.com): Based on how it hosts and delivers user-generated videos on its site, this site is perhaps the closest competitor of YouTube. The site gets over 120 million unique visitors monthly. DailyMotion offers three ways for you to make money. You can enroll in an affiliate-type program and earn money by sharing video links on your website or through your social media channels using DailyMotion's special widget; or you can rent your videos (for use by others) on a subscription basis. Or as with YouTube, you can make money earning ad revenue with your videos. DailyMotion provides an easy view of your earnings and engagement statistics through its Revenue Analytics tool.

Building social influence for dollars

Now you know about the different types of social media platforms and video networking sites, and can see some of the ways online entrepreneurs are cashing in on them. But you may be asking, *how* do you reach the point that you can capitalize on social commerce?

First, let's recap the primary ways you can earn money through social media:

>> **Ad revenue:** Earn money from showing ads to your followers. Depending on what type of social media platform you're using, there may be limitations to how ads are delivered. For example, videos may include ads that show up inside the videos themselves; other social media sites, or even a blog, might have ads show up in your profile or alongside the content.

>> **Sponsorships:** Brands pay you to sponsor, or be the highlighted advertiser of, your account for a limited period of time. Sponsorships can be for specific posts or videos, for email distributions to your followers, or for the sponsorship of your entire social media account or profile.

>> **Brand account take-overs:** If your influence is substantial, and you have a large community of fans and followers, brands may pay you to run their social media accounts for a few hours, or a full day. The idea is that your followers, as well as the brand's customers, know you're the one on their Instagram or Facebook account sharing photos and interacting with fans.

>> **Subscription services:** Especially with video, fans are often willing to pay monthly fees to watch your video or view your content. This has lucrative

earning potential because it is automatically recurring revenue. In other words, fans sign up once but their credit cards are auto-billed each month.

>> **Repackaging content:** Reusing what you've already created is an efficient way to increase earnings. Whether you are reselling photos or segments of your video, or other types of content that you've previously used, you retain the copyright but give buyers a limited-use license. The license permits people to use content for a specified fee, and you determine the parameters for how and when the content is used, thus the term "limited use."

>> **Selling direct:** As with any online retailer, social commerce earnings add up when selling products or services through a social media platform.

Before you get significant traction earning money from one of these types of revenue streams, it's important to have an audience that wants to be part of your community. You need social influence, or the ability to persuade others through your social media persona. In the examples we provided of social entrepreneurs and vlogging celebrities, you probably noticed that most all had several hundred thousand, if not millions, of fans and followers. That adds up to a lot of social influence. Your fans not only what to see you and watch what you do, but they also think your opinions are meaningful, especially when it comes to what products and services you use.

Is it necessary to have a large fan base in order to make money? That's almost always the case (unless you are repackaging your content) or selling products directly. The real question is *how many* followers qualify as a large enough fan base for you to exchange views for dollars? That's a tough question to answer because there's no definitive number.

Some social influencers on Instagram have had as few as 1,000 followers before receiving interest from brands. And many Instagram influencers agree that the turning point for brand interest is somewhere between 1,500 and 3,000 followers. For YouTube, and any other social platform, that number varies. Some of it is dependent upon the particular topic in which you specialize. The more niche, or specialized your content, the smaller the overall audience may be, and so a small number of followers may have a big impact.

Building your fan base

In the world of online business, we always like to point out the fallacies of the "build it and they will come" philosophy. Whether it's a new website, online store, or social media account, just because you have one of those things doesn't mean people will instantly flock to it and become visitors, customers, or fans. Like any business, developing a following of active users takes time, dedication, and persistence. Here are some of the ways to increase followers and build influence:

- **Stay active and consistent:** No matter what platform you want to be on and build a following, the number one most important factor for increasing fans is staying active. People don't have any reason to follow you or stay in touch with you if there's no content to like, share, or respond to. Not only that, but it's important to stay consistent — being active for three days in a row and then having no activity for the next two days means you aren't in front of your fans. It's similar to a newspaper having lots of stories in the paper for three days, but having only one article (or none!) the rest of the week. Readers would unsubscribe to the paper because there's nothing there to read. The same applies to your activity level on social media.

- **Be worthwhile:** It's not enough to put information out there on a regular basis. The content you create and share should be interesting, entertaining, or educational. And your content should match the interests of the type of fans or followers you want to attract. If you're growing a fan base of antique car enthusiasts, they probably don't care about cool new technology or apps, unless they specifically relate to caring for or buying and selling old cars.

- **Follow others:** It's amazing how many people on social media will follow you, if you follow them first. When connecting with followers for the first time, send them a thank you for the follow or tag them a post to welcome them to your community (others in your new follower's network are likely to follow you, too).

- **Communicate:** Having someone follow you is a great feeling, but if you never see her or hear from her again, you're likely to forget she exists. Equally important to having followers is to stay in touch with that follower by liking her posts, commenting on her posts, or sharing her posts. Engaging with your followers helps you build relationships and keeps you, and your brand, top of mind.

- **Display your genuine self:** If you've not spent much time on social media, it may seem confusing to you as to how to act. The best approach is to be true to yourself and talk or engage with others online, the same way you would talk to people offline.

- **Research other brands:** One of the great things about being on social media is that you often have more visibility into your competitors, or other brands with similar types of followers. Spend time following other successful brand accounts and see what type of content they share and how they engage with followers. This can provide some good ideas and strategies for you to emulate (but in your own voice, of course!). You can also interact with that brand's followers and like or follow those customers. So not only are you getting some creative ideas for your own social media site, but you're also (hopefully) gaining followers.

WARNING

Some social media platforms have third-party companies or individuals that advertise the ability to help you grow your followers in exchange for money. You might get a message from someone saying she can provide you with 5,000 new followers for $50, for example. Don't use these services! First, some of these companies are scammers that don't deliver users, but gladly take your money. Second, if you do get "followers," they are typically from fake accounts and not real people. Being successful with social commerce requires that you have active, engaged followers. Fake, non-existent followers won't do you a bit of good — and it can hurt your profile by having too many fake followers!

Gathering, Networking, and Promoting: Online Communities

Making the most of social commerce means getting involved. Sometimes, this takes you to places that may or may not have direct or in-platform selling options. There are lots of sites and communities that heavily influence your success with social commerce simply by influencing others. It's the offline equivalent of knowing all the networking hot spots (to meet and interact with new customers). It's a matter of knowing the online places where people are talking about where and how they buy, or what types of products are trending at the moment, and then making sure your store or products are being positively discussed by these active, vocal, and persuasive social customers.

Review sites

When was the last time you searched the Internet for product reviews before buying a specific product? Research shows that approximately 97 percent of online shoppers look to the Internet for recommendations and general product research before making a purchase. That's one reason websites that focus on product reviews are so popular. Of course, review sites focus on more than products. You also find reviews on places and services, from restaurants to day spas.

Regardless of what they're reviewing, these sites are yet another example of how social media influences behaviors — in this case, purchasing decisions. If you're selling anything, online or off, frequenting these sites is a good idea for several reasons. First, you can easily discover what customers have to say about the products you sell (or about your business). Second, you have the opportunity to interact with new and existing customers and get in on the discussion. On the other hand, if you have an interest in a niche market, you might consider launching your own review site. This strategy is popular when earning money through affiliate marketing programs, which we discuss in detail in Book 4, Chapter 2.

TIP

Many of the review sites provide business owners with a free profile page. Taking the time to complete this quick overview of your business is a good promotional opportunity. In addition to providing details about your business type and location, you can use the profile page to post specials or coupons.

Social cataloging

Social cataloging sites are similar to a virtual catalog. You can identify images that mean something to you, group them in one place (sometimes called a board or collage), tag them, and promote them as things you like. In some cases, you can link product images directly to product pages, or make products available for sale from within the site, itself. Primarily these sites focus on clothing and home goods, so what you can sell or promote is limited to those categories.

Social cataloging sites have evolved in only a few years, going from offering a Pinterest-style wish list for fans to becoming legitimate online catalog sites filled with super-active buyers. Whether or not you sell from these sites, another benefit is likely to come in the form of brand recognition and possible traffic referral to your site. Traffic from social cataloging sites could possibly provide enough eyeballs to generate ad revenue or affiliate-style commissions from product referrals.

Keep the following social cataloging sites on your radar:

>> **Chictopia** (www.chictopia.com): Users upload images of themselves wearing outfits from their favorite brands and offer links to buy those products. This community rewards users for engagement, such as liking photos, commenting, or sharing images. Reward points are traded for real products.

>> **Asos** (www.asos.com): The fashion brand, Asos, acquired an existing social cataloging site (Fashion Finder). Users upload looks, or images of themselves wearing specific outfits, and share those images using the hash tag #asseenonme. There is also a marketplace where other brands make their products available for purchase.

REMEMBER

As with any online community or social media platform, it's important to under-stand who the audience is that frequents the site and ensure that it matches your target customer. For example, Asos is filled with community members who shop small, trendy boutiques (think, less well known and not as pricey), whereas Poly-vore community members tend to shop for high-end designs, from clothing to furniture, and are willing to spend more. Similarly, while some or all of these social media sites and online communities may be new to you, most have been around for a long time and have experienced audience shifts. For example, Face-book has seen its younger users leave for Instagram.

As a social commerce business, it's easy to get started on these social catalog sites. While the specific sign-up and promotional actions you take may vary by individual site, here are the four must-do steps to begin putting the social into e-commerce:

1. Join the community.

The first step is to become part of the community — as a community member. Register (which may involve creating a personal profile) and begin exploring the site and getting comfortable with the way people interact and promote looks within the community.

2. Convert to a business profile.

Once you understand how the site works from the perspective of a community member, the next step is to sign up as a business, if this option is available. For example, Polyvore allows you to add "business" to your profile, which unlocks the ability to add products and clipping tools that let users choose your products to share in their style sets. Other sites may allow you create a profile that describes your business, and link to your online store.

3. Upload your product descriptions.

If the option exists, always upload products to the social catalog site so users can share the images. But even more important, add a short description (which also helps with search functionality to get your products found on the site). Include pricing as part of the description.

4. Engage with other users.

Perhaps the most important step, other than becoming a community member, is actively spending time in the site interacting with other members. This means liking or commenting on others' photos, following users, and even following other brands.

Presentation platforms

Plenty of community-based sites promote online socializing and sharing, but few of these networks, except LinkedIn, were created with businesses in mind. Given LinkedIn's success, sites that target the business customers and also provide a real service might just have potential as serious revenue generators. Presentation platforms are technically sites that offer a tool for businesses to publish, share, and archive business presentations. For example, a sales pitch developed in PowerPoint could easily be posted and viewed (publicly or privately) using one of these platforms.

Why classify presentation platforms as an online community? As mentioned, the capability to share, comment on, and circulate your published presentations in a defined space makes it a natural fit as a community. Your next question probably revolves around how to make money with this type of community. One possibility is that you could build your own niche presentation community and implement paid membership levels, similar to LinkedIn. But why go to all that trouble?

Instead, as a user of an existing presentation platform, you can use it as a tool to increase brand recognition and create your own presentation channel. From there, it's possible to capture leads (prospective customers!) and offer free or sample presentations as a way to send traffic to a site where your customers pay for access to more content. Not to mention, with the manner in which e-commerce is expanding to every corner of the online universe, we wouldn't be surprised to see click-to-buy functionality added directly into these types of tools. Take a look at the following presentation platforms that already attract lots of viewers:

>> **SlideShare** (www.slideshare.net): Offering a free account, SlideShare (now owned by LinkedIn) lets you post presentations developed in PowerPoint, as a PDF, or even as video — and generate leads from within your presentation. You increase the capabilities of this presentation network when you choose to upgrade to a Pro business account. Note that SlideShare is in the process of updating this program, so expect to see lots of changes and expanded options for generating revenue. SlideShare easily integrates with LinkedIn, which helps generate even more views.

>> **Prezi** (www.prezi.com): This presentation platform lets you create more of an interactive presentation that users can zoom in and out of, for example. The tool is easy to use and makes your presentation more engaging and user-friendly. Prezi offers different levels of paid accounts ranging from approximately $7 per month to $20 per month.

REMEMBER

Both communities offer the potential to make your online business more professional and visible. Although the money-making side of social networking sites and communities isn't always obvious, explore the possibilities and get creative. The sky is the limit on how you use social networks for your online success.

Chapter **3**

Evaluating the SaaS Model: Selling Software and Apps

E ven if you've never heard the term SaaS (which is pronounced like the word "sassy" but without the "y" on the end), you've likely used this type of service either in your business or personal life. SaaS stands for *software as a service* and it is delivered in the cloud. Whoa! The cloud? Yes, but not the type of cloud you see in the sky. Instead, when we refer to a service that is cloud-based, we mean that it is run over the Internet — so it's typically delivered, managed, and maintained offsite (not located at your physical site) and it is usually public (or shared by lots of people). SaaS is one of several categories within cloud computing. The idea of *cloud computing* is a pretty complex subject, but for our purposes here, we want to keep it simple and discuss it in very general terms. If you want to dive deeper into the subject, there are lots of information and opinions on the matter!

In a similar vein as SaaS is the mobile application (app) market. Delivered over the Internet, these apps are made for use on your mobile devices, from smartphones to tablets (such as the iPad). Whether you have an Android phone or prefer the iPhone, you've likely used lots of mobile apps for everything from scanning documents from your phone to monitoring the weather. All types of businesses, especially retail stores and restaurants, are rolling out mobile apps that make it easier to shop from your phone, receive special coupon offers, schedule in-store merchandise pickups, or order food for delivery. When you use Facebook or Twitter from your phone, or play games on your phone, all of it is done through mobile apps.

Online entrepreneurs have made a lot of money from creating and selling mobile apps and from developing and selling software as a service. In this chapter, we take a closer look at both the SaaS market and mobile app industry and show you why both of these areas still have plenty of room for you to get creative and *make bank* (that means earn a lot of money)!

Deciding to Deliver Online Services

If you've ever used TurboTax to complete your personal taxes, then you've used software delivered as a service. In fact, throughout this book we mention and recommend dozens of solutions, from shopping carts and credit card processors to website builders and data backup tools — all of which are examples of SaaS. Most people use cloud-based services today and don't even give it a second thought because it has become extremely common. In 2019, the SaaS market was set to hit $100 billion in revenues, according to Synergy Research Group. By the end of 2020, the global SaaS market is expected to hit the $157 billion mark, according to Statista.

Already, the SaaS market has seen consistent double-digit growth of 30 percent or more, year over year since 2013. Some analysts consider SaaS as a mature market, meaning there's not much more room for new growth or new competitors. Consider that some of the top U.S. companies already dominate the market, including Microsoft, Oracle, and Salesforce. You may be asking, if that's the case, then why are we including SaaS in this minibook about hot trends and market opportunities for small, online businesses? Within the broader software services market, you can still tap into other niche services areas.

One trend expected to see significant growth in the next couple of years is the *micro SaaS* business model. The micro market is defined by the following characteristics:

>> **Solopreneur:** The business is typically owned and managed by a single, founding entrepreneur or has fewer than five employees.

>> **Bootstrapped:** All the money it takes to start the business comes from the entrepreneur and is usually done in a very cost-conscious manner (translation: it's run on a shoe-string budget).

>> **Limited earnings:** While some businesses dream of multi-million (or billion) earnings, the micro SaaS model makes from $1,000 to $20,000, per month at most.

>> **No plans to scale:** The micro business is focused on its target audience and usually has limited features or capabilities — and it plans to stay that way.

>> **Remain self-funded:** Just as the solopreneur may have bootstrapped the start-up micro SaaS, there is no desire to seek outside funds from angel investors or venture capitalists in order to fuel expansion.

If you're interested in starting a small online business (which is very likely given you're reading this book), then the traits of a micro SaaS should easily ring true for you! To be successful in the micro SaaS market, there are some types of services or customers that are best to target. These include:

>> **Niche:** The software as a service addresses a very specific need within a much smaller market. You may not have a huge pool of customers, but you could be the preferred service that dominates that small space.

>> **Industry-specific:** No need to be everything to everyone. Instead of offering a service that works across lots of customer types, you focus on a particular area or customer, such as dentists (healthcare industry) or Realtors (professional services industry).

>> **Gap services:** A micro SaaS may address only a very specific need where another SaaS leaves off. So, you either fill in the gap or you offer a complementary service that extends the value of a larger, existing SaaS.

Putting the Software in the SaaS

Let's recap. SaaS is expected to remain a financially strong industry over the next few years. And there's a lot of opportunity to be had for a small, focused SaaS business. So far the news is all good, right? There's one small detail to discuss: how to develop software.

Here's the potential hiccup in your dream of starting a SaaS business: You have to provide usable software. If you're reading this chapter and you are *not* a software developer, a programmer, or a decent amateur developer, then it may be challenging for you to put down this book and immediately write a piece of software from scratch that's developed well enough (no bugs!) to make available to a paying customer. However, that doesn't mean you aren't capable of coming up with a fantastic idea — one that people are willing to pay for and that meets a real market need. So how do you transfer your idea into actual software? Here are some options:

>> **Take the self-taught route:** It's not inconceivable to think you can teach yourself how to code. We know plenty of people who have achieved this, and there are lots of resources available to help. Try reading one of these popular programming books to get started: *Java All-in-One For Dummies,* 5th Edition, by Doug Lowe (Wiley); or *Swift For Dummies*, by Jessie Feller (Wiley).

>> **Hire a pro:** There are lots of software developers who work as freelancers and are happy to get paid to turn your idea for a software service into a real product. There are also plenty of online sites to match developers with available projects. Check out these sites:

- Upwork (www.upwork.com)

- Guru (www.guru.com)

- Gun (www.gun.io)

- Toptal (www.toptal.com/freelance)

REMEMBER

When hiring a contractor or freelancer to create any type of content, from software applications to videos, you need a contract. Not only do you want to scope out the project and determine completion dates and payment terms, but you also want to get copyright details in writing. You may have to hire someone to execute on your ideas, but at the end of the day, you should own the complete rights to the software with no strings attached.

Understanding the SaaS Model for Making Money

Part of what makes software as a service a potentially lucrative business is the way in which you earn revenue. Most online businesses (or any business for that matter) are based on a one-time purchase. Even if you have a healthy dose of repeat customers, you probably don't have control over when or how often they come back to buy from you. That means your earnings are somewhat unpredictable, at least until you have enough buying history from customers to project your average daily or weekly sales. But the SaaS model is much like a subscription-based business in that customers agree to purchase your services every month, across a defined period of time. You know this revenue is going to show up in your business bank account every month, and this is called monthly recurring revenue.

As fantastic as it sounds to know exactly how much money is coming in every single month, there are some variances in this model that lend a bit of unpredictability. If you've ever signed up for cloud-based services, you probably know where we're headed with this.

First, SaaS companies usually offer several different pricing plans that range from a monthly pay-as-you-go option (with no service contract) to the option for a one-year or multi-year contract. In exchange for the customer committing to a longer term of service with a contract, there is a discount offered off the normal monthly fee. If the discount on multi-year contracts isn't a sweet enough deal, customers may prefer the month-to-month option. In this scenario, you're assuming the customer may stick with your service over a long period of time, but you don't know for certain.

TIP

There are ways to encourage customers to choose a multi-year contract option instead of a monthly plan. One strategy is to offer the monthly price but require that customers pay it in full for six months or for a full year at the time of registration. Instead of charging the customer's card for $10 each month, you charge $120 for 12 months; that way you still get a designated amount of money up front. The other strategy is to provide users with a free 30-day trial and at the end of the trial period offer a steeply discounted price on a multi-year contract if they sign up before the trial expires.

In addition to monthly and annual price plans, there's another pricing option that is sometimes at the heart of many SaaS businesses — it's free! This is referred to as the *freemium model.* You have a basic service option that is offered free, and you have add-on features or advanced (premium) services that are available for a larger monthly fee. The goal is to get a large number of customers to start using the product for free and then entice them with a more advanced service and features in the paid version. As you can imagine, the risk of this approach is whether or not you can convert enough free users to paid customers.

The next potential issue with the SaaS model is how much churn you have, or the rate at which customers drop off of your service on a monthly or quarterly basis. Churn rates could be higher if you have more customers on the monthly price plan and it's just easier to opt out of your service. But churn rates can also be impacted by the number of dissatisfied customers who drop your service because you've not delivered services as promised, have had technical issues or service interruptions, or you oversold the capabilities and the service or features don't work well or are too complicated to use. Whatever the reason, a high churn rate can take a big bite out of your projected monthly revenues. While rates vary by industry or service type, generally, SaaS businesses have a target churn rate of around 1 to 2 percent; but if your product isn't up to par, you might see rates double or triple that rate.

The other consideration that can impact your steady stream of incoming revenue is the amount of money it takes to get new customers. In the SaaS business model, the cost of acquiring a customer, or CAC, can be high compared to other types of online businesses. One reason for this is because there is a large amount of competition, unless you serve a specific niche, which means you may have to invest a lot more money for marketing, advertising, and sales. Complicating matters further is that it's relatively easy for customers to churn off, or leave, your service business. You could end up with a smaller base of loyal customers, so you not only need to gain brand new customers, but you may constantly have to replace existing customers.

If managing to get and keep more customers isn't enough to keep you busy, the last big factor in the SaaS model is the amount of money it takes to maintain your business. One of the big benefits of a SaaS business to your customers is the ease of use. Customers don't have to install or manage the software on their computers or in their networks. If something goes wrong, the SaaS provider (you!) is the one to fix it. That's great for your customers, but the flip side of that equation is that you are the one managing networks and maintaining services so they work around the clock. All of this network infrastructure and maintenance upkeep could add to up a pretty big bill each month. The trick is that you need to invest in these equipment and upkeep items first, even before you may have enough customers to cover those costs. This is why many SaaS businesses seek investors instead of self-funding.

If you can manage to keep costs low and wait for your revenues to catch up with your costs, you'll eventually be in really good shape with steady, predictable earnings.

SaaS TERMS YOU NEED TO KNOW

If you choose to deliver a software as a service, SaaS isn't the only acronym you're likely to hear. The SaaS industry has a lot of terminology that you may not have used previously. Here are some of the most common terms:

- **Freemium:** A combination of the words "free" and "premium," this is a pricing strategy for a SaaS business in which a basic service is available for free, but customers must pay to access a more advanced (or premium) version of the service.

- **Lifetime value (LTV):** Lifetime value refers to the amount of money a SaaS customer is worth to your business over the course of time (usually based on the length of contract terms).

- **Churn:** The term to reflect the rate or percentage of customers who leave your business across a set period of time, usually measured monthly, quarterly, or annually. You might have a churn rate of 3 percent quarterly — which reflects the portion of your total customer base that has "churned off" your services.

- **Monthly recurring revenue (MRR):** Monthly recurring revenue is the amount of money you take in every month for services actually provided. If a customer has paid a one-time set up fee for services, or has paid for a full year in advance, you do not count all of these funds as part of MRR. You only include the amounts for delivered services.

- **Annual contract value (ACV):** Annual contract value is the amount of money you expect to collect from a customer on a 12-month contract for your services, but it is the average of all yearly contracts.

- **Burn rate:** This is the calculation showing how quickly your SaaS model goes through cash to cover expenses.

- **Minimum viable product (MVP):** Minimum viable product represents the most basic version of your service (or product) that can be made available to early adopters, or those customers who are willing to try your service before it is fully developed.

- **Service level agreement (SLA):** Service level agreement represents the agreed upon terms of service between you (the SaaS business) and your customer using the service. It's a contractual obligation defining the specifics of how and when services are delivered, along with other reasonable expectations of service.

Creating Apps for the Mobile Customer

The number of smartphone owners has easily surpassed the number of PCs. According to Statista, the overall market penetration for smartphones will reach a rate of nearly 73 percent by 2021, which is significant. Of all the time people spend on digital (or online) media, adults spend an average of three hours per day on their mobile devices. And the vast majority of that time, 93 percent, is spent specifically on mobile apps. Mobile apps are a type of software that is created for use on a variety of mobile devices, including tablets and smartphones. With all this time spent on mobile apps, it's no wonder there have been billions of mobile apps downloaded worldwide.

More than 194 billion apps have been downloaded, as of the end of 2018. Even though only one-tenth of all apps are purchased, total worldwide app revenue reached $37 billion in the first half of 2019, and that's expected to continue to grow as mobile device usage expands. As enterprising app entrepreneurs, you could take a cut of this revenue; but, as with the SaaS market, the key is to find a smaller niche market to serve with a very specific use for your mobile app.

What types of mobile apps are people using? To answer that question, take a moment to look at your smartphone or that of friends. How many apps are installed on the device? What types are there and which ones are most used? As you might have predicted, gaming apps are by far the most downloaded, and account for nearly one-quarter of all available apps. And across all apps, iPhone users are most likely to pay for their app downloads. The most common price point is just over $1, but there are also spikes at the $4.99 and $9.99 price range. There are lucrative earnings potential in mobile apps, especially for games, but there are millions of gaming apps that also make little if any money. As with any endeavor, mobile apps are a business that requires having a solid, sought-after product, and marketing the product to make sure customers find you.

REMEMBER

Mobile apps like the gaming app examples we show you, potentially take in a lot of revenue, but it's not all necessarily from the cost of the download. Gaming apps have led the way in making add-on products and services available for purchase inside the apps. For example, you may download a popular mobile gaming app for a one-time fee of $2.99; once you start playing the game, you might also purchase virtual commodities (swords, gold, and special powers) to help you advance in the game. You could also purchase game "cheats" or tips to help you play better. All of this is counted toward the daily revenue that an app earns. As a mobile app developer, these are also examples of the ongoing development work you have to do (or pay for) to keep the game interesting and expanding. So, you have more than one-time development costs to create the game itself.

Games obviously aren't the only mobile apps getting the attention of users. Business apps make up nearly 10 percent of all available apps. Education is the next most popular category, followed by lifestyle and entertainment.

We should point out there are two main sources for downloading apps, depending on your type of mobile device. If you have an iPhone or iPad, the Apple App Store is your go-to source for apps. If you use an Android device, you likely use Google Play to get apps. The trends, of which apps are most popular and which ones generate the most revenue, match closely between the two app stores.

Budgeting and building apps

Making money with mobile apps is terrific if you happen to be a mobile developer. As with the SaaS dilemma, having a good idea for a gaming app or a business app only gets you so far — you have to develop the app, too! You can always hire a developer (check out the same resources we mention earlier for SaaS developers). Or, if you have some base-level programming skills and an interest in learning, you can teach yourself to develop mobile apps. To help you build your own, there are some resources available to make it somewhat easier.

Whether you have some familiarity with programming or are a complete novice, there are websites, apps, and toolkits (a collection of developer tools) that simplify the process of creating mobile software applications. Just like there are solutions that make it easy for you to build your own website, even though you don't know HTML, XML, JavaScript, or other languages, there are similar tools for building apps.

How much can you expect to pay to have apps built for you? If you're a savvy programmer, you can simply invest your time in building apps and it's especially cheap (or free!). Some development resources, like those listed in this section, charge nominal fees to access their app-building platforms, while others may offer free versions. If you're working directly with a hired developer, for example, then the range you may pay will vary widely. The payment range is largely dependent upon the complexity of the app and the time frame in which you want it. Prices for the completed project can rage from $50,000 to $500,000. As with any project-based contract with a developer, it's important to have the terms of the agreement carefully detailed at the outset.

Get started by checking out these resources:

>> **Appypie (**www.appypie.com**):** Code-free mobile app development that segments its app-building resources by category (church, retail, restaurants, and so on)

- » **Twilio** (`www.twilio.com`): Provides a set of development tools and coding short-cuts to develop communications and messaging apps

- » **QuickBase** (`www.quickbase.com`): Low-code development options available for business apps

- » **App Press** (`www.app-press.com`): Code-free options for developing a range of different types of apps

REMEMBER

When using low-code or no-code resources to help you develop an app, confirm the policy for reselling your app or using it for commercial, revenue-generating purposes. Some sites charge a fee if you plan to resell the app versus using it for yourself, or in your business.

Uploading apps for sale

The journey from coming up with a good idea for an app to developing a working mobile application available for sale is only part of the process of becoming an app entrepreneur. The final stage is to upload your mobile app to the appropriate app stores — Google Play (for Android) or the App Store (for Apple/iOS).

REMEMBER

As you may have realized, one of your first decisions in developing an app is whether it will be developed for only one mobile device platform or for both. Development is different for each, so if you want the app to be sold in both Google Play and Apple iStore, you are essentially building two different mobile apps. There is an annual fee for developers and contributors to participate in each of these application stores. It's $99 for Apple and $25 for Google.

Generally speaking, whether selling in Google Play or in Apple, it helps to follow these tips before officially submitting your mobile app for review:

- » **Test and retest:** The app must work, so complete a thorough testing process before submitting for third-party approval from an app store.

- » **Understand app store policies:** Educate yourself on the complete process for publishing an app in the store, and understand all policies so that you don't get caught with a violation that could halt or delay the approval process.

- » **Spell out app details:** From knowing what type of audience rating your app has to pricing, you want to have these details decided before submitting an app for approval, as they will be part of the application and review process.

- » **Prepare promotional material:** Save some time by having promotional images, videos, and app descriptions ready to go once you gain approval.

» **Complete store listing:** Follow guidelines for each app store so that you have all the information written down and ready to use for the in-store app description that users see when perusing the app store.

For specific details on the process of uploading an app for review, visit each of these stores:

» **Android for developers** (https://developer.android.com)

» **iOS for developers** (https://developer.apple.com)

Both app stores have specific requirements for accepting mobile apps into their stores. Getting your mobile app added to one of these busy online stores isn't difficult, but it does take patience. Not only does it take a while to hear back from the stores with their approval for your app, but the review process within each app store can be tedious. Once you load your app into the store, it can take quite a bit of time to gain final approval to offer the app for sale — sometimes as much as several months!

Chapter **4**

Generating Opportunities through the Generations: Millennials, Boomers, and Beyond

In this chapter, we take a look at carving out niche markets around segments of the population that are grouped together based on age, or the time period in which these consumers were born. Finding a small but lucrative subset of a larger market is the goal of any niche business. Some of the more popular niches that continue to withstand the test of time involve whole generations of a consumer base, including baby boomers, millennials, and Generation Z — and each of these categories keeps spinning out even smaller niche opportunities within the niche!

A record number of people were born between 1946 and 1964, and they eventually received the baby boomer label. The first generation large enough to have significant (and identifiable) influence on jobs, homes, and the economy, baby boomers at one time represented one of the fastest-growing markets. Not to mention, they have enjoyed an overall level of prosperity that has long made them a viable customer for many online business concepts. Considering this generation has been around long enough to be thoroughly sliced and diced into smaller niches, you may question whether any untapped market opportunity still exists. That's the beauty of segmenting a market by generation-based consumers. As consumers age and transition to different stages of life, their interests and needs evolve, which opens up new possibilities for businesses who serve them. For example, the baby boomer generation is retiring in record numbers and beginning to feel their age — this opens up new niche markets for everything from recreational activities to healthcare.

As we indicate, baby boomers are no longer the only generation with large numbers and very specific needs and wants. With more than 74 million individuals considered "millennials" (those born in the 1980s to early 1990s), they are now the largest living generation, having recently taken that title away from boomers. We discuss millennials in greater detail later in this chapter, but for now, just know that millennials have also surpassed baby boomers as the largest segment of employees in the U.S. workforce and are having kids of their own.

Speaking of children, on the heels of the millennials is Generation Z — loosely defined as those kids and young adults born in the mid-1990s to late 2000s. The approximate 15-year span that defines Gen Z is made up of consumers that total approximately 70 million. This is roughly the same size as the millennial generation. As you may have guessed, children make up a fairly large market of potential online customers, and there's no reason why you can't take a piece of that market — as long as you can keep them interested in what you have to offer.

In this chapter, we show you how to tackle the marketing strategies that help you tap into this young Gen Z market. There's no limit to the type of niche you can carve out to serve any of these diverse population segments.

Understanding the Baby Boomer Market

When baby boomers hit the big Five-Oh, they became part of another interesting demographic — the over-50 market, with projections putting that total market size (not only baby boomers) at nearly 76 million in the United States as of 2019. Today, most baby boomers are in their 60s (and beyond) and have been making news for their impact on the American workforce. Estimates show baby boomers are retiring at a rate of 10,000 per day, leaving large gaps in the workforce, and especially depleting the more experienced senior management roles. The aging baby boomer market has both pros and cons for online businesses targeting this niche market.

On one hand, the boomer group has earned a reputation for spending billions of dollars — online and off. However, some analysts wonder if members of this aging population, now headed into their Social Security–funded years, will still help fuel the economy with their buying habits or start to become a financial burden. So far, research indicates that the boomers' spending will remain strong. Not only does this generation control nearly three-fourths of all U.S. disposable income, but also its members are set to inherit $15 trillion in the next two decades, according to Nielsen. That is a lot of money sifting through the wallets of baby boomers!

Before targeting the over-60 customer base, you need to know some things about this group. Most importantly, you should monitor the changes in this group's traits and buying behaviors as the boomer population shifts and adjusts with time. For now, consider boomers to be lucrative customers, and take a look at these common traits. They are

>> **Open minded:** Research indicates that boomers are willing to try new products, regardless of who makes them. Like everyone else, they have their favorites, but these consumers aren't bound by brand alone. This flexibility means that you have room to introduce alternative products or services to boomers, and they're likely to receive the message.

>> **Value conscious:** Everyone likes getting a good deal, especially consumers over the age of 50. We're not talking about bargain basement shopping, though. Research shows that although this group is willing to spend money, boomers want to know that they're receiving a value in return. That value can range from a quality product for the price to a fantastic experience that makes the money worth spending. Again, consider that the tendency toward shopping for a value may only increase as this market segment reaches retirement age or if general economic conditions change for the worse.

>> **Influenced by peers:** Friends tend to have lots of opinions about their buying experiences, and boomers seem particularly interested in hearing from their comrades. And those opinions frequently influence the boomers' final buying decisions.

>> **Self confident:** Friends and family aren't the only ones with valuable opinions. People over 60 trust themselves, too. A person's experience with a product or service greatly affects future purchasing decisions. That's not to say that you can't make an honest mistake and be forgiven. But this group thinks carefully before spending more money at your site if you've already let boomers down.

>> **Research advocates:** Before buying, this market wants the scoop on products. And boomers are willing to invest whatever time necessary for a prepurchase investigation.

>> **Willing to spend:** As we mention, baby boomers have plenty of disposable income and they have a propensity to spend it. Some recent data indicates that their debt load is increasing as they spend more on kids and grandkids. As you consider where baby boomers are spending, don't overlook the fact that they are actively spending and taking on debt for others.

Designing your site to attract aging customers

Typically, website design trends apply across the board. For instance, we see sites adopting a very specific (and similar) look and structure, prompted by the need to be mobile-friendly. Even within these mobile responsive design templates, there's room for customization, and sometimes you need to make design decisions based on your target customer. That's the case with an older baby boomer customer. By making a few conscientious decisions, you can improve your site's appeal to this aging demographic.

Background and colors

Research shows that your site for the more mature customer is better served by sticking to some standard color rules:

>> **A white background color works best.** White is simple and crisp, and it makes text easy to read.

>> **Certain elements need color.** Captions, headlines, and ads can use color — use brighter, bolder selections.

>> **Black text reads well.** Stick with black text for articles and product descriptions, versus the trendy lighter gray you often see for text today.

>> **Minimize your use of blue and green.** Avoid using too many blue and green tones, especially from the lighter color palettes.

>> **Use only a few colors.** Keep the number of color selections to a minimum.

>> **Maximize your use of contrasting colors.** They're more pleasing to the eye, and they make information on your site pop.

Text and fonts

The prevailing mindset says that if you target older consumers, you have to use huge text on your site. This idea isn't exactly true. The overall goal is to increase the readability of your site. Follow these tips for better readability:

>> **Avoid placing text on top of blocks of color.** Use black text on a neutral (preferably white) background.

>> **For primary text, such as main content, use a slightly larger font.** Try 12 or 14 point.

>> **To grab attention in headlines and captions, use a large font.** Try 14 or 16 point.

>> **Use case wisely.** Place captions in ALL CAPS for emphasis, but use lowercase letters for other text.

>> **Use leading appropriately.** Add extra spacing between lines of text so that your content isn't cramped.

>> **Choose a sans serif font for your text.** Arial and Helvetica are good choices.

REMEMBER

If you're hesitant to move away from popular website design trends, you can opt to implement only subtle design tweaks and let your site visitors make adjustments to screen resolutions and font displays on their end.

Links and buttons

Every spot on your website serves a purpose, especially links and buttons. URLs placed on the site serve as links to help visitors move within your website. Buttons also guide people through your site's structure. You can enhance the functionality of these features, making it easier for boomers to get around, by using these tips:

REMEMBER

>> Visually differentiate between links that the user has or hasn't visited.

Having a link change color after a user clicks it is a common method to indicate a link that has been clicked.

>> Place a series of links in a bulleted list.

>> Be descriptive when labeling links. Use keywords and specific phrases to describe the link, as opposed to using the phrase *Click here*.

>> Make the clickable areas of buttons and graphics larger than the button or graphic itself. A consumer should be able to click the mouse on a target area that surrounds the image (as opposed to clicking exactly on the image itself).

Site structure

The key word for organizing your site is *intuitive*. You want boomers to be able to easily (and instinctively) locate information and products throughout your site. To make your site structure boomer friendly, follow these guidelines:

>> **Location, location, location.** Keep your most important information or content in the upper-middle areas of each page of your site, especially the home page.

>> **Limit scrolling.** Not all online shoppers appreciate excessively long web pages.

>> **Avoid excessive clicking.** Don't make shoppers click or double-click excessively to navigate through your site.

TIP

Try incorporating expandable menus in your site to show page options. Usually, these submenus appear whenever your mouse cursor moves over a specific button or link. Unlike with drop-down menus, you don't have to double-click to open expandable menus.

>> Display a directory of topics (shown as a group of links) at the top of your pages. When you group link choices and make them all visible at one time, your visitors can easily move throughout your site.

Many of these design rules for the older market translate to good design for everyone. For the most part, these guidelines come from a lot of research done on boomers. Organizations such as AARP now promote these design tools as recommended standards for this market.

Keeping baby boomers buying from you

As their active lifestyles demonstrate, boomers are far from decrepit! And although they may qualify for the classic senior discount at many businesses, you can use a number of better ways to reward those customers who fall in the more mature age range:

>> **Provide enhanced service.** Excellent customer service is a plus for any age group. This market is no exception. Dazzling your customers with extreme care and attention is better than any $5-off coupon.

>> **Offer targeted promotions.** Rather than give a general discount, you can create a personalized promotion that zeroes in on the interests and needs of each special consumer.

>> **Give out loyalty rewards.** Boomers may be open to trying new brands, but don't hesitate to reward them when they decide to stick to yours. Frequent-buyer discounts, special giveaways, and other product-based rewards help convince customers to come back to your site.

Finding a niche in the baby boomer market

Accepting a gold watch upon retirement and settling into a comfortable recliner is no longer the status quo. This generation is bursting at the seams to stay active, fit, and involved. Although, older baby boomers have different preferences from the younger consumers in this generation. One of the biggest differences is the interest in healthcare services and products by baby boomers in their 70s. Whereas those still in their 50s and 60s have a strong propensity for wellness and beauty products, specifically anti-aging products. Here are areas with great niche appeal to the baby boomer market:

>> **Convenience:** The do-it-yourself (DIY) trend is passé for boomers. Many of them think that the convenience of having someone else do tasks is worth the price. Any type of product or service that saves time is a winner in this market.

>> **Cosmetics:** On average, boomers consider themselves 12 years younger than their actual birth date indicates. Both men and women are willing to invest in helping their outsides appear as healthy as their inner selves feel.

>> **Customization:** Boomers are a diverse bunch who often reject any type of labels. You can't pigeonhole this group into any single category. One 65-year-old may be retiring while another is launching a new business. Those two people may be the same age, but that doesn't mean that they're experiencing the same things. The good news is that this individuality opens up another lucrative online market opportunity for you. Customization, specialization, a niche within a niche — call it what you like. Focusing your product base to a boomer's current lifestyle circumstances, rather than to an age-based generalization, often equals profit.

>> **Home experience:** Thanks to the interest in second homes, vacation properties, and a desire to live well in a primary residence, boomers have many houses to maintain. This demand creates a lucrative market for stylish household appliances, upscale linens, entertainment products and services, and many other household items. Big-box retailers like Lowes and Home Depot have seen healthy sales from baby boomers, and there's no reason you can't create an online business to focus on a niche within this area of interest.

>> **Healthcare:** For boomers already in their 70s, there's an enhanced focus on anything related to maintaining or treating your health. Baby boomers also

don't mind spending money on convenience, or any product or service that makes it easier to manage their health.

>> **Recreation:** Boomers can always find time for play. Recreational items, ranging from RVs to Vespa scooters (and everything in between), fit nicely with the active, adventurous lifestyle of most boomers.

TIP

You don't have to sell a 16-foot RV to find success in the recreation category. Instead, focus on a smaller niche, such as specialized accessories for the large vehicles.

>> **Pets:** It's true that the pet industry is a lucrative market that can support many different niche businesses. But baby boomers play a big role in the pet industry, accounting for nearly half of all pet-related spending. That opens the door for some interesting online concepts geared toward older pet owners.

>> **Travel:** Helping boomers explore exotic locations has proven to be a good strategy for several online travel sites. Any product or service that makes traveling more comfortable and enjoyable can result in a winning e-business for you. In fact, every year baby boomers spend more than $120 billion on leisure travel, according to AARP; this includes "once in a lifetime" destinations and travel to warm destinations. You don't have to be an online travel agency to take advantage of this trend; instead try to imagine services or products that would complement these highly mobile baby boomers.

The moral of this story is simple: You have an unlimited number of market opportunities when you're wooing baby boomers, so use your imagination and have fun with this exciting group of online consumers.

Figuring Out What Millennials Want and Delivering It

Unless you've spent the last couple of years hiding under a rock, you probably already know a few things about millennials. Politicians need them to vote, the entertainment industry wants them to watch movies and stream shows on Netflix, and e-commerce sites expect them to snap, chat, tweet, like, and share their favorite products with all their friends and followers. Considered to be in their early 20s to mid-30s, millennials are now considered the largest and most influential living generation, overtaking baby boomers in size; millennials account for more than 25 percent of the U.S. population.

This generation has also suffered through some disparaging labels, such as being lazy, underemployed, disrespectful, self-centered, and demanding. The research paints a different picture. This is not a generation of slackers, but they do have specific expectations from brands and they spend a lot of time on social media sharing their opinions and experiences — the good, the bad, and the ugly! They're also an instant-gratification type of consumer — meaning they don't like to wait.

Online businesses are a perfect fit for this consumer. Not to mention, millennials are expected to have $1.4 trillion in collective spending power in 2020 and beyond. That buying power makes millennials a sought-after niche consumer. However, this generation is now in the workforce and paying off significant student loan debt, and are often cited as "living paycheck to paycheck" with little net worth. Even so, millennials don't mind spending on trendy beverages, dining out, entertainment, and games. When targeting this influential generation of shoppers, here are some other important traits to take into consideration:

>> **Self-service options required:** As an online business, you want to provide excellent customer service, but millennials don't want that or anything else to disrupt the buying process. This generation wants to decide when and how they need assistance when buying online (or off).

>> **It's all about the journey:** Millennials focus on the experience that comes with everything they do, whether that's shopping, eating, or travelling. When catering to this niche, you're likely to earn these online shoppers' loyalty if you create a unique or special environment around buying from your store.

>> **Tech, tech, tech:** It's very likely this group of consumers are shopping from a smartphone, so your online store better deliver a seamless mobile experience. It's also a given that you'll use the latest technology to enable purchasing, servicing, and marketing to these super tech-savvy shoppers.

>> **Cause-centric brands appreciated:** Millennials not only have a generous heart, they also want to shop with online brands that share their passion for making the world a better place. Cause consumerism, or businesses that support social good, came into the spotlight with companies like Toms (www.toms.com), which donates a pair of shoes to charity for each pair of shoes purchased. Millennials have an affinity for this type of business model, and it's paying off for newer social good brands like FlexWatches (www.flexwatches.com), which is winning over online shoppers with its commitment to charitable giving that is tied to specific watch styles.

REMEMBER

To be successful with this type of approach to wooing millennial customers, you need to be sincere about your support to a cause. It goes beyond making occasional donations to nonprofits; millennials expect your business to be centered around giving, and the cause to truly be at the foundation of your business model.

>> **Be the brand:** Similar to wanting to have a unique experience when shopping, millennials want to be actively involved with your brand. It's not only about providing consumer-generated content, but rather helping influence the way your products are created or selected, and being an intimate part of the process somewhere along the way from start to finish. Think of this as going a few steps beyond customers giving feedback. If you can provide this niche market a sense of ownership in your online brand, you'll be rewarded with long-lasting loyalty.

>> **Social currency rules:** It shouldn't be a surprise that this socially adept generation of consumers take to social media, often when shopping online and off. They take to social platforms (including Instagram, Snapchat, and YouTube) to share their experiences with your brand, communicate with your brand, and learn about your brand from peers. If you're going to focus on a niche with millennial consumers, then you want to integrate social media into all aspects of your company, and do it well.

Getting Online with the Digital Kids: Generation Z

Often described as the younger siblings of the tech-savvy millennials, this is the first generation to grow up completely digital. Gen Z kids have never known what it's like to live in a world without the Internet or without social media. Even the younger side of this market segment, those kids under 10, are comfortable with technology; they have likely been playing video games and using smartphones since starting pre-school.

The older segment of Gen Z has some specific traits that you want to consider when trying to market to them, especially online. The Gen Z teens and young adults tend to share the following traits:

>> They are adept at communicating via social media, but, similar to millennials, prefer platforms like Snapchat and Whisper — and shy away from Facebook.

>> They are guarded with online privacy, having seen older generations disclose too much online.

>> They are entrepreneurial; this generation prefers to own a business as opposed to work for one, but is still practical when it comes to earning a living.

>> They are risk-averse and generally cautious.

After learning all these traits, you may be curious as to what type of customer an older Gen Z would make. In actuality, they are likely to be a loyal, repeat customer. The caveat is that you must treat them fairly, offer a solid product (or service) at a reasonable price, and respect their privacy when marketing to them online. But what customer wouldn't you treat this same way? When focusing on the younger side of Gen Z, privacy is also a huge concern. To understand the privacy regulations when marketing to this group, let's look at the way in which younger children are further divided into three distinct groups, based on age:

>> **Kids:** Although children who are 7 or younger don't always have enough independence to shop by themselves, they're influential in their parents' final purchasing decisions. Parents want to please their offspring and usually give 'em what they want. And keep in mind that marketers only consider kids 5 and older as part of Gen Z, so this group is a very small segment, but still counts!

>> **Tweens:** Children between the ages of 8 and 12 are considered a target market unto themselves. These kids have outgrown "baby" items and are starting to emulate the trends made popular by their older counterparts (teens).

>> **Teens:** Ranging in age from 13 to 17 (some marketers go all the way to 18), this group is typically more mature. Savvy-shopping teens usually have greater decision-making abilities with less adult input. And many teens have hefty amounts of money to throw around, from working part-time jobs or from receiving an allowance from their parents (or both).

All three age groups are adept at using computers. Tweens and teens are particularly comfortable surfing the Internet and embracing technology for multiple purposes — including shopping online, downloading apps and music, and playing online games. According to a 2019 *Taking Stock with Teens* report from Piper Jaffray Cos, teens (ages 12 to 17, with an average age of 16) frequently shop online, with a self-reported spend of $2,600 per year on products and services. That number breaks out to 45 percent of girls and 54 percent of boys with online shopping habits. Fast forward to the 2019 report, and we get a closer look at overall online habits. Gen Z teens:

>> Shop at specialty stores and boutiques over large retailers, but Amazon is the preferred online destination

>> Watch more YouTube and Netflix versus traditional television and cable

>> Communicate using social media and prefer Instagram and Snapchat

>> Prefer smaller, independent brands over large brands, particularly with fashion and beauty care

>> Care about social causes, especially the environment

Other interesting take-away points from this niche group of online spenders are the uses of mobile devices and digital streaming. Mobile devices are an important part of teens' lives, and they use smartphones and tablets for everything from online research to online shopping. The majority of teens prefer an iPhone.

Similar trends have been identified by Pew Internet and the American Life Project study, including these facts:

>> Nearly all teens (95 percent) use smartphones and nearly half indicate they are online "almost constantly."

>> When it comes to socializing, teens actively use a social networking site, and prefer Instagram, YouTube, and Snapchat.

>> It's not all fun and games; approximately 62 percent of teens look to the Internet for news, current events, and political information.

TIP

Pew Internet has a lot of good research to help you better understand the market of kids and teens online. You can access more facts about Gen Z teens and Internet usage for free on its website at http://pewinternet.org/topics/teens-and-youth.

Attracting a fickle customer

Perhaps one of the toughest challenges in selling to kids is simply keeping them interested. Kids are often among the first consumers to get excited about a new product and help it skyrocket to success. Unfortunately, their enthusiasm can pass quickly, and they're equally willing to shun an item after they tire of it. This behavior does not mean that an online store targeted to kids will be short-lived. Rather, it requires you to stay in tune to kids' interests and trends and be prepared to keep adding new products.

To decide which products your online business should promote to children, given this level of market uncertainty, you can search for items in one of the following broad categories. At least for the next few years, these product areas are expected to remain hot, hot, hot for kids of all ages:

>> **Technology:** Kids love technology. Think about where iTunes would be today without its young audience of fans. The fantastic fact about kids and technology

is that this relationship usually helps create other industries and products, too. You may not have created iTunes or the iPhone for that matter, but you can easily sell accessories or products to go along with these popular tech trends. In this example, think in terms of everything from custom cellphone covers to apps. Technology and anything related to it equals opportunity in the kid market.

>> **Interactive services:** Kids use the Internet in a big way. Their expertise and the amount of time they spend online will only increase over the next decade. That's why any service (for fun or otherwise) delivered by way of the Internet has a shot at success with kids. Online gaming, streaming videos, and binge-watching TV (on-demand) are all activities that rocketed into full-blown industries of their own, thanks in large part to the kid market.

>> **Sports:** Kids and sports are almost inseparable. A record number of kids now play on local sports teams, and sports span the gamut of this market, appealing to young kids, tweens, and teens. Whether you sell sports gear online or promote e-books targeted to improving your game, even your most fickle kid customer can't resist this category.

>> **Customization:** Kids like having the option to customize a popular product to their specifications. From shoes to jewelry, tweens and teens seem particularly fond of slightly tweaking a mass-produced item and calling it their own. This area has potential to grow, especially as more brand-name retailers offer online customization of products.

>> **Décor:** This product category is definitely hot right now, including stylish home products to decorate kids' bedrooms or teens' dorm rooms, and fun accessories that dress up school lockers and a teen's first car. Decorating personal space feeds into the desire of children to make things their own.

Keeping 'em coming back for more

No matter what you choose to market to kids, you have to deal with the issue of how to keep those little shoppers coming back to your site. Follow these guidelines to help turn your young customers into repeat buyers:

>> **Add products.** It almost goes without saying — introduce new products, and do it often. Period.

>> **Offer a twist.** You can update older products by offering them in new colors or styles. Or after you identify a particular product that sells well, offer companion products.

>> **Change your site.** In addition to the products you sell, the site itself needs a frequent face-lift. You don't have to redesign your site. Instead, try adding fresh images, updating content, and switching colors occasionally.

- >> **Create a community.** As the popularity of social networking sites demonstrates, kids thrive on interacting with other kids. Sites that (safely) offer the opportunity for kids to communicate online or that can build a sense of identity for a particular group keep kids coming back.

- >> **Let them socialize.** With 95 percent of teens regularly flocking to social media sites, keeping kids interested in your site means letting them connect and share the way they want. Integrate social networks into your site and provide a way for teens to share your site's information over these same networks.

- >> **Grab opinions, give rewards.** You can include quick polls, top-ten lists, and other surveys that solicit the opinions of your customers on your site. (These features also help create a sense of community.) Kids also like to be rewarded for patronizing your site. Free downloadable games, coupons, loyalty shopping rewards, freebies, and giveaways are sure to please.

TIP

If kids like your site and your products, they tell their friends. Why not make it easy for them? Let your loyal customers pass along some of your site's freebies to their friends by way of email, text, or social media. If you make sharing easy, you attract more attention — and future customers.

Reeling in the parents

Like it or not, moms and dads continue to play a role in their children's purchasing habits, even as the kids approach early adulthood. How, or how much, you involve parents in the online selling process typically depends on two things: age and product.

Age

Exactly how old is your target customer? Generally, the younger the child, the more information you want to provide for parents:

- >> **Kids:** Parents usually have the final authority on all purchases when young children are involved. But don't forget that these kids (especially as they reach school age) are fairly avid computer users. Have sections on your site that meet the wants of the children, as well as a section that addresses the needs of the parents.

- >> **Tweens:** After a child enters the tween stage, the parent/child relationship begins to change and your site has to respond appropriately. Parents still have a great deal of control, but their input becomes more of a filter. At this age, kids and parents are truly making decisions together. If you're marketing to tweens, you don't have to devote an entire section aimed at parents, but you may want to reassure adults that you're safely marketing to kids.

>> **Teens:** If teens are your market, you probably don't need any messages targeted to parents. However, you should actively communicate to this audience on social media sites, especially Instagram, Snapchat, and YouTube. Teens are particularly tuned into social media influencers, like David Dobrik and Kylie Jenner (both well-known YouTube personalities and celebrities).

TIP

If you have a product that appeals to more than one targeted age range, divide your site by age. Create sections for each age group so that kids and parents can quickly find the appropriate spot and start buying!

Product

The type of product you sell can determine how you involve, or market to, parents. One of the best examples of a product deciding the parents' role is clothing. Rarely do young children visit online clothing sites. In most cases, parents do all the shopping. Therefore, you might have a site designed in fun, age-appropriate colors because it matches the tone of the product line, but you're ultimately selling to parents.

Reading the small print: Important policies to consider

We can't cover the basics of selling to kids without sharing one of the biggest rules of running an online business: Always clearly post privacy policies and terms of agreement for your users. (You can find more details on these policies in Book 1.)

Posting and following a privacy policy is the number-one rule when you're running a site targeted to kids. The Children's Online Privacy Protection Act (COPPA), passed by Congress in 1998, oversees children's privacy on the Internet.

The primary goal of COPPA is to ensure that you're acting responsibly when you collect information online from children under the age of 13. In a nutshell, you can't request even a hint of personal information from a child without first notifying the child's parents and getting their permission. If you have one of the following two types of websites, COPPA applies to you:

>> **Children's site:** You have content, products, or services specifically designed for children. Your site also

- Is a *for-profit,* or commercial, website
- Collects personal information from children under the age of 13

>> **General site:** Your online business can offer any type of product or service, but COPPA applies if you

- Have a section on your main site targeted to kids or specifically designed to appeal to kids or have content types (such as video) targeted to kids

- Knowingly collect personal information from a visitor under age 13

Generally, you have to follow seven basic requirements for communicating with preteens, using the COPPA rule:

>> **Post your privacy policy.** Make your site's policy on protecting a child's personal information easy to spot on your home page. Don't be afraid to use a little extra real estate to make this policy stand out.

REMEMBER

No matter which type of site you run, always clearly post a privacy policy on your site for customers to read.

>> **Notify parents.** When children want to receive fun stuff from your site (or you want information about them), obtain parental permission first.

TIP

You're allowed to collect a child's name and his or her parent's email address to request parental consent. Check the Q&A portion of the Federal Trade Commission's COPPA site for businesses (www.business.ftc.gov/documents/0493-Complying-with-COPPA-Frequently-Asked-Questions) for the lowdown on getting parental consent.

>> **Protect data.** Any information you collect must remain private, secure, and protected. It's your obligation!

>> **Offer a choice.** After you notify parents that you want to collect information about their children, make sure they know they can say no.

>> **Provide access.** At any time, a parent can request to take a look at the information you have on file for their children. Be sure to open those files if a parent asks!

>> **Keep in touch.** Stay in contact with parents. Give them the opportunity to *opt out,* or discontinue receiving information.

>> **Allow participation.** No matter what, you can't restrict a child's access to your site if a parent doesn't want to give up personal information.

WARNING

If you fail to comply with COPPA, you and your site can be penalized by the Federal Trade Commission (FTC). If you make the necessary changes, you still have to pay a fine.

In 2019, YouTube (and its parent company, Google) settled a COPPA violation case with the FTC. The company was ordered to pay $136 million to the FTC and $34 million to the State of New York because YouTube allegedly collected information or data from children (in the form of cookies, used to track Internet activity of users) and then used that to target the children with ads, and did not notify parents under the requirements of the children's privacy law. It's the largest settlement of a COPPA violation to date.

In response to the settlement, YouTube is updating its requirements for COPPA compliance for video content creators who have channels or post videos to YouTube. The new policy, effective January 2020, requires all content creators to designate whether the video posted is "made for children." The content creator, regardless of geographic location or type of video content being shared, must select the designated box stating whether the content is created for children. Videos created for children will not appear in search results and will no longer have personalized ads served, which means advertising revenue for those content creators is likely to drop. YouTube says it's also using machine learning tactics to do its own analysis of whether a video is made for children. Even if the content creator didn't designate it as such, YouTube gets the final say and will subsequently remove the video if it finds that it is made for children and not designated as such. Those content creators violating the children's privacy law are also subject to fines from the FTC.

As you can see, this rule may have significant financial impact on all types of content creators making income from videos posted to YouTube. Given the fact that the YouTube policy is so new, and there has been an incredible amount of backlash about it from content creators, it'll be interesting to see how this policy continues to evolve and be updated. In the meantime, the takeaway is clear: You must understand COPPA and follow the rules of the privacy policy, especially if your content or website potentially targets children under the age of 13.

TIP

You can avoid tempting the Federal Trade Commission (FTC) to slap fines on you by deciding not to collect personal information. Instead, get parents involved. Communicate directly with moms and dads if you have messages for their children.

With everything that you have to worry about, selling to kids can seem a little overwhelming. If you take the time to plan your strategy, however, and make sure that your legal *i*'s are dotted and *t*'s are crossed, the kid's market, no matter which generation they belong to, is truly a fun one!

11

E-Commerce Advanced

Contents at a Glance

Chapter **1**

Mapping the Digital Buyer's Journey

nformation is power. There's little debate that a well-educated buyer is a smart buyer, and the Internet has truly empowered today's consumer online and off. That means that how and when a purchase is made has changed significantly in the last two decades. For example, despite the complexity of many business-to-business (B2B) purchases, Gartner Research shows that buyers spend only 19 percent of their time meeting with a vendor (the seller) when considering a purchase. And only 5 percent of their time may involve an actual salesperson! Why? Consider that analysts also estimate that as much as 70 percent of B2B buyers have already made or narrowed their decision to buy before seeking late-stage sales assistance from your business. For business-to-consumer (B2C) buyers, that number jumps to as much as 90 percent! Of course, this difference in buyer behavior isn't too surprising. A B2C purchase is often less complicated (buyers simply complete the online check-out process) compared to a B2B purchase (which might require actively engaging a salesperson to complete the sale). It's more important than ever before for online businesses to understand where and when buyers are getting information and how that influences their final buying decisions.

In this chapter, we walk you through the stages typical online buyers go through when making a purchasing decision, how they are collecting information about your brand, and what you can do to influence the modern buyers' journeys.

Deconstructing the Path of an Online Buyer

When talking about the *pathway* a buyer takes, we simply mean that there are typical stages a consumer goes through as part of the decision-making process. It's important to understand this process so that you have a better chance of influencing the buyer at each stage — even if you cannot directly reach or engage the buyer at the earliest of these stages.

You may be wondering how can you influence buyers if you can't actually communicate directly with them? The answer to that question is based on where buyers consume information, and from whom. Before the proliferation of the Internet, salespeople (whether B2B or B2C) primarily controlled the buying process and could guide a prospective customer through the sales process, telling the buyers what the company wanted to, when they wanted to (through product brochures, demonstrations, and advertising). As we shared earlier, B2B buyers are far less likely to even engage a salesperson in the buying process today. That's a big shift in behavior!

Talking to prospective customers was also a one-way communications process via advertising, with brands *pushing out* information to the consumers through TV commercials and magazine and newspaper ads, for example. There was little opportunity for buyers to control the flow or type of information they received from brands.

Today, the buyer may evaluate a company or brand long before the brand is aware of that buyer. The buyer gets that information from product review websites, social media conversations, online communities, competitors, peers, friends and perfect strangers — and the vast majority of this information-gathering process occurs online. Let's take a look at each stage of the buying process and see how a consumer's view of a brand evolves during the online discovery process:

>> **Awareness:** In this first stage, the consumer doesn't yet understand that he or she is starting the path to becoming someone's buyer. The consumer doesn't even realize he has a problem or a need that your product or service can solve. Let's use the example of a young male who has been scratching his face more and more after he shaves. He's mildly aware of it, and maybe irritated by it, but he doesn't spend a lot of time thinking about it. Then, he gets on the social media forum site called Reddit and explores different conversation threads. He comes across a discussion in which others are complaining about their faces being irritated after shaving and asking for opinions about what might be causing it. The responses range from the itchiness being caused by a skin

condition that requires medical treatment to reactions to certain skincare products. Several guys on the thread mention using a product called Dr. Carver's Post Shave Cream that they bought online from DollarShaveClub.com (www. dollarshaveclub.com). They rave about how much it helped fight irritation after shaving. The young male buyer considers that this might be part of his problem, but he's not ready to buy — yet. He's still discovering that he might have an issue.

» **Consideration:** Once a buyer decides he has a problem, he is ready to start actively looking for a solution. Following our male buyer, he decides his shaving process and the lack of quality products is creating a skin condition, but he's not yet made up his mind as to which solution is best. He's already been introduced to one product and a site where he can buy it, but being a savvy consumer, he's not ready to commit. Instead, he begins actively looking for other products that might work. In this stage of the buying process, he's doing a lot of detailed research about specific products and vendors, reading online reviews, watching product videos, and comparing the different types of shaving and facial care products for men — including pre-shave products like shea butter and oils. He may also come across reviews of your online business that specializes in men's healthcare products, and he adds that to his list to consider, in addition to Dollar Shave Club.

» **Decision:** Once the buyer enters the final stage, his decision is almost made. He's already narrowed down the type of product he wants and is fairly certain where he will buy it. In our scenario, the young male buyer is leaning toward a bundle package of Dr. Carver's Shea Butter and Post Shave Cream. He's now spending a lot of time on the Dollar Shave Club site comparing prices and trying to understand the specifics of the buying process. He likes that this monthly subscription service delivers products to his door every month without hassle. And, he can get his facial care products plus a free first shipment of razors as part of the subscription service. He signs up for the free monthly delivery service trial and adds on the bundled facial care products.

As part of the decision stage, buyers are actively taking sales-oriented actions. In B2B, this means buyers are requesting sales quotes and demos from sales representatives. In B2C, customers are signing up for free trials and starting to put products into their online shopping carts for consideration, or saving products to a favorites' list or "save for later" list, which allows customers to designate products of interest within the e-commerce site. This type of feature also gives your online business a view of the specific products buyers are interested in and you can use this information to market to them later, should they abandon their shopping carts or leave the site without buying.

» **Advocacy:** Also referred to as the *loyalty* stage, this stage sometimes gets left off when discussing the buyer's journey because the "buy" decision has already been made. We're including it here because it is an important part of the ongoing cycle that not only represents repeat sales from existing customers, but is also an important part of boosting new sales. In this post-buying stage, our young male buyer received his first subscription box from Dollar Shave Club. The Post Shave Cream really helped reduce the irritability he had after shaving, and he was especially impressed with the Dollar Shave Club experience — receiving his subscription box, the way it was packaged, and the fun personality of the brand that seemed to mirror his lifestyle and interests. He's so excited about his experience that he goes back to the Reddit thread where he first learned about the product and the site, and he shares his own experience. Plus, Dollar Shave Club offers a $5 credit for every referral he gets, so he posts a special code in the thread comments that incentivizes new buyers, while rewarding him. As part of the advocacy stage, your online business needs to continue talking to existing customers, keeping them excited about your brand, and providing incentives and loyalty programs that encourages sharing and recommending your brand.

Monitoring the Flipped and Fluid Digital Sales Funnel

In days of yore, the stages of the buyer's journey that we describe in the previous section also mirrored what was considered the *traditional sales funnel.* Shaped like an upside-down pyramid, as shown in Figure 1-1, the flow of browser to buyer was simple and straightforward, but that's no longer thought to be the case.

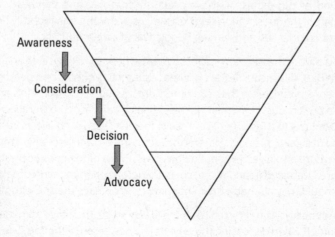

FIGURE 1-1:
The traditional sales funnel was a direct route to purchase.

Previously, it was assumed that there were large numbers of prospective buyers in the awareness stage. As your sales and marketing efforts were realized, the number of prospects slowly filtered down as they made a linear progression through the next stages of the funnel. Your salesperson introduced the key information a prospect might need to essentially guide or *pull* the prospect through the funnel. Eventually the prospect becomes a buyer and then an advocate of your product or service. Just as we illustrated in our example of that young male buyer looking for shaving products, he seemed to take a direct path from discovery to purchase.

TECHNICAL STUFF

When learning about the buyer stages as they relate to the sales funnel, you hear it described based on the physical location in the funnel. The awareness stage is considered the top of the funnel (or ToFu). The consideration stage correlates to the middle of the funnel (or MoFu). And the decision and advocacy stages are considered the bottom of the funnel (or BoFu).

But the modern buyer's journey is a bit more complicated. As we mention at the beginning of this chapter, buyers already know quite a bit about you before interacting with your website or your sales team. In addition, they have lots of sources for and types of information they receive. The modern buyer, not the brand, now controls the buying process.

There's lots of debate around today's sales funnel — what it looks like, how buyers move through it, and if it even exists. However you choose to describe its existence, most experts agree on the following when describing the digital sales funnel:

>> Buyers no longer move in a linear progression through the stages, but move in and out of the various stages in a fluid, and sometimes repetitive, nature (as shown in Figure 1-2).

>> Brands no longer control the process, but instead influence it through content, awareness, and advocates.

>> Buyers may skip stages, especially in an e-commerce environment, where it's easy to go from awareness to decision stage, especially when offered an immediate incentive to purchase (for example, having brand advocates distribute $10 off codes in social media channels for prospective buyers who are just in the awareness stage).

>> Movement through the funnel no longer occurs from a single platform or device (such as from the desktop), but instead occurs in an omnichannel environment — moving between the desktop, tablet, and smartphone, and by visiting social media, websites, and bricks-and-mortar storefronts.

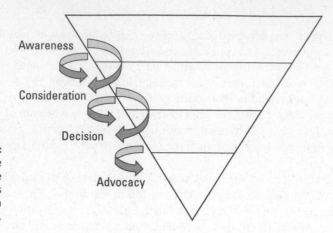

FIGURE 1-2:
Buyers move
in and out of the
various stages
of the modern
sales funnel.

What does this all mean for your online business? When it comes to tracking buyers through the sales funnel, it's important that you understand how and where buyers are converting, and making sure you have buyer-specific content that is appropriate for each stage of the funnel (which we discuss in more detail in Chapter 2 of this minibook).

Putting It All Together: The Buyer, the Conversion, the Channel

Now that you understand the buyer's stages and how they relate to the sales funnel, you're ready to construct the buyer's journey for your online business. Think of this process as taking a road trip. You use a map (or GPS or Google Maps) to plan the drive from your starting point to your destination. You'll need to also consider who else is taking the trip with you. You may want to drive your passengers straight to your destination, but depending on their personalities and desires, they may want to stop along the way. So, you'll want find out what their goals are for stopping (eating, adventure, shopping) and plan on the places along the route to eat, take bathroom breaks, buy souvenirs, or explore a new destination. And, it may not be realistic to identify every possible stop, because along the way you might meet others who recommend a restaurant or activity not on your list; or you may see some information that convinces you to alter your travel plans and take out time for a completely different activity. You'll eventually get to your destination, but there may be some unplanned stops along the way. Now, let's apply this process to the online buyer's journey.

Modeling buyer behavior

The more you know about your buyer, the better you can meet her needs while she searches for your products or services. This means you also need to understand *how* she buys. Knowing who your buyer is and how she moves through the purchase process provides a model that you can then replicate and apply to other (future) buyers. By the way, rarely will you have only one type of customer. Even in a niche business, you tend to have different *buyer personas* (or the people who make up your different customer segments). We show you how to create detailed buyer personas in the next chapter, where we discuss content marketing. For now, start thinking about how to describe your different buyers in order to create a profile for each one. To get you started, you might consider the following questions for each type of buyer:

>> Are they male or female?

>> How old are they? What is their age range?

>> What are they interested in? What are their hobbies?

>> How do they use your product — what need does it solve?

>> Is there a specific time or season they buy from you?

As you see from the questions, creating a buyer persona entails answering a wide range of questions that tells a story about that particular buyer. Some of this information you can get from customer data you have on file (in your customer relationship management, or CRM, software). Other questions you may have to answer by interviewing existing customers, or sending surveys to collect details about what motivates them to buy from you. The more you know about what makes your different types of buyers tick, the easier it will be to understand how they might move through the sales funnel and what information you need to provide them to arrive at a final buying decision.

Mapping critical conversion points

Speaking of knowing what information to introduce to a buyer, you also want to understand specifically where to introduce this information. *Conversion points* are those places online (and sometimes offline, if you also have bricks-and-mortar location) where buyers are directly engaging with your brand. Typically, this is a trackable action that your buyer takes to indicate interest or likelihood to purchase. Throughout this book, we discuss using a call to action (CTA) on your website, which prompts your visitor to respond to an offer. A CTA is simply a conversion point for your buyer.

Conversion points can be on your website, or may be delivered through other vehicles or sites. While there are plenty of places where your buyers may be influenced, keep in mind that conversion points are those engagement opportunities that you construct and control. You want to create offers (to prompt the conversions) for every stage of the sales funnel and for every type of buyer persona. Here are some example conversion points:

>> **Landing page on your website:** This is the page people will first come to or "land" on your website, and it may include an offer for a free trial or a white paper, for example.

>> **Landing page off your website:** Instead of driving buyers to your site (where they can wander from page to page), you may want to try and force a conversion by showing only a specific offer and not include navigation to the rest of your site. This is often used with pay-per-click ads (like Google Ads).

>> **Paid ads:** This includes Google Ads, Bing ads, retargeting ads, and paid social media ads.

>> **On-site offers:** Throughout your website, you are likely to offer different types of calls to action. You may have several on a single page, or may have them on your company's blog. It's possible that you might have customized offers that pop-up on a particular web page that provides content to a particular buyer persona.

>> **Email:** When sending communications to your database of prospective and existing buyers, you want to provide offers that will elicit a conversion.

>> **Mobile apps:** Whether you introduce an offer through a paid opportunity through someone else's app, or you create a mobile app specifically for your site, mobile apps can be effective conversion points.

>> **Branded social media channels:** Although buyers may find out about your site via social channels and online communities, you can provide conversion points through your company's social media channels.

Triggering the social influencer

Just as the Internet opened up a new world of exploration for buyers, the proliferation of social media has created equally incredible opportunities for the online buyer. Particularly significant about social media channels is that they are interactive, include heavy peer influence, and conversations and interactions often happen in real-time.

Data shows that more than 80 percent of purchasing decisions are influenced by social media. And your buyer's peers have the greatest amount of influence at the bottom of the sales funnel (at the decision and advocacy stages). Although, these social influencers aren't only friends and family persuading your buyers where to shop or what to buy. Social media channels, including forums and online communities, are filled with strangers whose opinions are considered equally, and sometimes more valued by your buyers than those opinions of friends and peers, especially at the top of the sales funnel (like in our example of the young male buyer and the shaving cream products). If this sounds odd that a perfect stranger can have so much influence, consider the popularity and persuasiveness of online product reviews. How often have you changed a buying decision after reading reviews from other customers? Influence within social media works the same way.

As the final part of tracking the buyer's journey, social media is an important component. In the analogy we used of planning a road trip, we said that some of your pit stops would be influenced by people (often strangers) you meet along the way. In the buyer's journey, social media is where much of that unexpected influence occurs. While you can't control this engagement, there are things you can do to better use social media along the buyer's journey:

>> Encourage advocates, your loyal customers, to share their experience on social media (for example, provide social media sharing links alongside customer reviews so customers can easily share their opinions on Facebook or Twitter; or ask them to take a picture of them with your product and share on Instagram).

>> Reward advocates for unsolicited mentions of your brand in social media; this can be as simple as a public thank you or a retweet of their comment, to sending them some type of swag or branded product.

>> Monitor conversations and respond (even if the comments are disparaging, research shows that buyers appreciate when a brand publicly responds to people's comments).

Mapping the buyer's journey comes down to this: understanding as much as possible about *who* is buying, anticipating *what* their needs are, knowing *why* they are buying, identifying *where* they look for information, and determining *how* they are influenced along the way to making their final decision.

Chapter **2**

Getting Personal with Content Marketing

A s consumers, Google has taught us that we can quickly find almost any type of information we want when conducting online searches. And, we can expect that the content showing in the search engine results page (SERP) will closely match what we asked for in our search query. As online marketers and online businesses, Google has made it clear that if we want our websites to rank well in search, it's up to us to provide high–quality content. Not only should the content *match* the searcher's intent (what she specifically wanted to know), but also it should *anticipate* what questions our buyers are asking.

For an online business, that doesn't mean Google expects you to be a mind reader. But search engines do require that you know your customers extremely well. You must also understand what content buyers find most helpful and anticipate how those content needs change during different stages of the buyer's journey. Sounds simple, right? Trust us, it really is not that difficult. In this chapter, we show you how content marketing and personalization can work wonders for your website and help meet the needs of search engines and customers.

Delivering the Goods with the Right Content Approach

As an online business, you use content to help drive quality visitors to your website. And search engines, not just Google, then deliver search traffic based on the content that best matches the information request of the customer. This is the goal of *content marketing.*

Creating useful, interesting content for your website pays. Consider that content marketing leaders get eight times more website traffic than those who don't use content well, according to technology pioneer, Neil Patel. What kind of content works best? Well, the short answer is that you need a mix of content types, styles, and lengths, which we discuss later in this chapter. But one interesting fact is that while consumers' attention spans are fading, it's still the longer form content that captures more site visitors. Top ranking content in Google is between 1,140 and 1,285 words, according to Searchmetrics (www.searchmetrics.com). However, the length is also influenced by industry. For example, Searchmetrics found that content for financial sites ranked better in Google when it was longer and more in-depth in quality, compared to camping and destination (travel) industries, which required shorter content. The takeaway is that SEO-friendly content must be of high quality and provide information that is relevant and of interest to your site visitors. Not only does Google see that as favorable, but Searchmetrics found that visitors are actually reading the content, spending nearly 40 seconds on long articles (which is a really long time in the online world!). Plus, readers then end up staying longer on the website that hosts the content.

If that's not enough to prove the value of good content, think about this: Quality content generates three times as many leads compared to that of traditional outbound marketing tactics; and content marketing costs 67 percent less, according to Demand Metric (www.demandmetric.com). Of course, long-form articles aren't the only requirement for creating an effective content marketing strategy. *Personalized content* is an increasingly important component for online success. And when delivered through your website, personalization is specifically referred to as *web personalization.* Let's define these three concepts more clearly, because you'll want to incorporate all of them:

>> **Content marketing:** The process of developing and distributing content of all types that attracts, obtains, and engages a target audience for the purpose of achieving marketing and general business goals, and specifically contributes to brand awareness, lead generation, and revenue growth.

>> **Content personalization:** A marketing strategy (as part of content marketing) that utilizes content written for a specific audience or persona, while aligning an individual piece of content's purpose to the needs of that persona. Content personalization can also apply to smaller segments of text within a larger piece of content. For example, in an email that is written for a general business audience, there may be one paragraph or even a single sentence within the email that is dynamically changed (according to the recipient). The majority of the email is the same for all recipients, but the piece of dynamic content with the email changes to address different buyers by job title or industry, for example. The key to personalization is that you know enough about your audience to segment them into different buckets so that you can personalize how you to talk to them.

>> **Web personalization:** Web personalization is the same as content personalization but it happens specifically online, and it can vary by channel or device. In this case, personalized content is delivered *from your website* to the desktop or to a mobile device, and it can also occur within a web app or a mobile app. It takes content that is written for a particular segment or buyer persona, and matches it to those segments that come to your website. For example, an online pet store may have a website visitor enter the site who has previously been identified with a product interest in dogs. That website visitor is shown content (coupons, special offers, and articles) only about dogs. If there's enough data to know the type of dog breed or the size of dog the website visitor has, then those offers and articles may be further personalized to the specific breed. The level of web personalization you offer is dependent on how much you know about the customer and how personalized your content is.

Developing Buyer Personas

Creating truly useful content starts with understanding as much as possible about the person who is consuming that content. You may have a website that sells to parents, but that's a very broad category of buyer. You might have a mom of twin toddlers looking for parenting information on your website. She has very different needs than the father of a 14-year-old teenager who is also searching for parenting advice. But both of these buyers are your target customers. You likely have products that appeal to each of them. However, if all your content is based generally about being a parent, it's going to be tough to convince these two different buyers to remain interested and shop with you. Your job is to provide both of them specific information that most closely matches their needs or interests.

If you have any type of store (online or off), you already understand the necessity of this customer analysis when stocking up on inventory. If you don't know who is coming to your store and what they are buying, or why they are buying it, then you're essentially guessing as to what products you should keep in stock. The same approach is needed when developing buyer personas for the purpose of creating content. If you're not familiar with the term "buyer personas," it's simply a profile of your different types of customers that describes as much as possible about who they are and what they want. You might have only two to three different types of customers, but you may also a dozen different customers.

TIP

Getting started developing buyer personas doesn't need to be complex. Create no more than three to five personas for your most frequent or important buyers.

Before you get started writing a profile of each of your best customers, you must have a substantial amount of information about those customers:

>> **Use your gut.** If you've already been in business for a while, you probably have a general sense of the different types of people who make up your customers. You may talk to them frequently and know a good bit about their personal lives, or you may only know them based on the products they buy from you. Perhaps there are some types of buyers who you tend to sell to more often. Use this general knowledge of your business to start categorizing the different types of existing customers.

>> **Analyze all the data.** Go digging through all your data sources, from website analytics to CRM (customer relationship management) software records. Look for trends or common traits and buying signals across all your customers. Once you identify patterns, group that information together to form a buyer persona.

>> **Check out competitors.** It's probable that some of your competitors have already gone through the process of creating buyer personas. You can tell by the different types of content offered on their website. Spend some time going through the competitor's website and blog and take note when there are articles, ads, or offers that seems to target a specific type of buyer and then see if you can see similar buyer profiles from your customer base.

>> **Talk to your buyers (all of them!).** One of the best ways to get detailed information about your customers is to talk to them. And this includes the people who buy from you regularly, those who visit your website and talk to your sales team but never buy, and those customers who bought only once or twice and never came back to you. By talking to the customer directly, you uncover more detailed information about what motivates them, how they found your website, or why they bought from you over someone else. You can access a larger percentage of customers by sending them an online survey, but you also need to call and talk directly to half-a-dozen customers or more to get a better sense of what makes your buyers tick.

TIP

You can increase the likelihood of getting customers to speak with you or complete your survey by offering them an incentive for spending time with you. You can give them a gift card for a free cup of coffee or a discount on their next purchase from you. But we almost guarantee that you'll have better and bigger response rates if you provide some small incentive or thank you for their time.

Speaking of getting your customers to hand over the keys to their personas, you might wonder what type of information you need to know. This can vary a bit depending on whether you sell B2B (business to business) or B2C (business to consumer), but generally you want to segment them into some common types. For example, in B2B, it may be important to know what their job titles are; that's because IT roles (or technical job roles) might show an interest in your product or service for very different reasons than business owners or executives. In B2C, you may want to know it's a parent who works full-time outside the home, or a stay-at-home mom or dad. While both of these parents are your customers, they are motivated to buy from you for different reasons. While this is not an extensive list, following are some of the most common data points you might want to know to start creating a buyer persona:

>> Job role or title

>> Industry in which the person works (healthcare, education, and so on)

>> Product interest

>> Geographic location

>> Age

>> Do they have kids (how many, what age)

>> Income range (either individually or by total household income)

>> Own pets (what kinds, what ages)

>> Hobbies or interests

>> Type of car they drive

>> Own or rent a house or lease an apartment

>> How often they buy from you (or from competitors)

>> Why they buy certain products or services (what drives that need or want)

>> What problem they want to solve when considering your website or products or service

>> Role in buying process (in B2B, do they have authority to buy or do they influence the purchase)

Once you have sufficient information, it's time to create a buyer persona. Start by sorting through all the data and interviews and look for common points of interest or common data points. You should be able to quickly begin grouping buyers into categories based on the similarities you uncovered. A buyer persona is actually a fictional customer who is made up of all the real data you collected from those different customer types you uncovered. So, for each buyer persona, you get to create a character.

Start by giving him or her a name and then identify this customer's buying category, such as "Serina, working mom of teenagers," or "Bob, stay-at-home dad of preschoolers." Another key persona for your online business may be "Geraldine, grandmother." Then, for each of these named personas, continue adding information that details who they are, describes their lives, and shows details about when or why they might buy from you. You'll also want to include information about where they go (online and off) to get news, parenting tips, and advice about their households. The objective is to figure out who influences them or what other online communities (forums, social media) or websites they depend on for information.

When trying to decide what or how much information to include in a buyer persona, imagine you are at a party with potential investors for your business. You've invited several of your top customers to meet the investors so they have a better idea of who is buying from you.

Consider how you might introduce each buyer to the investors so that they feel confident you know about your target market and your buyers. For example, you might say: "Joe, this is one of our top customers, Mary Steady. She has her hands full working full-time and raising two teenage daughters. Although she considers herself to be very cost conscious, she doesn't mind spending a little extra to shop with us. In fact, Mary buys from us frequently not only because of the quality of our products, which is super important to her, but also because it's convenient. She doesn't have to add another trip to the store to her already busy day. Instead, she orders online and knows everything will be on her doorstep with 2 to 3 days. She first discovered our site after a popular parent blogger mentioned it in an article."

As you see, a buyer persona contains not only basic facts about the shopper, but also it tells a story about your customer's life and how your product or service fits into her world. Once you get to know your different types of customers, you can give them content that will be interesting and helpful specific to that buyer persona.

Creating Content for Storytelling and Consumption

There's a reason content has the reputation of being King in the world of online marketing. Content, in all forms, has the capability to evoke specific actions, or reactions, from readers. And the content creator has the opportunity to shape what those actions or responses should be based on the desired intent. In other words, every piece of your content should serve a specific purpose. If done well, the content should net the desired outcome. When it comes to content marketing, your job is to align the right piece of content (purpose) with the right person (buyer) at the right time (buyer stage) so that you successfully tell your brand's story and lead that reader (or online shopper) down the path to become a buyer.

Content framework

In order to understand how best to use content, it helps to categorize it, or determine what type of content goes into which bucket. At the highest level of categorization is the framework. The information you create falls into one of these specific frameworks:

>> **Educational:** This content is focused on discovery, or helping the buyer to learn something new. Educational content could include an article about industry trends, or it might be a video that discusses the history behind the popularity of a particular product or category of products. The content should be of a high level.

>> **Instructional:** Similar to educational content, this type of content also revolves around learning, but it is detailed and usually product-specific. Instructional content includes product "how-to's" and "tips" or shortcuts for using the product or service.

>> **Entertaining:** Sometimes the purpose of content is to generate awareness and one way to do that is to entertain the reader or viewer. Capturing the attention of the prospective buyer is challenging, and providing fun, funny, or interesting content that entertains is one way to do that. Videos, memes (images with captions that are shared via social media), and lighthearted blog posts are all examples of content that can be entertaining for an online audience.

>> **Persuasive:** Ultimately, you want the online shopper to buy from you, and you need content that convinces her to do so. Usually, persuasive content provides a specific reason to use your product (a benefit). That message may get relayed by hearing from an existing customer in the form of a testimonial, review, or case study, or from an expert outside your company.

>> **Promotional:** There are plenty of times when you need content to shine a bright spotlight on your brand or product. Its sole purpose is to speak to your product and show why it is better than competing products. This type of content can be created by you or by your customers who have turned into advocates for the product or for your brand.

Now that you understand what makes up the content framework, let's look at another way to organize content based on who creates it.

Content segments

Today's online buyers are savvy shoppers. But they are also heavily influenced by others, including peers, trusted advisors (from analysts to bloggers), celebrities, family and friends, and strangers (people leaving product reviews, for example). When researching products and services, there is one information source that online shoppers tend to rank toward the bottom on the trust meter — the brand! This is especially true for paid advertisements, but it applies to content as well. Whom do shoppers trust? Research indicates that friends and family top the list as most trusted, followed by online reviews, and then third-party experts.

Yes, that means your company or brand can crank out a lot of content that *tells how great your product is,* but at the end of the day the buyer may be skeptical about its value, simply because it came from you. Notice the emphasis we put on the phrase "how great your product is" — that's because blatant, in-your-face promotional content usually isn't taken at face value, but other types of content produced by your brand can still be highly trusted. Buyers expect you to say only good things about your product, and that means they have to go other places to figure out potential problems or downsides to your solution. Customer reviews usually help fill in that gap, by providing a more balanced user perspective the looks at both the pros and cons of a product.

On the other hand, if your brand writes articles about industry trends or common problems and how to solve them (without directly naming your product as the solution), buyers are more receptive to hearing from you. Similarly, if you share information from your existing customers (case studies and testimonials, for example), buyers are also more trusting, especially if they can identify with your customer and see similarities to themselves.

While it's understandable that a direct sales pitch isn't always seen as the most accurate, you still have to talk about yourself and your products at least some of the time. The bottom line is that you need to produce content pieces that fall into all three of these content segments:

>> **Brand-generated:** This is content produced by your company. It includes both *branded* information (names the company, product, or service) and *un*branded (discusses trends, problems, or solutions but without specifically mentioning your company name or product name).

>> **Customer-generated:** This is content that is created by a customer or the public without help from your brand or company (although you can encourage the development of the content). This type of content usually mentions the brand name or product name, but it's from the perspective of the customer. An example of this are the Doritos commercials shown during the Super Bowl each year that are created by fans. Even though the brand requested the content and held a contest to find the best commercial, it's still the fan or customer who created it without direction from Doritos.

>> **Third-party validation:** In both B2B an B2C, there is a lot of content that is generated about a brand from someone other than customers or from the brand. This content comes from analysts, experts, celebrities, or others considered knowledgeable or influential about your product or service. These third-party content creators are not part of the brand, but sometimes the company can use (and pay for the use of) the content if it is favorable to the brand or product. (Think in terms of paid celebrity endorsements, or even the recent trend of paying bloggers and social media influencers to create content about the brand.)

Content types

The last category addresses the specific format of the content, or the way in which it's packaged for consumption. You want to have a wide variety of content types, but here are some of the most common types to add into your content marketing strategy:

>> Video

>> Images/pictures

>> Memes (images with text on top)

>> Articles

>> White papers/guides

>> Product demos

>> Infographics (using images or graphics as a way to show data or research)

>> Testimonials

- >> Online tools (savings calculators, free trials, and so on)

- >> Interactive quizzes

- >> E-newsletters

- >> Blog posts

- >> Social media posts

TIP

Sometimes it feels like you never have enough content. You can stretch out the content you already have by repurposing it, or repackaging it into a different content type. For example, you may have a video testimonial from a customer. You can take that same information and write it as a customer case study. Or you can pull out a specific customer comment from the video and use it as a stand-alone quote — add the quote to an image and create a sharable picture for social media.

REMEMBER

Content may have a shelf life. Blog posts about a new product, or articles that center on a current event or news will eventually no longer be relevant because it happens on a specific date or time period. To help increase the staying power of your content, consider adding some "evergreen" content into the mix. Evergreen means that it stays fresh, or relevant, indefinitely (or, at least for a very long time!). To give content the evergreen treatment, avoid using dates in the article. For instance, instead of referring to "Winter 2020," simply say "winter" or refer to "the colder months." Similarly, avoid referencing a specific event that could also date the content. The more general way your content is written, the better chance it has to live a long life online as a piece of evergreen content.

Aligning content to intent

As you can see, there are all types of content that serves a wide variety of purposes. For content to be effective in helping convert browsers to online buyers, you need to next match each piece of content to the appropriate stage in the buyer's journey.

The buyer's journey represents the path a prospective buyer takes on her way to becoming your customer. That journey is segmented into four stages: awareness (not yet aware of having a need or desire for a product, just exploring); consideration (aware of a need, researching options); decision (choosing a solution, comparing options); and advocacy (loyal customer, sharing experience with others and open to repeat purchases for self). We discuss the buyer's journey in detail in the previous chapter if you want to learn the nitty-gritty details, or need a refresher.

When you're ready to map out, or align, your content, start by considering your prospective customer's *intent* at each stage of the buyer's journey. What is it that they want or need to accomplish? What are their goals? How does your product or service meet that goal, or help in achieving the goal? Then, look at the best type of content that can not only address the buyer's intent at that particular stage in the shopping process, but also convince or entice the reader to move to the next stage. For example, let's say a buyer is shopping for a floor rug and trying to decide what kind. She has already found a vintage rug your online store has for sale, but is hesitant because she's unfamiliar with how to care for it, or if it will hold up to wear and tear from her kids and pets. This shopper is in the "decision" stage and if she has access to content that is instructional and promotional, it could help her finalize the decision to buy. In this case, you could provide a quick one-minute video from your company that shows how to care for vintage floor rugs. You might also show a review from other customers who speak to the sturdiness of the rug and its capability to hold up in high-traffic rooms, despite it being an antique. We like to use an Excel spreadsheet or Google Sheets to identify what content is needed at each stage of the buyer's journey. You can also tag which personas might need the content most at each stage. When your existing content is mapped out in this way, it's also a good way to reveal gaps in your content, or what type of content you need more of to ensure there's something available for everyone at every stage. In Table 2-1, we show you an example of how to map out your content framework, segments, and types to the buyer stage.

TABLE 2-1   **Align Your Content to Each Stage of the Buyer's Journey**

Stage	Awareness	Consideration	Decision	Advocacy
Goal	Exploration, entertainment (Not yet aware of need)	Researching, looking for a solution (Recognize a need)	Comparing solutions/products (Addressing need)	Sharing results (Committed to brand)
Content Framework	Entertaining Educational	Educational Persuasive Instructional	Instructional Persuasive Promotional	Persuasive Instructional
Content Segment	User generated Brand generated (unbranded)	Brand generated (branded) Third-party	Brand generated (branded) Third-party User generated	User generated Brand generated (both)
Content Type(s)*	Infographics Videos (fun) Trend articles E-books	White paper E-newsletter Webinars Online reviews	Free trial Demo Video (how-to) Testimonials, case studies	Video (testimonials) Video (product tips) Online reviews Social sharing

(continued)

TABLE 2-1 *(continued)*

Stage	Awareness	Consideration	Decision	Advocacy
Persona	Decide which of your personas are most likely interested in each stage of content.			
Vertical	Identify a specific vertical market that matches content you have to offer.			
Name of content	This is where you identify the exact content you will use.			

These are examples of the type of content that could fit with each buyer's stage. You could have more or less for each stage.

REMEMBER

As much as you want a prospective buyer to move effortlessly and in a linear manner through all the buyer stages to become a passionate, loyal customer, that's not realistic. A buyer may start the buying process at any one of the stages. And he may move in and out of several stages before actually becoming a customer. Having the appropriate content available for each stage of the journey is the best way to ensure you brand (or product) remains a consideration throughout the entire buying process.

Launching the Personalization Effort Online

Having content available for each stage of the buyer's journey is a critical step in any content marketing strategy. But why stop there? If you want to really increase your chance of influencing the buyer with content, then the information should be personalized as much as possible to that buyer. By "personalized" we mean that the content addresses challenges, needs, or desires that are specific to a particular buyer. If your customer is the office manager for a doctor's office tasked with shopping for an online appointment service, you want to provide her with content that talks specifically about her industry, healthcare. Your content should discuss patient needs, for example, when talking about how easy it is to use the service. Compare that scenario to another customer type. You might also do a lot of business with hair salons. For that buyer, you want content that addresses the hairdresser's customer, or perhaps how an online appointment service can help a salon have fewer cancellations. As you see, personalized content is just that — it is written with a particular buyer's needs in mind and speaks the language of that buyer, or her industry.

For online businesses, content personalization primarily occurs via your website, also known as web personalization. As with any online system, you need to make sure that all your online systems communicate in order to pass the right information (or, in this case, the right content) to the right website visitors, at the right time. Let's take a look at some of the backend system considerations, as well as some online tools that can make personalization easier for you to accomplish on your site.

Integrating systems

Just as you may have a backend inventory management system that needs to relay information to your shopping cart, there are other systems you may use to talk with customers. And in content personalization, it's important that these systems or tools integrate, or communicate, with one another to pass along pieces of information that lets you personalize your content. Here are some of the systems and tools that are likely to be involved in the web personalization process and need the capability to communicate with one another:

>> **CRM:** Your customer relationship management software holds a treasure chest of information about your buyers and your prospective buyers (or leads). You may use Salesforce (www.salesforce.com) or SugarCRM (www.sugarcrm.com) for this functionality. Whichever solution you choose, you want to make sure it has the capability to integrate with the other tools we mention in this section.

>> **Marketing automation software:** If you're a large online retailer or B2B company, you might send out a lot of email to customers and have a complex structure for communicating with them and nurturing them on a regular basis. You might use a system like Marketo (www.marketo.com) or Eloqua (from Oracle). Even if you are a smaller online business, you probably use email software such as Constant Contact, MailChimp, or Pardot (from Salesforce). Like a CRM, your marketing automation software also keeps a lot of information about customers and prospective buyers that is helpful in personalizing content.

>> **Website and analytics:** Using a tool such as Google Analytics, you are able to track an incredible amount of information about visitors to your website and the actions they take while on your site. Also within an analytics program, you might set up goals and conversion points that you track based on types of campaigns or users. This is some of the data that you might need to coordinate with a personalization tool to know when and where on your site to deliver personalized content.

>> **Paid ads:** You may use Google Ads, Bing ads, or other tools to create and manage your paid advertising efforts. It's possible to set up paid ad campaigns to deliver personalized content based on certain actions a visitor takes on your website.

REMEMBER

A benefit of marketing automation software is that most solutions offer a way to personalize messages within your email. As part of your mass email you may still be able to use a person's first name in the email so that it looks like it's been created especially for that customer. Or, you may be able to use dynamic content functionality. This allows you to change out small amounts of text within an email so that the text can be customized to a certain recipient.

Categorization: One thing is not like the others

As you begin to implement a personalization strategy in your content and on the web, you first need to decide how to segment your audience or visitors. If a visitor has never volunteered information about herself to you (by filling out a form or creating a customer profile), then getting information starts with cookies. When it comes to the web, you're able to use cookies, or a tracking code, to identify some things about your visitors and follow them around your site. If they leave and return, you are still able to use the cookie (unless the user clears his web browser cache, which would remove any cookie tracking).

TECHNICAL STUFF

Cookies are small text files that are encrypted and stored on the user's computer. There are different types of cookies that keep information on the user's web activity and preferences. Session cookies may track specific page activity on a website (like what items the user has added to a shopping cart). Permanent cookies hold information (like passwords or login details) even after the user shuts down the browser. And third-party cookies are tracking cookies used to collect specific information about the user. A site enables the use of cookies through the use of code that is placed on the website; the site's privacy policy must clarify what and how cookies are used.

Even if you're not familiar with implementing this process on your website, you've very likely been "cookie'd" yourself. Have you ever visited an e-commerce shop and looked at a specific product? After leaving the site without purchasing, you've probably noticed an ad for that exact product or website show up in your Facebook feed and in ads on other websites. Or, if you return to the site, you may see content or offers that are based on your previous browsing behaviors. Similarly, with the use of cookies, you can now decide some of the ways you want to segment or group your website visitors. First, there are two general types of visitors to consider:

>> **Known visitor:** These are people who have been to your website before and completed some type of sales form, signed up to receive your emails, created a customer profile, or taken similar actions so that you now recognize them (because they are in your CRM system or marketing automation system). The more you know about these visitors, the more options you have to segment them, such as by product interest.

>> **Unknown visitor:** Just like it implies, these are visitors who have never provided you with enough personal information to identify them to you. Instead, you'll depend on the information passed through an IP address (or other third-party solutions) to allow you to segment by geographic location or industry (in B2B), for example.

TIP

You can use web personalization tools to help you collect information in stages from unknown visitors, without sacrificing conversion rates on your offers. For example, you may start by showing an offer for free content that a visitor can download after submitting her email address. That's such a small amount of information visitors are more likely to provide it, thus converting on the offer. The next offer she sees asks for additional information, such as full name and job title. Eventually, you're able to construct a full profile of this visitor, or use other third-party tools to help fill in the blanks — but you end up with a known visitor.

Depending on whether you are targeting known or unknown visitors, here are some examples of other ways you can segment visitors to offer more personalized content:

>> Geographic location

>> Referral source (where they came from before getting referred to your site)

>> Organic source (from search engine) or paid source (from AdWords)

>> Product interest

>> Industry (usually specific to B2B)

>> Job role (B2B)

>> Income level (B2C) or company revenue (B2B)

>> Company size (B2B)

>> Demographic information (lives in a certain state or zip code)

>> Psychographic information (are parents of toddlers or teens or are pet owners)

As you see, the more information you have access to about your visitor, the more specific you can get with segmenting.

WARNING

There are existing and new rules surrounding online privacy, including the type of data that can be collected and stored for use as it pertains to an individual. There are also rules about when and how to notify website visitors about the way you collect and use an individual's data. These rules are not guidelines but legal requirements, and organizations (or websites) that break the law could be prosecuted and fined large amounts of money. We discuss online privacy and data regulations in Book 5.

While there are so many different ways you can segment your audience, or site visitors, it's only effective if you have content appropriate for that segment. If you're an online stationery store and want to target parents to buy graduation announcements, you need to have content that speaks to that buyer persona. In this example, you might want to offer a checklist for planning a graduation party, or offer a guide that discusses how to prepare your senior for college. Without specific content for your target persona, the purpose of personalization is lost.

TIP

As you build out your content, you'll want to keep a list of what you have available. There are lots of expensive content management solutions out there, which may be appropriate for a large, complex site, but they're also expensive. Instead, use a good old, reliable spreadsheet (or Google Sheets) to develop and track your inventory. As part of the content inventory, you'll want to include the following: type of content, when it was created, buyer persona(s) targeted, buyer stage, where it's promoted, and link to where the content is online.

Choosing personalization tools

One of our favorite things about having an Internet business is that there is almost always no shortage of online tools to help manage and grow your business. This is certainly the case with content personalization for the web. Here are some of our favorite solutions that make it easy to use personalization on your site in an effort to increase conversions — and revenue!

>> **Triblio** (www.triblio.com): Considered an Account Based Marketing (ABM) tool, Triblio allows you to show personalized content and offers on your website to prospective buyers. You can provide your content to known and unknown website visitors, as well as show personalized content to targeted buyers (specific leads or accounts you are trying to influence and sell to). Triblio also works with email or marketing automation platforms and Google Ads.

>> **Folloze** (www.folloze.com): Account-based marketing is also a core capability for this personalization tool. But one of the things we really like about Folloze is the unique method for delivering personalized content to buyers. Folloze lets you create content boards that contain many different pieces of content all designed for a specific buyer. Think of it in terms of a Pinterest-style layout of a board (or online page) that groups your content in one easy to access place. Figure 2-1 shows an example of a personalized board from the Folloze website. Another benefit of this tool is that it not only tracks who engages with or visits the board, but which pieces of content they interact with; and it lets you see who the prospective buyer is who is viewing the board. You can put a link to a Folloze board in an email, on a page of your site, or just about anywhere.

>> **Evergage** (www.evergage.com)**:** This content personalization tool monitors your site visitors' intent in order to know which content to show them. In addition to tracking what places of offers get clicked, Evergage also tracks how much time is spent on each page, where the visitors' computer mouse hovers, and how they scroll through a page. Looking at a host of data points as they occur on your site in real-time, or why a visitor is actually on the site, the tool uses machine-based learning to make recommendations and decisions on which content to deliver to the visitor. Evergage is designed for large e-tailers and other sites with heavy traffic, and can identify the users and what purchases or interests they've had on other sites and then recommend similar products or content to be shown on your site.

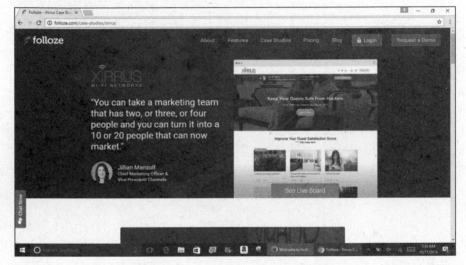

FIGURE 2-1:
Create a custom board to deliver highly personalized content to buyers using Folloze.

There are plenty more web personalization and account based marketing tools available. And, you don't have to start out using the tools, which can range from several hundred dollars per month to several thousand dollars monthly. These tools are a significant investment. But to compete online today, offering a one-to-one personalized approach to marketing with content and product offers is quickly becoming a necessity in order for you to remain competitive.

Chapter **3**

Listening to the Voice of the Customer

Have you ever shopped with an online business and had a really frustrating experience? Perhaps you had every intention of purchasing something from the site but encountered an annoying inconvenience, like having to create a lengthy new customer profile before checking out. In the end, you bailed, abandoning your shopping cart and leaving the site because the buying process was interrupted. You never contacted the company to explain why you left. And later, when the business studied its site's analytics reports, it simply showed that a site visitor made it all the way to check-out and then left before registering as a customer and completing the purchase. This knowledge gap between what the customer actually thinks and the story that a site's data tells can be filled by a concept called *voice of the customer,* or VOC.

Structured VOC programs have long been part of the product development process for companies, because the intent of VOC is to formally collect a customer's *requirements.* This helps redefine processes and influence product design. In the online business world, VOC has similarly become a way to collect specific information directly from the customer in order to modify the online buying experience. The customer's viewpoint, combined with other digital data points (such as website statistics), provides a more complete picture to guide decisions about everything from site design and product or service offerings, to customer service processes and payment options. While VOC may seem like something only large e-commerce sites might implement, it can be effective, and relatively simple to use in small online businesses, too. In this chapter, we explain how to use VOC to improve your site's functionality and, ultimately, your revenue.

Using VOC to Determine the Customer Experience

Let's face it. There are a lot of business and tech terms that get thrown around these days. It's challenging to keep up with all the trendy terminology, and sometimes it's down right confusing when figuring out which ones are really important to your business. VOC and customer experience (CX) are two examples of terms that can lead to lingo uncertainty. In this case, it can be even more difficult to understand because these concepts must actually work together to be truly effective for your business. So, let's clarify. A VOC program provides a means for soliciting specific information or requirements from your online customers. CX represents all the interactions a customer has with your business throughout the customer's entire online relationship with your brand. You use all the VOC feedback you receive to help improve the customer's experience. See, it's actually pretty simple!

REMEMBER

The customer's experience with your online brand can begin well before you become aware that the customer is engaging with you. CX includes every point of the buyer's journey, including awareness, consideration, purchase, and loyalty, as we discuss in Chapter 1 of this minibook. That's why it's even more important to understand what customers expect, so you have the opportunity to better influence their overall experience.

A bricks-and-mortar business has the advantage of being in front of its customers every day. Its employees can talk with the customer directly and ask questions like, "Were you able to find everything you were looking for today?" "Did anyone assist you?" "Was the store clean and were the products easy to see?" "Are you planning to shop with us again?" Similarly, if a customer has a complaint, suggestion, or general observation, it's very easy for her to seek out a manager and give that feedback. As an online business, you may have visitors who browse your site, even coming and going multiple times in a single day, and you may never know what they were looking for, why they never made a purchase, or why they kept returning but not spending. Without hearing from the customer, and with access to limited digital data, it's difficult to make improvements to your website that are meaningful to your prospective customers.

Getting customer experience right matters. Research indicates that improving customer satisfaction across the entire buyer's journey (all CX interactions) can result in a 15 percent increase in revenue and a 20 percent decrease in the customer service costs. Plus, positive customer experience leads to improved customer loyalty (and repeat customers). Interestingly, more than half of customers (and as much as 86 percent in some surveys) say they are willing to pay more for a better customer experience; yet only 1 percent of customers say businesses consistently meet their needs.

Delivering a consistent, positive customer experience across the online buyer's journey requires the following:

» **Identify your customers.** Understand who your customers are and what motivates them to buy. It's helpful to create buyer personas that detail each type of customer you serve. We discuss this in more detail in Chapter 1 of this minibook.

» **Get real-time customer feedback.** When possible, collect data from your customers while they are in the process of interacting with you.

» **Include employees.** Not only do you want to collect employees' feedback about processes and customer interactions, but also they should be properly trained to deliver a consistent experience (whether that's packing orders or servicing customers).

» **Improve technology.** Your online customers frequently interact with you through the solutions you use (shopping cart software, inventory management systems, and online chat services, just to name a few). You must continuously invest in better, user-friendly technology that provides the best possible customer interactions.

» **Build relationships with your customers.** You don't have to be in a physical location to interact with customers; it also happens through email, social media, community forums, and online chat. Use these interactions to form a positive bond with your customers.

» **Measure your success.** How do you know if your efforts are working if you don't track your progress? In addition to tracking website analytics and changes in revenue, follow up purchases and interactions with customer success surveys that allow customers to quickly rank their satisfaction.

As you may have noticed, many of these requirements for delivering a good customer experience requires you to get information from customers — VOC. Managing the customer experience process and knowing where to make improvements can't be based on your guesses (even educated guesses!) as to what's important, or what may be broken — you must get information from the customer, based on the customer's viewpoint.

Types of customer feedback that matter

So, what type of customer information should you collect, and how do you get it? When it comes to data, there are two types that consistently matter: structured data and unstructured data. For this purpose, the first type of data, structured, is just as it sounds: It's a more formal and organized approach to getting information. You have more control over how, when, and where you collect the information. The other data type, unstructured, comes from sources in an unorganized manner and you don't have control or influence on how the information is provided. Following are the types (or sources) of customer data:

> » **Structured**
>   - Surveys
>   - Interviews (phone or in-person)
>   - Call center (customer service) recordings
>   - Web logs
>   - Polls
> » **Unstructured**
>   - Social media
>   - Forums
>   - Online reviews

Tools for collecting and analyzing VOC data

Given that there are so many different ways to gather customer feedback, it can be overwhelming to develop a formal VOC strategy, especially if you have limited resources. Fortunately, as VOC and customer experience have evolved in the digital world, there are also tools available to help collect and analyze customer feedback. Most of these tools also enable you to collect the data in real-time, as customers are interacting with your site, which boosts the usefulness of the feedback. Here are some of the top VOC tools:

>> **Feedbackify** (www.feedbackify.com): A simple solution that allows you to receive real-time feedback from your website visitors. Users simply click on a widget on a website page and can provide feedback in the forms of ratings and comments on a form (which you customize for your site). In addition to being easy to deploy and use, it's also inexpensive at $19 per month for all features.

>> **UserVoice** (www.uservoice.com): Designed for use with product development, this VOC tool is particularly useful for online businesses that want serious feedback on features, functionality, or new products. UserVoice operates as a forum and allows customers to vote on and discuss suggestions and send feedback in "tickets." It's easy for users to access and doesn't require registration. This more robust solution is a bit more expensive at approximately $500 per month. It does offer a free trial, but you have to go through the sales team to set up the trial.

>> **Poll Everywhere** (www.polleverywhere.com): This tool extends beyond your website, to anywhere you are interacting with customers. It allows you to easily create polls (several format options are available) and then lets customers respond or vote from their smartphones, social media, or web browsers. If you're working with focus groups or sending polls through email, this is an ideal and affordable solution at $19 per month.

>> **UserZoom** (www.userzoom.com): If you have a large, complex online business there are solutions, such as UserZoom, that tackle all areas of usability, user experience (UX) design, and customer research. Although it has solutions for the finance and healthcare industries, it also specializes in large retail and e-commerce solutions, serving company such as Kohl's and Urban Outfitters. Because it's built for really large organizations, this is a robust but pricey option that starts at several thousand dollars per year.

REMEMBER

A/B testing is a method for comparing which one of two website elements performs best. In digital marketing, A/B testing is frequently used to determine what CTA (call to action) on a website gets more clicks. For example, if everything is the same (the images, the offer, and so on) except for the text on the CTA button, you would show some of your website visitors an offer with a CTA button that has the text "Buy Now" and show other website visitors the same offer but with a CTA button text "Add to Cart." You could then determine which button text prompted more visitors to place products into shopping carts. Once you had a winner, that option would be the text to use permanently (or until you tested another batch of text).

ASKING FOR REASONS WHY CUSTOMERS LEAVE

When it comes to collecting customer feedback, don't forget about *former* customers. They are likely to have specific and honest feedback about everything from process issues to customer service failures with your website. As with any VOC data, the best way to uncover the reason why a customer left (and all the other dirty details) is to ask. Whether you hire a professional or take on the task yourself, you can get the scoop from a former customer in several ways:

- **Email survey:** An email message targeting former customers can be a quick way to deliver a brief survey. Keep your survey limited to three to five questions. Start by asking for the last time the customer remembers purchasing from you (because he might not realize that he's considered a lost customer). Then start determining the possible reasons for the absence.

- **Direct mail:** Mailing former customers a more extensive survey is a legitimate way to uncover the details of why they left. You can also use direct mail to invite customers to call and talk to a customer service manager about their experiences with you. In both cases, getting a response requires offering some type of incentive (such as a gift card) in exchange for their time.

- **Call:** In Internet-based companies, picking up the phone to contact customers is often a forgotten option. Although some former customers might not appreciate the intrusion, you might find that feeling is the exception and not the rule.

- **Focus groups:** Gathering a small group of former customers and questioning them in depth can be revealing. Knowing how to extract the answers you're looking for takes experience, so we advise hiring a professional marketing firm for this endeavor.

Listening and Taking Action: Time to Redesign

Once you've talked with customers, past and present, and collected feedback from surveys, social media, and by using VOC tools, the next step is to actually do something with all that information. As an online business, the majority of customer feedback will most likely revolve around your website, including specific pages of your site, such as the home page, search functionality, or backend systems (that customers can experience), like your shopping cart. You've probably asked customers specific questions around the structure and design of your website, too.

These are some of the most important components affecting the online customer experience and the buyer's journey, in terms of how customers engage with your site and how they flow through your site to critical conversion points. We discuss this in more detail in the first chapter of this minibook.

TIP

When designing general surveys and questionnaires, divide them into sections that allow you to focus on certain areas of the business one at time. For example, one segment of questions should be only about customer service, and another segment about shopping cart functionality. This keeps the information organized and makes it easier for you to sort through results and then apply the answers to those matching business segments.

Of course, we can't tell you exactly what or how you need to improve your website — that's why you're talking to customers. On the flip side, just because one or two customers didn't like the colors you use throughout the site, for example, that doesn't mean you should redo your entire color scheme. Instead, it's important to look for recurring problems or similar suggestions across all customer feedback to validate that it's not just one person's opinion, but is an actual issue that is impacting overall customer experience.

As you look for common threads in the feedback, know that there are also some general guidelines you'll want to consider as part of a redesign to improve customer experience with your site:

>> **Watch the competition.** Spend some time examining sites that handle graphical design well, to see how the sites are built. If the sites are using new techniques, take notes and find out whether the new design is showing up in more than one place. Check out your competitors' sites to see which designs they're using. Compare those designs to your site design, to see whether other designs look more appealing.

REMEMBER

Your competitors can evaluate your site just as easily as you can evaluate theirs. Spend some time evaluating them routinely, to see how quickly they respond to a new situation. Your goal is to have other sites respond to your changes rather than play catch-up with their redesigns.

>> **Check for consistency.** Go to your business home page and make sure that all your category and subcategory pages have the same design and graphics. As websites change, not every page is updated. You might have added to your website some new sections that don't incorporate the latest site design. If you don't check for consistency, you might have four or five versions of your design coexisting on your site and confusing your customers, which reflects poorly on your company image.

>> **Test for compatibility.** If possible, test your current site on different devices and with different Internet browsers. Microsoft Internet Explorer is still used, but other dominant web browsers continue growing in popularity, including the Mozilla Firefox web browser (www.firefox.com), Google Chrome browser (www.google.com/chrome), and Apple Safari browser (www.apple.com/safari). If you see errors while using an alternative browser, find out the cause and update your site accordingly. Similarly, you must test how your site appears on different screen sizes of desktop computers as well as on devices such as smartphones and tablets.

>> **Familiarize yourself with new technologies.** Many times, the limitations your site faces are due to the technology available to you. As the web becomes more sophisticated and Internet browsers can handle new tools and devices, your options for implementing advanced design techniques on your site begin to expand. One example is the need for *responsive* web design, which allows your site to automatically change to fit the device being used to view it (such as a smartphone or a tablet). Talk to your website designer or do some research on the Internet to see which new technologies are reaching the mainstream. (The site www.webdesignledger.com has helpful articles.)

The point is to identify what's working, what isn't working, and what's possible to implement in your site design. After you have an idea of what you want to do, you have to create some different scenarios for your redesign. They can range from simple page updates to a slightly redefined user interface to a complete tear-it-all-down-and-start-over total site makeover. Weigh these scenarios against your current available budget and your overall plans for the site. After all, if you're going to completely change your business model, for example, you might want to delay any site design changes until then.

TIP

If your resources are limited, focus immediately on any errors that are occurring and all wildly inconsistent web pages. When you have more time and resources, you can work on updating your web page styles.

Increasing Appeal

Have you ever walked past a storefront and wondered what was sold inside the building? A dimly lit store with an abstract name, a window covered in a painted design or a series of posters, or a confusing display can be quite misleading. Imagine the difference you experience if the store has a clear view inside, an inviting entrance that encourages you to walk in as well, and informative signs that clearly display pricing, selection, and store hours. A powerful redesign doesn't just look new — it's also appealing to your customers.

Although some websites are chock-full of information and deals, if users can't easily find what they're looking for — or understand what they're seeing — they move on to one of the competitors. Websites that appeal to customers make their information clear, concise, and easy to find.

Giving your site a fresh design

It's true that design trends change, but some trends clearly take hold and determine what makes a website modern and fresh. When looking for trends to apply to your own website, pay attention to elements that not only make a big splash but also relate to other widespread functionality changes (such as mobility and video). Here are a few examples of design trends that are defining a new generation of websites:

>> **Hero image:** A large hero image on a home page is replacing the once popular sliding banner ad and carousel image. The hero image takes up a large portion of your page's real estate but also includes some text and important calls to action.

>> **Creative typography:** *Typography* is a fancy word for *fonts,* and the type or style of fonts you use is getting a lot of attention. Instead of using a plain style of text or using only one type of font throughout your website, online businesses are encouraged to get creative with font styles that have personality. Even if you have a B2B website with a more conservative tone or message, you can still use a variety of font styles or a more creative font style in some portion of your site to capture the attention of your customers. The trick with using interesting styles of typography is to make sure they don't interfere with the user experience and make it difficult for customers to read the information on your site.

>> **Videos instead of text:** We mention throughout this book that video is becoming an important part of website design — and marketing strategy. In many cases, video takes the place of lengthy text-based content.

REMEMBER

Some design trends have more staying power than others. Don't think that you have to immediately implement every trend that makes the rounds. Choose the ones that seem to have the greatest effect and endurance — and that work best for your website and your customers.

Adding content

People nowadays want to read good content wherever they go on the Internet. Quality content is also an important part of optimization to help your site rank well in search engines. E-commerce businesses that focus solely on selling products are finding that they have to add more information to entice people to check them out. But all online businesses must be mindful of the content they place on their sites — and today content includes not only words but also photos, graphics, and videos.

The key to satisfying both visitors and search engines is to provide meaningful and useful content. When placing words on the page, use clear, well-written, up-to-date, and accurate information that offers some value to the reader. Similarly, use good quality videos and photos that are helpful or interesting. Whatever type of content you use, it should contribute to (rather than take away from) the design and functionality of your website.

Look at the content on your site. Does it need to be updated? Could it be better written? Check out the information that people are reading on your site, and review the questions you receive from your browsers and customers. If you're not particularly skilled in editing, have some friends, employees, or colleagues look over your site and make suggestions. Does your site have dated or low-quality images? Does your site lack videos? Look for places on your site where videos and photos could add interest.

You should also look at potential ways you can add to your content, such as these examples:

>> **Add a section featuring reviews and recommendations for your products.** When customers have to decide what they want to buy, they like reading about other people's impressions, experiences, and opinions. When you provide reviews, you give customers a reason to come to your website and one less reason to look elsewhere when it's time to buy.

>> **Relate customer success stories and experiences.** When you highlight customers who have used your business, you provide a sense of validation to new customers by showing them that other buyers are happy with you. Videos are terrific vehicles for delivering customer testimonials or case studies because they can be quick, easy, and inexpensive to produce. However you feature these success stories, they also provide customers the opportunity to learn from each other, by sharing information on how they use your products. Sharing these customer experiences gives your business more value and helps you build repeat business.

>> **Provide articles you wrote for other sites.** One way you can market your business online is to write articles that have the effect of referring people to your business. Why shouldn't those articles appear on your own site first? See Book 6, Chapter 3 to find out how to write well-written articles.

TIP

If you don't have time to write articles, tap into free and low-cost article databases and freelance-writing services, such as Scripted (`www.scripted.com`) and Upwork (`www.upwork.com`).

>> **Tell the personal story of your business.** Customers are always interested in knowing more about the people who work behind the scenes in a business. You create a sense of trust and purpose when you add some personal information, because then you're putting a "face" to your clean, well-laid-out online business. Adding short biographies of you and key employees is an effective way to build credibility, especially for B2B websites. Adding to the biographies the ability to connect, follow, and engage with you on social media, such as Twitter or LinkedIn, is another way to help build trust with new buyers. If people get involved after learning more about the people behind the business or after hearing your story and the reason your business was created, their purchase becomes a form of support because they're buying from a real person who has goals, desires, friends, and a family.

>> **Add a blog.** If you have an e-commerce site or a service-based company, you might not think that a blog has a place on your website, but it's a natural fit for most sites. Blogs are a good way to keep a variety of content types (such as articles, videos, infographics, and photos) flowing on your website.

Creating a user community

You might have had the experience of turning to someone at a big department store and asking a question, only to find out that you're talking with a fellow shopper. Or maybe you overheard a conversation and you pointed another shopper to the correct aisle to find the item he was looking for that day. User interaction is a common aspect in the retail industry. Customers have a similar interest, which is why they're in the same store together. They can talk about their interests and how the products affect them, and even share advice about good and bad purchases.

In the online world, more businesses are adding virtual community meeting places to their websites or in social media sites. Mostly, these places take the form of forums, discussion boards, support boards, or full communities, where people can gather and discuss issues. Businesses provide a place for active discussions also by using social media, such as a Facebook page, a LinkedIn group, or even a Twitter chat group. For details on using social media to promote your website, see Book 6.

You, as a business owner, can enjoy several benefits by connecting your customers:

>> Customers might be quicker to respond to a new customer's question or concern and can give detailed answers.

>> Customers have one more reason to spend time — and their hard-earned dollars — at your site rather than at someone else's.

>> As browsers and customers hear about potential uses of your products from other customers, they might be more inclined to purchase those products themselves. Because they're already on your site reading about a product, your site is their first choice for making a purchase.

>> By keeping an archive of customer communications, you're building a knowledge database of questions, answers, and experiences that can help solve future customers' problems. It's another way to get ongoing feedback and can easily become a formal part of your VOC program.

You can find several free forum and community software tools. Look on the major search engines for a tool that works on the operating system for your web server (search for *online community software*). Talk to your web designer or IT staff to see whether they have access to any ready-made discussion board or online community software.

One way to encourage people to become active right away is to create certain events that revolve around a specific day or time. You can unveil your new chat room software by hosting a "town hall" or open meeting with your CEO or a visible board member, where customers and general browsers can ask questions and receive immediate responses. You or an employee can host a workshop where you explain a new feature or product that's being rolled out on your website.

Running a poll

You can also offer polls or surveys so that customers can vote on questions of the week (or month) that you devise. Make polls fun by asking about customers' favorite stories in the news, or have the polls tie in slightly to your business by asking people about their favorite products.

Again, use your polls and surveys as valuable customer research and part of an ongoing VOC program. Present a few new product lines and ask customers to vote on their favorites, where the winner of the poll results in your new product line. You add excitement and involvement for your users, and they feel like they have some ownership in your business.

If you don't have a software tool available for offering polls, check out one of the free or low-cost options, such as Poll Maker (`www.poll-maker.com`) or Poll Everywhere (`www.polleverywhere.com`).

WARNING

Update your poll regularly, to avoid making your site look stale and outdated. A 4-month-old poll turns off customers and makes your entire site look old and unprofessional.

REMEMBER

You can add polls, community forums, social media platforms, and other customer-engagement tools in several ways. For example, if your website is built on WordPress, you can use free WordPress plug-ins to easily add these types of tools to your site. If your site uses an e-commerce solution (or shopping cart), it may provide free access to similar tools, or APIs (application programming interfaces), as part of its standard marketing and promotional features.

Making Your Website Functional

Websites used to be limited in the functions they could offer customers. You could display *static* (fixed) web pages, have forms emailed to you with text fields of information, and have customers sign a guest book. Now your site can be fully interactive, where each web page is built or personalized based on a customer's specific needs. Your site can talk to other computer systems automatically, link to your own database to read or write information, and process everything from data to audio and video. These are all excellent ways to improve your site's customer experience.

When considering how to prioritize functional updates, especially those that are woven in with design updates, we recommend focusing on items that make your site more mobile-friendly. In the past, having a separate site for viewing on mobile devices was acceptable. Now, websites are expected to be designed for both desktop and mobile viewing, a process known as *responsive design*. Because a mobile-friendly site is critical to online business success, we discuss it throughout this book. But you can also learn more about responsive design in Book 3, Chapter 2.

In addition to responsiveness, a site optimized for mobile functionality may also mean eliminating or reducing the number of pop-up messages and forms on your site. These pop-up, or overlay, features typically do not function well in a mobile environment and interfere with the usability of your site. (And unless these pop-up boxes contain highly personalized content for your website visitors, you may find that they are an irritant to your customers and disrupt the customer experience.) Another element of mobile-friendly websites is the use of long, scrolling pages that are divided into segmented blocks of short text. This design change improves the functionality of a responsive website, making it easier for customers to find and view important information on your site.

REMEMBER

Just because websites can incorporate lots of complex functions doesn't mean that you should put all these functions on your site. Choose a series of functions that serve your business needs and your customer wants. The point of website functionality is to support the user experience and increase conversions.

Updating your website in a timely manner

As their websites become more and more complex, many businesses find that they rely on a single person or company to make all their site updates. This situation not only is a bad strategic decision (because it locks you into this entity if you want to keep using your own site), but can also seriously jeopardize your chances of keeping your customers.

Customers are looking for sites that are continually updated with fresh, important, current content. Businesses that want to succeed have to be able to respond to changes in the market quickly, go after new business opportunities, and satisfy a curious, fickle audience with varying demands. All these tasks require the ability to quickly update your site and its content, and relying on one person or business slows down the process. What if your web designer gets sick or is away on vacation? What if you have to post a critical announcement over the weekend and the web design company that handles your updates is closed? What if your designer is so busy changing someone else's site that your site isn't updated for weeks?

Your company should always be able to make some changes, especially content changes, to your own site. Why pay a web programmer lots of money to change some text? Instead, pay that person to develop a function where you and your employees can send changes to the site that are updated automatically. Or use a web-based site-building service or e-commerce platform that makes it easy for you to control most of your site's changes. Today's website solutions make it easy for someone with little or no knowledge of web programming and design to take a do-it-yourself approach with a professional result.

WARNING

If you allow your employees to update your company site, be sure to install some sort of screening process, where a serious change has to be approved by either yourself or a manager. You don't want an angry employee's changes plastered all over your site.

Building smart navigation tools

We talk repeatedly in this book about the importance of a good navigation system on your website. Maybe you have a vertical row of links or buttons along the left side of your page or a series of tabs along the top. Take it one step further: Determine how sophisticated your navigation bar is and whether it helps customers move around the site. One trend in web design is to eliminate sidebar navigation. Before jumping on this trend, we suggest that you carefully consider the effect of removing navigation or links in your sidebar. Does it help or hinder your customers' experience when using your site? You may find that the sidebar is a distraction to your customers and decide to do away with it.

No matter where your main navigation is, it's important to focus on using it to help customers move to and from pages in your site in a way that helps the buying process. When customers use the navigation bar to go to a particular section, for example, does the navigation bar tell them where they are on your site? Your navigation system should make it easy for a customer to move anywhere on your site from any page on your site.

One way that websites show a shopper's progression is to display the current web page's context within the entire site structure, called a *bread-crumb trail*. A user can return to a page by clicking the specific "crumb." Displaying a trail of crumbs shows customers how you group information on your site and how you establish a *hierarchy*, or order, of web pages. In addition, your customers can move up and down the hierarchy much more easily.

Your site navigation system should remain intuitive while being able to directly open the pages that customers need. They shouldn't need lots of explanation or training to navigate your site. A customer should be able to open your home page and instinctively know what to click or how to proceed.

As the owner or operator of your web business, you probably know your site by heart and can easily move around in it. What about new visitors, though? Gain a fresh perspective by having a stranger (or a friend who has never used your site) test your site. Or hire a company to handle this *usability study* for you. The point of a usability review is to gather a new visitor's impressions about what makes sense and what doesn't so that you can update your site and navigation system accordingly.

TECHNICAL STUFF

Usability, in the area of computer applications, refers to the effectiveness and ease of use that people find when they interact with the computer. If an element has high usability, people can easily learn about it and remember how it works, and they find it visually satisfying, efficient to operate, and helpful to use when things go wrong. Usability is a big part of customer experience!

Building your customer history

One reason that people still go to local shops and pay higher prices for products is the familiarity they feel when they're shopping in a store. The owners or employees know their shoppers' faces and call them by their names, so they can recommend new products because they know the shoppers' purchase histories and likes and dislikes, and can recommend products accordingly.

This high-service model works for many small businesses, and you can convert this familiarity to your site with some added functionality. Basically, you want to make customers' previous purchases (perhaps within a time limit, such as one or two years) available to them after they log in to your site. If the purchases are available to shoppers, they're available to you, the store owner, and you can provide analysis. From analysis come recommendations and suggestions, perhaps tied into an automatic marketing offer based on the customer's purchase pattern.

For example, if you know what your customer's previous orders are and you see that he's ordering something you predicted, you can offer similar goods at a package discount to encourage sales. When your customers can go back to your site and view their past purchases, they can answer questions on their own without involving you as much. They can also look up their order histories, and your shipping department can record the tracking numbers in your software or website tools. If your customers can answer their own questions or find answers without hearing back from you, you can focus on other customer service issues more quickly and efficiently.

Implementing this function means that your website software has to have both a way for customers to create their own accounts and a database to store customer information and order information so that it's ready to be displayed on your own website. The customer account should have some form of password protection and should potentially store customer address and payment information. You can integrate this software by looking for customer relationship management (CRM) software that works with your e-commerce software, such as Salesforce or SugarCRM. Or the e-commerce platform you use may already have this capability (as either an included feature or an API that you can add to the site), making it easy to suggest other products based on previous or current buying preferences.

Knowing these common website improvements and being able to balance potential updates with the feedback you receive from customers will make for a winning customer experience strategy.

Chapter **4**

Overhauling an Aging Online Business

How do you measure the success of your online business? As with any business, you should identify key performance indicators (KPIs) that closely match your primary objectives. These indicators may be based on profitability, sales revenue, or even customer service goals. One difference with an online business is that your KPIs are almost entirely based on your website. According to a poll of small-business owners, two of the biggest indicators of e-commerce success are positive feedback from customers and the amount of *traffic*, or visitors, the site receives. Making the traffic to your site truly count usually means ensuring you have the right type of traffic (or visitor) coming to your site, and then converting those visitors to customers. Perhaps that's why the survey also revealed that the number of sales leads and the amount of total online sales are important KPIs. However you choose to define success, understanding and tracking it is imperative.

Equally important is understanding that success has eluded you — and deciding that your online business needs an overhaul. This revelation is often the most important one you can make as a business owner and one of the most difficult to come to terms with. The sooner you confront the facts, the better chance you stand to reinvigorate sales. In this chapter, we show you the signs indicating that it's time for change, and we explain how to start putting your business back on the right e-commerce track.

Paying Attention to the Signs

Wouldn't it be nice if you could start your business, launch your website, attract lots of customers, make plenty of money — and never have to change a thing? If you've owned an online business for a while, you know that that's not the way it works. The Internet industry is constantly morphing, and so are the rules for growing a thriving online business. The secret of long-term online success is recognizing the signs of change — both good and bad — and being able to adapt, on a daily basis.

If your website has any of the following characteristics, you might need to reevaluate your business:

» **A drop in search engine rankings:** A good, high-ranking position on Google is often the lifeblood of an online business. If your site begins to slip or inconsistently maintains its position after several years on top, something is wrong. The problem might be an optimization issue related to the many changes search engines make in their algorithms to determine rankings. However, don't discount the possibility that your site is losing relevancy.

» **An outdated look:** The visual look of your site doesn't have to be considered a design relic from the dot-com era to be outdated. Site design and design functionality change quickly in today's online business environment. Black backgrounds and plain fonts, for example, have long been stripped from sites in exchange for white backgrounds and clean, crisp images and font styles. Today's sites must also be mobile-ready and *responsive,* or capable of automatically shifting for display on multiple device types. In other words, it's time for you to make changes.

» **A lack of ongoing maintenance:** You can work in your business every day and still overlook the simplicity of good site-keeping. Broken links, expired coupon offers, and irrelevant or dated content are all indicators that you haven't been paying much attention to detail. Not to mention, adding fresh or new content to the site on a regular basis is an important factor in search engine rankings. You want to show both Google and your customers that your site is continuously evolving.

» **Fluctuating market conditions:** All types of issues in the world influence your business, either positively or negatively. The fluctuations that most closely relate to your industry or customer base obviously affect it the most. Some of these factors are increased competition, changing product trends, regional or national economic indicators, supplier costs, customer demand, and pricing issues. A significant change in your market space can dictate a change in your online business operations.

>> **Overlooked technology upgrades:** Overlooking technology upgrades (whether you're updating antivirus software or installing a new version of a content-management system) is detrimental in the world of e-commerce. For an e-commerce business, adding customer service functionality and marketing capabilities is often entirely dependent upon upgrading or adding software. Allowing technology innovations to bypass you is a definite signal for change.

>> **Nose-diving profitability:** This factor isn't one of the more subtle signs that it's time for Plan B. When revenue falls, overhead increases, and your bottom line pays the price for it all, you know that regrouping is a necessity.

>> **A variation in visitors:** Is your site losing customers? Are your traffic counts falling or becoming less consistent? Or are you noticing an influx of visitors from a different traffic source, geographic region, or customer base — and you don't have products and services to relate to these new visitors? Fluctuations in site traffic and activity warrant a reaction.

REMEMBER

It's important to pay close attention to not only how much traffic your site receives, but also from what sources the traffic comes, and what *type* of visitors you receive. Your traffic might look normal, but some valid traffic may instead be fake traffic from a spam source — and doesn't do your site a bit of good! Or, you may get visitors coming from search engines (organic traffic) but immediately leave the site (bounce) because the site doesn't meet their actual needs — you're attracting the wrong visitors.

This list of signs pointing to change isn't exhaustive. It's a starting point, though, for conditions to search for in your own business.

To make sure that you don't overlook anything, conduct a thorough *business change evaluation.* This system first establishes a baseline for your business, based on your KPIs (such as sales, visitors, and available products). Using the baseline, you then can evaluate other possible influences on your business.

Your goal is to take a snapshot of all your business indicators and determine which ones are driving change. Create a checklist by following these steps:

1. **Write a detailed description of your e-commerce business.**

   Include as part of your description the specific products or services you sell both online and offline. This description should provide a complete picture of your business.

2. **Describe your existing customers.**

   Be sure to include as much classifying information as possible about your customers. Details such as age and household income are bonuses. If you don't know those types of details, classify customers according to their product interests or purchases, or even by how they found your site (such as ads, other site referrals, or offline).

3. **Break out your revenue structure.**

   List the ways or places in which you earn money. Break down the list by month for the past 12 months. Then complete a year-over-year comparison for the past 3 years (if the data is available). Show the numbers in percentages of total sales. If you have a bricks-and-mortar store, include revenue from your offline sales too.

REMEMBER

   If you're keeping up with your monthly profit-and-loss statements as part of your accounting procedures, you can pull these numbers directly from those statement histories.

TIP

   For a more immediate snapshot of what the numbers mean, show the results in the form of bar graphs or pie charts. This type of visual aid is often helpful for comparison purposes.

4. **Generate a traffic analysis of your site.**

   Break out the numbers in the form of a monthly comparison for the past 12 months, and then by year for the past 3 years. Include the total number of *unique* (different) visitors and *page views* (the number of pages requested within a particular period).

5. **Make a list of all areas that affect your business or influence change, either positively or negatively.**

   You can group the items by category as they apply to your site, such as marketing, sales, product development, or content.

6. **Categorize each item as positive or negative based on how it influences your site. Then explain why you chose that indicator. Beside the explanation, note whether you responded or reacted to the change.**

As you finish this section, you can identify areas where change is occurring and determine whether you have adequately adjusted to those new circumstances.

You might be tempted to believe that you already know this information or that this process is oversimplified. We can't emphasize enough the power of writing down this information in one place, for your review.

REMEMBER

The purpose of making a meaningful evaluation is to help you identify holes in your current online business strategy. Then you use the information to target a market weakness or opportunity that you might have overlooked.

Keep this completed chart on hand as you continue through the overhaul process. Figure 4-1 shows a sample checklist.

Business Change Checklist

Indicator	Type of Change (Positive/Negative)	Why?	Responded? (Y/N)	If Yes, How?
SITE				
Site design is outdated				
Dated/old graphics				
Broken links				
Content not fresh				
Expired coupons/offers				
Defunct affiliate programs				
New technologies released				
INDUSTRY/MARKET CONDITIONS				
Increase in competition				
Decrease in competition				
Fluctuation in economy				
Change in product/service				
Change in consumer demand				
Supply costs update				
Pricing update				
New vendors/partners				
Customer (profiles) different				
SEARCH ENGINE RANKINGS				
Dropped rank (out of Top 10)				
Removed from rankings				
Consistently moving down				
Inconsistent rankings				
Inconsistent rankings across various search engines				
Keywords outdated				
No active optimization activity				
Variation in site visitors				
Traffic/page views changing				
MARKETING				
Offline advertising reduced				
Less/more online advertising				
Changed # of referring links				
Updated promotions/offers				
OPERATIONS				
Major fluctuation in profits				
Outdated business plan				
Revenue resources altered				

FIGURE 4-1: Your checklist for evaluating change.

Qualifying for a Makeover from Lagging Sales

One no-fail indicator that your online strategy needs help is steadily falling sales. The issue always boils down to numbers — the number of products sold, the number of site visitors, and the last number on your bottom line. All these numbers are connected, and that connection has everything to do with sales.

The wonderful thing about the Internet is that you have immediate, and often real-time, access to online sales transactions. At any hour of the day, you can determine exactly how many dollars your website is generating. You then know whether your business is having a good day. What happens, though, when it's not a good day, or a good month?

If sales are down, start by asking yourself four basic questions:

» Do I need to pull in more website traffic?

» Do I need to attract more targeted types of visitors (those ready to buy from me)?

» Do I need to increase the number of repeat visitors and buyers?

» Do I need to convert more visitors to buyers?

Sure, sometimes you answer "yes" to all of these questions. Typically, though, your problem will stem more from one reason than the others. Addressing a sales decline most often comes down to an issue of acquisition, conversion, or retention. Either the number of people (or right people) coming to your site has decreased and your sales are affected, or the proportion of sales to the number of visitors is off because people are leaving your site before making purchases, or you aren't getting enough repeat visitors and customers to offset the high cost of acquiring new visitors. After you decide which issue is most responsible for weighing down sales, you can begin addressing the problem.

Increasing the number of visitors to your site

If you need to increase the number of visitors to your website, concentrate on these areas to give sales a lift:

» **Search engine optimization (SEO):** Reexamine the search engine optimization techniques used for your site (see Book 6, Chapter 6). SEO is a necessary part of ongoing site maintenance. If your site isn't optimized correctly, its chance for a solid ranking in the search engines goes out the window. In addition, customers searching for your specific site can be disappointed when it doesn't pop up in their search results. Perhaps you haven't provided the best possible information to make a match during a typical search request.

» **Marketing strategies:** Letting routine marketing activities slip in priority in the daily chaos of managing an online business is easy. Diminishing numbers of visitors are a wake-up call to get back to basic marketing concepts. Create an online newsletter, or send out a fresh round of promotional email to your existing customer database. You don't always have to dangle deep discounts in front of them. Sometimes they simply need a reminder that you're still out there!

» **Paid advertising:** Spend a little dough and pump up the number of site visits. Following are some areas where you should consider spending online advertising dollars:

- PPC (pay per click), such as Google Ads or Yahoo! Bing Network
- Mobile ads
- Display ads
- Retargeting ads
- Third-party sites, using banner ads, content sponsorships, or paid listings

If you're already spending money in these areas, look for new sites to place advertisements, or experiment with buying some different Google Ads with new keywords.

» **Linking opportunities:** When was the last time you asked someone to exchange links with your site? Spending an hour or two per month searching for sites that are compatible with or complementary to yours is still considered worthwhile. You may find sites that have already shared information about your site or products but are not yet linking to your site.

REMEMBER

Google continuously changes the algorithms that decide how sites are ranked in search engine results pages (SERPs). As part of those algorithms, if you break the rules or recommendations associated with SEO best practices, your website may be penalized, or dropped down in or booted out of the rankings. Link swapping is one of the areas that is affected by these changes, so it is important to always follow best practices.

TIP

Instead of swapping links, you can visit blogs that are applicable to your online business. Then leave comments to posts that include a link back to a specific page on your site (when allowed) or make sure your profile (that you set up to leave comments) references or links back to your website. The comments you leave on other sites may not rank high in search results, but they are a way to get awareness and possible traffic to your site from people reading the comments.

>> **Public relations:** Are you creating awareness of your site by engaging in effective public relations strategies? What was the date on the last press release you distributed? Reach out to a few reporters and suggest a story relating to your business. If you have an active blog on your site where you're creating interesting content, publications often republish blog posts (that are slightly tweaked) or use the content as the basis for a new article. When your site's traffic flow is slowing, now is not the time to be shy.

TIP

Not all news has to be based on good news. Think creatively and turn your *problem* into a relevant story idea that's timely and grabs attention. For example, a national report on decreased consumer confidence and spending could tie in nicely to a recent dip in sales for your site. Be sure to put a positive twist on how you're combating the issue. For instance, send the message that your site's competitive pricing is sure to win over customers now that they're more careful in their spending.

>> **Social media expansion:** Spend some time building the number of followers you have on Facebook, Twitter, and YouTube. Social media provides a good opportunity to not only monitor real-time conversations that relate to your online business, but also start conversations with customers and potential customers and keep people talking about your brand. Using paid social media ads is another way to take advantage of your social media networks — and they are often much less expensive than Google Ads. You can find more information about using social-networking sites to boost sales in Book 6.

REMEMBER

Using online paid advertising tactics, whether through pay-per-click or social media, allow you to target your audience. That means your advertising budget is more effective because you determine who and where your ads are shown to better ensure they are reaching visitors who are most likely to be interested in buying from your website.

>> **Offline promotions:** Whether or not you have a retail location, use traditional offline marketing to create an immediate boost in your online traffic.

TIP

Go to a networking event and hand out your business cards. Arrange for a speaking engagement at a meeting of a community organization or at a regional trade show. Create flyers or professional brochures and distribute them in stores that are complementary to (and not a competitor of) your site. Offline promotions also include the use of mobile marketing. Reach prospective buyers through their mobile phones and give them a discount code or other incentive to return to your website. You learn more about mobile marketing in Book 7, Chapter 4.

Converting more visitors to (repeat) buyers

Maybe the number and type of visitors to your site is on target. Instead, you need a boost in converting window shoppers into full-fledged buyers — and converting full-fledged buyers (existing customers) into repeat buyers. Or, you need to spend more effort bringing prior customers, those who haven't shopped with you in a while, back to buy again.

Keeping — or nurturing — good (existing) customers and enticing lost (prior) customers to return are not always easy tasks. Have you ever considered how much attention, time, and money businesses spend on marketing to attract new customers? With ongoing efforts to grow your new business, it's easy to understand how your existing customers might get overlooked or taken for granted. But continuing to do so often leads to lost customers and plummeting sales. Ignoring an occasional customer departure or two can be an expensive mistake for your online business.

Consider that gaining a new customer costs approximately five to six times as much as keeping an existing one. According to the "State of Retailing Online 2016" report, from Forrester. In 2016, the median average online order was $103, compared to $120 from a repeat customer. According to the "2019 State of Retailing Online" report from Forrester, 36 percent of online retailers said their average order value has decreased. However, 36 percent said that their repeat customer rate has increased, while another 38 percent said repeat customer rates remained steady. Given that over one-third of those e-tailers surveyed said that their new customer acquisition cost per order increased, it seems that spending money and time keeping customers provides a much better return on your investment (ROI).

So how do you convert more browsers to buyers? Focus on offering these features to start sales flowing in a positive direction again:

>> **Functionality and usability:** You might be surprised to discover how cumbersome shopping on your website can be. Viewers leave sites if they tire of trying to figure out how to check out. At other times, the problem is all about site design. In Book 3, we discuss how to update your site design and functionality to make it friendlier as part of the focus on creating a good customer experience.

>> **Content and CTA:** One issue that derails a sale quickly is a lack of useful content properly placed with the appropriate call to action (CTA). Ensure that your content, or web copy, provides customers with enough detail to get and keep their interest. To help encourage a buying decision, use a CTA that makes it clear what action the visitor should take next.

>> **Credibility:** Skepticism and uncertainty plague online shoppers, especially when buying from unfamiliar sites. Create trust and credibility by making customers aware of who you are and why your site is a safe place to shop.

TIP

Boost consumer confidence by displaying your contact information prominently throughout your site. Providing your phone number and physical address in addition to your email address shows customers that you can be reached for questions. For an added vote of confidence, clearly post privacy policies, FAQs, and return and exchange policies. Be upfront with customers about what they can expect when they do business with you!

>> **Customer reviews:** In addition to your own credibility, that same level of trust can be extended through the words of other customers. Data shows that the buying decisions of online customers are heavily influenced by the opinions of other buyers. When you allow buyers to rank the quality or value of a product (even if they didn't purchase it from you), write a review of the product on your site, or even link to a review offsite, other prospective customers will take notice.

TIP

Particularly if you have a service-oriented business, turn to the social-networking site LinkedIn to help boost credibility with recommendations. You can use LinkedIn to ask people in your network who have used your products or services to provide a written recommendation that remains on your LinkedIn profile — visible to the public. You can link to the recommendation from your website or place a duplicate of the recommendation directly on your website as an added testimonial. And don't overlook Facebook and other social-networking sites that allow your customers to leave comments and reviews.

>> **Product selection:** Sometimes, declining sales are a result of an outdated or limited choice of products. In Chapter 5 of this minibook, we discuss in greater detail the idea of expanding your product lines.

>> **Payment options:** Customers want not only a wider product selection but also payment options. Maybe your site is set up to accept payments only by PayPal. To attract and keep customers, you have to make buying easy and that often means you have to accept other methods of payment, such as credit cards, debit cards, and online check processing. See Book 4, Chapter 4 to find out the payment options you can offer.

>> **Affiliate programs:** You might be used to signing up for other sites' affiliate programs to add a little revenue. Why not create an affiliate program of your own? Products and services with more forgiving profit margins are ideal ways to boost revenue for both you and your online allies. Or, if you don't want to worry about tracking specific products, offer a flat percentage (or referral fee) on *any* sales that come through one of your affiliates.

TIP

>> **Pricing:** Drop by competitors' sites to find out what they're charging. A drop in sales can indicate that you're not keeping up with current pricing strategies.

To check out the competition, use online price-comparison guides such as PriceGrabber (www.pricegrabber.com) and ShopZilla (www.shopzilla.com). To more closely track sales from competing sites, check out competitor-price-monitoring software from PriceManager (www.pricemanager.com), Price2Spy (www.price2spy.com), and Profitero (www.profitero.com).

>> **Buying incentives:** Whatever you call them — coupons, discounts, free shipping, limited-time offers, loyalty rewards, subscriptions, or special sales — incentives to purchase often nudge browsers to act and entice existing customers to buy again. Free limited-time trials are another type of incentive that makes it easy for visitors to decide to try your product or service and get one step closer to buying!

>> **Upselling:** People in the restaurant business use this strategy to extract another dollar or two from customers at the time of purchase (for example, asking about dessert after a meal). You can do the same for online sales. Before a customer completes the check-out procedure, display another item and offer it at a one-time discounted price. You can use this same sales trigger to suggest products (based on prior buying preferences) to your returning customers as a way to increase the typical amount spent with your website. Impulse buys based on the power of suggestion are powerful.

Reengaging Customers to Spend with You, Again

We've said there's a lucrative ROI on marketing dollars when you focus on existing customers, and that includes those customers who bought once and never returned, or were frequent buyers who dropped off your radar. Maybe they left because of poor customer service, or simply haven't thought about your product or service again since that first order. Whatever the reason for your customers' departures, your objective is to win them back. Enticing customers to return means showing them that you've changed. You listened to their critiques and paid attention to what went wrong and, most important, you're ready to make amends.

Many marketing experts use the *lifetime value* (LTV) concept to quantify what a customer represents to your company. You may also see this concept referred to as the *customer lifetime value* (CLTV). Basically, to calculate a customer's relative value, you determine how much money the customer spent with you over a certain period and then factor in expenses and other considerations.

Unfortunately, we could fill an entire book explaining lifetime value. Instead, you need to understand why it's worthwhile to invest in winning back your customers, regardless of the dollar value of that effort. Winning back customers is worthwhile for these reasons:

>> **Cost:** If it costs you $100 to get back a former customer, it would cost at least $500 to win a brand-new customer.

>> **Profit:** Existing customers often account for more than three-fourths of a site's revenues.

>> **Familiarity:** Educating former customers on the benefits of your site takes less time than you might think. They're already familiar with your business, your products, and your service.

>> **Upselling:** After you win back a customer, you're more likely to increase the average value of his or her purchase or to upsell to another level of product or service. On the other hand, it takes more time to achieve the same result with a new customer.

>> **Referrals:** When you regain the value of a customer, you also net the value of all other customers that this one refers to you.

>> **Brand strength:** Loyal customers increase the strength and value of your overall brand.

A tailor-made offer

Inviting a lost customer to do business with you again involves far more than simply offering an apology for messing up the first time. More often than not, you just have to connect with your customer's needs again. What better way to do that than to present a personalized offer?

Being able to make this type of offer assumes that you have a database of good historical data that details the customer's preferences. (If you've built that database, this task isn't difficult.)

TIP

Most e-commerce shopping cart software now includes database functions for storing and acting on customer data. You can extend that capability by importing the data into a more powerful database (or customizing your own). Better yet, your e-commerce platform may also integrate with a third-party customer relationship management (CRM) program that your business can use to manage the customer experience, such as Salesforce or SugarCRM.

To customize an offer, start by looking at your customer's buying history. Review the products or services the customer bought most recently and frequently. If the data is available, you also want to find out which offers he or she responded to most often. Some examples are a percentage-off coupon code, an offer to buy one and get one free, a limited-time offer, the option to purchase on a deferred-payment plan, and the opportunity for free shipping. When you have this information, you're ready to create an offer tailored to the consumer's preferences!

TIP

For the best results, create the offer *after* you survey to determine the customer's reason for leaving. This way, the enticing offer you construct appeals to the person's present interests or needs and isn't based solely on old (and changed or outdated) buying habits.

A targeted offer

Customizing an offer for every departed customer might appear excessive. However, you can create ready-made targeted offers, such as these examples:

>> **Deep discounts:** An offer of a deep discount on the next purchase gives your customer a chance to experience the product or service again. You can include a coupon code to buy one item and get one for free or half the price.

>> **A reasonable discount on the next purchase:** Consider a 10 to 15 percent discount on the next purchase, depending on the price point of the product or service you sell.

>> **A gift card or free gift:** Offer cash up front with no strings attached — a $10 gift card, for example. Or send a small product as a gift to show a customer that you're serious about winning him or her back.

>> **Invitation to participate in an event:** For example, if you offer customers a special podcast or an informational webinar related to your site or product, they might just buy something from you.

Knowing Where to Start

When you're deciding which changes to implement and what types of offers to create for rebuilding customer loyalty, one source for making those decisions is your customers. An easy way to get feedback is implementing a customer survey. This is a quick way to get information not only on general customer service issues but also on the facts about your site, so you know where to make improvements. Keep these suggestions in mind when you're conducting this type of online research:

>> **Identify the basics.** Choose only the most critical information that you want to discover about your site. An all-inclusive survey becomes long and complicated, so choose only three to five areas. Including more areas in your survey warrants bringing in a professional to administer it.

>> **Keep it simple.** Web surfers have limited time and limited attention spans. Your best results come from keeping a survey simple and short.

>> **Offer an incentive.** Always thank customers for taking the time to share their opinions. Better yet, offer a small incentive (a discount on their next purchase, for example) in exchange for feedback.

>> **Select your customers.** Determine who will take your survey: potential customers or loyal customers who know your business.

Terrific online survey tools are available. Try SurveyMonkey (www.surveymonkey. com), which offers a full range of survey products and template options that start at less than $52 per month. The site also offers a free basic survey option that's ideal for quick surveys or for small sites. Another one of our favorite survey tools is SoGoSurvey (www.sogosurvey.com), which provides the ability to create surveys, polls, and online quizzes. It has a comparable pricing plan to SurveyMonkey, as well as a free version for its basic functionality and licenses available for students/ academics and nonprofits.

Chapter **5**

Expanding Products to Increase Stagnant Sales

I f you own a mature online business, you must master two tasks to maintain success. First, you have to nourish (or *feed*) your site in a way that keeps it healthy, productive, and growing. Second, you have to perfect your timing by creating a feeding schedule for your site and recognizing when it needs nourishment and care to expand.

The sale of products (or the lack thereof) is a good indicator of how well you're doing on both counts. If your site has been around for a while, you know that stagnant sales say a lot about your online business — and what they say usually isn't good.

If that's your situation now, this chapter is for you! We explain how to fine-tune the feeding schedule, adjust your inventory, and change your product mix to rev up your sales — at the right time.

Figuring Out When to Expand Your Product Line

With inventory, you're never deciding *whether* to drop a product; rather, you're deciding *when* to do so. Think about the last time you went grocery shopping. Did you notice that most food items had sell by (expiration) dates stamped on their packaging? If a product's sell by date has passed, the product shouldn't be purchased. Instead, it's eventually replaced on the store's shelves by a fresher product.

Most products (food or otherwise) have expiration dates, or at least life spans, because at some point, for whatever the reason, products are no longer valid. In marketing terms, a product's life span is referred to as its *life cycle* (see Figure 5-1).

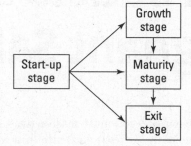

FIGURE 5-1: The four stages of a product's life cycle.

Typically, a product's life cycle is defined in four stages:

>> **Start-up:** As you introduce a product to the market, you're defining the product's place among your customers and building awareness for it.

>> **Growth:** In a product's expansion phase, you're increasing sales, developing the customer base, and exploring alternative markets for growth.

>> **Maturity:** When a product hits its prime, you have to protect its market share. You might notice more competitors at this stage. After a product hits its peak, try to eke out profitability for as long as possible.

>> **Exit:** In a product's stage of decline, its sales are steadily decreasing and interest in it has waned. You have to decide what to do with the product — eliminate it, repackage it, or update it.

REMEMBER

Not every product experiences all four stages of development during its life cycle. A product can move directly from the start-up phase to the exit phase, for example.

You can follow the upcoming steps to plot revenue and help determine when to phase out one product and introduce another. You have to decide when to drop a product, however. Unlike food items, not all products have sell by dates stamped on them. *Your* job is to determine when a product is past its prime. A logical starting point for determining when a product has outlived its shelf life is to conduct an inventory analysis. When you're ready to start this process, follow these steps:

1. **Make an exhaustive list of all your current product offerings.**

If you stock products, you can use a recent inventory list for this step, whether it's from your online inventory system or your own books. The most important task is to make sure that your list includes every product you offer on your site. Make a few notes about each product. You can include details such as

- Product locations on your website

- Product-specific promotional offers or coupons

- Other sites that link to specific products

- Ads or reviews that mention specific products

2. **Plot the sales history for each product.**

You should chart sales weekly, monthly, or annually. We suggest reviewing monthly sales over the past year. For older products, you can then chart annual sales for the preceding 2 or 3 years. (Likewise, for newer products, you might want to break the total monthly sales into weekly figures.)

TIP

When you're tracking a product's sales history, show the data in the form of bar graphs, line graphs, or other types of charts so that you can more easily visualize the product's progression in your overall inventory.

3. **Determine the percentage of sales for your inventory, by following this method:**

(a) *Divide the annual sale (in dollars) of the product by the total annual sales for all products.*

(b) *Multiply that number by 100.*

Your equation should look similar to this one:

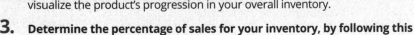
$7,525.00 (product X) ÷ $72,346.00 (total sales) = .10401 × 100 = 10.41%

4. **List the products in descending order.**

The list is then organized from highest to lowest percentage of sales.

5. **Match one of the four stages of the life cycle to each product.**

For example, products with sales that have steadily declined and account for a lesser percentage of your sales are probably in the Exit stage.

By the time you complete your list, you should see a clear picture of your inventory that shows how much, or little, each product has aged.

Limited appeal products

Just as some consumable products have a limited use, other products have limited appeal. Usually, you know that these products are temporary fads and that demand for them will wane after their novelty wears off.

Unless you're at least a certain age, you might not realize that someone once made millions of dollars by stuffing a rock into a box and selling it as a Pet Rock. Other examples of trendy products are T-shirts, bumper stickers, and coffee mugs printed with catchy phrases that reflect a current event. If you were selling a shirt with a witty slogan about the 2016 presidential campaign, for example, it naturally had a limited life cycle and should have been replaced by now.

Limited-use products

Before you axe all the products classified in the exit stage, as we describe in the preceding section, you have to consider a few other factors. As you might expect, sales history isn't the only indication of how well an item is selling or why its popularity is declining.

Some items — such as food, diapers, razors, or pet care products — have limited uses. After a product is consumed or applied, for example, it's all used up. Theoretically, this type of item should maintain a steady stream of sales because customers must replenish it.

If sales drop steadily, you have to consider the possibility that other factors are in play — for example, product quality, customer service, branding, or awareness (such as whether customers remember that they ordered a product from you).

Technology-based products

As technology advances, products become dated or defunct or their appeal lessens. If a new version of a technology-based product is released, the earlier edition can automatically be doomed for the clearance bin. Do your customers really want to purchase the Xmark1000 from you when they can have the advanced Xmark2000 for just a few dollars more?

Auxiliary products can force this change, too, as in the case of video games and game systems. The release of new games often coincides with the release of an updated game system. The catch is that the new games are compatible with only the new system. If the video games are popular enough, they drive sales of the updated game systems. In turn, the popularity of the earlier game system declines. Although the original system can take a while to become truly extinct, its value and marketability decrease.

Another example of auxiliary products changing has to do with smartphones. As Apple, Samsung, or other providers roll out new phones, these devices typically require new power chargers, carrying cases, and other auxiliary devices that are no longer "backward compatible" with older versions of the devices. Just like with video game systems, the sale of older device's auxiliary products can take a while to decline, but over time, most people will either upgrade or switch product lines.

You might decide that this type of product is in its final stage and should be replaced. Or, you might view it as a product entering its mature stage and decide to market the older system to a customer base that's more concerned with price and function than with the latest, greatest technologies.

Product marketing

Your marketing or promotional efforts can expand or shorten a product's life cycle. In fact, the theory of product life cycle is a marketing concept that's typically used in developing marketing campaigns for new products. By using the product life cycle concept, marketers can better respond to each stage of a product and increase (they hope) the overall product life cycle and its revenue.

Find out what you can do to prevent a decline in your product sales. Think about whether you actively promote products, and how often and in what ways you promote them. Before scratching a product from your inventory list, you might need to reevaluate your promotional strategy for that product.

Product positioning

Product positioning influences a product's sales and life cycle. Think about the physical location of an item (or, rather, its image) within your website. Do you rotate multiple products into premium spots on your site? Is a product positioned with similar items so that shoppers can easily find it? Or, is the product buried deep within your online store, waiting for someone to stumble over the right link? Even if a product is popular, if customers have trouble getting to it, your sales will suffer.

Price points

Setting the correct price for your product is essential. You can bet that a product that's priced incorrectly from the start will go straight to its exit stage in no time flat. As a product matures, though, its pricing also must be reevaluated.

Conversion rates

By using e-commerce (and effective analytic software), you're in the unique position of being able to track almost all your customers' movements, not just those initiating from ads. It's the equivalent of following someone around your store and watching as she picks up an item to look at it and then puts it down and moves on. You don't know exactly why she didn't buy it; you just know that she didn't. Online, when you direct a customer to a particular product page, you count it as a visit. If the visitor purchases the product, you count it toward a positive conversion rate.

You contribute to a higher or lower conversion rate for a particular product. Your site-design decisions, linking choices, and marketing efforts all factor into a conversion rate.

Suppose that your product has a history of low sales. You do a little research and find that even though the number of visitors to the product page is decent, the conversion rate is quite low. Do you cross the product off your list? Not yet.

Before you write off a product as a nonproducer, double-check all factors that affect the conversion rate. Here are two suggestions:

>> **Take a closer look at the product page.** Determine whether the page has enough information to allow a customer to make the decision to purchase — whether size and color options and the price can be quickly obtained, for example. Some critical details might be omitted from the description, or the product photo might be small or fuzzy or cannot be enhanced. If the page doesn't show up well on a mobile device, that could cause mobile buyers to give up. These factors can cause a potential buyer to remain a window shopper.

>> **Track all pages that link to the product page.** Find out, for example, whether customers expecting to find one type of product are finding a much different product when they click through to check-out. You don't want them to believe that they were misled or oversold.

Take a look at Book 6, Chapter 1 to find out how to calculate the conversion rate.

Replacement or Expansion: The Art of Culling Your Inventory

When you decide to drop products that aren't selling well, you can take two approaches to adjust or refresh your inventory, as described in the following two sections.

Replacing one product with another

One strategy for refreshing your inventory is to replace nonperforming products: Get rid of one product and immediately substitute it with a new one. Your replacement products should meet these criteria:

WARNING

>> **They're complementary.** Look for items that are a good fit with the theme or focus of your site. You want products that continue to be relevant to your target customer.

Resist the temptation to add products that require marketing to an entirely different customer base. That's almost the same as starting a brand-new business, and it can permanently derail you.

>> **They're price competitive.** The price points of replacement products should be within the range of your current pricing structure. You don't want to introduce a high-end luxury item if your site is more of a midrange store. Similarly, you want to search for products that can be competitively priced on the general market. If you can find the product from other online sources for significantly less cost, you will have difficulty competing.

TIP

Always compare prices before adding products. PriceGrabber (www.pricegrabber. com) lets you view current rates online for a particular item. Or download a price-comparison toolbar, such as PriceScout (http://pricescout.io) or PriceBlink (www.priceblink.com), which you add to your browser. These apps automatically display comparison pricing and relevant coupons when you search for products online.

>> **They're appropriate for markup.** Choose products that are priced right for you, too. An item can be costly to you if the wholesale price is too high, or if you have to buy a really large quantity to make the price feasible. These items throw off your normal markup strategy and leave you paying for it — literally!

>> **They're deliverable.** When you search for products now, the world is truly at your feet. You can send anything from almost anywhere and then resell it. If delivering a product to your customer becomes difficult or takes too long, however, it costs you business. Your site should feature products that can be quickly shipped to customers without hassles or delays.

Expanding your product line

You can refresh your inventory by simply expanding it. Here are a few expansion tactics:

REMEMBER

>> **Concentrate on expanding a particular product line.** Perhaps your inventory analysis reinforces what you already suspected: One particular brand of products sells particularly well. Suppose that you're a reseller of spa products (hair and skin care) and you realize that the three Bumble and Bumble brand products on your site consistently sell well. After dropping your five worst-selling products, you decide to expand the Bumble and Bumble line. You have no reason to search for other brand-name products; just build on the one you already have.

   Expanding on a popular line of products is also a useful marketing opportunity. Make the most of it. Promote not only the new products but also the fact that you're expanding the entire brand.

>> **Accessorize your bestselling products by adding items that complement one of your top products.** Perhaps you sell electronics and games and find out that the Xbox One X game system by Microsoft is one of your three best-selling products. When you beef up your inventory, concentrate on Xbox companion products. You can expand your line of Xbox video games, memory cards, controllers, and any other items that work with it.

   Accessorizing is similar to the promotional strategy of upselling. When you see a product that your customers want, add supplemental products that might also interest them.

>> **Scale back the number of your products.** This strategy narrows your focus so that you can concentrate on a select group of your top sellers, no matter which brand or category they're in. In other words, eliminate the dead weight. Then start promoting the heck out of your best-performing products to increase sales.

   For example, you might have 75 items for sale, and your inventory analysis shows that only a dozen of those products make up a clear majority of your sales. Combined, the other 63 items account for fewer than 15 percent of your total annual sales. If you get rid of the majority of your products and stick to the 12 bestsellers — along with marketing — you should see sales increase without the hassle of working with a large number of products.

Finding Alternatives to Spur Growth

No matter what strategy you use to replace products, you first have to find new ones (or opportunities) that shine. Fortunately, you can look in certain places to narrow your choices:

- » **Vendors:** If you already work with regular suppliers, ask them what's selling. Your vendors know which items they can't keep in stock because of demand and which ones are lagging. Suppliers usually have a good idea of which type of new products are coming in, and can suggest ones that fit well with your site.

- » **Customers:** Your customers know best. Or, at least they know what they're willing to spend money on. Do a little online polling or send a short email survey to find out which products your customers want to see on your site. They're usually quite willing to share an opinion or two. Also, see if there are any complementary services that you can offer on top of your existing product base that your customers would pay you to do.

- » **Competitors:** Check the clearance section of a competitor's site to see which items didn't sell, and take a look at deeply discounted items to see which items might be on their way out. Don't forget to see which items are being heavily promoted.

- » **Social media:** Nowadays, public opinion is easily measured by studying your social media channels. From Facebook and Twitter, to Instagram and Pinterest, see which products or services are getting referenced, liked, and shared with individual people's followers. Keep an eye on the conversations being generated as well.

- » **Online blogs and product sites:** A wide variety of blogs and sites are dedicated to every type of product. Often, these websites will include announcements about new products as well as rumors.

- » **Trade shows:** These events are filled with product distributors showcasing their latest product offerings. Often, you can even detect a theme for upcoming releases. For example, you can see which colors are hot or which product categories distributors are pushing. Not surprisingly, manufacturers are all usually pushing the same items, so you can easily spot the next trend, or even find a potential partner to offer something unique and make yourself stand apart from the competition.

REMEMBER

Trade shows and markets are also an opportunity to chat with suppliers and gather detailed information. The atmosphere is much more casual, and distributors and members of their sales force are eager to talk.

Of course, after you make your decision about which products to add, the real proof is in the pudding (as they say). With that proverb in mind, it certainly doesn't hurt to literally put your judgment to the test. You can run online tests for a product by using one of these methods:

>> **Forced placement:** Try featuring only a single product on your home page. This strategy forces visitors to view the new product so that you can more easily monitor click rates and conversions when you're introducing a product. If you're uncomfortable promoting one item, you can also place the promotion in a premium spot on your home page.

>> **Rotate promotions:** Alternatively, you can run internal promotions on your site and rotate new products with your popular staple items. Use banner ads, pop-up ads, product reviews, or testimonials, and then rotate the promotions throughout your site (not just on the home page).

>> **Email customers:** Introduce new products in an email campaign to your targeted customers. That way, you can quickly gauge customer reaction to your latest product selection.

>> **Keywords:** You can also place external advertisements to drive visitors for product testing. The most effective method is paid keyword searches. Because these target visitors are already searching for your particular type of product, or something similar, this method is an effective way to test the waters for purchasing behaviors.

>> **Sample offline:** Give a few samples to friends or family members, and ask whether they would buy the product or have bought one similar to it already. If so, find out where and for how much. You can even have an informal focus group check out your product online. You can watch as its members visit your site and search for the new product. Find out from them what they think of your product, whether the promotion you used was effective, and whether the product image on your site accurately portrays the product. Honest feedback offline can help put you on the right track online.

Even a well-researched and thoroughly tested product isn't a sure bet. However, implementing these strategies as part of your product expansion truly helps you beat the odds.

Chapter **6**

Transitioning a Small Site into Big Business

Truthfully, plenty of entrepreneurs are satisfied with their online businesses staying small. For the rest of us, growth is the carrot that's continually being dangled in front of us. In this chapter, we share the strategies and resources that allow you (and your site) to finally take a bite out of that carrot.

Seeking Out the Next Level of Your Business

Entrepreneurs can tell you that the process of growing your business almost always starts out the same way — by planning for it.

Before transitioning your online business to the next level, you have to identify exactly *what* that next level is. You have to put all your options under a microscope and decide which one makes the most sense to pursue. What are your choices? Well, each of the most common paths to growth has its advantages and disadvantages.

Expanding the business

An obvious choice is to add products or services to your existing site. The purpose is to use variety to attract a wider customer base while bringing in larger revenues. This strategy is certainly the one that many entrepreneurs implement regularly, whether they realize it or not. After you consciously identify it as your preferred growth strategy, you can become more aggressive and targeted with your actions.

Here are the pros of expanding your business:

>> You retain full control of the business, just like always.

>> You can try to sell more to existing customers to improve your finances.

>> You can explore different areas, which can be fun for an entrepreneur.

The cons of expanding your business are that they

>> Can take more time to show results

>> Add risks by entering a new market without a history of selling those new products.

>> Might require a large investment in back-end systems to support added inventory or a product base

We discuss ways to expand your product base in Chapter 5 of this minibook.

Acquiring other sites

Buying existing sites is another fairly typical development strategy. You can easily start by making a list of competitors' sites that might be worth purchasing. Also look at sites that complement your current business. These noncompeting sites offer products or services that are different yet still a good fit.

Of course, the larger or more established a site, the higher its asking price. Sometimes, a better strategy is to identify up-and-coming sites or sites that (like yours) have also remained small.

The pros of acquiring other sites are that they

>> Provide a quick way to expand or diversify

>> Prevent competitors from overtaking you in the market

>> Introduce your current site to a wider customer base

The cons of acquiring other sites are that they

>> Usually require substantial out-of-pocket cash

>> May come with unforeseen liabilities or pitfalls that would affect you after you acquire them

>> Sometimes aren't for sale, so it takes time to convince their owners to negotiate a price

Becoming an affiliate or a partner

Maybe you're not ready to purchase another company outright. A better solution might be to expand through partnering opportunities or affiliate programs. For example, you might partner with a national membership-based organization as the sole provider of a particular service or product.

Expanding your business through partnership agreements can be a good idea. You're typically unrestricted in the number of partners you have, and you retain control — and can cancel an agreement if the partnership doesn't work.

In a similar arrangement, starting your own affiliate program becomes a viable option. Unlike in a partnership, you're developing a specific program that another site can replicate in exchange for a commission.

Although an affiliate program is often associated with some commodity goods, e-books and other content products, it's a viable delivery method for almost any product or service. You even see traditional e-commerce stores offering a flat percentage of revenues to affiliate sites that sell their products by using links. Or you might see payroll services companies that create affiliate opportunities. In that case, the affiliate earns a flat dollar amount for every customer referral that comes through the site.

REMEMBER

To make affiliate programs attractive (and worthwhile) for others to participate in, you should have a viable product to promote and pay a decent commission.

The pros of going the affiliate or partner route are that they

>> Are relatively easy to set up

>> Are inexpensive to develop

>> Are compatible with almost any type of business (whether it's product-, content-, or service-oriented)

>> Can produce a quick return on sales

Here are the cons of going the affiliate or partner route:

>> Brand control becomes an issue (primarily with affiliates), as you lend your name for others to use.

>> Administrative duties increase (monitoring affiliate sales, cutting checks, and distributing 1099 forms, for example).

>> You're essentially marketing two companies now (your original concept and your affiliate or partner program).

In Book 4, Chapter 2, we discuss signing up for affiliate programs.

Going international

Expanding your operations outside your home country is a proposition that's both exciting and scary. This strategy becomes easier when you have, or a partner has, experience in working outside the United States. However, the return on the investment can be lucrative. Products can become oversaturated in the ever-competitive American market. Yet overseas, the product might be a relatively new and sought-after item with few — if any — distributors. Furthermore, external factors like politics and trade agreements between countries can add additional complications as you expand internationally; elements like unexpected tariffs can change the dynamic of how you can compete with overseas sellers, for example.

The pros of taking your business internationally are that they can

>> Have more opportunity for growth and increased sales in foreign countries

>> Achieve global name recognition

Here are the cons of taking your business internationally:

>> Language barriers can complicate the process.

>> Selling the product might require setting up foreign distributors and manufacturing plants.

>> Laws and regulations vary by country, which adds another layer of compliance.

Bringing in financial partners

Recruiting a financial partner might be a desirable option for your site. If you do it correctly, you end up with needed money for growth and a business partner who has expertise that you might not possess. Finding a financial partner is a little different from simply going out and finding money to support your expansion because you're taking on an actual partner in this scenario.

Unlike a bank or another lender, a *financial partner* is a person who has a say-so in your business. She participates in both operational and financial decisions. You can consider angel investors, depending on the arrangement, and venture capitalists as examples of investment partners (see Book 1, Chapter 4). More than likely, your financial partner will end up being a former coworker, a business associate, or a friend or family member.

The pros of finding a financial partner are that the person

>> Provides needed capital to upgrade and expand your site

>> Creates the opportunity for you to benefit from his connections as well

>> Introduces fresh, alternative ideas from an experienced financial partner

Here are the cons of including a financial partner:

>> You sacrifice some control (and ownership) of your business.

>> The situation can become ugly if you find out that you don't share a united vision for growth.

>> Your partner might bail out at an inopportune time.

TIP

An alternative to bringing in financial partners is to get a peer-to-peer loan or investment by using websites such as Prosper (www.prosper.com) or Lending Club (www.lendingclub.com), or trying funding programs through existing online payment processors, like PayPal Working Capital (http://www.paypal.com/workingcapital) or Square Capital (www.squareup.com/us/en/capital), where you can get an investment with a fixed interest amount in exchange for a portion of your future revenue over time. Recent changes in finance laws have allowed smaller companies to *crowdsource,* or raise funds from lots of small investors, rather than seek out a small number of large investors. Check out sites such as Fundable (www.fundable.com) or MicroVentures (www.microventures.com) for more information.

Going public

The good old days are connected with a bit of nostalgia. You might remember the heyday of the dot-com era, when companies went public with shares breaking Wall Street records. Well, going public remains a viable option for your Internet business, even if it takes more work (and a good battle against skepticism). Companies such as Google, GoDaddy, and LinkedIn certainly have proven that the dot-com magic is still viable.

Here's the catch: You have to follow the same game plan as any other company that wants to go public, which includes these tasks:

» Create a sustainable business concept that's capable of keeping shareholders happy over the long haul. Your financial statements must be in tip-top shape, and you must have a critical strategy in place to support sustained growth.

» Take a closer look at your employees, vendor partnerships, and customers, and then begin investing in some heavy hitters (if you haven't already).

» Attract executives who are knowledgeable about the process of going public, and who have substantial experience with recognizable companies. You also need to partner with, or sell to, big-name vendors and customers. The more attention your company gets, the higher your public stock will be.

The pros of going public with your company are that you

» Increase its net worth (you hope)

» Jump into the big leagues

The cons of going public with your company are that

» The process is complicated, time consuming, and expensive.

» You get no guarantees.

» A *venture capitalist* (a firm or person that prepares your company to go public) might ask you to step down as CEO or president if your skills aren't a match for taking your company public.

REMEMBER

You usually don't decide to go public overnight. If you're on this path, you will experience some lower-level rounds of fundraising first. During that time, you typically work with angel investors and work your way up to venture capitalists.

Passing on your company and retiring

For some owners, passing the company on to a family member might qualify as following an exit strategy rather than making plans for growth. We disagree. In this particular strategy, you're in essence growing your heir, who in turn grows the business. The first step is to decide whether you have a next-generation family member interested in taking over your business. Then you have to take an honest and objective approach to deciding whether that person has the necessary skills or talents. At this point, it's like hiring an employee whom you plan to groom for a management position. Obviously, it's not always easy to be objective.

The upside is that you might find an untapped resource who has a terrific energy level and pushes you.

The pros of handing off your business to someone else are that

>> You continue to have a lifeline to the business, even after you step away from it.

>> The person brings a fresh perspective that can accelerate your site's growth.

>> Your business stays within your family.

The cons of handing off your business to someone else are that

>> "Grooming" an heir can take several years.

>> You might hurt your relationship or cause increased tension in the family.

>> The business stays within the family. (Yes, this one is also a pro — family has a tendency to have both positive and negative aspects in running a business.)

Selling your site

Selling your site is considered an exit strategy. Yet, selling your site is sometimes the only way to grow it.

You might be tired, tapped out of money, and looking for a way out. Maybe you recognize that your site has fantastic potential and you lack the experience and knowledge to make it happen. You might also have a limited window of opportunity, or you simply might not have the resources to expand your site within that optimal time frame.

Keep in mind that developing a plan to identify a buyer is quite different from someone unexpectedly calling you with an offer. If selling is your strategy, preparing your business can take as long as 6 months to a year. If you have a smaller site, or have been lax in sticking to a management regimen, you need a few months just to clean up your organizational act.

Depending on your asking price and the current market, finding the right buyer can take another year (or longer). This time frame is where you see the difference between selling as an exit plan and selling as a growth strategy. When expansion by selling is your goal, finding the right buyer match is critical. A professional broker can help you identify key characteristics.

In general, you want to look for someone who has these characteristics:

>> A shared vision for your site

>> Experience in taking a business beyond the start-up phase or past the early-growth years

>> Peers in the industry who can substantiate her reputation and skills

>> Verifiable liquid assets and net worth to invest in the business beyond the purchase price

TIP

You can locate a reputable business broker through BizBuySell (www.bizbuysell.com). The site has a free, searchable database that's broken out by state.

You don't have to work with a professional to sell your site. However, a broker often has extensive contacts of potential buyers and can speed up the selling process. Regardless, selling your site might be the ideal opportunity for you.

Following are the pros of selling your company outright:

>> You receive a potentially large chunk of change for all your hard work.

>> The burden of growth is removed.

>> You can try something else.

Here are the cons of selling your company outright:

>> If you stay with the company, you lose control.

>> If you leave outright, you have to start a new business from scratch, find a job, or retire.

>> You have no guarantee that the buyer will succeed in growing the site.

>> Because payment terms might be spread out, realizing the full sale price can take a while.

>> The buyer may require you to sign a non-compete clause, which means you cannot compete with the buyer by starting another business in the same industry for many years. Given that your experience is heavily tied to the company you just sold, this could limit your opportunities in the future.

>> The business could go under before you collect all your money, leaving the site wiped out and you fighting in court for restitution.

Selling your domain

An alternative to selling your entire business is to sell only its URL. A popular domain name can fetch a pretty penny, which can help you expand your site.

Suppose that you have a limited amount of money to invest in any type of tools for growth. However, a key asset is your domain name. You can, in theory, sell the domain — to provide a needed influx of capital — and retain, as a condition of the sale, the rights to all content and services. That way, you move the content to another domain and use the money from the sale to build up the new site.

This strategy is particularly feasible if you already own a domain for a smaller site that has a similar theme or customer demographic. Of course, unless you have another domain name in your back pocket, starting over might be difficult.

WHAT TO DO BEFORE YOUR SITE GOES ON THE MARKET

Although the decision to sell might come easily to you, preparing your site for that transaction doesn't happen overnight. Check out this to-do list before you hang a For Sale sign on your business:

- Put your financial house in order with a set of audited financial statements.

- Meet with your accountant to discuss tax strategies for a sale.

- Have a professional valuation conducted to determine a feasible asking price.

- Contract with a business broker who has experience in selling Internet companies.

- Review all vendor agreements, equipment leases, and miscellaneous contracts, and then take a thorough inventory.

- Make sure that written policies and procedures are in place and are being strictly followed.

- Update all back-end functions (as long as doing so doesn't require a significant cash investment).

- Work on increasing the number of visitors to your site and the average length of time they spend there.

- Hire an expert in search engine optimization to improve your position at search engine sites.

- Step up your PR activities to get attention. (Unlike in the area of marketing, PR gives you more exposure for the money.)

The pros of putting your domain name up for sale follow:

>> The process is fast and can have a high monetary return.

>> You retain ownership of your content, products, or services.

>> You gain capital to reinvest in a new site.

Here are the cons of putting your domain name up for sale:

>> The purchaser of your domain can develop a competing site that uses your old URL.

>> The purchaser can use your domain name for a less-reputable type of site or as a gateway to a scam site.

>> You lose traffic, search engine rankings, and ratings for your previous site.

Dealing with Accidental Success

Ahh, sweet success. Admittedly, the term *accidental success* is a bit humorous. Ask any rock star or well-known actor about an overnight boost of fame. The honest ones don't hesitate to explain that years of hard work preceded their "accidental" good fortune.

The same concept holds true for any online business owner. Imagine finding yourself in the throes of a major public relations blitz, with skyrocketing sales following close behind. The reality is that you might be unprepared to handle the level of business that this scenario brings. But we guarantee you that your success is no accident.

How do you prepare for an onslaught of hard-won business? After all, if your site is merely mentioned on a TV talk show or featured in a short segment on one of the news channels, your URL can be rocketed into the glare of the spotlight (in an extremely good way). Before you know it, you would have back orders and your site would be bogged down from the jump in visitors. You wouldn't be able to get UPS to pull into your driveway fast enough. Lest this blitz of good fortune turn into your sudden demise, you had better be ready.

The following list describes both immediate and short-term actions you should take when opportunity comes knocking at your domain:

>> **Identify your pressure points.** Determine where the biggest demand for your time or resources is coming from. You might be beseeched by the media for interview requests and can't make it to the phone. More than likely, your production and distribution cycles have kinks, and you have to get (or keep) products stocked at the higher demand levels. Also, your customer service functions must handle the incoming request load. Maybe your biggest problem is figuring out how to pack and ship this steep increase in orders. After you identify your most immediate (and demanding) source of frustration, you can begin developing a solution.

>> **Hire temporary help.** When your manpower runs out of "man," you have to call in the cavalry. Going from a solo operation to one with a dozen employees, however, is daunting. Screening and hiring people and putting benefits in place take time. The solution is to hire temporary workers to provide an immediate boost to your productivity levels, without the hassle. Use a professional staffing agency to quickly add qualified and prescreened workers. An added benefit to this approach is that you can pull back on staffing levels if demand slows down.

>> **Outsource certain tasks.** After a sudden influx of orders, the most economical solution (for both the short and long terms) is to outsource some of your functions. As the owner of a small site, you're probably used to processing each order and then packaging and shipping the product yourself. Factor in a 50 percent to 75 percent increase in orders, and you can no longer physically keep up the pace. Combat the problem by finding a local call center that can take over functions related to customer service. Or try contracting with a distribution center to warehouse your products and handle order-packing and order-shipping functions. See Book 4, Chapter 7 to find an in-house or a third-party solution to your packaging and shipping dilemmas.

>> **Adjust the back end.** Another victim of your site's growing pains is the back-end function. From your shopping cart program to inventory control, the programs that were once suited for a start-up site can quickly become antiquated. To survive an unexpected sales rush, work with your vendors to make minimal improvements to your existing support systems. Then schedule time to research advanced products and features that can be better scaled to your new sales levels. We discuss all your back-end solutions in Book 4, Chapter 7.

>> **Seek funding.** The changes you have to make to your business require money. Even if you decide not to invest in new equipment or tools, you need money to handle inventory spikes and hire staff. One of the best things you can do is take a trip to your bank — or another lender. As long as your credit score is reasonable and your relationship with the bank is good, establishing a line of credit is an easy way to gain access to cash. A *line of credit* is basically a loan with a preestablished limit. Rather than take out the full amount at one time, you can withdraw money in smaller amounts only when you need it.

>> **Talk, talk, talk.** Now, more than ever, you need to communicate with vendors, distributors, employees, and customers. Take time out for daily or weekly 10-minute staff meetings. Take the opportunity to share operational changes and find out about problems that might otherwise fly under the radar in your stepped-up pace of activities. Let customers know about back

orders, shipping delays, and any other minor problems that are surfacing. The worst thing about overnight success is that if you don't address concerns effectively, you lose the customers who came to you during this crunch time of good fortune.

TIP

Take notes when you're talking to customers, especially when they have a positive comment or a success story concerning your product. Turn these stories into case studies or testimonials that you post on your website, and use them as offline marketing materials, too.

>> **Spend wisely.** We hope that your burst of success is proportionate to the rising number in your bank account. With years of hard work behind you, you might be tempted to splurge. Instead, think of this influx of funds as investment capital and put it back into your company as much as possible.

TIP

Meet with your accountant to review or update your financial strategy. A substantial increase in revenues, and subsequent expenditures, brings along plenty of tax implications. Ask your accountant to discuss your options to maximize the use of your money.

>> **Take it to the next level.** With momentum on your side, consider leveraging it a little further. With increased recognition and revenues, you have a good shot at negotiating partnering opportunities, developing another line of products or services, and riding out a wave of expanded publicity. Use your moment in the spotlight to further establish your site's brand and position it for the future.

Purposefully Making the Next Move

Whether your site is growing because of fate or strategy, your next move should be well thought out. Follow these strategies:

>> **Assemble an advisory board.** You might already have a formal board of directors that you assembled immediately after you incorporated. In that case, consider the value of expanding your board and adding individuals with specific expertise. If you're not comfortable bringing on directors, assemble a somewhat less formal *advisory board*. This group of professionals from your network meets regularly to review your business goals and provide guidance. Similar to when you have a board of directors, look for people with experience who complement your strengths and weaknesses.

>> **Update planning tools.** Growth means digging into that old business plan and marketing plan. You know which ones we mean — the ones you threw together half a decade ago because everyone said that you had to have them. Those people were right: You need both documents, even though they're long overdue for an update. Use the old plans as a foundation to reassess your current goals and strategies.

>> **Focus on long-term financial planning.** In addition to working more closely with your accountant, seek input from a financial planner or a CPA who specializes in your industry. You're no longer simply moving from one tax year to the next. As both your company revenue and personal income increase, you want to make calculated decisions about your money.

>> **Stay current.** It's all about the research. Growing companies tend to put up walls around themselves. By not paying attention to what's happening in the world around them, they are quickly outpaced by more innovative businesses. The best way to ward off this curse is to become a vigilant researcher:

- Watch for developing trends.

- Read business and trade publications.

- Talk with peers in your industry.

- Attend trade shows.

- Skim the Internet for information that might affect your site.

- Keep an eye on your competitors.

>> **Find a mentor.** You might not want to invite your closest competitor to have coffee with you, and getting the CEO of Google on board might be a little far-fetched. You can, however, look for sites that embody your philosophies and implement similar growth strategies. Approach the founder or president by email, and see whether she's open to answering some questions. (Be honest about why you're contacting her.) Striking up an online mentorship is easier than you might think.

>> **Participate in industry activism.** As a small-business owner, you have to focus primarily on your site. Your number-one priority is figuring out how to make your site work, which can be isolating at times. As you expand, you're in the position to broaden your horizon. Make a point of joining national industry associations or professional organizations in your local community. Get involved with issues that affect your business and your peers' businesses. Table 6-1 highlights a few of the national member-based organizations that cater to Internet professionals and small-business owners.

REMEMBER

Becoming active in your professional community and your industry associations is also a proven and powerful networking tool.

TABLE 6-1   **Associations for Online Business Professionals**

Organization	URL	Annual Membership Fee
Data Marketing & Analytics	www.thedma.org	$1,500
Entrepreneurs' Organization	www.eonetwork.org	$2,470
National Federation of Independent Business (NFIB)	www.nfib.com	$195
Search Engine Marketing Professional Organization (SEMPO)	www.sempo.org	$125

Index

Numbers

24/7 customer support, 155, 192, 517

52- or 53-week period, 118

80-20 rule, 441

1099 form, 90

A

A New Leash on Life (ANLOL), 674

A/B testing, 793

access point (AP), 364

accidental success, dealing with, 839–841

accidents, 344

account based marketing (ABM), 786

accountants, 127

accounting. *See also* recordkeeping
  balance sheet, 120–121
  cash basis method, 119–120
  e-commerce solutions, 572
  hiring professionals for, 126–132
  profit-and-loss (P&L) statement, 121–124
  software, 124–126
  tax year, 118–119

accounts payable, 120

accounts receivable, 120

accrued expenses, 121

action plan, 345–346

action timeline, creating, 14, 15

active donor base
  building from scratch, 674–676
  engaging passersby, 675
  establishing relationship, 675

existing supporters, 678–680

getting site noticed, 674–675

overview, 673

plans to reach donors, 677–678

reaching out those surfing for charities, 681–682

Active@ KillDisk, 373

address blocking, 278

address verification service (AVS), 278, 329

Adobe Acrobat, 79

Adobe Analytics, 463–464

Adobe Flash Player, 79

Adobe InDesign, 80

Adobe PDF Pack, 263

Adobe Reader, 262

Advanced Integration Method (AIM), 278

advertisers, 247

advertising. *See also* affiliate programs
  banner, 390
  classified, 414
  dayparts and, 388
  embedded, 265
  local, 542–550
  modal, 449–450
  paid, 413, 768, 783, 811
  pop-up, 449–450
  revenue, 388
  search engine advertising, 424–432
  social media, 545
  spending, 388

advisory board, 841–842

advocacy (loyalty) stage, online buying process, 763–764

advocate, in nonprofit organizations, 695

adware, 360

Adwords. *See* Google Ads

affiliate
  becoming, 831–832
  defined, 247
  network, 247

affiliate programs
  advertising programs, 241–242
  commission structure, 251
  converting visitors to repeat buyers, 814
  cookies, 251
  country of origin, 253
  details, 251–252
  finding, 249–250
  illegal, 253
  limits or exclusions, 251
  online vendors, 249
  overview, 245
  pay-for-performance networks, 249–250
  payment methods, 251
  penalties, 251
  questionable, 254–255
  recordkeeping, 251
  refunds, 251
  restrictive marketing strategies, 252
  retailers, 249
  scams, 255
  signing up for, 250–252
  sign-up fee, 254
  steps in, 246
  terminologies, 247–248
  tips, 246–247
  tracking, 251
  types of, 248–249
  videos, 265

affiliate traffic, 390

AffiliateWiz, 242

Aftcra, 227

age barrier, 9

aging online businesses, overhauling
- business change evaluation, 807–809
- converting visitors to repeat buyers, 813–815
- increasing number of website visitors, 810–812
- lagging sales, 810–815
- overview, 805
- personalized offers, 816–817
- re-engaging customers, 815–817
- signs of aging, 806–809
- targeted offers, 817
- where to start, 817–818

Airbnb, 232

Alexa, 2, 206

algorithms, 474

Alibaba, 298

Alipay, 273

ALS Association, 676

ALS Foundation, 649

ALT attributes, 481–482

Amazon
- 1-Click system, 442
- Associates, 250
- Best Sellers, 296
- FulFillment by Amazon (FBA) service, 587–588
- general discussion, 577
- logos on boxes, 433
- Prime, 585
- reviews, 399

Amazon Marketplace
- advantage of, 579
- business reports by ASIN, 587
- business reports by date, 586
- individual sellers, 580–585
- overview, 578

Professional Seller plan, 585–587
- referral fees, 579
- returns/refunds, handling, 587
- sales and orders by month, 587
- sales dashboard, 586
- transaction fee, 579
- variable closing fee, 579
- website, 12

American Academy of Attorney-CPAs, 129

American Bar Association (ABA), 112

American Express, 690

American Institute of Certified Public Accountants, 129

American Institute of Professional Bookkeepers, 128, 129

analytics software, 439–440, 573, 783

Android, 739

Android Pay, 273

angel investors, 45–47

Angelfish Digital Analytics software, 461

annual contract value (ACV), 735

antivirus, 373

App Press, 738

appendix, 34

Apple App Store, 737

Apple iCloud, 79

Apple Pay, 273

Apple Safari browser, 796

application service provider (ASP), 232

apps
- budgeting, 737
- building, 737
- creating, 736–739
- market for, 736
- prices, 736
- types of, 736–737
- uploading for sale, 738–739

Appypie, 737

architectural elements, in online store, 526

archived information, 424

articles, writing, 406–409, 798

Asos, 725

Association of Interactive Marketing (AIM), 680

at domain extension, 148

auction. See also eBay
- direct, 665–666
- nonprofit organizations, 663–666
- overview, 13
- promoting, 665
- third-party, 663–665

AuctionAnything.com, 666

Auctria, 666

author domain extension, 148

Authorize, 275

Automated Clearing House (ACH) processing, 277, 564

automated membership renewals, 690

automating routine tasks, 423

autorenew feature, 248

autoresponders, 423–424

Avid Mobile, 541

awards, 51

awareness stage, online buying process, 762–763

B

baby boomer market
- designing site to attract, 744–746
- finding niche in, 747–748
- overview, 742–743
- retaining customers, 746–747
- traits of, 743–744

back-end management
- adjusting, 840
- backend inventory management, 552

F

Facebook
  getting employees to like on, 689
  localized ads, 545–548
  reviews, 399
  setting up, 417–419
  social commerce, 13
  website, 710
Facebook Marketing All-in-One For Dummies (Vahl), 713
fact checking, 260
failing business, 499
family
  as investors, 44–45
  talking with, 14
Fashion Finder, 725
fax services, 71
feasibility study, 24–26
Federal Bureau of Investigations (FBI), 327
federal tax identification number, 86
Federal Trade Commission (FTC)
  complaints of online shoppers, 333, 370
  COPPA compliance, 756–757
  e-commerce regulation, 85, 331
  privacy policy, 60
Federation of Tax Administrators (FTA), 118
FedEx, 318, 319, 558
feedback. *See also* voice of the customer (VOC)
  customers, 240, 446–447, 792
  eBay, 617–619
  types of, 792
Feedbackify, 793
fees
  Amazon Marketplace, 579
  competition, 240
  credit card payments, 275
  Shopify, 602
  website designers, 182–183

fiber-optic Internet, 81–82
fictitious name registration, 97–98
52- or 53-week period, 118
file compression, 79
file storage and sharing programs, 79
filling the order. *See* fulfillment
filtering, 278
filters, Instagram, 636
financial freedom, gaining, 8
financial losses, minimizing, 370–371
financial partners, 833
financial requirements, 30
financials, 34
financing
  alternative, 49–52
  bootstrapping, 40–43, 96
  business plans and, 34
  crowdfunding, 50
  grants, 51–52
  high-interest loans, 51
  home equity loan, 50–51
  incubators, 52
  investors, finding, 44–49
  line of credit, 840
  online lenders, 51
  overview, 39
  retirement cash, 50
FindLaw, 112
Firesheep, 368
firewalls, 373, 375
FirstGiving, 688
fiscal year, 119
Fiverr, 184
fixed assets, 120
Flagship Merchant Services, 272
flash/USB drives, 264
FlexWatches, 749
flooding, 360
floor plan
  equipment list, 68
  furniture arrangement, 68–69

how to use space, 68
  sketching, 68
flyers, 433, 632
Foap, 720
focus group, 165, 794
Folloze, 786
fonts, 161, 745
Food and Drug Administration (FDA), 86
Form 2976-A, 319
forms
  1099 form, 89
  IRS Form 941, 116
  IRS Form 990, 668, 696, 699
  W-2, 90
  W-4, 90
  W-9, 89
  withholding forms, 115
Forrester, 8, 29, 299, 500
Forte, 277, 564
forum policy, 64
forums, 154
401(k), 50, 101
Foxy, 289–291
fraud, 329, 370–371
free gifts, 817
free limited-time trials, 815
freelancer
  hiring, 181–182, 732
  website designer, 181–182
freemium model, 733, 735
freeware, 42
frequently asked questions (FAQ) section, 437
friends, as investors, 44–45
frugal, becoming, 40–41
fulfillment. *See also* delivery
  back end maintenance, 320–323
  database, 320–321
  feeding orders to shipping department, 323
  in-house fulfillment model, 307–308

keyword(s)
ALT attributes, 481–482
in content, 200–203
density, 484
invisible, 479–482
long-tail keyword searches, 201
<META> tags, 479–481
product testing, 828
search engines and, 478–483
searches, 389, 414
spamming, 487
stuffing, 201, 478
tips, 202–203
visible, 482–483
Kickstarter, 50
kids, 751, 754
Kindle, 13
knowledge, 30
known visitors, 784
Koh's, 551
Kovter, 356
Kroc, Ray, 20

L

labor services, 232
landing pages, 158, 459, 532, 768
landlords, 92
laptop computer, vs. desktop, 75
LawDepot software, 35
lease to own strategy, in buying an existing site, 55
legal issues
bank account, 89
business licenses, 92–93
employee forms, 89–90
federal tax identification number, 86
health department permit, 86
overview, 85–86
resale certificate, 88
zoning, 90–92

Lending Club, 833
LexisNexis, 329
liability, 96
life cycle, of products, 820
lifestyle information, 469
lifetime value (LTV), 735, 815
limited appeal products, 822
limited liability company (LLC), 100
limited-time offers, 815
limited-use products, 822
line items, 121
line of credit, 840
LinkedIn, 237, 710, 715–716
LinkedIn Learning, 265
links
adding information to, 465–466
buttons or text as, 161
design for increased web traffic, 532
external, 390
incoming, 476, 478
opportunities, 811
qualifying, 248
reciprocal, 478
text inside, 483
in website design, 745
Linux server, 192
live chat, 523
live events, 632
LiveChat, 445
LivePlan software, 35
loans, high-interest, 51
local area network (LAN), 364
local organizations, 129–130
localization
defined, 542
Facebook, 545–548
geotargeting, 542–543
Google Ads, 543–545
social media ads, 545
Twitter, 549–550

location, store identity and, 527
logistics, 306–307
logos
affiliate programs, 252
in online store, 526
long-tail keyword searches, 201
Loop11, 167
loyalty rewards, 571, 815
loyalty stage, online buying process, 763–764
luxury items, 441
Lyft, 232
Lynda, 265

M

Mac computers, 76
Macy's, 530
MailChimp, 423, 604, 783
maintenance
inability, 498
lack of, 806
routine, 517
site performance, 559
malicious intents, 344
malicious intruders, 344
malware, 328, 343, 356–358
managed server, 196
management team, 34
market
analysis, 33
conditions, fluctuating, 806
identifying, 26, 27
target, 27
market research, 29, 298–299
marketing
asking for donations, 683–690
automation, 381
brand, 412–414
content, 200
cross-promotional, 690
digital, 380–382
e-mail, 571

organizational services, 232

org.nz domain extension, 148

org.uk domain extension, 148

orientation stage, in move to online store, 505–506

outages, 344

Outlook email program, 78

outsourcing, 309–314, 840

ownership
  of business, 96
  full, 43

P

page views, 455

paid advertising, 413, 768, 783, 811

Paint Shop Pro, 80

Palo Alto Software, 35

Pardot, 783

partners, becoming, 831–832

partnership deal, 414

partnerships
  agreement, 99
  general, 98–99
  proof of, 99
  switching to corporation, 102–103
  tax forms for, 115

pass-along marketing, 686–687

password generator, 355

passwords, 355

patents
  defined, 106
  professional assistance with, 112

path analysis, 466–467

pay by flat rate method, 241–242

pay by lead method, 241–242

pay per click (PPC), 242, 246, 430–432, 544

pay-for-performance, 248, 249–250

payment
  alternative methods of, 277–278, 563–564
  Bitcoin, 564
  checks, 278, 563–564
  credit card, 269–276
  deferred, 562–563
  electronic checks, 277
  extending options to virtual customers, 561–564
  fees, 275–276
  fulfillment houses and, 312–313
  gateways, 273–275, 284, 572
  gift cards, 277
  instant credit, 277–278
  multiple forms of, 518
  to nonprofit organizations, 659–660
  offline payment, 278
  options, 814
  overview, 12, 269
  Paypal, 277
  by phone, 278
  security features, 278–279

Payment Card Industry Data Security Standard (PCI DSS), 61, 87–88, 348

payment coprocessor, 175

payment processors, in e-commerce solutions, 568

PayPal
  as alternative payment, 277
  buy button, 175
  Credit, 278, 562–563
  Giving, 664
  Payments Pro program, 273
  signing up for, 610
  Working Capital, 51, 833

PaySimple, 70, 277

PC Magazine, 400

PCI Security Standards Council, 88

PDF (Portable Document File), 78–79, 262–263

peer-to-peer online campaigns, 648–649

Pepperjam, 250

periods of limitations, 133–134

peripheral components, inventory assessment of, 342

personal stories, 799

personalization
  content, 773
  integrating systems, 783–784
  launching online, 782–787
  tools, 786–787
  web, 772–773

personalized content, 772

persuasive content, 777

Pet Rocks, 10

Petplan, 704

pets, 748

Pew Internet, 752

Pew Research Center, 708

pharming, 360, 362

phishing, 343, 360, 361–362

phone, customer service, 523

PHP: Hypertext Preprocessor scripting language, 191

pick-and-pull sheets, 323

ping, 485

pins, 716

Pinterest, 13, 710, 716

Pitney Bowes, 317

PlayStation, 354

pledge, 58–59

plugs, 419

podcasts, 155–156

point of contact (POC), 695

points for improvements (PfI), 345

policies
  chat room policy, 64
  endorsement, 64

U

W

About the Authors

Shannon Belew: Shannon has been championing the benefits of online businesses and digital marketing for more years than she cares to admit. A passionate advocate for small businesses and start-up entrepreneurs, she loves using social media to spread the word about how to use an online presence to grow your business. She has owned several online businesses and currently leads an engagement marketing team for a global infracture software company. A freelance writer, Shannon has written for many online websites, magazines, and newspapers; she also has written several books about online marketing, e-commerce, and social media, including *The Art of Social Selling, Finding and Engaging Customers on Twitter, Facebook, LinkedIn, and Other Social Networks.* Shannon is a frequent guest speaker on webinars, radio shows, and other events, discussing topics such as digital marketing, content strategy, and social media marketing. As a former marketing and PR consultant, she has helped clients share their stories in such venues as *Inc. Magazine* and CNN. She hopes you'll help her keep the conversation about online marketing going by following her on Twitter (@shannonbelew) and connect with her on LinkedIn (www.linkedin.com/in/shannonbelew).

Joel Elad: Joel has authored or coauthored seven leading books in the fields of e-commerce, social media, and technology, including *LinkedIn For Dummies, Facebook Advertising For Dummies,* and *Starting an iPhone Application Business For Dummies.* He is the head of Real Method Consulting, where he provides consulting and advice for e-commerce companies and entrepreneurs. He sells online as a PowerSeller on eBay and runs several websites that focus on e-commerce and upcoming educational products. Through institutions such as the University of California, Irvine, the University of San Diego, and the Learning Annex, he has trained thousands of people on e-commerce and how to start a small business. He's a past contributor to *Entrepreneur* magazine and SmartBiz.com.

Dedication

Shannon: This book is lovingly dedicated in memory of my father, Ron "Baby Huey" Sanders. It has been an incredibly difficult year without him, but I was honored to have him serve as my inspiration and guide post for so many years. I share this tribute alongside my mom, Janice, and my children, who are filled with an entrepreneurial spirit of their own: my son, Holden, and my daughter, Wiley. And a very special thanks to Peter, who has brought me joy and adventure in a time when I needed it most.

Joel: This book is dedicated to the most caring woman I know, my mother; and the hardest-working man I will ever have the privilege of knowing — my father. Thank you both for showing me the value of planning, discipline, and love. You will always be my inspiration.

Authors' Acknowledgments

Shannon: My sincere thanks to the entire team at Wiley Publishing for making this book a reality, including Ashley Coffey and Elizabeth Kuball, who helped shape this project from the start and ensured we would bring the best to this book for our readers; my coauthor, Joel Elad, who is always the first person to jump in and help when needed; and the team at Waterside Productions, especially Carole Jelen, who keeps the light shining on all my projects. It's an honor to work with everyone. Thanks also to all those who choose to read this book and who aspire to become entrepreneurs. Your entrepreneurial spirit and dream for a brighter future makes this world go 'round, and your enthusiasm and energy for new endeavors continue to inspire me.

Joel: My biggest round of thanks has to go to the team at Wiley for their constant and amazing support of this title: Ashley Coffey, my coauthor Shannon Belew, and definitely Elizabeth Kuball, whose patience and guidance helped make this book possible. Thanks to my friends and contacts, including Anthony Choi, David Conde, Lynn Dralle, Greg Foreman, Greg Goldstein, and especially Doug Tondro, for the contacts, information, and support I needed along the way to fill in the gaps. Finally, I have to give a special acknowledgment to my usual coconspirator, Michael Bellomo, who put me on the path of being an author and keeps me going with a bizarre sense of humor mixed with a powerful dose of inspiration.

Publisher's Acknowledgments

Acquisitions Editor: Ashley Coffey

Project Editor: Elizabeth Kuball

Copy Editor: Elizabeth Kuball

Proofreader: Debbye Butler

Technical Editor: James Kelly

Production Editor: Mohammed Zafar Ali

Cover Photos: © sutthinon sanyakup/ Getty Images